SURPASSING
THE LOVE
OF MEN

Permission to quote has kindly been granted as follows:

Grateful acknowledgment is extended to Lovat Dickson and the Humanities Research Center, University of Texas, Austin, for permission to quote from Radclyffe Hall's unpublished letters and notes.

Grateful acknowledgment is extended to the Bancroft Library, University of California, Berkeley, for permission to quote from "A Beautiful Woman," an unpublished story by Harriet Lane Levy.

Grateful acknowledgment is extended to the Schlesinger Library, Radcliffe College, for permission to quote from the correspondence of Helen Morton and Mary Hopkinson.

Grateful acknowledgment is extended to the Houghton Library, Harvard University, for permission to quote from the unpublished diary of Sara Orne Jewett.

Grateful acknowledgment is extended to Butler Library, Columbia University, for permission to quote from the diary of Charlotte Cushman.

Grateful acknowledgment is extended to Mount Holyoke College Library/ Archives for permission to quote from the correspondence of Jeannette Marks and from her unpublished essay, "Unwise College Friendships."

From *Amy Lowell: A Chronicle,* by S. Foster Damon, published by Houghton Mifflin Company. Copyright © renewed 1963 by S. Foster Damon. Reprinted by permission.

From *The Complete Poetical Works of Amy Lowell,* published by Houghton Mifflin Company. Copyright 1955 by Houghton Mifflin Company. Reprinted by permission.

From Gertrude Stein, *As Fine as Melanctha,* published by Yale University Press. Copyright 1954 by Alice B. Toklas. Reprinted by permission from Yale University Press.

From Gertrude Stein, *Bee Time Vine and Other Pieces,* published by Yale University Press. Copyright 1953 by Alice B. Toklas. Reprinted by permission from Yale University Press.

Grateful acknowledgment is extended to Bonnie Zimmerman for permission to quote from her unpublished article, "My Whole Soul is a Longing Question."

Grateful acknowledgment is extended to Louis Crompton for permission to quote from his unpublished chronology on homosexuals and the death penalty.

Grateful acknowledgment is extended to Naiad Press and Margaret Porter for permission to quote from her translations of the poetry of Renée Vivien in *The Muse of the Violets*. Copyright © 1977 by Margaret Porter.

Grateful acknowledgment is extended to Virgil Thomson for permission to quote from our conversation regarding Natalie Barney.

I wish to thank the following journals for permitting me to reprint portions of my articles:

Journal of Popular Culture, "Lesbian Magazine Fiction in the Early Twentieth Century," XI, 4 (Spring 1978).

The Massachusetts Review, "Emily Dickinson's Letters to Sue Gilbert," XVIII, 2 (Summer 1977).

Conditions, "Radclyffe Hall and the Lesbian Image," I, 1 (Spring 1977).

Journal of Homosexuality, "The Morbidification of Love Between Women by Nineteenth Century Sexologists," IV, 1 (Fall 1978).

New England Quarterly, "Female Same-sex Relationships in Novels by Longfellow, Holmes, and James," LI, 3 (September 1978).

And I gratefully acknowledge the following for permission to reproduce several of the pictures:

The Bettman Archive, Inc., for Deborah Sampson (p. 1)
                            Havelock Ellis (p. 6)
                            Sigmund Freud (p. 6)
                            Alice B. Toklas and Gertrude Stein (p. 7)

The Trustees of Mount Holyoke College; The Mount Holyoke College Library/Archives for "Miss Marks and Miss Woolley" (p. 3)

Grateful thanks to J.-M. Lo Duca, Bibliothèque Internationale d'Erotologie, Paris, for "The Witches Sabbath" (p. 4)

Musée du Petit Palais, Paris, for "Sleep" by Gustave Courbet (p. 5)

Courtesy/The Bancroft Library, University of California at Berkeley, for "A.B.T. and Harriet Levy" (p. 7)

BBC Hulton Picture Library, London, for "Vita Sackville-West in 1924" (p. 7)

The cover of the August, 1967, issue of THE LADDER appearing on page 8 of the picture section is reprinted here with the permission of Barbara Grier for THE LADDER and Jane Kogan, artist, whose original painting, "Les Copains," was used in that cover.

Photograph of Kady and Pagan (on p. 8 of picture section) by JEB from EYE TO EYE: LESBIANS © 1979. Used by permission of the publisher, Glad Hag Books, P.O. Box 2934, Washington, D.C. 20013.

To Phyllis for everything

Acknowledgments

For their kind encouragement and assistance I wish to thank my colleagues and friends, Paula Bennett, Sandra Dijkstra, Ann-Marie Feenberg, Harold Karr, Jonathan Katz, Bill Moritz, Harriet Perl, Margaret Porter, Vivian Pollak, Joachim Ries, Tanya Rutter, Ken Seib, Allen Skei, Bonnie Zimmerman, Brigitte Eriksson, and my editor, Maria Guarnaschelli.

For their efforts far beyond their duties I wish to thank the Interlibrary Loan Librarians at University of California, San Diego, and California State University, Fresno, and the Huntington Library staff.

I wish to acknowledge my debt to Barbara Grier and Jeannette Foster, whose pioneering bibliographic works were indispensable to my own work. It is my fondest wish that I may be as helpful to future scholars as they were to me.

"Your love was wonderful to me, passing the love
of women."

David to Jonathan
2 Samuel, I,26

"I assure you, with a love "passing the Love of
Men," that I am yours . . ."

Lucy to Harriot
William Hayley's *The Young Widow*, 1789

"Davidean friendship, emulation warm,
Coy blossoms, perishing in courtly air,
Its vain parade, restraint, and irksome form,
Cold as the ice, tho' with the comets' glare.
By firmness won, by constancy secured,
Ye nobler pleasures, be ye long their meed. . . ."

of Sarah Ponsonby and Eleanor Butler
Anna Seward's *Poetical Works*, 1810

Contents

Introduction

This book began as a study of Emily Dickinson's love poems and letters to Sue Gilbert, the woman who became her sister-in-law. I believed I had found in the poet's writing irrefutable evidence that the grand passion of her life was not one of the ten or twelve men with whom she had been romantically linked by her twentieth-century biographers, but rather another woman. By the time I finished gathering my material, however, I realized that something was wrong: Although Dickinson had written the most passionate and sensual pronouncements of love to Sue Gilbert in the 1850's, there was never any suggestion that she felt the need to be covert about her emotions. If I had really uncovered a lesbian relationship, why could I not find any evidence of the guilt and anxiety, the need to keep secrets from family and friends, that I thought were inevitably associated with homosexuality before the days of gay liberation? Several critics suggested that the language of Dickinson's putative love letters to Sue Gilbert was simply consonant with the overinflated rhetoric that was fashionable in her day.

But what about the poems which picture her holding another woman's "sweet weight" on her heart at night, that describe her as the pet bird of a lady who throws her occasional crumbs, the queen of another queen? What about the evidence that immediately after Sue's marriage to Austin Dickinson, Emily, who viewed the event with painful ambivalence, had a nervous breakdown? Emily's love letters to Sue were not simply an example of Victorian rhetoric, but neither was this a lesbian relationship as such relationships have been lived through much of our century.

I decided to examine the work of her contemporaries to see if I might uncover traces of similar relationships in her day. Carroll Smith-Rosenberg's essay, "The Female World of Love and Ritual," suggested that I might find some, but I was not prepared to discover that it was virtually impossible to study the correspondence of any nineteenth-century woman, not only of America but also of England, France, and Germany, and not uncover a passionate commitment to another woman at some time in her life. I also found innumerable fictional examples of such female love relationships, all of them without any hint that the women involved had the slightest sense of wrongdoing, or any suggestion that such affection could be considered abnormal. I learned too that in various times and places in the nineteenth century, there were common terms to describe love relationships between women, such as "the love of kindred spirits," "Boston marriage," and "sentimental friends."

At first I assumed that this kind of romantic attachment was born in the Victorian era, when women were taught to fear premarital heterosexual love and sought other females for safe emotional outlets. But I soon discovered that the eighteenth century also had a term for love between women—romantic friendship—and that the term signified a relationship that was considered noble and virtuous in every way. I found romantic friendships not only in the eighteenth century but in the seventeenth century as well, and I came upon the genesis of the institution of European and American romantic friendship in the Renaissance.

These romantic friendships were love relationships in every sense except perhaps the genital, since women in centuries other than ours often internalized the view of females as having little sexual passion. Thus they might kiss, fondle each other, sleep together, utter expressions of overwhelming love and promises of eternal faithfulness, and yet see their passions as nothing more than effusions of the spirit. If they were sexually aroused, bearing no burden of visible proof as men do, they might deny it even to themselves if they wished. But whether or not these relationships had a genital component, the novels and diaries and correspondence of these periods consistently showed romantic friends opening their souls to each other and speaking a language that was in no way different from the language of heterosexual love: They pledged to remain "faithful" forever, to be in "each other's thoughts constantly," to live together and even to die together.

What surprised me most about these romantic friendships was that society appeared to condone them rather than to view them as disruptive of the social structure. I needed to find what it was that made such relationships, which have certainly been seen as threatening in our day, seem nonthreatening in other eras. I discovered that not all female same-sex relationships were condoned.

Transvestite women (i.e., those who dressed and often attempted to pass as men) who engaged in same-sex love were often persecuted and sometimes even executed. Why was a woman's choice of dress such a weighty factor in determining whether men would praise her love for another woman as being noble and beautiful or flog her for it?

An obvious answer was that if a woman dressed like a man, it was assumed that she behaved as a man sexually. If she dressed in clothes suitable to her sex, it might be assumed that she was not sexually aggressive, and two unaggressive females together would do nothing to violate men's presumptive property rights to women's bodies. But I found that the answer was in fact more complex: There were in several eras and places many instances of women who were known to engage in lesbian sex, and they did so with impunity. As long as they appeared feminine, their sexual behavior would be viewed as an activity in which women indulged when men were unavailable or as an apprenticeship or appetite-whetter to heterosexual sex. But if one or both of the pair demanded masculine privileges, the illusion of lesbianism as *faute de mieux* behavior was destroyed. At the base it was not the sexual aspect of lesbianism as much as the attempted usurpation of male prerogative by women who behaved like men that many societies appeared to find most disturbing.

It seemed to me, however, that most of the female romantic friends that I was studying probably did not have sexual relationships. Was that then the primary difference between romantic friendship and lesbian love? The definition of lesbianism became somewhat confused for me when I discovered that many of the lesbian cases cited by the early sexologists such as Havelock Ellis and Sigmund Freud (who were among the first to offer modern definitions of the term) were of Victorian and post-Victorian women whose love relationships were nongenital. If lesbianism was not a specifically sexual phenomenon to them, what was it? It appeared in many respects no different from the romantic friendships I had come across in earlier eras. Even the sexologists' evidence seemed to suggest that homo*sexuality* was generally no more appropriate a term to describe lesbianism than it was to describe romantic friendship. It became clear that women's love relationships have seldom been limited to that one area of expression, that love between women has been primarily a sexual phenomenon only in male fantasy literature. "Lesbian" describes a relationship in which two women's strongest emotions and affections are directed toward each other. Sexual contact may be a part of the relationship to a greater or lesser degree, or it may be entirely absent. By preference the two women spend most of their time together and share most aspects of their lives with each other. "Romantic friendship" described a similar relationship.

In discussing this notion with colleagues, I found that some of them, in our post-sexual-revolution day, had difficulty accepting my insistence that most female love relationships before the twentieth century were probably not genital, while others believed that those relationships were not genital, but could not accept the idea that they were nevertheless serious, that the women's professions of commitment to each other were real and not simply another example of sentimental excessiveness. Their difficulty, it appeared to me, had to do with their assumption that what is true of behavior and attitudes today has been true at all times.

But sexual patterns in general have altered tremendously over the centuries, and it could be demonstrated that people in Europe and the United States have probably become more sexual than they were in former times.[1] Even in our century it is apparent that great changes have occurred, particularly with regard to female sexual expression. For example, we can infer that in the nineteenth century, middle-class urban women seldom had sexual intercourse outside of wedlock from the information that among the 339 "illegitimate" mothers whose occupations were known in several London parishes during the 1850's, only three were "gentlewomen." Most were domestic servants. It was not until the beginning of this century that premarital sex became a significant reality in the lives of middle-class women who, with their increasing independence, began to see themselves as "like" (i.e., equal to) men, and therefore capable of sexual enjoyment, and having the right to that pleasure. Attitudes and experiences continued to change in more recent times. In the 1950's, when Alfred Kinsey was studying sexual behavior among unmarried women, only 20 percent of those he interviewed had had intercourse by the age of nineteen. In 1971 the number in a comparable sample had risen to almost 50 percent.[2] In 1969, 68 percent of Americans believed "it is wrong for people to have sexual relations before marriage." Four years later, in 1973, the number fell to 48 percent.[3] It is more difficult to trace sexual patterns of love between women, since lesbian sex leaves no evidence in "illegitimate" offspring, and there have been few surveys which deal with women's views of lesbian sexuality. But it might be assumed that female homosexual relationships followed a pattern similar to that of heterosexual relationships. Therefore, while there is abundant evidence of love between women in the diaries, correspondence, and fiction of other centuries, there are not many hints of sexual expression of that love.

My studies also led me to conclude that it is in our century that love has come to be perceived as a refinement of the sexual impulse, but in many other centuries romantic love and sexual impulse were often considered unrelated.[4] Certainly the degree of sexual expression among romantic friends must have varied, just as it does among women who are avowedly lesbian today. However, it is likely that most love relationships between women during previous eras, when females were encouraged to force any sexual drive they might have to remain latent, were less physical than they are in our times. But the lack of overt sexual expression in these romantic friendships could not discount the seriousness or the intensity of the women's passions toward each other—or the fact that if by "lesbian" we mean an all-consuming emotional relationship in which two women are devoted to each other above anyone else, these ubiquitous sixteenth-, seventeenth-, eighteenth-, and nineteenth-century romantic friendships were "lesbian."

But this conclusion presented me again with a major question: If these romantic friendships were in the quality and intensity of the emotions involved no different from lesbian love, why were they so readily condoned in earlier eras and persecuted in ours? Why were they considered normal then and abnormal now? From my work on Emily Dickinson, especially in observing how Martha Dickinson Bianchi, her niece, had bowdlerized Emily's *unselfconscious* love letters to Sue Gilbert when she prepared them for publication in the 1920's, I realized that society's view of love between women must have changed drastically in the sixty or seventy years before their publication. But to what were those changes due and exactly how were they manifested? Obviously the status of women had altered significantly during those years in the countries with which I was concerned. But why should that have effected a change in the permissibility of love between women? I recognized that the late nineteenth- and early twentieth-century sexologists who defined such love as a medical problem had something to do with the new views regarding these relationships. But why did they suddenly emerge at that particular time, and why were their pronouncements accepted so readily when fifty years earlier they would most likely have been excoriated and then ignored?

As I continued to look for romantic friendship in twentieth-century life and literature, I saw that openly expressed love between women for the most part ceased to be possible after World War I. Women's changed status and the new "medical knowledge" cast such affection in a new light. I discovered abundant evidence of female same-sex love, of course, but it was almost invariably accompanied by a new outlaw status. I was then led to investigate how that outlaw status affected the women who continued to love women despite twentieth-century societal taboos. I found that not only did twentieth-century lesbian literature by heterosexuals usually show love between women to be a disease, but that women who were professedly lesbian generally internalized those views. This was reflected in their own literature, which was full of self-doubts and self-loathing until the 1960's.

The 1960's ushered in both the sexual revolution and the new feminist movement. But why should those two movements have changed the attitudes regarding love between women? I found a contemporary analog to libertine society, which condoned rather than condemned lesbian sex because it made women sexier, in the swingers' parties where lesbian sex was encouraged as a "turn-on" for both men and women. But, more significantly, in lesbian-feminism I found a contemporary analog to romantic friendship in which two women were everything to each other and had little connection with men who were so alienatingly and totally different. It seemed to me that in a sense female same-sex love had come full circle. Of course, I discovered differences between romantic friendship and lesbian love, but the major difference had much less to do with overt sexual expression than with women's greater independence in the twentieth century: Now a woman can hope to carry on a love relationship with another woman for life. It can become her primary relationship, as it seldom could have with romantic friends of the past for economic reasons if no other. Because that appears to be the only distinction of importance between the two, I venture to guess that had the romantic friends of other eras lived today, many of them would have been lesbian-feminists; and had the lesbian-feminists of our day lived in other eras, most of them would have been romantic friends.

LILLIAN FADERMAN

July, 1980

PART I

THE SIXTEENTH THROUGH EIGHTEENTH CENTURIES

A.
Lesbianism in a Phallocentric Universe

CHAPTER 1

Lesbianism and the Libertines

In a sixteenth-century French work by Pierre de Bourdeille, Seigneur de Brantôme (1540–1614), entitled *Lives of Fair and Gallant Ladies,* which deals primarily with the amorous exploits of the females of the court of Henri II, the author includes a lengthy section on lovemaking between women. He tells of having gone with a group of ladies and their lovers to a gallery of the Comte de Chasteau-Villain where they saw many beautiful paintings. Among them was one that portrayed "a number of fair ladies naked and at the bath, which did touch, and feel, and handle, and stroke, one the other, and intertwine and fondle with each other, and so enticingly and prettily and featly did show all their hidden beauties." The painting was so sexually stimulating to a certain great lady of the group that, according to Brantôme, she lost all restraint of herself and, "maddened as it were at the madness of love," demanded that her lover take her home immediately, "for that no more can I hold in the ardour that is in me. Needs must away and quench it: too sore do I burn." Brantôme ends this section without any hint that he (or his readers) would find it unusual that a woman could be sexually aroused by a picture of other women fondling each other. He says only, "And so she did haste away to enjoy her faithful lover." [1]

In Brantôme's view women are usually ready to be sexual playmates—which is always delightful if you are a lover, but worrisome if you are a husband. Brantôme displays his and his society's ambivalence toward women's venereal appetite by describing all their sexual exploits with great excitement and gusto, but repeatedly call-

23

ing women who engage in illicit heterosexual relations whores. Although he appears seldom aware of the reason for this ambivalence, it seems to come down to the question of legitimacy, which for the upper classes at that time involved the issue of inheritance. A woman who cuckolded her husband could try to pass off as his a son conceived with her lover, a son who could make false claim to the husband's property. The fear of cuckoldry and men's apparent pleasure in giving other men horns was a virtual obsession in the sixteenth-century French court of Henri II and for centuries to follow.

Since *donna con donna* (Brantôme's words for lesbian lovemaking) cannot result in illegitimacy, there are many husbands, Brantôme claims, who "were right glad their wives did follow after this sort of affection rather than that of men, deeming them to be thus less wild." [2] In the next breath, however, he assures those men who are not husbands but who wish to cuckold that women who are permitted to indulge in *donna con donna* are not lost to them forever. Even Sappho herself, the mistress of them all, ended by loving young Phaon, for whose sake she died. To many women, Brantôme says, lesbianism is only an apprenticeship to sex with men. To others, it serves when men are not available and becomes uninteresting once they are. Most women who make love with other women will "if they but find a chance and opportunity free from scandal . . . straight quit their comrades and go throw their arms around some good man's neck." [3]

Donna con donna is also harmless because it does not involve penetration by a penis or insemination—"there is a great difference betwixt throwing water in a vessel and merely watering about it and round the rim," Brantôme quotes defenders of lesbianism as saying.[4] He believes that widows and unmarried women especially may be excused "for loving these frivolous and empty pleasures, preferring to devote themselves to these than to go with men and come to dishonour," by which he presumably means to find oneself with an illegitimate child.

The libertine poets of sixteenth- and early seventeenth-century France mirror Brantôme's attitudes. Sonnet XXXIII of Denis Sanguin de Saint-Pavin (1595–1670) describes, in terms borrowed from heterosexuality, two beautiful women loving each other, each trying desperately to satisfy the other: "Sometimes the lover is the mistress,/ Sometimes the mistress is the lover." Saint-Pavin calls them "These Innocents who deceive themselves,/ Searching in vain, in their loves,/ The pleasures which they refuse us." There is a tacit understanding that the women will soon escape from their frustrations to the arms of men, where they will finally find real sexual pleasure.[5]

"Elegy for a Woman Who Loves Another Woman" by Pontus de Tyard (1521?–1605) also emphasizes the frustration of lesbian love. The poem begins with the female speaker's discourse on how she wishes it were possible to join both beauty and honor in love. She had rejected the love of men because of her high ideals:

> I know our century too well:
> Men love beauty and laugh at honor.
> The more beauty pleases them, the more honor is lost.

But Cupid has ironically punished her disdain of heterosexual lust by forcing her to love another woman unrequitedly. In the beloved's hair he has tied an invisible ribbon which pulls the speaker to her; he enflames the speaker, and then he makes the beloved shun her after briefly encouraging her. Pontus de Tyard shares with Brantôme the attitude that love between two women cannot last long. One or the other woman will soon tire of it—and perhaps for that reason it need not be viewed with alarm by men.

But while de Tyard sees lesbian love as ephemeral and makes it clear that one cannot safely scoff at Cupid and heterosexual lust, he portrays the speaker as being poignantly if quixotically heroic. She had hoped with her beloved to ennoble love between women as Damon and Pythias, Hercules and Nestor, Aeneas and Achates once ennobled male love.[6] She is doomed to failure, but the writer hints at a secret admiration for her, not unlike the touch of admiration we see in Brantôme when he compares male and female homosexuals and declares: " 'Tis much better for a woman to be masculine and a very Amazon and lewd after this fashion, than for a man to be feminine, like Sardanapalus or Heliogabalus, and many another of their fellows in sin. For the more manlike she is, the braver she is." [7]

There were occasional poems during the late sixteenth and early seventeenth centuries which poked fun at lesbian love, such as "Tribades seu Lesbia" by François Mainard (1582–1646), in which the writer tells "Beautiful Phyllis" that if her finger knew how to urinate along with what else it knows it could pass for something unmentionable.[8] But there were no poems which matched the virulence regarding male homosexuality such as contained in "Against the Sodomites" by Mathurin Régnier (1573–1613), which he addresses to the "Rabid Sodomite, enemy of nature."[9] He depicts the sodomite engaged in what he views as the most shocking debauchery and antisocial behavior. Generally male writers looked at lesbian love with a compassion such as one might feel for a famished, whimpering creature, knowing it was in one's power to provide it with food and thus cure it of its sorrows.

Far and away, the most predominant attitude toward lesbian lovemaking in French libertine literature was that it was merely a prelude to heterosexual lovemaking. This was especially the case in literature that made no pretense at being anything but pornography, such as Nicolas Chorier's mid-seventeenth-century work, *Satyra Sotadica,* as well as writing which purported to be based on fact, such as Giacomo (Jacques) Casanova's *Memoirs.* Chorier presents this view in the most blatant terms: Two women discuss lesbian sex, act out their discussion, and having aroused each other they are joined by men who have sexual relations with them.

Jacques Casanova is a little more subtle in his eighteenth-century memoir, but he ends at the same goal. In Volume IV he is engaged to a young woman who has been put in a convent. He is also the lover of a nun in that convent, and he is happy to learn that the nun has initiated the young girl into the "mysteries of Sappho."[10] When Casanova meets the two women together he congratulates them on the "mutual inclination" they feel for each other, and is delighted to find himself a spectator to their lovemaking, "which made me laugh heartily." He says he would not have dreamed of troubling their sport, but instead excited them so that they would continue their display longer.[11] The women are content to share each other with Casanova, and he can only profit by their new sexual discoveries; but lest his young fiancée forget for a time what is really what, he gently reminds her (and the reader) that lesbian love cannot be taken seriously and will naturally bow before the claims of sex between a man and a woman: "Your mutual love is nothing but trifling nonsense—a mere illusion of the senses. The pleasures which you enjoy together are not exclusive . . . MM could no more be angry at your having a lover than you could be so yourself if she had one."[12]

The incident comes to a climax when the three find themselves in bed together. At first he is satisfied with "enjoying the sight of the barren contest of my two bacchanalians" and is amused by their efforts. But soon he becomes excited himself, "and consumed by the fire of voluptuousness, I threw myself upon them, and made them, one after the other, almost faint away from the excess of love and enjoyment."[13] Thus he assures his reader not only that he is superbly potent but also that lesbian sex is in no way threatening to men: It is a sterile game, the sight serves only as an aphrodisiac to the male spectator, and all the participants tacitly agree that the penis is the sine qua non of sexual pleasure.

There is little comparable erotic literature which includes lesbianism in sixteenth- and seventeenth-century England. What there is appears to have been borrowed from France, such as *A Dialogue Between a Married Lady and a Maid* (1688), which is primarily a translation of Chorier's *Satyra Sotadica*. For the most part, English writers seemed not to have been very aware of the possibility of sex without a penis. The educated, who were familiar with Sappho's love poetry, and were willing to recognize that both the speaker and the beloved of the poems were female, might have acknowledged that women of hot climes could invent all manner of lechery, but many would have doubted that Englishwomen were so inclined.

Even eighteenth-century medical manuals which deal with sexual problems generally do not admit lesbianism to their categories of abuses. In *The Ladies' Dispensatory; or Every Woman her Own Physician* (1740), a chapter on the horrors of self-abuse groups lesbianism with masturbation. The author seems to view it as a form of that problem, but does not single it out for special concern. He gives six detailed case histories of female masturbators and the effects their habits had on them: itching all over the body, numbness of the hands, frigidity, distension of the clitoris, racking pain in the back, fits, vomiting, nymphomania, infertility, and death. However, in one case a girl had been "taught the sin" of *masturbation* "by her Mother's Chambermaid, with whom she continued to practise it seven Years, they trying all Means to pleasure each other, and heighten the titillation." As a result of her activity her clitoris became enlarged, which the author sees as being a common effect of masturbation. She suffered none of the other horrors mentioned in the other cases, and that she had a partner in her sexual experiments was evidently considered not significant enough to comment on at length.[14] It seems never to have occurred to this author that such mutual masturbation was "lesbianism."

The most extensive discussion of lesbianism in eighteenth-century English literature appeared in 1749 in John Cleland's *Memoirs of a Woman of Pleasure* (*Fanny Hill*). Unlike Brantôme and Casanova, Cleland did not seriously claim to write about living people. His purpose was more patently to arouse than to record. He focused on the world of prostitution, which he depicted, in keeping with the pornographic genre, as being generally amoral (although Fanny's values ultimately become those of the great bourgeois world). Nevertheless, his view of lesbianism is the same as that in earlier French works: It is lightly regarded as an initiation into heterosexual intercourse. Phoebe, whose job it is to "break young girls" to the ways of the whorehouse, introduces Fanny to genital stimulation—but she reminds the girl (and the reader) that there is everything lacking in this act since the penis is lacking. "What a happy man will he be that first makes a woman of you!" Phoebe says. "Oh! that I were a man for your sake." After Phoebe exerts her talents Fanny recognizes that her appetite is whetted but of course cannot be satisfied in this situation. Fanny exclaims, "I now pin'd for more solid food, and promised tacitly to myself that I would not be put off much longer with this foolery from woman to woman." Phoebe's main sexual technique with Fanny is digital-vaginal stimulation—Cleland, with all his knowledge of sexual lowlife, seems to have had little idea of the role the clitoris played in female sexual response—but her fingers are not long enough to effect her partner's orgasm or to rupture the hymen. Thus Cleland suggests that what women can do together neither satisfies them nor robs them of the precious sign of their virginity. Men have no reason to regard lesbian lovemaking with anything other than amused tolerance.

How little women can do for or to each other is emphasized by Fanny's initial consummated heterosexual experience (appropriately enough in this pornographic romance, with the man who finally becomes her husband), which Fanny characterizes as "my ruin"—not of course because it has been her introduction to sex but because her hymen was ruptured. Since Cleland assumed women could not effect that rupture on each other, whatever they did together was not significant enough to constitute their "ruin" any more than it was efficacious enough to make them love each other.

Lesbian sex was not seen in such cavalier terms if it took on political overtones; that is, if it was engaged in by autonomous women, not for male delectation or *faute de mieux*, but as an expression of female independence. If women who appeared not to kick against the traces too much were found to engage in lesbian sex, in those times and places in which sexual expression was relatively open, such as the French court of Henri II, men were not especially disturbed. Men enjoyed a phallocentric confidence which ceased to be possible in the twentieth century. They could not believe that they were unnecessary to women in any way. First of all, it was universally acknowledged that women had to form bonds with men in order to survive. The claims of love between women could be seen as very slight in view of the overwhelming importance of the heterosexual bond. Secondly, in men's phallocentric world it was inconceivable that a woman's sexual pleasure could be significant if the male were absent.

If during these centuries a transvestite was caught in a lesbian sex act, however, men would neither smirk nor wink, since it would be one more infuriating indication that she rejected her prescribed role. But a woman who initiated lesbian sex, yet seemed otherwise not to demand male prerogatives, was generally met with no more than ambivalence—if her behavior was noticed at all. Perhaps lesbian sexuality was treated more tolerantly than male homosexuality because while male homosexuality meant a man might assume feminine behavior, which is inherently dispicable, female homosexuality meant that a woman might assume masculinity, which is inherently fine, as Brantôme suggested. As long as a women did not take her assumed masculinity too seriously, as long as she did not believe that it entitled her to any male social privileges, men must admire it somewhat, just as the Greek warriors were said to have admired the Amazons they defeated.

In twentieth-century pornography which deals with lesbian sex, frequently at least one of the females, generally the older woman, who is usually the aggressor, is criticized, either explicitly or implicitly, for her lesbianism. Her punishment, in fact, has often supplied the "redeeming social value" of the work. While there are some notable exceptions which will be considered, in the erotic literature of the sixteenth through eighteenth centuries, lesbianism is usually seen to function in an amoral universe. The women who indulge in lesbian sex are no more culpable than the other characters. Perhaps the difference in treatment may be accounted for in the measure in which women were and are taken seriously as independent or potentially independent human beings. Unlike in our century, it was seldom believed in earlier eras that non-procreative sexual behavior might carry over to autonomous social behavior, unless a woman flamboyantly demonstrated the connection, by transvestism for example.

CHAPTER 2

What Do Women Do?

If any women wrote lesbian sex literature during the sixteenth to eighteenth centuries, it has been lost to posterity. Had such literature existed, the descriptions of lesbian lovemaking would certainly have been different from the ones that are extant. Male writers who took it upon themselves to describe lesbian sexual activity in detail were ostensibly unable to conceive of any technique outside of what has come to be called the "missionary position" and vaginal penetration by some object. Regardless of the era or country, depictions of lesbian sexual techniques, based largely on male writers' knowledge of heterosexual lovemaking, shared the same unimaginative inaccuracies. Men could not absent themselves from their visions of any female sexual activity: If a man were not present in fact, one of those who was present must simulate him.

Brantôme says that there there are two ways to perform "*ces amours feminines*," and both copy conventional heterosexuality. One way is an imitation of the missionary position: "tribadism," or genital rubbing, with one woman atop another. The other method, to which he devotes more attention perhaps because it approximates heterosexual activity even more closely, involves the use of a dildo or *godemiche*, an artificial object shaped like a phallus with which one woman penetrates another.[1] Although Brantôme was not otherwise bothered by the *idea* of lesbianism, penetration by a dildo seems to have been disturbing to him, as it was to theological lawmakers during this period, possibly because in their minds it threatened to make the male superfluous, while tribadism was merely a child's imitation of an adult's game. Brantôme thus warns

31

that while lesbian sex "by rubbing . . . does not cause damage," the use of the dildo is dangerous, and he has known of women who have been injured by this method—those injuries he describes in some detail.

English literature contemporaneous with Brantôme does not demonstrate any more perception about the nature of lovemaking between women. In Book II of Sir Philip Sidney's *Arcadia* (c. 1580), a young man disguises himself as the Amazon Zelmane, and is thereby permitted friendly intimacy with Philoclea, daughter of the king, who does not know that Zelmane is a man. Philoclea falls in love with the Amazon, but is anguished since she cannot understand what her feeling for another woman means. At first she wishes they might live together all their lives, "like two of Dianas Nimphes," but she fears that other nymphs would join them and want to share Zelmane with her. Then she wishes that Zelmane were her sister because that natural bond might make her more special to "her," but if the Amazon happened to marry, even then she would lose "her." Finally she realizes that she and her beloved could live together forever without interference only if one of them were turned into a man. Believing the Amazon (and of course herself) to be immutably female, however, she laments not only that she will be unable to spend her life with Zelmane, but also that there is no way two women can sexually consummate their love:

> . . . it is the impossibilities that dooth torment me: for, unlawfull desires are punished after the effect of enjoying; but unpossible desires are punished in the desire itself. . . . The most covetous man longs not to get riches out of a ground which never can beare anything; Why? because it is impossible. The most ambitious wight vexeth not his wittes to clime into heaven; Why? because it is impossible. Alas then, O Love, why doost thou in thy beautiful sampler sette such a worke for my Desire to take out, which is as much impossible?[2]

Yet because love without a penis was an impossibility to sixteenth-century England, women were allowed to demonstrate the most sensual behavior toward one another without suffering the stigma associated with such behavior in more recent times. The chapter which follows Philoclea's lament contains an example of the kind of sensual expression that was possible. Philoclea and her sister Pamela are both frustrated in their loves. They decide to talk their sorrows out to each other, and, in order to "talk better" they lie down in bed together, but first:

> they impoverished their cloathes to inriche their bed, which for that night might well scorne the shrine of Venus; and there cherishing one another with deare, though chaste embracements; with sweet, though cold kisses; it might seeme that Love was come to play him there without darte; or that weerie of his own fires, he was there to refreshe himselfe betweene their sweet-breathing lippes.

The two women have taken off their clothes, they are in bed, they kiss, they embrace; Cupid, though arrowless (is Sidney using the missing dart to symbolize the phallus which is absent?), seems to be in the room with them, his presence is somehow connected to their tender kisses. Modern scholars have been at a loss as to how to read this scene. Iwan Bloch identifies it as "one of the earliest references to homosexual relations between women." [3] Jeannette Foster observes, as Bloch does not, that the two women were sisters (which she acknowledges would not invalidate his claim), but also that Bloch misread the "shrine of Venus" line, interpreting it to mean that they made elaborate preparation for a night of love. As Foster rightly points out, the line means simply "they released their own loveliness from their garments and laid themselves on the bed which was thus more 'inriched' than a shrine bearing an image of Venus herself." [4] Bloch's reading, furthermore, is inconsistent with the scene that precedes this one. Philoclea and Pamela cannot engage in homo*sexual* relations in Sidney's world because, as Philoclea has already told us, they do not exist. Love without a penis is counted among the impossibilities.

Something erotic, however, is definitely suggested in this scene. But in earlier centuries a relationship such as the one between Pamela and Philoclea, because it did not involve genital stimulation, would not have been considered sexual. A scene of this nature in a twentieth-century context would at least suggest the "lesbian tendencies" of the two women. It seems then that a narrower interpretation of what constitutes eroticism permitted a broader expression of erotic behavior since it was not considered inconsistent with virtue.

In later centuries as well, popular English notions regarding lesbian sexual possibilities (or impossibilities) appear to retain a phallocentric bias: Without a proper tool the job cannot be done. For example, Robert James's *Medicinal Dictionary* (1745), deals with lesbian sex under the entry "tribadism"—which, he implies, is the only erotic technique available to two women. But how do both women receive satisfaction by this method? James is forthcoming with an answer: In some women the clitoris "becomes so far prominent," he explains, that "they make Attempts to converse in a criminal manner with other women," rubbing their partners with their large clitorises, and thereby receiving as well as giving satisfaction.[5]

Obviously some male writers must have been informed by certain bold women that female sexual gratification was possible outside of the missionary position, but that knowledge is seldom revealed in literature about lesbian sex. In *Memoirs of a Woman of Pleasure* (*Fanny Hill*) John Cleland intimates that he knows about cunnilingus, but he does not suggest that the act can occur between two women as well as between a man and a woman, or that it can be carried to the point of orgasm.[6] Samuel Tissot, an eighteenth-century Swiss doctor whose work *Onania: A Treatise Upon the Disorders Produced by Masturbation* (1758) was translated into English in 1766, is one of the few writers who recognize the possibility of manual clitoral stimulation in lesbian sex. That act, he says, is even worse than masturbation because it sometimes causes "women to love other women with as much fondness and jealousy as they did men." [7] But other eighteenth-century writers seem to have placed this activity under the category of "masturbation" rather than lesbian sexual activity.[8]

Some English writers preferred, like Lucian in his *Dialogues of the Courtesans* (see p. 149), to leave out the details. Apparently they knew enough to reject the notion of a heterosexual model, but they claimed to believe that lesbianism involved esoteric mysteries, that it was a lost art, known only to women in ancient times, as Philip Massinger had the nymphomaniacal Corsica complain in his 1623 play, *The Bondman*:

> *Fie on these warres,*
> *I am starv'd for want of action, not a gamester left*
> *To keepe a woman play; if this world last*
> *A little longer with us, Ladyes must studie*
> *Some new found Mistery, to coole one another,*
> *Wee shall burn to Cinders else; I have heard there have been*
> *Such Arts in a long vacation; would they were*
> *Revealed to me.*[9]

Italy, which both France and England accused of exporting homo-sexuality to their countries,[10] was ostensibly no more knowledgeable about lesbian sex. A naïveté similar to that in Sir Philip Sidney's *Arcadia* with regard to the efficacy of love without a penis is revealed in sixteenth-century Italian literature. In Ludovico Ariosto's *Orlando Furioso* (1516), Book XXV, Fiordispina falls in love with Bradamant and laments the impossibility of her love. Bradamant, an Amazon warrior, dresses as a man, and after receiving a head wound, is shorn as a man. When Fiordispina declares her love, Bradamant quickly undeceives her by telling her there is a woman underneath the male garb. Like Philoclea, Fiordispina now grieves because she may "hope for no reliefe." [11] Fiordispina believes that her same-sex passion is unique in the history of the world:

> *Ah woe is me (she said) that I alone*
> *Should live in such despaire to be relieved.*
> *In passed times I think there hath been none,*
> *In time to come it will not be believed,*
> *That love should make by such a strong infection*
> *One woman beare another such affection.*[12]

She compares her love to other unorthodox loves: Nynus wished to copulate with her son, Myrrha was impregnated by her father, Pasyphae lusted after a bull. Yet all these women, Fiordispina laments, were more fortunate than she: Their passions could be consummated since their beloveds all had penises, and not even Dedalus, with all his artifice, could help her consummate her love.

After a sleepless night beside Bradamant, Fiordispina's erotic thirst has not abated, nor has she been able to think of a way it might be quenched. Fiordispina concludes that her only hope is in fervent prayer for some miracle that would "her bedfellow turne to a better sex." Her prayer is satisfactorily answered when Bradamant leaves and Richardet, Bradamant's brother who looks exactly like her, returns and pretends to be Bradamant now changed by a nymph whom she/he saved from a satyr. Fiordispina's passion can finally be gratified.

Male confusion about lesbian sex reached a peak at the beginning of the eighteenth century in Italy, when Lodovico Maria Sinistrari, a Franciscan who attempted to codify appropriate punishments for sodomy in *Peccatum Mutum* (1700), undertook to enlighten the clergy regarding sexual practices between women. Sinistrari observes that although moralists who treat of "this filthy vice" declare that "real Sodomy is committed between [women]," yet he has seen no one offer a credible explanation "as to how this takes place." Sinistrari ventures his own guesses. He rejects the assertion of other theologians that "if a woman gets upon a woman, and both fall to thrusting at each other mutually, it may happen that the seed of her on top may be injected into the natural vase of her laying under." Those theologians believe that "thus Sodomy is performed; but should the seed be not received into that vase, it is only pollution." Sinistrari takes issue with their argument, insisting, naturally with great seriousness, that sodomy cannot be performed that way because "woman's seed cannot be injected." [13]

He then quotes still other theologians who have distinguished between women who when they couple together merely rub each other and those who insert some material tool, for example of wood or glass. To these lawmakers, penetration was the essential act of venereal congress—without penetration there was no crime. If one woman penetrated another with a dildo, they were both to be put to death, as in the case of two nuns cited by Clarus. [14] But Sinistrari questions this definition of female sodomy too, since such a sexual act would leave one partner unsatisfied.

Finally he offers a definition of his own which explains how both women receive gratification: In some women the clitoris is very large. Those women can even sodomize a man, and some of them prefer to "run after women, and especially girls." Galen and Coelius corroborate this, Sinistrari says, by stating that the ancient Egyptians "cut off this bit of flesh in all virgins, that it may not grow out and thus enable them to conjoin with other women." Female sodomy consists only of a woman penetrating another with her clitoris. Any other act is "pollution," and "if pollution [the Confessor] can absolve them; if Sodomy he cannot." If a woman is accused of penetrating another with her clitoris, her body is to be inspected by a jury of matrons, and if her clitoris is sufficiently large and it is known that she lay with another woman, "there is a presumption that they made use of it for the heinous delinquency: just as it is legally presumed from a man's sleeping with a woman, that they have fornicated." The woman and her partner are to be tortured on the rack, and if it is discovered then that one did indeed penetrate the other, both are to be punished with death and burnt. [15] Of course, it is unlikely that many women were tortured or executed under laws based on Sinistrari's definition of a criminal lesbian act.

In our Masters and Johnson era it may be difficult to believe that such naïveté could have existed concerning the varied possibilities of sexual expression. But in earlier eras, when only men wrote about sex and women either did not tell men about their own feelings or were ignored, such an innocence should not be surprising. Even in more sexually sophisticated circles, such as the sixteenth-century French court, love between women was never described from a convincing female perspective. It was usually seen to be an imitation of heterosexual intercourse, and the closer it approximated intercourse, the more significant it became.

Most writers who attempted to deal with lesbianism regarded it primarily as a sexual act and were unwilling to give it the dimensions they might attribute to a serious male-female love relationship: admiration, concern for the beloved's welfare, tenderness, total involvement in the beloved's life. Their societies offered countless examples of love between women which had these characteristics, but unless that love clearly had a genital component, it was not lesbian—even if the two women indulged in all other manner of mutual sensual stimulation. Women themselves would probably never have arrived at a definition of lesbian love which was fixed only on the genitals any more than at a definition of lesbian sex which was fixed on penetration either through an artificial phallus or hermaphroditic miracles.[16]

CHAPTER 3

Eighteenth-Century Fantasy and the Lesbian Image

Not until Mathieu François Mairobert's *L'Espion Anglois* (1777–1778) was the subject of lesbian sex treated in extensive detail ranging over a hundred pages.[1] Mairobert's presentation is a prototype for pornographic literature focusing on sex between women: The principal women—one in her late twenties, the other a teenager—are both extremely beautiful; they have sex in a lavish setting with all manner of servants and devices at their disposal; bizarre practices such as flagellation are central to their lovemaking; jealousy is the primary emotion between the women; and a man finally wins the younger woman away from her older corrupter. Two hundred years later, these elements, or some modification of them, continue to be the main trappings of male conceived lesbian pornography.

Not only did Mairobert establish a pattern for a genre of pornography, but he also "created" lesbian history. It is difficult to understand how anyone reading Mairobert could confuse his wildly grotesque imaginings about lesbianism with fact. But several early twentieth-century writers did, and through them Mairobert's patently fanciful discussion of late eighteenth-century French lesbianism came to be taken as truth by many of our contemporary French historians.[2]

The narrator of the lesbian section of *L'Espion Anglois* is a young girl, Sapho, who had always had an obsession with sexual stimulation. When her mother catches her masturbating, she runs away to what she believes to be a convent but is actually a resort for whores. The madam soon takes Sapho to her house in Paris, where she discovers that Sapho "has a diabolical clitoris," and decides "she will be better for the women than the men." She rejoices because "our famous tribades" will pay the girl's weight in gold: Mairobert's concept of lesbian sex seems to have been like that of Robert James in his 1745 *Medicinal Dictionary*, that the active partner stimulated the passive one with her large clitoris. Madame Gourdan (who was an actual procuress of the period), having made her discovery, then writes to one of her customers, a wealthy, independent woman, Mme. de Furiel: "I have discovered for you a morsel fit for a king, or rather a queen, if one can be found that has your depraved taste." Sapho is then dressed in "a frock made in the style of the tribade costume; that is, open in the front and in the back from the belt to the stocking."

The rest of the work attempts to arouse the reader in the same far-fetched ways. Madame de Furiel, who is extremely beautiful, entertains Sapho in a lavish mansion, in which everything is intended to stimulate the senses, and there Sapho enjoys her first lesbian experience. After this initial sex scene we are told that in Furiel's home there is a temple of Vesta, "regarded as the founder of the Androgyne sect," where lesbians worship and have orgies after they have passed the initiation rite. This rite consists of an applicant being put in a room filled with various graphic examples of heterosexual erotic art and a lifelike statue of Priapus. At the foot of the statue is a lighly burning fire, which the applicant must tend. If she is distracted by these visions of heterosexuality for one instant, the flame will go out. She must endure this test for three hours over a period of three days.

Following the initiation rite, which Sapho passes, she attends a gorgeous banquet, after which a mass lesbian orgy is held. A medallion is given to the couple who can continue having sex the longest (Mairobert betrays here what is a distinctly and exclusively male sexual anxiety) and Sapho and Furiel are the winners. The orgy scene is followed by a proclamation from the actress Raucourt, the "president" of the lesbian club, which is entitled "Justification of the Androgyne Sect." This speech has been considered by modern scholars to be a serious essay by an eighteenth-century lesbian. Raucourt is made to observe reverently, for example, "The priesthood [of the androgyne] is perpetuated in our female monasteries of modern Europe, an emanation of the College of the Vestals" and "This expansive enthusiasm for the propagation of the cult of the goddess ought chiefly to devour a true tribade; she ought to wish that all her sex, if it were possible, would participate in the same happiness that she does." Raucourt's proclamation derives obviously much more from Mairobert's anti-Catholicism and ambivalent anxiety about lesbian proselytizing than from real life. The lesbian section of *L'Espion Anglois* ends when Sapho runs off with a man, is deserted by him, and finally takes a job with a madam who specializes in supplying whores to Catholic priests.

The literary connection between lesbianism and flagellation may have stemmed from *L'Espion Anglois,* since flagellation is such a central part of lesbian lovemaking here. In *Flagellation and the Jesuit Confessional* (1834), the author, Frusta, remarks that in Paris during the Revolution several lesbian flagellant associations had been discovered in which Sappho was honored as a protective goddess. His description of those "associations" borrows so heavily from the lesbian orgy scene in *L'Espion Anglois* that one suspects it was his main source. Frusta states that in these orgies Sappho's picture "adorned the altar in the hall where everything was calculated to make sense and fantasy reel. The orgies opened with flagellation and ended in the most shameful of sexual perversions. Deep hatred against men was the first principle." [3]

The vision of soft flesh striped with whip welts and of dominant females safely captured in the imagination that was elaborated in *L'Espion Anglois* apparently had widespread appeal to heterosexual males.[4] The English *Bon Ton Magazine* for December 1792 ran an article on a "female whipping club" which supposedly assembled in London's Jermyn Street every Thursday evening. There, the writer asserts, the ladies took turns whipping each other and otherwise mutually stimulating their pudenda. Despite these "factual" details of the time and place of the meeting, the language in which the activities are described places the club in the same realm of erotic male fantasy that Mairobert inhabited:

> Sometimes the operation is begun a little above the garter, and ascending the pearly inverted cone, is carried by degrees to the dimpled promontories, which are vulgarly called buttocks; until the whole, as Shakespear says, from a milky white, "Becomes one red"!! [sic] [5]

Mairobert's intentions in writing his extremely influential lesbian scene in *L'Espion Anglois* seem rather transparent. He was concerned principally with titillation: Just as a lesbian sex scene is almost compulsory in pornographic entertainment today, he made it so in his day. All the women in his lesbian episode are extremely beautiful and feminine in appearance, as are their counterparts in modern pornography, never unexceptional looking or masculine. But despite the beauty of the lesbians, they do not have the power to hold a young woman who will, in Brantôme's words two centuries earlier, at the first opportunity, "straight quit [her] comrades and go throw [her] arms around some good man's neck." The titillation which the male voyeur derives from the prospect of lesbian sex seems generally to be prodded by some anxiety that the women are lost to him—but the pornographer knows finally to alleviate that anxiety by assuring his reader that all Sapphos are ultimately conquered by Phaons, and thus creates "a happy ending," not necessarily for his female character, but for his male reader.

Mairobert's second intention seems to have been to shame specific independent women who did not fit his notion of womanliness. The lesbian characters in L'Espion Anglois were based largely on actual personages of the period—or rather they were fantastic caricatures of them—such as the actresses Raucourt and Souck, and Madame de Fleury, a leading social personality. Mairobert often used real names, particularly when the women had no great clout, or could not, because of their "immoral" professions as actresses,[6] conduct successful libel suits. Women who were titled or who were married to influential men appeared under thinly veiled names which members of their social sphere would have had no trouble recognizing. Madame de Furiel, for example, was Mme. de Fleury in real life,[7] but Mairobert's slight alteration was enough to protect him from charges of libel. These women wielded no great power, but neither were they content to lead retiring, secondary lives. Mairobert's disapproval of such women and his method of insulting them for their relatively atypical independence and aspirations were not of course peculiar to him or even to the eighteenth century. The charge of lesbianism has often been an important strategy for keeping restive women in check.

In The Toast (1736), an erudite, heavily footnoted British satire by William King, the central character, Myra, is meant to represent a certain Lady Frances Brudenell who outsmarted King in a substantial financial dealing.[8] Myra, who has "masculine" cunning, must also have masculine sex drives, King implies. He shows that having already proved herself "an indefatigable servant in venereal rites and ceremonies," [9] Myra has now been gifted by Venus with a set of male sex organs. She is at once pansexual, hermaphroditic, and a tribade. She leads a life of unrestrained lasciviousness with both males and females, though her favorite is the jewess, Ali.[10] Like Mairobert, King pretends that his enemy's aggressiveness in the world is explainable by her unnatural sexual appetite. To insult Myra by attributing to her a voracious bisexual libido seemed to King a fitting way to placate his gall at her independence and cunning.

King also hoped by this maneuver to make her an outcast, particularly among other women. Since she has a penis, he warns, women would not associate with her unless they were interested in sexual intercourse. Any intimacy with her, he hints, is as dangerous to their reputations as intimacy with a man would be: If some women "still continue to converse with the Hermaphrodite, as if she was a perfect woman, I am fully persuaded that they are not insensible of her Virility."

The same maneuver had been used several decades earlier against one Miss Hobart, a maid of honor in the Restoration Court of Charles II. Miss Hobart, who possessed a sharp tongue, a bold air, and an abrasive temperament, made herself a number of enemies among the men at court and was soon satirized in ballads as being a hermaphrodite. Anthony Hamilton reported in a 1713 work that "upon the faith of these songs her companions began to fear her." Her simplest actions were subsequently interpreted as attempts to molest. After a trick played on her by the libertine Lord Rochester, the author of *Sodom*, who had designs on one of Miss Hobart's few remaining defenders, Miss Temple, it was even believed that Miss Hobart was guilty of impregnating a maid whom she had fired.[11]

Among the political pamphlets which helped ignite the French Revolution is a whole group of accusations focusing on Marie Antoinette's supposed tribadism and her aggressive sexuality.[12] While Marie Antoinette's sex life provides the focus of the attack and even of the bizarre humor in these pamphlets, as was the case with Lady Brudenell and Miss Hobart, the real issue is their authors' hostility to the queen's power, which exceeded, according to them, the limit of what any woman should possess, and with which she and her minions were bringing the nation to ruin.

These pamphlets began circulating in the early 1780's and continued even after the queen's execution. Like the English satire on Lady Brudenell, they combine titillating accounts of the victim's sexual dalliance with other grievances of a completely nonsexual nature. In one dated 1792, for example, entitled "List of all the persons with whom the Queen has had debauched liaisons," approximately three dozen individuals are named, about half men and half women, including "a clerk of the War Secretary, . . . a son of the footman of the Ventadour family, . . . and a daughter of an actor.[13] In another, called "Admonishment to the Queen," Marie Antoinette is warned, "Don't summon anymore the too-amiable Swede, Fersenne; don't go anymore to visit the too-seducing Madame Lamballe in Paris; dismiss the valets and the wardrobe girls who still arouse your passion." [14] In some pamphlets she engages in bisexual acrobatics at the same time that she plots political intrigues against France.

One of the most infamous treatments of lesbianism in eighteenth-century literature is Diderot's *The Nun*, begun in 1760. This novel has all the virulent anti-Catholicism one would expect from its Enlightenment author and is based on an actual *cause célèbre* of the time,[15] concerning a young woman who had been forced to enter a convent. Suzanne Simonin, the heroine of Diderot's novel, is compelled by her greedy mother to become a nun, and her dramatic experiences at several institutions gradually educate her to the awful variety of corruption in convent life. At the first convent she enters Suzanne is tortured by sadistical nuns. During her final sojourn in a cloister the innocent heroine becomes the victim of a tyrannical mother superior's lechery. The vicious and pathological lesbianism Diderot depicts in this novel is markedly different from the gallant and light-hearted lesbianism that occurs in earlier French and Italian works about the pleasures and vices of convent life.[16]

Modern critics are mistaken when they suggest that Diderot's picture of lesbianism in *The Nun* is clinically correct and sympathetic, and an accurate reflection of the social attitudes of his day.[17] Rather, it is extremely revealing of the author's personal animosities and of his hostility towards the idea that women could hold positions of authority. Diderot wrote *The Nun* at a time when he "was most darkly suspicious of the relations between his mistress, Sophie Volland, and her sister," Mme. le Gendre.[18] The amount of time the two women spent together, and also the possible influence Mme. le Gendre exercised on Sophie's opinion of him, troubled Diderot deeply and he expressed his ambivalence about the relationship in letters. For example, he petulantly complained to an acquaintance about one long visit between Sophie and her sister, "It's been a century since I've seen my friend. Pleasurable parties, intended for other's pleasure, visits, spectacles, walks, dinners given and received have robbed me for the fifteen days since her sister has arrived." At another time when the two women were together, he complained to Sophie:

> I am obsessed and do not know what I write . . . I see by your scrawled letter that Madame le Gendre is or will be with you incessantly. I have become so suspicious, so unjust, so jealous; you tell me that so much. You endure so impatiently when one mentions some fault, that—I don't dare finish. I am ashamed of what is happening in me, but I don't know how to stop it. Your mother claims that your sister likes amiable women, and it is certain that she likes you very much; and then that nun for whom she had such a passion and then that voluptuous and tender manner with which she sometimes bends toward you. And then her fingers strangely pressed between yours.
>   Adieu. I am mad; do you wish that I were not? [19]

Diderot's exceptionally lurid treatment of lesbianism in *The Nun,* then, was quite probably affected by his own neurotic fears about Sophie's attachment to another woman [20] who threatened his influence on her.

Apart from Diderot's "philosophique" harshness toward Catholicism and his personal anxieties about his mistress, there is still another explanation for the grotesque character of the lesbian Mother Superior in *The Nun*: Diderot's antifeminism. Although Diderot critics have observed that he loved women and they occupied a central place in his work and his correspondence,[21] he, like many a chivalrous gentleman, loved them only in their place. Diderot's favorite Molière play, significantly enough, was *Les Femmes Savantes,*[22] a satire against learned ladies and the men who permitted themselves to be ruled by women. In his essay, "Sur les femmes," Diderot reveals his view of woman as, to borrow Simone de Beauvoir's term, "the other." Women are not the complex human beings insusceptible to facile categorization that he would grant most men to be; instead they are either "beautiful like Klopstock's seraphs," or "terrible like Milton's devils." [23] Not only does he deny women human complexity, he also denies them adulthood: "O women," he cries, "you are such extraordinary children." [24] While he pays lip service in this essay to the need for better treatment of women, he also makes it clear that he considers them vain, hysterical, designing, helpless, and generally stupid.

While Diderot the Encyclopedist urged greater freedom and self-determination for man, he did not urge the same for woman. The idea of a society ruled entirely by them, the convent, was probably as distasteful to him for that reason as it was for more progressive political and philosophical reasons. In a convent, women were almost entirely self-sufficient, and the head of the community was another woman. A father confessor visited the nuns periodically, but as Diderot himself suggests in *The Nun*, the priest had no real authority over the Mother Superior. When Suzanne tells her that the confessor has warned against the older woman's caresses, the Mother Superior is neither shaken by the priest's knowledge of her lesbian advances nor awed by his authority. She urges the girl to come to bed with her anyway, saying: "I am the one who rewards and punishes around here." [25] That confessor is soon gotten rid of. The Mother Superior's system of justice and privilege is invariably based on her feminine irrationality and her constantly vacillating likes and dislikes. She uses her authority to obtain personal power and to buy sexual affection. The whole nunnery falls into chaos because of her misrule. To Diderot, the convent was a place where the blind led the blind, and where the depraved led the innocent into depravity. It was the one French institution where women, who were at best incapable children, actually ruled.

Eighteenth-century literature in which lesbianism was treated explicitly seems to have often had a dual purpose. Frequently the author wished to arouse the male reader by the graphic depiction of lesbian sex, as do almost all the writers considered above. And since women themselves did not write erotic literature, the most bizarre male depictions of lesbianism went unchallenged.

But these works were usually more than erotic. They were based on actual personages, women who were, in every case, aggressive and unretiring, not at all like the conventional eighteenth-century ideal of femininity. These women had generally tread on the author's toes by their assertiveness; they had stepped out of line and behaved in an unwomanly fashion, either by attempting to outsmart a man, or by imposing themselves on male business, or simply by not extending to a man the deference he believed due him. What better way to shame such women than to attribute to them fierce sexual appetites at a time when it was not proper for women to have them? Lesbianism itself was seldom the focal point of attack in these works. Eighteenth-century men do not appear to have viewed lovemaking between nontransvestite women with much seriousness. The most virulent depictions of lesbian (or rather pansexual) behavior seem to have been rooted in the writer's anger at a particular woman's conduct in an area apart from the sexual. Her aggressive sexuality was used primarily as a metaphor.

CHAPTER 4

Transvestism: Persecution and Impunity

The female transvestite was not a figure in sixteenth-through eighteenth-century erotic literature and evidently presented a far more serious problem than women affording each other some sexual amusement. While a woman who engaged in lesbian sex posed no threat, at least to a libertine mentality, as long as she maintained all other aspects of her role as a woman, someone who both engaged in lesbian sex and rejected the other aspects of a female role *always* aroused societal anxiety.

The ephemerality of lesbian relationships was a notion cherished by male writers throughout the centuries. The Sappho-Phaon story (which many scholars reject as myth) was used as a reassuring prime example of lesbian transitoriness. One of the first encyclopedias, *Dictionary Historical and Critical* (first French edition, 1697; first English edition, 1710) by Pierre Bayle devotes most of its article on Sappho to a discussion of her desertion of women in favor of Phaon, with whom she was so infatuated that she leaped to her death from a Leucadian cliff when he did not reciprocate her passion. Bayle quotes at length from Ovid's "Epistle of Sappho to Phaon," the popular origin of the Phaon story:

> *No more the lesbian dames my passion move,*
> *Once the dear objects of my guilty love;*
> *All other loves are lost in only thine,*
> *Ah, youth ungrateful to a flame like mine.*[1]

Transvestites, who made lesbianism not just a sexual act but a whole life-style, did not hold out this tacit promise of change.

47

Even the slightest semblance of women (and men) rejecting their conventional garments was threatening because this implied that women ceased to be feminine (i.e., ruled) and men ceased to be masculine (i.e., ruling). William Harrison (1534–1593) in his *Description of England* complained that some women wore "doublets with pendant codpieces on the breast," and that he "met with some of these trulls in London so disguised that it hath passed my skill to discern whether they were men or women." And since many men's fashions had become feminized in turn, Harrison says, men were "transformed into monsters." [2] The next century in England saw a similar hysteria when fashions in dress again shifted to what was considered masculine for women and feminine for men. The author of a 1620 pamphlet, *Hic Mulier: or The Man-Woman: Being a Medicine to Cure the Coltish Disease of the Staggers in the Masculine-Feminine of our Times*, complained that society was going to the Devil because women had forsaken their "comely Hood, Cawle, Coyfe, handsome Dresse or Kerchiefe" and were now wearing mannish, broad-brimmed hats, masculine doublets, and "ruffianly short lockes." [3] This work set off a paper war regarding masculine women's and feminine men's fashions (for example, *Haec-Vir: or The Womanish Man* and *Muld Sacke: or the Apologie of Hic Mulier*). If fairly minor shifts in appropriate male and female dress caused such anxiety, one can imagine the horror that a full-fledged transvestite must have aroused.

Both literature and history indicate that a number of women disguised themselves as men in earlier centuries. Occasionally, as in the early decades of sixteenth-century England, women of some classes might have been able to achieve a degree of independence.[4] But for the most part in the sixteenth through the eigheenth centuries in England, France, Germany, and America women were restricted in the jobs open to them, in their freedom to travel without molestation, and in their general autonomy. If a woman craved freedom in a pre-unisex fashion era, when people believed that one's garments unquestionably told one's sex and there was no need to scrutinize facial features and muscle structure to discern gender, she might attempt to pass as a man. Novels such as Dr. Arbuthnot's *Memoirs of the Remarkable Life . . . of Miss Jenny Cameron* (1746), and the supposedly autobiographical *The History of Miss Kathy N———* (1757) suggest that such attempts were not as uncommon as might be expected.

If a woman passed successfully and was at all prepossessing, there was a possibility that she would be considered an eligible bachelor and receive serious attention from girls or their families. While some transvestite women ran from such attention, such as the late eighteenth-century English sailor, Mary Anne Talbot,[5] others could not or saw no reason to do so, or were happy with the attention. However, if a transvestite's community discovered that she was passing as a man and was romantically involved with a woman, her liberty and even her life were at stake.

In most cases of execution or other punishment for lesbianism, in both history and fiction, the accused was a transvestite. The first such instance is described in the early thirteenth-century extension of the French romance, *Huon of Bordeaux*, in which Ide, a woman in a man's dress, becomes a knight of the Holy Roman Emperor, and because of her skill is given the emperor's daughter in marriage. Not knowing how to extricate herself from this "privilege," she participates in a marriage ceremony with her enthusiastic bride, but of course she must finally tell the princess that she has not the proper equipment to fulfill her marital duties. When the emperor learns of this he condemns Ide to be burned to death, decreeing that he "wold not suffre suche boggery to be used." However, in this fictional story Ide is saved by a last-minute Iphis-like metamorphosis into a man.[6]

The laws and the writings of the theologians of this period suggest that a sentence of death by burning would have been considered appropriate in real life as well.[7] Saint Albertus Magnus (1206–1280) defined male and female homosexual sodomy as the worst sexual sin.[8] The laws of Orléans in 1260 codified the punishment for female sodomy in *Li livres de jostice et de plet*: A woman was to be mutilated for her first and second sexual offenses with another woman and burned to death for her third.[9] In the later Holy Roman Empire under Emperor Charles V (1519–1556), the law decreed that women who indulged in homosexual sodomy should be put to death by fire.[10]

It is doubtful, however, that women who did not change their female appearance suffered such penalties. The love poem to another woman written by the female troubadour Bieris de Romans, who lived during the period of *Huon of Bordeaux*, suggests no need to be covert about her affection, even to the slight extent of hiding behind a male persona. After praising Lady Maria's perfections, she implores her:

Thus I pray you, if it please you that true love
and celebration and sweet humility
should bring me such relief with you,
if it please you, lovely woman, then give me
that which most hope and joy promises,
for in you lie my desire and my heart
and from you stems all my happiness,
and because of you I'm often sighing.

And because merit and beauty raise you high
above all others (for none surpasses you),
I pray you, please, by this which does you honor,
don't grant your love to a deceitful suitor.

Lovely woman, whom joy and noble speech uplift,
and merit, to you my stanzas go,
for in you are gaiety and happiness,
and all good things one could ask of a woman.[11]

Although nothing is known of Bieris except for her sex, birthplace, and era, it would be safe to guess that she was not a transvestite if she managed to write such love poetry with impunity. Nontransvestite women had great latitude in the affection they could show toward other women. In a homosocial society in which it was expected that women would be close, affection might occasionally cross the border of the sensual into the sexual. Even in times and places which were not open to sexual variety, as long as those women practiced a modicum of caution to prevent a third person spying on them, they would have been safe. Transvestite women, on the other hand, would have put themselves under suspicion by their appearance alone if they did not "pass"; and if they tried openly to lead lives independent of men, they would have further enraged their societies. Any connection they had with other women would have come under scrutiny.

In nontransvestite women were careless enough to get caught *in flagrante delicto*, it appears that their punishments were fairly light. One such instance occurred in Plymouth in 1649. Goodwife Norman, the wife of Hugh Norman, and Mary Hammond were brought before the court "for leude behavior each with the other upon a bed." Mary Hammond received no punishment, and Goodwife Norman was sentenced "to make public acknowledgement . . . of her unchaste behavior."[12] That such leniency was not typical of Colonial America in the case of "serious" forms of homosexuality is evidenced by the fact that William Cornish was hanged in Virginia in 1625 and William Plain was hanged in New Haven in 1646 for homosexual activity.[13]

Transvestite lesbians do not seem to have been let off as easily as the two American women who were charged with "leude behavior." In 1566 Henri Estienne reported a case that had occurred thirty years earlier of a woman from Fontaines who, disguised as a male, worked as a stable boy for seven years, then learned to be a vineyard master, and being sure of a more comfortable economic status, married a woman. The two lived together for two years, after which time, Estienne says, the dildo that she used "to counterfeit the office of a husband" was discovered. She was arrested and, having confessed, was burned alive.[14]

Montaigne reports another execution of a transvestite lesbian in his 1580 *Journal de voyage*. Several years earlier, seven or eight girls from Chaumone en Bassigny had agreed to wear men's dress for the rest of their lives, presumably because transvestism gave them freedom of movement. They seem then to have left Chaumone in their disguises, and one of them, a weaver, went to Vitry. There she was able to pass as a man and win the respect and affection of the whole community. She became engaged to a woman from Vitry, but the match was broken off as a result of some misunderstanding between them. She then went to Montirandet and after a time married a woman with whom she lived for several months. According to Montaigne's sources, she employed, like Estienne's woman, a dildo in sexual intercourse. When a traveler from Chaumone recognized her, she was brought to trial "for the illicit inventions she used to supplement the shortcomings of her sex." Montaigne says she was hanged.[15]

A similar case occurred in early eighteenth-century Germany. Catharine Margaretha Linck, disguised as a man, served as a soldier in the Hanoverian, Prussian, Polish, and Hessian armies. In 1717, after her military service, she went to Halberstadt where, still disguised, she worked as a cotton dyer and married a woman. According to her trial transcript, she fashioned a dildo from leather and fastened on it a bag of pigs' bladders and two stuffed leather testicles. This was strapped to her pubis in order to perform coitus. When, after an altercation, her "wife" confessed to her mother that Linck was a woman, the outraged mother brought her before the law and she was imprisoned and tried. Her "mother-in-law" produced the dildo as evidence against her. She was executed in 1721.[16]

Still another case is cursorily reported in the anonymous English work, *Satan's Harvest Home* (1749), as having occurred in Turkey, where an "old Woman fell in Love with a Girl, the Daughter of a poor Man," after seeing her at the baths. When wooing and flattering did not win the girl's favors, the woman disguised herself as a man and established a new identity, pretending to be one of the *Chiauxes* of the *Grand Seignor*. She convinced the girl's father of her legitimacy and prosperity, and was given the girl in marriage. Of course, the girl discovered the woman's sex as soon as they entered the bridechamber, and she immediately informed her parents, who had the woman arrested. The governor sentenced her "to be pack'd away and drown'd in the Deep." [17]

In all these cases, the women did something which their societies seemed to regard as being far more serious than simply having sex with other women: They impersonated men. They claimed for themselves a variety of privileges ordinarily reserved for men—self-sufficiency, freedom to wander unmolested, freedom to explore occupations more varied than those open to women. By themselves their usurpations of male prerogatives might not have caused the women to be put to death; but, as we have seen, neither would most forms of lesbian lovemaking by themselves have been judged to warrant harsh punishment. The claim of male prerogative combined with the presumed commission (or, in the case of the Turkish woman, intended commission) of certain sexual acts, especially if a dildo was used, seem to have been necessary to arouse extreme societal anger.[18]

But despite societal disapproval, the combination of these social sins did not invariably mean that a woman would receive the death penalty. There is no record whatsoever of lesbian execution in England or America, or anywhere in Europe after the first quarter of the eighteenth century, although there were cases similar to Catharine Linck's in England in the 1740's and 1770's. In a sixpenny pamphlet, the novelist Henry Fielding, who was also a judge, relates the story of *The Female Husband: or the Surprising History of Mrs. Mary, Alias George Hamilton, Convicted for Marrying a Young Woman of Wells* (1746): Mary Hamilton, an adventurer who had in fact married women on three occasions, was sent to several towns to be publicly whipped and then imprisoned when her transvestism and use of a dildo came to the attention of the authorities.[19] In 1777 another female adventurer was brought before the courts of London for wearing male attire and marrying three different women. (The techniques employed in her conjugal bed are not discussed.) She was exposed in the pillory so that other women "might recognize her in the future" and was sentenced to six months in prison.[20]

Eighteenth-century French and German transvestite lesbians who wore men's clothes for the freedom they symbolized and did not seriously attempt to pass, or whose transvestism could be explained as an "honest mistake," were also treated less harshly under the law than Catharine Linck. Robert James's *Medicinal Dictionary* includes the story of Henrica Schuria, who served as a soldier, like Catharine Linck, under Frederic Henry, Prince of Orange, and fought in the siege of Boisleduc. After returning home, where she was of course known as a woman, she carried on an affair with a widow. James claims that she was so adept at lesbian sex "that, if the Laws of the Land had permitted, [the widow] would have married her, perhaps more cheerfully than she had done her deceas'd Husband, by whom she had had six children." When the dalliance was discovered it was ordered that Henrica be examined by midwives, who reported that her clitoris, when stimulated, extended the length of half a finger. James quotes "Johannes Poponius, a celebrated lawyer" as saying "that such Women should be punished by Death." But apparently since, unlike the other four women discussed above, she made no attempt to hide her gender from the community and did not use a dildo to "supplement the shortcomings of her sex," she was "only whipt with Rods," and then banished "far from the Partner of her crimes, who was, also, punish'd, tho' allowed to remain in the City."[21]

Anne Grandjean, a mid-eighteenth-century Grenoble woman, was similarly treated with comparative leniency. Her carpenter father had desired a son, and at fifteen Anne decided she would be one. She then convinced the simple town priest that she was in fact a boy, and with his consent she changed her name to Jean-Baptiste Grandjean. She courted the girls, and a short time later married a woman with whom she moved to Lyons. There another woman with whom Anne had earlier had an intimacy told the innocent wife that her husband was really a female. The wife then told a priest of Lyons, and as a result, Anne was exposed in the stocks and then imprisoned as a "defiler of the sacrament of marriage." She appealed to the Paris medical faculty, who upon examination declared her to be a woman with a touch of "hermaphroditism" (which probably meant that her clitoris was somewhat larger than normal). The parliament of Paris released her from prison, but also made her resume her female identity, annulled her marriage, and forbade her to have anything further to do with women. Perhaps she was not executed like her contemporary, Catharine Linck, because she was able to convince her judges that she had made an honest mistake which her Grenoble confessor had failed to help her correct, and because, like Henrica Schuria, she did not use a dildo.[22]

It can only be speculated whether the initial impulse of these transvestites was sexual or social, but many who left a record of themselves specifically claimed that they became transvestites in the first place because they desired greater freedom than women were permitted. For the most part, it does not appear that they had overwhelming libidinal interests in other women at the outset of their careers as impersonators, or that they were pushed to pass as males by the strength of their inverted sex drives. Those interests developed as their male roles developed and seemed to have been secondary in importance to their lives as masculine, i.e., autonomous, beings. Had they remained in their roles as females, in the right times and places they might have carried on lesbian sexual activity with impunity had that been their interest, although they would have continued trapped in women's circumscribed conditions. As transvestites, however, if caught they could usually expect prosecution. It would seem though that they were punished less for unorthodox sexual pleasures than for a usurpation of male prerogatives. What was most threatening to both Europe and America from the sixteenth to the eighteenth centuries was not lesbian sex by itself, but male impersonation and all that was implied in rejection of the feminine status.

Despite the vigorous prosecution described above, some transvestite lesbians of the same period remained untouched by the law. A woman of wealth and influence, such as the seventeenth-century queen of Sweden, Christina, could dress and (within some limits) behave as she pleased. Since women of her position were generally well known, they would make no attempt to pass, and their attire could be regarded as nothing more than eccentricity. A woman whose transvestism and relationship with another woman could be explained as having occurred out of sheer necessity rather than desire was also given considerable latitude, particularly if she were otherwise seen as a valuable member of the community, and especially if she were past childbearing age (which meant that her peculiarities had a minimal effect on the social structure). Finally, "characters"—flamboyant actresses, clowns, dramatic but harmless subculture types—could conduct themselves outrageously, at least in big cities like London or Paris. They were larger-than-life specimens, and their exploits could not be taken seriously. While a weaver or a cotton dyer or a stablehand could not hope to get away with much once her sex was discovered, a queen or an actress, or a public celebrity of any sort, usually lived under different rules.

In the seventeenth century Christina of Sweden, who dressed in men's clothing even while on the throne, abdicated in order not to marry. She settled for a time in Paris, where her masculine dress and sexual advances to women were recorded in the correspondence of numerous of her contemporaries, such as Count Palatine, the Duke de Guise, and Mlle. de Montpensier,[23] but she was accorded all the privileges and honors society believed due a woman of her exalted birth. The legend of her interest in women cannot be attributed to foundationless gossip. Her correspondence indicates how emotionally susceptible she was to other females. Her letters to Ebba Sparre, written while she wandered about Europe, show that she loved the noblewoman years before her abdication. For example, Christina wrote to Ebba from Pesaro, three years after leaving Sweden, "If you remember the power you have over me, you will also remember that I have been in possession of your love for twelve years; I belong to you so utterly, that it will never be possible for you to lose me; and only when I die shall I cease loving you." [24]

Her professions of attachment are not substantially different from the expressions of romantic friendship that will be examined in subsequent sections, but Christina's interest in other women appears to have been more consciously sexual than that of most romantic friends. The reputation of her erotic exploits lived on long after she did. In 1719, thirty years after Christina's death, Princess Palatine, mother of the Regent of Orléans, wrote that Christina once tried to "force" Mme. de Bregny "who was almost unable to defend herself." She added that it was thought that Christina was a hermaphrodite.[25]

Had Christina been born into the lower classes, her transvestism and masculine behavior would probably have caused an investigation; had she possessed no more discretion than she did, her sexual interests would have been discovered, and she would no doubt have suffered a punishment similar to those levied on the women previously discussed.

At first glance it is curious that Mary East, who had no advantages of birth or wealth, was not sentenced at least to a public whipping, as was her contemporary "George Hamilton" (see page 52). In the 1730's, having inherited some money, Mary and another young woman went to a small English town where they were unknown and became proprietors of a pub. Mary dressed in men's clothing and changed her name to "James How." She differed from "George Hamilton" in that she became a solid member of her community. Through scrupulous honesty, and hard work, "James" and her friend prospered in this pub and later in a larger one. The two were well liked everywhere, and "James" served in almost all the important parish offices. But eventually Mary was recognized by someone that she had known from home and was blackmailed. She paid her blackmailer for years and continued to live as James How, proprietor of a public house, model citizen, and husband. When her "wife" died after thirty-four years and her blackmailer hired ruffians to harass her further, she permitted a friend to seek protection for her from the magistrates of the district, hoping that her sex would not be discovered. Of course it was, but she was permitted to go free and her blackmailer was imprisoned—however, because she was exposed she felt compelled to give up her pub and go into retirement.[26]

It is probable that she was not prosecuted because when her true sex was discovered she was already an older woman, in her fifties, and therefore not considered a sexual being—and her mate was dead. Furthermore, the entire community maintained that she was completely honest and virtuous, and it must have been difficult for them to believe that a mid-eighteenth-century Englishwoman of such otherwise sterling qualities would be capable of sexual transgression. In fact, her neighbors were eager to convince themselves that she lived as she did not out of desire but pathetic necessity. Reports quickly circulated that she and the woman with whom she had shared her life had both once been disappointed in their fiancés and had met "with many crosses in love." For that reason they determined to remain single. They posed as man and wife only because two unmarried women could not otherwise live unmolested. According to these reports, Mary became the husband after the two tossed a coin and that part fell to her.

Other women who managed to live as transvestites without uncomfortable interference from the law generally were those who were able to cut such colorful figures that they were regarded fondly —they were humored and not taken very seriously. Mary Frith, who was something of a thief and a lowlife oddity with the proverbial heart of gold, was one such figure. Frith was the model for Moll in Dekker and Middleton's *The Roaring Girl* (1611), a figure in Nathan Field's *Amends for Ladies* (1618), and the subject of *The Life and Death of Mary Frith* (1662). It is not certain whether she was lesbian or bisexual, but Dekker and Middleton, her contemporaries, seem to speculate on those possibilities in their play: Mistress Gallipot says of her, "Some will not stick to say she's a man and some both man and woman," to which Laxton replies, "That were excellent, she might first cuckold the husband and then make him do as much for the wife" (Act II, Scene 1).[27] Whatever her sexual proclivities, her special status as a "character" placed her outside the law.

Actresses too had a special status, perhaps because their "peculiarities" could always be attributed to artistic temperament. In seventeenth-century France the most flamboyant and legendary was Mlle. de Maupin (on whom Théophile Gautier loosely based his nineteenth-century novel). Maupin, a singer in the Paris Opéra, frequently played men's parts. Her romantic involvements with women had been widely known, but she almost found herself in serious difficulty when, on a professional tour of Marseilles, the daughter of a rich merchant saw her on stage and fell in love with her. The two then ran off together. It is not known if anything sexual passed between them, but the girl claimed that as soon as she discovered Maupin's true gender, she escaped from her and informed the authorities. The actress was imprisoned and sentenced to be executed, probably under the sixteenth-century antisodomy law (which included lesbianism) of the Holy Roman Emperor Charles V. However, because of her stage popularity, public opinion was so much in her favor that she managed to have her sentence overturned and was able to return to Paris and resume her career. She even continued to dress on occasion in men's clothes, and the law no longer dared interfere with her.[28]

By the next century in England it had become common for actresses to play "breeches parts" on stage, a reverse of the Renaissance theater, in which boys played women's parts. Actresses and other theatrical types sometimes let their newfound freedom lap over into their personal lives—even if they were heterosexual. For example, Mrs. Centlivre, who was best known as a playwright, lived for years disguised as a boy with Anthony Hammond, a secretary of the navy. The most flamboyant of the transvestite actresses of this period was Charlotte Charke, daughter of the playwright and actor Colley

Cibber. As an actress she was able to cultivate eccentricity with impunity. In 1755 she wrote her memoirs, *A Narrative of the Life of
Mrs. Charlotte Charke (Youngest Daughter of Colley Cibber, Esq.)*,[29]
partly to blackmail her father into supporting her by threatening
to publish the work and shame him by the admission of her various
peculiarities—or, if he refused, to earn enough money through the
publication to support herself.

Charlotte relates in these memoirs her preference for men's clothes
since the age of four, her rejection of all housewifely education,
her penchant for male theatrical roles, and her decision to give up
women's dress permanently. While a lower-class woman would not
have dared make those admissions less than ten years after "George
Hamilton" was whipped and imprisoned, the public apparently was
entertained by such attitudes on the part of a stage personality—
who was anyway not a "real-life" human being.

Throughout the book her close relationships are with women;
and finally her closest and most enduring relationship, the one with
which she ends the book, is with a woman who becomes "Mrs.
Brown" to her "Mr. Brown" and shares her fortunes and misfortunes. Charlotte depicts them in a classic "butch/femme" relationship without the slightest trace of self-consciousness. "Mrs. Brown"
leaves all decisions to her, shows her deference in all things (even
when it is apparent that because of Charlotte's bad choices they
will go hungry for a while), and permits her to act as though she
were "the worthiest gentleman in the country" when they come
into a bit of money.

Charlotte claims she was often able to pass as a male, and outside
of London it was thought that the two women were husband and
wife. Surprisingly, she is totally confident that this confession will
not get her into trouble. Of course, unlike "George Hamilton" and
the London woman who was convicted in 1777, Charlotte never
attempted to marry "Mrs. Brown" legally. Nevertheless, she must
have relied a good deal on the privilege she knew her society would
grant to a flamboyant eccentric of a notable family. The Annual
Register between 1761 and 1815 cited fifteen cases of women who
had been prosecuted for dressing as males, and most of them did
not attempt to marry other women.[30]

In eighteenth-century America the most remarkable case of a
woman who impersonated a man was that of Deborah Sampson.[31]
Like Mary Frith, Deborah was a "roaring girl," a flamboyant personality. But it is most likely that she was not punished for imper-

sonation because she was married and a mother by the time her true sex was finally known, and she could also claim sympathy as a patriotic war hero, having fought as a soldier in the Revolution.

It was rumored that after Deborah's children were born she "refus'd her husband the rites of the marriage bed,"[32] but the Congressional committee which granted her a soldier's pension some years after her military service, declaring that the American Revolution "furnishes no other similar example of female heroism, fidelity, and courage,"[33] did not inquire into the felicity of her conjugal bond. Perhaps if she had not given up her transvestite ways by then, she would not have been so honored, but the committee members who looked at her case were able to convince themselves that her transvestism was merely an interlude, satisfactorily explained by her great patriotism which urged her to fight in the war for her country's independence.

In fact, as Herbert Mann, her biographer (who was her contemporary and worked largely from her own memoir notes) makes clear, she assumed male dress for the same reason that women generally chose to become transvestites—in reaction to the restrictions of the woman's role in her day, and not at all because her primary urge was patriotic. She had had several altercations in her Middleborough, Massachusetts, community regarding transvestism well before she became a soldier. On one occasion she stole a suit of men's clothes, enlisted in the army under the name of Timothy Thayer, took the bounty money she had been given, and went in drag to a tavern a couple of miles east of Middleborough, where she got roaring drunk "and behaved herself in a noisy and indecent manner."[34] Upon returning home, she "crept to bed with the negro [woman]"[35] who had helped her steal the clothes. The members of the First Baptist Church of Middleborough, which she had recently joined, were incensed at her behavior, as their records for September 3, 1782, show:

> The Church considered the case of Deborah Sampson, a member of this Church, who last Spring was accused of dressing in men's clothes, and enlisting as a Soldier in the Army, and although she was not convicted, yet was strongly suspected of being guilty, and for some time before behaved very loose and unchristian like, at last left our parts in a suden maner, and it is not known among us where she is gone, and after considerable discourse, it appeared that as several bretheren had

labour'd with her before she went away, without obtaining satisfaction, concluded it is the Church's duty to withdraw fellowship [i.e., excommunicate] untill she returns and makes Christian satisfaction.[36]

Deborah decided finally to enlist in the army in earnest both because she feared "lest punishment should overtake her" in her community as a result of the Timothy Thayer fiasco, and because her mother had been urging her to marry a young man whom Deborah described in her manuscript memoir as "having the silliness of a baboon."[37] After enlisting again, but this time in a different community and under the name of Robert Shertliff, she stayed with a captain in Medway while waiting to be called up. There a "love passage" occurred between her and a girl visiting the family.[38] This was the first of many love affairs with women during this period of her life. Mann states without comment that "her limbs are regularly proportioned. Ladies of taste considered them handsome, when in masculine garb."[39]

Deborah's sex was discovered by a sympathetic doctor when she was sent to a hospital with a near-fatal wound, and she was gently discharged. After her discharge she went to work on her uncle's farm, still wearing male attire and "flirting with the girls of the neighborhood."[40] Her eighteenth-century biographer, finding it difficult perhaps to reconcile her apparent transvestite lesbianism and his desire to depict Deborah in the most admirable terms, explains her relationship "with her sister sex" as a platonic friendship, which seem dubious in this case: "Surely," he comments, "it must have been that of sentiment, taste, purity; as animal love, on her part, was out of the question."[41]

A short time later Deborah married a neighboring farmer and had three children. Perhaps her desire for children explains her marriage, which was anomalous to everything that is known of her. Or perhaps she married realizing that as an indigent young woman, having no real education and no one to help her establish herself in a decent position, the prospects were not bright. In addition to the vision of a future of unglorious toil, she must have seen that her lean, handsome, beardless-boy appearance was starting to vanish under wrinkles and flaccidity: Time was running out for her as a young gallant. It is probable that many women who would have much preferred to remain lovers of women married for similar reasons throughout the centuries.

* * *

It appears then that while most women could not be transvestites with impunity, certain types were granted special prerogatives. Women like Christina of Sweden were, of course, generally above the law (although even she had to give up her throne for her unwillingness to conform to heterosexual custom). But other women who could "carry it off" with style also had the privilege of engaging in unorthodox behavior. Some of these women counted heavily on people loving a clown and being tolerant of its genderless oddity, and thus they risked being ostensibly open about their personal lives. But since they were often actresses or lowlife characters, their communities probably saw them as beyond the pale in any case. What they did could not set an example for the average woman. On the other hand, if enough women weavers or cotton dyers decided to eschew restrictive female dress and marriage, they could have a substantial effect on the social structure. The law moved decisively, as the evidence indicates, to quash such behavior.

Transvestites were, in a sense, among the first feminists. Mute as they were, without a formulated ideology to express their convictions, they saw the role of women to be dull and limiting. They craved to expand it—and the only way to alter that role in their day was to become a man. Only in convincing male guise could they claim for themselves the privileges open to men of their class. Transvestism must have been a temptation or, at the very least, a favorite fantasy for many an adventurous young woman who understood that as a female she could expect little latitude or freedom in her life.

PART I

THE SIXTEENTH THROUGH EIGHTEENTH CENTURIES

B.

The Enshrinement of Romantic Friendship

CHAPTER 1

The Revival of Same-Sex Love: Sixteenth and Seventeenth Centuries

In his essay "On Friendship," Montaigne writes that love between two men could cause them to "mix and blend in each other with so complete a mixing that they efface and never again find the seam that joined them." He claims that he and Éstienne de la Boëtie loved each other in that manner: Each loved the other's entire being, "which, seizing my whole will, led it to dive and disappear in his; which, seizing his whole will, led it to dive and disappear in mine, with a like desire, a like consent." Such love is mystical and magical, Montaigne concludes. Try as he might to categorize this love, it resists analysis because it is motivated by an "inexplicable and fatal force." The two men loved each other at first meeting, at first sight, "nothing from then on was so near to either of us as was the other." One merged in the other so truly that "we kept back nothing to be our own, to be either his or mine."

Montaigne distinguishes this love from homosexuality as practiced by the Greeks by pointing out that in the latter, there was generally a great disparity in age and vocation between the lovers, and that the relationship was often founded on the corporeal beauty of the youth alone. Thus friendship was rarely possible. For the same reason, he maintains, relations between men and women are generally inferior to those possible between two mature men. Heterosexual love, which is usually founded merely on desire, is easily weakened once desire is sated. But women do not make good friends for men for still another reason: Their ordinary capacity, Montaigne declares, "is not sufficient for that confidence and self-disclosure which is the nurse of this sacred bond." [1]

65

Montaigne's attitude toward male love was greatly influenced by ancient Greek and Roman writers whose works were important to the learned of the Renaissance and subsequent centuries. Most of these ancient sources made no solid distinction between love and friendship. Aristotle, whose work was basic reading for the educated man during the Renaissance, says in his *Nicomachean Ethics* that friendship is based on love for both the person and the character of the friend, on a desire to love rather than to be loved, and on intimacy (even to the extent of cohabitation). In *De Amicitia*, Cicero considers friendship more desirable than anything on earth, far surpassing mere heterosexual love. "He who looks on a true friend," Cicero says, "looks as it were upon a kind of image of himself," "a friend is a second self," and "true friendships are eternal." [2] Unlike modern attitudes toward friendship, the Greeks and Romans regarded it not as an amenity that might supplement fundamental needs but as fundamental in itself. [3]

Renaissance writers, also encouraged by an interest in Platonism, which in the Renaissance emphasized the importance of the soul over the body (and thus defused any potential concern about male homosexuality), borrowed these ideals of friendship with little ostensible modification. Sir Fridericke in *The Courtier*, for example, urges his reader to make friendship "endure until death . . . no lesse than those men of old time." [4]

These attitudes had especially great currency in Renaissance England. The language that English writers used to describe friendship was barely distinguishable from the language of erotic love. A 1577 poem by a British writer, Timothe Kendall, "To a Frende," is characteristic:

> *When fishes shun the silver streames:*
> *When darknes yields bright* Titans *beames,*
> *When as the bird that* Phoenix *hight,*
> *Shall haue ten thousand mates in sight.*
> *When* Ioue *in* Limbo *low shall lye,*
> *And* Pluto *shall be plast on hye;*
> *Then I will thee forsake my deere*
> *And not before, as shall appeare.* [5]

Two male friends are often described in Renaissance literature as sharing "one bed, one house, one table, and one purse" (William Painter, *Palace of Pleasure*, 1566), [6] or as being "neither separated at bourde, nor severed at bed" (Thomas Lodge, *Euphues Shadowe*,

1592).[7] While the Restoration rage for pederasty apparently put an end to this unselfconscious view of appropriate behavior between male friends, for female friends it continued during the next three hundred years.

Men in Renaissance literature about friendship generally marry women before the denouement, but their friendships continue with unchanged intensity and energy. Painter in *Palace of Pleasure*, for instance, observes that although one of the two friends has married, "their goodes were common betweene them, and the marriage did yelde no cause to hinder their assured amities." It is not clear what happened in the "one bed" Painter's friends had always shared; however, Renaissance writers usually avoided all discussion of a genital aspect in the same-sex love relationship. But since these "friendships" were modeled largely on the Greek and Roman, the Renaissance writers borrowed the ideals and vocabulary with which to describe them from those who wrote of same-sex love which was frequently genital. While many of the ancients could not conduct the most intense emotional relationships (outside of those between parent and child) totally divorced from a genital component any more than most of us today can, those in the Renaissance and subsequent eras could. Or at least they could repress the genital component or sublimate it through sentiment or constant proximity— and, in the case of some female romantic friendships, through erotic behavior which fell short of the genital.

Although literary examples of intense friendships between women during the Renaissance are not as numerous as those between men, the examples which do exist suggest that women were permitted emotional attachments as all-consuming as those between men. In Thomas Lodge's *Rosalynde*, for instance, Alinda accompanies her friend Rosalynde into exile, and she delivers to her a speech much like Ruth's to Naomi, chiding her for being melancholy even though:

Thou hast with thee Alinda a frend, who will be a faithfull copartner of all thy misfortunes, who hath left her father to followe thee, and chooseth rather to brooke all extremeties than to forsake thy presence. . . . As wee haue been bed-fellowes in royaltie, we will be fellowe mates in pouertie: I will euerbee thy Alinda, and thou shalt euer rest to me Rosalynd; so shall the world canonize our friendship, and speake of Rosalynd and Alinda, as they did of Pilades and Orestes.[8]

Perhaps there were fewer depictions of female friendships in the Renaissance because few women wrote for publication during this period, and while a male writer might know what went on between male and female or between male and male, he would have little way of knowing what occurred between female and female.

By the eighteenth century, when Englishwomen in comparatively large numbers were writing voluminous letters and diaries as well as poetry and fiction, literary evidence of intense friendship (indistinguishable from romantic love) between women became abundant. Harriet Bowdler spoke for her female contemporaries when she characterized romantic friendship in terms that were current in the literature of male writers in the Renaissance and in the Greek and Roman eras: It was a "union of souls, a marriage of hearts, a harmony of design and affection, which being entered into by mutual consent, groweth up into the purest kindness and most endearing love. . . ." [9]

There is ample evidence to suggest that romantic friendships between women flourished in the seventeenth century as well. For example, Mme. de La Fayette (the author of *The Princess of Cleves*), who has been depicted by historians as the lover of La Rochefoucauld, wrote to Mme. de Sévigné in 1691, "Believe me, you are the person in the world I have most truly loved." [10] In the same spirit another seventeenth-century novelist, Mlle. de Scudéry, wrote to Mlle. Paulet, when she went to Marseilles while her friend remained in Paris, that she had not had "one moment of tranquil pleasure since being away from you," and quoted a verse by Malherbe about Mme. d'Auchy as being applicable to her own state, "Where Caliste is not, there is my hell." [11]

In seventeenth-century England their class and intellectual counterparts had similar relationships.[12] These women learned from Renaissance writers the ideals of Platonism, in which perfect friendship was seen as superior to sexual love. Impassioned asexual love could thus take as its object a male or a female indiscriminately. For seventeenth-century women the object was not infrequently another woman.

The best literary record of seventeenth-century female romantic friendship in England is furnished by a poet, Katherine Philips, "the Matchless Orinda" (1631–1664). Had she written in the twentieth century, her poetry would undoubtedly have been identified as "lesbian." Her seventeenth-century contemporaries saw it as the finest expression of female friendship. Abraham Cowley celebrated her relationship with Anne Owen (the "Lucasia" of her poetry) in a poem of praise for "Orinda":

> The fame of friendship which so long had told
> Of three or four illustrious Names of old,
> Till hoarse and weary of the tale she grew,
> Rejoyces now to have got a new,
> A new and more surprising story,
> Of fair Lucasia's and Orinda's glory.[13]

Jeremy Taylor dedicated his discourse, "Offices and Measures of Friendship," to Katherine Philips, and many of her literary contemporaries held her up as a model of virtue for her commitment to romantic friendship.

"Orinda's" work, imbued as it is with the language and poetic conventions of her day, nevertheless reveals her passion, jealousy, sensuality, and tenderness for other women. Of course, these poems contain ample literary conventions, but her emotions cannot be viewed as simply "literary." They are reflected in her life, if we can believe not only such writers as Cowley and Taylor but also her own correspondence. For example, in a 1658 letter to a female friend, she characteristically exclaimed: "I gasp for you with an impatience that is not to be imagined by any soul wound up to a less concern in friendship than yours is, and therefore I cannot hope to make others sensible of my vast desires to enjoy you."[14] In content, there is little to separate both her letters and her poems from the writings of Sappho. As one might expect, Philips, who lived most of her life during the reign of the Puritans, does not dwell on the physical manifestations of her arousal as Sappho does; she is much more concerned with the ecstasy of her soul, but it is another woman who brings about this ecstasy and makes her feel complete. When she is unhappy with a beloved woman, her sorrow is like death (she probably was not using the term in a sexual sense, as was the poet by whom she was most influenced, John Donne). Women conquer her with their beauty and shoot her with "Cupid's Dart"; they set her "heart on fire," but the only culmination which she apparently knows to demand of such passion is to "speak our Love."

"Lucasia," to whom most of her poems are written, is described as the "dear object of my Love's excess"; she is "all my hopes of happiness."[15] In a poem entitled "To My Excellent Lucasia, On Our Friendship," Katherine declares that she had not lived until she loved Lucasia, who is "all that I can prize,/My Joy, my Life, my Rest," and neither a bridegroom nor a "crown-conqueror" can be as happy as Katherine is since "They have but pieces of the Earth,/I've all the World in thee." [16]

Although many of the poems emphasize her spiritual satisfaction in her beloved woman friend, Philips often draws on the language of Eros. "To My Lucasia, In Defense of Declared Friendship," for example, borrows heavily from the early seduction poems of John Donne:

> . . . *Before we knew the treasures of our Love,*
> *Our noble aims our joys did entertain;*
> *And shall enjoyment nothing then improve?*
> *'Twere best for us then to begin again.*
>
> *Now we have gain'd, we must not stop, and sleep*
> *Out all the rest of our mysterious reign:*
> *It is as hard and glorious to keep*
> *A victory, as it is to obtain.*
>
> *Nay to what end did we once barter Minds,*
> *Only to know and to neglect the claim?*
> *Or (like some Wantons) our Pride pleasure finds*
> *To throw away the thing at which we aim.*
>
> *If this be all our Friendship does design,*
> *We covet not enjoyment then, but power:*
> *To our Opinion we our Bliss confine,*
> *And love to have, but not to smell the flower.*
>
> *Ah! then let Misers bury thus their Gold,*
> *Who though they starve no farthing will produce:*
> *But we lov'd to enjoy and to behold,*
> *And sure we cannot spend our stock by use.*
>
> *Think not 'tis needless to repeat desires;*
> *The fervent turtles alwaies court and bill,*
> *And yet their spotless passion never tires,*
> *But does increase by repetition still. . . .* [17]

But for her the smell of the flower and the misers' buried gold are not sex, as they would be to John Donne. Incredible as it may seem from a twentieth-century perspective, despite the last quoted stanza, Katherine is requesting of her beloved only what is suggested in the title—that they *declare* their feelings, or as she pleads in the opening line, "O my Lucasia, let us speak our Love."

In poems to other women as well, Katherine uses the language of erotic love when she is really writing about a spiritual union manifested through verbal declarations and noble actions alone. In "To My Lady, Elizabeth Boyle," for example, she complains that Elizabeth, the "subduing fair," has used many a needless dart to conquer Katherine's undefended heart.[18] In "Rosania, Shadowed Whilst Mrs. Mary Awbrey," she explains that she loves Rosania so excessively that she is rendered speechless, and that Rosania's beauty "Would make a Lover of an Anchorite."[19]

Several of the poems suggest that these passionate relationships were often charged with conflict, jealousy, ambivalence, all the emotions which generally accompany an intense sexual relationship. In "Injuria Amicitae," for example, she demands to know of the "lovely" other woman, "What was my Offence?/Or am I punished for Obedience?" She complains of the beloved's "ingenious scorns" and views herself as burning Rome—the other woman is Nero, who set her on fire and now surveys her handiwork. The poem ends, "Yet I'll adore the author of my Death,/And kiss the Hand that robs me of my Breath."[20] And yet the title reminds us that in the author's view, she has been injured not by romantic love but by friendship.

It is impossible to be certain what Katherine Philips's passions meant to her, but we can be fairly sure that they were regarded by those who believed her to be a model of the perfect romantic friend as an expression of platonism which delighted not in physicality but in the union of souls and in philosophizing and poetizing. Men viewed these relationships as ennobling. Thomas Heywood writes that love between women "tends to the grace and honor of the Sex." His example of female friendship indicates that some men saw it not as frivolous but serious even unto death. He relates the story of Bona, "a sinless maiden," who lived a retired life in a convent. Bona, Heywood says, "had a bedfellow, unto whom above all others she was entired." When this bedfellow is lying on her deathbed, with all hope for recovery gone, Bona, who is in perfect health, prays to God that she will not survive her friend and that their bodies will not be separated in death. In answer to her prayer, both die on the same day and are buried in the same sepulcher. Heywood states that just as they shared one bed, they will share one grave and also "one kingdom" in heaven. He concludes by extolling their example of "mutuall love, amitie, and friendship."[21]

Naturally not all seventeenth-century men took romantic friendship as seriously as Heywood. Some who did not consider it especially ennobling approved of it anyway, since it gave them some voyeuristic pleasure. It was sweet and pretty—and not quite believable. According to the poet Edmund Waller, two young women who appear to be totally taken with each other present to the male nothing more than a tantalizing double vision of beauty: In Waller's 1645 poem, "On the Friendship Betwixt Two Ladies," Amoret and Sacharissa make a pair more "lovely, sweet, and fair," and more "choicely matched" than Venus' silver doves or Cupid's wings. Waller laments in the first stanza, "Tell me, lovely, loving pair!/ Why so kind, and so severe?/Why so careless of our care,/Only to yourselves so dear?" [22] But he decides that their ostensible love for each other is only cunning; they display their passion for male benefit in order to "control" men's love. They are like debtors who, not wanting to pay a debt (give themselves up to a man), avoid the law by signing away all their property (their store of love) to a friend. The debtor and the friend understand, of course, that the gesture is only a pretense. Waller implies that romantic friendship is charming to observe but has little substance, and it would not exist at all if women did not desire a playful tool with which to tease their male lovers.

Many men might have regarded romantic friendship between women as an analog (somewhat diffused by women's weaker natures and therefore not as powerful) to their own male romantic friendships. It would not have troubled them, nor would they have seen anything "abnormal" in it. If a man bothered to react to romantic friendship between women at all, he would have had no reason to discourage it, probably not even that of jealousy: he would have had little interest in claiming a woman's intense friendship for his own if he believed, as many did, that females had little capacity for such a "sacred bond" with males.

Because platonism assured romantic friends that what they loved so passionately in each other was the soul, theoretically it was irrelevant whether one chose for one's great love an individual of the same or the opposite sex. But in fact it was believed by women as well as men that such a bond might more easily be formed within one's sex. Since the union of souls was to have been foremost in these intense female romantic friendships, they were probably often without a realized genital component. Nevertheless, the record left by romantic friends of their attachments suggests that they frequently had sensual interest in the person of the beloved. That sensual interest, however, must have been within the realm of the acceptable, even in the era of the Puritans, since even in work intended for public perusal, the writer saw no need to hide her feelings. Perhaps it was assumed that what appeared to be sensual was merely an inevitable overflow of the spiritual, and that the overwhelming importance of the spiritual would keep eroticism in check.

These Renaissance and seventeenth-century views of romantic friendship were inherited by the eighteenth century. They explain in part why the men of the eighteenth century saw no reason for concern when so many women expressed intense love and eternal devotion to their women friends.

CHAPTER 2

The "Fashion" of Romantic Friendship in the Eighteenth Century

In *Sexual Life in England: Past and Present*, Iwan Bloch postulates that "fashion," not deep-seated pathological reasons (as our psychologically sophisticated era has insisted), often explains the development of a particular erotic taste. He uses as examples the sudden widespread interest in pederasty during the Restoration and the defloration mania in eighteenth-century England, which caused procurers to go to the most outrageous lengths to obtain virgins and/or help girls simulate virginity for their customers.[1] "Fashion" in the seventeenth, eighteenth, and nineteenth centuries dictated that women may fall passionately in love with each other, although they must not engage in genital sex. Unlike society's response to pederasty and the defloration of virgins, however, passionate love between women was socially condoned, originally because it was not believed to violate the platonist ideal, and later for more complex reasons. But while it is true that love between women was "in style," women's experiences of that love were no less intense or real for their social acceptability.

Elizabeth Mavor, whose *The Ladies of Llangollen: A Study of Romantic Friendship* shows that the institution reached a zenith in eighteenth-century England, specifically rejects the terms that Freud and other sexologists used to describe the type of love relationship that existed between the two subjects of her study; and she suggests that the term "romantic friendship," which was current in the eighteenth century, is not only more liberal and inclusive but "better suited to the diffuse feminine nature." These relationships could be Edenic, she points out, "before they were biologically and thus prej-

74

udicially defined." [2] Such passion in the eighteenth century was not believed to violate seriously any code of behavior, even when it was taken to such extremes that the women eloped with each other, as did the Ladies of Llangollen—Eleanor Butler and Sarah Ponsonby— in 1778. When Sarah's family discovered that she had run off with a woman instead of a man, they were relieved—her reputation would not suffer any irreparable harm (as it would have had her accomplice been male). Her relative Mrs. Tighe observed, "[Sarah's] conduct, though it has an appearance of imprudence, is I am sure void of serious impropriety. There were no gentlemen concerned, nor does it appear to be anything more than a scheme of Romantic Friendship." [3]

The English, during the second half of the eighteenth century, prized sensibility, faithfulness, and devotion in a woman, but forbade her significant contact with the opposite sex before she was betrothed. It was reasoned, apparently, that young women could practice these sentiments on each other so that when they were ready for marriage they would have perfected themselves in those areas. It is doubtful that women viewed their own romantic friendships in such a way, but—if we can place any credence in eighteenth-century English fiction as a true reflection of that society—men did. Because romantic friendship between women served men's self-interest in their view, it was permitted and even socially encouraged. The attitude of Charlotte Lennox's hero in *Euphemia* (1790) is typical. Maria Harley's uncle chides her for her great love for Euphemia and her obstinate grief when Euphemia leaves for America, and he points out that her fiancé "has reason to be jealous of a friendship that leaves him but second place in [Maria's] affection"; but the fiancé responds, "Miss Harley's sensibility on this occasion is the foundation of all my hopes. From a heart so capable of a sincere attachment, the man who is so happy as to be her choice, may expect all the refinements of a delicate passion, with all the permanence of a generous friendship."

Perhaps society felt obliged to permit such friendships even among married women because divorce was all but impossible, and a woman who was alienated by her husband might find comfort in a woman friend while doing no harm to the essential fabric of society. Such a woman would continue to be "virtuous," but if she received comfort from a male friend, male sexuality being what it is, she would no doubt soon become a "bad" woman. In novel after novel of eighteenth-century England, the heroine is trapped in a wretched marriage and pours out her heart to another woman who offers her love and understanding. In *The History of Lady Barton* (1771), the title character finds relief from a terrible marriage only in her correspondence with another female to whom she confesses the horrors of her married life, and Lady Barton rejoices despite that unhappiness because in her correspondent she has "a subject for my tenderness." To her, Lady Barton quotes a poem which she claims perfectly expresses her sentiments:

> Remote, unfriended, melancholy, slow,
> Where mountains rise, and where rude waters flow,
> Where e'er I go, whatever realms I see,
> My heart untravelled fondly turns to thee.
> Still to my Fanny turns, with ceaseless pain,
> And drags at each remove a lengthening chain.

Throughout this novel men constantly deceive and are in every way undependable, but women never forget that they can turn to each other.

Certainly in some eighteenth-century works, the female correspondent is no more than an epistolary device—a mere sounding board to whom the heroine may express herself according to the demands of the form, as may be seen, for example, in *Letters from the Duchess de Crui and Others* (1776), in which Mrs. Pierpont complains of her cruel husband in epistles to the Duchess. But in novels such as *The History of Lady Barton* and *Euphemia*, the same-sex love relationship is, to a greater or lesser extent, a central element of the tale.

Occasionally some writers, those who feared any manifestation of sensual expression, questioned the social code which permitted such intense expressions of affection between women. The anonymous author of *Satan's Harvest Home*, in a section on the fashion of same-sex friends kissing and hugging in public, complains that when he sees "two Ladies Kissing and Slopping each other, in a lascivious Manner, and frequently repeating it, I am shocked to the last Degree." However, he claims, that is not nearly as bad as two men showing similar affection to each other in public; and he then expresses a disbelief that Englishwomen would even be capable of becoming "criminally amorous" of each other (while men, he is certain, move inevitably from such public display of affection to the vice of sodomy).[4] But even such slight suspicions as this author voices concerning female same-sex affection are quite rare.

Discouragement of romantic friendship seems to have been rare, not only because society believed that love between women fulfilled positive functions such as providing a release for homosocially segregated girls and unhappily married women, but also because men generally doubted that these relationships would be very enduring in any case. In Samuel Richardson's *Clarissa* (1748), the Colonel observes to John Belford, "Friendship, generally speaking . . . is too fervent a flame for female minds to manage: a light that but in few of their hands burns steady, and often hurries the sex into flight and absurdity. Like other extremes, it is hardly ever durable. Marriage, which is the highest state of friendship, generally absorbs the most vehement friendships of female to female, and that whether the wedlock is happy or not." In William Hayley's *The Young Widow* (1789), Mrs. Audley complains to Cornelia (who calls Mrs. Audley a "second self" and one who "knows all my thoughts"), "The greater part of the [male] sex have no faith in female friendship." Hayley thus acknowledges men's scepticism regarding female relationships, but he allows the two women to prove men wrong.

Eighteenth-century fiction suggests that men also believed women carried on passionate friendships with other women so that they would have someone in whom to confide about their relationships with men. In Harriet Lee's *The Errors of Innocence* (1786), for example, Obrien says of Sophia and Helen, "Lady Helen is the mere sentimental correspondent every modern nymph adopts, as the Knights-errant of old did their squires, only to be the living chronicle of their own exploits." [5] But for the most part, the women characters of the eighteenth-century novel demonstrate that love for their romantic friend and not the ulterior motive of excitement about a male is the *raison d'être* of the relationship. Despite Obrien's crass assessment in *The Errors of Innocence*, Sophia, now a married woman (unhappily so, significantly enough), tells Helen, "to you I early gave my heart, nor have I ever wished to withdraw it: a similitude of feelings rendered the gift in some degree worthy of your acceptance, and the romance of youth has rivetted our friendship." The men could exclaim as much as they pleased about the slight quality of a love between two women. The women insisted that it was powerful and enduring.

The institution of female romantic friendship was at least as pervasive in eighteenth-century France as in England. Historians point out that the intensity of such relationships in France went far beyond the love a woman showed her family and far beyond "the commonplace courtesy of the heart, such as a woman bestowed on a dozen acquaintances." These same-sex friendships were marked by "a pervasive feeling, a vital illusion, a kind of passion." The women would pledge one another lifelong devotion. They would exchange "sighs and embraces, whispered effusions and tiny transports." Each would claim that there was no leaving the other, no living without her. They would address each other in letters as "my heart," "my love," "my queen," and wear each other's colors. They went only to suppers where they were both invited. They "sauntered through the Salons, hand in hand." And they wore portraits of their beloved women friends dangling from their wristbands. In the idiom of the day, a woman said that she had a "feeling" or a "passion" for another woman, or that the other woman was "appealing" to her.[6]

A French comedy of the period describes the trappings of these friendships, and shows also how male writers viewed them: The maid of the Marquise de Gemini enumerates the expenses her lady has gone through in order to carry on her passion:

> Eight hundred pounds for a desk! . . . A pretty sum for a letter to her dear Dorothy, her darling Viscountess; for, praise be where praise is due, my Lady has no better occupation than to dedicate all her days to her. She writes her regularly ten notes in as many hours! One large secretary, three hundred pounds! One secret portfolio. . . . A Group representing *The Confidences of Two Youthful Beings*, one hundred and twenty pounds! . . . And items for hair-rings, hair-watches, hair-lockets, hair-bracelets, hair-collars, hair-scentbags.[7]

French fiction also confirms the historians' observations regarding the pervasiveness of romantic friendship. In Rousseau's *La nouvelle Héloise* the intensity of the relationship between Claire and Julie often threatens to overshadow the very passionate heterosexual relationships in the story. Claire, in fact, admits to the man who is to become her husband, to his disbelief and tolerant amusement, that Julie is much more important to her than he can ever be, although she realizes that it would be proper if she would let him take precedence in her affection. To Julie she explains that she cannot marry M. d'Orbe because she loves Julie better, and she cannot distinguish between her love for a woman and what one is supposed to feel for a man. "Tell me, my child," she asks, "Does the soul have a sex? Truthfully, I scarcely feel mine . . . An inconquerable and sweet habit attached me to you from childhood; I love only you alone perfectly." Claire marries M. d'Orbe after all, but after his death she hopes only "to reunite myself to [Julie] for the rest of our days." And although she admits finally that her love for Julie has not excluded heterosexual interest from her life—she, too, has loved St. Preux, Julie's beloved (and Rousseau in his mystical fashion appears to suggest that it is fitting that two women who love each other so much should love the same man)—but that emotion has never equalled in her mind her love for Julie, who taught her how to feel: "The most important thing of my life," she writes to her romantic friend, "has been to love you. From the very beginning my heart has been absorbed in yours . . . and I have lived only to be your friend."

Twentieth-century scholars who have discussed these passages seem to worry about whether the two women are lesbian, or they point out that there is "undoubtedly some sexual ambiguity involved" in their relationship.[8] Rousseau shows us that his society generally did not concern itself with bald sexual analysis. Saint Preux is very happy to watch the two women tenderly kissing and to see the cheek of one upon the bosom of the other. While he claims to be jealous of "so tender a friendship," he finds it less threatening than beautiful and (like Casanova) exciting: "Nothing, no, nothing on earth is capable of exciting such a voluptuous sensibility as your mutual caresses; and the spectacle of two lovers has not offered my eyes a more delicious sensation."

Rousseau modeled the love between these two women on the passionate female friendships that he observed everywhere and that had long existed in France. The correspondence between Mme. de Staël and Mme. Récamier illustrates the intensity that was characteristic of romantic friendship in France throughout the eighteenth and into the nineteenth centuries. These two women devoted themselves to each other for years, even through their various heterosexual affairs,[9] and almost until Mme. de Staël's death in 1817. After their first meeting, Mme. Récamier records, "from then on I thought only of Madame de Staël."[10] Soon Mme. de Staël was writing to her, "I love you with a love surpassing that of friendship. I go down on my knees to embrace you with all my heart." When their relationship was several years old, Mme. de Staël reflected that it was impossible to separate her feelings for Juliette from those that she had experienced in heterosexual love; her love for Juliette, she says, "fills my imagination and spreads over my life an interest which one other sentiment alone has inspired in me." It is, in fact, impossible to see a difference in the language of love she uses in writing to Juliette and that which might be used in a heterosexual love letter:

> You are in the forefront of my life. . . . It seemed to me when I saw you that to be loved by you would satisfy destiny. It would be enough, in fact, if I were to see you. . . . You are sovereign [in my heart], so tell me you will never give me pain; at this moment you have the power to do so terribly.
>
> Adieu, my dear and adorable one. I press you to my heart. . . . My angel, at the end of your letter say to me *I love you.* The emotion I will feel at those words will make me believe that I am holding you to my heart. . . .[11]

Such a love was confessed without self-consciousness, since it was entirely within the realm of the socially permissible.

It is probable that many romantic friends, while totally open in expressing and demonstrating emotional and spiritual love, repressed any sexual inclinations, and even any recognition of those inclinations, that they might have felt for each other, since during most eras of modern history women were well taught from childhood that only men or bad women were sexually aggressive. But because it was believed that good women could generally be counted on to suppress sexual desires, even a puritanical society had little concern about allowing them fairly unlimited access to each other. Thus romantic friends are typically described in fiction as sharing "one bed, one purse, . . . one heart." [12]

Because it was thought unlikely that even their sensuality, which included kissing, caressing and fondling, would become genital, romantic friends were permitted to articulate, even during the most sexually conservative times, their physical appreciation of each other as professedly heterosexual women today would be ashamed to do. In *The Young Widow*, Lucy tells Harriot, her sister-in-law—again without the slightest trace of self-consciousness—that she is not to worry because her brother has fallen in love with a young Italian woman who resides with them: "If one of our family had been tempted to sleep with her it would have been your humble servant Lucy, and not the innocent Edward." It is Lucy's inability to understand what we might view as the implications of this statement and her innocence regarding erotic possibilities that permit her to make such a declaration. She concludes "as I am absolutely in love with her myself, and have not also the power of metamorphosing myself into a husband, I should most vehemently wish for Edward's success."

In the same innocent spirit, romantic friends sometimes made specific comparisons between their love and Eros, generally to the detriment of Eros, as in Sarah Ponsonby's "Song":

> *By Vulgar Eros long misled*
> *I call'd thee tyrant, mighty love!*
> *With idle fears my fancy fled*
> *Nor ev'ne thy pleasures wish'd to prove.*
>
> *Condemn'd at length to wear thy chains*
> *Trembling I felt and ow'd thy might*
> *But soon I found my fears were vain*
> *Soon hugg'd my chain, and thought it light.*[13]

Those comparisons usually suggest that there is no difference between romantic friendship and Eros with regard to the intensity or the all-consuming qualities of the love. For Sarah Ponsonby, who slept in one bed with her beloved Eleanor Butler for more than fifty years, the major distinction between the two loves was that Eros was "vulgar," while her romantic friendship was not.

A Note On Romantic Friendship and the Language of Sentiment

Modern scholars, whose sophistication regarding sexual "abnormality" was derived from the work of the late nineteenth- and early twentieth-century sexologists and their disciples, generally have explained love letters such as those that passed between Mme. de Staël and Mme. Récamier as examples of nothing more than the vocabulary of the day, a style that "came out of the sentimental extravagance of the Romantic and Gothic novel." [14] Such an analysis comfortably discounts the seriousness of the emotion these women felt for each other. It is not surprising that it has been our century's favorite explanation for the ubiquitous traces of passionate love between women before our day. How could a woman who ostensibly had male lovers, and was perhaps even married and a mother, have been in love with another woman? the scholars ask. She could not, because she was clearly heterosexual, and by definition a woman who loves another woman is homosexual! Therefore, if a woman pledged undying devotion to another, if she claimed that her world revolved around her female friend, that she lived for her and would die for her, she was not expressing profound emotion: She was only using the sentimental language of her day.

But even in a period of sentimentality, when feeling was often valued for its own sake and expressions of profound emotion were more common than genuine profundity of feeling, it is possible to make some distinction between superficial and artificial expressions of sentiment and the real thing.[15] The eighteenth century made these distinctions as a matter of course. Charlotte Smith, in her 1798 novel, *The Young Philosopher*, says of her heroine, "Her sensibility was not the exotic production of those forced and unnatural descriptions of tenderness that are exhibited by the imaginary heroine of impossible adventures; it was the consequence of right and genuine feeling." Fiction of the period contains numerous examples of forced and artificial expressions of love between women as well as those which were intended to be viewed as expressions of genuine feeling.

Not infrequently in the didactic novel of the eighteenth century, a false romantic friendship is placed side by side with a true romantic friendship, and the author shows the reader how to detect the difference. In Charlotte Lennox's *Euphemia*, the title character is given two romantic friends. One is Lady Jackson, who, Euphemia says, "loaded" her "with a thousand professions of friendship, and called it a misfortune to have known me, since she was to lose me so soon." Lady Jackson offers to buy Euphemia a small estate in the vicinity so that the two women may be together forever, and she cries to Euphemia, "Tell me you will accept my offer—tell me so, and make me happy." But Lady Jackson, Euphemia soon discovers, values feeling for its own sake, and her behavior does not match her expressions of sentiment. When, for example, she has the opportunity to buy back for Euphemia some family pictures which are being auctioned off, she claims she must go out of town that week. It does not take Euphemia long to understand that Lady Jackson's passion for their friendship does not go beyond the language she uses in speaking to her. Lady Jackson, she concludes, can be nothing more to her than "a companion in my amusements—one who returns my visits most punctually, never fails to send daily inquiries after my health if I am the least indisposed, and is a most strict observer of all the civil duties of life." Maria, on the other hand, is an exemplary passionate friend. When Euphemia must leave for America with her husband, Maria complains that she had hoped that they would forever "live in sweet society together," and never be separated except

by the briefest absences, "rendered tolerable by frequent letters."
She laments:

> You are going to leave me; and, too, probably forever. . . . All
> that now remains of the friendship, which was the pride and
> happiness of my life, will be the sad remembrance of a good I
> once enjoyed, and which is fled forever! . . . How shall I teach
> my heart to forget you! How shall I bear the conversation of
> other young women of our age and condition, after being used
> to yours! . . . I was happy, and I am so no more. I must lose
> you! There is no remedy! Tears efface my letters as I write!

Unlike Lady Jackson, Maria proves the sincerity of her sentimental language by her behavior, such as her readiness to make sacrifices
for Euphemia. Euphemia returns this devotion and the two women
are continually first in each other's thoughts. When Maria faints for
joy upon hearing that her beloved has returned to Britain, neither
Euphemia nor the reader is able to doubt her utter sincerity.

Like Charlotte Lennox, Anne Hughes in *Henry and Isabella* (1788)
makes a distinction between true passionate friendships and those
which are little more than acquaintanceships. While the former are
"warm," "tender," "sweet," and "lasting," and even exceed "the so
much boasted pleasures" of heterosexual love, the latter are "prudent," "sensible," ungenerous, and ultimately cold. They do not require complete commitment or total confidence, and they are thus
not to be trusted or valued.

A willingness to sacrifice anything for another woman's happiness
was one test of a genuine romantic relationship. Another was the test
of time—although many passionate friendships could not have lived
up to this ideal of longevity, since women were often physically separated by the marriage of one or both of them; and while they might
carry on an ardent correspondence, they were robbed of the joys of
proximity. The more fortunate Sarah Ponsonby wrote in her day
book about romantic friendship in general and her own in particular, "Esteem of great powers, or amiable qualities newly discovered
may embroider a day or a week, but a friendship of twenty years is
interwoven with the texture of life." A true romantic friendship,
according to Sarah, became a part of life and even life itself. Dura-
tion was an important indication of its profundity: "Those that have
loved longest love best," Sarah explained.[16]

The young Anna Seward, writing to a romantic friend about her
hopes for their future, contrasted the solid "foundation" of the

"fervent inclination" which she and her correspondent felt for each other to that of "the giddy violence of novel-reading misses, who plight their first-sight friendships with solemn earnestness, because they think it pretty and becoming to have plighted friendships. . . ." But those foolish young women, Seward says, should embroider a motto on their samplers:

> *We swear eternal troth—but say, my friend,*
> *What day, next week, th' eternity shall end.*[17]

These women had no difficulty in distinguishing sentimental gesture from true romantic friendship. When in both fiction and life, they told each other, "I love you," they meant precisely that. When they wept for sorrow or joy at the loss or the return of the beloved friend, their tears were real. They claimed to place each other above anyone else, and their actions frequently revealed that they did. Their language and behavior are incredible today: Thus such friendships are usually dismissed by attributing them to the facile sentimentality of other centuries, or by explaining them in neat terms such as "lesbian," meaning sexual proclivity. We have learned to deny such a depth of feeling toward any one but a prospective or an actual mate. Other societies did not demand this kind of suppression. What these women felt, they were able to say; and what they said, they were able to demonstrate. Their vows and their behavior may seem excessive to us, but they were no less genuine.

Women who were romantic friends were everything to each other. They lived to be together. They thought of each other constantly. They made each other deliriously happy or horribly miserable by the increase or abatement of their proferred love. They were jealous of other female friends (and certainly of male friends) who impinged on their beloved's time or threatened to carry away a portion of her affections. They vowed that if it were at all possible they would someday live together, or at least die together, and they declared that both eventualities would be their greatest happiness. They embraced and kissed and walked hand in hand, and some even held each other all night in sleep. But unless they were transvestites or considered "unwomanly" in some male's conception, there was little chance that their relationship would be considered lesbian.

CHAPTER 3

The Battle of the Sexes

In her book *The Ladies of Llangollen: A Study of Romantic Friendship* Elizabeth Mavor observes that romantic friendship reached a height in the eighteenth century because women of the middle and upper classes, "refined into awareness by Addison and Steele's *Spectator*, the poets of solitude, and Richardson's novels, found little cultural reciprocity from the more conservative gentlemen, and as a consequence of this sympathetic discrepancy turned to their own sex." [1] Her analysis offers one plausible explanation for the distance between men and women but their alienation was far more complex and far-reaching. Renaissance men and subsequent generations of males believed, along with Montaigne, that they could not share honesty with women. And for their part, women seem to have been convinced that they could not find that attribute in men—or at least that men would not be honest with them. There were, of course, exceptions. In the seventeenth-century novels of Madeleine de Scudéry, platonic, all-consuming friendship between men and women was viewed as a realizable ideal, and she herself enjoyed a forty-year "spiritual" relationship with the *Précieux*, Paul Pellisson, a man seventeen years her junior. However, like Montaigne, many women doubted the possibility of such a relationship and believed that they had to turn to other women for openness and honesty. The mutual distrust between men and women is not surprising in view of the homosocial societies in which they lived during the Renaissance and subsequent centuries up until fairly recent times.

By the eighteenth century, men and women had long been considered different species. Upper-class males and females were usually brought up separately, taught separately, and encouraged to function in entirely separate spheres. Typical of seventeenth-century women, Lady Anne Halkett reports in her autobiography that she cannot remember three times that she spent in the company of any man besides her brothers when she was a young woman.[2] Even when the educations and interests of men and women by some unusual circumstance were not dissimilar, it seems that through habit they separated themselves on social occasions, as Elizabeth Carter, the eighteenth-century bluestocking, writer, and translator of Epictetus, complains of a party she attended:

> As if the two sexes had been in a state of war, the gentlemen arranged themselves on one side of the room, where they talked their own talk, and left us poor ladies to twirl our shuttles and amuse each other by conversing as we could. By what little I could hear, our opposites were discoursing on the old English poets, and this subject did not seem so much beyond our female capacity, but that we might have been indulged with a share of it.[3]

The woman of ambition probably had the most reason to feel alienated from men because she took herself seriously while most men usually didn't. In eighteenth-century England such a woman was a rebel in a very real sense. Although in the Saxon, Anglo-Norman, and Medieval periods, during the Tudor era, and in part of the seventeenth century, women could find meaningful ways to occupy their time, after the Restoration and throughout the eighteenth century, they were encouraged to be idle.[4] Bluestockings and a few other women in the eighteenth century refused. The brightest and strongest of them, however, must have felt the most alienated. Lady Mary Wortley Montague observed, early in the eighteenth century, "There is hardly a creature in the world more despicable or more liable to universal ridicule than a learned woman." At about the same time in France, Mme. de Lambert, who conducted one of the foremost Paris literary salons, lamented the general hostility toward erudite females: "Shame is no longer for vices, and women blush over their learning only."[5] If Charlotte Lennox has given us an accurate picture in *Euphemia*, men found nothing so odious as a woman of achievement in any era. The character Mr. Hartley complains upon meeting the "learned and scientific Lady Cornelia

Classick" and "the Diana of our forests, the fearless huntress Miss Sandford":

> A man makes a silly figure in company with so learned a Lady, and her Amazonian friend. Talents so masculine, and so ostentatiously displayed, place them above those attentions and assiduities to which the charming sex have so just a claim, and which we delight to pay. Women should always be women; the virtues of our sex are not the virtues of theirs. When Lady Cornelia declaims in Greek, and Miss Sandford vaults into the saddle like another Hotspur, I forget I am in company with women; the dogmatic critic awes me into silence, and the hardy rider makes my assistance unnecessary.

Such unsympathetic views of exceptional women's gifts, or any women's desires to develop those gifts, date back well before the late eighteenth century. The *Précieuses* in seventeenth-century France, much like the eighteenth-century English bluestockings, formed salons where they could meet to discuss intellectual matters and escape from the frivolity of the court and the rest of their society.[6] These women were frequently ridiculed in satirical drama and poetry. For example, they were the main butt of the joke in two Molière plays, *Les Précieuses ridicules* and *Les femmes savantes*, and were also attacked in Molière's *The School for Wives Criticized* in the character of Climène. One of the most brutal depictions of these women is in a mid-seventeenth-century poem by Claude le Petit, "Aux Précieuses." He portrays them as being pedantic and prudish; he invites them to a brothel to see what it's really all about, and advises them that once they become aroused they ought to roll up the book and use it as a dildo.[7] The *Précieuses*'s eighteenth-century counterparts continued to be satirized in works such as Dorat's *Les Prôneurs* (*The Eulogists*), an attack on Mme. de Lespinasse in particular, whose salon was especially influential in establishing literary tastes of the day. Dorat says of her: "She speaks, she thinks, and she hates like a man."

Although a major attraction in most of the salons was one or two male intellectuals, the women took each other seriously as thinking human beings. The English bluestockings of the eighteenth century formed similar coteries. Their gatherings were attended by men like Samuel Johnson, Horace Walpole, Edmund Burke, David Garrick, and Samuel Pepys—but even more important, as Mrs. Elizabeth Montagu observed to her friend Mrs. Vesey in 1785, they were attended by "the best, the most accomplished, and most learned women of any times." [8] These women, who had such great intellectual pride in themselves and in each other, must have felt in constant conflict with their society, which attempted to discourage their pride on all levels. Even Samuel Johnson, a lion to many of the bluestockings, was disparaging toward female aspiration in general. It was he who compared a woman preaching to a dog walking on its hind legs: "It is not done well," he was supposed to have said, "but you are surprised to find it done at all." Horace Walpole, another favorite of the eighteenth-century salon, described Elizabeth Montagu (whom Johnson called "the Queen of the Blues") as "a piece of learned nonsense." Nor were women's intellects taken any more seriously by the male lions of the French salons. La Rochefoucauld, a great salon celebrity of the seventeenth century and a close friend of the novelist Madame de La Fayette, observed, "There are few women whose worth survives their beauty."

Lesser lights discouraged and disparaged women with aspirations even more. William Kenrick, in *The Whole Duty of Women* (1753), told them that what was most dear to them—their intellectual accomplishments—was entirely inappropriate and forbidden:

> Seek not to know what is improper for thee; thrust not after prohibited knowledge; for happier is she who knoweth a little, than she who is acquainted with too much. . . . It is not for women . . . to trace the dark springs of science, or to number the thick stars of the heavens. . . . Thy kingdom is thine own house and thy government the care of thy family.[9]

The great popularity of this work in the latter half of the eighteenth century attests to its uttering widely accepted sentiments. Even in America, where, according to La Rochefoucauld, women were allowed great independence, Kenrick's book was a success—between 1761 and 1796 it went through nine American editions.[10]

With such a lack of sympathy toward their pursuits, intellectual women discovered that if they were to receive any encouragement at all, it generally had to come from among themselves. Perhaps men would not take them seriously as thinking human beings, even those whom they lionized and whose reputations they helped make, but they would take each other very seriously. Their correspondence shows in what great regard they held each other (especially each other's minds), what respect and admiration they (and they alone in their day) had for the female intellect.[11]

The French *Précieuse* and the English bluestocking, women who had a great sense of themselves as autonomous beings, had good reason to mistrust men and marriage. The seventeenth-century *Précieuse* Madeleine de Scudéry, speaking in her own character in the novel *Cyrus* (Volume X), observed, "I am well aware that there are many fine men, but when I consider them as husbands, I think of them in the role of masters, and because masters tend to become tyrants, from that instant I hate them. Then I thank God for the strong inclination against marriage he has given me." Widowhood was to the *Précieuses*, as Abbé de Pure observed in his study of these seventeenth-century women, a "pleasant escape from captivity."[12] When their families and fortunes permitted them to avoid these entanglements, they did; but such freedom was rare. When they married—in some cases because of family pressures, in rare cases out of what they themselves later characterized as foolish passions— they often regretted it, frequently to the extent that it kept them apart from their women friends. Elizabeth Montagu, "the Queen of the Blues," who was married to a man twenty-nine years her senior—with whom she lived until his death at an advanced age, carrying on all the while a series of passionate friendships with women—expressed to a correspondent a bluestocking's view of marriage:

> I own it astonishes me when I hear two people voluntarily, and on their own suggestion, entering into a bargain for perhaps fifty years cohabitation. I am so much of Solomon's mind that the end of a feast is better than the beginning of a fray, that I weep more at a wedding than a funeral. . . . I desire my congratulations to your family on the wedding. Marriage is honourable in all, and I have an infinite respect for it, and would by no means be thought to make a jest of so serious a thing. It is a civil debt which people ought to pay.
>
> I have told your friend Black, that the more sickly he is, the more he wants a tender friend to nurse him. I think most Women make good Nurses, few perhaps very eligible Companions. I always advise as many of my female friends as are indiscreet, and as many of my male friends as are sickly, to marry; for the first want a Master, and the second a Nurse, and these are characters generally to be found in the holy State of Matrimony; the rest is precarious.[13]

Along similar lines, young Anna Seward, the poet, who never married, urged a girlhood friend, who was considering making what Seward believed to be a very dubious match, to think of the comparative joylessness of marriage. "If he should treat you after marriage," Seward argued, "with tolerable kindness and good nature, it is the best you have reasonably to expect. What counterpoise, in the scale of happiness, can be formed by that *best* against the delights you must renounce in the morning of your youth?" Seward offers her friend what she believes to be an exciting distraction to pull her out of the marriage snares that could deliver her to lifelong misery:

> Return to Lichfield to me for the remainder of the winter! We will banish all mention of Mr. L——, which is a much better method than abusing him. We will read ingenious authors, who shall rather give our minds new ideas from the stores of science and observation, than increase the susceptibility of our hearts.[14]

For these women there could be no love without respect. Because their intellect was so important to them, perhaps they required respect for that part of themselves more than any other part. Most males of the period were rendered incapable of giving women intellectual respect by the early inculcation of society's views regarding female inferiority, so such women sought intimacy with other women. Because women of their class and temperament generally did not engage in sex outside of marriage, it probably occurred to few of them that the intense emotion they felt for each other could be expressed in sexual terms—but that emotion had all the manifestations of Eros without a genital component. Perhaps the primary difference between the salons of seventeenth- and eighteenth-century France and England and the salons of Paris in the 1920's where lesbian love was openly expressed (see Part III, page 369), was that as a result of the late nineteenth-century sexologists, women in the 1920's knew they were sexual creatures and behaved accordingly. Before that time, good women knew that only bad women were sexual creatures. What these good women felt for the women they loved was, therefore, described as "passionate" or "romantic" *friendship*.

Of course, not all women of the genteel classes were concerned enough with their intellect to look to other women for the affirmation that men denied, but many did feel, for other reasons, an alienation from men. Because they were encouraged to live in an essentially homosocial environment, to distrust men, and to form close relationships only with other women outside of marriage, romantic or passionate friendship, which was pervasive among the female intellectuals, also became an institution among women in general throughout the middle and upper classes in France and England. It is easiest to trace these romantic friendships in the correspondence of the women intellectuals because their letters have often been preserved, whereas those written by women who did not distinguish themselves have usually been lost to posterity. In their cases, however, the fiction of the time indicates romantic friendship was prevalent in their lives, and shows that while they did not have the same motives as the *Précieuses* and the bluestockings to cherish other women, they had other powerful incentives.

When genuine communication occurred between a man and a woman in the eighteenth century, it seems to have been so rare that, if Jane Austen is representing her society faithfully, people had difficulty believing that the pair were not contemplating marriage: She shows in *Sense and Sensibility* (c. 1797) that everyone was positive Elinor and Colonel Brandon were engaged because they often talked together—what had a man and a woman to say to each other, after all? Their education and socialization led them in virtually opposite directions.

The alienation between men and women was further increased by the rules of the double standard which were forcefully inculcated in young women. Girls were taught to recognize the double standard as a fact of life [15]; as the first Marquis of Halifax advised his daughter at the end of the seventeenth century, "The world . . . is somewhat unequal, and our sex seemeth to play the tyrant in distinguishing partially for ourselves, by making that in the utmost degree criminal in the woman, which in a man passeth under a much gentler censure." He went on to warn her, "Remember, that next to the danger of committing the fault yourself, the greatest is that of seeing it in your husband. Do not seem to look or hear that way." [16]

Except during the interregnum period in England, men had little encouragement to bridle their ids, but women were constantly repressed by social mores. Patricia Meyer Spacks observes that such repression reached an apogee in eighteenth-century England. Women had virtually no freedom of emotional expression. They were obsessed with innocence, concerned about the danger of passion; they were angry at men, often longed to be males or children. But despite their anger, Spacks asserts, they accepted what they were taught and believed that their repression was simply "in the nature of things." [17] However, even though most women did not appear to question "the nature of things," they often found a way within the framework of social respectability to express themselves emotionally and even sensually.

The repression of sexual activity among middle and upper-class unmarried women was especially stringent, since virginity was a sine qua non of a good woman. It was the only thing she had by herself and apart from her family influence that could command a price. A woman's chastity in eighteenth-century England was called, appropriately enough, her "purse." [18] French and English didactic literature of the sixteenth and seventeenth centuries invariably advised women to be chaste,[19] but with the rise of the novel in the eighteenth century, the subject of female chastity became a mainstay of fiction as well. In England it was held dear not only by characters such as Richardson's Pamela (whose "virtue"—i.e., chastity—is ultimately rewarded by marriage to a rich gentleman) and the class of women she represented, but by some of the most enlightened minds of the day. James Boswell reports that Samuel Johnson observed, "Consider of what importance to society the chastity of women is. Upon that all the property in the world depends. . . . They who forfeit it should not have any possibility of being restored to good character; nor should the children by an illicit connection attain the full right of lawful children." [20]

Naturally the man in the street agreed with these views, even to the point of ludicrousness, as the letter-to-the-editor section of *Gentleman's Magazine*, December 1773, indicates:

> The writer has succeeded in seducing his loved one, but now is tortured by the fact that he cannot marry her, for he will always suspect that where he conquered, others can too; and yet, he still loves her and hates to continue to ruin her. "I am doomed, in spite of reason, to entertain suspicions of that virtue which melted before the flame of my love." [21]

Once having lost her precious chastity, a young woman might as well wring her bosom and die, Oliver Goldsmith tells us in *The Vicar of Wakefield* (1766). Lady Mary Wortley Montagu, the eighteenth-century traveler and letter writer, recognized as a young woman the terrible potential dangers to a female of any sort of heterosexual permissiveness, as she wrote to the man she eventually married: "All commerce of this kind between men and women is like that of the Boys and Frogs in L'Estrange's Fable—'tis play to you, but 'tis death to us—and if we had the wit of the frogs, we should alwaies make that answer." [22] Even loving parents of the period, fiction tells us, preferred a daughter's death to her heterosexual transgression. The father of the seduced and abandoned girl in Henry Mackenzie's *The Man of Feeling* (1771) proclaims, "Her death I could have borne; but the death of her honour has added obloquy and shame to that sorrow which bends my grey hairs to the dust."

Other countries were no more permissive than England. In France, although a married woman had more sexual freedom than her English counterpart, a girl of a respectable family had even less. At a young age she was sent off to a convent, where her mind and body were to be preserved in pristine condition, and she was usually not permitted to leave until her family had selected a husband for her and had made plans for the wedding. Diderot warns mid-eighteenth-century French girls who might not be segregated from men that they must not be fooled by those who tell them they love them. Girls who allow themselves to be seduced will lose everything worth having in the world, and will gain little more than a "thank-you" from the men they love:

> What do these words signify which are pronounced so easily and interpreted so frivolously: "I love you"? Actually they mean, "If you would sacrifice for me your innocence and your morals, lose the respect that you now have for yourself and get from others, walk with lowered eyes in society . . . make your parents die of grief, and afford me a moment of pleasure, then I will be very obliged to you for it.

He begs mothers to read this warning to their daughters,[23] and as a proper father he sternly warns his own daughter of such dangers.[24]

In eighteenth-century America, attitudes were not much more liberal. Moral values were largely shipped from Europe to the Atlantic seaboard, particularly through literature.[25] Herbert Mann, Deborah Sampson's eighteenth-century biographer, believed that his readers would forgive all the more shocking aspects of her transvestite exploits if they could be convinced that throughout them all she remained a virgin and was never tempted by the men with whom she came in such close contact. To emphasize his point, Mann included in an appendix the story of Fatima, who gave her body to a lover and who was abandoned by him when he was sated. Mann adds that a woman who loved Deborah (or any female) was much luckier than Fatima, who had the misfortune to love a man, because a female would leave the woman who had loved her with her hymen intact. Although Mann, who was writing for a more conservative American reader, would not intimate as Brantôme does in *Lives of Fair and Gallant Ladies* that for a virgin, lesbian love is preferable to heterosexual love because "there is a great difference betwixt throwing water in a vessel and merely watering about it and round the rim," his implication is the same—romantic intimacies between women are harmless, and if a virgin must be intimate with someone, she is far better off choosing another woman.

Because such a value was placed on the hymen, women found themselves in a confusing situation. Men, they were told, were sexual creatures, and a married woman proved her love and duty to her husband by allowing him to satisfy his appetite upon her. But an unmarried woman would place in peril her total human value if she thus proved her love to a man. Yet, that women would pay such a high price for giving up their virginity did not prevent men from asking it, as the *Gentleman's Magazine* letter indicates, and tricking women out of it, as countless eighteenth-century novels and magazine stories demonstrate.[26] In this way, men and women were placed in an adversary situation, and the girl who valued herself learned early to distrust men. Her parents helped by taking care that she circulated in an almost exclusively homosocial society and thereby avoided the dangers of heterosexual temptation. While a girl from the lower class could not be so sheltered, she too was in peril if she allowed herself to trust a man. In French and German villages of the sixteenth, seventeenth, and eighteenth centuries, some kind of "fornication penalty" (a fine or humiliating punishment) was almost universally levied by the town fathers or by a seigneurial court against any woman found to have had intercourse outside of wedlock.[27] The author of *Satan's Harvest Home* (1749) suggests that the English lower classes also placed great value on an intact hymen before marriage. If an unmarried woman from the country or from the city should be "ruined" she would soon join the prostitutes who filled the streets of London from White Chapel to Charing Cross.[28]

Eighteenth-century English and French writers and social historians leave us with the impression that since men and women were typically placed in adversary positions, little love was possible between them. Historians claim that "love" in eighteenth-century France, especially among the upper classes, was a game that only married women could play (but not with their husbands). To say "I love you" to a member of the opposite sex meant "*I desire you: to possess,* for men, and *to capture* for women, there lay the whole sport and utmost goal." [29] The literary record seems to support their thesis: Choderlos de Laclos's *Les liaisons dangereuses* (1780–1781) suggests through the character of Valmont that a man's greatest pleasure with a woman was to effect "her ruin"—but not simply to rob her of her virtue: The game must be prolonged and subtle and as vicious as possible. He laments when he fears that Mme. de Tourvel will give in to him too easily:

> Let her yield herself, but let her struggle! Let her have the strength to resist without having enough to conquer; let her fully taste the feeling of her weakness and be forced to admit her defeat. Let the obscure poacher kill the deer he has surprised from her hiding place; the real sportsman must hunt it down. . . . It is I who control her fate. [30]

In later references to his seduction of Tourvel, he uses the language of war—she is the "enemy," they engage in "battle," and he effects her "defeat." [31]

The fashionableness of the Marquis de Sade during this period suggests that Valmont was not a singular villain. Sade took the brutality that existed between the sexes to its gruesome conclusion: If it was enjoyable to torture a woman mentally and emotionally, would it not also be thrilling to torture her body? [32] Some of the worst excesses of the French Revolution, which occurred in the Marquis de Sade's day, revealed this male hostility toward and contempt for women: Not only was the beautiful head of the guillotined Mme. de Lamballe paraded about on a pole, but her pubic hair was also cut off and worn by some gentlemen as a moustache.

Nicolas Restif de la Bretonne, the author of *L'Anti-Justine* (1798), who claims he is writing "a book sweeter to the taste than any of Sade's," a "villain [who] never presents the delights of love experienced by men without accompanying them by torments and even death inflicted upon women," [33] offers an interesting illustration of how even one who understood the ugliness of Sade's views was apparently addicted to them. While the book's title, preface, and even epilogue all clearly attempt to counter the popular and "baneful *Justine,*" Bretonne describes extensively a man fantasizing having sex with a woman and then murdering her, following this with an entire chapter in which such a murder actually occurs —the woman dies after the man bites off her nipples and rips her vagina and anus so that "where there were formerly two holes, there is now but one." He then slices her apart with a scalpel and lancet, beginning first with her breasts and mons veneris.[34] The antisadistic author seems to have been convinced that the eighteenth-century reader of pornographic literature required at least one such scene in order to be aroused.

Although English writers of this period produced nothing to equal Sade,[35] the literature indicates that the cruel game between the sexes which historians and novelists describe was not peculiar to France. The most popular eighteenth-century novels, such as Samuel Richardson's *Pamela* (1740) and *Clarissa* (1748), are all about this game, and frequently it is treated as a light-hearted joke, which is made funnier by the agony or embarrassment of the woman. Tobias Smollett's *The Adventures of Roderick Random* (1748) illustrates this attitude: Roderick impregnates a servant, uses her assistance to get money from his employer so that he may leave, and never mentions her again; he stumbles into the bed of a woman who mistakes him for her lover, and though he hates her he opportunistically has sex with her; he beds a country girl with particular relish, thinking all the while of another who is unobtainable, etc. When Roderick is not expressing hostility toward a woman or deceiving her, other men are: Miss Williams, who has been driven to prostitution, tells Roderick how as a young girl she was seduced, impregnated, and then abandoned by a seemingly ingenuous, upstanding young man, Lothario, who had promised to marry her but married a rich woman instead. She miscarries as she tries unsuccessfully to kill him, but soon afterward she is comforted by a stranger, Horatio, who tells her that he killed her false lover in a duel out of pity for her. In gratitude she gives herself to Horatio, but soon discovers that Lothario lives, and that he and Horatio together invented the story of the duel so that Horatio might have the opportunity to enjoy her sexually for a while.

Such extravagant machinations in order to get a woman to bed were common also in the magazine fiction of eighteenth-century England. For example, *Lady's Magazine* ran an epistolary novelette during 1780, in which a country girl is seduced by a lord who promises to marry her and seals his promise by writing her a note which says that if he does not marry her within one month he will give her 20,000 pounds—but he purposely fails to date the note. She is impregnated of course, and then abandoned by the lord, who marries a wealthy woman. It is true that most of these examples of male hostility are taken from fiction, but the very frequency with which they appeared in novels shows that it must have reflected a common attitude. Men agreed as a society that unbridled sexual access to any women they desired should be denied out of respect for property rights; but unarticulated mores encouraged many of them to procure such access by any dissimulation necessary.

Nor could women automatically feel safe from male hostility once they were married, since among the upper classes at least, marriages were not often made with consideration to the parties' affections. Marriage was a commercial affair that replenished family fortunes and united family names. Love sometimes entered it, but only by accident. Forced marriages, arranged by parents, were so common in seventeenth-century England that the subject became popular fare in the drama.[36] In France from the sixteenth century to the end of the eighteenth century, marriage in the upper classes was often little more than a convention. Adultery for an upper-class male from the sixteenth century to the end of the eighteenth century, and for an upper-class female in the eighteenth century, was not even considered a moral offense,[37] although if proper discretion were not exercised, it may have been thought an offense against manners.

Eighteenth-century French marriage was strictly a "family matter," determined by the parents solely on the grounds of rank and fortune. The young woman was not even consulted, and she often learned that she was to be married by the unwonted stir in the house.[38] Among the middle classes, a woman could expect to be wooed and courted before marriage, but once married she found herself in a subservient position; for her, "to take a husband" generally meant "to take a master." [39] Women of the lower classes were even worse off, and could expect frequent beatings by their husbands. An eighteenth-century peasant's wife, according to one early nineteenth-century French historian, was valued far below his horse, since she was less important to livelihood.[40] "Lovelessness," he observes, was everywhere common to petty bourgeois and peasant marriages.

Upper-class marriage in eighteenth-century England was also made by parental decision, always with regard to fortune and rank, sometimes with regard to moral respectability, but often without regard to suitability of age or temperament or to the possibility of love between the bride and groom. The unhappiness resulting from such marriages provided material for numerous plots and subplots in the literature of the day. Commercial considerations in eighteenth-century fictional marriage always override romance. Even in the most sentimental stories, social and economic concerns had to be satisfied before love was permitted. Marriage was less a union of two lovers than of two people of complementary rank and fortune. "There was no good marriage without a good settlement."[41] The attitude was apparently ubiquitous in real life as well. Richard Steele, in a hope for reformation, complained that parents were most often concerned with "finding out matches for their estates and not their children."[42] Nor were things much better in America apparently, as the author of *Reflections on Courtship and Marriage* (attributed to Benjamin Franklin) shows in his outcry against arranged matches, insisting that marriage without union of minds, sympathy of affection, mutual esteem and friendship was contrary to reason, and no one should be compelled to it.[43]

Parentally arranged May-December marriages, which were often the basis of a tragic fictional plot, were common in real life too, both in France and America. Madame Geoffrin, who conducted one of the most influential literary salons in eighteenth-century France, was given in marriage at the age of fourteen to a settled, respectable man of forty-eight. She had a good dowry to bring to a marriage and could have attracted a much younger man, but her grandmother reasoned that since the girl was orphaned, it would be excellent for her to have a parent figure in a husband. In England the eighteenth-century bluestocking, Mrs. Elizabeth Montagu, was married at the age of twenty-two to a man of fifty-one. Wealth was usually the major consideration in such unions. In her autobiography the librettist Mrs. Delany tells of having been married by her parents at the age of seventeen to a man of sixty whom she abhorred. "The day was come," she complained, "when I was to leave all I loved and valued, to go to a remote country, with a man I looked upon as my tyrant—my jailor; one that I was determined to obey and oblige, but found it impossible to love."[44] But her parents felt that the match was a fine one, since the groom was much wealthier than they.

Mrs. Delany's weepy but unquestioning obedience to her parents' wishes seems to have been usual. In *Sense and Sensibility* (c. 1797), Jane Austen shows that many are shocked at Edward Ferrar's imprudence when he refuses to marry the wealthy Miss Morton, who was selected for him by his mother. For this uncustomary assertion of independence, his mother threatens to disinherit him. Although in *Sense and Sensibility* Austen is on Edward's side, in a juvenile work, *Love and Freindship* [sic], written when she was about fifteen, she evidently accepted the prevalent attitude that disobeying a parent's wishes was absurd. In this book she paints a satirical portrait of a young man who has been requested by his father to marry Lady Dorothea: " 'No, never,' exclaimed I. 'Lady Dorothea is lovely and engaging; I prefer no woman to her; but know Sir, that I scorn to marry in compliance with your wishes. No! Never shall it be said that I obliged my Father.' " Austen portrays those who approve his statement as being equally silly when they gush, "We all admired the noble manliness of his reply." When Sir Harry and Aemily in the novel *Female Friendship* (1770) marry without the consent of Aemily's father, the shock of such unprecedented insubordination kills him—and out of guilty grief Aemily has a miscarriage, and then a fever, and then dies.

Eighteenth-century novels like *Clarissa* and *Tom Jones* (through the character of Sophia Western) show that while a parent should not actually force a child into a marriage that was repugnant, and that the child might be justified in resisting parental tyranny, nothing could have justified marrying against the parent's will.[45] Thus, a daughter might resist a match that would make her miserable, but she could not on her own choose one that would make her happy if she had any sensitivity to society's rules. Love matches conducted with autonomy by young men and women of the genteel classes seem to have been very rare indeed.

Even the word "love" was not often used in relation to marriage among the upper classes, as both fiction and journals suggest. If a lady felt that the man she was to marry "valued" her, she was sufficiently lucky and to be envied.[46] When Clarissa in Richardson's novel rejects the man her parents have chosen for her and tells them that she prefers Lovelace, Mrs. Harlowe is shocked that her daughter could be so brash as to consider "the person." Clarissa was simply expected to marry the man her family had selected, and to consider neither what was appealing nor unappealing about him. Even the independent bluestocking Hester Chapone eventually accepted the wisdom of this point of view herself. She had married, as she characterized it, "for love," but she was not mature enough to have real discretion and taste. Great animosity immediately developed between her and her new husband. He died ten months after the marriage, to her apparent relief, and she accepted the prevalent opinion of her society on this matter ever afterward, advocating marriage by parental arrangement.[47]

Since the sexes were so dichotomized, a marriage between two equals was generally impossible. And because women of the upper classes were not free to choose their mates, it was recognized that they might find themselves wedded to someone incompatible with their own temperaments and moral tastes. If so, their only recourse was to close their eyes and ears to what was distasteful to them and carry on as best they could, as Lord Halifax advised his daughter at the end of the seventeenth century.

Although a husband and wife loathed each other, as was frequently the case in parentally arranged marriages that did not consider the feelings of the principals, they stayed married but led separate lives. Divorce could be obtained only by an act of Parliament, and was both costly and difficult. The upper classes looked on marriage with "cynical aversion." Married couples went together to social functions, but except for such occasions they saw little of each other. Men often congregated to the exclusion of women, and wives were left to get through the long day however they could.[48] English literature of the seventeenth and eighteenth centuries illustrates the custom. In Vanbrugh's seventeenth-century comedy, *The Relapse*, Amanda asks the happily widowed Berinthia (who had been forced to marry by a parent) how she and her husband lived together. Berinthia replies:

Like Man and Wife, asunder;
He lov'd the Country, I the Town. . . .
He the Sound of a Horn, I the Squeak of a Fiddle.
We were dull Company at Table, worse A-bed.
Whenever we met, we gave one another the Spleen.
And never agreed but once, which was about lying alone.

In the eighteenth century, Henry Fielding describes an upper middle-class marriage thus:

The Squire, to whom the poor woman had been a faithful

upper-servant all the time of their marriage, had returned that behavior by making what the world calls a good husband. He very seldom swore at her, perhaps not above once a week, and never beat her. She had not the least occasion for jealousy, and was perfect mistress of her time, for she was never interrupted by her husband, who was engaged all the morning in his field exercises, and all the evening with his bottle companions.

Were most genteel young women really willing to sacrifice their lives to their parents' wishes without question? Why else would they have agreed to marry under such circumstances? Perhaps because in the seventeenth and eighteenth centuries, when women had little hope of economic independence, marriage was actually the only way a girl could pass from the tyrannical control of her family into adulthood. Lady Mary Montagu, for example, seems to have married Edward Wortley for just that reason after a long correspondence with him which made it clear that on her side there was little love. Although they never considered divorce, after the first months of their marriage they seldom lived together, except when she went with him for a few years to Turkey where he served as ambassador.

Frenchwomen also believed that marriage was the only escape from family tyranny. Claire, who has just married M. d'Orbe, writes Julie in Rousseau's *La nouvelle Héloise*:

> If it had depended on me, I would never have married, but our sex buys liberty only by slavery and it is necessary to begin as a servant in order to be a mistress someday. Although my father never bothered me, I had annoyance from my family. To escape it, I married M. d'Orbe.

Claire's situation cannot be attributed to the dramatic demands of fiction. Madame Houdetot similarly confessed to Diderot, "I married, that I might live to go to the Ball, the Opera, the Promenade and the Play." Her contemporary, Mme. de Puisieux, also admitted that it was because she would be permitted to own by herself a gilded coach, fine diamonds, and good horses that she agreed to marry a most unprepossessing man.[49] Once an upper-class woman took a husband, she was in effect free to go her own way for the first time in her life, and her way frequently wended in an opposite direction from his. Receiving so little emotional sustenance from the intimacy of marriage, she often sought that sustenance in a romantic friendship with a beloved woman friend.

Elizabeth Mavor's observation regarding the eighteenth-century devotion to sensibility which overtook so many literate Englishwomen and separated them from men is useful as one explanation of why romantic friendships flourished then. But the concern with chastity, which made women suspicious of men; the education of males and females, which had opposite aims; the homosocial environment and the inhabitation of different spheres; and the marriages between virtual strangers also explain why these friendships flourished. The most important reason, however, is that society imposed no stigma on romantic love between women as it did in the twentieth century. Women had no reason to fear that their emotion was immoral or diseased, and so they could give expression to a passion that developed very naturally out of mutual admiration, respect, shared interests, shared aspirations, and encouragement to realize one's individuality rather than to fit into a prescribed role.

CHAPTER 4

Romantic Friendship in Eighteenth-Century Literature

By the second half of the eighteenth century in England, romantic friendships became a popular theme in fiction. Novels of the period show how women perceived these relationships and what ideals they envisioned for love between women. Those ideals generally could not be realized in life because most women did not have the wherewithal to be independent. In fiction, however, romantic friends (having achieved economic security as a part of the plot, which also furnishes them with good reasons for not having a husband around) could retire together, away from the corruption of the man-ruled "great world"; they could devote their lives to cultivating themselves and their gardens, and to living generously and productively too; they could share perfect intimacy in perfect equality.

The most complete fictional blueprint for conducting a romantic friendship is Sarah Scott's *A Description of Millenium Hall* (1762), a novel which went through four editions by 1778. The author was one of the fortunate few who was able to live her ideal of romantic friendship. Scott married in 1751, and the disastrous relationship lasted for only one year before she separated from her husband (and for some mysterious reason he not only returned her dowry but also provided her with a yearly income). In 1748 she had met Barbara Montagu, sister of Lord Halifax, at Bath. The two became such inseparable friends that Barbara accompanied Sarah on her honeymoon (it was not unusual for a bride to be accompanied by a friend in the eighteenth century), and lived with her and Mr. Scott during most of their short married life. After Sarah left her husband she went to Bath, where Lady "Bab" had a home. Then in 1754 the women took a house together in Bath Easton, a village about two miles outside of Bath. There they began a charity project for poor girls, which became the foundation of the *Millenium Hall* story. They lived and worked together until Lady Bab's death. Elizabeth Montagu, Sarah Scott's sister, when describing a visit to Sarah and Bab in a 1775 letter to Gilbert West, affords a glimpse of Sarah's life. Mrs. Montagu consciously refutes here the popular stereotypes of the unmarried woman and her dull, unproductive existence:

> Her conversation is lively and easy, and she enters into all the reasonable pleasures of society; goes frequently to the plays, and sometimes to the balls, etc. They have a very pretty house at Bath for the winter, and one at Bath Easton for the summer; their houses are adorned by the ingenuity of the owners. . . . My sister seems very happy; it has pleased God to lead her to truth by the road of affliction. . . . Lady Bab Montagu concurs with her in all things, and their convent, for by its regularity it resembles one, is really a cheerful place.[1]

Elizabeth Mavor, in her study of Sarah Ponsonby and Eleanor Butler, states that all serious female friends were familiar with Sarah Scott's novel, that it was the *vade mecum* of romantic friendship.[2] While *Millenium Hall* is not a faithful rendering of the actual lives of Sarah Scott and Barbara Montagu, it does show their ideals, and probably the romantic aspirations of many pairs of female friends during the eighteenth century.

The main characters of *Millenium Hall* are Miss Melvyn and Louisa Mancel, who had met in boarding school. They are both beautiful, genteel, and sweet. They love reading and making music, and studying geography, philosophy, and religion together. Scott says of them in their youth, "They seldom passed a day without seeing each other. . . . Their affections were so strongly united that one could not suffer without the other feeling equal pain."

After she leaves school, Louisa does menial work so that she can support herself while remaining close to her beloved. When Miss Melvyn is forced into marriage, she begs Louisa to live near her, and Louisa agrees, "since a second paradise would not recompense her for the loss of her society." However, the new husband, Mr. Morgan, is not so amenable and refuses even to let Miss Mancel visit, protesting, "I will have no person in my house more beloved than myself." The two women are devastated by the demand that they, who are so close, separate: "The connection of soul and body did not seem more indissoluble, nor were ever divided with greater pain." As Mrs. Morgan watches her friend walk off, she feels "more dead than alive." When a turning in the road robs her of the sight of Louisa, "as if her eyes had no more employment worthy of them left, they were again overwhelmed in tears."

Conveniently, Mrs. Morgan's husband dies a short time later, and the two women, who now have financial independence, are free to live together. They retire to the country, away from the corruption of city life, where they can enjoy "rational" pleasures together. They are soon joined by three other women, two of them romantic friends: Of Miss Selvyn and Lady Emilia it is observed that "neither of them appeared so happy as when they were together," and that they loved each other "with a tenderness."

All the women had been able to bring considerable amounts of money into their joint establishment, which becomes a model of happy, generous living. They are totally self-sufficient, even to the extent of keeping a vegetable garden for their own use. They devote their lives to "aesthetic pursuit and civilized enjoyment," but also to good works; for example, they employ only servants who have handicaps and would not be readily employed elsewhere, they open their estate as a refuge to the old and the deformed, and they also take in women of genteel poverty and give them useful training so that they may find jobs as governesses, companions, and housekeepers. They even establish a carpet and rug factory in their town, so that they can give employment to several hundred people.

The major heterosexual relationships in the book invariably end in unhappiness; the same-sex relationships are invariably happy. The fifth woman of *Millenium Hall*, Mrs. Trentham, sums up the apparent attitude of the author and her main characters with regard to eighteenth-century heterosexual marriage:

> To face the enemy's cannon appears to me a lesser effort of courage, than to put our happiness into the hands of a person, who perhaps will not once reflect on the importance of the trust committed to his or her care.

And yet the five owners of Millenium Hall provide dowries for young women and are proud that they celebrate at least two marriages a year at the Hall. Perhaps Scott felt that if she scandalized society by antimarriage views that were too shockingly unorthodox and threatening, her novel would not get a fair reading. It is likely that for that reason she permits the women to support marriage,

although (for the sake of consistency) not with overwhelming enthusiasm and not for themselves. As Mrs. Morgan explains:

> We consider matrimony as absolutely necessary for the good of
> society; it is a general duty; but as, according to all ancient
> tenures, those obliged to perform knight's service, might, if they
> chose to enjoy their own fire-sides be excused by sending depu-
> ties to supply their places; so we, using the same privileges, sub-
> stitute many others, and certainly much more promote wedlock,
> than we could do by entering into it ourselves.

However, in reality genteel women could enjoy unmarried bliss as
did the five at Millenium Hall only if they were financially independent, and few women of their class were. For most pairs of romantic friends, Millenium Hall was an unobtainable ideal. Eventually they would either have to settle into marriage, or they would be
tolerated in the homes of their parents or a relative. There were few
who could retire to the country and expect to receive financial (or
emotional) support from their families.[3]

But if women could not live forever in the unmarried bliss of romantic friendship, they loved to read about it: Even the mention of
such a relationship in the title of a work must have promoted its
sales—which would explain why a 1770 novel that uses friendship
between women as nothing more than an epistolary device was entitled *Female Friendship*.[4] Women readers could identify with the
female characters' involvement with each other, since most of them
had experienced romantic friendship in their youth at least. Mrs.
Delany's description of her own first love is typical of what
numerous autobiographies, diaries, letters, and novels of the period
contained. As a young woman, she formed a passionate attachment
to a clergyman's daughter, whom she admired for her "uncommon
genius . . . intrepid spirit . . . extraordinary understanding, lively
imagination, and humane disposition." They shared "secret talk"
and "whispers" together; they wrote to one another every day, and
met in the fields between their fathers' houses at every opportunity.
"We thought that day tedious," Mrs. Delany wrote years later, "that
we did not meet, and had many stolen interviews." [5] Typical of many
youthful romantic friendships, it did not last long (at the age of
seventeen Mrs. Delany was given in marriage to an old man), but it
provided fuel for the imagination which idealized the possibilities of
what such a relationship might be like without the impingement of
cold marital reality. Because of such girlhood intimacies (which were

often cut off untimely), most women would have understood when those attachments were compared with heterosexual love by the female characters in eighteenth-century novels, and were considered, as Lucy says in *The Young Widow*, "infinitely more valuable." They would have had their own frame of reference when in those novels, women adapted the David and Jonathan story for themselves and swore that they felt for each other (again as Lucy says) "a love 'passing the Love of Men,'" or proclaimed as does Anne Hughes, the author of *Henry and Isabella* (1788), that such friendships are "more sweet, interesting, and to complete all, lasting, than any other which we can ever hope to possess; and were a just account of anxiety and satisfaction to be made out, would, it is possible, in the eye of rational estimation, far exceed the so-much boasted pleasure of love." Of course, women's passionate friendships were not always lasting, because a husband had the sole legal right of choosing a domicile, and he might if he wished take a woman miles and even countries away so that she would never see her romantic friend again. But despite that sad possibility, the novels generally agree that romantic friendship had all the sweetness, excitement, and intensity that heterosexual love at its best might have, and few of the anxieties and dissatisfactions.

The bliss and flawlessness of romantic friendships are perfectly illustrated in *Danebury: or The Power of Friendship* (1777), an anonymous poem "by a Lady." *Danebury*—which is about two passionate friends, Elfrida and Emma—opens with a quotation in praise of friendship from Akenside's "Pleasures of Imagination":

> *In all the dewy Landscape of the Spring,*
> *In the bright Eye of Hesper or the Morn,*
> *In Nature's fairest Forms is Aught so fair*
> *As virtuous Friendship?*

The love between Emma and Elfrida may be "virtuously" ungenital, but the two are nonetheless lovers, with one mind, one heart, and considerable sensuality between them. They live together in perfect harmony:

> *If Emma's bosom heav'd a pensive sigh,*
> *The tear stood trembling in Elfrida's eye;*
> *If pleasure gladden'd her Elfrida's heart,*
> *Still faithful Emma shar'd the larger part.*

The action of the poem concerns a battle between the West Saxons and the Danes, in which the Danes are defeated (and the women's region is thus renamed Danebury Hill), but in the midst of the battle Elfrida saves her father by catching the arrow that was meant for him in her own "gentle breast." She appears to be dying, but in a scene that suggests Christina Rossetti's later "Goblin Market," Emma saves her beloved friend by sucking the poison from her breast and taking it into her own body:

Friendship, a bold, a generous act design'd.
While death-like sleep her friend's sensations drown'd,
She suck'd the poison from the throbbing wound!
Resign'd herself a victim to the grave,
A life far dearer than her own to save.

Emma is then rescued from the clutches of death by herbs which Elfrida's father administers, and the two young women continue in their blissful, harmonious friendship.

In the eighteenth-century literary works which take romantic friendship as a major or minor theme, women find a good deal to like as well as love in each other. They regard themselves as whole people, as they were seldom regarded by men. They love each other for their strengths and self-sufficiency rather than for their weaknesses and dependence. Typically, Juliana, who is described as being "romantic in her notions of friendship" in *Henry and Isabella,* is enchanted with Lady Frances for the "commanding nobleness" of her "figure and manners," her "winning affability," "her understanding," and the "justness and generosity of her sentiments." Lady Frances loves Juliana for her "beauty of person," and for her "taste, understanding, and knowledge," as well as her "sweetness of temper, and goodness of heart." One would be hard put to find in any eighteenth-century novel a description of a man's love for a woman which contains such a complete combination of physical, mental, and spiritual virtues.

But although these fictional romantic friends are willing to sacrifice everything for each other, even life itself, marriage to a man is frequently regarded as necessary—women are tricked into it, forced into it, occasionally choose it for reasons the novel does not dwell upon. The writers were reflecting reality: Seldom could a woman go from girlhood into a lifelong primary commitment to a romantic friend. There would be great pressure on her to marry, and unless she was a true rebel, like Sarah Ponsonby or Eleanor Butler, she would probably bend to that pressure. Despite such a heterosexual entanglement, however, in many of these novels the marriage is portrayed as secondary to the friendship in the minds of the female characters: If the marriage interferes with the perfect intimacy of the romantic friends at the present time, it will not always do so.

Women were not often forced to give up such friendships once they were married unless, as in *Euphemia*, in which the title character is dragged off to America by her husband, a separation of the friends was central to the plot. In such a case the resolution would usually show the friends reunited. Perhaps society was not overly disturbed by the literary depiction of perfect, all-consuming female friendships, since the marriage of one or both of the female friends was inevitable, and none of the writers could have been accused of attempting to subvert marriage and the social structure. Female friends could live together, as do the two pairs in *Millenium Hall*, only if they had a good reason for not being married.

Also perhaps society did not object to the theme of passionate friendship in literature because it appealed to male voyeurism. Eighteenth-century English writers, except for pornographers, were more restrained than Casanova or St. Preux (see page 79) in their admission of arousal by female-female love, but their male characters seemed to share with the real and fictional Frenchmen (and express presumably for the male reader) a voyeuristic pleasure in observing the affection of romantic female friends. In *Anecdotes of a Convent* (1771), Lord Malcolm, seeing the tenderness between Louisa and Julia, exclaims, "How amiable . . . is friendship in your sex, Ladies! It is a noble sentiment in itself, but when dressed in female softness is irresistible" (J.M.S. Tompkins in *The Popular Novel in England* cogently asks, "Irresistible to whom?").[6]

By the mid-eighteenth century, romantic friendship was a recognized institution in America too. In the eyes of an observer such as Moreau de St. Méry, who had just recently left Revolutionary France for America and must have been familiar with the accusations of lesbianism against Marie Antoinette, the women of her court, and most of the French actresses of the day, women's effusive display of affection for each other seemed sexual. Saint Méry, who recorded his observations of his 1793–1798 journey, was shocked by the "unlimited liberty" which American young ladies seemed to enjoy, and by their ostensible lack of passion toward men. The combination of their independence, heterosexual passionlessness, and intimacy with each other could have meant only one thing to a

Frenchman in the 1790's: that "they are not at all strangers to being willing to seek unnatural pleasures with persons of their own sex." [7] It is as doubtful that great masses of middle- and upper-class young ladies gave themselves up to homosexual sex as it is that they gave themselves up to heterosexual sex before marriage. But the fiction of the period corroborates that St. Méry saw American women behaving openly as though they were in love with each other.

Charles Brockden Brown, the first professional American novelist, shows a particular interest in such love relationships. His early untitled fragment about the romantic friendship between Sophia and Jessica [8] demonstrates what Americans considered to be within the realm of the "natural" in female same-sex love, in contrast to St. Méry's observation about the "unnatural." In this fragment, Sophia and Jessica, both in their early twenties, exchange letters asserting their love:

> I want you so much. I long for you. Nay, I cannot do without you; so, at all events, you must come. . . . You shall dine, sup, and sleep with me alone. I will have you all to myself.
> (SOPHIA TO JESSICA)

> What I feel for you I have not felt since I was sixteen, yet it cannot you know be love. Yet is there such a difference brought about by mere sex—my Sophia's qualities are such as I would doat upon in man. Just the same would win my whole heart; where then is the difference? On my word, Sophia, I see none.
> (JESSICA to SOPHIA)

Jessica seems to have been destined to see a difference, since there is some suggestion that the love between the two women in this unfinished work was to be, as Brantôme said about sex between women, an apprenticeship to heterosexuality. Because Jessica has learned to respond to the person of Sophia, she has been prepared to respond to a man. Upon meeting Colden, to whom she is powerfully attracted, she writes her friend, "Such eyes, Sophia! They often made me think of yours." While not enough of the fragment is finished so that we can be sure of what Brown actually intended to do with the heterosexual relationship (the man's name—Colden—is certainly inauspicious), there are enough clues to suggest that he thought to make it a central aspect of the novel.

Of course, both women, typical of romantic friends, vow never to marry. They assure each other of the exclusivity and superiority of their love and swear that they could never love men as they love each other:

> Truly, truly, thou art an admirable creature, Jessy, and I love thee, that I do. A friend! Till this age, and till I knew thee, I never had a friend, and shall never have another, of either sex; for surely the world contains not such another creature as thou: at least in the form of *man*. Single, then, Jessy, shall I ever be.

They talk about living together in sweet retirement in the country, an ideal of romantic friendship which we saw in *Millenium Hall* and will see more of in the story of Eleanor Butler and Sarah Ponsonby.

Their attachment is by no means simply ethereal. They claim to "have fallen in love with" each other, and speak often of the physical as well as the moral perfections of the other. There is a definite sensuous element in their love. Jessica, for example, refers to one of her most joyous experiences of their *conversational* intimacies— which took place in a bed:

> You honoured me once, you know, with your company for one night. How delighted was I . . . Shall I ever forget that night! We talked till past three; and such unbosoming of all your feelings, and all your pleasures and cares, and what you called your foibles; spots in the sunny brightness of your character. Ever since that night I have been a new creature; to be locked in your arms; to share your pillow with you, gave new force, new existence to the love which before united us; often shall we pass such nights when thou and I are safe together at Wortleyfield [where they plan to "retire"].

The height of bliss for these two romantic friends is to share secrets and to open their souls to each other, to "speak our love" as Katherine Philips wrote a century earlier. That is best done, however, "locked [in each other's] arms," in the dark on a bed. But since decent women of the eighteenth century could admit to no sexual desires, and decent men would not attribute such desires to them, the sensual aspect of their relationship goes no further in fiction, as it probably would not in life.

A male's relationship with another male was more likely suspected to have the worm in it. Even Brown, who viewed love between women with such indulgence, appears to have had quite different ideas about love between men.[9] In another fragment, "Memoirs of Stephen Calvert," [10] a character describes the "depravity" of a man whose "associates were wholly of his own sex," and speaks of being "frozen with horror" at witnessing him with other men. What Brown intended finally to do with his homosexual male character is not known, but it is certain that he never regarded love between women in the same manner nor permitted any of his characters to express such distaste toward it.

Brown's novel *Ormond: or the Secret Witness* (1798), for which the Jessica fragment may have been a false start, presents a complete full-length treatment of love between women. Robert Hare has suggested that Brown was influenced in his portrayal of the love relationship between Constantia and Sophie by Rousseau's depiction of Julie and Claire's love in *La nouvelle Héloise* and by William Godwin's description of Mary Wollstonecraft's "ruling passion" for Fanny Blood in his *Memoir* of her.[11] But it was not necessary for Brown to turn to literature to discover romantic friendship between women; he needed only to look around him.[12]

The American ideals of romantic friendship were no different from the English according to *Ormond*. The important intimacy in the lives of Brown's two heroines is with each other, despite the fact that one of them is married. Men are treated with suspicion or barely treated at all. The women's fondest dream is to be together. A sensual aspect in their relationship is hinted at, but their great joy is in mere proximity and in "speaking their love."

The narrator of *Ormond* is Sophie Courtland, who had been raised with Constantia and who now tells Constantia's story. The two had been separated for four years while Sophie traveled in Europe after inheriting a good deal of money. During that time Constantia's once-wealthy father lost all his money and his health and Constantia became his supporter and comforter. With his death she finds herself quite alone, with the exception of the company of two women to whom she is briefly attracted before she discovers their faults. Constantia has also been attracted to and then quickly repelled by a type of gothic villain with supernatural powers— Ormond. Meanwhile, Sophie has married, but she returns alone to America to find Constantia and take her back to Europe. After a blissful reunion between the two women, Constantia goes to make a sentimental farewell to her childhood home. She again encounters Ormond, who locks her in a room and threatens to rape her. She vows to kill herself first, but when he retorts, "Living or dead, the prize that I have in view shall be mine," she kills him. Sophie arrives and releases her friend from the room. The two women go off to England together.

Constantia is not without some heterosexual feeling. At some point she is aroused by Ormond and upset by her discovery of "a passion deeper and less curable than she suspected." But nevertheless she cures it quickly, since she believes him to be an unsavory character. She knows that he has seduced and abandoned at least one young woman, and therefore she decides that "every dictate of discretion and duty" enjoins her to have nothing to do with him. Her passion for Ormond is somewhat of an anomaly in her life, since she had had little interest in men earlier and had even decided that she would prefer not to marry. Brown, himself a feminist,[13] attributes feminist arguments to her in this regard:

> Now she was at least mistress of the product of her own labour. Her tasks were toilsome, but the profits, though slender, were sure, and she administered her little property in what manner she pleased. Marriage would annihilate this power. Henceforth she would be bereft even of her personal freedom. So far from possessing property, she herself would become the property of another. . . . Homely liberty was better than splendid servitude.

She rejects not only Ormond, who may or may not have been willing to engage in a relationship as orthodox as marriage, but also an unnamed young man who courted her in the days of her father's prosperity and a character by the name of Balfour.

While she is generally suspicious of men, Constantia feels sympathy for and attraction to women. When she first sees Martinette in a music shop, she is haunted by her beauty and demeanor, which make a "powerful impression" on her. She has fantasies of their friendship and intimacy; "her heart sighed" for such a relationship, and she becomes "daily more enamoured" of Martinette. Helena, the young woman whom Ormond has seduced and abandoned, Constantia loves "with uncommon warmth." Her longing for Sophie, from whom she is separated for the first part of the novel, is characterized as being "pregnant with such agonizing tenderness, such heart-breaking sighs, and a flow of such bitter yet delicious tears, that it were not easily decided whether the pleasure or the pain surmounted."

Sophie has married a young man, Courtland, during her stay in

Europe. While her affection for her friend Constantia is depicted in terms that twentieth-century popular novelists might use to describe that of a lover, her affection for her husband is portrayed in terms that today would be considered appropriate for a friend: We are told that there is between Sophie and Courtland "a conformity of tastes and views," and this gives rise to "tenderness," as compared with the passion between the two women. It would perhaps have been considered unseemly to depict such fiery intensity between a woman and a man, but detailed descriptions of the greatest passions between a woman and a woman were apparently not thought so. In any case, Brown makes absolutely no suggestion that passion existed between the husband and wife.

Although she is married, Sophie returns alone to America to look for Constantia. She claims that she would like to spend her life with Courtland in England, where her maternal family lives, but first it is "indispensable" to be reunited with Constantia and bring her to England too. "If this could not be accomplished," Sophie says, "it was my inflexible purpose to live and die with her." At the conclusion of the novel the two women go together to England, where Courtland is waiting; and presumably they will be a *ménage à trois*. However, Constantia decides not to sell her childhood home because she hopes "that some future event will allow her to return to this favourite spot without forfeiture of [Sophie's] society." It is not clear what that event might be, but she seems to want to preserve inviolate the place where the two women were once happy together without interference from other parties.

The relationship between Constantia and Sophie has nothing in common with "friendship" in a contemporary sense. The two women are totally involved with each other. As an initial sign of the intensity of their love, Brown depicts Constantia fainting for joy when, after their long separation, she hears Sophie's familiar voice singing in an adjoining room (cf. Maria's fainting in *Euphemia* when she hears that her beloved friend has returned from America). When, prior to this reunion, Sophie thinks that Constantia has died in the plague, "all hope of happiness" in this world disappears, and she desires only "to join my friend" in death, where they will never be separated. Once the two women are finally reunited, their ecstasy is overwhelming, as Sophie reports:

> The appetite for sleep and for food were confounded and lost amidst the impetuosities of a master passion. To look and to

talk to each other afforded enchanting occupation for every moment. I would not part from her side, but ate and slept, walked and mused and read, with my arm locked in hers, and with her breath fanning my cheek. . . . O precious inebriation of the heart! O pre-eminent love! What pleasure of reason or of sense can stand in competition with those attendant upon thee? . . . Henceforth, the stream of our existence was to mix; we were to act and to think in common; casual witnesses and written testimony should become superfluous. Eyes and ears were to be eternally employed upon the conduct of each other; death, when it should come, was not to be deplored, because it was an unavoidable and brief privation to her that should survive.

Although the love between the two women is intoxicating and all-consuming, Brown does not suggest that it is genital, anymore than do other eighteenth-century authors who deal with romantic friendships. In fact, Sophie seems specifically to discount the genital possibilities of their passion by saying that nothing occurred during their nights in bed together that was "incompatible with purity and rectitude." But Sophie clearly considers herself, as does Ormond her rival, to be Constantia's lover in all other ways. For example, Ormond complains to Constantia that he knows she was about to write him "that thy affections and person were due to another." When Sophie contemplates a union between Constantia and Ormond, she remarks, "I could not but harbour aversion to a scheme which should tend to sever me from Constantia, or to give me a competitor in her affections."

Perhaps it is an indication of the relative independence of the eighteenth-century American woman that the heroine of this novel, unlike her English counterpart, is permitted to reject all her suitors and remain unmarried to the end of the book with no husband in sight—or perhaps the conclusion merely reflects the feminist convictions of the author that women should have such freedom. The love relationship between the two women goes beyond what Brown hints at in his earlier fragment about Jessica and Sophia, in which Jessica appears to be developing a strong heterosexual interest as the work breaks off. In *Ormond* the female-female love, despite the title of the work, is the central and most powerful relationship in the book, and it provides the happy ending.[14]

* * *

Helen Williams's novel, *Anecdotes of a Convent* (1771), shows how far romantic friendships could go without being thought questionable, i.e., sexual. A subplot concerns Louisa, a lovely young woman who has just returned from a French convent where she had been sent to be educated. She is in a deep depression. Julia, one of the epistolary narrators, tells us that Louisa's "sorrows flow from the loss of a female friend." When at dinner Louisa's father inquires after Miss Merton as the friend "whom you was so wrapt up in at the convent," Louisa "turns pale and sinks off her chair." Julia learns after this scene that Louisa stayed at the convent two years longer than her parents had intended her to "because she could not be brought to leave the nunnery whilst her friend remained in it." Julia, who finds Louisa's sorrows only somewhat excessive, comforts her as she lies in bed crying and sighing, and finally she learns Louisa's story:

The first day at the convent Louisa met Fanny Merton: "I raised my eyes on her," Louisa says, "and felt as if my soul at that instant had darted through my breast into hers, there to take up its residence forever." Fanny returns her affection. She is an active young woman whose attention could be fixed by nothing but Louisa and books, "both of which were her passions . . . [and] tender only to me, the business of her life was to oblige me." When another attractive, lively girl comes to the convent, Louisa fears that she will be a rival for Fanny's affections, "and I looked on her, for that reason, with some degree of coldness," but Fanny remains faithful.

Louisa is completely enthralled by her relationship. When she is taken to Paris she can enjoy nothing of the diversions; in the midst of the loveliness and grandeur, "I sighed in my heart for the hour which was to restore me to my friend Miss Merton." As the years go by, the intensity of her affection becomes greater still. The two wish only to be together every minute. When Louisa's father calls her home, "I trembled at the apprehension of being separated from my friend," and she convinces him she must stay at the convent longer.

When the Father Confessor attempts to get Louisa to convert to Catholicism, he uses the argument he believes will reach her the deepest: "Should you not be very sorry, after this life, to go to a place where your friend Miss Merton [who is Catholic] can never come. . . . You must *both* be of the same religion my Dear, or you can never meet in another world." Louisa, who misses his Catholic-chauvinist meaning, nevertheless responds, "No place can be a heaven to me where she is not." When it appears that Fanny will be called home, Louisa reports, "I could not sleep, and I would not eat, so that in a few days I look'd like the picture of death, and had hardly the strength to crawl about the house."

All of this behavior is considered within the limits of appropriateness to passionate friendship. It is only after Fanny embraces her "violently," stifling her with kisses, that the reader is supposed to suspect that here is not the usual passionate friendship. Finally it is learned that Frances Merton is really Francis Merton, who had been at birth placed in a convent by his Catholic mother, who did not want to honor the agreement with her Protestant husband that he would raise a boy child as a non-Catholic. In the reverse of Ovid's story of Iphis, at Francis's birth his mother told her husband that the boy was a girl. Francis, never having been informed of the difference between male and female, also believed himself to be a girl.

Once he discovers his sex, he can ask Louisa to marry him. But it is significant that their love is viewed as unchanged, except for the possibility of its permanence now. Francis asks, "Will you not love me as well as you did when you were ignorant of my sex? Yes, I know you will—you must—my heart is not alter'd by the change, why then should that of my beloved Louisa's?" The only distinctions, then, that are made between romantic friendship and heterosexual love in this eighteenth-century novel are that the latter is manifested by "violent" embraces and kisses, and that no one can separate the heterosexual lovers. These are also the major distinctions in most other novels of the period that deal with both romantic friendship and heterosexual love.

So many of these fictional works were written by women, and they provide a very different picture of female intimacy than the usual depictions by men. The extreme masculine view, which is epitomized in Casanova's *Memoirs*, reduced female love to the genital, and as such it could be called "trifling." But love between women, at least as it was lived in women's fantasies, was far more consuming than the likes of Casanova could believe. Women dreamed not of erotic escapades but of a blissful life together. In such a life a woman would have choices, she would be in command of her own destiny; she would be an adult relating to another adult in a way that a heterosexual relationship with a virtual stranger (often an old or at least a much older man), arranged by a parent for considerations totally divorced from affection, would not allow her to be. Samuel Richardson permitted Miss Howe to express the yearnings of many a frustrated romantic friend when she remarked to Clarissa, "How charmingly might you and I live together and despise them all."

CHAPTER 5

Romantic Friendship in Eighteenth-Century Life

The twentieth-century scholars' difficulty in accepting the notion of fulfilling romantic friendship in the literature of other centuries is surpassed by their difficulty in accepting it in women's actual lives. What is one to make of the letters from Mary Pierrepont (later Lady Mary Wortley Montagu) to Anne Wortley in 1709:

> My dear, dear, adieu! I am entirely yours, and wish nothing more than it may be some time or in my power to convince you that there is nobody dearer [to me] than yourself . . .

> I cannot bear to be accused of coldness by one whom I shall love all my life. . . . You will think I forget you, who are never out of my thoughts. . . . I esteem you as I ought in esteeming you above the world.

> . . . your friendship is the only happiness of my life; and whenever I lose it, I have nothing to do but to take one of my garters and search for a convenient beam.

> Nobody ever was so entirely, so faithfully yours. . . . I put in your lovers, for I don't allow it possible for a man to be so sincere as I am.[1]

One commentator, who asserts that these letters carry "heart-burnings and reproaches and apologies" which might make us, the readers, "fancy ourselves in Lesbos," assures us that appearances are deceiving, that Mary was not really telling Anne that she loved her, but rather that she knew Edward, Anne's brother, would read what

119

she had written her, "and she tried to shine in these letters for
him." [2]

If there is no male figure hovering in the background to whom
the women's passion could be attributed, modern observers offer a
convenient twentieth-century explanation of the "peculiarity" of
the women's interests in each other. They thus refuse to recognize
that the emotions which late nineteenth-century and early twentieth-
century sexologists taught us to label "morbid" were perfectly commonplace in an earlier day: One writer, for example, describing
Queen Anne's intense devotion to Sarah Churchill and other
women, reflects that one "has a sense of something in Anne's emotions that suggests the abnormal." He further compounds his and
the reader's confusion about love between women by pointing out
that Anne's sister Mary seemed to have a similar passion for Frances
Apsley, for in a letter she sent to Frances before her wedding, Mary
wrote:

> I have sat up this night . . . to tell my dear dear dear dearest
> husband [Frances] . . . that I am more in love with you every-
> time I see you, and love you so well that I cannot express it no
> way but by saying I am your louse in bosom and would be very
> glad to be always so near you.[3]

Like many historians of his day, he fails to observe that so many
records of correspondence between women of that period contain
some such evidence of same-sex love.

As eighteenth-century novels demonstrate, women did not need
a male audience to speak passionately to each other; nor did they
consider themselves (nor were they considered by others) "abnormal"
because they loved other women—and what we know of middle and
upper class women's lives through the extant correspondence and
diaries indicates that those novels reflected reality. (It is indeed unfortunate that lower-class women, who generally were illiterate, have
left so little record of themselves and the meaning of romantic
friendship in their lives.) All the language and sentiments of romantic friendship—vows to love eternally, and to live and die together;
wishes to elope together to sweet retirement; constant reassurances
of the crucial, even central role these women played in each other's
lives—are found in the actual letters and journals of the time.

The great "success story" of romantic friendship is that of Sarah
Ponsonby and Eleanor Butler, "the Ladies of Llangollen." Sarah

and Eleanor were two upper-class Irishwomen who managed to run off together and share thereafter every waking and sleeping moment (until one of them died fifty-three years later), just as countless women prayed (fruitlessly, in most cases) in their letters to their own romantic friends that they might be able to do. In 1778, Sarah and Eleanor, both of wealthy, titled families, eloped. They dressed in men's clothes for the elopement, hoping thereby to be less conspicuous on the road. When they were pursued and foiled in their escape by their families the first time, they ran away a second time. Finally their relatives were convinced that nothing would change their minds, and they let the two women be. Eventually Sarah and Eleanor were even given small stipends, and in 1787 Sarah received a pension from the king. They settled in Wales, and in 1780 procured a cottage in Llangollen Vale. In no time at all they established a marvelous garden. With very little money but wonderful taste and imagination, they redecorated the cottage (which they christened Plas Newydd), and their home became a shrine to romantic friendship in their generation and in later generations.[4]

The local papers referred to them as "the Irish Ladies who have settled [here] in so romantic a manner"; their home was "the Fairy Place of the Vale" and a "rural and sylvan-like retreat of those Ornaments of their sex."[5] They were admired and befriended by the Duke of Wellington, William Wordsworth, Robert Southey, Josiah Wedgewood, Edmund Burke, Hester Thrale Piozzi, Sir Walter Scott, Lady Caroline Lamb, and many other notables of the day. Few poets who knew them were not inspired to record their romantic friendship in verse. Wordsworth, for example, declared after visiting the ladies in 1824:

> *Glyn Cafaillgaroch, in the Cambrian tongue,*
> *In ours the Vale of Friendship, let this spot*
> *Be nam'd where faithful to a low roof'd Cot*
> *On Deva's banks, ye have abode so long,*
> *Sisters in love, a love allowed to climb*
> *Ev'n on this earth, above the reach of time.*[6]

The poet Anna Seward wrote enough verses about the "Davidean friendship" (cf. David and Jonathan) of the two women to fill a small volume. She praised Eleanor, with a hint of envy, for her "firm, free step" which permitted her to lead her "loved friend" to their blissful retirement, away from the "irksome" life to which women of their class were usually subject: "By firmness won, by

constancy secured/Ye nobler pleasures. . . ./The life of Angels in
an Eden lead." [7] And years after their deaths they continued to be
celebrated in myth and bad poetry for as long as romantic friendship was honored by society:

> *Once two young girls of rank and beauty rare,*
> *Of features more than ordinary fair,*
> *Who in the heyday of their youthful charms*
> *Refused the proffer of all suitors' arms,*
> *Lived in a cottage here rich carved in oak. . . .*
> *Then none were known to come unto their door*
> *That was not welcomed with kind words or more.*
> *These ladies to each other kind and true,*
> *Around Llangollen's vale, like them were few . . .*
> *As they through life together did abide,*
> *E'en now in death they both lie side by side. . . .*
> *Beloved, respected by the world were they,*
> *By all regretted when they passed away.*[8]
>
> (REVEREND J. PRITCHARD, D.D., c. 1856)

It was known by everyone that Sarah and Eleanor shared every
part of their lives with each other. Ostensibly "heterosexual" acquaintances would close letters to one of them enjoining her to "give
my love to your better half." [9] Their relationship was considered
not only socially permissible but even desirable. One reason it was
so revered was that it was thought to be nongenital—or rather the
sexual possibilities of a life in a shared bed were not thought of at
all. Women envied them because they seemed not to have to be
bothered with what many eighteenth-century females considered the
duty and burden of sex. Romantic men admired them because they
seemed to keep by choice that "crown of their virtue"; they lived
together because they were too spiritually pure to be sullied by the
physical; they were Protestant nuns. Their society was happy to see
them as the embodiment of the highest ideals of spiritual love and
the purest dreams of romantic friendship.

If there had been many female couples who emulated their life-
style with success, the Ladies would probably have been regarded
as a threat to societal norms. But how many women would have
had their energy and strength, which were required not only to
fight family pressures to marry an appropriate title and estate, but
also to elope not once but twice, and finally to convince relatives
that they must provide them with financial support? It would be

safe to guess not many. Thus no one could believe that Sarah and Eleanor would serve as models for a dangerous new life-style. They were, in modern parlance, the "token blacks" of same-sex love.

Perhaps also they would have been viewed with more alarm had they been social rebels in any other areas of their lives. But they were as unimaginatively conservative as the most staunch upholder of the "Great Chain of Being" could have wished. They prayed incessantly for the health of crazy King George; at the start of the French Revolution they feared only for the safety of the nobility; in 1802 Eleanor recorded in her journal that the ladies in Paris were "so indecently naked that the sight is disgusting to the last degree"; [10] and they dismissed a servant who had worked for them for three years when it was discovered that although she had no husband she was pregnant. The Ladies were hardly "radical types." Their class must have reasoned, consciously or not, that anyone who propounded such correct political opinions and stringent "moral" views could not have been sexual in an unorthodox way.

Probably they were not. Eleanor's journal is filled with references to Sarah as "my Heart's darling," "my sweet love," "my Sally," "my Beloved." [11] It often speaks of the two being in bed together, but usually in connection with illness:

> I kept my bed all day with one of my dreadful Headaches. My Sally, my Tender, my Sweet Love, lay beside me holding and supporting my Head.

> Rose at Eight after a tedious night spent in coughing and with a most dreadful head ache. My dearest, my kindest love did not sleep even for one moment the entire night but lay beside me watching and lamenting my illness and soothing by her tenderness the distressing pain of my Head.[12]

Of course, even had there been a sexual relationship between them, it is doubtful they would have committed a discussion of it to paper. But their generally rigid, inhibited, and conventional views regarding undress and evidence of sexuality suggest that it is unlikely that as eighteenth-century women, educated in the ideal of female passionlessness,[13] they would have sought genital expression if it were not to fulfill a marital duty. Since they had no sexual duty to a husband, who, as they would have seen it, would be "driven" by his male nature to initiate the sex act, they were probably happy to be oblivious to their genitals.

There may have been some slight suspicion in 1790, perhaps fostered by Eleanor's near-transvestite appearance, that their relationship was unorthodox. The *General Evening Post* hinted as much in an article on July 24, entitled "Extraordinary Female Affection," which observed that these two "daughters of great Irish families" were living in retirement in "a certain Welsh Vale" :

> Miss Butler, who is of the Ormonde family, had several offers of marriage, all of which she rejected. Miss Ponsonby, her particular friend and companion, was supposed to be the bar to all matrimonial union, it was thought proper to separate them, and Miss Butler was confined.
>
> The two Ladies, however, found means to elope together. . . .
>
> Miss Butler is tall and masculine, she wears always a riding habit, hangs her hat with the air of a sportsman in the hall, and appears in all respects as a young man, if we except the petticoats which she still retains.[14]
>
> Miss Ponsonby, on the contrary, is polite and effeminate, fair and beautiful.[15]

The article infuriated the Ladies, who immediately canceled their subscription to the paper and wrote to Edmund Burke asking if the author could be sued. Perhaps they wanted Burke's assistance because they knew he was not only opposed to the harassment of homosexuals, but had also had experience in suing for libel when he was himself accused of homosexuality.[16] Or perhaps the Ladies had had no reason in the past to pay attention to issues involving homosexuality,[17] and they called on Burke only because he was an influential friend. At any rate, he informed them that it was generally difficult to get redress in libel suits, but that they should be consoled in knowing "that you suffer from the Violence of Calumny for the virtues that entitle you to the esteem of all who know how to esteem honour, friendship, principle, and dignity of thinking, and that you suffer along with everything that is excellent in the world." He went on to assure them that their libelers "make no impressions except those of contempt on any person living." [18]

Burke was right. Despite the newspaper article, no one among their acquaintances seemed to believe that their relationship was of the forbidden variety. The homophobic Mrs. Thrale wished in her diary in 1789 that the French sapphists might be thrown "into Mount Vesuvius," and wrote again in 1790, 1794, and 1795 of the "strange propensity" which existed in England "for unspeakable sins," and of the scandalous relationships that certain women carried on with each other.[19] But Mrs. Thrale was a close friend and neighbor to the Ladies, visited them frequently, and wrote them cordial letters. In her correspondence with others, she refers to them as "fair and noble recluses" and "charming cottagers."[20] Perhaps she distinguished between the lesbians she excoriated in her diary and the Llangollen Ladies because they seemed to follow to the letter the prescriptions for romantic friendship: They retired to the country,[21] they communed daily with nature, they spent their days reading and tending their garden in contrast to the worldly ladies of the French court and the London theater and Bath society. Mrs. Thrale must have believed that surrounded by such natural, moral influences, Sarah and Eleanor could not possibly desire what would give "Offence towards God and Reason and Religion and Nature."[22]

We do not know whether or not their relationship was genital, but they were "married" in every other sense. We have no similar clear pictures of other same-sex marriages during the eighteenth century because few journals such as Eleanor's detailing women's lives together have survived, nor were there others who attracted so much popular attention and became to such an extent the subject of diarists and poets. Through correspondence and memoirs, however, we can piece together other stories that corroborate how ubiquitous the ideas of romantic friendship were among literate eighteenth-century women. This material reveals all the romantic sentiments which have come to be publicly associated with heterosexual love alone in the twentieth century. Romantic friends courted each other, flirted, were anxious about the beloved's responses and about reciprocity. They believed their relationships to be eternal, and in fact the faithfulness of one often extended beyond the death of the other. The fondest dream of many romantic friends, which was not often realized, was to establish a home with the beloved. To that end they were willing to make the greatest sacrifices, and were devastated if their hopes were disappointed. There is nothing to suggest that they were self-conscious about these passions or saw them as being abnormal in any way.

Elizabeth Carter, one of the leading bluestockings of the period and the much praised translator of Epictetus, illustrates in her correspondence with Catherine Talbot, another writer, the nature of courtship and the mood of romantic tension that often existed between passionate friends. Both of these women decided very consciously not to marry men. Elizabeth felt compelled to care for her widowed father, and Catherine, an invalid, was cared for by her mother. But it is doubtful that they would have been interested in heterosexual marriage even if their familial situations had been different. For example, no longer a young woman in 1749, Elizabeth was still plagued, as she characterized it, by those who desired to make matches, and she complained to Catherine, "As I have been convinced that one is not perfectly secure on this side of an hundred, it will be quite prudent in me, by way of precaution, to learn to swim, having run away from matrimonial schemes as far as dry land goes, my next step must be into the sea." [23] Elsewhere she characterized marriage to a man as being oppressive and suppressive:

> If I have suffered from the troubles of others, who have more sense, more understanding, and more virtues than I might reasonably have expected to find, what might I not have suffered from a husband? Perhaps be needlessly thwarted and contradicted in every innocent enjoyment of life; involved in all his schemes right or wrong; and perhaps not allowed the liberty of even silently seeming to disapprove them.[24]

Her relationship with Catherine, which lasted almost thirty years until Catherine's death in 1770, elicited no such complaints. Elizabeth thought of Catherine, as she repeatedly said in her letters during the 1750's and 1760's, as "one of the dearest and most distinguished blessings of my life." [25]

It was love at first sight. Only a short time after meeting Catherine, Elizabeth wrote to a Mr. Wright, who had introduced the two women (and then apparently congratulated Elizabeth on being so well liked by Catherine at a recent meeting):

> I do not know whether you ought to congratulate me upon my good success last Sunday, for what have I gained by it? Only a new addition to my impatience, which really was very strong before, but is now out of all bounds of moderation. Miss Talbot is absolutely my passion; I think of her every day, dream of her all night, and one way or another introduce her into every subject I talk of. You say she has a quarrel against my fan sticks; give me the pleasure, if you can, of knowing she had no objection to the paper. You will see her tomorrow (a happiness I envy you much more than all your possessions in the skies).

Pray make her a thousand compliments and apologies for my haunting her in the manner I have done, and still intend to do, though I am afraid she will think me as troublesome as an evil genius, a species of being she never could be acquainted with before.[26]

The language and the sentiments here are what the twentieth-century reader might expect to find only in a letter from a male lover about his inamorata. Women in the eighteenth century thought such passions commonplace and appropriate enough that they could confide them to a third party—in this case a male who was not even a particularly intimate acquaintance.

Elizabeth courted Catherine with a tension that, again, has been considered appropriate in the twentieth century only in a heterosexual relationship. In the beginning she apparently did not even dare write her directly—a half year after their initial meeting, she seems still to have been sending letters through Mr. Wright: "As I heard Mr. Wright mention his design of writing to you, I could not resist the temptation of taking that opportunity to torment you with a melancholy proof how much you are the subject of my thoughts. . . . It has cost me at least half an hour's laborious study to compose the Introduction [to this letter]." [27]

After this open confession of her infatuation, Catherine on her part seemed to reveal herself more to Elizabeth, and even admitted that she felt the same tension about their relationship. If it cost Elizabeth a half hour to frame the introduction of a letter to someone who Catherine said could be sure "would receive anything of her writing with a great deal of pleasure," then Elizabeth could imagine how "I have been racking my brains for an answer ever since I received it." [28] From this point on, Elizabeth addressed her pasionate love letters directly to Catherine:

People here are not in the least danger of losing their wits about you, but proceed as quietly and as regularly in their affairs as if there was no such person in being. Nobody has been observed to lose their way, run against a door, or sit silent and staring in a room full of company in thinking upon you, except my solitary self, who (as you may perceive in the description) have the advantage of looking half mad when I do not see you, and (as you know by many ocular proofs) extremely silly when I do.[29]

Since Catherine's tone was generally more reserved, and presumably also her behavior toward Elizabeth,[30] such a fever pitch did not continue indefinitely—it is highly unlikely that such fervor could have continued throughout the almost thirty years that their relationship lasted. But the letters make clear that the two women continued to love each other, although in a calmer way, until Catherine's death. On the first anniversary of their meeting, Elizabeth, borrowing from Petrarch, wrote:

> *Benedetto sia il giorno, e'l mese, e'l anno*
> *E la stagione, e'l tempo, e'l hora, e'l punto.*
> And St. James's Church, and Mr. Wright, and the particles *yes* and *no*, and every other person that contributed to make me happy in the sight and conversation of Miss Talbot.

Five years later she was still celebrating the anniversary of their meeting with enthusiasm. And even ten years afterward, Elizabeth was begging Catherine for a lock of hair and thanking her profusely on its receipt.[31]

Their love was not without the usual psychological complications which play a greater or lesser part in any close relationship between two people. For example, although Catherine attempted for years to dampen Elizabeth's overwhelming ardor, once she seemed to succeed, she regretted the loss of that tribute to herself. When Elizabeth admired the beauty of other women or seemed to form other passionate attachments, Catherine chided her, sometimes jokingly, sometimes at least half seriously, and sometimes passive-aggressively and with perfect seriousness. For example, in 1763, after receiving a letter from Elizabeth, who was vacationing in Spa where she reported she saw many lovely women to admire, Catherine responds, "What heads and hearts folks have at Spa! I have just received yours of the 31st, in which you talk to me of a belle Hollandaise and a Chanoinesse angelique, for neither of whom do I care. And say no more of la Baronne than if no such amiable being existed. I begin to suspect this is really the case, and that she is only *un être d'imagination*, whom you dreamt of on the inspiring bank of the Geronstere Spring." Catherine also complains in this letter (with how much humor?) that a mutual acquaintance has assured her that the Baroness was not a figure of Elizabeth's imagination, but rather that "you are only fallen in love with another woman, and the first is forgot. A pretty gentleman you will come home indeed, fi volage!"[32]

Catherine seems to have been particularly concerned about Elizabeth's friendship with Mrs. Montagu—who was Catherine's friend too, but not her romantic friend. When Elizabeth Carter traveled with Elizabeth Montagu, Catherine's letters were always reserved or half-jokingly angry. In one letter she hopes that when the two return to England, Montagu will leave Carter alone for a while:

> . . . [I] shall disinterestedly enjoy the thoughts of you reposing at home, after so many fatigues, till January; though I dare say Mrs. Montagu, who had had you with her all this while, cannot help being unconscionable enough to grumble at not bringing you on directly with her.

In the same letter she apologizes for having written to her insipidly while Elizabeth was traveling, but she explains that she liked almost no one in Elizabeth's party, and "I have felt genée when I have writ to you as one does when talking in a mixed company." She promises that now that Elizabeth is alone again, "I feel easy and can write nonsense." [33] At other times when Elizabeth is traveling with Mrs. Montagu, Catherine's letters are passive-aggressive in their resentment: "It would really be much for my peace if all my friends would stay as quietly at home as I do . . . but there are you and Mrs. Montagu, ascending and descending mountains, fording torrents, and crossing seas." [34]

Catherine and Elizabeth never broke away from their parental homes and, in Elizabeth's case, the responsibility for a parent. One can only speculate on the reasons why the two women never attempted to live together. Even if they could have managed financially to establish a household, Elizabeth could not have braved the criticism that would have ensued—not, of course, because she was living in a lesbian relationship, but because, without the justification of heterosexual marriage, she had deserted her widowed father who needed her assistance. Had she gone to raise a family of her own—to fulfill the first call of nature and society—that would have been understood and accepted. But if she had gone to live in romantic friendship and neglected the vital duty to a parent, she would most certainly have been castigated. In the less-passionate Catherine's case, perhaps it was primarily her poor health and the tender nurturing that she received from her mother (who outlived her by many years) which rendered her incapable of seeking a life such as that of Eleanor Butler and Sarah Ponsonby. But although

Elizabeth and Catherine had no marriage as the Llangollen Ladies did, they were most surely "lovers."

Since eighteenth-century English heterosexual marriage among the upper classes was so often an affair of the purse rather than of the heart, it is probable that many married women took lovers (although that action would not have been as readily condoned as it was in France). Other women took romantic friends. Elizabeth Montagu was one of the latter.[35] One of her strongest attachments was with Elizabeth Carter. Their relationship began while Catherine Talbot was still alive, and continued with some intensity after her death.

Mrs. Montagu complains throughout her correspondence of her husband's "churlishness." Finally she says she has given up trying to get a decent human response from him, and "as I consider him now as retired to his inactive chimney corner for the rest of his life, I teach myself to endure to hear without replying to it whatever he pleases to utter, just considering it as the hail and hoarfrosts engendered by unkindly climates which fall equally on the bountifull, the beautiful garden, or the desert." There is nothing to him but an "acid spirit," she laments, and wonders "how I can have the scurvy when I have been in a regimen of acids many a year." [36]

In contrast, the letters indicate that her romantic friendship with Elizabeth Carter was affectionate, warm, and generally joyous. Her biographer, Reginald Blunt, characterizes her as having a "passionless level of unswerving common sense . . . [with] a stern watch upon her heart . . . a finger on her pulse . . . self possessed and [guarded]." [37] If she was those things with the rest of the world, she was not with Elizabeth Carter, to whom she wrote upon not hearing from her for a few days, "I have felt very fretful and disappointed at receiving no letter from you since I came home. Not that there was any manner of reason why I should think you would write; but reason belongs only to the head, and expectation is the partage of the heart." [38] The two women thought about each other constantly, cared always for the amount of affection in the other's heart, reminded each other at every opportunity that they were first in the other's emotions. For instance, after visiting a castle that she and Mrs. Montagu had once seen together, Elizabeth Carter writes, sad that she had not been with her this time: "I saw and thought for you as well as myself, (how seldom is it that I see or think without you!)" [39] Several months later, when Mrs. Carter in her travels passes not far from Mrs. Montagu's home, the latter complains, "If you were at the distance of an hundred miles, it might, and must be endured, but to consider that we are within view of the same smoke, and within the sound of the same bells, and yet that I am in such a state of total ignorance about you, as if you were in the bottom of one of your mines, is insufferably vexatious. I long my dear friend, to know how you do, what you do, and what you think of, and whether among other things you think of me." [40] When Mrs. Montagu stays at Mrs. Carter's home while the latter is away, she reports that she seeks her dear presence everywhere, is haunted by her, and complains, "I know not how in this room to accommodate my thoughts to solitude and silence, which every moment convey a repetition of disappointment." [41] During the early 1760's, when their attachment was at its most intense, they long, always with great feeling, for each other's presence: "Are you in your dressing room alone, my dear friend, and wishing for me, with as much impatience as I am wishing for you?" [42]

Mrs. Montagu complains of depression and illness in 1764, but she prays to keep living "because it is an object to you," and because Mrs. Carter has promised they would be together, to grow old together. That promise "throws a lustre over declining life, and my sun sets in purple, and in gold." [43] The two women must have planned for a considerable time their future "retirement" when they would both be free. A year later Mrs. Montagu writes her friend on this same idyllic subject:

> I cannot express how tenderly I feel myself obliged to you for so kindly placing me in the charming spot which your imagination is planning. Old age in such a retreat, and under such circumstances as you describe, is a calm moonlight evening. . . . You cannot think how delightfully I have lost myself in reveries ever since I received your letter; how I have wandered with you along the side of the river, and listened to the cascade while you were resting on the green bank, and the little rock.[44]

Although both women lived into their eighties, they did not retire together. Both Carter's father and Montagu's husband lived until the 1770's. After Mr. Montagu's death, Elizabeth Montagu settled a pension of one hundred pounds a year on Elizabeth Carter, but by that time their passionate feeling toward each other had cooled. Duty won, as it must have many times during this era, over romantic friendship. But for Mrs. Montagu at least, her romantic friendship gave her the emotional sustenance to live through a disagreeable marriage. And since such a relationship was socially condoned in England more than a liaison with a male lover would have been, she neither was viewed by others nor had to view herself as an immoral woman.

Although duty or economics or custom or the wavering commitment of one partner prevented many eighteenth-century women from establishing a marriage like Eleanor Butler's and Sarah Ponsonby's, lifelong faithfulness in the heart was not uncommon. Perhaps the most moving example is that of the poet Anna Seward. Like Elizabeth Carter, Anna Seward lived with her father, a rector, who was wealthy and an invalid. Her duty to him until his death in 1790, when she was in her forties, provided her with an excuse not to marry, but it is doubtful that she would have married in any case. A letter to a friend, written when she was in her early forties, expresses happiness with her "single blessedness" and registers a familiar eighteenth-century complaint regarding men:

> Men are rarely capable of pure unmixed tenderness to any fellow creature except their children. In general, even the best of them, give their friendship to their male acquaintance, and their fondness to their off spring. For their mistress, or wife, they feel, during a time, a tenderness more ardent, and more sacred; a friendship softer and more animated. But this inexplicable, this fascinating sentiment, which we understand by the name of love, often proves an illusion of the imagination; —a meteor that misleads her who trusts it, vanishing when she has followed it into pools and quicksands, where peace and liberty are swallowed up and lost.[45]

Even though such sentiments were expressed often in her correspondence, twentieth-century biographers have typically felt compelled to provide her with the most flaming heterosexual romances. For instance, one observes that while it is true that in youth she declined many offers of marriage, "in middle age [she] gave the passionate and unremitting devotion of her heart to a man she could not marry."[46] Another scholar, with evidence gathered admittedly only "from a few lines in letters written thirty years later," asserts that in girlhood Anna had an affair with a young man who "had singled her out from the bevy of girls. . . . There were sighs, glances, notes, pressings of the hand."[47]

In fact, the most enduring and passionate attachment of her life,

if Seward's own letters and poems can be believed, was to Honora
Sneyd, a woman nine years her junior whom she had known since
early girlhood. Anna loved her to distraction through Honora's
marriage to Robert Edgeworth (the father of the novelist Maria
Edgeworth) in 1773 and to Honora's death in 1780, and then
mourned her in poems and letters almost to the very day of her own
death approximately thirty years later.

Anna and Honora had lived together in Anna's father's home for
fourteen years during their childhood and young womanhood. In
a letter written long after Honora's death, Anna described those
early years (1766 to 1771) as paradise: Honora's proximity "made
Lichfield an Edenic scene to me." [48] But then Honora's father, in a
better emotional and financial state than he had been in when he
asked the rector to care for his young daughter years before, called
her to his home. Anna observes, "The domestic separation proved
very grievous; but still she was in the same town; we were often
together; and her heart was unchanged." [49] Two years later Honora's heart was changed. She married Edgeworth (who had only
recently lost a wife) despite Anna's pleading with her not to. Anna's
fury and grief over Honora's desertion are reflected in numerous
poems she wrote that year. In "Sonnet XIII, July 1773," she begs
for sleep, which would "charm to rest the thoughts of whence, or
how/Vanish'd that priz'd Affection." [50] In another sonnet written
during the same month, she accuses Honora of ingratitude, which
has killed "more than life,—e'en all that makes life dear." [51] In
"Sonnet XIX, to ——" she addresses Honora directly with anger:

> Farewell, false Friend!—our scenes of kindness close!
>   To cordial looks, to sunny smiles, farewell!
>   To sweet consolings, that can grief expel,
>   And every joy soft sympathy bestows!
> For alter'd looks, where truth no longer glows,
>   Thou hast prepared my heart;—and it was well
>   To bid thy pen th'unlook'd-for story tell,
>   Falsehood avow'd, that shame, nor sorrow knows.
> O! when we meet,—(to meet we're destin'd, try
>   To avoid it as thou may'st) on either brow,
>   Nor in the stealing consciousness of eye,
> Be seen the slightest trace of what, or how
>   We once were to each other;—nor one sigh
>   Flatter with weak regret a broken vow! [52]

In another poem, she weeps because Honora's "plighted love is changed to cold disdain!"[53]

It does not come as a surprise that one of Seward's twentieth-century biographers speculates that she was so upset over Honora's marriage because she may have desired "to marry Edgeworth herself. She was thirty years old—better suited to him in age and experience than Honora. Was she jealous of the easy success of her foster sister? Would she have snatched away, if she could have done so, the mature yet youthful bridegroom, so providentially released from his years of bondage?"[54]

Not only is there not one shred of evidence that Seward had any interest in Edgeworth, but her letters and poems show the absurdity of this heterosexist fantasy, since Anna was completely, obsessively, and romantically in love with Honora. In "Epistle to Miss Honora Sneyd.—Written, September 1770," Anna calls her "my life's adorner."[55] In "Honora, An Elegy," written while Honora was staying in Shropshire for a month, Anna speaks of her great anxiety in this short separation: "Honora fled, I seek her favourite scene/With hasty step, as I should meet her there;/The hasty step and the disorder'd mien/Fond expectation's anxious semblance wear." She calls up Memory to impart "the dear enduring image to my view," and asks Honora, "Has she not drawn thee, loveliest on my heart/In faithful tints, and permanent as true?" Memory then provides her with a picture (as "vivid, and perfect, as her Anna's love") of Honora's physical and sensual beauty: the "soft luxuriance" of her "waving locks," her lovely brow, which is fair no matter what mood she is in, her "vermeil lips," and her "melting" tones. Honora was Anna's muse, her inspiration, and the subject of a vast number of her poems. It was probably with wishful recollection of Shakespeare's "Not marble nor the gilded monuments" that Anna promised to immortalize her:

ELEGY

Written at the Sea-Side
and addressed to
Miss Honora Sneyd

I write, Honora, on the sparkling sand!
The envious waves forbid the trace to stay:
Honora's name again adorns the strand!
Again the waters bear their prize away!

So Nature wrote her charms upon thy face,

The cheek's light bloom, the lip's envermeil'd dye,
And every joy, and every witching grace,
That Youth's warm hours, and Beauty's stores supply.

But Time's stern tide, with cold Oblivious wave,
Shall soon dissolve each fair, each fading charm;
E'en Nature's self, so powerful, cannot save
Her own rich gifts from this o'erwhelming harm.

Love and the Muse can boast superior power,
Indelible the letters they shall frame;
They yield to no inevitable hour,
But will on lasting tablets write thy name.[56]

Although many of the poems written during Honora's lifetime refer to Anna's powerful "Affection" for the younger woman, there is no sense that their relationship went beyond the acceptably sensual to the genital. Anna seems so unguarded in her involvement with Honora, so entirely and guiltlessly public—and it is difficult to believe that a woman reared in her conservative environment and continuing to be comfortable in it, would have been open about any nonmarital relationship that was sexual.[57] But it cannot be assumed, of course, that because it probably had no genital expression, this passion was not deep and intense. It had all the manifestations of an ideal romantic friendship: The two women shared for years their most intimate secrets, as well as one bed, one board, and one purse. Many of Seward's poems are pastoral, picturing the two women in nature, among the fields and groves, in bowers or under the "vernal sun," where they celebrate their "Friendship," a word which appears repeatedly. Other poems suggest their joy in learning together. The most exciting days are those in which their ardent spirits explore together both "Science' bright fanes, and Fancy's fairy bowers." Despite the nine years' difference between them, the relationship is apparently one of complete equality and totally shared sentiments, such as few eighteenth-century women hoped to find with men. Theirs was a marriage, and Anna believed she had good reason to expect permanency.

Anna's first reaction, when Honora married Robert Edgeworth, was to excoriate her "false friend" in poem after poem. From the point when she learned Honora was dying of consumption, however, she again idealized her, and Edgeworth became the villain. In Sonnet XXXI, she cries, "O, ever Dear! thy precious, vital powers/Sink rapidly," while Edgeworth's "eyes gaily glow,/Regardless of thy life's fast ebbing tide;/I hear him, who should droop in silent woe,/Declaim on actors, and on taste decide."[58] In the sonnet that follows, her hatred of Edgeworth grows even more virulent as she tries to assuage her anger at Honora's desertion seven years earlier:

> *Behold him now his genuine colours wear,*
> *That specious false-one, by whose cruel wiles*
> *I lost thy amity; saw thy dear smiles*
> *Eclips'd; those smiles, that used my heart to cheer,*
> *Wak'd by thy grateful sense of many a year*
> *When rose thy youth, by Friendship's pleasing toils*
> *Cultured;—but Dying!—O! for ever fade*
> *The angry fires.—Each thought, that might upbraid*
> *Thy broken faith, which yet my soul deplores,*
> *Now as eternally is past and gone*
> *As are the interesting, the happy hours,*
> *Days, years, we shared together. They are flown!*
> *Yet long must I lament thy hapless doom,*
> *Thy lavish'd life and early hasten'd tomb.*[59]

Her hatred of Edgeworth, and her conviction that were it not for him Honora would have lived and been hers forever, grew with the passing years after Honora's death. In a poem written six years later, for example, Anna laments that Honora's grave is "By faithless Love deserted and forgot." Anna, however, cannot forget. She ends the poem happy for Sleep which permits her to be with the other woman again: "Come to my dreams, my lost Honora, come!/ Back as the waves of Time benignly roll,/Shew thy bright face to my enchanted soul!"[60]

Anna's mourning grew more intense with the passing years and there are many poems written long after Honora's death praising her youth and beauty, and telling of how happy the two women had been together long ago. They describe the poet as forever haunted by the vision of Honora. Even in a poem written not long before Anna's own death (about thirty years after Honora's), she still weeps because she shall no more see "Thy speaking eyes, that cheer'd my soul!"[61]

Anna's obsessive sorrow was clearly not literary alone, since her life shows that she lived that sorrow. Four years after her friend's death, when she briefly met a woman whose features were "so like my lost Honora," she wrote that she wept uncontrollable tears.[62] Even the value in which she held her friends is determined, at least in part, by whether or not they knew Honora, as she wrote to a Mrs. Powys in 1802: "Your kind bosom is a mirror which reflects my happiest years, and on your memory their sweetest delights are written. Friends of later date may be admired, esteemed, beloved, but unconscious of Honora, cannot be dear to me as yourself." [63]

Nor can Anna's immoderate grief be attributed simply to the sentimentality of the age which also made the graveyard school of poets so popular. She had also lost to death a young, beautiful, intelligent sister, who was just about to marry. The two had been extremely close and loving. Anna mourned for a period, expressed her grief in letters and a few poems, but as the years passed her loss was assuaged. Her obsession with the dead Honora, though, seems to express a tragic depth of feeling that has little to do with sentimentality and is not characteristic of her behavior with others.[64]

Because of the loss of her great romantic friend, it was both painful and fascinating for her to make the acquaintance of Sarah Ponsonby and Eleanor Butler. Anna's letters and poems express her melancholy admiration and envy. She met the two Ladies in 1795, and they remained close friends until her death, for which they were provided mourning rings by a stipulation in her will. Anna's letters to others in the mid-1790's discuss at great length Sarah and Eleanor's home, their devotion to each other, and the respect they receive from all levels of society. The Vale where they live, Anna wrote in 1796, is consecrated three times "by valour, by love, and by friendship." [65] No doubt the Ladies' love for each other reminded her of her own for Honora. When, in October 1797, Anna happened upon a picture by Romney of "Serena, reading by candlelight," which "accidentally formed a perfect similitude of my lost Honora Sneyd's face and figure," she immediately purchased it and sent it to Llangollen, telling Sarah and Eleanor how much she wished that Honora's "form should be enshrined in the receptacle of grace and beauty and appear there distinctly as those of Lady E. Butler and Miss Ponsonby, are engraved on the memory and on the heart" of Anna.[66] This gesture was perhaps her way of living out a fantasy: Anna would identify herself with Eleanor and Sarah, and Honora (or at least her artistic embodiment) would live in their temple dedicated to love between women.

Her poems to the Llangollen Ladies are filled with her beloved, here usually implicitly, and with how the love between Eleanor and Sarah makes her think of what she has lost. In "Llangollen Vale," she envies their "sacred Friendship, permanent as pure" and their strength when young to resist all that would sunder them: "In vain the stern authorities assail,/In vain persuasion spreads her silken lure."[67] Implicit here is her sorrow and resentment that Honora had been snared by the "specious" and "false" Edgeworth. In another poem, "To the Right Honourable Lady Eleanor Butler," she praises Eleanor (the older of the two and the one with whom Anna especially identified) for her valor and fortitude:

> *Thou, who with firm, free step, as life arose*
> *Led thy loved friend where sacred Deva flows*
> *On Wisdom's cloudless sun with thee to gaze . . .*

She envies in their relationship "The blest reality of Hope's fond dream,/Friendship, that bliss unshar'd disdains to know,/Nor sees, nor feels one unpartaken woe." [68] They embody everything she had wanted in her romantic friendship with Honora—a shared life of total devotion amidst learning and the joys of nature, in a true "Eden," as Anna calls their home in several poems, of innocent sensuality and perpetual bliss.

Correspondence and memoirs of the period indicate that it was the ambition of many romantic friends to set up households together: Those households would differ from ordinary heterosexual arrangements in that the two women would be always inseparable, always devoted; their relationship would be truly intimate, based on no consideration other than their love for each other. Mary Wollstonecraft, seeing the failure of heterosexual marriage in her parents' home, craved from her youth a permanent attachment to another female. In 1773 she wrote to her first romantic friend, Jane Arden, when it appeared that their relationship was near the end because of Jane's infidelity, "Love and jealousy are twins. . . . I could not bear the thought of C——'s rivalling me in your love." In case Jane had missed the fact that Mary felt disappointed and betrayed by her, she enclosed a contemporary essay which defined friendship as "the most solemn, sacred union, displaying itself in all the offices of true affection and esteem.—Happy beyond expression is the pair who are thus united." [69] Some time afterward Mary formed another romantic friendship which, she hoped, would match the ideal described in that essay and which would endure as her first love had not. She was happy to write Jane that Fanny Blood was the "friend whom I love better than all the world beside."[70]

Mary's love for Fanny might have started on the rebound, but it soon grew and developed a tremendous power of its own. William Godwin (the social philosopher who was the father of Mary's second child [Mary Shelley] and, for a brief time before her death, her husband) describes her initial meeting with Fanny as love at first sight: "Before the interview was concluded," Godwin writes, Mary "had taken in her heart the vows of eternal friendship."[71] The two became inseparable. Mary admired Fanny's ostensible accomplishments and sympathized with her in her unhappy domestic situation, which was not very different from Mary's own. Before long, however, Mary outstripped Fanny in accomplishments, and she became the leader and lover in their relationship, while Fanny was a passive recipient of her attentions.

They were separated for over a year, when Mary's ne'er-do-well father moved the family to Wales. During this time Mary could think only of a permanent life with Fanny. She wrote Jane, this time with all sincerity, "The roses will bloom when there's peace in the breast, and the prospect of living with my Fanny gladdens my heart:—You know not how I love her." She went on to say that she had given up everything "that would interfere with my determination of spending my time with her," and hinted that since she was "on many accounts . . . averse to any matrimonial tie," she would not marry a man, but would stay with Fanny forever.[72]

In 1780, when Mary was twenty-one, she went to live with the Bloods at Walham Green, south of London, and for two years found herself in a constant struggle to help Fanny's family out of debt and poverty. Finally, Mary had reason to believe that she and Fanny could leave the Bloods' home and live together alone. She took it upon herself to find a place for them. Godwin reports in the *Memoirs* that she did this through "infinite exertions." She then sent a note to Fanny saying that "a house was prepared, and that she was on the spot to receive her." But Fanny's response was only an "enumeration of objections to the quitting of her family, which she had not thought of before, but which now appeared to her of considerable weight."[73] However, even as late as 1783 Mary was still pursuing her dream of their life together, and she finally convinced Fanny, by then suffering noticeably from consumption, to open a school with her. Although their first venture, in Islington, was a failure, their second, in Newington Green, was somewhat more successful. However, the scheme was short-lived. Mary now realized that Fanny had none of the moral or physical strength needed for a life pledged to romantic friendship.

Godwin says that it was Mary's recognition of her friend's disturbing "morbid softness of temper" and her unsuitability for the fray of an independent life that made Mary "advise Fanny to accept the proposal of Hugh Skeys, who was then living in Portugal where Mary hoped Fanny's consumption might be alleviated." Godwin has no doubt that Fanny married Skeys only on Mary's advice, although later biographers, perhaps unduly influenced by Mary's sketch of Ann in her novel *Mary: A Fiction*, conjecture that Fanny had been pining for Skeys for years.[74] Whatever the truth, Mary remembered Fanny's marriage (or wished to remember it and therefore reported it to Godwin thus) as having taken place not because Fanny loved another better but because Mary desired it out of pique with her friend's weakness as well as concern for her illness. Their relationship did not entirely end with the marriage and Fanny's departure for Portugal. Toward the end of 1785, Fanny was due to deliver a baby, and Mary went to Lisbon to offer support and assistance. Fanny died in Mary's arms on November 29, 1785, after bearing a child who also did not live.

Godwin describes Mary's love for Fanny as "so fervent, as for years to have constituted the ruling passion of her mind," and calls her "the chosen object of Mary's attachment."[75] He explains the lifelong impact of the relationship on Mary, presumably as she reported it to him: It formed her personality, Godwin believes. Because she failed in her youthful passion, being unable to establish a life with her first beloved, she came to expect failure from all her endeavors.[76]

Throughout Mary's short life she never was able to forget her first powerful involvement. She always wore a locket with Fanny's hair. In 1794 she named her first child Fanny, "in remembrance of the dear friend of her youth, whose image could never be erased from her memory."[77] In 1796, a year before her own death and eleven years after Fanny's, she wrote in *Letters from Norway* that she still recollects "looks I have felt in every nerve, which I shall never more meet. The grave has closed over a dear friend, the friend of my youth; still she is present with me, and I hear her soft voice warbling as I stray over the heath."[78] Her autobiographical novel, *Mary: A Fiction* (1787), is largely concerned with her unhappy love for Fanny. Mary, who becomes involved with a man after the death of Ann (Fanny) in the novel, openly states that "had Ann lived, it is probable she [Mary] would never have loved [a man]."

Not surprisingly, in the case of Mary Wollstonecraft too, twentieth-century scholars have refused to accept what was entirely acceptable in her time and was regarded by husbands as a fact of life: Women's passionate attachments to other women. Faced with the information that in 1785, after Fanny's marriage and death, Mary underwent a horrible depression and complained in a letter to Fanny's brother, George Blood, "My harrassed mind will in time wear out my body. . . . I have lost all relish for life—and my almost broken heart is only cheared by the prospect of death. . . . I almost hate the Green [her last home with Fanny], for it seems the grave of all my comforts,"[79] the unfailing response of modern scholars is *chercher l'homme*. One biographer, even after remarking how much Fanny's health had worsened at the Green, and noting that as Mary's reason for encouraging her to marry Skeys, refers to the above letter to George Blood and asks, "What had happened [to cause Mary's depression]? Surely her father's difficulties could not suddenly have plunged her into such a despondent state; nor could loneliness for Fanny or George."[80] His explanation is that Mary was madly in love with the Reverend Joshua Waterhouse and had been spurned by him.

He admits that there is no concrete evidence to prove this hypothesis, but reasons that "sometheing drastic" must have happened "to provoke such despair"—and in the twentieth century the loss of a much-loved woman friend is not regarded as "drastic." He quotes a letter which Mary wrote to George Blood six months after Fanny's death: "My poor heart still throbs with selfish anguish. It is formed for friendship and confidence—yet how often it is wounded." The biographer points out that the next sixteen lines have been obliterated by a later hand, and he suggests that they must have referred to her affair with Waterhouse. "Surely the censor did not go to such pains to conceal Mary's lamentations on the death of her friend," he asserts. It must have been Mary's love for a man the censor was trying to hide.[81] However, considering Godwin's complete honesty regarding Mary's affairs with other men and himself, it is doubtful that a considerate censor would wish to spare her the embarrassment of one more youthful affair. What is more likely is that the letter was censored by someone more recent who, aware of the twentieth-century stigma regarding "lesbianism," wished to spare

Mary that accusation, as, we will see, Martha Dickinson Bianchi did in censoring Emily Dickinson's letters. The discomfort that many modern biographers feel in the face of irrefutable evidence of their female subject's love for another woman is very clearly stated by a Wollstonecraft biographer of the 1970's who, after discussing Mary's attachment to Fanny and pointedly distinguishing it from lesbianism, introduces earlier theories on Mary's affair with Waterhouse with the statement, "In spite of these emotions and professions [to Fanny], a certain secret disloyalty to Fanny did take place. It is rather a relief to discover it [sic!]." [82]

The facts of Mary's life during this period cannot relieve twentieth-century homophobic anxiety. Her actions and her later revelations to Godwin show that she was absolutely sincere in wanting more than anything else during the time she knew Fanny to establish a marriage with her. Mary's failure to attain this objective accounts for her intense depression and, as Godwin himself suggests, her negative outlook during the rest of her life.

How are the passions of these eighteenth-century romantic friends distinguishable from "lesbianism"? If one believes that lesbianism is primarily a sexual phenomenon, there is no similarity. But women who identify themselves as lesbian generally do not view lesbianism as a sexual phenomenon first and foremost. What romantic friends wanted was to share their lives, to confide in and trust and depend upon each other, to be there always for each other. Sometimes their relationships were tense and as fraught with ambivalence as any demanding emotional relationship is. Almost always they envisioned themselves together forever. In these ways, surely, there is little to distinguish romantic friendship from lesbianism. [83]

If eighteenth-century romantic friends had lived in the twentieth century, however, they would have had to deal very consciously with the "sexual implications" of their attachments. To have disregarded them, as they could in a pre-Freudian era, would have been impossible. The knowledge that there was a label society could apply to passion between women would also have been inescapable, as it was not in the more reticent eighteenth century. Whether or not they chose to act on their understanding of sexual possibilities, they would have had to consider if they could tolerate, emotionally, the application of the label to themselves. And they would have realized, had they openly manifested the same level of involvement with one another, that the term "lesbian" would probably be applied to their relationship, regardless of whether it was really sexual. If they could not tolerate the label, they would have felt themselves under tremendous pressure to "get cured." If they could not be cured, they might have come to internalize the conviction that their love, which was no different from what they were able to think of as noble and fine in their own day, was degenerate and diseased.

PART II

THE NINETEENTH
CENTURY

A.
Loving Friends

CHAPTER 1

The Asexual Woman

In 1811 Miss Marianne Woods and Miss Jane Pirie, mistresses of a girls' boarding school for daughters of the wealthy in Drumsheugh, a town near Edinburgh, Scotland, sued Dame Helen Cumming Gordon for libel. Dame Gordon, whose natural granddaughter had attended their school, had had reason to believe that the two women engaged in "improper and criminal conduct" with each other, and she had informed the parents of all the girls at the school of her suspicions. As a result, every last pupil was removed. The two women claimed in their lawsuit that they had no notion of what Dame Gordon meant in her accusation, but they had lost their life savings and livelihoods because of her defamation of their characters.[1]

Dame Gordon's sixteen-year-old granddaughter, who was born in India, the only child of her deceased son and an Indian woman with whom he had lived, was sent to the newly opened school to be prepared for entrance into society. Dame Gordon's first intention had been to have the girl trained for a trade, but perhaps because of her anguish over her dead son and consequent anxiety over his offspring, she changed her mind and decided to educate her as she would a granddaughter who had legal claim to her family name and who was born of a British woman.

In the beginning Miss Cumming appeared to be very happy at the school and to be fond of her two mistresses, although occasionally she complained that she was too severely punished for minor infractions. As the oldest girl in the school, she was the bedfellow of Miss Pirie, and they shared a dormitory-like room with several other girls, who all doubled up in beds, as was usual in a nineteenth-century school.

The rest of the pupils slept in another dormitory room with Miss Woods and her bedfellow, the second oldest girl, Miss Munro.

After some time Miss Cumming complained to her grandmother that she had been kept from sleeping by strange goings-on in her bed: In the middle of the night Miss Woods would come into their room, get into bed on Miss Pirie's side, climb on top of Miss Pirie, and shake the bed. Occasionally Miss Cumming would overhear conversations between them:

"Oh, you are in the wrong place," Miss Pirie said one night.
"I know," Miss Woods answered.
"Why are you doing it then?"
"For fun," Miss Woods said.

Another night Miss Pirie implored Miss Woods, "Oh, do it, darling." And still another night, upon leaving the room, Miss Woods said to Miss Pirie, "I think I have put you in a fair way to sleep." Dame Gordon did not stop to confront the two women with the accusation before she informed the parents of all the other girls that their children were in grave danger at the school and must be removed immediately. It was quite enough evidence for her that Miss Munro corroborated the story: Miss Pirie had several times climbed into the bed Miss Munro shared with Miss Woods, mounted Miss Woods, and shaken the bed, keeping Miss Munro awake just as Miss Cumming had been kept awake.

In 1819 the House of Lords delivered a judgment in favor of the two women, who were then entitled to claim financial remuneration from Dame Gordon. The judges were of course swayed by the implausible accusation that two women who could make any arrangements that would suit them in the school chose to behave in such a manner with a third person in close proximity. They were undoubtedly also swayed by the fact that the main witness against the women was "coloured" and illegitimate, and that her future was in a sense at the women's mercy: They reasoned that she must have thought that if she did not do well at the school she would again be sent to learn a trade, and that fear must have made her resentful and anxious to find a way out of their domination. The judges suggested that Miss Cumming, having been raised in the lascivious East, had no idea of the horror such an accusation would stir in Britain, and hoped only to be removed from the school herself when she complained of the women's activities.

But the judges were most swayed in their judgments by their unwillingness to believe that women above the lower class were sexual creatures, that they would willingly indulge in sexual activity for the gratification of their own appetites and not for the sole purpose of procreation. If a decent woman would not engage in illicit sexual activities with a man, whose great sexual impulse might have a seductive effect on her, she would certainly not do so with another woman, who, like her, could have no overwhelming sexual drive. As Lord Gillies stated in his judgment, "No such case was ever known in Scotland, or in Britain . . . I do believe that the crime here alleged has no existence." [2]

In order to prove that lesbianism existed, the lawyers for Dame Gordon had included in their presentation a number of historical works, including Lucian's "Dialogues of the Courtesans." In this work Leana admits to Clonarium that she had been living with Megilla, a woman from Lesbos, neither a man in disguise nor a hermaphrodite, who made love to her. When Clonarium asks, "What did she do? How? That's what I'm most interested to hear," Leana responds, "Don't enquire too closely into the details; they're not very nice; so, by Aphrodite in heaven, I won't tell you." [3] Here the dialogue ends. Since even Lucian, living in immoral times, did not know how such an act could be conducted, one of the judges reasoned that this in itself was proof that even then women did not engage in sex together: Lucian did not know what two women could do in bed simply because there was nothing they could do in bed. [4]

The lawyers for Woods and Pirie based their major argument on that opinion. After establishing the good character of both these women, they demanded, "Is it no violent improbability that no less than *two* such persons should at last have been guilty of a crime so utterly abandoned, that it is totally unknown, and even doubtful if it can exist?" [5] That argument settled the case, in effect. Could two people engage in venereal activity though the male sex is absent? one judge asked. "Could murder be committed by hocus-pocus or paw-wawing?" Without an instrument the act is impossible, the judge decided. "Copulating without penetration of the female, or the gratification of wild and unnatural lust committed in sport [i.e., in mere imitation of heterosexual intercourse], and in the course of long chit-chat and whispers [e.g., "You are in the wrong place," etc.], appear to me to possess much of the same character [as murder committed by hocus-pocus],—much like charging a rape as committed *en gaieté du coeur*, and in the course of small talk." [6]

The women's lawyers had an easy task since the judges, like most men in Britain, were predisposed to believe in the genteel woman's essential asexuality. Lord Meadowbank explained to the others that he had been to India, and he would venture to guess that Miss Cumming had developed her curiosity about sexual matters from her lewd Indian nurses, who were, in contrast to British women, entirely capable of obscene chatter on such subjects—although it was based merely on imagination and obviously exhibited no knowledge of the possible.[7] Lord Boyle, on the other hand, did not believe tribadism impossible among savages, but certainly improbable in civilized Britain: He proclaimed that "however well known the crime here charged may be amongst Eastern nations, this is the first instance on record, of such an accusation having ever been made in this country."[8] Lord Justice-Clerk Hope, in his more colorful manner, asserted that he could believe the accusation against the two women as much as he could believe "that a person heard thunder playing the tune of 'God Save the King.'" No British woman was capable of such action, he said. "There is not a prostitute so blasted as these women are described by Miss Cumming." Being certain of the purity of the women whom he knew intimately, he was convinced of the purity of these two women of respectable birth. "I have no more suspicion of the guilt of the pursuers," he stated, "than I have of my own wife."[9]

The judges were further prejudiced against Dame Gordon by a particular detail in the evidence given by her granddaughter, the dialogue with regard to being "in the wrong place." What British woman of respectable family would engage in sodomy, and lesbian sodomy at that? Lord Justice-Clerk Hope's outraged statement again seemed to sum up the feeling of most of the other judges: "I would rather believe Miss Cumming, and almost Lady Cumming [Gordon] herself perjured, than I would believe the statement about *the wrong place* to be true, especially with regard to women of good character. This is stated of women alive to all the fine feelings of Christian morality . . . To commit sodomy with a woman,—a double unnatural crime: Can it be believed of such persons? Is character, and such character, to be of no weight here?"[10]

The lawyers for Woods and Pirie felt it crucial to establish their characters as unimpeachable, and therefore attributed to them all the important moral values of their day: The women were Christian, they were sober and industrious, and, most of all, they were capable of enduring and self-sacrificing friendship. To be willing to involve oneself in totally committed female friendship was an indication of the seriousness of one's moral character. Paradoxical as it seems to us today, it would have been self-defeating for the women's lawyers to argue that Miss Woods and Miss Pirie had only a cold business relationship. They sought to establish that the women loved each other with great, unquestioning intensity, knowing that the judges would agree that such overwhelming love (which was ennobling) would not permit the demon of sex (which was debasing) to wend its way in. The lawyers offered as evidence of the "purity" of these women a letter which, in the twentieth century, might well have been used by Dame Gordon's lawyers as proof that the two women were in love and hence probably lovers. It appears that Miss Woods and Miss Pirie had frequent fights, often about Mrs. Woods, Marianne's aunt, who helped manage the school, and about the financial arrangements of the school. On one occasion after an argument, Miss Pirie confided her anguish to a woman friend. She wrote of Marianne:

> . . . circumstances have arisen to shake my faith in my friend's affections for *me*. I always loved *her* as my own soul: and would willingly have laid down my existence to increase her comforts, till my confidence in her sincerity was so cruelly shaken.
>
> When I give way to doubts I feel miserable beyond description . . . How should I act? I can *never* conquer my affection, should she even declare herself my enemy. I have loved her for eight years with sincere and ardent affection, and have accustomed my mind to contemplate her as the model of very virtue. And if I cannot regard her as superior to everything unworthy of a great and exalted mind, I feel misery must be my portion in this life. You must aid me with your advice, as you can enter into my feelings and, perhaps, administer an opiate that can assuage the heart-rending sorrow I frequently experience. Pardon this incoherent production. Permit me to see you when convenient . . .[11]

The women's lawyers used as further proof of their purity the fact that Miss Pirie had presented Miss Woods with a Bible—and they pointedly included in their evidence Miss Pirie's inscription, which we would see today as a statement of love not at all inconsistent with the feelings of a lover, homosexual or heterosexual:

> Accept, my beloved, of that book, which can give consolation in every situation; and, dearest *earthly* friend, never open it without thinking of her, who would forego all friendship but her God's, to possess yours. Ever your own . . .[12]

The Woods and Pirie case points to a major paradox: Because throughout much of the nineteenth century in Britain and America, sex was considered an activity in which virtuous women were not interested and did not indulge unless to gratify their husbands and to procreate,[13] it was generally inconceivable to society that an otherwise respectable woman could choose to participate in a sexual activity that had as its goal neither procreation nor pleasing a husband. Because there was seemingly no possibility that women would want to make love together, they were permitted a latitude of affectionate expression and demonstration that became more and more narrow with the growth of general sophistication and pseudosophistication regarding sexual possibilities between women. A twentieth-century judge could never declare as Lord Justice-Clerk Hope did in the early nineteenth century, "according to the known habits of women in this country, there is no indecency in one woman going to bed with another." [14]

Understanding this nineteenth-century view of women, their lawyers did not attempt to prove that Miss Pirie or Miss Woods never climbed into bed with the other and embraced. Instead they argued that a man and a woman in bed together may be suspected of venereal congress, and perhaps even if two men were in bed together without good reason, "an unnatural intention may often be inferred." However, "a woman being in bed with a woman cannot even give a probability to such an inference. It is the order of nature and of society in its present state. If a woman embraces a woman it infers nothing." [15]

To have accepted that such behavior infers something sexual would have called into question the most strongly held beliefs of the era regarding women. It would have raised an issue which touched the very foundation of society, that of female venereal appetite. Not just the reputation of two women was at stake here, but the reputation of every respectable British woman. If these two British women, of decent background, good Christian education, and admirable attainments, were possessed of such blatant sexual drives, was the wife of Lord Justice-Clerk Hope free from those drives? Lord Meadowbank declared that the interest of the entire public was at stake here, "for the virtues, the comforts, and the freedom of domestic intercourse, mainly depend on the purity of female manners, and that, again, on the habits of intercourse remaining as they have hitherto been,—free from suspicion." [16]

The House of Lords found the behavior of these two women free from suspicion, and affirmed their right—even their *obligation*—to intimacy. A woman who is not capable of the tenderest feelings and deepest intimacy toward her friend is lacking in an essential human component. Lord Gillies complained that Dame Gordon's lawyers had tried to make them believe "that wherever two young women form an intimacy together, and that intimacy ripens into friendship, if ever they venture to share the same bed, that becomes proof of guilt." If that be the case, he declared, "where is the innocent woman in Scotland,—if any such is known to your Lordships, she is not known to me. I hope none such will ever be known to me, whose intimacies do not ripen into friendship, and whose friendship would not permit her to sleep in the same bed with her friend when necessary." [17] The women's lawyers had not even suggested that their sleeping together was in any way necessary, but it is significant that one of the judges embellished his analysis of the situation to be consistent with his views of the purity of this and all female friendships, and was not corrected by his fellow judges.

It is true that the Woods and Pirie trial was held in Edinburgh, which was in general less sophisticated than London or Paris, but with regard to lesbianism, an accusation such as that against the two respectable Scottish women would probably not have been taken any more seriously in most cosmopolitan centers around 1811. If the women had been actresses or prostitutes or of the decadent aristocracy, it would have been conceivable that they were prone to any sort of debauchery. But they were schoolmistresses, capable of great sentiment (which indicated delicacy of feeling), and they were from good middle-class families.

Such naïveté toward same-sex love did not, of course, extend to male homosexuality, even in Scotland. There were at least four cases of Scottish men, all from respectable families, who were persecuted for homosexuality at about the same time the Woods and Pirie trial was held.[18] In 1810 in London, one year before the Woods and Pirie trial, two men were sentenced to death and seven others were imprisoned for homosexual relations.[19] Six of the latter were also required to stand in the pillory, where they were pelted by thousands of spectators with dead cats, mud, and offal until they were almost completely buried. In contrast to the complete silence of the Edinburgh papers about the Woods and Pirie case, the crime and ordeal of the men were reported in detail with great relish by the London papers.[20]

In the male view, it was incredible that women such as Woods and

Pirie could be capable of blatant sexual exhibitionism, since they did not even possess a sexual appetite; a sexual act without a male initiator, one which required autonomous drive, would be unthinkable. The eighteenth century believed a good woman was sexually dormant, and the nineteenth century promulgated that idea with a vengeance. Particularly in Britain and other countries in which the middle class grew in influence,[21] that view of female sexuality, which we have come to call "Victorian" (not because Queen Victoria invented the view, but because she reigned during the time it was at its height), characterized the times. Departure from such a view was a conscious, specific (often violent) reaction to middle-class "morality."

If men defined lesbianism as just sex between women, they could believe that they never encountered a lesbian in decent society. But what was devotion, or affection, or even an exclusive commitment between two women? It was not, as Alfred Douglas said of male homosexuality later in the century, the love that dared not speak its name. It was the love that had no name, unless it were a sentimental one like "romantic friendship," even if the intensity of the relationship made the term "friendship" inaccurate and misleading.

Some of the most sophisticated individuals, such as Flora Tristan, the nineteenth-century French writer and reform leader, who spent most of her life in Paris and who worked for a time in London, knew no name whatever for passionate love between women. In 1839 she wrote to another woman, Olympe, "For a long time I have desired to make a woman love me passionately—Oh! how I wish I were a man so I could be loved by a woman. I feel, dear Olympe, that I have reached a point where the love of no man could satisfy me—perhaps a woman's could? . . . Woman has so much power in her heart, in her imagination, so many resources in her spirit." But Tristan believed, despite her longings and her blatant flirtation with Olympe, that she would never find a woman to love her passionately, since "the attraction of senses cannot exist between two people of the same sex." [22] Despite the attraction that existed between her and Olympe (who had written her that she made Olympe "shiver with pleasure," that she hypnotized her and put her in ecstasy, and that she, Olympe, loved her), both women were trained to deny the evidence of their feelings. They could not be experiencing "the attraction of senses," since such attraction "cannot exist between two people of the same sex."

If a cosmopolitan Frenchwoman of the first half of the nineteenth century could ignore her own sensations and those of another woman, we may be sure that the general public had no conception of the potentials of love between women. In Victorian England as well as in France, few seemed to know of such possibilities; and some of those who knew—or thought they knew—something of lesbian sexuality believed it was in the public interest to keep the knowledge from spreading. For this reason the British critic, John Morley, blasted Swinburne's 1866 work, *Poems and Ballads*, in the *Saturday Review*. Morley angrily wrote, "The only comfort about the present volume is that such a piece as 'Anactoria' [in which Sappho complains to a fickle woman lover] will be unintelligible to a great many people, and so will the fevered folly of 'Hermaphroditus,' as well as much else that is nameless and abominable."[23] His review is essentially devoted to the plea that such matters should remain nameless and arcane lest young women learn what they should not know.

In America even in the late 1890's, knowledge of the potential of female same-sex love was limited. A medical doctor, Allan McLane Hamilton, wrote in 1896 that "until within a comparatively recent period the mere insinuation that there could be anything improper in the intimate relations of two women would have drawn upon the head of the maker of such a suggestion a degree of censure of the most pronounced and enduring character." He speaks of a "case" of lesbianism that had come to his attention only a few years earlier when such "mental perversion was not of the recognized kind." Hamilton attributes the new knowledge regarding lesbianism especially to Théophile Gautier's *Mademoiselle de Maupin* (which had been translated into English and published in America in 1890) and to other French and German novels of the period. But although he "knew all about" sex between women, it is doubtful that had he advised the judges of the Woods and Pirie case the women would have been found any more culpable. A lesbian, Hamilton wrote, was "usually of a masculine type, or if she presented none of the 'characteristics' of the male, was a subject of pelvic disorder, with scanty menstruation, and was more or less hysterical or insane."[24] Since neither Woods nor Pirie was masculine or reported menstrual problems or was accused of insanity, they could not have been frolicking with each other on a bed.

Although lesbianism was first identified as a "medical problem" in Germany, and by the end of the century numerous books had been written on the subject, many German authors were no more perceptive or accurate about the potential of love between women than the

American doctor. The same confusion existed in the popular mind in Germany: Good women had no sex drive; therefore, there could be no sexual relationship between them. New medical "knowledge" said that abnormal women—those who were masculine or hysterical —might engage in unorthodox sexual practices, but what of normal-looking, healthy women? By 1900 the confusion was intensified by the militant New Woman's growing commitment to other women, as the German novel by Elisabeth Dauthendey, *Of the New Woman and Her Love: A Book for Mature Minds* (1900), dramatically illus trates. The central character, Lenore, a New Woman, refuses to form a relationship with a man because men have not yet evolved as highly as women. She rejects the "impure advances of sapphists," but she falls in love with Yvette. A climactic scene shows the two women thus:

> Without a sound, in the silent ardor of deep, blissful joy we lay in each other's arms.
> And the breath of our beating pulses was just enough to let us speak the beloved name—
> "Lenore"—
> "Yvette"—

The author does not say what distinguishes this love from the love of sapphists, but it is clear that for her the term "sapphist" or "lesbian" cannot apply to a woman who is healthy and normal looking, regardless of how her passions are engaged and what her commitments are.

To the very end of the century then, the sexual potential of love between decent, healthy women was still unacknowledged by many seemingly sophisticated authors: sound women were asexual. It was doubtful enough that they would concern themselves with any form of sexual satisfaction, but that they would seek sexual expression without a male initiator was as credible as claiming to hear the thunder play "God Save the King."

CHAPTER 2

Kindred Spirits

Throughout much of the nineteenth century, women moved still farther from men as both continued to develop their own even more distinct sets of values. Men tried to claim exclusively for themselves the capacity of action and thought, and relegated women to the realm of sensibility alone. Women made the best of it: They internalized the only values they were permitted to have, and they developed what has been called the Cult of True Womanhood.[1] The spiritual life, moral purity, sentiment, grew in importance. But with whom could they share these values?

In America and England during the second half of the nineteenth century, as more women began to claim more of the world, the reasons for bonding together against men who wished to deny them a broader sphere became greater. When men wrote about female attachments in literature, they tended to see the same sentimental pictures that were prevalent in eighteenth-century fiction: Two sweet females uplifting each other morally, but ultimately entirely dependent on men whether that dependence brought them joy or tragedy. What they did not see was how female relationships could sustain a woman intellectually and make her strong enough to engage in the battle for more of the world. But they also did not suspect—any more than the women themselves did—that such an emotional and even physical closeness was "lesbian," at least in a twentieth-century definition. They did not treat it as an abnormality because it was common enough to be a norm.

Since men and women occupied separate spheres, particularly among the great middle classes, they considered themselves virtually

157

different species. Men believed a woman could command no rational thought as a man could, although, at her best, she dwelt in the realm of the heart and might be an "Angel in the House," as the English writer Coventry Patmore calls her in his mid-nineteenth-century poem. But whatever she was, she was not male and thus not as human as man. The observation regarding women that Tennyson's protagonist makes in "Locksley Hall" (1842) was probably echoed by many men: "Nature made them blinder motions bounded in a shallower brain: woman is the lesser man."

Men saw women as what Simone de Beauvoir has called "the Other," and for that reason they could attribute to them magical properties (sometimes beneficial, sometimes dangerous) which the real human beings, men, do not have; e.g., they believed that if a syphilitic man raped a virgin he would be cured.[2] Such absurdity was not limited to folk wisdom. For example, in 1878 there was a serious debate, which lasted over several issues among correspondents in the *British Medical Journal*, about whether or not ham would be spoiled if cured by a menstruating woman. Several of the doctors who joined the debate agreed that it would.

Such views of women as being something other than human were by no means peculiar to Britain. G. J. Barker-Benfield shows that in nineteenth-century America, the estrangement between men and women was even worse than in Britain, since it had an immediate practical purpose in men's minds: The American male must not be distracted from his "desire of prosperity" by the softness and seductiveness of the female. He "had to be above sex" to succeed. Stronger bonds were formed between father and son, and male and male in general, because men needed the assistance of other men to realize their ardent material passion.[3] Male "muscle values" and "rational values" were fostered to the exclusion of women. The converse of this situation was, of course, that mother and daughter, and female and female, also formed stronger bonds largely based on "heart values," since male-directed society permitted them little else.

Female chastity which was held to be vital in earlier centuries took on even greater importance in nineteenth-century America, since an unchaste woman could distract a man from his larger purpose. Accordingly, an 1808 writer warns young men to test the virtue of a woman whom they wish to marry by making sexual advances to her. If she does not respond with "becoming abhorrence," she is not a proper girl and would not make a good wife.[4] In this way women were taught to deny any heterosexual urge. The lesson was often extended to sexual appetites not only outside of marriage but in marriage as well. By the mid-nineteeth century a number of authorities warned that even in lawful marriage, too much intercourse caused the male "general debility, weakness, and lameness of the back" as well as a predisposition to "almost innumerable diseases." It afflicted the female with "uterine inflammation, and ulceration, leucorrhea, deranged menstruation, miscarriage, barrenness as well as debility, hysteria, and an endless train of nervous and other diseases." [5] Since heterosexual indulgence was declared to be dangerous to both social standing and health, we can believe the author of *Plain Talk on Avoided Subjects* (1882) when he states that not infrequently so great a shock is administered to a young woman's sensibilities on her wedding night "that she does not recover from it for years" and that she often "forms a deeply rooted antipathy" toward heterosexuality.[6]

Women understood that they must not be open with men. They must not show heterosexual feeling even to a beloved fiancé before marriage, and once married they must be very restrained or they risked grave disease. They knew too, in an era when birth control was not effective and when the risks of childbirth were high, that heterosexual intercourse might mean they were taking their lives into their hands. To love a man meant pain and burdens and potential death. What Nancy Cott has called "passionlessness" was soundly impressed upon them.[7] Since middle and upper-class women were separated from men not only in their daily occupations, but in their spiritual and leisure interests as well,[8] outside of the practical necessities of raising a family there was little that tied the sexes together. But with other females a woman inhabited the same sphere, and she could be entirely trusting and unrestrained. She could share sentiment, her heart—all emotions that manly males had to repress in favor of "rationality"—with another female. And regardless of the intensity of the feeling that might develop between them, they need not attribute it to the demon, sexuality, since women supposedly had none. They could safely see it as an effusion of the spirit. The shield of passionlessness that a woman was trained to raise before a man could be lowered with another woman without fear of losing her chastity and reputation and health. Men too were encouraged to form intense friendships with other men. Thoreau was speaking for his time when he observed in his mid-nineteenth-century essay, *Friendship*, that intimacy was much more possible "between two of the same sex" than "between the sexes." [9]

William Taylor and Christopher Lasch ("Two 'Kindred Spirits':

Sorority and Family in New England, 1839–1846") and Carroll Smith-Rosenberg ("The Female World of Love and Ritual: Relations Between Women in Nineteenth Century America")[10] have amply demonstrated that deeply felt friendships between women were casually accepted in American society, primarily because women saw themselves, and were seen as, kindred spirits who inhabited a world of interests and sensibilities alien to men. During the second half of the nineteenth century, when women slowly began to enter the world that men had built, their ties to each other became even more important. Particularly when they engaged in reform and betterment work, they were confirmed in their belief that women were spiritually superior to men, their moral perceptions were more highly developed, and their sensibilities were more refined. Thus if they needed emotional understanding and support, they turned to other women. New England reform movements often were fueled by the sisterhood of kindred spirits who were righting a world men had wronged.[11] In nineteenth-century America close bonds between women were essential both as an outlet for the individual female's sensibilities and as a crucial prop for women's work toward social and personal betterment in man's sullied and insensitive world.

What was the nature of these same-sex bonds that so many twentieth-century historians have observed? Margaret Fuller, an early feminist, saw same-sex love as far superior to heterosexuality. She wrote in her journal in the 1840's, "It is so true that a woman may be in love with a woman, and a man with a man." Such love, she says, is regulated by the same law that governs love between the sexes, "only it is purely intellectual and spiritual, unprofaned by any mixture of lower instincts, undisturbed by any need of consulting temporal interests." Presumably what she means by "lower instincts" is stark sex, and by "temporal interests" the practicalities one must take into consideration when choosing a spouse. To a nineteenth-century woman the first must have been ugly and the second an embarrassing necessary evil. While the unpleasant aspects of heterosexual love are lacking in love between women, nothing of value or joy is, at least as Fuller experienced that love herself. She admits to having loved another woman "passionately": "Her face," Fuller writes, "was always gleaming before me; her voice was echoing in my ear; all poetic thoughts clustered round the dear image. This love was for me a key which unlocked many a treasure which I still possess; it was the carbuncle (emblematic gem!) which cast light into many of the darkest corners of human nature."[12]

Female autobiographies and memoirs throughout the century suggest that Fuller's elevated view of passionate love between women was not atypical. Anna Cogswell Wood, for example, recounts her thirty-three-year relationship with another woman, characterizing it as a "true friendship" which "unites in its pure flame all other loves, that of parent and child, of brothers, as well as of the chosen companion." [13] Her relationship with Irene Leache is indistinguishable from a perfect marriage. She rhapsodizes for four pages over the eyes of the other woman, but spends more time discussing their happy life together, which was much like that of the Ladies of Llangollen. "Before six in the morning we were in the garden, where, seated under a pear tree, we passed the hours between sunrise and breakfast occupied with a book and needlework or with conversation." [14] Wood prizes her relationship with Irene Leache especially because it permitted her to develop, to blossom forth; Leache, she says, had the "power to draw beauty out of the commonplace" and to make her do it too; she stirred her "inmost depths." Through her relationship with the other woman, Wood was able to grow in ways she had never before imagined, even to perceive "sublimity in abstract thought, because love completed my circle of existence and raised things to their highest power."[15]

Nineteenth-century women were taught to expect to find what Fuller and Wood did in their love relationships with other females. Love between women could be both passionate and spiritually uplifting. It could cast one into a state of euphoria and yet unlock the secrets of life and the intellect. William Alger in *The Friendships of Women* (1868) cites one historical example after another of love between women (in America and Europe), which was characterized by the same enthusiasm described in Wood's memoir—a love which "largely constituted the richness, consolation, and joy of their lives." Typically the women wrote each other, "I feel so deeply the happiness of being loved by you, that you can never cease to love me," "I need to know all your thoughts, to follow all your motions, and can find no other occupation so sweet and so dear," "My heart is so full of you, that, since we parted, I have thought of nothing but writing to you," "I see in your soul as if it were my own." They did not need to play games with each other such as in heterosexual relationships—they shared perfect trust: "I fear no misunderstanding with you; my gratitude alone can equal the perfect security with which you inspire me." [16] Alger encourages his unmarried women readers to form such relationships, and promises that passionate friendships bring to life "freshness, stimulant charm, noble truths and aspirations."[17]

What made a male writer so sensitive to the glories of romantic friendship between women? Alger's motives were mixed. Writing in 1868, shortly after the American Civil War had increased even further through male mortality the large surplus of females, he recognized that many women would remain unmarried. He drew for them the solace of passionate friendship as a "rich and noble" resource which would occupy them and compensate happily for the lack of a family.[18] But he also saw female friendship as a means of keeping women in their place by encouraging their self-image as primarily sentient beings, too pure for the material world. Alger believed that women must stay out of men's sphere, but how to convince them that "it is simple blindness to fail to see that the distinctively feminine sphere of action is domestic life, and the inner life,—not the brawling mart and caucus," especially if they had no husbands and families?[19] Women needed some diversion that would occupy their time and emotion. In his chapters entitled "Friendships of Women with Women" and "Pairs of Female Friends," Alger offers the solution of romantic friendship which permits women to be emotional, spiritual creatures together. Perhaps this trivializing view of romantic friendship accounts for why American men continued to be fairly tolerant of it throughout much of the twentieth century.

Englishmen were also tolerant, undoubtedly for the same reasons, since England too had a large surplus of women and a generally strong determination to restrict them to their proper sphere.[20] In fiction the male view of romantic friendship was largely unchanged from what it had been the century before: Men found it charming and delightful and quite unthreatening. George Meredith, for example, in *Diana of the Crossways* (1885) presents Antonia (the Diana of the novel) and Lady Emma Dunstane as two lovely creatures who see no way out of the round of their tragic relationships with men, despite the fact that they have a powerful love for each other. Antonia tells Lady Dunstane, "Be sure I am giving up the ghost when I cease to be one soul with you, dear and dearest." She calls her "my beloved! my only truly loved on earth!" Like eighteenth-century heroines, they often talk of the possibility of a classic friendship between women, "the alliance of a mutual devotedness men choose to doubt of." However, also like eighteenth-century heroines, even Diana the chaste must attach herself to a man, even though she resents those forces "natural and social" which urge her to "marry and be bound." Although Meredith attributes feminist sentiments to her, he renders her incapable of acting on them. Throughout her unhappy marriage, she continues to think of Emma, again like in an eighteenth-century novel, as "the next heavenly thing to Heaven that I know." Male-female relationships are always a dismal failure in this novel, but the romantic friendship endures and offers refuge and sustenance to the end. It does not, however, go beyond the pattern we have already observed in most of the novels of the previous century.[21]

But Englishwomen, like their American counterparts, often viewed romantic friendship as much more. For instance, to Edith Simcox, the writer and reform leader, her passionate involvement with George Eliot (Mary Ann Evans) was not only emotional and uplifting, it was sensual, intellectually stimulating, and, in fact, her great reason for being. In Simcox's autobiography she states that she loved Eliot "my Darling, lover-wise"; [22] she speaks repeatedly of kissing her "again and again," of murmuring "broken words of love." Eliot seems to have had little interest in Simcox as a lover, but she admired her as an intellect and cheered her on to achievements. Although Simcox lamented that "my life has flung itself at her feet—and not been picked up—only told to rise and make itself a serviceable place elsewhere," she vowed to take the life Eliot directed her toward and make it constructive. Much of her social work, her zeal on behalf of the oppressed, her almost religious commitment to causes were stimulated by the desire to please Eliot.[23] As Bonnie Zimmerman remarks in her study "My Whole Soul is a Longing Question: Edith Simcox and George Eliot," Simcox's love for Eliot, while unrequited, provided fuel to keep her writing, organizing, and lecturing. Edith Simcox founded a cooperative shirt-making factory, served on the London School Board, started a lodgers' league, organized trade unions for women and men, and lectured extensively on topics such as socialism, women's work, suffrage, and conditions in China. She wrote for intellectual journals and political newspapers, and she published several books. Such Herculean efforts by a woman born in the mid-nineteenth century were possible because she took Eliot for her muse and her model.[24] In a patriarchal culture like Victorian England, the worship which a romantic friend bestowed upon the object of her love, and her desire to be worthy of that love, may have been one of the few stimuli which motivated achievement in a woman's life.

In the same vein, women with ambition to make a name for themselves looked for kindred spirits to appreciate their achievements and sympathize with them for the coldness with which the world greeted their efforts. Such a relationship might be crucial to offset society's hostility, or what was at best society's indifference. It was thus charged with a warmth, a fervor, a passion that went beyond simple friendship. The letters of the nineteenth-century English writer, Geraldine Jewsbury, to the wife of Thomas Carlyle, Jane Welsh Carlyle, are representative. Jane, who prided herself on her intellect, was, according to her, generally neglected and disparaged by her husband. She complained constantly of her loneliness and feelings of worthlessness. Geraldine gave her both the affection and encouragement she needed. Her letters to Jane are those of a lover, such as Thomas Carlyle had neither the inclination nor the desire to be. They indicate also the frustration Geraldine must have felt in loving a woman who was bound in Victorian marriage: "O Carissima mia . . . you are never out of either my head or my heart. After you left on Tuesday I felt so horribly wretched, too miserable even to cry, and what could be done?" (July 1841); [25] "I love you my darling, more than I can express, more than I am conscious of myself, and yet I can do nothing for you . . ." (October 29, 1841); [26] "I love you more than anything else in the world. . . . It may do you no good now, but it may be a comfort some time, it will always be there for you" (May 1842); [27] "If I could see you and speak to you, I should have no tragic mood for a year to come, I think, and really that is saying no little, for I have had a strong inclination to hang myself oftener than once within the last month" (c. 1843).[28]

Geraldine craved a Llangollen-like existence with Jane, which was unattainable, even if Jane had wished it, since she was legally and socially tied to her husband. But she begged Geraldine to come live near her—to which Geraldine responded that what she truly wished was "a cottage in the country with you," and painted a picture of an idyllic life in such a setting.[29]

It appears that Geraldine had heterosexual relationships, but she often informed Jane that they were insignificant compared with her love for Jane, "You are of infinitely more worth and importance in my eyes. . . . You come nearer to me." [30] Jane was usually furious over these heterosexual attachments, minor as they were.[31] But although it was sometimes stormy, the love between the two continued for more than twenty-five years until Jane's death in 1866.

Their love was reinforced by a mutual struggle to transcend the role allotted to Victorian women. Jane flagged in that struggle often, too overcome by Carlyle's overbearing personality to summon the energy to assert herself. Geraldine, who believed she was the luckier of the two because she was independent and could earn a livelihood through her writing, frequently exhorted Jane to such a healthy pursuit. In one letter, for example, she points out that Jane is depressed because she has no occupation. Writing would be ideal, but Geraldine understands that her friend will get no encouragement at home. She takes it upon herself to provide the encouragement:

> It is not . . . altogether for your own sake that I am anxious you should set to work upon a story or a book of any kind that you are moved to do. You have more sense and stronger judgment than any other woman I ever knew or expect to know. . . . Do not go to Mr. Carlyle for sympathy, do not let him dash you with cold water. You must respect your own work and your own motives; if people only did what others thought good and useful, half the work in the world would be left undone.[32]

Jane could not write because she felt that she would be ridiculed by her husband, and that in any case he would dwarf any production of hers. Geraldine, who had no such problem, nevertheless saw a similarity between herself and Jane, which perhaps bound them initially: While Geraldine had no husband to discourage her efforts, she had the world. However, she believed that the world was slowly changing, and that women of the intellectual caliber of herself and Jane were making it change. But their great tragedy was that the world had not yet changed enough—they were New Women before the era of the New Woman, as Geraldine suggests to Jane in a letter of 1849:

> I believe we are touching on better days, when women will have a genuine, normal life of their own to lead. There, perhaps, will not be so many marriages, and women will be taught not to feel their destiny *manqué* if they remain single. They will be able to be friends and companions in a way they cannot be now. . . . I do not feel that either you or I are to be called failures. We are indications of a development of womanhood which as yet is not recognized. It has, so far, no ready made channels to run in, but still we have looked, and tried, and found that the present rules for women will not hold us—

that something better and stronger is needed. . . . There are women to come after us, who will approach nearer the fulness of the measure of the stature of a woman's nature. I regard myself as a mere faint indication, a rudiment of the idea, of certain higher qualities and possibilities that lie in women, and all the eccentricities and mistakes and desires and absurdities I have made are only the consequences of an imperfect formation, an immature growth. . . . I can see there is a precious mine of a species of womanhood yet undreamed of by the professors and essayists on female education, and I believe also that we belong to it.[33]

Geraldine saw that they were both out of place in their era, and that a remedy for their dislocation was to provide love and encouragement for each other while they awaited a new day.

If Geraldine could have written a novel about women's lives and their relationships with each other about fifty years from the time of the above letter, it probably would have resembled Florence Converse's novel *Diana Victrix* (1897), in which the world has become more ready for New Women, they need not feel themselves *manqué* if they remain single, and their love for each other can take on revolutionary dimensions as it could not in 1849.

Unlike Meredith's "Diana," Enid and Sylvia, the American Dianas of Converse's novel, never feel compelled to form a connection with a man. While one of them is tempted for a time to engage in a heterosexual liaison, she sees it ultimately as destructive and rejects it. The other, although she is pursued by a likable man, can think of no reason for marrying him—the "natural and social forces" of Diana of the Crossways do not exist for her. As the title of Converse's book suggests, Diana, embodied in these two women, can now be victorious to the end. However, for women without a profession and an overwhelming desire to succeed in this world, the concept of Diana generally fails: Converse presents a foil character, Rosa Campion, who envies the relationship between Enid and Sylvia and wishes she had one too. But Rosa was born into great wealth and has had no reason to focus her energies on external accomplishments such as would confirm the conviction that a woman need not marry to feel herself complete. She reluctantly admits, "I am afraid I should feel as if I hadn't managed my life cleverly if I did not marry. I should feel ashamed of myself." Enid, however, speaks for the author when she tells Rosa, "I have been sorry for married women oftener than for old maids."

Converse is open about the physical closeness between her two heroines. For example, she places Enid and Sylvia in bed together and tells us, "Enid had her arms about her and was saying a great many things very softly in the dark." Male writers had often depicted such scenes. What they generally did not depict, however, and what women writers who lived the experiences themselves could depict, was strength and encouragement to achieve in the world which romantic friends of the late nineteenth century could give each other. Converse shows these women sustaining each other as a husband generally could not and would not. Not only do they encourage each other's worldly successes, but, when the relationship is at its best, they nurture each other in ways wives were taught to nurture husbands. Converse finds such relationships between professional women to be characteristic of her times, and she clearly indicates that she is not talking about Longfellow's "rehearsal in girlhood of the great drama of woman's life," but rather about solid, permanent attachments: "As a woman advances towards thirty unmarried, her women-friendships possess more and more a stability, an intensity, which were lacking in the explosively sentimental intimacies of her youth; they are to her instead of many things." Despite a woman's successes in the world, or perhaps because of them, she desperately requires the nurturing love that another woman can give her.

Nineteenth-century men, who generally did not have convenient labels to fall back on (i.e., lesbianism or perversion), simply could not understand such relationships. When a man proposes to Enid, she tells him she cannot marry him for two reasons: First of all, she is devoted to her work. This he doesn't understand, but he understands her second reason (which is inextricably bound up with her first) even less:

> "I do not need you. It is true I have no man friend whom I enjoy as much as I do you, but I have a woman friend who is dearer to me. . . . I share with her thoughts that I have no wish to share with you. I give to her a love surpassing any affection I could teach myself to have for you. She comes first. She is my friend as you can never be, and I could not marry you unless you were a nearer friend than she. You would have to come first. And you could not, for she is first."
>
> "And this is all that separates us," said Jacques, in a tone of

amazement. "Only a woman?"

"The reason the woman separates us," said Enid, "is because the woman and I understand each other, sympathize with each other, are necessary to each other. And you and I are not. It is not simply her womanliness, it is her friendship. There might be a man who could give me the inspiration, the equalness of sympathy, I find in her,—there might be,—some women find such men. But there are not yet enough for all of us."

She expresses a mortal fear that a man would make her give up her work and offer "only his love in return, his love and his amiable domestic tyranny!", and she tells Jacques that his domestic tyrannies and the role they would cast her in would be destructive to all she values most—while her life with another woman gives her energy for what is most important to her:

> For a moment, because I was tired, I thought I wanted you— your home. But I do not! . . . I am not domestic the way some women are. I shouldn't like to keep house and sew. . . . It would bore me. I should hate it! Sylvia and I share the responsibility here, and the maid works faithfully. There are only a few rooms. We have time for our real work, but a wife wouldn't have. And, oh, I couldn't be just a wife! I don't want to! Please go away! I have chosen my life and I love it.!

Enid is the New Woman, whose number is "increasing every day." The New Woman is firm in her purpose in life (in Enid's case she is a writer and lecturer involved with improving the lot of the masses), and nothing can distract her. As a human being she needs love, but she knows she must find it in a relationship that will strengthen her purpose instead of interfering with it.

Through the character of Jacques's father, Converse warns men away from the heroic New Woman while still encouraging respect for her. She is like Joan of Arc, he says: "That kind is not to be possessed by one man; she belongs to a cause. . . . [She is] to be worshipped—the great, the universal woman—but that is a different affair from a wife."

The novel ends happily with Enid and Sylvia in domestic bliss and in the joy of their professional success. Sylvia surfaces from a long depression, caused first by her feeling that she did not have enough talent to be a fine writer and then by her ambivalence over an unworthy man. At the conclusion Sylvia publishes a novel about a New Woman similar to Enid (who marries at the end of Sylvia's novel only because "the public are more used to it"—but as Enid joyfully reminds Sylvia, "sometimes . . . I don't marry, even in books"), and presents Enid with a copy of the novel, which is dedicated to her.

But such a revolutionary aspect of romantic friendship went largely unobserved by American male novelists of the nineteenth century. Instead, their view was of sentimental and comfortably ephemeral relationships. Henry Wadsworth Longfellow's treatment of two female protagonists in *Kavanagh* (1849) and Oliver Wendell Holmes's presentation of a similar set of characters in *A Mortal Antipathy* (1885) are representative. Longfellow's Cecilia and Alice are permitted to indulge in a boundless affection for each other, sharing the kind of intimacy the eighteenth-century novel portrayed. The two were bosom friends at school, and afterward, "the love between them, and consequently the letters, increased rather than diminished." Longfellow is gently satirical about their verbal effusions, which he considers to be characteristic of female friendship. He has difficulty in understanding of what, specifically, intimacy between two young women might consist, so he limits himself generally to showing them baring their hearts: "These two young hearts found not only a delight, but a necessity in pouring forth their thoughts and feelings to each other." However, he also plays occasionally with the notion of a sensual relationship between his two heroines. In one scene he borrows imagery from *Cymbeline* and "The Eve of St. Agnes" to suggest a delicate sensuousness between them. Cecilia has just purchased a carrier pigeon to hasten delivery of their urgent communications (which Longfellow presents as nothing more than girlish secrets):

> "I have just been writing to you," said Alice; "I wanted so much to see you this morning!"
> "Why this morning in particular? Has anything happened?"
> "Nothing, only I had such a longing to see you!" And, seating herself in a low chair by Cecilia's side, she laid her head upon the shoulder of her friend, who, taking one of her pale, thin hands in both her own, silently kissed her forehead again and again . . .
> "I am so glad to see you, Cecilia!" she continued. "You are so strong and beautiful! Ah, how I wish Heaven had made me as tall, and strong, and beautiful as you are!"

"You little flatterer! What an affectionate, lover-like friend you are! What have you been doing all morning?"

"Looking out the window, thinking of you, and writing you this letter, to beg you to come and see me!"

"And I have been buying a carrier-pigeon, to fly between us and carry all our letters."

"That will be delightful."

"He is to be sent home today; and after he gets accustomed to my room, I shall send him here, to get acquainted with yours;—a Iachimo in my Imogen's bed-chamber, to spy out its secrets."

"If he sees Cleopatra in these white curtains, and silver cupids in these andirons, he will have your imagination."

"He will see the book with the leaf turned down, and you asleep, and tell me all about you."

Longfellow depicts such sensuous exchanges, making it clear that they are not very serious. While Alice and Cecilia are in love with each other, they both fall in love with a young minister, Kavanagh, and naturally the heterosexual love is more overwhelming. Longfellow can thus characterize love between two women as "a rehearsal in girlhood of the great drama of woman's life."

Oliver Wendell Holmes offers an identical explanation of the passion between Lurida and Euthymia, his two heroines. "The friendships of young girls," he remarks, "prefigure the closer relations which will one day come in and dissolve their earlier intimacies." After assuring the reader that all will end right, he presents the two women as a perfect couple:

The two young ladies who had recently graduated at the Corinna Institute remained, as they had always been, intimate friends. They were the natural complements of each other. Euthymia represented a complete, symmetrical womanhood. Her outward presence was only an index of a large, wholesome, affluent life. . . . She knew that she was called The Wonder by the schoolmates who were dazzled by her singular accomplishments, but she did not over-value them. She rather tended to depreciate her own gifts, in comparison with those of her friend, Miss Lurida Vincent. The two agreed all the better for differing as they did. The octave makes a perfect chord, when shorter intervals jar more or less on the ear. . . .

It was a pleasant thing to observe their dependence on each other.

He even suggests, as Longfellow did, a sensuous element in their attachment in brief exchanges:

> "It is a shame that you will not let your exquisitely molded form be portrayed in marble . . ." [Lurida said]. She was startled to see what an effect her proposal had produced, for Euthymia was not only blushing but there was a flame in her eyes which she had hardly ever seen before.

Despite their mutual involvement, the forces "natural and social" move the two young women toward a heterosexual selection. Both marry, although Lurida (who wanted to be a doctor until she discovered she could not stand the sight of blood) protests to the zero hour.[34] By 1885, when Holmes wrote this novel, New England women who were happy in their romantic friendships and had some sort of professional ambition did not need to opt for marriage. Their friendships often became lifelong relationships which were a source of great support in their occupational struggles. But Holmes was a romantic writer who had no interest in recognizing a revolutionary life-style for women.

There is yet another manifestation of the failure to recognize the revolutionary potential of romantic friendship: It is curious that so many English and American writers of the nineteenth century presented such explicit sensual descriptions of the affection between two female characters. In 1928, Radclyffe Hall's novel, *The Well of Loneliness*, was censored, although she shows nothing more about the physical relationship of her two female characters than one kissing the other's hand "very humbly" in a brief scene which concludes, "and that night they were not divided." In the 1860's, at the height of the Victorian era, Christina Rossetti could describe the two heroines of "Goblin Market" thus without the slightest fear of public objection:

> *Golden head by golden head,*
> *Like two pigeons in one nest,*
> *Folded in each other's wings,*
> *They lay down in their curtained bed:*
> *Like two blossoms on one stem,*

Like two flakes of new fall'n snow . . .
Cheek to cheek and breast to breast
Locked together in one nest.

It was probably not the almost precious quality of the description alone that saved Rossetti from contumely. Thomas Hardy in *Desperate Remedies* (1871) presented, without being threatened by the censors, an even more detailed description of his two female characters in a bed:

> The instant they were in bed Miss Aldclyffe freed herself from the last remnant of restraint. She flung her arms round the young girl, and pressed her gently to her heart.
> "Now kiss me," she said. . . .

When Miss Aldclyffe discovers that the girl, Cytherea, whom she hired as a lady's maid, loves Edward Springrove, she cries:

> "Cytherea, try to love me more than you love him—do. I love you more sincerely than any man can. Do, Cythie: don't let any man stand between us. O, I can't bear that!" She clasped Cytherea's neck again. . . . "Why can't you kiss me as I kiss you? Why can't you!"

Although Miss Aldclyffe's kisses are described, in spite of her passionate outburst, as being "motherly" (and Hardy sees no contradiction in that description), the sensual element in her interest in Cytherea is overt. For example, before Miss Aldclyffe hires the inexperienced Cytherea, she has some initial concern that it might be boring to instruct her in her duties as a lady's maid, but then she decides it will be worthwhile "in order to have a creature who could glide round my luxurious indolent body in that manner, and look at me in that way—I warrant how light her fingers are upon one's head and neck." Most surely an author who had written forty or fifty years later this explicitly would have had to stand trial for obscenity and would have found the pressure on him so uncomfortable that he would be forced to take a night boat to the Continent. But perhaps such descriptions were permissible in the nineteenth century because that era did not have our passion for placing people in sexual categories.

Widespread twentieth-century pseudoknowledge about sexual matters, beginning with the writings of the French aesthetes and the German sexologists in the middle and late nineteenth century, has made self-described sophisticated individuals certain that they understand what "lesbianism" is and how to identify it: Two women holding one another in bed, breast to breast, is "lesbianism"; one woman begging another to love her more than she loves a man is "lesbianism." To provide a label which has been charged with the connotations of sickness or sin, and then to apply that label to a particular situation, renders that situation sick or sinful regardless of its innate attributes.

But in nineteenth-century English and American writing, behavior and emotions were not as facilely defined as they are now. Even by 1912, Edward Carpenter, who was very familiar with the sexologists' theories, spoke nevertheless for the nineteenth century when he observed that "no hard and fast line can at any point be drawn effectively separating the different kinds of attachment." He states what any nineteenth-century person must have known, that there are "friendships so romantic in sentiment that they verge into love," and that there are "loves so intellectual and spiritual that they hardly dwell in the sphere of passion." He considers this phenomenon to be indicative of the immense diversity of human temperament in matters relating to sex and love.[35] The twentieth century has rejected such subtleties by insisting that a woman is either a lesbian or she isn't; and if she is, she is abnormal; therefore a woman who loves another woman passionately is abnormal.

Such a pat definition would probably have mystified the nineteenth century. Not having the "knowledge" of the French aesthetes or the German sexologists as a guide, writers could present the most passionate love scenes between two women and not be concerned that they were dealing with "abnormality." The American writer Elizabeth Wetherell can therefore show her young heroine in the popular girl's book, *The Wide, Wide World* (1852), as being ecstatic over the possibility of spending two nights in a row together with an older girl. Wetherell can tell the reader, "There was a long silence, during which they remained locked in each other's arms," and she can have the older girl request of her young friend, "Come here and sit in my lap again . . . and let your head rest where it used to."

Similarly, Louisa May Alcott, whose fame rested on her moral stories for children, can show in *Work: A Story of Experience* (1873), two young women, Christie and Rachel, casting amorous glances at each other. Christie "woos" Rachel "as gently as a lover might," proffering flowers and compliments. She tells Rachel, "I only want to feel that you like me a little and don't mind my liking you a great deal." When Rachel seems encouraging, Christie is ecstatic: "'Then I may love you, and not be afraid of offending?' cried Christie, much touched. . . . Then Christie kissed her warmly, whisked away the tear, and began to paint the delights in store for them in her most enthusiastic way, being much elated with her victory." The two women live together after Christie proposes to Rachel: "I must love somebody, and 'love them hard,' as children say; so why can't you come and stay with me?" Rachel's presence gives Christie purpose and happiness. When the two are separated for a time, and Christie believes she has lost Rachel for good, she marries. But at the conclusion Rachel, who it turns out is the sister of Christie's husband, comes back into her life. Christie's husband conveniently dies in the Civil War, and the two women presumably remain together forever. There is nothing covert about such relationships in nineteenth-century American fiction. The writers show the women laying bare their emotions in front of any third party without the least suggestion that there is any reason to hide such emotions.

In nineteenth-century American life as well, such intense emotional bonds were not unusual, and the expression of those feelings was often committed to paper. But what the nineteenth century saw as normal, our century saw as perverse. Twentieth-century biographers have not infrequently bowdlerized the letters of their nineteenth-century subjects in order to "save" those subjects' reputations. Emily Dickinson's letters to Sue Gilbert, the woman who became her sister-in-law, and the edited version of those letters by her niece, Martha Dickinson Bianchi, are perhaps the most dramatic illustration of this point. Emily's love letters to Sue were written in the early 1850's. Bianchi's editions appeared in 1924 [36] and 1932.[37] Because Bianchi was Sue's daughter, she wished to show that Emily relied on Sue, that Sue influenced her poetry, and that the two were the best of friends. But working during the height of the popularization of Sigmund Freud, she must have known to what extent intense friendship had fallen into disrepute. She therefore edited out all indications of Emily's truly powerful involvement with her mother.[38] For example, on February 6, 1852, Emily wrote Sue:

> . . . sometimes I shut my eyes, and shut my heart towards you, and try hard to forget you because you grieve me so, but you'll

never go away. Oh you never will—say, Susie, promise me again, and I will smile faintly—and take up my little cross of sad—*sad* separation. How vain it seems to *write*, when one knows how to feel—how much more near and dear to sit beside you, talk with you, hear the tones of your voice; so hard to "deny thyself, and take up thy cross, and follow me"—give me strength, Susie, write me of hope and love, and of hearts that *endured*, and great was their reward of "Our Father who art in Heaven." I don't know how I shall bear it, when the gentle spring comes; if she should come and see me and talk to me of you, Oh it would surely kill me! While the frost clings to the windows and the World is stern and drear; this absence is easier; the *Earth* mourns too, for all her little birds; but when they all come back again, and she sings and is so merry—pray, what will become of me? Susie, forgive me, forget all what I say.[39]

Bianchi reproduced only these lines of the passage:

. . . Sometimes I shut my eyes and shut my heart towards you and try hard to forget you, but you'll never go away. Susie, forgive me, forget all that I say.[40]

In the letter of June 11, 1852, Bianchi tells us that Emily wrote:

. . . Susie, forgive me darling, for every word I say, my heart is full of you, yet when I seek to say to you something not for the world, words fail me. I try to bring you nearer, I chase the weeks away till they are quite departed—three weeks—they can't last always, for surely they must go with their little brothers and sisters to their long home in the West! [41]

But the complete letter reads:

. . . Susie, forgive me Darling, for every word I say—my heart is full of you, *none other than you in my thoughts*, yet when I seek to say to you something not for the world, words fail me. *If you were here—and Oh that you were, my Susie, we need not talk at all, our eyes would whisper for us, and your hand fast in mine, we would not ask for language*—I try to bring you nearer, I chase the weeks away till they are quite departed, *and fancy you have come, and I am on my way through the green lane to meet you, and my heart goes scampering so, that I have much ado to bring it back again, and*

learn it to be patient, till that dear Susie comes. Three weeks—
they can't last always, for surely they must go with their little
brothers and sisters to their long home in the West! [42] (Italics
mine)

Bianchi also includes an affectionate note that Emily sent to Sue
on June 27, 1852:

> . . . Susie, will you indeed come home next Saturday? Shall I,
> indeed behold you, not "darkly, but face to face"—or am I
> *fancying* so and dreaming blessed dreams from which the day
> will wake me? I hope for you so much and feel so eager for
> you—feel I cannot wait. Sometimes I must have Saturday be-
> fore tomorrow comes. [43]

But what Emily really said in that note places their relationship in
quite a different light:

> . . . Susie, will you indeed come home next Saturday, *and be
> my own again, and kiss me as you used to?* Shall I indeed be-
> hold you, not "darkly, but face to face" or am I *fancying* so,
> and dreaming blessed dreams from which the day will wake me?
> I hope for you so much and feel so eager for you, feel that I
> *cannot wait, feel that now I must have you—that the expecta-
> tion once more to see your face again, makes me feel hot and
> feverish, and my heart beats so fast—I go to sleep at night, and
> the first thing I know, I am sitting there wide awake, and
> clasping my hands tightly, and thinking of next Saturday, and
> "never a bit"* of you.
>
> Sometimes I must have Saturday before tomorrow comes. [44]
> (The words "fancying," "cannot," and "now" are italicized in
> the Johnson edition. All other italics are mine.)

Bianchi must have felt that if she did not censor the letters, her
aunt's literary reputation could be at stake. Since love between
women had become in her day an abnormality, if Emily Dickinson
were suspected of lesbianism, the universality and validity of her
poetic sentiments might even be called into question, just as Amy
Lowell's were in the 1920's. [45]

But it would not have occurred to Americans (and to most of the
English) of the previous century to regard such sentiments as abnormal. Perhaps love between women was permitted to flourish un-
checked in the nineteenth century because the fact of the New

Woman and her revolutionary potential for forming a permanent bond with another woman had not yet been widely impressed upon the popular imagination, as after World War I when New Women emerged in great numbers. It was then that love between women came to be generally feared in America and England. The emotional and sensual exchanges between women, which correspondence and fiction tell us were a common form of affectional expression for centuries, suddenly took on the character of perversion.

CHAPTER 3

New Women

Love between women could take on a new shape in the late nineteenth century because the feminist movement succeeded both in
opening new jobs for women, which would allow them independence, and in creating a support group so that they would not feel
isolated and outcast when they claimed their independence. Living
situations which would have been impossible earlier became feasible
now. A young woman could reject marriage in pursuit of a career
and not feel as Geraldine Jewsbury did in 1849 that she was an
"imperfect formation." While her family might object, as families
often did, that the only truly fulfilling path for a woman was marriage, she nevertheless had a plausible reason for not marrying—
and she could make enough money to care for herself, so that while
her family's objection might be emotionally painful, it could not
starve her into marriage. The wistful desire of Clarissa Harlowe's
friend, Miss Howe, "How charmingly might you and I live together," in the eighteenth century could be realized in the last
decades of the nineteenth century. If Clarissa Harlowe had lived
about a hundred and fifty years later, she could have gotten a job
that would have been appropriate for a woman of her class. With
the power given to her by independence and the consciousness of
a support group, Clarissa as a New Woman might have turned her
back on both her family and Lovelace, and gone to live "charmingly" with Miss Howe. Many women did.

Although there were isolated feminists in earlier centuries in
both Europe and America, it was not until the mid-nineteenth

century that a feminist movement emerged. Reasons for the growth of the movement varied in the United States, Britain, France, and Germany (for example, the great loss of American males during the Civil War and the emigration of men from England meant that large numbers of women would not marry and would be forced to agitate for education and jobs to support themselves), but several explanations apply to all four countries. One was the growth of the middle class: Since women of this class were less affected by tradition or the virtual threat of starvation, they could make their own ideals. They could, with courage, write a new script for woman's life. They were not forced into a marriage of convenience for the sake of merging great estates and titles as were their aristocratic counterparts, nor were they forced into a marriage of necessity for the sake of sheer survival as were their lower-class counterparts.[1]

The women in all four countries also knew of the French Revolution, which in its original intent was a liberation movement on a large scale. The Revolution inspired the American Judith Sargent Murray to publish a women's-rights essay in 1790, "On the Equality of the Sexes." It also inspired the *Declaration of Rights of Woman and Citizen* (1791) by the French dramatist Olympe de Gouges, and *Vindication of the Rights of Woman* (1792) by Mary Wollstonecraft. While Germany had no such spokeswomen, a young male student, Hippel, wrote a manifesto of German feminism in 1790. In the nineteenth century, women were aroused further to feminism by the birth of humanitarian and betterment movements such as abolitionism, socialism, and various forms of utopianism in which women participated and through which they began to understand that they were no more free than slaves or workers or other oppressed groups.

In addition, the opening of higher education to women in the nineteenth century, for which the early feminists agitated, meant that an even stronger group of women would emerge who had been trained to think about ideas and to articulate them, and who had also been led to hope—not by public encouragement especially but by their own laborious efforts at study and their sense of justice—that worldly success was attainable for women. In the United States, Oberlin College became coeducational in the 1830's; in 1837 Mt. Holyoke, the first real women's college in America, was established.[2] By 1880 forty thousand women, over a third of the entire student population, were enrolled in institutions of higher learning.[3] The United States was the leader in opening higher education to nineteenth-century women, but other countries slowly followed. In England in 1848, Queen's College was opened, and in 1869, Girton, where the plan of study was modeled after that of Cambridge, was established. The University of London began granting women B.A. degrees in 1878. Victoria Lyceum, the first women's college in Germany, opened in 1869, although it did not grant a degree. German-speaking women were able to get a degree from the University of Zurich, which began to accept females in 1867, but it was almost thirty years later before they could receive degrees from German universities: In 1895 the University of Göttingen began granting degrees to individual women, and the University of Heidelberg admitted women to their Ph.D. program. However, by the first decade of the next century, approximately one thousand of the University of Berlin's fourteen thousand students were female. In France women were admitted to some universities in the late 1860's. In 1880 the Society for the Propagation of Instruction Among Women established the first women's college, the College de Sévigné. Many of these college-educated women turned their attention to women's problems, further swelling the ranks and providing the leadership for the women's movement.

Another reason for the rise of feminism is one that has already been touched on: the general homosociality of nineteenth-century society, which gave women of the middle class plentiful leisure to meet often and share grievances. In America, proper women were not only excluded from favorite male pleasure haunts such as saloons, clubs, and sporting matches, but apparently they seldom even attended such public events as fairs, if the observation of an English captain who visited America in the 1840's is correct: He found only nine women in a crowd of thousands at a Massachusetts fair,[4] which meant of course that thousands of women may have had only themselves and each other for adult company. A similar observation was made by Frances Trollope, another English traveler. She claimed to have observed during her 1827–1831 visit that almost "all the enjoyments of men are found in the absence of women. They dine, they play cards, they have musical meetings, they have suppers, all in large parties, but all without women." At the few heterosocial gatherings she witnessed, "the women invariably herd together at one part of the room, and the men at the other . . . The gentlemen spit, talk of elections and the price of produce, and spit again." The women, according to Trollope, talked of clothes, sermons, and dyspepsia[5]—but knowing the nineteenth-century woman's penchant for baring her heart to other women, we can be sure they often talked of subjects more stirring to them.

It is curious that these English writers felt obliged to comment on American homosociality, since relationships between the sexes were not appreciably different in England. One anonymous English author, writing in 1857, pointed out that in the middle classes it was virtually "impossible . . . for the sexes to break ground on any but the most commonplace topics of conversation," since they had in common almost no pursuits, interests, tasks, or sentiments. Only two of the same sex could communicate meaningfully.[6] Nor is there any reason to think that the relations between the sexes were different elsewhere. In his discussion of the petty bourgeoisie of eighteenth- and nineteenth-century France and Germany, Edward Shorter shows that a complete lack of communication was typically a feature of the relationships between the sexes even within marriage.[7] Novels of the period suggest the same distance existed between men and women of the higher classes. The title character of Théophile Gautier's *Mademoiselle de Maupin* (1835) observes that men and women are entire strangers to each other, that men's existence is as foreign to women "as if they were inhabitants of Saturn or of some other planet a hundred million leagues from our sublunary ball." They are like "a different species," she remarks, "not the slightest intellectual link exists between the two sexes."

Finally, a reason for the rise of feminism was that initially, growing industrialization and "prosperity" limited even more the few jobs that had been open to women. Baking and brewing, for instance, were now large-scale operations carried on almost everywhere in factories, and in some places men had entirely replaced women in such work.[8] Servant positions, which would have been thought suitable for a female while her family belonged to the lower class, were no longer suitable if they moved into the middle class. Women of the middle class had little in which to invest their energies.[9]

A large group of educated, articulate women, who saw the possibilities of organizing for social betterment and were not tied to old traditions, who were raised believing that men and women were different species and could share nothing but family, who could not marry and had no work to occupy them, made inevitable the growing strength of feminism in the latter half of the nineteenth century.

Charlotte Brontë's plea to English fathers in her novel *Shirley*

(1849) indicates that in the middle of the nineteenth century some women still looked to men to deliver them from their plight:

> Men of England! Look at your poor girls, many of them fading around you, dropping off in consumption or decline; or, what is worse, degenerating to sour old maids, envious, backbiting, wretched, because life is a desert to them: or, what is worst of all, reduced to strive, by scarce modest coquetry and debasing artifice, to gain that position and consideration by marriage, which to celibacy is denied. Fathers! cannot you alter these things? Perhaps not all at once; but consider the matter well when it is brought before you, receive it as a theme worthy of thought: do not dismiss it with an idle jest or an unmanly insult. You would wish to be proud of your daughters and not to blush for them: then seek for them an interest and an occupation which shall raise them above the flirt, the maneuverer, the mischief-making tale-bearer. Keep your girls' minds narrow and fettered—they will still be a plague and a care, sometimes a disgrace, to you: cultivate them—give them scope and work—they will be your gayest companions in health; your tenderest nurses in sickness; your most faithful prop in age.

But having received no deliverance, they began to look more and more to each other and to organize a cohesive and angry feminist movement.

The first semblance of an organized movement began in 1848, the year before Brontë's plea was published. In that year in the United States, the Seneca Falls convention was called, Englishwomen founded female-suffrage organizations in Manchester and Sheffield,[10] and Luise Otto-Peters began organizing a German feminist movement.[11] In France there had been even earlier attempts to organize feminists within radical groups, such as the Saint-Simonians, which in the 1830's published journals with titles like *La femme nouvelle* and *La femme libre*[12]; and in 1848 French feminists even attempted to get elected to the Second Republic. However, unlike the movement in other countries, the French effort lost momentum instead of gaining it throughout the last decades of the nineteenth century, and Frenchwomen did not even receive political enfranchisement until 1945.[13]

Nineteenth-century middle-class women were by and large raised with the notion that they would marry and take care of a family.

But during many decades in Europe and America, women out-numbered men by the hundreds of thousands and even the millions. Their plight was intensified because they were cut off from jobs that had been open to them in previous centuries and the careers which women of their class could enter were overcrowded or required un-usual talent (for example, novelist). Since they were middle class, it was unlikely that they would inherit enough money to be self-sufficient, and it would have been a disgrace for them to take a position as servant or factory worker. As their number grew by vir-tue of the rising middle class, their agony and their fury grew, and so did their feminism.

The "redundant" or "superfluous" woman, which is what un-married women were called in nineteenth-century England, became a social problem of vast proportions. In Germany at the turn of the century, for instance, there were three million unmarried women [14] (and only 10 percent of them had inherited sufficient means to live).[15] A German novel by Gabriele Reuter, *Aus Güter Familie (A Girl from a Nice Family* [1895], subtitled *A History of a Young Girl's Suffering*), dramatically depicts the plight of a woman whose entire education is directed toward one goal: to mold her into a perfect wife. She is unassuming, nurturing, frugal, unobtrusively intelligent, extremely well mannered, and a marvelous housekeeper. Yet she never manages to catch a suitable husband. Since she has been trained for nothing else, she becomes a pitiable spinster, en-tirely dependent on the generosity of her brother. Reuter claimed that her purpose in writing the novel was not just to show the life of her heroine, Agathe Heidling, but the fate of thousands of such women (millions would have been more accurate), who were raised with the one goal of marriage in mind, and whose lives were thus rendered tragic.

In America during the second half of the nineteenth century, several factors contributed to the increase of single women, par-ticularly the Civil War, which depleted the number of marriageable men by three million, and the development of the West and of large industrial centers, which drew young men in much greater proportion than women from rural areas, villages, and small towns to new job opportunities. The situation was similar in England—men of marriageable age left not just rural areas and small towns but England itself: They emigrated to areas of the growing Empire where work was plentiful. About five million young people, mostly men, left Britain between 1830 and 1875, and a huge surplus of women was created. In 1851 there were 2,765,000 unmarried women in England; 24.86 percent of the women of marriageable age under thirty were unmarried according to the census of that year.[16] The number of unmarried women in England increased more than the proportionate population growth with each census—i.e., 2,956,000 in 1861 and 3,228,700 in 1871—and in 1881 in some areas of England (such as Kensington), females outnumbered males by approximately 150 percent. In London the ratio of females to males was 112 to 100.[17] How were those women to live? Most of them needed to support themselves. Unmarried women made up the bulk of the female labor force in England: In 1861 there were three and a half million working women, two and a half million of them unmarried.[18]

Feminists used these figures to show that humanity and decency demanded that more jobs be opened which would allow women to be self-supporting while maintaining their pride. As Clara Collet remarked in an angry essay of 1892, "If anyone objects that women who are intensely interested in work which also enables them to be self supporting are less attractive than they would otherwise be, I can make no reply except that to expect a hundred women to devote their energies to attracting fifty men seems slightly ridiculous." [19] Such logic did not stop antifeminists from objecting that if women were too happy in their work, the institution of marriage would be destroyed, as would the world; [20] but women continued working anyway, usually out of sheer necessity.

There were few decent jobs open to women anywhere until the last decades of the century. In eighteenth-century America, as the public record indicates, women still owned small businesses, and were printers, munitions-makers, blacksmiths, and medical workers; in the nineteenth century they were essentially barred from all these areas as the nation grew. The ideal image for a middle-class woman was that of a lady of leisure whose primary work was supervising the servants. But if she had no male to pay servants she could supervise, she was in trouble. The author of an 1860 American study, *"Woman's Right to Labor": or, Low Wages and Hard Work,* observed that society condemned a lower-class woman to "marry, stitch, die, or do worse" (i.e., be a prostitute).[21] If she were raised in the middle class, she had even fewer choices: She could marry, teach, or die.[22] But teaching salaries in the first six or seven decades of nineteenth-century America bolstered the position of those who believed that women should either marry or die. For example, in New York in 1853, women received one-tenth of the salary given to men teachers. In other states they fared a little better: In the mid-1860's, when women teachers outnumbered men two to one, the average salary in six states was $444 per year for male teachers and $210 per year for females.[23] However, the situation began to change after the Civil War, when women's status was recognized by the National Teachers Association as equal to men's and they began gradually to receive equal pay.

English middle-class women had a similar struggle throughout the century, and teaching remained the one profession open to large numbers of them. Their situation began to show signs of improvement from about 1870 onward, when they were given some political rights which allowed them to fill public positions, including those of overseer, guardian, churchwarden, sexton, governor of a workhouse, medical officer of a workhouse, surveyor of highways, inspector of factories, member of a school board, and member of a parish council. They were also slowly permitted into business offices. The 1871 census lists no women secretaries. In 1891 there were 17,865.[24] In 1872 women were admitted to positions in the British post office, although at salaries lower than those of male postal workers. An increasing number of clerical jobs began to open to women in civil service and business, because an industrialized nation bent on imperial expansion meant more trade and more paper work.[25]

In America, with the invention of the typewriter in 1873 and the opening of the Bell System in 1876, further employment opportunities were created for women, especially after it was found that boys tended to be restless and impatient at such work. And, of course, women who knew little of union organizing could be paid much less than men. One American writer in 1879 estimated that women in such positions were paid from six hundred to nine hundred dollars per year, while men in comparable positions received from twelve hundred to three thousand dollars.[26] But despite such injustices, by the beginning of the next century it could be asserted, equally for England and the United States, that "no middle class woman of average intelligence . . . is unable to earn a living if she chooses to do so." [27] In view of Charlotte Brontë's complaints in *Shirley* just a little over fifty years earlier, women's progress was considerable.

Even some prestige professions such as medicine began to open up in the second half of the century.[28] The American Elizabeth

Blackwell became a medical doctor in 1849 and began practicing in 1851 in New York. In 1868 she established a practice in London. During the Civil War, females were allowed to serve as doctors in the army.[29] In 1869 Sophia Jex-Blake, the first English woman doctor, complained that women in Italy, Germany, France, and Russia could study medicine, while they could not in England; [30] however, over the next few years they were allowed into some English medical schools and by 1895, 264 women were registered as doctors,[31] not a phenomenal number, but an indication that a very motivated woman could enter the profession.

Undoubtedly a woman needed immense motivation in order to try. Sarah Orne Jewett's 1884 novel, *A Country Doctor*, has a ring of truth in its portrayal of a young woman, Nan Prince, who wishes to become a doctor and is told by her only relative, "I could not believe my ears,—a refined girl who bears an honorable and respected name to think of being a woman doctor! If you were five years older you never would have dreamed of such a thing." Nan's only encouragement comes from the doctor who was her foster father. However, Jewett permits her to stay on her path, to refuse to consider offers of marriage (which have not the slightest interest for her anyway), and to attain her goals. The novel ends with Nan, one of the few truly happy "old maids" in nineteenth-century literature, saying, "O God . . . I thank thee for my future."

The attainment of a professional career was to a nineteenth-century woman a pearl of great price, and many could not be thrown off their course by the too-consuming and, to them, dispensable distractions of heterosexuality. Considering the great commitment it must have taken for a nineteenth-century woman to be willing to pioneer and to be able to achieve eminence in a particular career, it comes as no surprise to learn that of the 1,470 biographies of the most distinguished women of their era collected by Frances Willard and Mary Livermore in 1893, more than 25 percent of their subjects never married and one-third of those who did were widowed early and remained single; in other words, more than half spent most of their lives unmarried.[32] Of the 977 women appearing in the 1902 edition of *Who's Who*, almost half did not marry,[33] and of women who received Ph.D.'s in American universities from 1877 to 1924, three-fourths did not marry.[34] While some professional women were willing to split themselves between a career and the demands of a nineteenth-century marriage, and others might have agreed with Julia Ward Howe that "marriage, like death, is a debt we owe to nature," [35] at least as many would have agreed with Louisa May Alcott, whose 1868 article on independent spinsters was entitled "Happy Women," [36] and who said of herself, "I'd rather be a free spirit and paddle my own canoe."

In an era before effective birth control and when so many social forces converged to teach women that a wife's place is by the hearth, many ambitious women must have seen heterosexual marriage and success as being entirely incompatible. Heterosexual marriage generally meant that a woman must submerge her own ego to care for her husband and children. Charlotte Cushman, the American actress, whose long-term relationships were all with other women, recognized this in 1861 when, after twenty years on the stage, she confided in a letter to a friend how lucky she felt herself to be because "at a period in my life when most women (or children, rather) are looking to but one end in life," she did not seek a male "counterpart," but sought rather to perfect her talents. Her escape from heterosexuality permitted her, she said, to give "my entire *self* to my work," as she never could have if she had been married to a man.[37]

Many achievement-oriented women like Charlotte Cushman could not submerge their egos as required by heterosexual marriage. Yet as products of their era they were sold on the virtues of monogamy, although they often rewrote the script: Their long-term partners were other women; they divided duties not on the basis of sex-role stereotypes but on the basis of natural talents or inclination or time; and they pooled emotional, physical, and financial resources not better to enable one of them to go out into the world and strive, but to allow them both to do so. To all intents and purposes they were married, but their marriages fostered rather than hampered their pioneering activities toward worldly success while also fulfilling all their personal needs.

The early life pattern which both Robert Riegel (*American Feminists*, 1963) and Barbara Welter (*Dimity Convictions*, 1974) have observed as being characteristic of nineteenth-century feminists is identical to the one that many psychoanalysts have attributed to lesbians (before the new lesbian-feminist movement): Both tended to be the only or the oldest child in a family; the father molded the daughter's education and character, while the mother was impassive and uninvolved; the girl and her father developed close ties; and the girl, sensing her father would have preferred a son (as did most men in a patriarchal society), attempted to compensate him, in a relationship fraught with ambivalence, by developing what was viewed as masculine attributes and interests. Perhaps those characteristics were found in both representative early feminists and representative early lesbians because those women were potentially one and the same. Many feminists could and did find other women to live with and love, and thus became lesbians; and any woman who identified herself as a lesbian, once she thought about women's problems, realized she had always understood those problems on a gut level—she was a natural feminist.

A female who was the first-born or the only child in her family, having received for a period of time all the attention her parents could give, naturally developed a sense of herself and an ego strength which normally only boys have the opportunity to develop. An impassive mother presents a perfect model to a girl with a healthy ego of what she does not want to be. She would cherish the opportunity to develop into a more independent being through a "male-style" education. Her anger toward a patriarchal society, and the patriarch closest to her, would follow once she understood that society viewed her, regardless of how she saw herself, as a member of the second sex. She would reject marriage and strive for a career which she believed her education had put into her reach. If she felt the need for a partner in life, another woman would be a logical choice. Whether, as an independent, ambitious nineteenth-century woman, she began as a lesbian or as a feminist, it was very possible that she would end as both.

An unpublished story by Harriet Levy, an early friend of Alice B. Toklas, written probably around the beginning of the twentieth century, suggests how closely the New Woman and the new possibilities of love between women might be aligned in women's minds everywhere by the turn of the century. The story, entitled "A Beautiful Girl," opens as the narrator, an American, is sitting in the lobby of a Paris hotel. She is approached by a smart-looking Austrian woman, an opera singer, who tells her she reminds her of a friend with whom she traveled for many months. "We were very happy together," she says. The narrator understands that the woman is inviting her to some intimacy. She is direct while seeming indirect and ostensibly says very little that is personal except to ask the narrator whether she is alone in Paris. The narrator is ambivalent. She is "deeply moved" by the woman, but she is also frightened. She decides to play ignorant: "What was she saying to me? I did not know. And yet at the same time I did know. I knew and I grew tense with knowing that I must not let her know that I knew. I must not let her suspect that I knew." She succeeds in her ruse, and the other woman leaves with apologies, though nothing overt has been said. What the narrator knows has been communicated to her in code: The Austrian woman tells her that the friend with whom she traveled was a New Woman, "moderne," and then surveying the narrator tells her that she too seems "moderne . . . so moderne." [38] The woman's interest in a person who is "moderne" (the word is apparently used here as the word "gay" was used between women before the 1960's, when its meaning was still relatively secret) indicates that women who wished to form attachments with other females saw a connection between such relationships and the New Woman.

In 1912 Edward Carpenter, the socialist reformer, observed in the women's movement "a marked development in the homogenic [homosexual] passion among the female sex," despite the reigning sexologists' theories that true inverts are born, not made. Carpenter postulated that women's growing consciousness of their oppression brought about a strained relationship with men. They were becoming more unwilling to ally themselves unequally in marriage, and, Carpenter said, this distrust of men caused them to draw more closely together and to cement alliances of their own. "It is pretty certain," he concludes, "that such comrade-alliances—of a quite devoted kind—are becoming increasingly common, and especially perhaps among the more cultured classes of women who are working out the great cause of their own sex's 'liberation.' " [39] Women were not, of course, becoming *more* interested in their own sex—they had always been interested, and especially in the eighteenth and nineteenth centuries. But the women's movement now provided a body of thought which articulated why male-female relationships were generally unfair to women; and the expanded work opportunities for late nineteenth-century women had by this time also given them the possibility for enough economic independence to act on their convictions rather than to suffer and be silent as in the past.

CHAPTER 4

Boston Marriage

The term "Boston marriage" was used in late nineteenth-century New England to describe a long-term monogamous relationship between two otherwise unmarried women. The women were generally financially independent of men, either through inheritance or because of a career. They were usually feminists, New Women, often pioneers in a profession. They were also very involved in culture and in social betterment, and these female values, which they shared with each other, formed a strong basis for their life together. Their relationships were in every sense, as described by a Bostonian, Mark DeWolfe Howe, the nineteenth-century *Atlantic Monthly* editor, who had social contact with a number of these women, "a union—there is no truer word for it."[1] Whether these unions sometimes or often included sex we will never know, but we do know that these women spent their lives primarily with other women, they gave to other women the bulk of their energy and attention, and they formed powerful emotional ties with other women. If their personalities could be projected to our times, it is probable that they would see themselves as "women-identified-women," i.e., what we would call lesbians, regardless of the level of their sexual interests.

Henry James intended his novel *The Bostonians* (1885), which he characterized as "a very *American* tale " (the italics are James's), to be a study of just such a relationship—"one of those friendships between women which are so common in New England," he wrote in his *Notebook*.[2] Briefly, the novel concerns Olive Chancellor, a wealthy young feminist, who discovers in Verena Tarrant an un-

190

tutored, charismatic personality whose oratorical abilities could advance the Women's Cause. She tutors her and forms a passionate attachment to her, which Verena, who has always been a leaf in the wind, half returns. When Olive's southern cousin, Basil Ransom, comes on the scene, Verena is also swayed by his interest in her. It is he who carries her off; but his victory is Pyrrhic, and James hints that the couple will be unhappy.

In his treatment of the relationship between Olive and Verena, James is describing a Boston marriage. From Olive's perspective we learn that Verena is "what she had been looking for so long—a friend of her own sex with whom she might have a union of soul," and she implores Verena, "her face . . . full of eagerness and tenderness . . . 'Will you be my friend, my friend of friends, beyond everyone, everything, forever and forever?'" During the happiest period of their union, one character tells us, Olive and Verena "love to be together; it seems as if one *couldn't* go out without the other." Although Verena is passive in the relationship, her reflection on leaving Olive for Basil indicates that she felt herself to be as completely involved in the union as she, who had never been capable of undivided commitment to anything, was able to be:

> Olive would never get over the disappointment. It would touch her in the point where she felt everything most keenly; she would be incurably lonely and eternally humiliated. It was a very peculiar thing, their friendship; it had elements which made it probably as complete as any (between women) that had ever existed. Of course, it had been more on Olive's side than on hers, she had always known that; but that, again, didn't make any difference. It was of no use for her to tell herself that Olive had begun it entirely and she had only responded out of a kind of charmed politeness, at first, to a tremendous appeal. She had lent herself, given herself, utterly, and she ought to have known better if she didn't mean to abide by it.

Twentieth-century critics, flagrantly misreading James and his time, have no doubt that James is presenting a study of a disease.[3]

F. W. Dupee, for example, sees in Olive Chancellor "pretty distinctly a case of perverse sexuality,"[4] and Louis Auchincloss notes that *The Bostonians* contains a graphic picture of "Olive Chancellor's lesbianism," which he describes as a "mental malady."[5] Such contemporary responses to the character have created a gen-

erally accepted, clear-cut interpretation of the novel: Olive, a lesbian, has entrapped Verena, who is basically a normal woman, in
an unnatural relationship. Basil Ransom, "a man, a real man," as
Auchincloss calls him,[6] comes along to "rescue Verena from an
unnatural union"[7] and restore her to a world that is "natural and
unspoiled."[8]

James would have been puzzled by this neat categorization and
interpretation of his complex drama. If we can read *The Bostonians*
with a pre-twentieth-century perspective, it becomes clear that
James intended that there be neither heroes nor heroic rescues in
this ungentle novel. Certainly he makes great fun of Basil's antagonist, Olive Chancellor: "The most sacred hope of her nature was
that she might someday . . . be a martyr and die for something,"
he tells us and shows her as being humorless to the point of (as her
first name suggests) drabness; he also satirizes the women who surround Olive. But Basil does no better than his chief antagonist or
her army of feminists. He is frequently merely silly and smug.
James observes of him, "though he thought the age too talkative
. . . he liked to talk as well as anyone." Basil's view of women is
laughable, even in a nineteenth-century context; and surely James
was laughing when he wrote:

> That was the way [Basil] liked them—not to think too much,
> not to feel any responsibility for the government of the world
> . . . if they would only be private and passive, and have no
> feeling but for that, and leave publicity to the sex of the
> tougher hide! Ransom was pleased with the vision of that
> remedy.

Nor does James suggest that by winning Verena, Basil is rescuing
her from a terrible fate; instead a much better argument could be
made that in leaving with Basil, who has little respect for the
woman he loves, Verena embraces a terrible fate. James explains
that Basil's method of bringing Verena closer is "to drag her former
standards in the dust." He makes her endure humiliation not for
her ultimate happiness but for his use; when she laments, "It's a
remarkable system that has no place for us," Basil confesses, "No
place in public. My plan is to keep you at home and have a better
time with you there than ever." The reader will be reminded of
Torvald's attitude in Ibsen's *A Doll's House*,[9] or perhaps of James's
own earlier male chauvinist, Gilbert Osmond, in *Portrait of a Lady*

—a selfish, manipulative man who tried to force a woman into the role of obedient wife.

James tells us that Basil feels toward Verena a "merciless devotion," but his behavior indicates he is more merciless than devoted. Basil is like a beast toying with its prey, recognizing "that however she might turn and twist in his grasp he held her fast. The emotion she had expressed . . . was only one of her instinctive contortions; he had taken due note of that—said to himself that a good many more would probably occur before she would be quiet." He finally conquers Verena by pulling her out of the auditorium just as she is about to make the most important speech of her career. James uses violent imagery to describe Basil's state of mind in this scene:

> There were two or three moments during which he felt as he could imagine a young man to feel who, waiting in a public place, had made up his mind, for reasons of his own, to discharge a pistol at the king or the president.

It is Verena as the embodiment of the women's cause that he is waiting to assassinate. Or, if he will not symbolically kill her, he will subdue her by muscle, figuratively and literally:

> . . . he saw that he could do what he wanted, that she begged him, with all her being, to spare her, but that so long as he should protest she was submissive, helpless. What he wanted, in this light, flamed before him and challenged his manhood . . .

> "Olive, Olive!" Verena suddenly shrieked; and her piercing cry might have reached the front. But Ransom had already, by muscular force, wrenched her away, and was hurrying her out.

A usual critical interpretation of Basil's victory is that he rescues Verena "from an unnatural union with Olive, brings back, one might almost say, the vernal recognition of her place in the rhythms of nature." [10] But if James meant us to believe that Verena is going off to vernal bliss, his conclusion is very puzzling. He tells us that Verena is in tears, and he finishes the novel:

> It is to be feared that with the union, so far from brilliant, into which she was about to enter, these were not the last she was destined to shed.

David Howard has astutely pointed out that Verena's relationship with Basil is "limiting and destructive (far more so than the relationship with Olive). And what it limits or destroys is what James's lyrical tone in presenting her so often manifests . . . her 'gift,' what is responsive and vivifying in her nature," [11] and without which Verena is little more than a stick of sugar candy. It is Olive who encourages her to use her natural "gift" and expand it by involving herself in a cause that she will ultimately understand not merely intuitively but intellectually.

While Olive is as obsessive and as manipulative as Basil in her relationship with Verena, James shows us that Verena blooms when she is in Olive's company: She is happy and, even better, feels herself to be wonderfully productive under Olive's tutelage. Verena and Olive are depicted working together with "an effort as religious as never to be wanting in ecstasy." During this period, James suggests, Verena changes from a submissive girl to a woman who is radiant with her sense of accomplishment:

> Verena was thoroughly interested in their great undertaking; she saw it in the light of an active, enthusiastic faith. . . . She expanded, developed, on the most liberal scale. Olive saw the difference, and you may imagine how she rejoiced in it; she had never known a greater pleasure. Verena's former attitude had been girlish submission, grateful, curious sympathy. She had given herself, in her young, amused surprise, because Olive's stronger will and the incisive proceedings with which she painted her purpose drew her on. Besides, she was held by hospitality, the vision of new social horizons, the sense of novelty, and the love of change. But now the girl was disinterestedly attached to the previous things they were to do together; she cared about them for themselves, believed in them ardently, had them constantly in her mind. Her share in the union of the two young women was no longer passive, purely appreciative; it was passionate, too, and it put forth a beautiful energy.

Verena herself characterizes her time with Olive as "happy, active, fruitful," and their efforts together as "splendid"; James also shows us through Basil's candid statements regarding male-female relationships that Verena will have to deny that gift which, as she developed it, permitted her to experience "a beautiful energy"—she will be someone who is "submissive, helpless" under Basil and with whom *he* will have "a better time."

Twentieth-century critics have overlooked such an apparent reading of this novel because in our label-prone post-Freudian society, "lesbian" is "sick," and if Olive can be called a "lesbian," then her love for Verena is certainly "perverse." "Heterosexuality," on the other hand, is "mature" and "natural" and brings "fulfillment"; and even if we are told that a young woman is destined to shed many tears in a particular heterosexual relationship, since that relationship is "normal" it is certainly preferable to Olive's "mental malady." James, however, believed that a romantic relationship between two women was not of itself sick. It had the potential to be constructive and fulfilling, and could permit the self-actualization of the women. Of course, those possibilities might be negated by the limitations and complexities of the individuals involved, but James shows that is certainly also true of a heterosexual relationship.

James had no prejudices against same-sex love.[12] In 1885, before the popularization of the sexologists, he would have had no reason for viewing love between women as a "mental malady" and an abnormality. He considered it (as he says himself) as a very common, "American" phenomenon.

James had observed it at close range in Boston and in his own family. The one positive relationship in his sister Alice's life was with Katharine Loring. Alice, raised in a household with the formidable Henry James, Sr., as well as Henry the novelist and William, had as a young woman been plagued by psychosomatic illnesses and was a recluse. In 1878, when she was thirty, she suffered a nervous breakdown, as had her two olders brothers some years before. A year or two later Alice met Katharine, who was active in Boston charities and betterment organizations, and whose energy and health, in startling contrast to Alice's own condition, immediately attracted Alice. She described Katharine in a letter to a friend as having "all the mere brute superiority which distinguishes man from woman, combined with all the distinctively feminine virtues. There is nothing she cannot do from hewing wood and drawing water to driving runaway horses and educating all the women in North America."[13] Henry James observed the difference Katharine Loring made in his sister, who had shown no desire to have serious human contact with any individual before. He wrote his mother that Katharine "appears to unite the wisdom of the serpent with the gentleness of the dove," and that she was "the most perfect companion" that Alice could have found. To Alice he expressed delight in Katharine's "noble qualities." [14] Between 1881 and 1884, as he got to know Katharine well, James became more and more grateful for her relationship with Alice. He was certainly not one who could have seen a Boston marriage as a "mental malady" in his 1885 work. Not long after the publication of *The Bostonians,* James wrote to his aunt regarding Katharine's love for Alice that "a devotion so perfect and generous [was] a gift of providence so rare and so little-to-be-looked-for in this hard world that to brush it aside would be almost an act of impiety." [15]

Katharine and Alice did not have a proper Boston marriage since Katharine kept house for her father in Beverly, Massachusetts, and spent much time caring for a sickly sister, Louisa. When in 1884 Katharine decided to take her sister to England for medical reasons, Alice was determined to go along. She and Katharine remained there until Alice's death in 1892.

For much of the time Katharine lived with her sister in Bournemouth and Alice lived near Henry in London, until Louisa's eventual recovery freed Katharine to be with Alice more. Alice, perhaps in unconscious competition with Louisa for Katharine's attention, was often sick, although it was not until 1891, some months after the doctors diagnosed Alice's illness as cancer, that Katharine came to live with her and to nurse her. Alice ironically noted in her diary for March 22, 1891, "Through complete physical bankruptcy, I have attained my 'ideal' as nurse calls it, and we are established since March 12th in a little house on Campden Hill." But she added with content, "We decided a little while ago that I could not go out of town, or become the prey of the landlady, so that a house to ourselves was a necessity, and a possibility with Katharine at hand, who had only to wave her magic wand, and in three weeks from our decision we found ourselves delightfully settled, she, after her usual manner, having levelled all the rough places and let sunlight into the dark corners of suggestion." [16] Although Alice was aware of her impending death, she said of 1891, which she spent almost entirely with Katharine, "This year has been the happiest I have ever known." [17] Gay Wilson Allen in *William James: A Biography* claims that William's wife saw the relationship between Katharine and Alice as being "suspiciously Lesbian." [18] Whether she did or not, it is certain that the James family was thankful to Katharine for giving Alice her only happiness, and that Alice regarded Katharine as her one piece of good fortune in this life.

Alice's romantic friendship was beset with frustrations until the year before her death, but there were happier, quite perfect Boston marriages in the nineteenth century. A model Boston marriage existed between the novelist Sarah Orne Jewett and Annie Fields, which lasted for almost three decades. For many years during that time the two women lived together a part of each year, separated for another part of the year so that they could devote complete attention to their work, traveled together frequently, shared interests in books and people, and provided each other with love and stability.

In 1854, when Annie Fields was nineteen, she married a middle-aged widower, James T. Fields, the American publisher of Dickens and an editor of the *Atlantic Monthly*. James Fields died in 1881. According to Mark DeWolfe Howe, Annie Fields's friend and biographer, James Fields, just before his death, saw Sarah Orne Jewett as the ideal friend to fill the impending gap in Annie's life and encouraged the relationship between the two women.[19] It is impossible to know whether Howe, writing in 1922 at the height of Freudian awareness, was being truthful or whether he was attempting in this way to stave off accusations of "perversity" against his friend. It is noteworthy that when Annie Fields wanted to bring out a volume of Sarah Jewett's letters after Sarah's death, Howe, according to his daughter Helen, "laid a restraining editorial hand across her enthusiasm." He suggested that Annie omit four-fifths of the indications of affection between them "for the mere sake of the impression we want the book to make on readers who have no personal association with Miss Jewett. . . . I doubt . . . whether you will like to have all sorts of people reading them wrong." Helen Howe says that her father was probably "distressed to have to recognize the sentimentality in Sarah."[20] What probably distressed him, however, was what the two women's romantic friendship laid bare for the world to see: Such a love was common and appropriate behavior in the century in which the two women had spent most of their lives (and he saw it himself as common and appropriate at that time);[21] but it suddenly became "abnormal" in a twentieth-century context, although nothing about the nature of the relationship had changed.

Jewett's most assiduous biographers have been unable to find a trace in her life of even the slightest interest in a heterosexual love

affair or marriage. Francis Matthiessen reports that one day John
Greenleaf Whittier asked her, referring of course to heterosexuality,
" 'Sarah, was thee ever in love?' She answered, with a rush of color,
'No! Whatever made you think that?' and Mr. Whittier said, 'No, I
thought not,' and again she laughingly explained that she had more
need of a wife than a husband." [22] In her clever story about role reversal, "Tom's Husband," [23] Jewett showed heterosexual marriage
to be destructive to women because they merge their identities in
their husbands, lose interest in things outside the house, feel themselves growing rusty and behind the times, suspect their spouses can
get along pretty well without them, regret having missed much of
life, and generally believe they are failures. Jewett would have none
of that in her own life.

She was a conscious, articulate feminist as early as the 1880's, when
she argued that marriage was not good or possible for all women.
Since there are a majority of women in any civilization, she wrote,
some must be "set apart by nature for other uses and conditions than
marriage." As society "becomes more intelligent," she continued, it
will recognize the fitness of some persons and the unfitness of others
for matrimony, and it will let women who choose to remain single
follow the life and pursuits which they see as being most valuable
for themselves.[24] For herself, Jewett required another individual
who could give her intense devotion without holding the reins too
tightly, someone who would let her work when she needed to work
and give her affection and diversion when she needed those—but also
someone who led a separate life as important as Jewett's was to her,
so that Jewett would not feel that she had placed another person into
the position of Tom in "Tom's Husband." It was not likely that
there were many nineteenth-century men who could have filled her
requirements.

Like most women of her era, Jewett had several romantic friendships when she was young, which she recorded in the diary she kept
from the time she was twenty-two until she was thirty. In an unpublished, undated essay, "Outgrown Friends," she speaks of the development of affection between friends to the point where it becomes
indistinguishable from love.[25] Her diary entries suggest that the high
state of excitement usually attributed to romantic love characterized
her friendships with other young women. In an 1871 entry about
Kate Birckhead, for example, Jewett wrote, "When I heard her voice
on the stairs . . . it gave me the queerest feeling. I have longed to

see her, to be with her, for so many months that I could not believe it was real. My dear dear darling Kate!" and she declared, "I love her so perfectly." [26] Many of her friendship poems, which seem to be addressed entirely to women, are similarly indistinguishable from love poems. In an 1880 poem, originally entitled "Love and Friendship," Jewett refers to the previous year, at the end of a happy summer which the two women spent by the sea, "When we gave ourselves to each other/Before you went away." She laments:

> *How little we knew my Darling,*
> *All that the year would bring!*
> *Did I think of the wretched mornings*
> *When I should kiss my ring*
> *And long with all my heart to see*
> *The girl who gave the ring to me?* [27]

Until Annie Fields was free to establish a Boston marriage with her, most of Jewett's love poems talked about renunciation of the beloved woman, as do the love poems that her contemporary, Emily Dickinson, wrote to other women.[28] She assumed that in the course of time the other woman, who often did not have the stimulus of a career such as Jewett had projected for herself early in life, would marry. The poet would have to content herself with memories and with love at long distance. Her gentle, pathetic poem, "Together," which appeared in the May 1875 *Atlantic Monthly*, is concerned with such frustrations, of which Jewett sentimentally tries to make the best:

> *I wonder if you really send*
> *Those dreams of you that come and go!*
> *I like to say, "She thought of me,*
> *And I have known it." Is it so?*
>
> *Though other friends walk by your side,*
> *Yet sometimes it must surely be,*
> *They wonder where your thoughts have gone,*
> *Because I have you here with me.*
>
> *And when the busy day is done*
> *And work is ended, voices cease,*
> *When every one has said good night,*
> *In fading firelight, then in peace*

> *I idly rest: you come to me,—*
> *Your dear love holds me close to you.*
> *If I could see you face to face*
> *It would not be more sweet and true;*
>
> *I do not hear the words you speak,*
> *Nor touch your hands, nor see your eyes:*
> *Yet, far away the flowers may grow*
> *From whence to me the fragrance flies;*
>
> *And so, across the empty miles*
> *Light from my star shines. Is it, dear,*
> *Your love has never gone away?*
> *I said farewell and—kept you here.*

Many nineteenth-century romantic friends, like those a hundred years earlier, had to be content with no more. Jewett was ultimately luckier.

In her 1877 novel, *Deephaven*, she depicts an idyllic romantic friendship between two young women in a New England coastal village called Deephaven. At the end of the summer one of the women suggests "we should copy the Ladies of Llangollen" and settle in Deephaven permanently, away from the distractions of Boston. But the two women agree that sweet as such a life would be, they would miss the luncheon parties, and symphony concerts, and visits, and fairs, and reading club, and the Children's Hospital of Boston. Sarah managed to win for herself the best of both worlds.

In 1882, the year after James Fields died, Sarah and Annie went to Europe, a trip which they repeated a number of times during their life together. Upon their return in the autumn of 1882, Sarah began the schedule she was generally to adhere to for years to come. Several months of each year she spent alone in South Berwick, Maine, where she had been born. She returned there to write full time. The rest of the year she spent with Annie in Boston or Manchester. During Sarah's absence, Annie, too, was occupied with authorship and with her social interests, but she wrote Sarah almost daily—sometimes letters, sometimes only affectionate little notes.

Jewett's letters to Annie show how perfectly the relationship worked for them. In her 1911 edition of the correspondence, Annie comments in Victorian language, but with no less a ring of truth, that the letters show "the portrait of a friend and the power that lies in friendship to sustain the giver as well as the receiver." [29] If the letters reflect a true picture of their relationship, Sarah was able to bring so much energy and concentration to her writing because she had the assurance of Annie's love behind her, and she knew that when she emerged from her self-imposed prison in South Berwick that Annie would welcome her. The correspondence does not indicate a flaming passion, but a wise, steady, fruitful Victorian romance:

> Here I am at the desk again, all as natural as can be and writing a first letter to you with so much love, and remembering that this is the first morning in more than seven months that I haven't waked up to hear your dear voice and see your dear face. I do miss it very much, but I look forward to no long separation, which is a comfort.[30]

> I shall be with you tomorrow, your dear birthday. How I am looking forward to Thursday evening. I don't care whether there is a starlight or a fog. Yes, dear, I will bring the last sketch and give it its last touches if you think I had better spend any more time on it. I want now to paint things, and drive things, and *kiss* things [italics are Jewett's]. . . . Good night, and God bless you, dear love.[31]

The letters also indicate that the two women had a support group of other couples who were engaged in "Boston marriages," both in Boston and elsewhere: Elizabeth McCracken, author of *The Women of America*, and her friend; two women with whom they went to Europe in 1892; the novelist Vernon Lee (Violet Paget) and Kit Anstruther-Thomson; Willa Cather and the woman with whom she lived for forty years, Edith Lewis.

It probably would have astonished Jewett that Mark Howe saw anything to censor in her letters to Annie Fields. In the context of her time, her love for Annie was very fine. But Willa Cather, who was almost twenty-five years her junior and came of age in a different environment, knew that what Jewett's generation would have seen as admirable, hers would consider abnormal. There is absolutely no suggestion of same-sex love in Cather's fiction. Perhaps she felt the need to be more reticent about love between women than even some of her patently heterosexual contemporaries because she bore a burden of guilt for what came to be labeled perversion. The Cather characters that are suspiciously autobiographical, such as the narrator in *My Antonia*, appear as male whenever they show love interest in females. Jewett, whose own writing Cather greatly admired, noted the falsity of this characterization, even in the younger woman's early fiction, and warned her against it. For example, after reading Cather's "On the Gull's Road," which appeared in *McClure's* in 1908, she wrote the younger writer, "The lover is as well done as he could be when a woman writes in the man's character,—it must always, I believe, be something of a masquerade . . . and you could almost have done it as yourself—a woman could love her in the same protecting way—a woman could even care enough to wish to take her away from such a life, by some means or other." [32] The letter must have made Cather blush—but Jewett probably would not have known what she was blushing about.

In her own writing Jewett did not feel the need to use the word "man" when she meant "woman." Her story "Martha's Lady," which first appeared in *The Atlantic Monthly* in October 1897, could never have been written by Cather—not because Cather did not wholeheartedly believe in its basic premise about the redemptive power of love, but because the two principals were female. Jewett treats this fact entirely without self-consciousness. Her own Boston marriage confirmed her belief that love—perhaps any kind of love, but especially between women—had the power to foster the most praiseworthy ambition and to bestow the energy to carry that ambition out. The love described in "Martha's Lady" demands renunciation, but Martha anyway reaps those benefits of love which Jewett seems to have valued most in her "marriage."

At the beginning of the story, Helena Vernon, a lovely young Boston woman, comes to visit her spinster cousin, Miss Harriet. Miss Harriet's new maid, Martha, is unskilled, graceless, dull, and indifferent to everyone until the arrival of her mistress's new guest, who is just Martha's age. A responsive chord is immediately struck in each young woman. When Helena wishes for some cherries, Martha climbs the cherry tree "like a boy" to procure them for her. She later overhears Helena praising her to Miss Harriet, and Jewett tells us, "From that moment, she not only knew what love was like, but she knew love's dear ambitions," and she begins to look "almost pretty." Helena soon leaves to marry, but Martha hears news of her from time to time, and, like the speaker in Jewett's poem "Together," lives with her close by every day even though she is a great distance away. Martha's entire personality changes through her love for Helena. She becomes eager to learn and to be competent, then spiritual and strong and a comforter of the troubled and sick. The story ends forty years later, when the widowed Helena returns to her cousin's home and is reunited with Martha.

Jewett's focus is on love—what would be called lesbian love in our times—and how it can better a person. When Martha first learns of Helena's marriage, she feels a "sense of loss and pain," and "her idol seemed to be less her own since she had become the idol of a stranger." But "love at last prevailed," and Martha is content that Helena seems happy. Martha's love makes her "unconsciously beautiful, like a saint," and a model of goodness and gentleness. Jewett compares her to a picturesque, lonely tree which gives shelter to unnumbered lives while standing quietly in its place; "there was such a rustic homeliness and constancy belonging to her," she writes, "such beautiful powers of apprehension, such reticence."

Both women are sixty when Helena returns, but Jewett's conclusion is appropriate to a love story. Martha, upon hearing that Helena will come back, "wondered that she could speak as usual, there was such a ringing in her ears." When she sees the beloved woman she is startled, because in her mind's eye Helena had always been twenty as she was when she left: Helena "is an old woman like me!" Martha cries; Jewett says, "She had never dreamed it would be like this; this was the one thing she could not bear." But looking at Helena's unchanged eyes, Martha is enthralled again. The story ends as Helena suddenly has a moving insight into Martha's passionate love for her through the years and begs the other woman, "Oh, my dear Martha! Won't you kiss me goodnight!"

As romantic as the conclusion is, Martha's great reward for her faithfulness is not her reunion with Helena and the kiss, but the metamorphosis of her awkward, unreflective character into something sensitive and fine through her ability to love. Late nineteenth-century America, and even (or rather, especially) proper Boston, believed that there was such potential in love between women. Perhaps because it was assumed (at least by those outside the relationship) that love between women was asexual, unsullied by the evils of carnality, a sex-hating society could view it as ideal and admire, and even envy, it as the British had admired and envied the Ladies of Llangollen a hundred years earlier.

CHAPTER 5

Love and "Women Who Live by Their Brains"

Employment opportunities for most middle-class or lower middle-class women were not extensive in the last decades of the nineteenth century. Louisa May Alcott shows in *Work: A Story of Experience* (1873) that a woman who wants to be self-supporting must usually choose a career from a short list—schoolteacher or governess, lady's maid or companion to an invalid, actress, seamstress, small-business assistant, or nurse. However, a woman with exceptional ability could make her way in the late nineteenth century as she seldom could have in earlier periods. She could dream of being a professional artist, a writer, a reform leader, or a doctor or professor, and have some glimmer of hope that she might realize that dream. These opportunities, limited as they were, created a whole new class of females—an elite who maintained that position not by virtue of their connection to a powerful father or husband but solely by their own efforts.

These women were very conscious of their elite positions. They viewed themselves as pioneers, and as such they assumed the right to create a whole new life-style. Their living arrangements had to assist rather than hinder their professional pursuits. It would have been impossible for them to form unions with men, who would demand what nineteenth-century husbands were taught they might reasonably expect from wives, and the unceasing responsibility of child care would have diverted time and energy from the pursuits to which they wanted to dedicate their lives. Their practical reasons for not marrying were strong enough, but their emotional reasons were even more compelling. Society saw heterosexual unions in measuring-stick terms: In a suitable marriage the male was more of everything—he was older, taller, stronger, richer, smarter. It was inculcated in a girl that she must be less of everything than the man with whom she would spend most of her earthly existence. Her daily life was to be a constant reminder of her junior status. A nineteenth-century woman with an ego strong enough to envision being an earthly success would have difficulty accepting an unexamined, a priori definition of herself as inferior to her lifemate. Even if her husband did not assume superiority over her, society would nevertheless attribute that superiority to him, and she would have to live with the injustice. Then, too, these New Women lived in an era when women saw other women as kindred spirits and men as the Other. To spend their lives with a kindred spirit had been the dream of countless romantic friends. In the late nineteenth century it was finally possible.

In their romantic friends many women sought equals who were striving for their own earthly crowns, but there were among them also couples of transvestites and their feminine partners such as existed in earlier centuries. There were nineteenth-century British, American, and French women, too, who might have said of their own Boston marriages, as a turn-of-the-century German woman wrote of her same-sex marriage, "My lovely, dear wife bustles in our cozy home like a true German hausfrau, and I work and care for us both, as an active, vital husband."[1] Having been raised in a society in which roles were bestowed on a person from the day of birth, it would have been impossible for all these women to escape the idea which had been so assiduously impressed on all of them—there must be a masculine and feminine in every pair. Later it even became politically useful to claim to be a man trapped in a woman's body. However, most of these women, who had a violent aversion to being molded into an "appropriate role," would have had no interest in adopting a life-style based on the false role patterns from which they had escaped, even if it meant they could take the superior position. What they felt they needed was a mate with whom they could share the happiness and misery of their struggles, who would understand what those struggles were since she was engaged in them too, and who could share on an equal basis the excitement of the new ideas which surrounded them.

The Irish writer, Edith Somerville, observed, "The outstanding fact, as it seems to me, among women who live by their brains, is friendship. A profound friendship that extends through every phase and aspect of life, intellectual, social, pecuniary. Anyone who has experience of the life of independent and artistic women knows this."[2] One reason a single profound friendship was so vital to these women was that their pioneer experiences of "living by their brains" could be lonely and frightening in the extreme. They learned, again from Victorian society whose dogma idealized marriage, that one's spouse helped combat loneliness and fear. The individual solution of monogamy was the only conceivable one for most of them—except, of course, that they altered the rules by making the two principals female.

Somerville's own romantic friendship was poignant though somewhat bizarre: It ended only with Edith Somerville's death in 1949, long after the death of her friend, Violet Martin, in 1915. The two women were writers. During Violet's life they collaborated on numerous books. After her death they continued to collaborate, according to Edith, who claimed that she was able to communicate with Violet nightly.[3] All Somerville's books written after Violet's death were published under the names of E. O. Somerville and Martin Ross (Violet's pen name). After Violet died, when Edith alluded to her it was never in the past tense alone. For example, in a 1917 book Edith stated, "Martin and I, like our mothers before us, were, are, and always will be Suffragists, wholehearted, unshakable, and the longer we have lived the more unalterable have been our convictions."[4] In the last essay which Edith wrote, three years before her death in 1949 at the age of ninety-one, "Two of a Trade," she says of their first meeting in 1886, "I suppose our respective stars then collided and struck sympathetic sparks. We very soon discovered in one another a comfortable agreement of outlook in matters artistic and literary, and those collided stars lit for us a fire that has not faded yet."[5] As late as 1947 she was still celebrating Violet's birthday. (Her notion that Violet was still alive on another plane and that they could communicate with one another is less bizarre when placed in the context of the great interest in Ireland during the late nineteenth and early twentieth centuries in mysticism and the occult. Her most illustrious contemporaries, such as William Butler Yeats, would have found nothing far-fetched in her ideas.)

Somerville's biography is an almost perfect composite of the characteristics that Riegel and Welter identified in the nineteenth-century feminists, except that her mother was not a frail, impassive woman. Edith was the first born, and at prayers was placed between her father and grandfather, suggesting an "heir apparent";[6] she was encouraged in "masculine" activities; and in the 1870's, when few women were given higher education, she was sent to college.

Violet was also brought up with a fine sense of herself and her capabilities, both intellectual and physical. She was an expert rider and served more than five years as the head of a hunting society. One biographer suggests that as a young woman she was interested in a confirmed bachelor,[7] but it was not likely that a late nineteenth-century woman of her independence, tastes, and talents would seek heterosexual marriage even if the bachelor had changed his mind.

The two women were second cousins, but they did not meet until Violet was twenty and Edith twenty-four. By then the latter was a professional artist, but after their third meeting they decided to collaborate as authors, and Edith gave up her art career. In *Irish Memories*, written more than thirty years after their first meeting, Edith commented, "If I did indeed loose my hand from its first grasp, it was to place it in another, in the hand of the best comrade, the gayest playboy and the faithfullest friend that ever came to turn labour to pastime, and life into a song." They wrote thirteen volumes together, beginning with the novel *An Irish Cousin* (1889). Edith wrote sixteen more books after Violet's death, all of them published under both their names.

In *Irish Memories* and "Two of a Trade," Edith discusses their method of collaboration: One—or both simultaneously—would come up with a proposition, argue it, then modify and approve it. Then whoever was holding the pen would write the idea down, and together they would revise it.[8] After Violet's death, Edith says in "Two of a Trade," the technique of writing "has had to be changed, and, to a certain extent, modified," but they have always relied on each other, "whether on this plane or another." Here she is lyrical and mystical about their joint efforts:

> Sometimes the compelling creative urge would come on both, and we would try to reconcile the two impulses, searching for a form into which best to cast them—one releasing it perhaps as a cloudy suggestion, to be caught up by the other and given form and colour, then to float away in a flash of certainty, a completed sentence—as two dancers will yield to the same impulse, given by the same strain of music, and know the joy of shared success.

Because of the fundamental sympathy between them, she concludes, "there was never a break in the harmony of our work nor a flaw in our mutual understanding." [9]

In her autobiographical works Somerville makes no attempt to hide the intensity of her involvement with her collaborator. She speaks of the relationship overtly as a union, which she and Violet selected as others select heterosexual marriage. For most boys and girls, she says, the flirtations and emotional episodes of youth "are resolved and composed by marriage." But "to Martin and to me was opened another way, and the flowering of both our lives was when we met each other." [10] It would be safe to guess that by 1917 a Victorian woman probably could not have spoken so openly about her love affair with another woman had she been burdened by the memory of shared carnality. Geraldine Cummins, her biographer and companion from 1927 (although clearly not a true successor to Violet who still lived for Edith), observes that she had "definite views" on the "evils of sexual immorality and considered the Irish Roman Catholic Church wise in its condemnation of misdemeanors of this kind." [11]

This is not to say, of course, that women of Edith's class did not sometimes have carnal relations with other women. But it would have been astonishing, considering the Victorian antipathy to sexual expression of any kind, if such relations could have been carried on free of guilt and without an imagined cost to the "purity" of their love. As most of the women of her class would have perceived it, sex (outside of the demands of heterosexual marriage) inhibited the spiritual aspect of a union, which was far more important. The diary of Minnie Benson (wife of Edward White Benson, the Archbishop of Canterbury in the mid-nineteenth century), which reveals her guilt over her sexual relationship with another woman, Lucy Tait, is probably representative. She wrote in 1878:

> Once more and with shame O Lord, grant that all carnal affections may die in me, and that all things belonging to the spirit may live and grow in me. Lord, look down on Lucy and me, and bring to pass the union we have both so blindly, each in our own region of mistake, continually desired.[12]

To Edith and Violet, too, the spiritual aspect of their union was of vital importance, and what interfered with it in their view would have been eliminated. For all its lack of carnality, however, Edith and Violet saw their relationship as a perfect marriage. They believed that without their union, whatever worldly success they had as women who "live by their brains" would have been impossible.

The two women who wrote under the name "Michael Field,"

Katharine Bradley and Edith Cooper, had a similar relationship. Like Somerville and Ross, they were related by blood—Katharine, who was fourteen years older, was Edith's aunt, and the two lived in the same household while Edith was growing up. In 1878 when Edith was sixteen, she joined Katharine at University College, where they studied the classics and philosophy together. They were feminists from their childhood and youth, rejecting the passive, inconsequential roles their society allotted women. As a symbol of this rejection, they seldom used their female names. When she was a child, Edith took the name "Field," presumably because of her love of nature. Once on a visit to Dresden, she had an illness which caused her to lose some hair, and a German nurse dubbed her "little Heinrich," which then became Henry. Katharine matched her with the name Michael.[13] Soon after they began to write together, they combined each nickname into a pseudonym, probably because they guessed that women's work was, even in the 1880's, still not taken entirely seriously. According to some biographers, they were right in their assumption. Their first collaboration, published under feminine or neuter pseudonyms (Arran and Isla Leigh), was virtually ignored. Subsequent volumes of poetry and drama published under the name of Michael Field were quite successful, until it was discovered that Michael Field was two women. Their work then returned to oblivion,[14] though it was highly praised by such contemporaries as Robert Browning and George Meredith.

Since the two women were independently wealthy, however, their lack of success could alter neither their resolve nor their life-style, as they characterized it in a poem of the 1890's, "My love and I took hands and swore/ Against the world, to be/ Poets and lovers evermore." [15] Although biographers have attributed some brief heterosexual interests to them,[16] it is clear that the major interest in their lives was each other—and inextricably connected with that was the shared excitement in being New Women and poets. Their poetry and their journal both indicate that theirs was a union of love and work—and that love and work were interrelated was a source of great joy to them. In their journal they observed of Robert and Elizabeth Browning, "These two poets, man and wife, wrote alone; each wrote, but did not bless and quicken one another at their work; *we are closer married*" (the italics are theirs).[17] Again they used the language of marriage to describe their method of working together in a May 1886 letter to Havelock Ellis, who wanted to know which of the two wrote a particular piece:

As to our work, let no man think he can put asunder what God has joined. . . . The work is a perfect mosaic: we cross and interlace like a company of dancing summer flies; if one begins a character, his companion seizes and possesses it; if one conceives a scene or situation, the other corrects, completes, or murderously cuts away.[18]

Their literary productions were bound as closely as their lives for as long as they lived. Even on those rare occasions when one composed a volume separately, it was published under the name of Michael Field, as for example, Edith's *Poems of Adoration* (1912) and Katharine's *Mystic Trees* (1913)—only two poems in the latter are by Edith.

What was the nature of their personal relationship, if even for a moment it can be separated from their professional relationship? Katharine sometimes spoke of her very motherly feelings toward Edith,[19] but some of Edith's journal entries suggest an extremely sensual if not outright sexual interest in Katharine.[20] Their earlier poetry, especially in Book III of *Underneath the Bow*, which is a series of love poems to each other, reveals the all-consuming quality of their bond; for example, "Constancy":

> *I love her with the seasons, with the winds,*
> *As the stars worship, as anemones*
> *Shudder in secret for the sun, as bees*
> *Buzz round an open flower: in all kinds*
> *My love is perfect; and in each she finds*
> *Herself the goal. . . .*

And yet, like Edith Somerville, they were generally so completely without self-consciousness in their public declarations of mutual love, that from a twentieth-century perspective it is hard to believe that their love was not—as a Victorian would phrase it—innocent. Although they thought of themselves as aesthetes, unlike their contemporary Oscar Wilde, they would have been shocked to think they were shocking. If they saw something unorthodox about their relationship, they would have been more reticent in their poems to each other.

Their volume of verse, *Long Ago* (1889), inspired by fragments of Sappho's lyrics, gives little hint of any consciousness about the possibility of sexual expression between women; the emphasis in these poems, in fact, is on the heterosexual Phaon myth. It is possible, of course, that Katharine and Edith were not more definite about Sappho's homosexuality because they feared the censors, but it is at least as likely that they treated Sappho's "lesbianism" in a vague manner because they saw it in terms of their own love for each other, which was not as clear-cut as we would see it today. While Sappho's feeling for Phaon is patently erotic, just as it is in Ovid's poem, her love for women is almost impossible to define given our twentieth-century choices. It is sometimes sensual, but the sensuality is usually mixed with strong maternal emotions. Perhaps the poems in this volume which deal with love between women give us the most valuable insight into the relationship between Katharine and Edith, especially from Edith's perspective:

> *Atthis, my darling, thou did'st stray*
> *A few feet to the rushy bed,*
> *When a great fear and passion shook*
> *My heart lest haply thou wert dead;*
> *It grew so still about the brook,*
> *As if a soul were drawn away.*

> *Anon thy clear eyes, silver-blue,*
> *Shone through the tamarisk-branches fine;*
> *To pluck me iris thou had'st sprung*
> *Through galingale and celandine;*
> *Away, away, the flowers I flung*
> *And thee down to my breast I drew.*

> *My darling! Nay, our very breath*
> *Nor light nor darkness shall divide;*
> *Queen Dawn shall find us on one bed.*
> *Nor must thou flutter from my side*
> *An instant, lest I feel the dread,*
> *Atthis, the immanence of death.*[21]

While it is hard to pin down exactly how they conceived of love between women, either in their poetry or in their lives, it is certain that they saw it as the single most important factor in their existences. In 1907 it caused them to convert to Catholicism, for the same reason that Alice B. Toklas, a Jew, converted several decades later—because the Catholic religion held out hope of an afterlife where she would be reunited eternally with Gertrude Stein, her beloved. If their poetry is a true indication, Katharine and Edith believed that their religious conversion altered their love only to intensify it. In the poem "Lovers," Katharine wrote: "Lovers, fresh plighting lovers in our age,/Lovers in Christ. . . ./One thing is plain:—that we can never part./O Child, thou hauntest me in every room;/Nor for an instant can we separate;/And thou or I, if absent in a tomb/Must keep unqualified our soul's debate." [22] In another poem one of them stated: "Beloved, now I love God first/There is for thee such summer burst/Where it was stirring spring before." [23]

The saddest tribute one paid to her love for the other was her inability to outlive her. Edith learned she had cancer in 1912. She lived until December 1913. While nursing Edith, Katharine developed cancer herself—a perfect example to support the theory that the genesis of cancer is related to grief and loss. Katharine kept her own illness a secret from Edith, not wishing to add to her burden, but she outlived Edith by little more than half a year. It was a happier tribute, for her readers at least, that Katharine wrote the most moving poetry of her career at this time, almost all of it relating to her great love and sorrow, as in "Caput Tuum ut Carmelus":

> I watch the arch of her head,
> As she turns away from me. . . .
> I would I were with the dead,
> Drowned with the dead at sea,
> All the waves rocking over me!

> As St Peter turned and fled
> From the Lord, because of sin,
> I look on that lovely head;
> And its majesty doth win
> Grief in my heart as for sin.

> Oh, what can Death have to do
> With a curve that is drawn so fine,
> With a curve that is drawn as true
> As the mountain's crescent line? . . .
> Let me be hid where the dust falls fine!

Twentieth-century biographers, unable to understand the scope of their commitment to each other and ignoring the autobiographical poem in which they swore to be "poets and *lovers* evermore" (the italics are mine), have observed, like Mary Sturgeon, that Katharine and Edith, "in honouring their vow to poetry, gave life . . . 'a poor second place.' " [25] However, the record they left indicates that in their marriage neither their life nor their work (they) would have found it absurd to discuss them as separate entities) was forced to take a second place.

The perfect, absolute equality in the relationships between Somerville and Ross and the Michael Field women, while not unique, was not attained in all Boston marriages. As Sarah Jewett observed, professional women had no need for a husband but plenty of need for a wife, and if they did not establish a relationship with someone like Annie Fields, who was strong enough to hold her own, one of the pair sometimes became helpmeet to the other more accomplished or more famous consort. An English example of such a "marriage" was that of the novelist, Marie Corelli (who was for forty years, during the last decades of the nineteenth century and the first decades of this one, "Queen of the Best Sellers") and Bertha Vyver. Corelli (born Mary MacKay), who turned to fiction after a brief and not very successful musical career in order to earn money, was probably astonished at her phenomenal literary success, beginning with her second novel. Her works were publicly praised by Lord Tennyson, George Meredith, William Gladstone, and Oscar Wilde; she was the only writer Edward VII invited to his coronation; she was translated into most European and even some Asiatic languages; she was invited to lecture at intimidating gatherings such as the Philosophical Society of Edinburgh. At a time when most midde-class women still did nothing outside of their housewifely jobs, Marie Corelli must have felt under terrific pressure as she stood in the limelight. She needed someone who would sustain her while she battled to keep a position that was relatively new for a woman. What husband would have subsumed his own existence under hers for the sake of her continuing success? Bertha Vyver, the daughter of a French countess and by some accounts a talented painter, gave up her own pursuits to help promote Marie Corelli's career.

Bertha, who was one year older than Marie, came into the writer's life permanently (her mother had been a family friend when Marie was a child) when Marie was twenty-three. Bertha was convinced of Marie's genius, and convinced Marie herself. Since Corelli's literary talents are far from impressive by objective standards, the merit of their *folie à deux* is dubious in terms of benefit to society,[26] but Marie approached literature as a business, just as most popular male writers have for centuries. Her motive was no more laudable than theirs—but literary men had been able to support themselves through their wits, while few women before her era had managed to do so.

She did what any word-oriented person who had no interest in teaching and hated starving would have dreamed of doing. And it was Bertha's assistance which permitted her to do it.

In Bertha Vyver's account of their relationship in *Memoirs of Marie Corelli* (1930), written six years after the novelist's death, it becomes clear to what extent she encouraged Marie to think of herself as gifted and charming and lovely. She created "Marie Corelli" just as Alice B. Toklas can be said to have created Gertrude Stein. She was both mother and lover to the writer, who cultivated an image of perpetual girlishness and wrote Bertha letters during brief absences saying, "Your little wee one embraces you fondly and sends you tender kisses, and wishes you were here to sing '*Il était un petit navire!*' to soothe her poor head." [27] Bertha kept house for her, cared for Marie's invalid father until his death, stayed at home to take care of business so that Marie could vacation (after the father's death in 1889 they were free to travel together), and put herself at Marie's disposal in all things.

On her part, Corelli apparently supported Vyver and gave her a share of prestige at one remove. At public gatherings they were a recognized couple. One acquaintance reports that at parties "they did not dance but spent most of the evening with their arms around each other looking on at the rest." [28] Fairly early in the relationship Marie expressed the hope that Bertha would always regard "home" as the place where she was and as "a place where there is always love and unity." [29] Their bond was symbolized by Corelli in a large stone fireplace in the music room of their home on whose mantel she had carved in elaborate design her initials and Bertha's, intertwined.[30]

Like any proper, unreflecting Victorian wife (and mother), Bertha had little conscious resentment of her generally secondary position. In the *Memoirs* she innocently quotes a most peremptory letter from Marie, written before the death of her father, when Bertha went to pay a brief visit to her aunt at Liège:

> I have just got your letter saying you are not coming till October 5th. I confess this is a most bitter disappointment to me, for I had been calculating the month from Thursday to Thursday. Dear Ber, would you feel it very hard if I ask you to come home by Saturday, instead of delaying it so long? If you knew how really suffering and worn out I am, I am sure you would come. I cannot bear to contemplate actually nearly another fortnight

to wait. So, dear Ber, do come home if you can. Surely your aunt will not persuade you to remain when she knows the circumstances. I am so fearfully lonely and Papa becomes so fretful and unmanageable. I do not wish to appear selfish, but I feel that I shall be really ill if this nervous strain goes on much longer. I have one of my splitting headaches today and a very bad cold into the bargain—trotting after the housekeeping, feeling ill and ready to tumble each minute. Housekeeping wouldn't suit me. I feel wretchedly done up today. Oh, I do pray you will come home next week; do not let me pass two more Sundays before I see you. Do, do come to oblige me. —Your sorrowful wee one.

Bertha's comment on that letter is "after such earnest pleading, I yielded easily." [31]

Bertha outlived Marie by approximately twenty years, but she continued to fashion her life around her love until she herself died. She turned their home into a virtual museum, preserving everything intact as it was on the day of Marie's death, even stopping the clock at the hour she expired; she preserved and displayed all Marie's manuscripts in museum fashion on glass-covered tables, except for the manuscript of one of Marie's novels, *The Sorrows of Satan*, which she presented to the trustees of Shakespeare's birthplace, being sure, no doubt, that her beloved would someday rank with that immortal.[32] Despite Marie's poseur quality and her self-absorption, she must have recognized that it was a fine thing to have such a faithful, loving human being in her corner.

In America the author Alice French, who wrote under the name Octave Thanet, and Jane Crawford, her companion of almost half a century, also had a relationship in which the energies of both went into the career of one. Octave, who for thirty years was among the highest-paid writers in the United States, also came to literature as a business—and her success in it was due at least in part to the nurturing support that Jane gave her.

At the height of the first wave of the feminist movement, Octave had little feminist consciousness. Although her mother had actively supported Elizabeth Cady Stanton, Octave did not even favor female suffrage. One effect of the predominant antiwoman attitude of the world of the nineteenth century was that many women who wished to use their talents to make a claim on that world were forced to dissociate themselves from their gender. Octave seemed to view humanity as having three sexes—men, women, and Octave Thanet. While a feminist might have been disturbed at the notion that another woman, by choice or not, was effaced in order to promote her, Thanet saw only the model of heterosexuality around her and never questioned its morality.

She and Jane Crawford had been girlhood friends. When Jane left their hometown of Davenport, Iowa, to be married, Octave was crushed. But Jane returned a few years later after her husband's early death, and the two women established a lavish residence together and became monogamous companions until Jane's death in 1932 (Octave died less than two years later). Jane made a home for Octave in every sense, not only encouraging her work but also providing a female presence which was a necessary counterbalance to the masculine persona Octave assumed as armour against a world she saw as hostile to female aspiration.[33]

In France the nineteenth-century artist Rosa Bonheur had a similar relationship with Nathalie Micas. Although Nathalie thought of herself as an inventor of sorts and even attempted to market a railway brake of her own design, most of her life was spent giving support to her renowned friend. Rosa too had little feminist consciousness. She had been determined early in her life to achieve and seeing only masculine models of success, she began by identifying with them and ceased to think of herself as a woman, which in mid-nineteenth-century France meant someone who is passive and impotent. Her persona was ultimately genderless. In her *Reminiscences* she recalls that because her father was a member of the Saint-Simonians, a utopian group which believed in the equality of the sexes among other things, she was educated along with her brothers when young, and this "masculine" education permitted her to develop freely as females of her era seldom could. Such freedom itself (to society in general and thus to her when she saw how the world thought) was "male." She says regarding her early education:

> The influence it had on my lifework cannot be exaggerated. It emancipated me before I knew what emancipation meant and left me free to develop naturally and untrammelled. . . . So from the very start a masculine bent was given to my existence.[34]

In order to maintain that masculine freedom, it seemed logical to her, as it did to women of other centuries, that she should adopt masculine garb. Unlike many of her predecessors, she did not attempt to "pass," and her fame would not have permitted her to do so in any case. But a contemporary of hers, Paul Chardin, observed that her studio costume, a peasant smock and man's trousers, "helped the illusion that she might be of the male sex." [35] However, he does not examine her motives: that a masculine guise served to remind her that she had chosen to be unfettered by conventional femininity, and that she would devote herself to being an artist (which was almost invariably a masculine pursuit) rather than to being a woman. The legend regarding Rosa Bonheur's transvestism is that she began dressing in male attire to facilitate her art study in the slaughter-houses. It is true that in order to keep a long skirt from being soiled, she would have had to lift it with one hand while balancing her art materials with the other, and that would have been terribly awkward, but the symbolic meaning of male garb to an ambitious nineteenth-century woman cannot be overlooked.

Nathalie Micas, with whom Rosa lived from the 1840's, when both women were in their twenties, to Nathalie's death in 1889, seems to have been a woman of great but erratic energy. She claimed to have medical and even surgical skills, which she practiced on her neighbors as well as her animals. And she invented dozens of devices, among them her Micas railway brake. She even attempted painting, to Rosa's amused encouragement. However, as another acquaintance, the Princess Stirbey, observed, her real job was to play the role of a great artist's wife:

> On the whole, it was a necessary and beneficent part. Rosa Bonheur could never have remained the celebrated artist she was without someone beside her, at each instant, to spare her the material cares of the household, the daily worries of existence, and to help her also with moral and physical support, as well as advice in many things relating to her art [such as the sale of pictures]. Nathalie made herself small, ungrudgingly, so that Rosa might become greater.[36]

Rosa herself observed before her death in 1899 that Nathalie had been not only a helpmeet, but a "well-beloved friend. She was my equal in everything, and my superior in many things," but the examples she gives serve to point up Nathalie's protective abilities, which permitted Rosa to go about her business of being an artist, unburdened by the world; for example, "She preserved me from being spotted by the mud that was thrown at me." [37] Few male artists would have turned their backs on such nurturing and love had it been offered them, and Rosa was unable to, since she was under double pressure: to succeed in a most difficult endeavor, and to succeed despite the fact that she was a woman.

There can be no doubt of their love for and passionate commitment to each other, but their relationship was modeled along heterosexual lines which have been most useful to men's aspirations for success in the world. After Nathalie's death Rosa was confirmed in her view that it was difficult if not impossible to continue working at the same level of energy without such nurturing. About ten years later, at the end of 1898 and only months before her own death, she found a similar relationship with a minor American artist, Anna Klumpke. At this time she wrote to an acquaintance that her health and spirits had finally returned, "since I have found a kind, excellent friend who takes care of me and has cured me of my discouragement and misanthropy." [38] Rosa joked about the nature of their union: "My wife has much talent, and the children don't prevent us from painting pictures," [39] but beneath the humor was more than a grain of truth. There were, of course, other women artists who had no wives, but it might be argued too that they generally did not make so great a splash as Bonheur, at least partly because they had no one to devote her life to nurturing them and promoting their talents.

Whether or not many women artists took wives, a good number of them believed that heterosexual relations were incompatible with their goals. A love relationship with another woman, on the other hand, whether a "butch-femme" arrangement or a relationship of equals, had the potential of encouraging their achievement. "Diana and Persis," an unfinished story by Louisa May Alcott about two women, a sculptor and an artist, suggests that some ambitious women may have thought these points through. The sculptor, Diana, an ardent feminist, is uninterested in the pleasures of youth and the honors of being a beauty and a member of the weaker sex—"Bread and the right to work was all she asked of the world." When the younger Persis complains that she sometimes lacks a motive to keep her going, Diana warns, "Don't look for it in marriage, that is too costly an experiment for us. . . . Do not dream of spoiling your life by a commonplace romance."

Although Alcott believes a heterosexual marriage is too costly for a woman artist, a Boston marriage is ideal. In an 1883 novel, *An Old Fashioned Girl,* she presents just such a marriage and shows how it promotes the work and the well-being of Rebecca, a sculptor, and Lizzie, an artist, who are described as being "all alone in the world, but as happy and independent as birds; real friends, whom nothing will part."

Diana and Persis are not as fortunate. There is a passionate and tender attraction between them: "Diana kissed [Persis's] face and let it go reluctantly as if peculiarly conscious of the charm just then," and Persis calls her "my chosen goddess Diana," but the two decide to separate for a time while Persis goes to Europe to study art. They plan that Diana will join Persis as soon as she is able, perhaps in a year. In her letters Persis writes, "Come, oh come to your Percy, oh my dearest Diana." However, Persis gets sidetracked. She meets a kindly businessman who promises her that if they marry he will in no way interfere with her career. But Alcott shows that even with the most sympathetic husband a woman artist cannot combine marriage with her work. In a short time Persis's studio is full of dust and her artistic ambition, despite her denials, has disappeared. Alcott says, "something of the youthful audacity was gone and the eyes that looked so pleasurably into the future for herself began to wear the tender anxiety of a mother's eyes." While Diana, who comes to visit, is discussing with Persis's husband the possibility of combining work and motherhood, Persis "was thinking what they should have for breakfast since morning would inevitably bring that dreadful question." [40]

Alcott never finished the story, perhaps because Persis was modeled after her artist sister, May, who died at the birth of her first child during the time Alcott was in the midst of this work. But although the novel is unfinished, it is fairly certain from the extant chapters that the author would have shown Persis's work as an artist becoming inconsequential under the demands of marriage and motherhood.

Alcott's views of the best life for a woman who was serious about her art were bolstered by what she saw in the life of successful professional women. Living in Boston, she was surrounded by "Boston marriages," but she probably knew also that such arrangements existed everywhere. In the 1860's she became friends with the American sculptor Emma Stebbins and her mate, a leading American actress, Charlotte Cushman (who is Miss Cameron in *Jo's Boys*). Through them she may have heard a good deal about the Roman colony of women artists who gathered around the sculptor Harriet Hosmer,[41] with which Emma and Charlotte were intimately connected. Hosmer, the most famous woman sculptor of the nineteenth century, observed in no uncertain terms in 1854:

Even if so inclined, an artist has no business to marry. For a man it may be well enough, but for a woman, on whom matrimonial duties and cares weigh more heavily, it is a moral wrong, I think, for she must either neglect her profession or her family, becoming neither a good wife and mother nor a good artist. My ambition is to become the latter, so I wage eternal feud with the consolidating knot.[42]

However, she tied the knot for a time with at least two other women.[43] Although no biographer has yet been able to furnish evidence that Louisa May Alcott had such relationships herself, it is certain that she avoided heterosexual marriage just as firmly as Hosmer, seeing it as incompatible with her goals.

Charlotte Cushman's odyssey in search of a perfect mate must have been repeated many times by nineteenth-century professional women who did not, like most of the women we have looked at so far, love once and forever. Cushman, who opens her memoirs with the sentence "I was born a tomboy," [44] early developed what were considered "masculine" tastes but what were in reality those that any intelligent, energetic young person would prefer if allowed to grow without intimidating restraints: She valued exercise over passivity, working with her hands and mind to playing with dolls (she cracked open a doll's head so that she could examine its brains), and taking a leading rather than a subservient role in games. Since her society defined those healthy choices as masculine, she began to think of herself in those terms—which meant that she developed "masculine" aspirations: to have a career, to make a good deal of money, to be independent. In the mid-1830's she set out to discover a profession that would permit her to retain her sense of herself. She had little choice: She could be a singer, a writer, or an actress. At the first she failed miserably in 1835. In 1837 she wrote a story which was published in *Godey's Lady's Book*, but she recognized that she possessed no great genius in that area. However, about the same time she made a very successful debut as an actress. Acting then became her life's profession.

Her desire to be a success in some area became even more compelling, because she took it upon herself to support her debt-ridden family. Like Louisa May Alcott—who also undertook the support of her family, since her father, Bronson Alcott, repeatedly failed in all his business ventures—exigency became a further stimulus to achieve what was already a much-desired goal. Charlotte sensed early that a heterosexual connection would distract her from her aims, and since her personality demanded that she, and not the individual to whom she was connected, be prime, she did not miss what she "gave up." With women, on the other hand, she could share what most passionately interested her, such as her love of the arts; she could treat them as kindred spirits, and a love relationship with them would not threaten her view of her own potential.

Her early emotional bonds were all with women. The most powerful relationship began in her mid-twenties with Rosalie Scully, a painter, who was two years younger than Charlotte, gentler in temperament, and conventionally feminine, although she was attempting to be a professional artist. As Charlotte's diary and the letters between them indicate, their tie grew stronger throughout the early 1840's as Charlotte built her reputation on the American stage. By 1844 Charlotte was recognized as a leading actress in America, much of her fame being attributed to her spectacular success in "breeches parts," a not uncommon undertaking for actresses in the nineteenth century. Her next logical step, with regard to her fame and her earnings, would be to go to London and conquer the British theater audiences as well. She was reluctant to leave Rosalie, but the two agreed that an English debut was necessary for Charlotte and that the separation would be short, perhaps only six months.

In Charlotte's diary for 1844–1845, which she took to England with her, "Rosalie Scully" is written on the flyleaf in Rosalie's hand —perhaps the painter thus hoped to be daily in Charlotte's memory. Charlotte did not need such assistance in the early months of her absence. In her entry for October 27, 1844, she calls herself "wretched" with the "memory of all that I had left, pouring upon me words of regret at the steps I had taken. . . . Such wretched thoughts that it were better if I could not think. . . . I hear her sigh for her absent friend. I feel almost her arms about me and then weep again, till I almost wish I could sleep away six months. . . . Shall I ever make sufficient money to have her with me always? . . . Only my God can know how dear, how very dear she is to me . . . the one bright spot of my existence, the one hope that bids me toil on."[45] Other entries during this voyage are equally pitiable. In the entry for November 11, she speaks of being fascinated with the walk of a woman in a nearby cabin because it is so like Rosalie's. On November 14, she writes of her nighttime sorrows and how she lay "thinking of dear Rose for more than an hour, speaking to her,—calling on her in the most endearing manner and hoping for an answer—I only saw her lips move to kiss me! and almost sprang up from my berth at the fair thought of my usual reply to that sweet Expression from her. I sank back again and started imagining I had her head upon my shoulder. I dropped asleep." [46] Her diary during this time indicates also that she kept up a constant correspondence with Rosalie.

In the nineteenth century, married heterosexuals had a religious and/or civil bond between them that they were conditioned to hold sacred. In addition to that conditioning, for most people the law made divorce virtually impossible. Once a commitment of marriage was made, all the forces of society converged to see that it was kept. Women who loved each other had, of course, no such social encouragement to consider their mutual pledges sacred and immutable. Their constancy depended only on the constancy of their affections. Charlotte, a young woman alone in a strange country, an immediate stage success, her vanity and her loneliness appealed to by many women "who came to 'kneel' at her feet," [47] formed a relationship with the English poet Eliza Cook.

Cook, as androgynous and self-assertive and flamboyant as Charlotte herself, wooed the actress with love sonnets.[48] But perhaps her greatest appeal was that, unlike Rosalie, she appeared to be able to stand on her own. Charlotte felt that her most basic and undeniable obligation at this time was to earn enough money so that within "five years more" she would have enough, perhaps $50,000, on which to retire and, she wrote her mother, "that will, if well invested, give us a comfortable home for the rest of our lives." [49] Although Charlotte loved Rosalie, she would have been, if not a drain on that goal, at least no help, since Charlotte had already decided that if they were to continue together it was Charlotte who would have to support them. Because she had convinced herself at the start of her career that she needed success not for herself but for her family, her commitment to Rosalie was not strictly consonant with her early goals. At about the time of the Cook affair Charlotte brought her whole family to England, but for some reason Rosalie was not sent for or could not come. She was also becoming dimmer in Charlotte's mind's eye, as her diary entries show—she is unable to dream of Rosalie when she wishes to, she mentions her less and less often, she gets caught up in the great social whirl of London.

It is not surprising, therefore, that without the hindrance of society's sanctions such as a husband might have in a similar situation, Charlotte, thousands of miles away, permitted herself to be seduced by Eliza Cook. Yet, incredible as it seems, when Rosalie in Philadelphia heard the news of the passionate friendship the two women were conducting in London and apparently upbraided Charlotte for it, Charlotte wrote a brief entry in her diary for May 10, 1845, "Letter from Rose breaking my heart." [50] Charlotte's resolution to the problem was taken out of her hands some months later when she was notified that Rosalie was dead.

Charlotte Cushman and Eliza Cook were too much alike. Their romantic friendship could not last long, since each had to possess the limelight. Charlotte required someone who could stand on her own but was more subdued in her behavior both in the world and toward the person she loved. In 1848 Charlotte thought she had found her lifelong friend in Matilda Hays, a woman two years older than Charlotte, who, largely inspired by Charlotte, had recently developed an interest in going on the stage. The two probably met through Geraldine Jewsbury, who had known Matilda since the 1830's when Matilda was translating George Sand's stories and helping the French author gain a reputation in English-speaking countries.[51] At just about the time Charlotte met Matilda, Charlotte's sister, who had been playing Juliet to Charlotte's Romeo, decided to retire from the stage. Charlotte trained Matilda, who was willing to put aside her writing career, to be her new Juliet. Initially Matilda received some very fine reviews of her acting, and it looked as though she would be a great stage success. Her victory was short-lived, however. When the two women returned to America and Matilda made an American debut in 1849, the talent that she had demonstrated earlier seemed to vanish. Perhaps it was eaten up by the force of Charlotte's very dominant personality. Whatever the reason, the two then decided that Matilda, instead of being Charlotte's leading lady, would be her confidante and companion. Matilda would earn her keep by supplying a sense of home for Charlotte in her travels.[52]

Joseph Leach, in his definitive biography of Charlotte Cushman, observes that from that time on, Matilda was a disappointment to Charlotte. As she came more and more to resemble a Victorian wife, her "nerves" got worse and worse, and she complained constantly that nobody understood her.[53] Charlotte felt that she had made some commitment to Matilda, however, since it was she who had proposed the new form of their relationship, and continued for years to try to make a success of an intimacy that had started on a somewhat equal footing and wound up as role-ridden as a Victorian heterosexual marriage. In 1852 they went to Rome where to all appearances they attempted to maintain something of their initial bond. Elizabeth Barrett Browning, who knew them there, wrote that the two women had a "female marriage," and that Charlotte and Matilda "have made vows of celibacy and eternal attachment to each other—they live together, dress alike." [54] But the situation deteriorated in Rome, where Matilda was surrounded by talented women—actresses, writers, sculptors—who were a constant reminder to her that she had failed. For a while it seemed that she might attach herself to Harriet Hosmer—but that bond would have presented the same problem to Matilda, who was bitter at the realization that her own talent was not equal to her ambition. Finally the difficulty resolved itself after years of agony in the healthiest way it could for a woman of Matilda's psychological makeup. She left Charlotte to return to England, where she had been offered a writing job on a new magazine, *The English Woman's Journal*,[55] which would permit her to try once again to realize her aspirations as an independent woman.

It is not clear how Charlotte viewed her involvements. Emma Stebbins, her biographer and longest companion, states openly regarding her relationships with other women, "for all her life long, her friendships were of the nature of passions." [56] But as open as Stebbins's comment is, and despite the fact that young women swooned around Charlotte's stage door, confirming any notion she may have had regarding her attractiveness to her sex, Charlotte did not feel intrepid in her amorous pursuits. She writes in her diary, for example, of meeting "the loveliest woman I ever looked upon. . . . Such eyes such hair such Eyebrows: Mouth nose chin. . . . What a lucky thing I am not of the other sex for a heavy mortgage would have been made upon her from this hour. As it was it almost deprived me of my dinner." [57] Apparently Charlotte had some awareness that not all women were interested in friendships that "were in the nature of passions," but since she spoke so freely about her loves to people like Robert and Elizabeth Browning and to her own family, it is doubtful that she considered them unorthodox.

In her next, and last, serious relationship, Charlotte was more careful to choose a mate who would really suit her own temperament. She had learned by now that what she required was a woman whose talents and strength she could respect, a person who was aggressive and confident in her work, who was in all ways independent, and yet who would not compete with her as a "character." In 1857 she was fortunate in meeting Emma Stebbins, then forty-one years old, about Charlotte's own age, and a sculptor, who had all the attributes Charlotte sought. Their relationship worked on every level. Not only could Emma encourage Charlotte in her work and provide intelligent companionship in her leisure, but she too was engaged in important work; she too received adulation and critical acclaim and could consider herself a professional success. In addition, Charlotte could help Emma's career in a way which would not detract from Emma's own accomplishments. Emma was assertive as an artist, but shy as a saleswoman. Therefore, Charlotte acted as Emma's sales agent, a role Emma had hated to play.

Emma's general self-sufficiency meant that the women could be apart without "nerves" and recriminations such as Charlotte had experienced in other love relationships. And Emma's own professional success also meant that Charlotte would mature by learning how to give up her own immediate pursuits occasionally and follow Emma if she wanted to be with her. As an example, for several months in 1861 Charlotte traveled alone, pursuing her career on the American stage; when Emma received a Horace Mann commission and had to return to Rome in order to finish her work, Charlotte accompanied her. They were, as Charlotte saw it and explained to her nephew and his bride, a perfect team: Emma's needs completely encompassed her own and were totally comprehensible to her. "I love her very much," she wrote her young relatives, "she is the finest nature I have ever been thrown in contact with, the very truest and dearest of human beings." [58] The relationship continued for almost twenty years until Charlotte's death in 1876.

What she sought in a romantic friend seems to be what most woman-identified professional women of the next few decades thought to be their ideal too—a woman who understood the demands of their occupational life because she worked under such demands as well, and who could give support and sympathy when needed, who was self-sufficient to the extent that she had a whole life of her own, but who also had energy for another, more intimate life with an equal.

Romantic friendships of this nature were especially common among academic women at the end of the nineteenth and the beginning of the twentieth century. In many colleges and universities a woman could not marry a man and remain on the faculty. It is doubtful that most of these pioneering women would have wanted to even if they could have, for the reasons discussed at the beginning of this chapter, but the regulation in any case encouraged women to have little to do with men. In the very challenge of entering a field that had been largely forbidden to women anywhere in the world there must also have been something which drew them to each other—in anxiety over their success, in defiance of a society that had kept women from the academies for so long, in wonder at finding other brave, intelligent beings like themselves. In his mid-nineteenth-century comic poem about higher education for women, "The Princess," Tennyson has Princess Ida say of her learning mate and herself that they would be "two women faster welded in one love/Than pairs of wedlock." Much to his probable dismay, he may well have been observing correctly the sentiments of many women pursuing learning together.

Perhaps another reason academic women were drawn to each other is that while they may have been confident of their own intellectual abilities, like the *femmes savantes* and the bluestockings of the seventeenth and eighteenth centuries, they had no reason to believe that men would take those abilities seriously. They craved respect for what they had invested so much of themselves in, and when they received respect—especially from a sympathetic being equally endowed with gifts of the intellect—they responded with gratitude and love. One of the most dramatic examples is found in the early nineteenth-century correspondence between two German women, Bettine von Arnim and Caroline von Günderode. Their letters, translated by Margaret Fuller in 1842 because she recognized that their views of women learning and women loving were similar to her own, were written in 1805–1806, when Bettine was in her early twenties and Caroline was about eight years older. They discuss literature and philosophy and religion and nature—and their love for each other, which is woven in and out of their esoteric dissertations. Bettine writes to Caroline, for example:

> Thou shinest on me with thy intellect, thou Muse . . . I hold thee dear,—whistle before my window in the black midnight, and I tear myself away from my moonlight dream, and go with thee. Thy Schelling's philosophy is to me, indeed, a pit; it makes me giddy to look down and see where I might break my neck, trying to find my way through the dark gulf, yet for thy love I would creep through on all fours.[59]

While Caroline took Bettine's efforts to learn seriously, the men

who surrounded her told her, "First, I am to acquire domestic virtues; secondly, where do I think to find a husband if I learn
Hebrew?" [60] It is no wonder then that she saw Caroline as a refuge
from the world's hostility and insanity, her reason for existing—for
it was only with Caroline that she might be who she wanted to be—
and the great passion of her life, as Bettine tells her:

> If thou wert not, what would the whole world be to me? No
> opinion, no human being has influence over me but thou. I am
> dead already, if thou dost not bid me rise up and live on and
> on with thee; I feel with certainty my life wakes up only when
> thou callest, and will perish if it cannot continue to grow in
> thee.[61]

The need was mutual. Caroline writes to Bettine, "Thou art my bit
of sun that warms me, while everywhere else frost falls upon me." [62]
Although after Caroline's early death Bettine found a more illustrious correspondent in Goethe who also encouraged her intellectual
interests, his view of a thinking woman is betrayed in the title of
their published letters, *Correspondence with a Child,* which began
in 1807 when Bettine was twenty-two.

In America the number of women's colleges that opened during
the last half of the nineteenth century meant not only that many
educated women would emerge but also that jobs would be available
for some of them to educate other women. A woman who became a
professor in the late nineteenth century was aware of the widespread
social views she was up against, even if she had escaped from internalizing them: Not only had she taken herself out of the home, where
she belonged, to become educated, but now she was helping other
women do the same. In 1895, just as education for women was really
coming into its own, there was a great public outcry when a survey
revealed that more than half the graduates of women's colleges remained spinsters. There had been at that time a general agreement
that every married couple in America needed to produce at least
three children for the Republic to survive, and higher education for
women (and all who were connected with it) was now held account-
able for these women's escape from their patriotic duty.[63] The academic woman must have been under considerable pressure. Although
there were in society at large many who were sympathetic to her
efforts, she would not have had to look very far to find many more
who were not. Of course, it would be her healthy impulse to form

an intimate bond where she might get the most support and under-standing—with one whose struggles and interests were similar to hers.

Anna Mary Wells, the author of a study of a romantic friendship between two academic women, Mary Woolley and Jeannette Marks, observes that in women's colleges of the late nineteenth and early twentieth centuries, "twosomes were an established institution on the faculty." [64] The relationship Wells explores began when the two women met at Wellesley College in 1895—at that time Jeannette Marks was a student and Mary Woolley, a professor of Biblical history. It lasted through Mary's presidency at Mt. Holyoke College from 1901 to 1937, where Jeannette taught and wrote books, through Mary's retirement, and to her death in 1947.

Jeannette Marks's comment on the Ladies of Llangollen in her book *Gallant Little Wales* gives insight into why she formed an at-tachment with Mary Woolley. She remarks that "they loved inde-pendence and did not love their suitors. Many things drew them together." [65] As Wells shows, Marks and Woolley had a love affair and then a marriage, regardless of whether or not it was genital (she guesses it wasn't). It was widely known and apparently accepted on the Mt. Holyoke campus before the two women lived together that one would visit the other every evening in order to kiss her good-night,[66] and once they did live together in the president's house, all knew that Jeannette was Mary's life partner.

The relationship was not without complications, particularly for Jeannette, the younger of the two, whose own accomplishments never quite equaled those of her illustrious partner, under whose shadow she feared to be hidden. Her conflict is apparent in a 1902 letter to Mary Woolley:

> Dearest, if I say I will come next summer, will you take care of me and help give me a chance to do the work I long to do? . . . If I give all to you and give up the idea that I must pro-tect myself from you, will you really care for my work as well as loving me? . . . I cannot be happy away from you, yet sup-posing I should be worthless because I have given in to you? [67]

But although she never achieved the fame of Mary, who in 1930 was named one of the twelve greatest living women in America and appointed by the President of the United States to be the only woman member of the Geneva Arms Conference in 1932, Jeannette's anxi-eties were not well founded, as they might have been had she the care of a house and children and concern over a husband's career to distract her. During their fifty-two year relationship, she headed the English Literature Department at Mt. Holyoke for two decades, she founded the famous Laboratory Theater, and she published almost twenty books. While she too had a "measuring-stick" problem similar to one that might exist in a heterosexual relationship, her recognition that ultimately she was reliant on herself permitted her to solve it probably more satisfactorily than even her most ambitious counterpart in a legal marriage could have.

It is not surprising that similar pairs of academic women make up the history of American women's colleges around the turn of the century.[68] They chose a living arrangement that was the most workable for women "who live by their brains," and the most desirable for those who not only considered other women "kindred spirits," as females of their society generally did, but who also had the wherewithal to act on their convictions.

When Marks and Woolley established their union in 1895, they saw it, and it was still seen by many other Americans, as fitting perfectly into the tradition of romantic friendships in women's colleges. Over the next few years such a tradition became suspect, and even those who participated in it had to view it in a different light. An unpublished 1908 essay by Jeannette Marks, "Unwise College Friendships," suggests how painful the new view of love between women must have been to romantic friends, and what self-loathing women must have developed as they tried, whether only publicly or in fact, to alienate themselves from their strongest emotions.

In her essay Marks sees love between women as something that is "unpleasant or worse," an "abnormal condition," a sickness which requires "a moral antiseptic." We can only wonder at and feel sorry for the confusion and internalized contempt that would cause a woman to describe in that way her own deepest ties and what was apparently a source of her greatest strength. Marks writes that such loves "cannot be fumigated out of the college because they are brought in from the outside world, from an incomplete or unwholesome home life, or as the result of ill health," and she asserts in contradiction to her whole life that the only relationship that can "fulfill itself and be complete is that beween a man and a woman." It is clearly not lesbian genital sex alone which she attacks here, but rather romantic, or as she repeatedly calls it, "sentimental" friendship—that is, the very type of relationship that was so ubiquitously encouraged in the nineteenth century, and which she knew from girlhood, whether or not she knew lesbian sex.[69]

Marks's essay was never published, perhaps because in America romantic friendship was still not widely viewed with the horror which by 1908 characterized the European attitude. Possibly at that time American editors would still have been puzzled by Marks's vituperative tone. Her homophobic battle did not stop with the article, however. Three years later, in 1911, in *A Girl's Student Days and After,* she speaks again of the dangers of romantic friendship, although in a more subdued key. "There is no denying," she observes, "that there is great temptation to violent admirations and attractions in school," but, she warns, "a friend is too absorbing who takes all of one's interest to the exclusion of everything else; there should be interest in other people, other activities as well as in one's work. Such a friendship can only make a girl forget for what she has come to school." [70] In 1926 and 1927 she was considering the possibility of writing a book on homosexuality in literature, in which an emphasis would be on insanity and suicide associated with same-sex love.[71]

For reasons that will be discussed in the following chapters, such self-alienating behavior was not uncommon among twentieth-century women who lived in love relationships with other women before the rise of the lesbian-feminist movement in the early 1970's. Perhaps if these women carried remnants of Victorian sex hatred within them, they distinguished their relationships from "perversion," as Jeannette Marks may have, by refraining from genital activity. Or perhaps, as twentieth-century women who were also convinced that continence was unhealthy, they did not refrain and hated themselves and their lovers all the while. Those who remained whole persons and were not driven to insanity or suicide in an atmosphere that forced them to deny or loathe a love that was central to their lives were miracles indeed.

PART II

THE NINETEENTH CENTURY

B.
The Reaction

CHAPTER 1

The Rise of Antifeminism

The first glimmerings of a feminist movement in the nineteenth century immediately awoke an antifeminist movement. Surprisingly, many of the most articulate antifeminists were women who in some cases felt they had invested their whole beings in the old system and were chagrined suddenly to discover a new crop of women arising to tell them that they had "done it all wrong"; in other cases, as professional writers they cynically wrote to what they saw as the prevailing taste, hoping to make a fortune (as Mrs. Sarah Ellis did from her popular antifeminist tracts) and ignoring the fact that if antifeminists had their way, they would be cooking, cleaning, and nursing instead of writing antifeminist tracts. Elizabeth Lynn Linton, for example, a woman who by her own admission had grown up as a tomboy, was separated from her husband, and made a fine living as a novelist, essayist, and public figure, asserted in the preface to her 1883 collection, *The Girl of the Period and Other Social Essays*, "a public and professional life for a woman is incompatible with the discharge of their [sic] highest duties or the cultivation of their noblest qualities." [1]

There were, of course, plenty of males who attempted to nip feminism in the bud. The Prince's father in Tennyson's poem *The Princess* is speaking for many nineteenth-century men (although Tennyson implies he is something of an extreme) when he says, "Man for the field and woman for the hearth;/ Man for the sword and for the needle she;/ Man with the head and woman with the heart;/ Man to command and woman to obey;/ All else confusion." In America, G. J. Barker-Benfield observes, men thought it was

233

vital that women be kept in their places, since men believed their manhood was continually threatened by constant competition and anxiety over failure in the anarchic world of Jacksonian democracy.[2] Women had to be pinned to a secondary status for the sake of male ego survival. If women joined the competition, men would have no respite.

In England very popular antifeminist tracts began to appear in the 1830's. Although there was no organized feminist movement until the next decade, there were enough individual women around who spoke of legal equality and more independence to warrant a reaction. Mrs. Sandford was uttering society's official attitude against overt and covert female rebels in her 1831 book, *Woman in Her Social and Domestic Character*:

> There is something unfeminine in independence. It is contrary to nature, and therefore it offends. A really sensible woman feels her dependence, she does what she can, but she is conscious of her inferiority and therefore grateful for support. . . . In everything that women attempt they should show their consciousness of dependence.[3]

In any area in which a woman might wish to challenge her dependent role—education, marriage, occupations—scores of writers rose up to tell her she could not, and that if she did she would be hurting those dearest to her. For some years, Sarah Stickney Ellis complained in 1838 in *The Woman of England: Social Duties and Domestic Habits* (published a decade before women were allowed any higher education in England), women had been too concerned with the cultivation of mental faculties, leaving themselves no time for domestic usefulness. As a result, "the character of the women of England assumed a different aspect, which is now beginning to tell upon society in the sickly sensibilities, the feeble frames, and the useless habits of the rising generation." [4]

American women were given the same warnings in the popular books and magazines of the period. Even feminist writers learned that if they wished to write for and be read in the popular magazines, they had better modify their views to accord with the prevailing attitudes. For example, throughout the 1840's and 1850's, the articles that appeared in women's magazines such as *Godey's Lady's Book*, which was sympathetic to the struggle for higher education for women, invariably emphasized the point that such education was never to be attained at the expense of domestic virtues. "On what does social well-being rest but in our homes?" the authors typically reminded the readers.[5]

The women of America were also admonished that if they did not stop their drive to become educated and assertive, they would turn into men, whether in fact or in everyone's view of them. The anonymous author of the article, "Female Orators," which appeared in *The Mother's Magazine* in 1838, observed of intellectual women, "The Amazonians are their own executioners. They have unsexed themselves in public estimation, and there is no fear that they will perpetuate their race." [6] Henry F. Harrington, in an article entitled "Female Education," published in *Ladies Companion* the same year, warned that women who seek education are "semi-women" and "mental hermaphrodites." [7]

With the rise of an organized national feminist movement in America in 1848, literature which insisted that women must be silent and subordinate proliferated. A wife should busy herself only with trivial domestic matters unless called upon by her spouse to do otherwise, the author of *The Lady's Token: or, Gift of Friendship* (1848) advised: "Wait till your husband confides in you those of a high importance—and do not give your advice until he asks for it." [8] Some of the most reputedly enlightened minds of the era soon joined the attack, as is evident for example in a hostile and antifeminist article by Henry James, Sr. (the father of the novelist) which appeared in *Putnam's Magazine* in 1853.[9]

Education continued to come under particularly strong fire, since it was the chief enemy of the conservative forces: If women learned how to manage in the world as well as men, if they learned about history and politics and studied for a profession, of course they would soon be demanding a voice and a role outside the home. The medical doctors soon discovered that education was dangerous to a female's health. Dr. Edward Clarke in *Sex in Education; or, A Fair Chance for Girls* (1874) pointed out that a great variety of illnesses had suddenly beset the middle-class American girl because she was forcing her brain to use up the blood which she needed for menstruation.[10] The author of a *Popular Science Monthly* article observed in 1888 that since a woman's cranium is smaller than a man's and her brain is six ounces lighter, to educate her means to curse her with "nervousness, hysteria, hypochondriases, and insanity, . . . emaciation and other diseases, the offspring of an exhausted constitution." [11]

The London *Saturday Review* for February 7, 1857, in an article about the United States National Women's Rights Convention, which had been held annually from 1848 until the Civil War, suggested that if feminists were so smart they should "form a Grand United Female Railway Association to be stocked and engineered by women of experience in Bloomer costume." [12] But the British also had their own feminists to be outraged about. Satirical cartoons abounded in the periodicals, showing women breaking down the doors of offices, crocheting while they sat behind business desks, leaving husbands with screaming babies while they went off to take care of business. The popular writer, Dinah Craik, assured her readers that equality of the sexes was simply not in the nature of things: "A pretty state of matters would ensue! Who that ever listened for two hours to the verbose, confused inanities of a ladies' committee, would immediately go and give his vote for a female House of Commons?" [13] Such vituperative criticism continued throughout the century.

With women's increasing gains, modest as they were, the anxiety about gender distinction became more pronounced and somewhat confused. Horace Bushnell, for example, argued in 1869 that women should not be given the vote because they were so unlike men that they almost constituted a separate species.[14] Other writers said that the problem was that women were becoming too much like men, and the differences would soon be almost indiscernible. Elizabeth Lynn Linton knew that her complaint would be cheered by large segments of society when she wrote in her 1885 novel, *The Autobiography of Christopher Kirkland*:

> Equal political rights; identical professional careers; the man's virile force tamed down to harmony with the woman's feminine weakness; the abolition of all moral and social distinctions between the sexes;—these are the confessed objects of the movement whereby men are to be made lady-like and women masculine, till the two melt into one, and you scarcely know which is which.[15]

If things continued as they were going, the whole world would soon be topsy-turvy; the most sacred values of society would become as extinct as dinosaurs. Women's votes, the *Saturday Review* declared in 1871, would "endanger the institution of marriage and the family." [16]

Such anxieties were not, of course, limited to England and America. In France the emergence of a feminist movement in the first half of the century[17] brought predictable reactions. For example, while women's gains in formal education were quite scanty, writers such as Balzac hoped to see them stay that way: "I could more willingly tolerate a woman with a beard," he remarked, "than one who pretends to learning."[18] In Germany during the 1860's, though Marx had observed in *Das Kapital* that "the fact of the collective working group being composed of individuals of both sexes and all ages, must necessarily, under suitable conditions, become a source of humane development," the German Workers Association staged a massive campaign to keep women out of jobs, arguing that working women contributed to the "destruction of the family" and placed that institution in "a wretched state," its most ideal possession—the wife and mother—being removed.[19]

There can be no doubt that the slightest indication that women wanted to break out of some aspect of their traditional roles caused society great anxiety throughout the nineteenth century. As women actually began to make gains in achieving a modicum of independence during the middle and late 1800's, the degree of social anxiety rose proportionately. Those gains suggested to society (which is always by and large conservative and slow to alter a long-held system of values unless pushed to change quickly by the emergence of a powerful revolutionary force) that civilization—i.e., "the world as we know it"—was in grave danger. It is true enough that feminist gains had the potential of shaking the traditional family structure: If women could hope for an education and jobs and political equality, they had no need to marry unless they truly desired to. At a time when it was feared both in America[20] and England[21] that the birth rate was dipping dangerously low, young women could coolly choose whether or not to come to the aid of the Republic or the Empire— and many of them chose not to.

If they gained all the freedom that feminists agitated for, what would attract them to marriage? Not sex drive, since women still were not acknowledged to have one; possibly the longing for children—but women had been having children since the world began, while they were only just starting to be able to live like full human beings: a pretty heady prospect for a young woman with a pioneering spirit. Perhaps love for a man might draw a woman to marriage, although with the battle of the sexes raging even more virulently than ever, how could that magnet be relied on? But the desire for a home, the desire to share life with another human being, and loneliness, and the fear of living alone and dying alone—these might certainly draw a woman to marriage. However, if women on a large scale now had no hindrance in their freedoms, they might find kindred spirits, other women, and provide homes and solve the problem of loneliness for each other.

For the first time, love between women became threatening to the social structure.

Romantic friendship was not widely discouraged in England and America until the theories of the late nineteenth-century sexologists, which originated in Germany, became common knowledge at the turn of the century and later, and provided a weapon against same-sex love. But there were already suggestions of protest in the 1840's and throughout the century from a few writers who feared that love between women might replace marital love.[22] French "concern" developed earlier, perhaps because the French aesthete writers from the 1830's on delighted in exploring whatever had the potential to astound the bourgeoisie (it became a slogan: *épater le bourgeois*), and flaunted exotic images of sex between women in their poetry and prose. Combined later with the "knowledge" furnished by the sexologists and the annoyance of feminism, French anxiety about the potentials of female alliances rose to a fever pitch by the end of the century. To some extent it influenced the views of other countries as well. For example, according to an American psychiatrist writing in 1896, it was French romances that helped to open his eyes with regard to perverted sexual appetites which could cause a woman to entertain for another those emotions she should feel for the opposite sex alone.[23]

These factors taken together—the concern over the ramifications of women's increasing independence; the sexologists' theories which came along at a most convenient time to bolster arguments that a woman's desire for independence meant she was not really a woman; and the poetry and fiction of the French aesthetes which provided anxiety-provoking images of the sexual possibilities of love between women—guaranteed that romantic friendship, which had been encouraged by society in the past, would now be seen in a different, and most antisocial, light.

CHAPTER 2

The
Contributions of the Sexologists

In 1869 Carl von Westphal, a German psychiatrist, published a case study of a young woman who from childhood on preferred to dress as a boy and play boys' games, and had always been attracted to women,[1] like the transvestites of the eighteenth century, from Henrica Schuria who was given a public whipping to Deborah Sampson who was given a congressional pension. But Westphal identified her as a "congenital invert," whose abnormality was not acquired, not the result of a desire to transcend the boring, passive lot of women, but rather the result of hereditary degeneration and neurosis. She became a new type, and doctors began flooding the medical journals with papers on women like the one in Westphal's study.

Westphal's study came at an interesting time. As we have seen, women who demanded an education and job opportunities were called "unsexed" and "semi-women" as early as the 1830's, and as females gained more freedoms, there was ostensible concern that the distinction between the sexes would be obliterated. Westphal's article received some international attention not only in the medical journals but in fiction and in life as well.[2] Specious as that explanation was, it "explained" why some women had such a grave craving for independence from men. While Westphal's article was not circulated enough to have widespread influence on people's views, the works of those who were inspired by him were. Whether or not the process was a conscious one, those opposed to women's growing independence now could hurl, with credible support behind them, accusations of degeneracy at females who sought equality, and thereby

239

scare them back to the hearth with fears of abnormality. A lesbian, by the sexologists' definition, was one who rejected what had long been woman's role. She found that role distasteful because she was not really a woman—she was a member of the third sex. Therefore, she did not really represent women. All her emotions were inverted, turned upside down: Instead of being passive she was active, instead of loving domesticity, she sought success in the world outside, instead of making men prime in her life, she made first herself and then other women prime. She loved womankind more than mankind. Of course, love between women had been encouraged or tolerated for centuries—but now that women had the possibility of economic independence, such love became potentially threatening to the social order. What if women would seek independence, cut men out of their lives, and then find solace from loneliness by making what should have been "a rehearsal in girlhood of the great drama of a woman's life," the drama itself? Love between women was metamorphosed into a freakishness, and it was claimed that only those who had such an abnormality would want to change their subordinate status in any way. Hence, the sexologists' theories frightened, or attempted to frighten, women away from feminism and from loving other women by demonstrating that both were abnormal and were generally linked together.

While accusations of lesbianism did not entirely stop the feminists' progress over the last hundred years, it slowed it down significantly. Throughout much of our own century, women have been actively discouraged from achieving in the world by the argument that the drive to achieve means that a woman is abnormal and unfeminine.[3] When the feminist movement was reborn in the 1960's, its opponents tried hard to bring about its early death by hurling the "lavender herring" at it: Only lesbians would participate in such a movement, so if you're not a lesbian you'd better get out. . . . Or are you a lesbian? Certainly it frightened some women away from feminism. Even the founder of the National Organization for Women, Betty Friedan, was beset with anxiety because she feared that lesbianism, or rather the public's suspicion of its existence, would destroy feminism. Friedan went to great trouble to deny that women who love women are a significant part of the women's movement—until feminists defused the issue by proclaiming that it was fine to love other women, and continued their demands for better jobs and better laws.

* * *

The two most influential disciples of Westphal were Richard von Krafft-Ebing (*Psychopathia Sexualis*, 1882) and Havelock Ellis (*Studies in the Psychology of Sex: Sexual Inversion*, 1897). Both writers cast love between women in a morbid light and associated it with behavior which had nothing to do with same-sex love but did have a great deal to do with the insanity of some of the patients they examined (who in these cases happened to focus their primary interests on women, just as other female psychotics have focused their primary interests on men). Ellis, for example, began his discussion of female homosexuals in the nineteenth century (in the chapter entitled "Sexual Inversion in Women") with the story of Alice Mitchell, whom he called a "typical invert," who "cut [her lover's] throat." This he followed by two other cases of lesbian murder and attempted murder. Next he stated, "Homosexual relationships are also a cause of suicide among women"—with the apparent implication that heterosexual relationships are not.[4] Although Ellis suggested throughout his study that many talented and gifted people have been homosexual and that (ostensibly disagreeing with Krafft-Ebing) homosexuality is not necessarily linked with morbidity, the emphases in all his case histories of women lead the reader to precisely the opposite conclusion.

Krafft-Ebing's work, by which Ellis was largely influenced, expanded on Westphal's study, pointing out that lesbianism was due to "cerebral anomalies," that it was the sign of "an inherited diseased condition of the central nervous system" and a "functional sign of degeneration." This inherited condition he consistently referred to as "taint."[5] While later writers such as Iwan Bloch, Magnus Hirschfeld, and John Addington Symonds agreed that homosexuality was congenital, they rejected Krafft-Ebing's views that the condition was also pathological,[6] but Havelock Ellis largely accepted those views,[7] and it was his book on sexual inversion that remained for years one of the most influential treatises on homosexuality written in English.[8] Hence, it was primarily through Krafft-Ebing and Ellis's writings that the twentieth century received its stereotypes of lesbian morbidity.

Both writers developed a category of the "true invert," which they distinguished from prepubescent homosexual behavior and *faute de mieux* homosexuality. The main way to distinguish normal women from true inverts, Ellis argued, was that normal women, when given the opportunity to have relationships with men, would bring their "normal instincts . . . into permanent play."[9]

Ellis, like his predecessor, generally ignored the role of social pressure in establishing this "normal instinct," although he occasionally hinted, without taking the point to its obvious conclusion, that socialization and peer pressure or support might have something to do with whatever sexual feelings the nineteenth-century woman ultimately accepted as being appropriate for herself. With regard to the subsequent marriage of women who had regularly fallen in love with their female classmates when they were students, Ellis observed that once they participated in "practical life," they learned to understand "the real nature of such feelings," and they developed a subsequent distaste for them" [10] and a taste for men and marriage. But it is obvious that throughout much of the nineteenth century, women were obliged to marry if they could for economic reasons alone, and by the late 1890's, when many women no longer needed to get married since they could support themselves, they learned from the outside world that loving another female was considered perversion ("the real nature of such feelings"), and thus they realized they must repress those emotions.

Ellis largely ignored the significance and the "normality" of romantic friendship, which was still socially acceptable in mid-nineteenth-century England when he was growing up.[11] However, he saw the connection between feminism and love between women. He claimed to support women's rights, but he was ambivalent at best: The women's movement, he said, has "involved an increase in feminine criminality and in feminine insanity. . . . In connection with these we can scarcely be surprised to find an increase in homosexuality, which has always been regarded as belonging to an allied, if not the same, group of phenomena." The women's movement taught women to be independent and to disdain "the old theory which placed women in the moated grange of the home to sigh for a man who never comes," Ellis pointed out; but such independence often led to homosexual behavior, especially if women took jobs, since at work they would come into frequent contact with like-minded women and they might "find love where they find work." He was quick to state in this regard that a woman who has been led to homosexuality through feminism is very likely not a real lesbian, but only a "spurious imitation" unless she was born with the "germs" of inversion. In such a case, the women's movement might "promote hereditary neurosis." [12] He also singled out women of the professional and middle classes (in apparent contradiction to his earlier points about violent lesbian lowlife) as being most prone to inversion—at least 10 percent of them are "abnormal," he guessed.[13]

How, according to Ellis, can one distinguish between the "spurious imitation" of the lesbian and the "true invert"? His case histories established the criteria: One common phenomenon appears with almost uniform consistency in true inverts—the tendency of these women to have had girlhood crushes on other females. A second phenomenon, which *is* consistent in all his case histories, is congenital taint:

> Case XXIX, Miss S.: ". . . She belongs to a family in which there is a marked neuropathic element."
>
> Case XL, Miss M.: ". . . There is a neurotic element in the family."
>
> Case XLI, Miss B.: ". . . Among her brothers and sisters, one is of neurotic temperament and another is inverted."
>
> Case XLII, Miss H.: ". . . Among her maternal relatives there is a tendency to eccentricity and to nervous disease."

In insisting on the prevalence of congenital taint among homosexuals, Ellis seems to have ignored the common sense of his supposed collaborator, John Addington Symonds, who pointed out that at that moment in Europe there was probably not a single person who had inherited no neuropathic stain whatsoever.[14] Ellis also seems to have ignored his own observation that "normal" girl children frequently indulged in same-sex crushes and erotic play.

A third phenomenon which, according to Ellis, distinguished "the actively inverted woman" from females who have schoolgirl crushes and *faute de mieux* lesbians, is "a more or less distinct trace of masculinity."[15] But despite this assertion, when Ellis described the physical characteristics of the subjects of his case histories, he often admitted that "the general conformation of the body is feminine" or that "her person and manners, though careless, are not conspicuously man-like."[16] The seeming discrepancy is explained with the statement that such masculinity "may, in the least degree, consist only in the fact that she makes advances to the women to whom she is attracted."[17] This somewhat contradicts Ellis's theories about *faute de mieux* homosexuality in schools and prisons, since it means that at least one of the women in any same-sex love relationship is probably the real thing.

Ellis never suggests that the difference between a "true invert" and a normal female lies in the invert's interest in genital sex with other women. One would, in fact, be hard put to find a difference between Miss M. (whom Ellis identifies as a "true invert") and a woman who was a "romantic friend." He quotes Miss M. as saying, "I love few people . . . but in those instances when I have permitted my heart to go out to a friend I have always experienced most exalted feelings, and have been made better by them morally, mentally, and spiritually. Love is with me a religion. The very nature of my affections for my friends precludes the possibility of any element entering into it which is not absolutely sacred." So what makes her an invert? A year previous to her interview with Ellis, she had come across a translation of Krafft-Ebing's book. Before reading it she had no notion that her sentiments were anything other than a manifestation of love for a particular person, but from the book she learned that "feelings like mine were 'unnatural and depraved' and 'under the ban of society.' " [18] One wonders how many romantic friends, who had felt themselves to be perfectly healthy before, suddenly saw themselves as sick, even though their behavior had in no way changed, as a result of the sexologists' formulations.[19]

Although most of his case histories pointed in another direction, Ellis repeatedly tried to associate lesbianism with transvestism, from the beginning of his chapter "Sexual Inversion in Women," when he referred to sixteenth- and seventeenth-century women who were executed for dressing in male attire and using dildos. This association is emphasized by his report on the Countess Sarolta V. (appendix E of his book), based on a medicolegal account published a few years earlier in Friedreich's *Blätter für Gerichtliche Medicin*. The totally bizarre case of Countess Sarolta is briefly referred to in the "Sexual Inversion in Women" chapter as being *"in most respects so typical"* (the italics are mine) of true lesbians.[20] Sarolta came from a family which had always been remarkable for eccentricity. One aunt was hysterical and somnambulistic; another aunt "lay in bed for seven years on account of an imaginary fatal illness," but at the same time gave balls; a third aunt believed that the console in her drawing room was bewitched; and a fourth aunt would not allow her room to be cleaned and would not wash or comb herself for two years. Her mother was "nervous and could not bear the moonshine." Her father's family was "generally regarded as rather crack-brained."

Sarolta's father educated her as a boy and his two sons as girls. The sons were dressed in women's clothing until they were fifteen.

The father traveled extensively with Sarolta, insisting usually that she dress as a man. In 1888 at the age of *twenty-two* (Ellis observed that until that point her affairs had been typically brief—in conformity with a stereotype of flightiness he wished to establish—with the exception of one previous relationship that had lasted for *three years!*), she met a woman who believed her to be a man. The following year they were married. Sarolta deceived her bride's family by stuffing handkerchiefs or gloves into her trouser's pocket to produce the appearance of male sexual organs and by urinating in a standing position. When she was arrested because of some financial difficulty with her father-in-law, one of her greatest concerns was about having to give up her masculine garments in jail.

Ellis emphasized that Sarolta "recognized the morbidity of her sexual inclinations," i.e., her love for other women. And he concluded by reiterating the expert opinion on her case that her "incriminated actions" were "due to her marked and irresistible sexual impulse." Through this incredible case, which he specifically called "typical," Ellis established the mystique of the "true lesbian," a mystique which was subsequently accepted by many lesbians themselves who then became transvestites and "butches" because such behavior demonstrated *ipso facto* that they were the genuine article, that they must be taken seriously and not forced into heterosexual patterns.

While Ellis devoted a section of his work (Appendix D) to establishing how entirely common erotic love between young women was in his day, he pointedly invalidated the seriousness of such love relationships by describing them as "school-friendships of girls"—although some of the females included in this study were women in their twenties, and although he admitted, "these friendships are often found among girls who have left school" [21] and thus cannot be considered "school-friendships" at all.

Appendix D, "The School-Friendships of Girls," begins with an Italian study by two medical men, Obici and Marchesini, who observed female pupils between the ages of twelve and twenty in late nineteenth-century Italian normal schools.[22] They discovered that the "flame" (or "rave," "spoon," "crush"—i.e., same-sex infatuation or love among young people) was in every college "regarded as a necessary institution," [23] and that although it was often nongenital, "all the sexual manifestations of college youth circle around it," and "all the gradations of sexual sentiment" were expressed within it.[24]

Obici and Marchesini made clear that such a relationship was in no way simple friendship. Its beginning generally took the form of "a regular courtship": The one who was struck first would take frequent walks in the garden when the other was likely to be at her window; she would pause on the stairs to see her beloved pass; she was filled with "a mute adoration made up of glances and sighs"; she would send her beloved flowers, little messages, and finally "long and ardent letters of declaration." [25]

The two doctors had read over three hundred love letters which had been "carefully preserved by the receivers." From these letters they concluded that the "flame" generally arose from a "physical sympathy," an admiration for the physical form and style of the beloved. The letters themselves are "full of passion; they appear to be often written during periods of physical excitement and psychic erethism."

Obici and Marchesini specifically enumerated almost a dozen points which distinguished these relationships from ordinary friendships, among them: the frequent exchange of love letters; anxiety to be together, to embrace and kiss; persistent jealousy; exaltation of the beloved's qualities; determination to conquer all obstacles to the manifestation of the love; and pleasure of conquest.[26]

In addition to the Obici and Marchesini study, Ellis cited similar research from England and America. His English informant also distinguished between a friendship and—as it was commonly known in English girls' schools and women's colleges—a "rave": The young woman with a rave often had several intimate friends for whom she felt affection without the emotion, the pleasurable excitement, and the more or less erotic response characteristic of a rave. Those who had afterward fallen in love with men said that the emotions called forth in both cases were similar.[27] The American study of such relationships was carried out at Clark University in Worcester, Massachusetts, by E. G. Lancaster, and published in *Pedagogical Seminary*, July 1897. Lancaster studied the emotional lives of over eight hundred teachers and older pupils. Although his research questionnaires contained nothing about same-sex love, Lancaster reported that a large number of his respondents voluntarily offered information about their homosexual experiences, which led him to conclude that love of the same sex was very common especially among young people, that such emotion was not in any way "mere friendship," but rather "the love is strong, real, and passionate" and contains "the same characteristics of intensity and devotion that are ordinarily associated with heterosexual love." [28]

Lancaster also observed that "raves" among females were in some schools so much a "fashion" that "hardly anyone [was] free from it," and any student newly entering the school "would soon fall victim to the fashion." Occasionally there would be a "lull in the general raving," and after an interval it would appear again "in more or less of an epidemic form." [29] Ellis once more did not take this point to its logical conclusion: It would seem that homosexual passion or lack of it might often be dictated by what one's immediate environment admits as an appropriate passion, in the same way that large-breasted women are "in" with regard to male heterosexual interest in some eras and "out" in other eras. Erotic love has perhaps far less to do with innate instinct and more with "fashion" than most sexual theorists have recognized.

Obici and Marchesini estimated the frequency of flames in normal schools at about 60 percent—to which a collaborator added the observation that of the remaining 40 percent half did not indulge "because they are not sufficiently pleasing in appearance or because their characters do not inspire sympathy," [30] i.e., as much as 80 percent of all the females described in the study would have liked to or did experience romantic relationships with other females.

Since of this 80 percent none of the subjects were specifically known to come from neuropathic families or to be "masculine" in any respect, how did Ellis explain the apparent frequency (i.e., "normality") of same-sex love? He pointed out that while there is "an unquestionable sexual element in the flame relationship," such a relationship cannot be regarded as an absolute expression of "real congenital perversion of the sex-instinct." [31] That it is a spurious imitation of homosexuality is evidenced not only by the fact that these females eventually slip into a heterosexual life-style, but also by the fact that the phenomenon is so widespread. He seems to reason thus: If the majority of females experience this type of same-sex love, it cannot be "abnormal," but neither is it real. Real inversion is something else—identifiable by characteristics which the majority of these young women do not share. In this way Ellis rejected as being "spurious imitations" all manifestations of same-sex love that proved it was entirely common; he characterized as being indicative of "true inversion" any trait that could be identified as morbid— a marked neuropathic heredity, a strain of violence, a penchant for transvestism—and he coupled these ills with feminism.

His immediate disciples, such as Thoinot, who saw apparent flaws in Ellis's theory dealt with those flaws not by calling the theory into question but by building on it. For example, how could one explain the phenomenon of a woman who was married and had children but who later became sexually involved with another woman? She suffered from a congenital inversion which did not show itself until late in life; i.e., "retarded inversion," as Thoinot called it in 1898.[32]

The sexologists thus created a third sex, which, they said, was characterized by a neurotic desire to reject what had hitherto been women's accepted role, and by an emotion which they called "inverted"—an emotion that had for hundreds of years been recognized as normal. Their theories had considerable impact on the medical profession and on women themselves. In the preface to the twelfth edition of *Psychopathia Sexualis*, Krafft-Ebing observed that his book's great "commercial success is the best proof that large numbers of unfortunate people find in its pages instruction and relief in the frequently enigmatical manifestation of sexual life." As a result of Krafft-Ebing's pioneering efforts, between 1898 and 1908 in Germany alone more than a thousand articles and books on homosexuality were published.[33] The impact of the sexologists' theories around the turn of the century was also shown in the formation of groups like the Scientific Humanitarian Committee, which was devoted to explaining the third sex to the world.[34] Although it was to be another decade or two more before the general public would become aware of the sexologists' theories, views toward love between women had already begun to change significantly.

Men who loved men were happy to accept the scientific explanation that their feelings were due to a congenital problem, because it was expedient. During the nineteenth century and even into the twentieth century, throughout much of Europe and America there were laws that made sexual relations between men illegal (women were largely ignored by nineteenth-century law, although in Austria they risked the same punishments as men). Those laws implied that the reason homosexuality was illegal was because it was a vice. The congenitalists, however, showed that it was not a vice but a condition with which one was born. This meant that it was neither sinful nor catching, and the laws against it were superfluous.

But why did women accept and, like Ellis's Miss M., internalize such views of love between women? Perhaps because to resist would have taken more self-confidence than fledgling full human beings (which women were just becoming around the turn of the century) could muster. How could they have told a great portion of the medical profession, which had intimidated women even to death throughout the century,[35] that it was all wet, or that its motives, conscious or unconscious, were suspect. Or, perhaps women accepted the congenital theory because, ironically it attributed a seriousness to independent women which they had never been granted before: Yes, they were different; they needed to make their own livings, they had no interest in men or marriage, and they preferred the company of their own sex—because they were born that way, and no amount of threatening or cajoling or tempting would change them. Thus while the sexologists' theories discouraged feminism on the one hand by linking it to abnormality, on the other hand they gave to strong feminists who would not be diverted from their goals a staff which helped them continue in their direction unmolested—or so they hoped.

By the beginning of the next century, some feminists wore "inversion" as a badge of which they were proud. In a 1903 German novel by Aimée Duc, *Sind es Frauen?* (*Are These Women?*), the author repeatedly insists through her characters that women like these must never marry, that they are intended for another life. While their love is given only to other women, that other life takes its shape not primarily through love but through work. One character is a doctor, another a medical student, several are studying for Ph.D.'s. They reject "romantic love" such as women indulge in with men because, as one says, "I believe that being in love makes you unfree, and I think that the highest good is to maintain the freedom of one's self." Another asserts that the person who is occupied "intellectually very intensively and energetically doesn't have very much time to think about the fulfillment of love." Women's major problem, they agree, is that they suffer "from lack of work and intellectual training and therefore [they] become such easy victims of unhappy love." The characters' arguments are pure feminism, but they have already been taught by the sexologists that normal women do not think that way and that they have such sentiments only because they are congenitally different. They are happy enough to accept the label of themselves as "Krafft-Ebingers," as one woman says, as long as it permits them to retain their "own intellectual and physical freedom and also preserve for ourselves, who aren't breeders, our human rights!" Their compromise is logical: Before the sexologists, every attempt would have been made (if not by relatives and friends specifically, then by general inculcation through society) to convince such women that as soon as they found the right men they would give up their pretentious pursuits and raise a family. Without the sexologists' theories about why some women were different, they may have believed themselves that with time their "normal instincts" would win out, and so they may not have been able to give so much of their whole-hearted energies to their pursuits.

The sexologists rescued them, in effect, by furnishing what appeared to be a plausible theory explaining why they should be allowed to pursue their goals in peace. Of course, they also loved women—but so did most other women. It was not their homoeroticism that made them willing to call themselves Krafft-Ebingers but their desire for freedom.

The sexologists' theories and women's increasing mobility soon created a separate self-conscious society of women who now identified themselves as "inverts." [36] In Germany, where the impact of the first theorists, who were for the most part German, was felt earliest and most strongly, a new lesbian society was flourishing by the turn of the century. Xavier Mayne observed in 1908 that in German cities "where the 'Emancipation' of feminine interests has obtained," there were lesbian assemblies and artists' balls attended "by the best element of female aesthetic life" and other professional women.[37] Many of these women had had their first ties with the women's movement. Now they emerged as a separate society, which was still feminist, and they began to call on the women's movement to come to their aid, since the two were inextricably linked.[38] The response was quite favorable.[39]

Not all feminists viewed themselves as lesbian, of course, although it was pointed out that the strongest and most energetic leadership came from women who also called themselves homosexual.[40] It would seem that some feminists identified themselves as homosexual and others as heterosexual not because of congenital differences and early traumas or the lack of them, but rather because of the immediate chance circumstances of their lives; for example, were they able to maintain emotional ties with a romantic friend or had she married? Had they met a sympathetic male who promised to assist them in their feminist goals, or had their suitors attempted to talk them out of all that nonsense? Had they met within the movement a compatible woman, unencumbered and with the same goals, who was open to intimate friendship? The desire for one kind of genital sex over another was not the major issue in their "sexual identification." Nor would it have occurred to most of them, all of whom were raised in a Victorian era, that genital sex could be the major issue.

It would not be possible for most women of our era, with all our post-Freudian, Masters and Johnson sophistication, to conceive of an *erotic* love relationship without genital sex. Turn-of-the-century women could easily imagine such a situation. Vida Scudder, a writer and a Wellesley College professor, and the lifelong romantic friend of the novelist Florence Converse (*Diana Victrix*), was probably representative of many women who were born in the Victorian era. Writing in 1937, as an old woman, retired for ten years from the Wellesley faculty, she looks back on her friendships, and especially on her romantic friendship with Florence Converse: She observes that such a relationship "approaches nearer and nearer to that absolute union, always craved, never on earth at least, to be attained," [41] and that "more than any other sublunar forces, it initiates us into the eternal. When it has not been born of illusion, it can never die, though strange interludes may befall it, though loyalty may need to be now and again invoked to supplement desire. Its drama normally knows no end, for death sets the seal on the union. . . . In the Ever-Living land, lover and beloved move together." [42] In her Victorian psyche, her passion, which combines the mystical with the erotic, must stop short of the genital if it is to remain fine. But apparently that was no burden to her or to many other women who had learned to ignore the "sexual instinct" in the nineteenth century. Scudder protests that the emphasis on sex in our lives is overdone. Freud, she says, is responsible, "and he has much to answer for." She confesses to being puzzled that one should find it necessary to "pay so much attention to one type of experience in this marvelous, this varied, this exciting world. . . . A woman's life in which sex interests have never visited, is a life neither dull nor empty nor devoid of romance." [43] Her romances, she admits, have been with other women.

Elisabeth Dauthendey reveals in *Of the New Woman and Her Love* (see page 156), that confusion arose for some women when they tried to cope with the notion of genital sex as a component of love between women. Dauthendey shows that women who wished to escape the grossness of men and to pursue careers formed love relationships with other women. And they shared a bed together and the "ardor of deep blissful joy." But, Dauthendey says, such love has nothing to do with the "impure advances of sapphists." The confusion was compounded when even some of those who accepted the label "sapphist," such as Ellis's Miss M., also would have nothing to do with genital sex, since it would interfere with their "most exalted feelings." To many middle-class "proper" women raised in the nineteenth century, whether they identified themselves as "normal" or "inverted," genital sex remained the great bugaboo which, circumstances permitting, they preferred to ignore or deny.

Considering the models of inversion that Krafft-Ebing, Havelock Ellis, and their disciples presented (e.g., Alice Mitchell, the "typical invert" who cut her lover's throat), it was inevitable that many women fled into heterosexual marriage or developed great self-loathing or self-pity if they accepted the label of "invert." By the early twentieth century, European popular literature, influenced largely by the sexologists, was referring to "thousands of unhappy beings" who "experience the tragedy of inversion in their lives," [44] and to passions which "end in madness or suicide." [45] In the popular imagination, love between women was becoming identified with disease, insanity, and tragedy. It soon became a condition for which women were advised to visit a doctor and have both a physical and mental examination.

In view of this, it is astonishing that many women managed to keep their equilibrium so well. It must have taken an unusual amount of strength and maturity. Perhaps their lives as independent, whole women with serious concerns in the world helped them to develop those qualities, and to see themselves as healthy and productive, despite society's assessment of their life-styles. Although such women never seemed to appear in sexologist case studies, the "contrasexual" author of an autobiographical essay published in a German homosexual yearbook for 1901 was probably representative of many women of her class: She relates one professional success after another in her life and her excellent fortune in her beloved companion. She ends by exhorting others to her own optimism and sense of well-being:

> Take this courage, my sisters, and show that you have as much
> right to exist and to love as the "normal" world! Defy this
> world and they will tolerate you, they will acknowledge you,
> and they will even envy you! Raise the weapons! You must and

will succeed. I've done it. Why shouldn't you all, every single one of you, succeed? [46]

But voices such as hers were drowned in the sludge of medical literature and popular novels that were published over the next decades.

CHAPTER 3

Lesbian Exoticism

At the beginning of the chapter entitled "Sexual Inversion in Women," Havelock Ellis refers to a number of examples of lesbianism taken from French literature, together with some from French life, and makes little distinction between them. He mentions Diderot's *The Nun*, Balzac's *The Girl with the Golden Eyes*, Zola's *Nana*, Belot's *Mademoiselle Giraud, My Wife*, and fiction or poetry by de Maupassant, Bouget, Daudet, Mendès, and Verlaine.[1] In 1890, shortly before Ellis began "Sexual Inversion in Women," he went to Paris for three months with the aesthete British writer, Arthur Symons, and met other French literary men who dealt with homosexuality in their work.[2] Ellis's theories regarding love between women were influenced not only by what he saw, or thought he saw, in English life, but also by what he read in French fiction and what he discussed with its creators. Those literary images, which became incorporated in Ellis's views and in the views of the many who regarded his work as "medically" accurate and reliable, were based on a reaction by male French writers to some dramatic signs of female independence, as well as those writers' fascination with exoticism and their express desire to shock the stiff, prudish bourgeoisie.

It is no coincidence that nineteenth-century novels dealing with the sexual possibilities of love between women began to appear in some number with the first glimmerings of a feminist movement in France during the late 1820's and the 1830's.[3] Henri Latouche's *Fragoletta* (1829) deals with a woman who disguises herself as a man and seduces another woman. This book was followed a few years

The Memoirs of Casanova. Illustration by Chauvet. A late nineteenth-century privately printed edition of this eighteenth-century work.

THE

Female Husband:

OR, THE

SURPRISING

HISTORY

OF

Mrs. *MARY*,

ALIAS

Mr GEORGE HAMILTON,

Who was convicted of having married a YOUNG WOMAN of *WELLS* and lived with her as her HUSBAND.

TAKEN FROM

Her own MOUTH since her Confinement.

—— *Quoque id mirum magis esset in illo ;*
Fæmina natus erat. Monstri novitate moventur,
Quisquis adest : narretque rogant. ——
OVID Metam. Lib. 12.

LONDON:
Printed for M. COOPER, at the Globe in Pater-
noster-Row. 1746.

Title page of *The Female Husband* (1746) by Henry Fielding.

IN DEBORAH SAMPSON'S CASE, THE LASS WHO LOVED A
SOLDIER HAD A RUDE AWAKENING

Deborah Sampson, a soldier of the American Revolution. Woodcut. (THE BETTMAN ARCHIVE)

Anna Seward

LLANGOLLEN BLUE GUIDE SHEETS

PLAS NEWYDD
and the LADIES

Eleanor Butler and Sarah Ponsonby
from the portrait by Mary Parker

The Ladies of Llangollen

Mary Wollstonecraft

Maria Corelli

Edith Sommerville

Miss Marks and Miss Woolley (MOUNT HOLYOKE COLLEGE LIBRARY/
ARCHIVES)

Mademoiselle de Maupin—
A Third distinct sex—
The body and soul of a woman
The mind and power of a man.

(*Above left*) The Marquise de St. Réal and Paquita. "Meurs! Souffre mille morts! s'écria la marquise." From *The Girl with the Golden Eyes* (1835) by Honoré de Balzac. Illustration by Louis-Edouard Fournier. (*Above right*) *Mademoiselle de Maupin* (1835) by Théophile Gautier. Privately printed by The Pierre Louÿs Society, 1927. (*Above*) "The Witches Sabbath" by Sir John Lindsay, 1898.

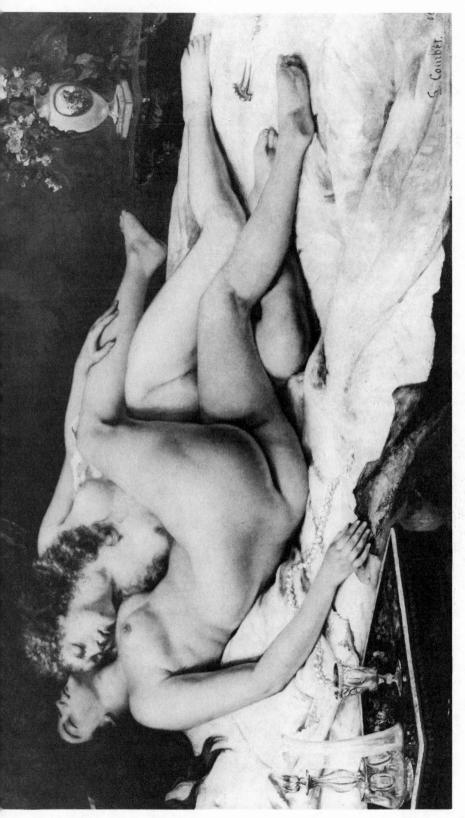

"Sleep" by Gustave Courbet, 1866.

"Si je la vois, mon coeur s'arrête." ("When I see her my heart stops.")
The Songs of Bilitis (1894) by Pierre Louÿs.

octeau.
karika-
keines
ibrigen
rch die
ιumiers
ιrzt der
Медizin
Auf die
ʒe ihrer
ck ver-
ᴇn Mit-

ᴇn, dass
Aerzte-
ᴇtwa 20
ist sehr
ı Kritik

Sigmund Freud, a drawing by
Jean Cocteau.

Havelock Ellis

(*Above left*) Alice B. Toklas and Harriet Levy. COURTESY, THE BANCROFT LIBRARY. (*Above right*) Alice B. Toklas and Gertrude Stein (THE BETTMAN ARCHIVE)(*Below left*) Vita Sackville-West, 1924. (*Below right*) Colette and Willy, her husband.

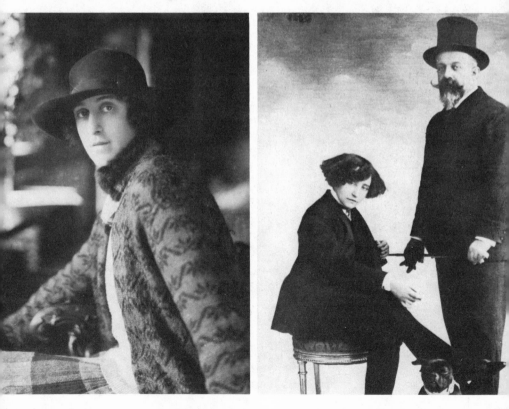

The Ladder
a Lesbian Review

acme

August, 1967

(*Left*) *The Ladder.* August, 1967, cover. (*Below*) "Kady and Pagan," PHOTOGRAPH BY JEB © 1979 FROM *Eye to Eye: Portraits of Lesbians.*

later by two other novels with androgynous female characters who made love to other women—Théophile Gautier's *Mademoiselle de Maupin* and Honoré de Balzac's *The Girl with the Golden Eyes.* Mario Praz in *The Romantic Agony* suggests that the frequent literary appearance of the transvestite woman who seduces another woman was due to George Sand: For the cliché of the transvestite lesbian to be created, he postulates, it is necessary that a particular figure make a profound impression on the popular imagination, as Sand did in Paris in the early 1830's.[4] "Thanks especially to George Sand," Praz says, "the vice of Lesbianism became extremely popular."[5]

However, the appearance of Latouche's book two years prior to Sand's arrival in Paris suggests that even before Sand's figure became so well known in French literary circles, there were fears about women who refused to be simply feminine. But Sand became the embodiment of those fears. Not only did she refuse to be hampered by women's clothes and to take the passive role in her various relationships with the effeminate men who became her lovers, but she was also an articulate feminist. In *Letters to Marcie* (1837), six fictional letters regarding woman's plight, she complained, "In heroic days you might have been Joan of Arc, Madame Roland, Héloise. But what might you be today? Try to find a single position anywhere in the social hierarchy, on any level of government or industry, which you might think of occupying without being ridiculous. Only the role of artist is open to you," (letter I), and "Women are allowed a deplorable education. That is men's worst crime. Masculine abuses against women are everywhere, supported by the most sacred institutions. Men have even played upon women's most innocent and legitimate emotions. They have been able to enslave and degrade women, and now they claim that women's condition was established by God and is part of immutable law," (letter VI). In her autobiography, *Story of My Life* (1854–1855), she railed further against the double standard, masculine insensitivity, and unjust marriage and property laws.

In addition, she conducted several well-publicized romantic friendships with women, beginning with the actress Marie Dorval in 1833. Speculation about Sand's erotic practices may have been especially encouraged by the first edition of her novel *Lélia* which was published the same year. In this work Pulchérie confesses to Lélia that she watched her as she slept and received "my first lesson in love, my first sensation of desire." No doubt Paris, whose moral fiber was bourgeois no matter how hard the artists tried to rebel against it, gleefully believed that someone as promiscuous and unconventional as Sand would not neglect to do the most shocking things with another woman as well as with men, given the opportunity.[6] Tongues must have wagged later in her career also when Sand frequently dined with the scandalous poet-actress Adah Isaacs Menken, and both women wore men's clothes.[7] Such behavior was disturbing even to the most enlightened French, who preferred not to be confused about sex roles. It caused Victor Hugo, for example, to complain that Sand "cannot decide whether she is female or male."[8]

But feminism and the dramatic, disturbing figure of George Sand (who was known personally by writers like Gautier, Balzac, and Zola) do not alone explain why suddenly the lesbian became almost a stock image in a certain school of nineteenth-century French literature. This was largely due to the hostility of the aesthetes to middle-class morality: *Épater le bourgeois* became the artist's cry from the 1830's onward. This hostility was forcefully articulated by Théophile Gautier, whose *Mademoiselle de Maupin* (1835) became the bible of aesthetic-decadent literature,[9] and whose title character became a prototype of the lesbian in literature for decades afterward. The literary image by which Gautier was immediately influenced in his characterization of Mlle. de Maupin was that of Fragoletta in Latouche's novel. Gautier even transposed into a poem, "Contralto," a section of his predecessor's novel which deals with a statue of a hermaphrodite: "Is it a young man? is it a woman?/. . . Love, fearing to be infamous,/Hesitates and suspends its opinion./. . . To make such accursed beauty,/Each sex gives its gift." The poem hints why, in a work dedicated to shocking the bourgeoisie, Gautier would choose as his heroine a person who could pass equally for a man and a woman, who could have sexual relations with a male, and, minutes later, visit the bed of a female for, presumably, similar relations. What could be more infamous, more accursed, more shocking to the bourgeois mind which cannot deal in ambiguities than an individual who is not completely masculine or completely feminine? And what could be more shocking —and more titillating—to the artist himself, who was also brought up as a bourgeois and retained the mark of those values on his psyche? The artist thumbed his nose at those values in an attempt to exorcise them from within himself, but he believed nevertheless that sexual ambiguity was "infamous" and "accursed."

In his 1835 preface to his novel, Gautier expressed his disgust at the "rehabilitation of virtue undertaken by all the journals" in France of his day. France, which before the July Revolution had been a country ruled by *joie de vivre*, did an about-face, Gautier lamented. It was now ruled and ruined by the bourgeois temperament (and by Louis Philippe, who was called the Bourgeois King). The artist needed to stand apart, to assert himself, or he would be drowned in the bourgeois surge of power. He could distinguish himself most from the bourgeoisie by attacking what they held most dear—their morality (i.e., their antisexuality).[10] Virtue, Gautier exclaimed in his preface, is a grandmother, and he preferred something coquettish and a little immoral. "But it is the fashion now to be Virtuous and Christian," he complained. "People have taken a turn for it. They affect Saint Jerome as formerly they affected Don Juan. . . . They speak of the sacredness of art, the lofty mission of the artist, the poetry of Catholicism." Gautier's response to their boring ideals was to jar them by the most shocking and novel images conceivable. What would be more upsetting to them than the idea of a lovely woman from a good class behaving like a sexual creature?—two such women behaving like sexual creatures, together! To Gautier and his aesthete-decadent disciples, the lesbian became a fabricated fantasy image of what would most upset (and arouse) the reader—an image as consciously contrived as the dead woman in Edgar Allan Poe's "The Philosophy of Composition," who would be "the most poetical topic in the world," since she would be the embodiment of what is most melancholy (death) and what is most beautiful (a woman).

Gautier chose to ignore love between women as expressed by so many of his middle-class contemporaries. His emphasis was on the wild and exotic. Gautier's lesbian, a beautiful young woman who looks equally stunning when dressed as a man, flaunts her sexual nature and refuses classification in either of the two sexes (which the French much preferred to think of as being strictly discrete categories: *vive la différence*). Mademoiselle de Maupin explains that traveling in male guise, with a young girl as her companion, she has been happy to pay her "little darling" all the attentions which women normally require from men, such as assisting her on difficult roads, holding her bridle or stirrup, defending her if anyone insulted her, undressing her and putting her to bed, "in short, doing everything for her that the most impassioned and attentive lover does for a mistress he adores." If a man had

shown her such attentions, Maupin declares, it would have dis-
pleased her extremely, since her feminist pride is much better
suited to playing an active rather than passive role in a relationship.
Yet she is a *femme fatale* as far as men are concerned, and the hero
of the novel, d'Albert, falls madly in love with her. He is permitted
to bed her once and taste bliss, to make his longing all the more
poignant (but also to assure the reader that like all women she is
attainable). However, unlike the typical nineteenth-century heroine
who becomes pregnant and dies of grief afterward, Maupin rides off
into the sunrise, having first stopped to show off her newfound
knowledge of genital sex to d'Albert's old mistress, Rosette, who is
also in love with her. Maupin explains that she belongs to a "third,
distinct sex, which as yet has no name." She has "the body and soul
of a woman, the mind and power of a man, and . . . too much or
too little of both to be able to pair with either."

There is a certain jejune quality that underlies the creation of
Maupin, who is calculated to outrage. She is shocking only if one
is disturbed by female independence and sexual ambiguity. But
it is doubtful that Gautier understood much about those attributes
as they existed outside his fantasy. Gautier phallocentrically has
Maupin initially assuming male dress and independence, not in
logical protest against the acknowledged inanity of her female existence, as did the transvestites discussed in Part I of this book,
but only because she believed that men led a very different life
when not in the company of the virgins, and she wished "to be
able to see men and study them thoroughly before giving my heart
to any among them." (She is so disgusted by what she sees that she
becomes unable to love them.) [11]

At about the same time Gautier's book was published, Honoré
de Balzac produced a similar image of a lesbian in his sensationalistic novel, *The Girl with the Golden Eyes* (1835). But he approached his character from a different direction: Unlike Gautier,
he did not claim to have found the French, and especially the Pa-
risians, too virtuous and Christian, but saw them, as he wrote in
The Girl with the Golden Eyes, as being too "universally tolerant."
Anything is acceptable in their world, he complained, and thus
corruption flourishes in it.[12] Like Gautier, he looked for an objective correlative that would be most shocking to his readers, but
Balzac's avowed purpose was to jar his readers out of their moral
complacency by demonstrating an apogee of the corruption he
claimed he saw everywhere, to goad them to change. The two au-

thors, one aiming to criticize prudishness and the other to criticize immorality, fabricated the same image in the conviction that it had the most potency for their purposes. It seems that whether the French adhered to the values with which they were raised or frantically repudiated them, the idea of strong female sexuality (the zenith of which was double female sex), which challenged all they had been taught to hold sacred, always had the power to unsettle them as it could never unsettle their counterparts in our era.

One literary historian has suggested that Balzac's lesbian character in *The Girl with the Golden Eyes* was inspired by the real-life George Sand–Marie Dorval episode, that Balzac and Gautier probably discussed sapphism together, and that Gautier's work, which was written first, must have influenced Balzac.[13] Whether that is true or not, like Gautier, Balzac's original literary source for the lesbian character was probably Latouche's *Fragoletta*, which Balzac mentioned with great enthusiasm a number of times in his own writing.[14]

In *The Girl with the Golden Eyes*, Balzac presents the Marquise de St. Réal as an androgynous, all too independent and worldly woman, a Fragoletta. Her relationship with Paquita, the title character, is sexual and exists on no other plane. As one indication of how low society has fallen, the Marquise literally buys the beautiful Paquita from her mother when she is twelve years old, and can do with her as she wishes, unhampered by the forces of social decency. When Paquita becomes a woman, the Marquise takes her to Paris and there holds her prisoner in a room "built for love," i.e., sex. It is even soundproofed so that the Marquise can avariciously guard the "accents and music" of their carryings-on. Balzac's fantastic descriptions of lesbian sex and its trappings are reminiscent of the lesbian orgy scenes of the eighteenth-century *L'Espion Anglois*. The images of lesbianism in both works were born in the male imagination and were intended, for all the conflicted authors' supposed moralistic disapproval, to arouse the reader sexually. Balzac goes even a step beyond *L'Espion Anglois*, in which nothing more violent than sexual flagellation is shown. In *The Girl with the Golden Eyes*, the voluptuous, sexy Marquise brutally murders the voluptuous, sexy Paquita after telepathically discovering that she has been unfaithful with a man. The man, Henri de Marsay, who is actually the Marquise's identical half-brother, plays the voyeur to the exciting murder scene and is the center of identification for the reader.

These contrived, literary representations of lesbianism became in France, and decades later in other countries, a major image in the reading public's mind. Based as it was not on reality but on male fantasy, it nevertheless influenced many other male writers to create similar images. In time, those images were internalized and became self-fulfilling, as will be seen in the lives of twentieth-century, literary-minded women such as Renée Vivien.

One major writer who may have been influenced by *The Girl with the Golden Eyes* and *Mademoiselle de Maupin* was Charles Baudelaire.[15] Baudelaire dedicated *Les Fleurs du Mal* to Gautier and even wrote an admiring pamphlet on him and his works. While he did not express such boundless affection for Balzac, the insatiability, jealousy, and torment bound up with lesbian love in his poems are suspiciously reminiscent of the relationship between Paquita and the Marquise.

Enid Starkie, biographer of Baudelaire, points out that his lesbian poems were written during his "apprenticeship," from the time he was twenty-one until he was twenty-five, "when he set out to shock his contemporaries." [16] In 1846 his publisher had announced that the poems would soon be issued in a volume called *Les Lesbiennes*. If it is the same volume that finally appeared in 1857, the title was chosen not to represent the subject matter of the poems (there are only three that are explicitly about lesbians), but for maximum disturbance effect. When *Les Fleurs du Mal* was published, Baudelaire received the notoriety he sought in an obscenity trial which singled out two of his three lesbian poems, along with four others, as being pornographic. *Les Fleurs* quickly became a *succès de scandale.*

If we can believe that Baudelaire's remarks about his book were not made cynically, it is apparent that, like Balzac, he was confused about what he was doing. From his earliest manhood he enjoyed discomforting others with his unorthodox behavior. He loved to refer publicly to himself as "the son of a defrocked priest," to talk about "the time that I murdered my poor old father," and to tell a woman, interrupting himself while narrating another of his incredible stories to an enthralled crowd, "Mademoiselle, you who are crowned with sheaves of such golden corn, and who listen to me with such eager interest, do you know what I long to do? I long to bite into your white flesh, and, if you will permit me, I'll tell you how I'd like to make love to you! I'd like to take your two hands, bind them together, and then tie you up by your wrists to the ceiling of my room! When that was done, I'd kneel before you in worship, and kiss your snow white feet." [17] But while he longed to express his hostility to philistine propriety and ordinariness, he was nevertheless born a bourgeois Catholic and, as Rimbaud observed in *Une Saison en Enfer,* "*on est esclave de son baptême.*" Baudelaire's confusion about the stance he wished to take toward bourgeois, Catholic morals and values is evident when he exclaimed regarding *Les Fleurs,* "I am extremely proud of having produced a book which expresses horror and terror of vice," and when he wrote to his mother that the work was "based on Catholic inspiration." [18] On the one hand, he relished the notion that through his book he could shock the bourgeoisie. But on the other hand, he believed to the very depths of his being, as we cannot in our era, that the sex and the dope he wrote about were truly shocking, that to indulge in either one immediately, immutably dehumanized and damned a human being. Only a puritanical or a "Victorian" age could have produced the poems of *Les Fleurs du Mal,* with their ambivalence, their voyeurism, their expressed fear of damnation, and their childish wallowing in the deliciousness of "sin." [19]

Several Baudelaire biographers have suggested that the three women with whom he had affairs before he wrote his lesbian poems —Jeanne Duval, La Pomaré, and Mme. Stoltz—all had lesbian tendencies, but the poems are less concerned with living beings he might have known than with erotic fantasies. The women he writes about present a tantalizing, infuriating image for the voyeur who watches from a distance. They are the most appealing creatures in his scheme of values, as he hints in poem number 24:

I love you as I love the vaults of night, . . .
Love you the more, most fair, for fleeing me. . . .
I press to the attack, I scale and storm,
As on a corpse a wormy choir will swarm;
And covet, beast implacable and cruel,
Your very ice, that is my ardour's fuel! [20]

In the poem "Lesbos," [21] which was probably intended to preface the aborted *Les Lesbiennes,* the women exchange "kisses, languorous or wild,/Luscious as melons, hot as Phoebus' flames," but they seem to be performing for the speaker, who says he has been haunted by such images since childhood and announces without explanation, "For Lesbos, out of all on earth, chose me/To sing the secret of these virgins fair." The speaker sees Lesbos as "Fairer than

Venus," who "well can envy Sappho's cheer," but the lesbians are also accursed. Their kisses have "beguiled" them, they engage in "sterile ecstasy." Finally, however, phallocentric justice intervenes: "Manful" Sappho is conquered by Phaon. The author describes her suffering, her "death-pale charms," and the "screams of torment" that rise from Lesbos at night. But he claims to be not unsympathetic to her plight, and he even hints at admiration for lesbians, whose "daring hearts" (with which he could identify through his own struggle against the moral views he loathed even while they continued to be lodged in his psyche) win them pardon by "endless martyrdom." Nevertheless, despite his sympathy, he cannot transcend his horror at (and fascination with) the image of wild, erotic, exotic desire between women which he has pulled from his imagination. Their love is "frenzied mirth combined with dark despair," although it is never clear why lesbianism must be frenzied, or why it brings dark despair in Lesbos, a world outside of bourgeois Christianity. The same ambivalence is apparent in the first (uncensored) "Doomed Women" poem.[22]

The second "Doomed Women" poem, subtitled "Delphinia and Hippolyta,"[23] emphasizes even more than the other two his vision of sex and sin in love between women. The poem opens with an image of young Hippolyta, lounging, as lesbians often do in male fantasy, "in cushioned fragrancy" and "dejected wantonness," dreaming of the skilled lesbian caresses that "lifted her veil of virgin modesty." Baudelaire intimates here that lesbians have esoteric sex techniques to which men will never be privy, "diversions most obscure." Delphinia, her wicked lesbian lover, an older woman, watches her like "a beast that, after marking with its teeth,/Then gloats at leisure on its hapless prize." It soon becomes apparent that Delphinia is a wild-eyed sadist and Hippolyta her "pallid victim" in their inevitable sadomasochistic lesbian relationship. Delphinia assures Hippolyta that she loves her and warns her that she must never sleep with men, who will hurt her with their clumsiness and cruelty, but Delphinia is herself far more merciless than the men of her admonishments.

Hippolyta knows in her soul that the two women have "committed deeds unnatural." But caught in her desire even while she realizes that she is sinking into death and hell, she becomes a monster like Delphinia. Here the narrator interjects, "On, on, you wretched victims, thus begins/The steep descent to torment without end!" Their pleasures, he says, will sire their own chastisement, since women are insatiable and nothing lesbians do can drown their "rabid cravings"—their "sterile dalliance" only maddens their thirst for more. He ends by suggesting they will attempt to flee the infinite lesbian sexual cravings they bear within themselves, which are impossible to gratify and just as impossible to escape from, and he exhorts them to "Go, roam like wolves the wilderness through/ On, you disordered beings, do your worst." The women in these poems generally become victim and monster both, since Baudelaire attributes to them wild sexuality, which is a horror to the bourgeois Catholic side of him and a brave rebellion to the aesthete radical side of him.

The notoriety of Baudelaire might have influenced other French writers and artists as well in their depiction of love between women. Gustave Courbet's painting entitled "Sleep" (1866) is representative of the exotic, erotic image that became popular as a result of *Les Fleurs*: Two young women with expressions that suggest sadness or torment, even in their slumbers, are naked together upon a bed. The right leg of the dark-haired one is draped over her friend's waist, the left thigh touches her friend's pubes. The blond girl caresses the other's leg with her right hand. Her chin is on her lover's breast. On a table within hand's reach are a wine decanter and a wine glass (empty, of course), and a string of pearls with one end resting in the glass and the other on the bed—probably they were used for "diversions most obscure." The two girls might easily be Hippolyta and Delphinia.[24] The dark one has Delphinia's "wild mane," the blond one has a more "fragile loveliness" and an expression which suggests that she is dreaming of the "leaden fears" of which Hippolyta speaks.

Perhaps because of Baudelaire's notoriety, the lesbian theme became especially popular in underground literary pornography of the 1860's,[25] such as *Un été à la campagne* (1867) and *L'école des biches ou moeurs des petites dames de ce temps* (1868). Several reissues of Sinistrari's 1700 work even appeared in the last decades of the nineteenth century, as for example, *De la sodomie et particulièrement de la sodomie des femmes distinguée du tribadisme*, published by Liseaux in 1879.

Baudelaire's influence is most directly traceable in the anonymous *Un été à la campagne (A Summer in the Country)*, which was published—and probably written by—Baudelaire's own publisher and friend, Auguste Poulet-Malassis. That Poulet-Malassis should undertake such a venture after the legal persecution of *Les Fleurs* indicates that the obscenity trial must have been good for his business, despite the fact that he was fined a hundred francs.

A Summer in the Country, an epistolary novel, takes place, unlike Baudelaire's poems, in the amoral universe of pornography. But although the characters do not become moral monsters as Baudelaire's lesbians do, the external view of them—both bewitchingly feminine, one dark and the other light, the seducer several years older but still delectably young, and both tied together by nothing but sex—is identical to that in Baudelaire's second "Doomed Women" poem. The author probably had that poem in mind while writing the book, and seems to have borrowed from it (and possibly from Courbet's "Sleep," which appeared the year before) to set the scene of the poem "A Stormy Night" which Adèle of *A Summer in the Country* sends to her woman lover. That poem begins:

> *It was an August night; through curtains fell*
> *Faint light of moon on boudoir elegance,*
> *Light on two sleeping beauties, as they lay . . .*
> *. . . You sense*
> *Perspiring flesh and bones that melt away.*
>
> *Two girls asleep: not much concealed*
> *By bedclothes on this sort of sweltering night.*
> *They share the bed in charming postures.*[26]

Baudelaire's scene is similar:

> *In the pale light the fading lamps dispersed,*
> *Hippolyta, in cushioned fragrancy,*
> *Dreamed of the skilled caresses which had first*
> *Lifted her veil of virgin modesty . . .*
> *Delphinia, calm and blissful, lay beneath*
> *Her consort's feet . . .*

Both couples exist in the same suspended world of imagination where they are forever young and beautiful (although, in Baudelaire's poem, ultimately tormented), surrounded by opulence, free from all realities such as the effects of aging or the need to work to earn money to buy their luxurious trappings.

Baudelaire may also have influenced other French and English writers of his era whose reputations—and thus whose images of lesbianism—survived well into the twentieth century, including Verlaine, Swinburne, and Louÿs. Verlaine's poem, "Sappho," [27] published not long after his enthusiastic reviews of *Les Fleurs*,[28] depicts the Greek poet in the same state she is seen in Baudelaire's "Lesbos," sick with her passion for Phaon, forgetful of the lesbian rites of her cult, seeking refuge in death. The emphasis in most of Verlaine's other lesbian poems, as in Baudelaire's, is on sex and sin—but of course the women are always young and lovely and arousing as they shuffle off to hell.[29]

The English writer, Swinburne, especially seems to have been influenced by the lesbian images in the work of Baudelaire and his predecessors.[30] While his lesbian poetry evokes *Les Fleurs*, the lesbian portions of his novel, *Lesbia Brandon* (1877), echo Gautier and Balzac. *Mademoiselle de Maupin* was for Swinburne "the golden book of spirit and sense,/The holy writ of beauty" and "the most perfect and exquisite book of modern times." [31] It was this work which confirmed for Swinburne, according to his biographer Randolph Hughes, his interest in the theme of sexual ambiguity and the artistic power in it.[32] Swinburne was equally familiar with Balzac's novels about sexual ambiguity,[33] and he referred to *The Girl with the Golden Eyes* a number of times in *Lesbia Brandon*. Like Gautier, Swinburne deals with cross-dressing (in this novel a male, Herbert, cross-dresses as a female, and Lesbia, whose name is prophetic, falls in love with his sister Margaret through his feminine image) and with the charms and horrors of paganism. Like Balzac, he shows that lesbianism leads to death and destruction. The title character, frustrated in her lesbian love, sees Margaret as Proserpine and "death incarnate." In tribute to her, Lesbia kills herself off gradually with the help of opium and eau de cologne, which she drinks. Her death-room scene is like the lesbian lovemaking scenes in aesthete-decadent literature: All is shadows, cushions, and the overpowering fragrance of perfume and flowers. Even though she is almost a corpse, "Her beauty of form was unimpaired." Her decadence is so unregenerate that even as she is about to expire she wishes that Herbert would dress as a woman again so that she might once more experience the passion she has for his sister.

The basis of her problem, Swinburne makes clear, is that she has too much intellect. Her father admits, "If my daughter had been a boy she'd have been . . . at Eton. . . . She's half-male as it is I think sometimes; don't know where she got all her brains." He confesses that he allowed her governess to give her "a boy's training and do a boy's lessons," and now, instead of taking an interest in cooking and cleaning, she "turns out verses." Her independent spirit makes her lesbianism inevitable, just as her lesbianism makes her suicide inevitable. Swinburne was another refugee from the bourgeoisie who could not rid himself of his conventional attitudes regarding appropriateness and sin, even while ensconced in the aesthete-decadent camp.

Pierre Louÿs's treatment of lesbianism is based on the same attitudes and also suggests the same literary predecessors and their offspring.[34] Despite Louÿs claim that he intended *The Songs of Bilitis* to be a challenge to "bourgeois moral prejudice," he was basically no freer of that prejudice than his predecessors and contemporaries. Although he defends love between women in his preface, proclaiming that "whatever men may think," it has "more of true passion than invoked viciousness," [35] in the poems which follow he generally shows it to be promiscuous, fickle, narcissistic, sadomasochistic, and childishly based on a heterosexual model.[36]

The love between women in these poems, as in those of Louÿs's predecessors, exists primarily on a sexual plane. In the poem "Psappha," for example, Sappho, who was in fact the head of a school for young ladies and taught them fine arts, is here a "butch" who wanders the streets looking for girls to pick up. Immediately upon her arrival in Lesbos, Bilitis is accosted by the poet and taken to bed. Sappho is described as having "virile breasts," and "narrow hips," and her hair is "cut like that of an athlete." In the morning Bilitis does not even stay to exchange addresses. She stealthily climbs over the body of her sleeping sex partner to slip out of bed, fearing "lest I touch her hip and she will take me as I pass." [37] Where the sex relationship between women is not modeled on heterosexuality, it is, contradictorily, narcissistic: Women love other women because in them they see themselves. Bilitis, still a neophyte in the poem "Counsels," is told by another woman that lesbian sex is superior because "if thou hast an ardent soul, thou wilt see thy beauty, as in a mirror, upon the bodies of women, thy lovers." [38]

Despite Louÿs's dedication of the poems "to the young girls of the society of the future," the poems are more apparently intended for the male reader. "Penumbra," for example, appeals to male voyeurism all the more keenly as Bilitis graphically depicts the most personal intimacies between herself and Mnasidika while bragging that men will never know how the two women carry on.[39] The relationship between Bilitis and Mnasidika ends, in familiar assurance to male readers, when a Phaon comes along and takes Mnasidika from Bilitis, who is given the poignant, provocative lament:

And, above all, if my despair is a perpetual torture, it is because I know, moment by moment, how she swoons in the
arms of another, and what he demands of her and what she
gives.[40]

At the end of the series of *Songs*, Bilitis, who has become a courtesan,
is ancient (although she is not yet forty), exhausted by Eros, and she
drinks too much. Such are the pitfalls of lesbianism, even in Sappho's
day, according to Louÿs.

In the light of the real lives of the women that have been examined in other chapters, the torment, the drunkenness, the hell, and
the havoc of love between women, whether genital or not, seem to
have existed more in male literature than in reality. The limited
definition of love between women as lesbian sex, accompanied
usually by frustration and sorrow, is born in male fantasy. Even for
women whose love for other females in all probability had a sexual
component, lesbian love was a good deal more than lesbian sex.
The poet-actress Adah Isaacs Menken, the friend of George Sand
and later of Swinburne, who was considered one of the most scandalous figures in her day and undoubtedly not a stranger to lesbian
sex, suggests in her own poems dimensions of lesbian intimacy
which never appeared in aesthete-decadent poetry, but which we
would expect to have existed knowing the lives of so many nineteenth-century women who loved women. Her poems, while far less
interesting as literature than Baudelaire's or Swinburne's, are probably much closer to the truth:

> *Speak to me tenderly,*
> *Think of me lovingly.*
> *Let your soft hands smooth back my hair. . . .*
> *Let my lonely life creep into your warm bosom, knowing*
> *no other rest but this.*
> *Let me question you, while sweet Faith and Trust are fold-*
> *ing their white robes around me . . .*
> *The Storm struggles with the Darkness.*
> *Folded away in your arms, how little do I heed their*
> *battle! . . .*
> *The darkness presses his black forehead close to the window*
> *pane and beckons me without.*
> *Love holds a lamp in this little room that hath power to blot*
> *back Fear.*[41]

Charlotte Cushman and Emma Stebbins, Katharine Bradley and Edith Cooper, Edith Somerville and Violet Martin, all would have understood most intimately what this poem is about. But had they read the works of the nineteenth-century aesthete-decadents which purported to describe love between women, they would have thought those females as strange and terrifying as they were to their creators and heterosexual readers, since the characters of those poems and novels had absolutely nothing to do with their lives and loves.

CHAPTER 4

Lesbian Evil

The exotic image of the lesbian which was created by the ambivalent attitudes of the French aesthetes (the lesbian was a demon to their bourgeois Catholic side and a rebel and martyr to their artist's side) became an image of pure evil in the hands of the nonaesthete writers of the nineteenth century. For them lesbians were tormentors and seducers of the innocent. The dubious pity and occasional admiration that were expressed by the writers discussed in the preceding chapter never appeared in the works of the nonaesthete authors.

The first nineteenth-century poem which has been widely thought to deal with lesbian evil, Samuel Taylor Coleridge's "Christabel," probably did not. "Christabel," which was started in 1798, never completed, and published first in its unfinished form in 1816, caused a great stir upon publication, and was, together with Byron's "Parisinia" (whose subject is incest), pronounced obscene: Both were said to be "poems which sin as heinously against purity and decency as it is possible to imagine." [1] Twentieth-century critics, armed with their knowledge of the sexologists and French literature, have assumed that the "obscenity" to which the nineteenth-century critics referred when lambasting "Christabel" must have been lesbianism.[2] But an examination of other reviews by Coleridge's contemporaries suggests that the "heinous sin" which shocked them was not Geraldine's putative lesbianism, but rather that Geraldine was, they believed, a man in disguise.[3]

There were a number of nineteenth-century works which did indeed deal with lesbian evil, but they came later in the century and

277

were influenced by other forces discussed in previous chapters. One of the earliest fictional treatments of unmitigated lesbian evil occurs in Adolphe Belot's novel, *Mademoiselle Giraud, My Wife*. Jeannette Foster suggests that the book was accepted in *Le Figaro* for serialization in 1870 probably with the intent of capitalizing on Westphal's work on lesbianism which had just attracted so much attention in medical circles. Belot must have been familiar with that work, since he mentions in his novel the disturbing French casualness regarding love between women contrasted with the serious concern it elicits in Germany.[4] But while he may have been conversant with "medical" opinions regarding lesbians, he was also familiar with Balzac's *The Girl with the Golden Eyes*, as he remarks in a prefacing statement,[5] and he seems to echo Balzac (and also Baudelaire) in his images of lesbian evil rather than the sexologists—although he never relieves his condemnation of his lesbian villain by pity as his literary predecessors did.

He tells his story from the point of view of a young man who marries a woman, Paule, who behaves toward him like a comrade and gives him every polite consideration but keeps him out of their bedroom at night. He slowly discovers that she has no interest in consummating her marriage with him because she is a helpless prisoner of lesbianism, locked in a fatal passion for an evil seductress, Berthe de Blangy, whom she met as a girl in boarding school, and who, once they became adults, cleverly vitiated all of Paule's attempts to free herself. When Paule finally does manage to extricate herself, it is too late—she dies of a brain fever brought on by too much sex. Berthe at the conclusion is drowned by the narrator, who thus rids the world of a monster. The two women step out of the pages of Baudelaire: One is blond, the other brunet; both are young and beautiful; and of course they are sexually insatiable, even to the point of self-destruction.

Belot makes an interesting commentary on eighteenth-century attitudes toward romantic friendship from the standpoint of the "wiser" nineteenth century in France. Before the narrator proposes to Paule he observes, as many a fiancé did in eighteenth-century literature dealing with romantic friendship:

> Her animation in speaking of Madame de Blangy and the joyous light that had come into her eyes when the countess appeared, had impressed me particularly. A young girl who was capable of such friendship, must—I believe—be capable of loving

in a ravishing manner. There must be, in her heart, treasures of tenderness and love that would prove rare jewels in a wife.

But in view of what Balzac and Baudelaire and Westphal had already expounded, Belot implies that his narrator certainly should have known better and portrays him as rather imbecilic when he still "doesn't get it" after Berthe tells him it would be a disaster if he married Paule. In France at least, innocence regarding the potential of love between women was virtually at an end by this time—although it persisted until much later in England and especially in America.

It is instructive to compare Belot's view of boarding schools with that of an American writer who wrote about the same time. Belot warns that since young girls are herded together and come to depend on a special friend for love and affection which they can get from no other source, eventually they seduce each other; and try as they might, they cannot shake off the destructive yoke of their passion until they leave school. If by some chance they meet again, it is fatal; they are trapped in hell.[6] In contrast, the American William Alger, whose *The Friendships of Women* was written only two years before Belot's novel, can still regard boarding-school romantic friendships as one of the loveliest experiences of a girl's life:

> School girl friendships are a proverb in all mouths. They form one of the largest classes of those human attachments whose idealizing power and sympathetic interfusions glorify the world and sweeten our existence. With what quick trust and ardor, what eager relish, these susceptible creatures, before whom heavenly illusions float, surrender themselves to each other, taste all the raptures of confidential conversation, lift veil after veil till every secret is bare, and, hand in hand, with glowing feet, tread the paths of paradise![7]

Many American writers, in contrast to the French, retained this ideal view of youthful romantic friendship until the end of the second decade of the twentieth century.

In Belot's novel, Paule marries the narrator because her parents wish her to. They threaten to place her in a convent if she does not marry; and having no possibility of supporting herself, she sees no alternative. But her heart and soul were imprisoned by Berthe when they were boarding-school maidens together, and now Paule cannot free herself, no matter how much she hates Berthe and wishes to leave her (although finally, just before Paule dies, the narrator's masculine devotion helps her save her soul). The women's lesbian passion is depicted with familiar trappings (see Mairobert, Balzac, and Baudelaire): Their rendezvous apartment is decorated in black and red satin, Louis XV chandeliers, rosy candles, small Venetian mirrors on the walls, and erotic artwork. All the books on the shelves —those of Diderot, Balzac, and Gautier are mentioned by name—are lesbian. In the closet hangs a cashmere cloak, lined with the same shade of deep red satin which decorates the apartment, and a black satin dressing gown. The garments are "still impregnated with subtle perfumes." There are Turkish cushions everywhere and—naturally—"the sun never penetrated the room." [8]

The outcome of Paule's passion is just what Baudelaire promised it would be in his second "Doomed Women" poem: As she is dying, Paule has ghastly hallucinations, obviously about the overdose of lesbian sex which killed her. The narrator reports: "She appeared to be struggling against a phantom which she tried to push away with her hands, and which returned incessantly. Hoarse cries escaped from her throat. . . . 'Go away! go away! Wretch! Lost! I am afraid, I am afraid!' " [9] She is the embodiment of Baudelaire's "disordered being" who has traveled "the steep descent to torment without end." [10]

Belot claims that his purpose in writing this novel is to warn women away from such fatal pitfalls. He admonishes those who would be silent about vice that to allow it to live in the shadow encourages it. Vice must be exposed, he declares—and particularly that vice which may appear to be simply friendship between women and which thus "passes for virtue." In his day, he implies, romantic friendship is no longer innocent as it once may have been. He asks, "How many have been lost because there was not found a man strong enough, or with enough authority to cry out: 'Beware! a new vice has just been hatched, a new leprosy has come into your midst!' Not being warned, [they] could not defend themselves; the vice grew, the leprosy extended." [11] Belot offers the strength and authority of his own voice to cut off this "new vice" at an early stage—and he offers also a concrete solution which anyone who happens to meet a lesbian is encouraged to try: The narrator, after Paule's death, encounters Berthe at a seaside village. Berthe goes swimming in rough waters, and, pretending to save her, the narrator actually drowns her. He soon receives a congratulatory note from Berthe's husband: "I understand and I thank you in my name and in the name of all honest people, for having ridden us of this reptile." [12]

Belot's intense hatred of lesbianism seems less sincere than sensationalistic. Berthe is not a real person to him—she is the embodiment of esoteric sin, fascinating and repulsive. Unlike the aesthete-decadents, however, he cannot admit his fascination. It is never his express purpose to undermine orthodoxy but rather to defend it. Yet he incorporates the most decadent and provocative props into his portrait of lesbianism. One suspects that he (and *Le Figaro*) were capitalizing on the late nineteenth-century Parisian interest in "vice," an interest which was dramatically characterized by the number of French books which appeared using that word or a related one in the title: Victorien du Saussay, *L'Ecole du Vice*; Joséphin Péladan, *Le Vice Suprême*; Serge Paul, *Le Vice et l'Amour*; J. de Merlin, *Vice, Crime, Amour*; Jean Lorrain, *Le Vice Errant*; Jules Davray, *L'Armée du Vice*; Georges Brandimbourg, *Croquis du Vice*; Dr. Fauconey, *Les Vices Féminins*; and Saint-Medard, *La Volupté Féroce*; Louis Besse, *La Débauché*; Victor Joze, *Paris-Gomorrhe*; Paul Bouget, *Crime d'Amour*; Catulle Mendès, *Méphistophéla*.

Belot's censorious tone was taken up over the next decades by a number of French writers, including Catulle Mendès,[13] Joséphin Péladan,[14] Émile Zola, Guy de Maupassant, and Alphonse Daudet. The association of lesbianism with vice and unmitigated evil may have been partly due to a concern over the rapidly declining French birthrate and the fear of anything which might promote that decline. By the end of the century, the birthrate had dipped so dangerously low compared with that of bordering countries that the demographer Bertillon, head of the Statistical Institute of the City of Paris, calculated that within seven years "every French soldier would be faced by two enemies." He was referring especially to recent governmental figures showing that the French birthrate was only half that of Germany and was continuing to decline.[15]

All of the above novelists were undoubtedly familiar with the aesthete-decadent literature of their predecessors, and their images of the lesbian derive partly from it. But they probably also derive from their experiences of Parisian lowlife in the 1880's and 1890's. In *La Gynandre* (1891), Péladan observed that it was only within the last decade that the "vice" of lesbianism had become so popular.[16] Through the character of Tammuz, he specifically attributes its popularity to the sensationalistic stories of authors who have nurtured the cult of Lesbos, and seems to suggest that lesbian life has patterned itself after such (male-authored) lesbian literature. The real lesbians to whose lives he and other men were privy were the ones that lived in public—in the bars and cafés that welcomed prostitutes; many of them apparently indulged in lesbianism as an escape from the heterosexual grossness and brutality they experienced daily in their profession. An anonymous late nineteenth-century English writer characterized what was probably a universal experience among prostitutes:

> *Men fire our persons for the night,*
> *Keep us awake, and kiss and teaze,*
> *But ah! how different the delight*
> *I have in cuddling dear Elise.*[17]

In France of the 1880's and 1890's, the haunts of the prostitutes became fashionable meeting places for writers and artists. The favorite of Toulouse-Lautrec and Conder, for example, was the Rat Mort in Pigalle, where the colorful prostitutes had the added panache of their interest in lesbianism, which they openly displayed.[18] Laure's restaurant in Zola's *Nana* (1880), where the prostitutes went to relax and to flirt with each other, also had its counterpart in reality. It is probable that it was his observation of such Parisian haunts that caused Pierre Louys to associate prostitution and lesbianism, both in his poem cycle, *The Songs of Bilitis*, and in his novel, *Aphrodite*. In any case, lesbianism among prostitutes was apparently so widespread by 1887 that some attempt was made through the Municipal Council of Paris to halt it.[19]

The lesbians in Zola's *Nana*, Maupassant's "Paul's Mistress" (1881), and Daudet's *Sappho* (1884) are all prostitutes or better-paid courtesans. The lesbian prostitutes that congregate in Laure's restaurant in *Nana* are vice-ridden, and their physical ugliness is a manifestation of their moral ugliness. Laure herself is a fat, "monstrous creature," who resembles "an old image of Vice, whose face has been worn and polished by the kisses of the faithful." She lords it over a "tribe of bloated women." When young females enter the restaurant, the old prostitutes are "excited by the sweet scent of their youth," and they jostle each other out of the way to get at the new meat. Nana's friend, Satin, who introduces Nana to Laure's, has an affair with Madame Robert, who gets "absurdly jealous" when Satin makes love to others, and Madame Robert beats her. Before long, Satin and Nana begin an affair of their own, which is constantly interrupted by their heterosexual as well as homosexual promiscuity and by their bickering and violence.

It comes as no surprise to learn that Zola wrote the sententious preface to a later edition of Belot's *Mademoiselle Giraud, My Wife*. He calls Belot a "moralist" and congratulates him for "courageously" depicting "the monstrous friendship of two old schoolfriends." Zola admonishes the readers (the book had already "attained the enormous sale of 30,000 copies") to "cease to hide this book; place it on all your tables, as our fathers placed the rod with which they chastised their children. And, if you have daughters, let your wife read this book before she separates herself from those dear creatures to send them away to school." [20] The lesbian portions of *Nana*, which end with Satin's predictably early death, similarly constitute a cautionary tale.

The lesbian prostitute of Guy de Maupassant's "Paul's Mistress," who is as corrupt as those in *Nana*, is contrasted with the innocent young Paul. The story takes place in a resort outside Paris, La Grenouillère, where "all the scum of society, all its well-bred debauchery" [21] may be seen. Such a society tolerates everything, de Maupassant implies, even the vice of lesbianism. When four lesbian residents arrive at the resort in "butch" and "femme" guise, the crowd cheers them on, calling "Lesbos! Lesbos! Lesbos!"—as if, de Maupassant says, "these people, this collection of the corrupt, saluted their chiefs like warships which fire guns when an admiral passes along the line." Lesbianism is the chief of all vices. The women do not feel insulted or upset by the salutation, and they respond with cheerful equanimity. Could de Maupassant really have believed he was writing about actual human beings who inhabited the same earth as he?

Paul alone, the only decent man in the bunch, de Maupassant suggests, is disgusted and exasperated at the sight of the lesbians. "It is shameful!" he says, with an anger reminiscent of Belot's. "They ought to be drowned like puppies with a stone about the neck." But no one else in this corrupt society feels as he does—and a sign of their great corruption is their tolerance.

The moral corruption of the women is manifested, like Laure's, in their physical unpleasantness. Strangely enough, Paul's mistress, Madeline, a prostitute whom he worships without reason, becomes enamored of the ugliest of them, the fat one who waddles, "swelling out her wide trousers with her buttocks and swaying about like a fat goose with enormous legs and yielding knees." The two women go off to the bushes together (sic), and Paul discovers them in "a crime against nature, a monstrous, disgusting profanation." He escapes from this corrupt world by drowning himself in the river. The story ends on what de Maupassant intended to be the most chilling and anxiety-provoking note (although in earlier eras the identical statement would have been considered mere fact): Madeline, who is shocked at Paul's suicide, puts her head on the shoulder of the other woman, "as though she had found a refuge in a closer and more certain affection, more familiar and more confiding," and the two go off together.

Similarly, the prostitute-model of Alphonse Daudet's *Sappho* makes a "shipwreck" of the life of her young male lover, Gaussin, although his tragedy stops short of death. She gives him the "most disturbing anxieties" [22] with her lesbian affairs, which she herself describes in reference to one of her female lovers as "the vilest, the most monstrous" vice. While she assures him, "Have no fear . . . your love has cured me of all those horrors," he knows he can never be sure of her, and her nickname "Sappho," given to her when she posed for the bust of the poet whose name "has become the label of a disease," is intended to be prophetic.

Through novels like these, lesbianism and lowlife came to be linked. It is not unlikely that some of their authors actually observed in lowlife lesbian haunts, where love between women was openly displayed, the jealousies and violence and debauchery they wrote about—but they could have observed the same in similar heterosexual haunts, except that the principals, instead of being female and female, would have been male and female. Of course, the writers would not have attempted to pass those observations off as representations of heterosexual life, but merely as examples of the life of a particular element of society, explainable by their poverty and social injustice. However, the habits and misfortunes of the prostitute lesbian, grossly exaggerated through fiction, became those of "the lesbian" in the writers' view and hence in their readers' view, since there was, by the last decade of the century, little to counterbalance that image in French literature. The widespread, salacious interest in the mysterious subject of love between women was fed by scores of novels, each one based apparently on the myths of the previous one, although an occasional author probably took a trip to a lesbian bar to see "how they really lived"—and found the representations of Zola and the others to be true enough. Mario Praz observes of turn-of-the-century France, "Of all the monstrosities which pullulate in the fiction of this period, Lesbians are among the most popular." [23] But the likes of Rosa Bonheur and Nathalie Micas, who were certainly lesbians and certainly not—aside from

Rosa's genius—a unique couple, were nowhere to be found in French novels of the day.

One would think that the gross views regarding lesbian evil in nineteenth-century French literature would have been considered exaggerated, that no one would have believed such incredible excesses, as practiced by Sophie in *Méphistophéla* or Paule and Berthe in *Mademoiselle Giraud, My Wife*, could exist in reality. But even some of the most sophisticated readers apparently took those depictions as fact—and their views of female-female relationships were colored to conform to fiction. The Swedish author, August Strindberg, is a most dramatic illustration of this point. In *A Madman's Manifesto* (which was actually written in French under the title *Le Plaidoyer d'un Fou*), he accuses his first wife, Siri von Essen, of almost every one of the monstrosities about which he probably learned through the sensationalistic French fiction that was published before he wrote *A Madman's Manifesto* in 1887 as well as through his fascination with decadence, with which he believed himself to have become especially familiar when he stayed for ten months in 1880 in an artists' village near Paris.[24] Siri, whom he repeatedly calls a lesbian, although he accuses her also of being promiscuous with innumerable men, comes under Strindberg's suspicion regardless of what she does: If she expresses too much interest in him (or any other man), she is a "brazen whore"; if she displays no sexual interest in men, she is "abnormal" and "depraved."

It is impossible to know whether or not Siri actually had sexual relationships with other women (the daughter of Strindberg and Siri denied it in her account of their marriage published in 1956), but Strindberg's recitation of her affairs stretches credulity beyond even the most willing imagination. He is depicting not a living woman, but one of those moral monsters of French literature. For example, Siri debauches a servant girl: First she plied her with liquor, then she "undressed her with her eyes"—Strindberg sees all this through a keyhole—and "she drew closer to her, placed her head on the very developed breasts of that new 'friend' and took her by the waist and asked her to kiss her."[25] Strindberg claims also to have surprised Siri at another time "with her hands plunged into the bodice of an open-bloused maid, with her avid lips near to the breasts dazzling with a pearly whiteness."[26] She debauches children as well. In Switzerland she seduces a fourteen-year-old girl—Strindberg observes them kissing and bathing together.[27] At a party in Germany, drunk, she gathers about her two girls of fifteen and one of fourteen, "gloating licentiously over them and kissing them on the mouth, in the way which lesbians are accustomed between themselves." [28] Naturally she carries on disgracefully with a myriad women of her own age and class as well. Befitting all such tortured demons, she has dreams at night which cause her to "moan atrociously." [29]

It is possible that Siri might have displayed a good deal of warmth toward her women friends, and even loved them passionately, and still—this was in the 1880's, when many people continued to think romantic friendship was a noble institution—had no idea of the import of Strindberg's paranoid fury. Siri, in fact, openly admits to loving women but is, or perhaps only pretends to be, confused by Strindberg's accusations. Regardless of how much sexual knowledge she actually possessed, she thought that presenting her relationships with other women as romantic friendships should be a satisfactory explanation for her husband. Strindberg complains of her protestations of innocence, "What was the use of explaining to her that the law condemned crimes of this nature to hard labour? What was the use of convincing her that those touchings, exciting the pleasure of the recipient, were, in medical books, classed among the vices? It was I who was debauched, since I was instructed in all those vices! And nothing was able to drag her from her innocent games. She was one of those unconscious villains which it would be better to lock up in institutions of special education for women, rather than keeping them in one's home." [30]

At the root of Strindberg's fury is his hatred of feminism—and it was French decadent literature which supplied him with his "weapon" (his accusations of vice and sickness) against women who wished to be independent. Siri is herself torn regarding her craving for independence. Before she divorces her first husband and marries Strindberg, she tells the writer that she envies his bachelor state: "To be one's own master, to have one's own interior, to be free of all control! Oh, I'm mad on freedom! This state of marriage is infamous." [31] But being unable to support herself as an independent being, she marries again and has three children with Strindberg (although he doubts his paternity).

Strindberg begins *A Madman's Manifesto* by an admission that he greatly resents his wife when she mourns over her lost career as an actress. He is infuriated when she laments, "Isn't it sad? . . . that existence of a woman, without a goal, without a future, without an occupation! I will die of it." Being a "*mother* equal to her task," he sententiously tells her, should keep her busy.[32] He is especially upset when she befriends professional women who encourage her to resume her career and, he suspects, to lose respect for the marriage bonds. He complains, "Under the influence of her odious companion she had learned that married woman is a slave, who works for nothing for her husband."[33] He speaks of his own joy in being in Germany, "land of soldiers, where the regime of the patriarchate was still in force," and where Siri "did not feel at home. No one had understood her silliness on the alleged rights of women"; the Germans had just forbidden girls to attend university lectures, and all state employments "were reserved for man, the provider."[34] Strindberg writes here in all seriousness:

> To want to unseat man, replace him by woman, going back to matriarchy, to dethrone the true master of creation, he who created civilization, spread the benefits of culture, the progenitor of great thoughts, of the arts, of the crafts, of everything, to raise the dirty beasts of women who have never taken part in civilizing work—or almost never—with a few futile exceptions— that was to my mind a provocation to my sex. And at the very idea of seeing those bronze-age minds, those anthropomorphs, semi-apes, that horde of evil-doing animals coming to the forefront, the male rose up within me. . . . Woman is not at all a slave since she and her children are fed from the work of man. Woman is never subjugated since she chooses her role, since nature has bestowed her lot upon her [sic], which is to remain under the protection of man during the accomplishment of her maternal functions. Woman is not the equal of man in intellect and man is not the equal of woman in the realm of procreation. Woman is thus superfluous in the great work of civilization since man understands his business better than she. . . .[35]

He also claims that it was the heroic masculine element in him that impelled him to write *Married,* the book which Siri loathed and in which she felt personally attacked.

Thus Strindberg's anxieties over feminism stimulated his anxieties over his wife's intimacies with other women (which in an earlier era would have been considered normal and perfectly respectable): He needed to construe those intimacies as being necessarily sexual (i.e., evil), and hence he exaggerated them in the grossest manner. He was aided by both French literature and, as he says, "medical books," which put a sexual construction on all such intimacies (even when the women denied any genital interest). Because, like most men of his era, he was fundamentally sex-hating, anything that hinted of sex was necessarily a vice (even within marriage— Strindberg complains with disgust that Siri, in bed with him, "turned into a brazen coquette when very excited"); [36] and between two females, who conspired against male dominance, laughing at marriage and motherhood, and seeking to claim new rights for themselves, it was the worst vice of all. His train of associations must have been repeated many times in male minds during the late nineteenth century and after.

Two years after Belot's *Mademoiselle Giraud, My Wife* appeared in *Le Figaro*, the Irish writer Joseph Sheridan LeFanu published a short story, "Carmilla" (1872), which seems to equal Belot's work in its depiction of lesbian evil. [37] It tells of a pretty young vampire who preys on other pretty young females, most notably the narrator of the story, Laura, who, at the age of twenty-seven, recalls her encounter with Carmilla eight years before.

When, at the beginning of the relationship, Laura asks to know more about her, Carmilla responds, "The time is very near when you shall know everything. You will think me cruel, very selfish, but love is always selfish. How jealous I am you cannot know. You must come with me, loving me, to death; or else hate me, and still come with me, *hating* me through death and after." Later Carmilla tells Laura, as her "hot lips" travel along Laura's cheek, "You are mine, you *shall* be mine, and you and I are one forever." In 1872, however, it was still conceivable that, aside from Carmilla's most extravagant utterances about hating, her behavior might be considered appropriate within the framework of romantic friendship— apparently Laura sees it as such. After Carmilla holds her close and whispers her affection to her, Laura observes in her narrative, "Young people like, and even love, on impulse. I was flattered by the evident, though as yet undeserved, fondness she showed me. I liked the confidence with which she at once received me. She was determined that we should be very dear friends. . . . I was delighted with my companion."

Some twentieth-century critics such as Peter Penzoldt point out "the technical term 'lesbian' is never used, and it is doubtful whether LeFanu ever knew it, or was aware of the true nature of what he was describing." [38] In fact, LeFanu may have been somewhat confused in his intent. He has the father of another of Carmilla's victims exclaim that he cannot understand why "Heaven should tolerate so monstrous an indulgence of the lusts and malignity of hell." His terms are suspiciously close to those that Belot and Swinburne and others used to describe lesbianism. And yet LeFanu also shows that Carmilla, in her original manifestation, was heterosexual, the beloved of a man who loved her so dearly that although she had been infected with vampirism, he lied concerning the whereabouts of her corpse and hid her coffin so that her body would not be mutilated in a ritual to destroy her vampire power. LeFanu does not hint at bisexuality in Carmilla's original manifestation nor suggest why she became interested in preying exclusively on women.

It is possible that LeFanu, who was of French background and familiar with the language, may have known French writings regarding lesbianism, especially that of Belot, whose *Mademoiselle Giraud, My Wife* came out very shortly before LeFanu began writing "Carmilla," and that of Baudelaire, whose poem, "The Vampire's Metamorphosis" (number 6) immediately followed "Doomed Women: Hippolyta and Delphinia" (number 5) in *Les Fleurs du Mal* (perhaps the serial order of the Baudelaire poems created an association in LeFanu's mind). He was probably also familiar with the poems of Swinburne, who himself expressed great admiration for his stories.[39] Perhaps, then, he was influenced by those writers, or perhaps, as Penzoldt suggests, he did not understand that what he described might be seen as "lesbian lust." He may have thought only to show romantic friendship as a vampire would conduct it—taken to the extreme of bloodsucking—and the victim's father may only have been referring to vampirism rather than lesbianism when he spoke of "the lusts and malignity of hell."

It is more certain that when LeFanu's compatriot, George Moore, wrote *A Drama in Muslin* in 1886, he was familiar with both the French writers (whose naturalistic novels, especially those of Zola, fascinated him) and with the early sexologists.[40] Like Belot, Moore depicts a passionate friendship which begins in a girls' school and develops into a monstrosity as it continues into adulthood. The lover, Cecilia, is a physically deformed young woman: Her physical deformity is a sign of her mental deformity, just as in Zola and de Maupassant's lesbian characters. Cecilia claims that she has no interest in marriage because her real interest is in "beautiful things" and God, but in fact she simply hates men. She writes to Alice, her beloved, "Women are pure, men are obscene animals. Their love is

our degradation. Love! a nice name they give it. How can a sentiment that is merely a gratification of the lowest passions be love?"
Moore's explanation of her antipathy is "scientific." Cecilia's father
was an old man and her mother had a great loathing for him during
conception and pregnancy; hence her hatred was planted and left to
germinate in Cecilia's misshapen body, and Cecilia's emotions were
"the almost inevitable psychical characteristics that a human being
born under such circumstances would possess." When she tells
Alice, who was born "normal," of her passion for her, Alice responds, "Cecilia, dear, you shouldn't talk to me like that; it is absurd. Indeed, I don't think it is quite right," although she says she
can't herself explain "about how it is wrong." She merely has a "normal" woman's instinct to squelch such passionate talk from another
woman—of course, this "instinct" was entirely absent in earlier
literature about romantic friendships.

Cecilia tells Alice almost exactly what two characters of (coinci-
dentally) identical names told each other in Longfellow's *Kavanagh*
about forty years before. The Alice of the earlier novel says to
Cecilia, "I had such a longing to see you. . . . You are so strong
and beautiful! Ah, how I wish Heaven had made me as tall and
strong and beautiful as you are," and Cecilia happily accepts her
kisses. In the later novel, Cecilia says to Alice, "It seems like heaven
to see you again. You look so nice, so true, so sweet, so perfect.
There never was anyone so nice as you," but such passion makes
Alice uneasy—she feels she is confronted with abnormality, irregu-
larity: the narrator remarks that it "revealed thoughts in Alice's
mind—thoughts of which Alice herself was not distinctly conscious,
just as a photograph exposes irregularities in the texture of a leaf
that the naked eye would not perceive."

At the end of the novel, when Cecilia realizes that her love is
fruitless, she goes into a convent, first telling Alice, "Ah, if you knew
the lofty hopes that were once mine, of the ideal life I once dreamed
to live with you; a pure ecstatic life untouched by any degrading
passion, unassailed by any base desires." In earlier novels of romantic friendship her sentiments would have been seen as unquestionably noble and would have been very familiar to the
women readers. By 1886, in the hands of an "informed" writer such
as George Moore, they are the utterings of a deformed crazy.

Such negative views of romantic friendship did not appear in the
United States until a decade later, and it was only gradually and
well into the twentieth century that these sentiments were common

enough to be reflected in the pages of the popular magazines. Apparently it was not until the 1890's in America that real fear about love between women began to appear in the medical profession, the courts, and finally in fiction. In 1890 Gautier's *Mademoiselle de Maupin* was first published in America by the Chicago firm, Laird and Lee. The following year the same publisher brought out Belot's *Mademoiselle Giraud, My Wife*. By 1892 the Post Office Department decided that lesbian pornography had gotten so out of hand that they undertook to destroy tons of it.[41] Significantly, it was about that time that doctors began to report hearing (often at second hand) of cases of women who, for example, practiced "the orgies of tribadism with other women after getting them under the influence of drink."[42] When in 1892 Alice Mitchell, a young Tennessee woman, who had a history of insanity, murdered Freda Ward, her female beloved, in order to "make it sure that no one else could get her,"[43] there was real proof that the French did not lie about the excesses of lesbianism. As a result of the murder, it was suggested by at least two doctors in 1893 that all "sexual perverts" be "asexualized."[44] Even boarding-school crushes became suspect, as a Dr. Edward Mann wrote in 1893, borrowing the language of Krafft-Ebing:

> In one instance I have known of this morbid sexual love for a person of the same sex, starting probably, with some one girl, of a faulty nervous organization, in a young ladies seminary,— almost assume the form of an epidemic (genesis erethism),— and several young ladies were brought up before the faculty, and were told that summary dismissal would follow if this were not at once dropped. The terrible mischief which was thus arrested, and doubtless originated with an insane girl, in this case evidently assumed an hysterical tendency in others not insane, but who might have easily become so if they were neuropathically endowed, as they doubtless were.[45]

The Mitchell case made a long-lasting impression on the legal profession as well as on the medical profession. As late as 1930 a law writer observed "Freda Ward's killing and trial of Alice Mitchell still live in the history of famous cases taught young lawyers and in the world anthologies of sex psychology and sex pathology."[46] In 1950 *Sexology* published an article about the two women entitled "Lesbian Love Murder."[47] For decades the case helped to provide an image of love between women which quite eradicated the image of romantic friendship, even among schoolgirls.

In the United States before the 1890's, not only romantic friendships of the nature described in Chapters II A, 4 and II A, 5 were socially acceptable, but even transvestism was fairly widely tolerated. In 1855, for example, Lucy Ann Lobdell published her memoirs, *Narrative of Lucy Ann Lobdell, the Female Hunter of Delaware and Sullivan Counties, New York*, in which she openly talked about her life as a transvestite and connected it with her feminism.[48] There were also a sizable number of women who fought in the Civil War in male guise and who, in some cases, even had love relationships with other women; these were generally reported with as little consciousness of wrongdoing as we have seen in the biographies of Deborah Sampson, their Revolutionary War counterpart.[49] Dr. Mary Walker, a transvestite who unlike the others did not attempt to pass, although, she wore the male uniform when she served in the Union Army as a surgeon, was presented with a Congressional Medal of Honor by President Johnson in 1866.[50]

By the 1890's, however, the behavior of any of these women might have caused considerably more concern. Two fictional works published in 1895 indicate that "wisdom" about lesbianism was spreading among the popular fiction writers in America. Mary Wilkins Freeman's short story, "The Long Arm," suggests that the Alice Mitchell case probably left an association in the public mind between lesbianism and violence. In the light of her own close friendship with Mary Wales and her generally unfortunate experiences with men, it may be somewhat difficult to understand Freeman's motives in writing "The Long Arm."[51] But as will be seen in an examination of the twentieth century, such self-loathing, self-alienating behavior was not uncommon among women writers. "The Long Arm" is about romantic friendship gone wrong—or, rather, it is viewed in the light of the emerging end-of-the-century American attitudes which show it to be wrong. Phoebe Dole and Maria Woods, two dressmakers, have lived together for forty years. Maria sews well, but it is Phoebe, the aggressive one, who handles all the business arrangements. As the story opens, the narrator, Sarah Fairbanks, reports that her father, with whom she lived next door to the women, has just been murdered and that it is her intention to find the murderer. The police are stymied, since no motive which can be matched with a likely suspect is discernible. Before long, Sarah finds a wedding ring with the motto "Let love abide forever" and two dates, the present one preceded by another, forty years earlier. She discovers that her father had proposed to Maria before he married Sarah's mother, and that "this sweet, child-like woman had always been completely under the sway of [Phoebe's] stronger nature. The subordination went back beyond my father's original proposal to her; she had, before he made love to her as a girl, promised Phoebe she would not marry; and it was Phoebe who, by representing to her that she was bound by this solemn promise, had led her to write a letter to my father, declining his offer, and sending back the ring." When Sarah learns that her father had recently renewed his offer and that Maria had accepted, she has her suspect. Phoebe, once confronted, admits, "I stopped [the marriage] once before. This time I knew I couldn't unless I killed him. She's lived with me in this house for over forty years. There are other ties as strong as the marriage one, that are just as sacred. What right had he to take her away from me and break up my home?"

There are so many similarities between Freeman's story and the Alice Mitchell case that one wonders if Freeman hadn't seen newspaper accounts of the actual murder in the two or three years before she wrote "The Long Arm." While Phoebe kills not her lover but her lover's lover, she is, like Alice Mitchell, the masculine one in the relationship between the two women; like Mitchell, her motive for murder is fear that her beloved will be separated from her; like Mitchell, she is apparently insane and shows no remorse over the murder (Sarah says, "I cannot describe the dreadful calmness with which that woman told this to me. . . . I believe in demoniacal possession after this"); and like Mitchell, she dies a short time after being institutionalized. Finally, just as it was believed that Mitchell's relationship with Freda Ward was not genital,[52] we learn that Phoebe has a downstairs bedroom and Maria has the one upstairs. The suspicion of genital sexuality was not even necessary for some to cast romantic friendship in a horrid light by now; its intensity alone was enough.

Passages of Mary Hatch's novel, *The Strange Disappearance of Eugene Comstock* (1895)[53] also indicate that the author may have been familiar with the Mitchell case.[54] Whether she was or not, there is no doubt that she was familiar with the French literature about lesbianism which had recently been translated into English. She has her transvestite lesbian villain (a late nineteenth-century Mlle. de Maupin) admit that as a very young woman she went to Paris and "plunged into the wild excesses of that gay capital." There, she says, "it mattered nothing to me whether men or women were my companions, as I cared for neither. However, several women cared for me, and a duel was the result."

In her female guise she is Rosa Cameron, a feminist, an independent, large, but attractive woman who nevertheless contrasts dramatically with Gracia Hilton "with her lovely feminine ways." While Howland, the hero of the novel, regards Rosa as "the most fascinating creature I ever saw," his intuition is at work: He admits, as Laura does of Carmilla in LeFanu's story, "yet she repells at the same time," and he sees something "sinister" about her. Rosa's familiarity with a great number of languages, as well as "metaphysics, quaint philosophy, and current topics" immediately makes her suspect enough.

Among Rosa's many roles once she gets to the United States is that of a bank bookkeeper, Eugene Comstock (in which guise she makes off with the bank's money), and that of a daring robber, Captain Dandy, head of a feared band of villains. At the same time, she is the mistress of the bank's cashier and persuades him to let her rob the bank. Among her other treacherous deeds, she breaks the heart of an innocent young girl who falls in love with her. She also admits, when her identity is exposed, just before her suicide, that she would not have traded her evil life for that of a normal woman even had she had the opportunity. She remarks: "To sit in a parlor and do fancy work, and welcome a husband from his daily toil, to get his meals, to attend to his clothes, bah! It fills me with disgust." Hatch attributes all her misdeeds and faults to the fact that, like Ovid's Iphis, she was raised as a boy until she was twelve because her father wanted a son, and after his death it was too late to change. While Gautier's Maupin is an intriguing creature whom neither men nor women can resist, transplanted on American soil sixty years later, she becomes a tormented neurotic, handicapped by her unfortunate intelligence and learning. While she may attract, she also repels in the same measure. If she can ruin a life, she will.

Nevertheless, in America such images of lesbian evil were not common in fiction that dealt with love between women. A novel like Florence Converse's *Diana Victrix* (1897) could exist side by side with *The Strange Disappearance of Eugene Comstock*. On the Continent, however, and to a lesser extent in England, where literature about evil lesbians was all the rage and where hundreds of doctors were turning their attention to the disease of love between women, the perception of romantic friendship as a noble institution which society had no reason to discourage and every reason to encourage, was quite dead by the end of the nineteenth century.

PART III

THE TWENTIETH CENTURY

A.

Sophistication

CHAPTER 1

The Last Breath of Innocence

In 1908 it was still possible for an American children's magazine to carry a story in which a teenage girl writes a love poem in honor of her female schoolmate, declaring:

> My love has a forehead broad and fair,
> And the breeze-blown curls of her chestnut hair
> Fall over it softly, the gold and the red
> A shining aureole round her head.
> Her clear eyes gleam with an amber light
> For sunbeams dance in them swift and bright!
> And over those eyes so golden brown,
> Long, shadowy lashes droop gently down. . . .
> Oh, pale with envy the rose doth grow
> That my lady lifts to her cheeks' warm glow! . . .
> But for joy its blushes would come again
> If my lady to kiss the rose should deign.[1]

If the above poem had been written by one female character to another in magazine fiction after 1920, the poetess of the story would no doubt have been rushed off to a psychoanalyst to undergo treatment for her mental malady, or she would have ended her fictional existence broken in half by a tree, justly punished by nature (with a little help from a right-thinking heterosexual) for her transgression. Much more likely, such a poem would not have been written by a fictional female to another after the first two decades of the twentieth century, because the explicit discussion of same-sex love in most popular American magazines by that time was considered

297

taboo. In the early twentieth century, however, popular stories often treated the subject totally without self-consciousness or awareness that such relationships were "unhealthy" or "immoral." With the spread of those attitudes which originated in Europe, within the next decade or so such declarations became prohibited in America. But in the early twentieth century, not only *St. Nicholas* but periodicals like the *Ladies' Home Journal* and *Harper's* could carry passionate tales of love between women.

America may have been slower than Europe to be impressed by the taboos against same-sex love for several reasons: (1) Without a predominant Catholic mentality the country was less fascinated with "sin" and therefore less obsessed with the potential of sex between women; (2) by virtue of distance, America was not so influenced by the German medical establishment as other countries were, such as France and Italy and, to a lesser extent, England; (3) there was not so much clear-cut hostility, or rather there was more ambivalence to women's freedom in a land which in principle was dedicated to tolerance of individual freedom. Therefore, romantic friendship was possible in America well into the second decade of the twentieth century, and, for those women who were born and raised Victorians and remained impervious to the new attitudes, even beyond it.

There were early twentieth-century equivalents to nineteenth-century writers like Alexander Walker and Henry Guernsey [2] who feared any form of sensual discovery on the part of women. Thomas Shannon, for example, in the book *Perfect Girlhood* (1913) warned that girls must never be allowed to sleep with their hands inside the blanket, to sit on their own feet, or to sleep at each other's houses. [3] But such warnings suggested no more sophistication than that found in the 1740 work, *The Ladies Dispensatory: or Every Woman her Own Physician,* in which sex between a young woman and her maid is placed in the category of masturbation. [4]

In America it took the phenomenal growth of female autonomy during and after World War I, [5] and the American popularization of the most influential of the European sexologists, Sigmund Freud, [6] to cast the widespread suspicions on love between women that had already been prevalent in Europe.

In her novel, *We Sing Diana* (1928), Wanda Fraiken Neff shows that the change in attitude toward female relationships took place just around the time of World War I. In 1913 her heroine was a student at a women's college, where everyone engaged in romantic friendships, which were considered "the great human experience," and a violent crush on a particular woman teacher had run to such epidemic proportions that she was called "The Freshman Disease." In 1920, when the heroine returns to the same college to teach, the atmosphere is entirely different. Now undergraduate speech is full of Freudian vocabulary. Everything is attributed to sex. And "intimacies between two girls were watched with keen, distrustful eyes. Among one's classmates, one looked for the bisexual type, the masculine girl searching for a feminine counterpart, and one ridiculed their devotions."

A comparison of two autobiographical works written at a fifteen-year interval, *The Story of Mary MacLane by Herself* (1902) and *I, Mary MacLane: A Diary of Human Days* (1917), provides another literary illustration of the change in attitudes during so short a period. In the first autobiography the young narrator asks in nineteenth-century fashion, "Are there many things in this cool-hearted world so utterly exquisite as the pure love of one woman for another?" [7] She then goes on to explain that she loves Fanny Corbin, her former teacher, a woman a dozen years older than Mary, "with a peculiar and vivid intensity, and with all the sincerity and passion that is in me." Like many a romantic friend before her, she has dreams of retiring with her beloved, whom she calls the "anemone lady," to a Llangollen-like retreat, "some little out-of-the-world place . . . for the rest of my life." [8] Quite without self-consciousness, Mary can cry to Fanny in 1902, "My dearly-loved anemone lady, I want you so much—why aren't you here!" [9] and she can speak of feeling in her presence "a convulsion and a melting within." [10] Her devotion is in no way distinguishable from romantic love. She even goes as far as to admit, "I feel in the anemone lady a strange attraction of sex," and to ask the reader, "Do you think a man is the only creature with whom one may fall in love?" [11] Despite such declarations and her worldly stance throughout the book, there is no indication that love between women is taboo, that what she feels has been attributed to sin or sickness.

Fifteen years later, such naïveté was no longer possible. In her 1917 book MacLane observes with authority borrowed from German and French writers, "The Lesbian sex-strain as an effect is reckoned a pre-natal influence" and "to each other [lesbians] are . . . victims, preyers, masters, slaves." Although she admits, in the hope of shocking, "I have lightly kissed and been kissed by Lesbian lips," she is quick to add, "I am too personally fastidious . . . to walk in direct repellent roads of vice even in freest moods." She refers to love between women as "contraband" and "twisted." While it is her primary intention to *épater le bourgeois* in this book, and she speaks of lesbianism in subsequent pages in exotic terms, she is consistently careful to make it clear that she is not really a "Lesbian woman," one of those "whose predilections are warped: who lives always in unrest: whose inner walls are streaked with garish heathen pigments: whose copious love-instincts are an odd mixture of mirth, malice, and *luxure*." [12] MacLane assumed or hoped, no doubt, that her readers would have long forgotten her 1902 confessions about the "sincerity and passion" of her love for Fanny Corbin, which included even "a strange attraction of sex." Perhaps in the light of her newfound wisdom she had forgotten them herself. Her shift in attitude is a mirror of the shift throughout society.

American fiction of around the time of MacLane's first book frequently presents New Women, engaged in activities which had only recently become accessible to them and conducting old romantic friendships. The heroines are often students in a women's college or they are preparing for a career or they are professionally engaged, often as artists, teachers, or nurses, the "women's professions." The love relationships in these stories are conducted without a hint that Krafft-Ebing or Baudelaire existed.[13]

A popular collection by Josephine Dodge Daskam, *Smith College Stories*, which was first published in 1900 and reissued a number of times in the following years, reflects the ordinariness of emotional involvements between women. In "The Evolution of Evangeline," for example, the older girls invite the younger to all-women dances. When one older girl, Biscuits, is obliged to invite Evangeline, who is not attractive to her, "visions of the pretty little freshman she had in mind on filling out her [dance] programme flashed before her with irritating clearness." When another freshman is disappointed in her hope of being escorted to the dance by her favorite sophomore, the narrator observes, "the little freshman cried herself to sleep, for she had dreamed for nights of going with Suzanne, whom she admired to stupefaction." [14] It is assumed in Daskam's universe, just as it generally was in nineteenth-century novels, that these loves would be superseded by heterosexual attachments. But while Daskam's characters are at Smith College, their passions are primarily for each other.

In a 1909 novel, Clarissa Dixon's *Janet and Her Dear Phebe*, the New Women conduct a nineteenth-century romantic friendship with all the old lack of restraint, oblivious to French and German images of female love. Although Janet and Phebe become teacher and nurse, they are also nineteenth-century women; and feminism, such as that of the heroine of *Diana Victrix*, does not exist in the world of this novel. As women, they must marry. But despite the fact that these two passionate friends of childhood are engaged to men (at the ages of twenty-seven and twenty-eight, respectively), their main attachments are to each other. The girls had been separated years before by their fathers' quarrels, but each spent a good deal of her adult life looking for the other. Finally Janet goes to a favorite spring where the two had gone together, and there she writes on a rock, "The love of Phebe and Janet was written upon this stone." Just as she finishes, Phebe miraculously appears, having also come there to relive her past happiness with Janet. At the conclusion of the novel Janet tells Phebe that it would be lovely if they could get lost together, just as they did when they were children, but Phebe replies, "Now that I have found you and you have found me, we could not be lost though we wandered throughout the whole universe. Our sun shall not set; we shall lose knowledge of darkness." Their impending marriages are a fact of female life in this 1909 novel, no less than marriage had been throughout the preceding century, but their mutual romantic involvement dims all else.

Jennette Lee, like Josephine Daskam, also uses a women's college setting in a relatively late story (1919), "The Cat and the King," which was published in the *Ladies' Home Journal*.[15] The probable lack of sophistication of most *Journal* readers explains perhaps why love between women could be treated in such positive terms at so late a date. When the freshman of this story, Flora, sees her idol, Annette, the narrator observes:

> To the freshman gazing from her walk, it was as if a goddess, high-enshrined and touched by the rising sun, stood revealed. She gave a gasp of pleasure.

Certainly one might point out that such a description is a relic of the sentimental rhetoric of an earlier day, but Lee retained the attitudes toward the *fact* of love between women as well, as the action of her story illustrates. Flora has a crush on Annette, who is a senior and the captain of the college ball team. When Annette hurts her ankle and is hospitalized in the school infirmary, Flora decides the best way to meet her idol is to feign a strange illness and to be hospitalized too. But on Flora's first day in the infirmary, Annette is released. A kindly woman doctor discerns the problem and help-fully devises two ways to get the girls together: She employs Flora in her lab where Annette also works, and she has Flora placed on the ball team. The doctor exits from the story, telling Flora happily, "You are to report at once to the captain—in her room."

It is inconceivable that such a story would have been printed in a magazine like the *Ladies' Home Journal* a decade or even a few years later. In a more psychoanalytically aware society, the rapture that Flora expresses over her beloved would be considered appro-priate only if that beloved were of the opposite sex. When Flora's roommate assures her, "You can live if you don't make the team [and thus lose the opportunity to be near Annette]. Other folks do," Flora responds, *"I can't!"* [italics are Lee's]. In the infirmary, when the doctor says, as she is taking Flora's pulse, that Flora will have a bed near Annette, the pulse speeds up so that the doctor "started and glanced sharply down at the wrist under her fingers." When Flora is in Annette's presence, she looks at Annette "adoringly," watches her "with devoted happy eyes," and gazes "at the beloved face." When Annette is released from the infirmary sooner than Flora expected, Lee writes, Flora "subsided, a bundle of sobs, under the tumbled clothes." It is doubtful that post-World War I college women, who were probably readers of more sophisticated fare, could maintain such innocence about the sexologists' pronounce-ments regarding love between women. But the readers of *Ladies' Home Journal* apparently still could.

In view of modern pseudoknowledge, even more inconceivable than the *Ladies' Home Journal* story is fiction published in a chil-dren's magazine. "The Lass of the Silver Sword," which appeared serially in *St. Nicholas* during 1908–1909, is set in a girls' boarding school. As in "The Cat and the King," the older girl, Carol Arm-strong, who is eighteen, is loved by the younger Jean Lennox: The narrator states that "Jean had fallen in love with [Carol] at first sight." Again, the description of her involvement is one that the reader might expect to find in contemporary popular magazines only if the subject were male and female:

> Alas! the course of true love never did run smooth! Jean had not dared to confess her admiration to anyone but Cecily Brook, whom she had pledged to keep her secret. Now and then she made offerings of candy and flowers anonymously, leaving them on Carol's desk, and so far all Carol's attempts

to play detective had failed, and it looked as if her admirer would remain forever unknown.

But, as a prank, two other girls steal Jean's notebook, which contains "poems and stories, and *odes*" to Carol, and having discovered "she's dead in love with her," they send the notebook to Carol. Carol is delighted by the discovery, as she tells Jean, "To think I might have gone on to the end of school, and never found you out, you dear!"

Although there is some vague suggestion of heterosexual interests in the story, the real emotional center is the relationship between Jean and Carol—and frequently when it appears to have shifted slightly, in fact it has remained the same. For example, Jean has written a novel in which Carol is the protagonist. A scene from the work is cited in which Carol is happily awaiting the approach of a handsome young man with the knightly name of Arthur de Lancy. But just prior to the discussion of this fantasy, Jean has talked about forming with her other school friends an order of knights, The Silver Sword, of which she is to become the leader. It is likely the author is suggesting that Jean fantasizes herself as a King Arthur or a Lancelot, and that she herself is Carol's love interest in her seemingly heterosexual fictions.

The physical affection that Jean and Carol exchange is totally without the self-consciousness that would be inevitable in a post-Freudian era. For instance, at one point in the story "Carol came in, caught Jean, whirled her around, pulled her down on a cot, and gave her a warm kiss." At a later point Carol pulled Jean "into her lap and hugged her tight. 'You precious little Jeanie Queen! I never saw anything so dear as you in all my life.'" Most significantly, there is nothing covert in their relationship. All the other characters understand that these two are devoted to each other—and their popularity does not suffer: Jean is elected to head the Order of the Silver Sword, and Jean and Carol organize a girls' camp which their classmates are eager to attend. Although this is an adolescent friendship and could be dismissed as an emotional phase, subsequent treatments of strong attachments between girls were considerably toned down, presumably because the authors feared they would be encouraging homosexuality. Most later authors did not dare write that one girl pulled another down on a cot and gave her a warm kiss.[16]

In several popular early twentieth-century magazine stories depicting adult relationships between two females, at least one is an artist who is committed to her work, which explains why she failed to marry when other women did. But unlike the early twentieth-century French image of the bohemian woman artist (and later American prototypes), these women's choice of profession is not an explanation for eccentric amorous tastes, since their same-sex love is not regarded as eccentric. The treatment of the love relationship is completely sympathetic, usually without the slightest hint that in some parts of the world such love had been frowned on for decades. O. Henry's short story, "The Last Leaf," which first appeared in *Strand Magazine* in 1906, is an example.[17] His two characters, Sue from Maine and Joanna from California, meet in New York. They both support themselves as artists and live together. They are New Women, extremely career-conscious and without any intention of marrying. Their unfeminine modernism is underlined by their choice of new names: Joanna is called Johnsy and Sue is Sudie. Nowhere does O. Henry suggest that he disapproves of their aspirations or their conduct.

As the story opens, Johnsy is severely ill with pneumonia. The doctor informs Sue that her friend's chances of recovery are one in ten, and that she will live only if she has a strong desire to fight for her life. In the dialogue that follows between Sue and the doctor, O. Henry clearly validates the women's independent life-style and even their relationship. He shows the doctor to be pompous and insensitive when he tells Sue:

> "Your little lady has made up her mind that she's not going to get well. Has she anything on her mind?"
>
> "She—she wanted to paint the Bay of Naples some day," said Sue.
>
> "Paint?—bosh! Has she anything on her mind worth thinking about twice—a man, for instance?"
>
> "A man?" said Sue, with a jew's-harp twang in her voice. "Is a man worth—but, no, doctor, there is nothing of the kind."

O. Henry tells us not only that men are not of amorous interest for these women, but also that the two are almost everything to each other. And when Sudie fears that Johnsy is dying, she implores her, "Dear, dear! . . . Think of me if you won't think of yourself. What would I do?" The only other area of importance in their lives is their art. When Johnsy recovers she tells her mate with serious conviction, "Sudie, some day I hope to paint the Bay of Naples."

There is no hint in this early twentieth-century piece of popular magazine fiction that the two women will be distracted from their interest in each other and their profession by what the doctor unimaginatively calls something "worth thinking about twice—a man, for instance."

Perhaps O. Henry could afford to be so sympathetic because women had not achieved independence in significant numbers by 1906: It was not yet socially threatening if occasional independent women—those who, for example, could eke out a living as artists—chose to devote themselves to each other. Most American women still had little possibility of becoming independent in a fulfilling profession; they must and would marry, regardless of their youthful emotional ties.

The general inevitability of marriage for ordinary women who had no extraordinary calling is described in another story about women artists which appeared in *Harper's Magazine* in 1912, "The Beautiful House." [18] Like O. Henry, the author is very sympathetic to an extraordinary character, Mary Hastings, who remains unmarried, and to her love for Sylvia Brunton (who leaves her for a man); however, the lack of permanence in such relationships is emphasized not only in the action of the story, but even in the somewhat heavy-handed symbolism. Sylvia and Mary find a beautiful house, which they both love and hope to inhabit together. The caretaker explains that the house is called "Love o' Women" because "it won't last long." And, in fact, the house burns to the ground as Mary loses Sylvia to her handsome male cousin, Evan Hardie.

Mary, a thirty-five-year-old woman, is consistently described in positive terms: She is "handsome" and has a "dignity of carriage that went beyond her years." She suffers from none of the characteristics that popular literature has so often attributed to the "old maid":

> Spinsterhood suited her temperament and had not faded her vitality in the slightest degree; indeed, her independence and the passage of time had marked her only with a finer gravity of bearing. Her occupation gave her abiding content, she was an able and even distinguished landscape painter, and her sufficient income was increased by the sale of her sketches that she liked least. Her best work she either kept or gave away.

Like the two women in O. Henry's story, she is a committed artist. Sylvia, on the other hand, is not committed to her art; and, as far as the reader can see, she is not economically independent. She merely plays at being a New Woman. She is described as "one of the time-markers," who thinks she wants to be an artist because she has an "overpowering sense of the responsibility of life that comes to the serious young [we are told that she is between twenty and thirty], a trust of years and opportunity which must be met, it seemed to her, and met instantly, and which she had all too hastily supposed was an obligation to paint pictures." Sylvia attended an art school where "Mary Hastings saw her, and in a manner fell in love with her." On her own level, Sylvia seems to return the affection, and they continue for a while in perfect intimacy; "and then to intensify their communion they found the House, which gathered together the threads of their love, and held it as a body should its soul." At this point Sylvia seems as involved in the relationship as Mary. It is she who convinces Mary that they must have the "beautiful house":

> "We could come here together," Sylvia went on. "Just whenever we wanted to. Just you and I, Mary beloved," she almost whispered, "wouldn't you like it?"
>
> Her slender hands lay out along the table, palms turned up. Mary gathered them in her own hands and kissed them.
>
> "I should—like it!" she said, whimsically insistent on the moderate word.

But despite her "adoration" of Mary, and her insistence that she "can't possibly do without seeing" Mary frequently, Sylvia is after all only a "time-marker" who seems to be waiting to pass on to something else, while Mary, "although she did not perceive it," soon permits herself to "picture their relationship to each other . . . crystalized and enduring."

The relationship is not without an erotic element, at least in Mary's mind: For example, as Sylvia admires an old bust in the garden of the beautiful house, "Mary thought of nothing else but how adorable Sylvia looked there, with the transparent pink of her skin against the old gray stone head." Mary's love is certainly what would be called "homosexual" in more recent times, but since— living in a less sophisticated time—the author did not use terms suggesting "perversity" or "abnormality," Mary is the most sympathetic character, while Sylvia appears to be a flibbertigibbet; and Evan is silly and insensitive—looking at the beautiful old ivy in the garden, for example, "he stopped and became serious. 'If you were to strip down that ivy,' he said with animation, 'you could have a fives-court here.' "

Sylvia goes off with him in perfect contentment, with "the happy security of a bird that drops upon its nest," while Mary mourns. However, the author's point is clearly not that all women need and want a heterosexual relationship, but that most women do not have Mary's resources: her strength, her commitment to her art, and, not the least of these, her ability to support herself. Because women like Mary are rare, it is probable that the "love o' women" will be impermanent: not because it is inherently flawed, but because most women require the "happy security" of a "nest" (i.e., marriage and family).

In Helen Hull's "The Fire," which appeared in *Century* magazine in 1917,[19] the older character, Miss Egert, is again a self-supporting artist, an unmarried woman who is perfectly happy with her lot despite the fact that she must battle her brother's "attempts to make [her] see reason" and the community's suspicion of her independence. The author is completely sympathetic to her and makes us admire her strength, her gentleness, and her joy in beautiful things.

Cynthia Bates, her young art student, loves her. Cynthia's mother becomes suspicious of the relationship, believing that it causes Cynthia to "drift away from us, your head full of silly notions," and she forbids Cynthia to continue her art lessons and even her visits to Miss Egert. Her opposition is complex: She fears that Cynthia will develop under Miss Egert's influence values that will make her unsatisfied with the unimaginative, staid, routine-ridden lives of her parents, that she will lose hold over Cynthia, who is beginning to worship art and beauty, which are alien to Mrs. Bates. But, as suggested in the discussion of Mary MacLane's second book, French and German views were gradually filtering down into popular consciousness in America. Affection between women was becoming suspect. Hull's story hints that Mrs. Bates fears not only Miss Egert's artistic influence on her daughter but also the possibility of an erotic relationship between them. "What were you doing when I found you?" she yells at her daughter. "Holding hands! Is that the right thing for you? She's turning your head." When Cynthia protests that they were talking about beauty, her mother is outraged:

Beauty! You disobey your mother, hurt her, to talk about beauty at night with an old maid! . . . Pretending to be an artist . . . to get young girls who are foolish enough to listen to her sentimentalizing . . . I've always trusted you, depended on you; now I can't even trust you.

And there does in fact seem to be an erotic element in their relationship which is inextricably mixed with their roles as the mentor of beauty and courage and the devoted pupil, as their farewell scene indicates:

> Cynthia's fingers unclasped, and one hand closed desperately around Miss Egert's. Her heart fluttered in her temples, her throat, her breast. She clung to the fingers, pulling herself slowly up from an inarticulate abyss.
>
> "Miss Egert,"—she stumbled into words—"I can't bear it, not coming here! Nobody else cares except about sensible things. You do, beautiful, wonderful things."
>
> "You'd have to find them for yourself, Cynthia." Miss Egert's fingers moved under the girl's grasp. Then she bent towards Cynthia and kissed her with soft, pale lips that trembled against the girl's mouth. "Cynthia, don't let anyone stop you! Keep searching!" She drew back, poised for a moment in the shadow before she rose. Through Cynthia ran the swift feet of white ecstasy. She was pledging herself to some tremendous mystery, which trembled all about her.

Although Cynthia bows to her mother's pressure and gives up Miss Egert, it is made clear that she will not give up Miss Egert's influence, which is portrayed as entirely positive and constructive in contrast with the pathetically narrow ideals that Cynthia's parents try to impose on their daughter.

Love between women, openly treated, was dead as a popular literary theme in America by the 1920's. It might still have been found however in art magazines like Margaret Anderson's *Little Review*.[20] It could also be treated in more popular magazines as well as other media, if the subject matter was sufficiently disguised, as in Gertrude Stein's "Miss Furr and Miss Skeene," which appeared in *Vanity Fair* in 1922. The story is a play on the word "gay," which was not yet widely understood to mean homosexual—only those who had become a part of what was by this time a flourishing lesbian subculture would have known what Stein meant by her description of gay Georgine Skeene and Helen Furr.

While Stein disguised her subject matter through a highly stylized language, other authors disguised theirs by locating romantic friendship in some far-off kingdom in the distant past, as Edna St. Vincent Millay did in her play *The Lamp and the Bell* (1921). Despite the setting, her character Bianca was probably modeled on Charlotte

Babcock, the woman Millay loved when she was in her early twenties, while Beatrice was probably Millay.[21] In the play one character observes of Beatrice and Bianca, "I vow I never knew a pair of lovers/More constant than those two." The women tell each other, "You are a burning lamp to me, a flame/ The wind cannot burn out, and I shall hold you/ High in my hand against whatever darkness," and "You are to me a silver bell in a tower./ And when it rings I know I am near home." Like the nineteenth-century romantic friends in Longfellow's *Kavanagh* and Edith Arnold's *Platonics*, both women fall in love with the same man. Beatrice sacrifices her feelings so that Bianca can marry him, although it is clear that even after the marriage the two women are more to each other than a man can ever be to them.

Elizabeth Atkins states in her biography of Millay that the poet was really writing of college women's relationships, and that while the play purports to be set in the kingdom of Fiori years ago, it is really set in Poughkeepsie-on-the-Hudson around 1913–1917, when Millay was a student at Vassar.[22] While Longfellow and Arnold and most others who wrote about romantic friendship in the nineteenth century and earlier set their scene in their own place and century, Millay felt compelled to send her characters to an Italy of long ago, although the theme of the play in no way demands such a setting. By 1921 it was necessary to place romantic friendship at a distance, where it could be attributable to the peculiarities of time and location in order to make it safe.

This must have been extremely puzzling to women who grew up in the Victorian era. For some, as indicated in the discussion of Jeannette Marks, it must have brought on a painful alienation from self. Others attempted to ignore the absurd new rules for affectionate expression between women, but they must have felt placed in a defensive position if they were aware of contemporary attitudes. It was probably unusual when a literate woman such as Vida Scudder could state without self-consciousness in 1937 regarding romantic friendship that "more than any other sub-lunar force, it initiates us into the eternal. When it has not been born of illusion, it can never die, though strange interludes may befall it, though loyalty needs be now and again invoked to supplement desire. Its drama normally knows no end." But she was seventy-six at the time, far too old to believe that anyone viewed her with suspicion or that she must or could change her views.

Undoubtedly Vera Brittain, an English expatriate who made her home in America, was more typical. In *Testament of Friendship: The Story of Winifred Holtby* (1940), Brittain discussed her romance with Holtby "which continued unbroken and unspoilt for sixteen incomparable years."²³ She quotes Winifred saying to her, in Marguerite's words to Faust, "I need thee every hour!"²⁴ Brittain admits that when she decided to marry, Winifred became "pale, tired and restless" and left England herself "so as not to be 'left.'"²⁵ But Brittain is aware that such statements have a sexual implication in her day, and she decides to meet it head on. At one point she complains, "Sceptics are aroused by any record of affection between women to suspicions habitual among the over-sophisticated," and she refers to legends that were current about them in their neighborhood.²⁶ Later she is even more direct in a reference to "the scandalmongers who invented for [Winifred] a lurid series of homosexual relationships,"²⁷ and throughout she feels obliged to remind the reader of the harmless and socially beneficial effects of same-sex love: "Loyalty and affection between women is a noble relationship which, far from impoverishing, actually enhances the love of a girl for her lover, of a wife for her husband, of a mother for her children."²⁸

What disturbs Brittain, of course, is the possibility that her readers would see in her love a congenital taint, or arrested development and the evil little countenance of sex. Anna Cogswell Wood, telling a very similar story only a few decades earlier (*The Story of a Friendship: A Memoir*, 1901),²⁹ had no notion that there was anything in her book which could be negatively construed. But Brittain was right to be chary if suspicions disturbed her: What contemporary reader could piece together Brittain and Holtby's friendship with the composer Ethel Smythe (who was notoriously lesbian), the evidence of Holtby's passionate letters to another woman,³⁰ and the fact of Brittain's long-standing fascination with *The Well of Loneliness*,³¹ and not conclude that the two women had a lesbian relationship?

Similarly, Doris Faber's recent efforts to show that Eleanor Roosevelt and Lorena Hickok maintained a passionate romantic friendship but were never sexual together will be met skeptically by her readers. Faber gives ample evidence of Hickok's love relationships with other women. She shows that Hickok made advances to a female colleague in a hotel room and that she was self-conscious enough to advise against carrying *The Well of Loneliness* around in public. Faber quotes letters between the First Lady and Hickok, such as, "I want to put my arms around you and kiss you at the corners of your mouth. And in a little more than a week now—I shall."³²

Despite this, she passionately insists on the "purity" of their friendship. However, in a sex-conscious age a relationship like the one between Hickok and Roosevelt will surely be considered sexual, particularly if it is made so clear that one of the principals is sexually knowledgeable. While some decades earlier Hickok and Roosevelt themselves might have been able to think of their excitement over each other as a manifestation of their spiritual longing, in the early 1930's, at the height of their relationship, post-Freud and post-*Well*, and as two worldly, literate women, they no longer had the luxury of innocence. At the very least, they would have been compelled to discuss the psychosexual implications of their love and to deal with them.

Our century has a passion for categorizing love, as previous centuries did not, which stems from the supposedly liberalized twentieth-century view of sex that, ironically, has created its own rigidity.[33] In our century the sex drive was identified, perhaps for the first time in history, as being the foremost instinct—in women as well as men—inescapable and all but uncontrollable, and invariably permanently intertwined with real love. As a result, romantic friendships of other eras, which are assumed to have been asexual since women were not given the freedom of their sex drive, are manifestations of sentimentality and the superficial manners of the age. Throughout most of the twentieth century, on the other hand, the enriching romantic friendship that was common in earlier eras is thought to be impossible, since love necessarily means sex and sex between women means lesbian and lesbian means sick.

There is plenty of anecdotal proof that love between women cannot exist without self-consciousness in our era, and that regardless of its noble qualities it is given a label which, until lesbian-feminists reclaimed the word in recent years, meant sickness. For example, one young woman, writing in the feminist journal *Ain't I a Woman* in 1970, told of her close, affectionate and even physical relationships with other girls in high school, which she did not recognize as abnormal until she read *Life and Love for Teenagers*, whose authors described such feelings and "prescribed psychiatric counselling though they also stated that prognosis for cure was very low." While previously she had believed her romantic friendships were a strength in her life, now she felt "hopelessly dirty and sick. I became suspicious of any uncontrollable emotions and motives my strange new self might have."[34] Sidney Abbott and Barbara Love in *Sappho Was a Right-on Woman* (1972) quote a similar experience:

In my marvelous new feelings for her I felt I had discovered myself. I went walking, celebrating sun, sky, and trees, and myself as somehow the center of it all. Then I stopped as if I had come on the edge of a chasm there in the woods. A word came clawing up from the depths of my mind. I didn't want the knowledge that was coming, but my wish didn't stop it. The horror of the word burst upon me almost before the word itself—sick, perverted, unnatural, *Lesbian.*[35]

It is not clear whether or not these relationships had a specifically genital component, but in any case the young women felt guilty. It is not the proof of *sex* between women that they sensed their society would disapprove of but their love and devotion as viewed in the context of twentieth-century pseudoknowledge and female autonomy.

An experiment conducted by two Palo Alto, California, high school girls for a family-life course illustrates the point. For three weeks the girls behaved on campus as all romantic friends did in the previous century: They held hands often on campus walks, they sat with their arms around each other, and they exchanged kisses on the cheek when classes ended. They expressly did not intend to give the impression that their feelings were sexual. They touched each other only as close, affectionate friends would. But despite their intentions, their peers interpreted their relationship as lesbian and ostracized them. Interestingly, the boys limited their hostility to calling them names. The girls, who perhaps felt more anxiety and guilt about what such behavior reflected on their own impulses, threatened to beat them up.[36]

A whole area of joyful, nurturing experience which women of other centuries enjoyed freely has thus been closed in our liberated times. To demand it has meant to put oneself beyond the pale and to accept the label which has carried dreadful meanings with it. But life beyond the pale has had its value too for those who have managed to retain their sanity. It has freed them to create new modes of being and relating to each other such as eighteenth- and nineteenth-century romantic friends could not, since they were permitted to remain in the prison of convention. Madame de Staël saw her passionate attachment to Juliette de Récamier only as the love of two creatures who suffered because they were of their society and their society demanded that women be weak and suffer. But twentieth-century romantic friends, lesbians beyond the pale and prison of their society, could experience their relationships as liberating, freeing them from the restrictive conventions of female heterosexuality, and giving them the opportunity to decide for themselves what love is and what woman is. It was this liberating aspect of lesbianism that ultimately became so appealing to many feminists in the 1970's, who began to covet for themselves the label that had earlier brought with it mixed blessings.

CHAPTER 2

The Spread of
Medical "Knowledge"

Krafft-Ebing continued to be a major influence on sexologists well into the twentieth century. By the 1920's, however, Sigmund Freud essentially replaced him. Their differences with regard to the "causes" of same-sex love amounted, in the simplest terms, to the argument of nature vs. nurture. Krafft-Ebing maintained that the true invert was born with his or her condition; Freud maintained that it was childhood trauma which was primarily responsible for the condition. But both grouped male and female same-sex love together as one entity, quite ignoring the differing social conditions that would convince a man or a woman to accept a homosexual identification. Both also agreed that same-sex love was a problem with which the medical profession ought to be concerned, and whether it was a sign of congenital defect or of blocked development, it was undesirable.

Regardless of studies conducted in the first third of the century which showed that love between women was normal even statistically and that even those who indulged in a genital expression were at least as healthy as those who did not, the sexologists maintained that women afflicted with love for other women were abnormal. Freud's disciples encouraged them to get medical help in order to be cured of their condition. What had been widely recognized as natural now became widely viewed as neurotic, a subject for medical conventions and psychiatric journals, a problem that necessitated help by a professional trained in dealing with mental diseases.

Freud captured the popular imagination especially in America as previous sexologists had not. A jingle which appeared in the Febru-

314

ary 1924 issue of *Harper's Magazine*—"Our lives would not be so complex/ Without suppressed desires and sex"—is typical of the easy usage of Freudian terms and the popularized understanding of Freudian theories which were pervasive in America in the 1920's. Through the mass dissemination of Freud's medical wisdom, the country became obsessed with sexual expression and its perversion. It would not have been necessary to read Freud's essays on "The Sexual Aberrations" or "The Psychogenesis of a Case of Homosexuality in a Woman" in order to know that love between women was now an indication of childhood trauma and arrested development. Writers of popular literature, who may or may not have gone back to the original source themselves, regurgitated the information for mass delectation.

Krafft-Ebing's theories were not dead with the advent of Freud, but they continued and were often modified by those who saw themselves as the "inverts" he described. While Krafft-Ebing regarded same-sex love as a congenital defect, disciples like Magnus Hirschfeld argued that although it was congenital, it was not necessarily a defect. In fact, among some homosexuals (generally men) a cult of homosexual superiority developed that viewed the invert as the man of the future, a member of an elite. As the moral voice in A. T. Fitzroy's *Despised and Rejected* (1918) states:

> [Those] who stand mid-way between the extremes of the two sexes are the advanced guard of a more enlightened civilization. They're despised and rejected by their fellow men today . . . but I believe that the time is not so far distant when we will recognize in the best of our intermediate types the leaders and masters of the race. . . . From them a new humanity is being evolved. . . . The human soul complete in itself, perfectly balanced, not limited by the psychological bounds of one sex, but combining the power and the intellect of the one with the subtlety and intuition of the other.[1]

Women, who had little experience in challenging the experts, were for the most part too intimidated to claim such superiority for themselves.

In Germany the first organized homosexual movements emerged appropriately enough on the tail of the sexologists' pronouncements. Efforts (which some women supported) soon began to educate the public to accept those congenitalists' theories that appeared to place those who identified themselves as homosexuals in a positive light. Most homosexual spokespersons maintained the homosexual's lack of choice in orientation, but they assured the public that in all other ways the homosexual was sound. Elisabeth Dauthendey's 1906 pamphlet, *The Uranian Question and Women,* is typical of this stance. Dauthendey lists "facts" regarding lesbianism such as:

> *1.* Uranianism is no one's fault since it is due to a disorder of empirical natural laws.
>
> *2.* Like all other deformities or functional disorders, it deserves compassion and not contempt.
>
> *3.* It is definitely compatible with intellectual functioning.
>
> *4.* It is never the result of exterior causes or training but always congenitally conditioned.[2]

Popular fiction also came to the aid of the cause by presenting upstanding, moral people whose one problem is their inversion. In a 1901 Danish novel, which created considerable interest among German homosexuals, the author asks in the title, *Whose Fault Is It?,* referring to the heroine's inversion. The novel's response is that it is no one's fault. Nina, a likable if pathetic person, was born with her problem, as even her body attests: "No visible swelling of her breast indicated that she was a woman, her facial features were sharply delineated, and her eyes were strong and self-assured, as is only seldom the case with a female." When Jünger, the protagonist, falls in love with her, he decides her proclivities are really "a sort of sickness" from which "she might be healed" with proper care. But he soon learns that she cannot help herself, that she follows an inborn instinct which causes her to be sexually aroused by women. He finally believes her when she cries, "You don't know how great the passion is which burns in my breast. . . . I cannot live without kissing a woman."[3] The book's pro-invert message was somewhat revolutionary in popular fiction. The French had already observed that lesbianism must be taken seriously and that men must have no illusions about converting lesbians from their desires. But the German sexologists provided material now for the argument that lesbians were driven to their desires by their genes, and that they were no more immoral than they were changeable.

Even in the 1920's some Krafft-Ebing disciples continued to disseminate his ideas. Auguste Forel, for example, a leading Swiss psychiatrist, in his 1925 edition of *The Sexual Question: A Scientific, Psychological, Hygienic, and Sociological Study*, used Krafft-Ebing's classification of sexual psychopathology without any reference to Freud's theories which had reached the height of their popularity in Europe and America at that time.[4] Radclyffe Hall, in preparation for writing *The Well of Loneliness* (1928), compiled a set of notes based on "the latest and revised editions of the works of the highest authorities on sexual inversion, exclusive of the psychoanalysts." Her authorities were all Krafft-Ebing disciples such as Havelock Ellis, Iwan Bloch, and Magnus Hirschfeld.[5]

Nor is Krafft-Ebing's congenital inversion theory dead today: transsexuals are the modern "congenital inverts." They, and some of the medical men who work with them, are convinced (as their earlier counterparts were) that they are trapped in the wrong bodies. Most are also fixated (as were their earlier counterparts) on the notion that there is "appropriate" masculine and feminine behavior and that same-sex love is sinful. Thus if a woman loves a woman it must be because she is really a man.

It is not difficult to see the less-than-honest motives behind the acceptance of one set of theories over another. The practicing analysts generally championed Freud because his views held out the possibility of "cure" for same-sex love, and "cure" was their business. Forel, the director of the insane asylum of Zurich, argued that when sexual perversion is recognized in children and adolescents who are born with their abnormality, they should be isolated—i.e., placed in an insane asylum and treated "as a patient afflicted with a nervous affection who is thereby dangerous to himself and others." [6] Radclyffe Hall, an avowed lesbian, saw in Krafft-Ebing's disciples enough flexibility to argue that while same-sex love was hereditary, its victims might nevertheless be productive citizens. She seized on the congenitalists' theories because (before the days of advanced plastic surgery) they alone dismissed all efforts to change the direction of the invert's love interest. They sanctioned her rejection of insipid feminine behavior together with her preference for "masculine" pursuits: She was, after all, a man trapped in a woman's body. It was Radclyffe Hall, more than any other writer, who was responsible for bringing the congenitalists' theories to popular fiction and thereby disseminating them widely years after they were no longer the most accepted theories among medical men.

Hall believed that her novel would provide lesbians with a moral and medical defense against a society which viewed same-sex love as immoral or curable. If a female argued that she *chose* to center her life on another female, she laid herself open to accusations of immorality, she willfully flew in the face of the conventions of her day. If she accepted the psychoanalytical theory that something had happened to her in childhood to cause her aberration, she had no excuse not to seek a cure which would undo the trauma and set her straight. But if she maintained that she was born with her "condition," although some might consider her a freak she could insist, as Hall actually did, that God created her that way, that she had a purpose in God's scheme of things even if she was a freak. Unless a lesbian accepted the congenitalists' theories, her grounds for not changing were indefensible if she did not live in a society totally committed to the principle of free choice—and Hall knew that her barely post-Victorian society had no such commitment.

The Well of Loneliness is the most famous lesbian novel that has yet been written. For decades it provided for many (even for women who loved women) their only literary image of lesbianism, and it pretended to medical accuracy. But Hall's earlier novel, *The Unlit Lamp* (1924), is very different from her 1928 *succès de scandale*, which describes congenital maiming and "the haunted, tormented eyes of the invert." *The Unlit Lamp* is the story of a woman who missed happiness because she did not leave her mother, whom she regarded as her responsibility, to go off with another woman. The title is taken from Robert Browning's poem about two similarly frustrated heterosexual lovers, "The Statue and the Bust":

> *And the sin I impute to each frustrate ghost*
> *Is—the unlit lamp and the ungirt loin.*

While *The Unlit Lamp* gives some vague Freudian explanation for Joan's and Elizabeth's interest in each other, it does not suggest that they suffer from a congenital problem. In fact, in this book the choice of another female as love object seems to have its roots primarily in feminism and in a rejection of the sexist and heterosexist values of society. Love between women and feminist consciousness seem to be as inextricably bound together in this early novel as they are for contemporary lesbian feminists. When Joan at the age of fifteen announces to her father that she intends to be a doctor, he responds, "An unsexing, indecent profession for any woman, and any woman who takes it up is indecent and unsexed. . . . I'll have none of these new-fangled women's rights in my house; you will stay home like any other girl until such time as you get married. You will marry; do you hear me? That's a woman's profession!" Joan learns her feminism from Elizabeth, who complains, "But surely . . . a woman's brain is as good as a man's. I cannot see why women should be debarred from a degree, or why they should get lower salaries when they work for the same hours, and I don't see why they should be expected to do nothing more intellectual than darn socks and have babies."

The primary cause of Joan's unhappiness is shown to be not that she was born in the wrong body, but that she was born in the wrong time, and that without a support group she lacked the courage of her feminist convictions. Toward the end of the novel, Joan, who is now middle aged, sees all around her young women (usually with female friends) who, perhaps aided by the circumstances of World War I, made better choices than hers:

> Active, aggressively intelligent women, not at all self-conscious in their tailor-made clothes, not ashamed of their cropped hair; women who did things well, important things; women who counted and would go on counting. . . . But she, Joan Ogden, was the forerunner who had failed, the pioneer who got left behind, the prophet who feared his [sic] own prophecies. These others had gone forward, some of them released by the war, others who had always been free-lances . . . and if the world was not quite ready for them yet, if they had to meet criticism and ridicule and opposition, if they were not all as happy as they might be, still, they were at least brave, whereas she had been a coward, conquered by circumstances.

Hall recognizes here the connection between female same-sex love and feminism. She shows that women often determine not to marry, that their affections go to other women—not because they are men trapped in women's bodies but because they reject prescribed roles, and they require a relationship in which the partner will say, as Elizabeth says to Joan, "I not only want your devotion . . . I want your work, your independence, your success." [7]

A short time later, however, Hall began experimenting with the theme of congenital inversion. Her story, "Miss Ogilvy Finds Herself," is about a woman who learns through a dream before death that in a previous life she had been a man. In her present incarnation she is a man, too—but she is trapped in the wrong frame. A respite came during World War I when she was permitted to do a man's job as an ambulance driver, but for the rest of her life she lives with an awareness that she has no place in a two-sex universe. Hall's major purpose was apparently to raise sympathy for the woman with "masculine" predilections and energy who is capable of contributing to her society, who is put to work when society needs her, but is cast aside as a misfit at all other times:

> Poor Miss Ogilvy. . . . Poor all the Miss Ogilvies back from the War with their tunics, their trenchboots, and their childish illusions! Wars come and wars go but the world does not change: it will always forget indebtedness which it thinks it expedient not to remember.

As an apology for inversion, "Miss Ogilvy" was a trial run, and even in that story the reader can detect some feminist awareness in Hall's complaint regarding women's social and professional limitations. *The Well of Loneliness* is a full-fledged development of the congenital-inversion theme. She retains for Stephen Gordon's history Miss Ogilvy's stint as as ambulance driver during World War I, but she drops all hint of feminist awareness—"normal" women are silly, evil, or weak in *The Well*—perhaps because she thought feminism would only detract from her congenital-inversion argument. Despite the perception in *The Unlit Lamp* that lesbianism is "caused" by woman's natural affinity to other women, coupled with her protest against society's desire to stick her into a marriage as quickly as possible and make a nonentity of her, in *The Well* Hall adheres strictly to the nineteenth-century sexologists' theories. She even persuaded Havelock Ellis to write a few scientific prefatory words to the novel.

Hall was concerned with presenting a polemic that would convince heterosexuals that homosexuals need and deserve their "merciful toleration" and their "better understanding," [8] that society ought to leave homosexuals in peace and stop trying to condemn them or convert them. She believed her purpose was best served not by arguing that women chose to be lesbians for good reasons, or that they could be healthy, happy, and good company, or that their lifestyle often permitted them to be more productive than heterosexual women, but rather by persuading heterosexual readers to feel sorry for them.[9]

The reviews of her novel show that Hall was right in believing that she would be more likely to get a sympathetic reception, at least from "liberal" reviewers, if she presented her heroine as a woman who was trapped not by the facts of her environment (or even by arrested development from which one could be cured with enough psychoanalysis) but by a terrible accident of birth. A typical positive 1928 review praised Hall's presentation of "the dreadful poignancy of ineradicable emotions, in comparison with which the emotions of normal men and women seem so clear and uncomplicated, [which] convinces us that women of the type of Stephen Gordon, in so far as their abnormality is inherent and not merely the unnecessary cult of exotic erotics, deserve the fullest consideration and compassion from all who are fortunate enough to have escaped from one of nature's cruellest dispensations." [10]

As an apologist for the invert, Hall shows Stephen Gordon to be of superior moral disposition despite her congenital problem. Stephen takes to heart the instruction from Puddle, her governess: "Have courage; do the best you can with your burden. But above all be honorable. Cling to your honor for the sake of those who share the same burden. For their sakes show the world that people like you and they can be quite as selfless and fine as the rest of mankind. Let your life go to prove this." But Stephen's heroism and nobility are overshadowed by her self-pity and self-loathing, which are explainable by Hall's conviction that tolerance would be most effectively wrung out of her heterosexual readers by eliciting their pity. When Stephen discovers that she has been deceived by Angela, a "normal" woman with whom she had been having an affair, she cries out to her deceiver, "I'm just a poor, heartbroken freak of a creature who loves and needs you much more than its life." Her suffering reaches a bathetic height when she realizes that even her dog perceives that she is not a genuine article and favors a real man, her rival Martin, "not being exactly disloyal to Stephen, but discerning in the man a more perfect thing, a more entirely fulfilling companion. And this little betrayal, though slight in itself, had the power to wound." To arouse sympathy, Hall creates the impression that such suffering is merely a matter of course for the lesbian; that it is part of her makeup along with "the terrible nerves of the invert, those nerves that are always lying in wait"; and that inversion is a congenital *defect*. After reading Krafft-Ebing, Stephen laments, "And there are so many of us—thousands of miserable, unwanted people . . . hideously maimed and ugly— God's cruel; He let us get flawed in the making."

Hall pleased the "liberal" critics who were sympathetic toward congenital inverts to begin with. But despite her efforts to create a pathetic picture of creatures who begged only for pity and understanding, those who began with prejudice seem not to have been affected. James Douglas, the editor of the *Sunday Express*, declared, "I would rather give a healthy boy or a healthy girl a phial of prussic acid than this novel. Poison kills the body, but moral poison kills the soul." And he classed Hall with "the decadent apostles of the most hideous and loathesome vices [who] no longer conceal their degeneracy and their degradation." [11] In America the judge who first considered the novel at an obscenity hearing in 1929 stated, "The book can have no moral value since it seems to justify the right of the pervert to prey upon normal members of the community," and he concluded that it was "antisocial and offensive to public morals and decency." [12]

There was probably no lesbian in the four decades between 1928 and the late 1960's capable of reading English or any of the eleven languages into which the book was translated who was unfamiliar with *The Well of Loneliness*. Del Martin, co-author of *Lesbian/ Woman*, has called it a "Lesbian Bible." [13] It was widely used in college abnormal psychology classes, and was the only lesbian novel known to the masses. But many lesbians who read the book during Hall's day and after felt angered and betrayed by it. An American sociological study of lesbians in the 1920's and 1930's indicated that "almost to a woman, they decried its publication." They believed that if the novel did not actually do harm to their cause, at the least it "put homosexuality in the wrong light." [14] The responses of individual lesbians were similar. The artist Romaine Brooks, for example, called *The Well* "a ridiculous book, trite, superficial" and Hall "a digger up of worms with the pretention of a distinguished archaeologist." [15] Violet Trefusis in a letter to her lover, Vita Sackville-West, declared the book a "loathesome example," and said she longed herself to write a story of same-sex love in response that would be very different.[16]

Nor has the novel brought much satisfaction or joy to women in more recent times. It has often served to label for a woman what her love for another female has meant to society in the twentieth century, and it plays a sad, prominent part in many an individual lesbian history. For example:

> My mother gave me *The Well of Loneliness* to read and told me that if I continued to write and receive [love] notes like that [which she had just discovered], I would end up like Stephen in the book. [When I returned to school] my mother

kept sending me letters and telling me to be sure and remember the book she'd given me to read, and not to be sinful.[17]

I had found a copy of *The Well of Loneliness* in the library, and for the first time in my life, I felt a certain shame about my feelings towards women.[18]

The Well has had generally such a devastating effect on female same-sex love not only because its central character ends in loneliness but—and much more significantly—because its writer fell into the congenitalist trap. She believed that if she argued that some women were born different, society would free them to pursue their independence; instead, her popular rendition of "congenital inversion" further morbidified the most natural impulses and healthy views. It reinforced the notion that some women would not marry not because the institution was often unjust, that they sought independence not because they believed it would make them whole people, that they loved other women not because such love was natural—but instead because they were born into the wrong body. To be born into the wrong body was freakish. Many a woman must have decided to tolerate even the worst heterosexual inequities rather than to view herself in such a way.

Freudianism, with its theories of arrested development, was equally discouraging about love between women, since it too treated same-sex love not as a natural impulse and a choice made in healthy response to one's environment but as a failure to develop along normal lines—in this case not as a fetus but as a child.

In "The Sexual Aberrations"[19] Freud divided women who love women into "butches" and "femmes" no less than Hall did with her "invert" and "mate of the invert." He declared that "the active invert" generally exhibited both physical and mental masculine characteristics and looked for femininity in her love object. Neither he nor Hall seemed to be aware that if some lesbian relationships were based on such patterns it was because women were emulating the only examples of domestic situations available to them in a patriarchal culture, that they often felt compelled to force themselves into these roles and did not assume them by inborn or trauma-acquired impulses. The great popularity of both authors also served to promulgate further the notion that a lesbian relationship required a "butch" and a "femme."

In a later work which focuses exclusively on an eighteen-year-old female, "The Psychogenesis of a Case of Homosexuality in a

324 * SURPASSING THE LOVE OF MEN

Woman," [20] Freud insists on lesbian masculinity. Seen in the light of our day though, what was "masculine" to Freud appears to us as his subject's desire to free herself from her status as object and also, her just anger at the limited lives women of her time were compelled to lead. She is damned for her most admirable qualities. For example, Freud admits he can find little physical masculinity in her, but "some of her intellectual attributes could be connected with masculinity; for instance, her acuteness of comprehension and her lucid objectivity."

How did the young woman develop this problem? The psychogenesis of her case is twofold. When she was sixteen she wanted her father to give her a baby, and instead he gave one to her mother, so out of subconscious guilt and anger she turned her sexual feeling away from men. Also she saw her older brother's penis and wanted one. It is interesting to note how Freud combines his discussion of her penis envy with her feminism:

> The girl had brought along with her from childhood a strongly marked "masculinity complex." A spirited girl, always ready for romping and fighting, she was not at all prepared to be second to her slightly older brother; after inspecting his genital organs she had developed a pronounced envy for the penis, and the thoughts derived from this continued to fill her mind. She was in fact a feminist; she felt it to be unjust that girls should not enjoy the same freedom as boys and rebelled against the lot of women in general.

But he never draws the obvious conclusion: It was not her brother's penis that she envied but his male freedom, not the uses to which he could put his penis but what that bit of flesh symbolized to the world.

The homosexuality of Freud's subject did not include sexual relations. She had never gone beyond kisses and embraces. Freud compares her love of a woman to Dante's love of Beatrice, "Hoping little and asking for nothing." The subject spoke often of "the purity of her love," and had visions of retiring with her beloved, rescuing her from the ignoble circumstances of her life. The major difference between this young woman's love and the romantic friendships which absolutely "normal" women of earlier centuries experienced was that the former was viewed in the context of forty years of medical exploration of abnormality.

Although Freud reiterated both in this work and later that he doubted adult homosexuality might be cured,[21] many medical men, pouncing on the idea that if homosexuality was not congenital it was not fixed, were quick to promise that they could convert homosexuals to heterosexuals.[22] Some even claimed that their experience over the years "absolutely confirms" their belief that same-sex love is nothing more than "a psychic disease and is curable by psychic treatment"[23]—i.e., a lengthy analysis which takes the patient back at least to puberty if not to the embryo in order to rework problems which caused him or her to be emotionally arrested. Freudians made themselves further indispensable to the same-sex love sufferer by again selecting what was useful in their mentor's writings and rejecting what was not. For example, while Freud observed in "The Sexual Aberrations" that "inversion is found in people who otherwise show no marked deviation from the normal . . . whose mental capacities are not disturbed," his immediate disciples often declared, "We will never find a homosexual who has not other stigmata of a neurosis."[24]

However, the studies done by nonpsychiatrists of that time, who had nothing to gain from a discovery of widespread neurosis, tell a very different story. One such study was conducted by Robert Latou Dickinson, a gynecologist who collected data on his patients' sexual experiences while he treated them for various gynecological problems. His work began in the nineteenth century and continued until 1920. Dickinson does not discuss women who had romantic friendships with other females without genital contact. Of the 350 women for whom he compiled complete sexual histories, he was told or he inferred that twenty-eight had had genital relationships with other women—eighteen admitted to sexual experience (he does not say what caused him to make inferences about the other ten). He observes of those twenty-eight women: "Good health and steady occupation is the rule; appearance, dress, and social status are without idiosyncrasy and above the average."[25] He states that he could find no nervous breakdowns, no evidence of maleness of feeling, and no evidence of congenital cause. What he did find is that they were often the only or the oldest daughter (see Robert Riegel and Barbara Welter, page 187), that a good many of them were college graduates and engaged in the professions or in business, and that their relationships with their lovers went beyond sex to financial and protective elements. Furthermore, their accounts of love between women "followed the pattern of Victorian ideals and perfectionism," and in that sense they "lagged behind the contemporary practice and tradition of love," which was more cynical and less romantic. In short, and in startling contrast to the picture painted by the Freudians, the lesbians Dickinson studied were extremely productive and healthy members of their community, out of sync only by virtue of their idealism.

In a study of a lesbian-identified social community in Utah during the 1920's and 1930's, it was also found that "the group seemed remarkably well-adjusted to society" and that "in all respects except sexual behavior, the women as a group were probably far less alienated from society than the average contemporary woman, if only because of better education and their jobs which threw them more into the societal mainstream than the traditional married woman." [26] The women of these studies were primarily middle class, and their socioeconomic position explains in part their good adjustment to society. Very possibly a study of financially and culturally deprived lesbians who lacked their privileges would have shown that neurosis and maladjustment were prevalent. But a study of heterosexual women thus deprived would probably have yielded the same results. Compared with middle-class heterosexual women, however, the lesbians of these studies were extremely successful in their ability to function both on a personal and societal level.

A 1929 study drew conclusions similar to those of Dickinson and the Utah study. Katharine Bement Davis (*Factors in the Sex Life of Twenty-two Hundred Women*) conducted nationwide research among women *assumed* to be "normal" when they were invited to participate. More than half of them, 50.4 percent, indicated that they had experienced "intense emotional relations with other women." About half of those experiences were accompanied by sex or were "recognized as sexual in character." [27] Most of the women who had had homosexual experiences viewed themselves as healthy in spite of the psychiatric establishment of the 1920's. Only 13.6 percent of those with lesbian experiences saw them as "a sexual problem requiring solution." [28] While 77.3 percent of Davis's entire sample claimed to be in excellent health, 78 percent of those who admitted having homosexual physical experiences regarded themselves as being in excellent health. [29]

Those with same-sex love experiences were also better educated and more productive than those without: For example, 65.4 percent of those with homosexual physical experiences (H II) had been gainfully employed as adults; 64.6 percent of those with homosexual experiences that were limited to the emotional (H I) had been gainfully employed; but no more than 56.4 percent of those with neither homosexual physical or emotional experiences (Others) had been gainfully employed.[30] She also found that 87.7 percent of H II were college graduates, as compared with 77.7 percent of H I and 69.1 percent of the entire sample. [31] What this appears to mean is that the more independent, aggressive, and determined a woman was, the more likely she was to have engaged in lesbian experiences.

It is noteworthy that Davis recognized a distinction between H I and H II experiences. Fifty years earlier the possibility of widespread H II experiences would have been admitted by no one. Fifty years later in our sexually liberated day, the claim of H I experiences is met with incredulity, since popular wisdom insists that all intense love impulses between adults are necessarily sexual. Love between women in a post-sexologist age has become either sex between women or nonexistent, despite the fact that in many of the lesbian case histories presented by the sexologists (about a third of Havelock Ellis's cases and Freud's only case which he discusses in detail) the women never had genital contact with other women. Since the twentieth century carried for so long the burden of Victorian antisexuality, love between women, assumed to be sexual, was therefore shameful.

Studies such as those by Dickinson and Davis received little attention. Mass literature, even when it had scientific pretensions, instead of examining such scientific studies, often borrowed from fantasy fiction to describe female sexual relations (which became foremost in the public mind with regard to love between women). Xavier Mayne, for example, in *The Intersexes: A History of Similisexualism* (1908), observed that a lesbian often chooses a career like dressmaker, milliner, dealer in fine underwear and hosiery, and costume designer so that she "can come into intimate bodily contact with beautiful women. Appetizing girls innocently can titillate daily her sexualism. . . . [These professions] are recognized as a screen for Lesbian bawd in many great cities." [32] A Dr. Maurice Chideckel devoted chapters of his 1935 book, *Female Sex Perversion*, which purported to be a scientific study, to subjects such as "Tribadistic Orgies of Lasciviousness" and "The Promiscuousness of Tribadists." [33]

During the 1920's in America, all types of sexual activity outside of marriage increased significantly.[34] This sexual revolution is attributable in large part to the violent (though ambivalent) reaction against the Victorian "purity" of the preceding generation, as well as to the liberating effect of Freud's views on the compulsive power of the sexual drive. From the 1920's on when women loved other women, they were forced to examine their sexual motives; and where none existed that were powerful enough to act on before, in a climate which insisted that humans are sexual or they are repressed, it is likely that many who sought such motives found them. Hence there were probably more overt sexual exchanges between women at this time than in previous eras. But such sexual exchanges alone do not signify whether or not a woman chose to identify herself as a lesbian. In response to the heterosexual environment which she found stifling and in recognition of the natural affinity between women, a woman might see herself as lesbian without having had any sexual experiences with other females, as Ellis's and Freud's cases did. Or she might have had numerous such experiences for pleasure or diversion, and still not regard herself as a lesbian.

While there has always been a great divergence among women who identify themselves as lesbian with regard to their interest in sex, just as among heterosexually identified women, the popular view has pretended that sex is the lesbian's primary interest. That has probably seldom been the case, not only because women's sensuality is generally broader than the specifically sexual, but especially because women have chosen lesbianism for far more complex reasons than sexual drive. In the past, few wrote about their lesbianism or discussed it publicly. Today they do write about it and discuss it, and almost to a woman they discount sexual attraction as being of overwhelming importance in their decision to become lesbians. Sociologists who study lesbians typically discover, as did Donna Tanner (*The Lesbian Couple*, 1978), that "the women in this study stated that they valued romance, affection, hugging and kissing, and don't regard the sexual act as the focal point of the relationship," [35] or, as did Barbara Ponse (*Identities in the Lesbian World*, 1978), that their respondents' emphases were not on sex but on the quality of their interactions: "They referred to the dimensions of mutuality and closeness, particularly emotional closeness, in describing their relationships." Ponse concludes that in the lesbian community "lesbian" is an essential identity that goes far beyond sex. [36]

It is no doubt unlikely that many women born into a sex-conscious era can conduct a lesbian relationship today without some sexual exchange. The pressure is on in our culture to be sexual if we want to be physically and mentally healthy, and even women who identify as lesbian have been affected by such popular wisdom. But in many relationships the sexual exchange is like signing a pact of mutual trust. What is important is not the signing of that pact but the exchanges of support in day-to-day life. The frenzied "use it or lose it" concern expressed in the David Reuben best sellers is foreign to a lesbian relationship, in which neither partner has to worry about possible vanishing sexual potency.

Avowed lesbian writers testify from firsthand experience and observation to the sociologists' findings. They refuse, first of all, to accept the definition of a lesbian as simply a woman who has sex with other women. Del Martin and Phyllis Lyon (*Lesbian/Woman*, 1972) assert, "a number of lesbians never have any sex at all." [37] Sally Gearhart (*Loving Women/Loving Men*, 1974) points out that not only have many self-identified lesbians not had lesbian sexual experiences, but a number of heterosexual-identified women have indeed had lesbian sexual experiences. Gearhart declares, "We do not become lesbians by leaping into bed with another woman," but rather lesbianism is the result of a woman's discovery that she can and does love women coupled with her refusal to be exploited in a heterosexist system.[38]

Lesbians now often express fury at the popular wisdom which defines lesbianism in terms of sex. Judy Grahn remarks ("Lesbian as Bogey Woman," 1970), "Men who are obsessed with sex are convinced that lesbians are obsessed with sex. Actually, like any other woman lesbians are obsessed with love and fidelity. They're also strongly interested in independence and in having a life work to do." [39] Nina Sabaroff ("Lesbian Sexuality: An Unfinished Saga," 1975), similarly claims, "It isn't just 'good sex' we want, but good friendships, work, knowledge. . . . I no longer believe that sex is an overpowering drive. This kind of sexuality—the kind that takes over your life—must be exposed as part of the patriarchy that feeds it." [40] Those lesbians who see sex between women as a vital part of their bond refuse to separate it from other aspects of the relationship as male-authored lesbian literature does. Mary Daly ("Sparking: The Fire of Female Friendship," 1978) states that "female identified erotic love is not dichotomized from radical female friendship, but rather is one important expression/manifestation of friendship." In this mystical essay Daly sees such expression as only one form of energy exchange between women which can assume many different shapes and colors. She too finds that friendship is the primary element of female same-sex love.[41]

In the 1970's women began to define lesbianism for themselves. Previously the medical experts had made the definitions—generally on the basis of what they observed in their patients who came to them in the first place of course because they were troubled, not necessarily about their sexual orientation. Therefore, the doctors could say with some measure of truth that all their lesbian patients were sick, as though all their heterosexual patients were not. Throughout the 1950's and 1960's, the medical profession largely ignored Kinsey's findings about the statistical frequency—i.e., "normality"—of lesbian experiences, and his discovery that everyone is capable of responding "homosexually" if freed from the "powerful conditioning" of "social codes," [42] since their treatment of homosexuality was dependent on creating sickness where none existed. Based on their experiences with disturbed persons, they then wrote that lesbians were "severely disturbed persons"; [43] that lesbianism was "an illness, the symptom of a neurosis"; [44] that lesbians wallow in self-pity, continually provoke hostility to ensure more opportunities for self-pity, and collect injustices; [45] that they are excessively dependent and fixated on the mother-child relationship; [46] and that they are unscrupulous vampires: "Once they get hold of a victim they do not let go until she is bled white." [47] All agreed, of course, that treatment is necessary.

It is to be hoped that recent studies which indicate how emotionally healthy self-identified lesbians are will forever put to rest such clichés,[48] but since studies published in the 1920's and 1930's presented a similar image of lesbian health, it is difficult to believe that statistical evidence can have much effect in changing popular opinion. If love between women has become more acceptable since the early 1970's, it is due partly to the American Psychiatric Association's 1973 resolution (after pressure from the very healthy gay liberation movement) to remove homosexuality from its list of mental disorders (as odd as it is to think that mental sickness or health can be decided by vote). Acceptance is also due to the new morality of this era, which recognizes that people can have intimate relationships outside of sanctified marriage and yet remain moral. It is due too to the almost universal admission that procreation is not and cannot be the primary goal of love in an overcrowded world. Lesbians have been allowed to share to some extent in the sexual freedom heterosexuals have claimed for themselves. But the most significant factor in the change of the lesbian image is her articulate insistence on defining herself, not to beg tolerance from the heterosexual as Radclyffe Hall attempted to do—but for herself and others like her. Lesbians have wrested the definition of love between women away from the medical profession and reclaimed it. Although it is impossible for twentieth-century women to return to nineteenth-century sexual innocence, and women no longer need end their same-sex love relationships by marriage, love between women as defined by women in our era has more in common with eighteenth- and nineteenth-century romantic friendships than with medical pronouncements on female homosexuality.

CHAPTER 3

Keeping Women Down

When women's increasing freedom began to threaten to change the world—or at least parts of Europe and America—many who had vested interests in the old order were happy to believe the medical views of lesbians as neurotic and confused and to believe that women who wanted independence usually were lesbians. It is no coincidence that many laypersons discovered the congenitalists' theories when the women's movement first began to achieve some success at the end of the nineteenth century. After World War I, when large numbers of women had participated in the war effort and had proven by their stamina and determination that there were few biological reasons for keeping women down, laypersons discovered Freudian theories. It is doubtful that any of the theories regarding female homosexuality would have been offered or have enjoyed such currency a hundred years earlier, since independent women presented no significant threat at that time. Throughout the late nineteenth century and the twentieth century, where women's demand for independence was the strongest and when it was most within their grasp, the conviction that female same-sex love was freakish or sick was at its most pronounced.

The apostles of natural female passivity and those who pretended to see disaster if the "course of nature" were changed were rampant at the beginning of the twentieth century. They declared with what was by now becoming wishful thinking, since women were proving otherwise, "Woman does not wish to be treated as an active agent; she wants to remain always and throughout—this is just her womanhood—purely passive, to feel herself under another's will. She demands only to be desired physically, to be taken possession of, like a new property."[1] They felt compelled to reassert again and again man's natural superiority, and fairly early in the century they believed they could claim proof of woman's inferiority in her failure to accomplish anything great, despite her years of opportunity "thanks to the modern movement of the emancipation of women."[2] Occasionally male hysteria about increasing female freedom was not even hidden by pretense of reasoned arguments about female passivity and male superiority. Irrational fear that the male sex was breathing its last was openly expressed. In 1904 one writer, for example, complained about feminist literature that not only did it exalt women above men, but it also gave girls the impression "that the male sex is destined to shrink away in time to the relative proportion which the spider husband has to his gigantic spouse" or to emulate the water fleas, among which the "He's diminish ever to a vanishing point." The author then proclaims, "And if any think that I exaggerate, let them get some of this literature and read it, when they will grant that, according to all the laws of deduction and logic, this is precisely that unto which these Women-Righters are tending."[3] The fear continued in the next decades. H. L. Mencken, for instance, depicted "Women-Righters" as "man-eating suffragettes."[4]

Much early twentieth-century popular fiction did what it could to encourage women's "natural passivity" and to convince them that they had better believe that a husband is a necessary lord and master. The silly woman lawyer of Brand Whitlock's *Her Infinite Variety* (1904) loses a wonderful fiancé because of her feminism. In Helen Winslow's *A Woman for Mayor* (1909), her central character, the first female mayor in America, is not so silly. Although she has been a fine mayor, she gives up her political career when her term is finished, declaring, "Say what you will, woman was not meant for this kind of thing." In Henry Harrison's *Angela's Business* (1915), the female assistant principal, like the lady mayor, also leaves her career, without a backward glance of regret, in order to marry. She is contrasted with an older woman, a feminist, Miss Hodger, who never had such good sense. Harrison's old maid steps right out of the eighteenth-century pages of Smollett and Fielding: "A tall figure . . . [with] a flat chest, a tangled mane of sorrel hair and a face somewhat like a horse's." In presenting such a revolting spinster, the twentieth-century author's intent, like that of the eighteenth-century satirists, was to discourage young girls who might be tempted to ignore society's precepts about the necessity of marriage.

Such depictions rapidly multiplied after World War I, when it seemed that women had a firm and unshakable foothold on the ladder of equality. English and American women played particularly strong roles in their countries' war efforts. They demanded freedoms in return for their patriotism. Those freedoms were viewed with horror by traditionalists, who prophesied the death of the family and even of the world as a result of women's liberation.

World War I caused some breakdown in the separation between male and female occupations. Women served not only as nurses and clerks, but they also worked in the arms factories and the metal trades, they managed heavy equipment, and they drove ambulances and buses. What had been exclusively manpower became womanpower too.

In both America and England, female patriotism was excessive at times: For example, even before war was declared, some women put on military uniforms and drilled in female camps.[5] They felt perhaps that whether or not that war would make the world safe for democracy, it would usher in a new order, and that if their services were seen as necessary, what they long desired could not be denied them. As soon as America declared itself in the war in the spring of 1917, Carrie Catt, the head of the National American Women's Suffrage Association, pledged patriotic support. Women enlisted in the war effort and signed petitions for suffrage simultaneously. Three states gave females the right to vote in presidential elections that year. At the end of the war, all adult women in America were rewarded with suffrage. In England too, women over thirty were given the vote in 1918 (although younger women had to wait until 1928 before they were enfranchised). Englishwomen were also rewarded in 1919 with the Sex Disqualification Removal Act, which meant that women could no longer be disqualified from holding public office or civil or judicial posts by virtue of their gender.

The popular response to these freedoms was to inveigh against them or to very pointedly ignore them. Sidney Ditzion (*Marriage, Morals, and Sex in America*) observes that while masculine fears grew in proportion to the number of women entering better-paid commercial jobs after World War I, media men who interpreted femininity for public consumption soothed male paranoia by adhering to the old pictorial and literary stereotypes: While American women had undergone radical transformations in actuality, they still retained their old look on magazine covers, where their hands were usually filled with mirrors, fans, flowers, or babies; and inside the covers too, they were seldom active or individualistic. The writers maintained, Ditzion observes, "that women's best use for their freedom was to give it up as fast as they could in marriage." [6]

Novelists presented the same appeal. A 1919 American novel, Nalbro Bartley's *A Woman's Woman,* shows what happens when a woman forgets that her province is the home and her only concerns are her family. Densie, a middle-aged mother of three, scorned and neglected by her husband and her two oldest children because she is old-fashioned, decides as soon as the century turns that she will cease to be a nineteenth-century woman and become a twentieth-century one. To that end, she starts a business and she becomes a phenomenal success. But she pays a price: Her husband loses confidence in himself and becomes sullen and morose because "she had trespassed on his territory, driven him from it—into nowhere"; her older daughter, who is a feminist, has a nervous breakdown when her roommate leaves her; her younger daughter wastes her life on a cad who turns out to be a German spy; and her soldier son, Kenneth, who had no mother at home to teach him right from wrong when he was a child, is fatally wounded while escaping the guardhouse in order to meet a woman. It is this latter tragedy which makes Densie see the error of her ways. She promises her surviving family, "Mummy will try to make a home for you all—but it will be too late for Kenneth." Lest the reader did not get the point before, here the author intervenes:

> Densie realized that once more she must provide a home, that a home is the veritable job of creation. . . . Densie had been tempted by the modern enemy of women—the home-destroying spirit—and she had yielded. She should have withstood the enemy, weathered the difficulty, the stings of ridicule, the pricks of neglect—but kept the home. It was a sacred duty in which she had temporarily failed.

The appeal to guilt was one method of keeping woman in her place. Another, which was observed to some extent in the nineteenth century, became a full-fledged tactic in the twentieth century: Women who did not wish to stay in their place were depicted as masculine, therefore abnormal, i.e., lesbian. The link between feminism and "sexual abnormality" was made not only in America and England but in Germany and France as well. In early twentieth-century fiction and nonfiction, feminism was seen to destroy the distinctions between the sexes, and it was argued that since feminists obliterated the attraction of opposites by taking on themselves the characteristics of the opposite sex, lesbianism was an inevitable outgrowth. As Maria Janitschek's heroine complained in *Mimikry: Ein Stück modernen Lebens* (1903), the newest "sign of the times" was each sex's increasing inclination toward its own sex. This is because feminism has made women more like men and men more like women. Since women and men no longer complement each other, females have forgotten what they were supposed to look for in a mate. A woman now "finds in woman more what she needs than in man." In the revealingly entitled *Feminismus und Kulturuntergang* (1927), Dr. E. F. W. Eberhard is even more hysterical in his observation that feminism is bringing about the destruction of civilization and that lesbianism is its tool. In his section on "Tribadie und Frauenemanzipation," Eberhard claims that the women's movement is led by "men women," who are not real women at all. Although he grants that there are heterosexuals in the movement, he maintains that the "men women" make up a strong nucleus of the organization, influence the direction it takes, and "fan the flames," keeping the women agitated. It is they alone who have infected other women with the desire to be free of men and independent. They seduce the normal young women in the movement and spread lesbianism. One cannot underestimate their danger, Eberhard declares. It is possible to combat them only if "woman remains in her household circle." Her education must preserve her femininity and discourage any masculinizing influence.[7]

French writers had long warned that women's desire for independence was connected with lesbian desires, but in post-World War I fiction it became virtually impossible for a heroine to express feminist philosophy without having a lesbian experience to accompany it.[8] The heroine of Victor Margueritte's *La Garçonne* (1922) suggests that women's new desires are not natural to them but merely a response to male excesses. She believes that it is only centuries of male despotism which made the women's movement inevitable, that women would never have thought of equality had men not driven them to it. But now, to pay men back, they demand not only work and social liberation but the right to have babies by whomever they wish and the right to sleep with women as well as men. Typically, while seeming to defend his heroine in the liberated 1920's, Margueritte is also shocked at the libertine remarks he places in her mouth. But he seeks to excuse her behavior by having another

character explain that we are all "the playthings of forces that sur-
pass us in strength," that she is only a pathetic product of her
liberated times.

Early in the twentieth century in England, Edward Carpenter
identified feminism with lesbianism. In *Love's Coming of Age* (1911)
Carpenter, ironically himself a homosexual and a revolutionary,
said that women become feminists because they are not normal.
Their maternal instincts are not very strong since they are not
real women and therefore do not "represent their sex." They are
"mannish in temperament," "ultra-rationalizing and brain-cultured,"
and lesbian.[9] Perhaps this association between feminism and lesbianism was made so blatantly in 1911 because around 1910 the
feminist movement began to become really militant in England and
hence more threatening. Once it was seen that even with Edward VII
dead and a new king on the throne of England, women would still
not be enfranchised; and when the Conciliation Bill, which would
have given a million women the vote, was vetoed in November 1910,
the suffragists decided to start throwing bricks and make complacency impossible. Antifeminists must have considered that whatever would scare women away from the movement was fair play. And
to associate feminism with what the experts had called morbid
would surely scare women away.

It is possible that the English movement was indeed made up
largely of women who loved women. Not only might they have
learned from the previous century that love between kindred spirits
was normal, but also Englishwomen with an independent bent were
furious that their simple demands for complete citizenship were
turned down. They identified men as the enemy and each other as
the ally. And by the end of the first decade, there were enough women
in middle-class professional positions to present role models to those
who wished to live their lives without husbands.[10] George Dangerfield (*The Strange Death of Liberal England*) speculates that because
of her political disappointments, the prewar suffragist reacted violently to "the unlived female life" and decided that it was necessary
to overthrow the personal security that had kept women lurking
behind male coattails for so long. To recover her womanhood the
suffragist believed she must "go out into the wilderness, there to
elope with herself and her sisters," just as among certain primitive
tribes, he says, marriageable girls would spend some time in the
woman-house to learn the wisdom of women. Dangerfield suggests
that it was this mystical yearning "to recover the wisdom of women"

that was responsible for the development of the "homosexual movement," whose inception among the suffragists he mysteriously sets at 1912.[11] Whether the feminists' decision to become lesbians was as consciously motivated and clear cut in 1912 as Dangerfield suggested about twenty-five years later is questionable. But there is every reason to believe, judging from contemporary feminism and its encouragement of love between women, that the first wave also encouraged this emotion as a natural outgrowth of healthy self-love. Armed with the club of "abnormality," antifeminists then chose, as Carpenter did, to put as freakish a construction on such love as possible.

In America the earliest twentieth-century association of feminism with lesbianism was made by a psychiatrist, a Krafft-Ebing disciple named William Lee Howard. In his novel, *The Perverts* (1901), Howard's diseased Ph.D. feminist, Mizpra, who delights in causing misery, is born with her twisted personality, having come from degenerative stock. Although it is not clear that she is a lesbian, it is evident that she is an independent woman—and Howard believes that there is no difference in psychosis between the two:

> The female possessed of masculine ideas of independence, the viragint who would sit in the public highways and lift up her pseudo-virile voice, proclaiming her sole right to decide questions of war or religion, or the value of celibacy and the curse of woman's impurity, and that disgusting anti-social being, the female sexual pervert, are simply different degrees of the same class—degenerates.

As a psychiatrist, Howard was familiar with the literature on "degeneration" that most Americans would have had little access to, but he had no immediate followers. Over the following decades however, with the popularization of Freud, many more writers associated feminism and lesbianism.

They were not congenitalists like Howard. Instead they believed that nurture created the individual. Their particular attack was often on women's colleges, which took women out of the home and kept them out by virtue of the feminist indoctrination they gave to their students. In those women's colleges, according to some writers, a female is led to homosexuality because she is taught to engage in athletics, encouraged "to masculine ways of feeling, dress and sentimentalisms," and permitted to "muscularize her mind beyond the harmonious vigor to make her man's companion."[12] Parents were repeatedly warned that in segregated schools the less self-reliant females became dependent upon the ones with stronger personalities, and in that way both were spoiled for future heterosexual relationships.[13] Both fiction and nonfiction confirmed that women graduate from women's colleges "into life long homosexuality."[14]

But the antifeminists believed it was not women's colleges alone which fostered lesbianism. It was the times. Some complained that with increasing female freedom, which encouraged women to develop not only athletic skill, executive ability, and professional success but even to develop boyish figures, the secondary sex characteristics were becoming so modified that lesbianism was inevitable. Others warned that when women enter men's territory (i.e., "public life, politics, education, the professions, business"), they try to act like men and hence they are ruined for men.[15] Lesbianism was, William Carlos Williams observed in 1932, the "knife of the times,"[16] and it was killing women and castrating men.

World War I increased female freedom and mobility. World War II, which not only demanded the services of Rosie the Riveter and her sisters, but also made space for women in professional schools such as had never been available before,[17] threatened to eradicate all the social distinctions between the sexes. Predictably, when the men returned from overseas, the women were encouraged to step down and return home. Accusations of lesbianism were used as the whip to make them gallop there more quickly. The technique is reflected in *Modern Woman: The Lost Sex* (1947), which became a classic source book for those who wished to argue that healthy women were happy only in the kitchen and nursery. The authors, Lundberg and Farnham, depicted feminism as "an expression of emotional illness, of neurosis . . . at its core a deep illness."[18] Throughout their book, beginning with Mary Wollstonecraft as the mother of feminism, they characterized the feminist impulse as an aspect of lesbian sickness. Women are feminists because they are lesbians, and they are lesbians because they were arrested in their development. The authors' message is clear. But they are even more specific in their warnings: Lesbians, who are probably the only women who would wish to do so, have a good deal more to say about public and institutional policy than is socially desirable. Since they are "distorted personalities," they project their distortion onto society.[19] They must be dislodged from their positions. In fact, no unmarried woman should even be allowed to teach school because she might set a poor example for children.[20]

Their attacks on feminism by associating it with "abnormality" enjoyed great currency throughout the following decade. Some of the most respected sociologists and psychologists spoke about the importance of keeping women in the home and maintaining traditional sex roles.[21] Women were scared into retreat unless they could cope with a self-image of abnormality. A mid-1950's survey of the most prestigious women's colleges showed that students were choosing a major based on how well they thought it would "enrich family life" and that alumnae had become overwhelmingly "family oriented." [22]

History repeated itself, or tried to, in 1970 when *Time* magazine took it upon itself to discredit the new feminist movement by publicizing the bisexuality of Kate Millett, the woman that *Time* had earlier made a feminist leader. In an article entitled "Women's Lib: A Second Look," [23] *Time* called into question feminists' "maturity, morality, and sexuality," while hopefully pointing out that Millett's disclosure of her bisexuality was bound to "cast further doubt on her theories, and reinforce the views of those skeptics who routinely dismiss all liberationists as Lesbians." But by then feminists had learned from history. At a mass meeting in New York, which had originally been scheduled around the issues of child care and abortion, all the women attending donned lavender armbands, just as the Danes had donned yellow armbands during World War II when Hitler demanded that Danish Jews be turned over to him. What the women understood, according to leaflets they handed out to the press, was that it was not sexual preference that was under attack but any values "that fundamentally challenge the basic structure of patriarchy," and that *Time* was using the old scare tactic against feminism by associating it with lesbianism. The leaflets declared that the tactic would no longer work. All feminists were prepared to stand together now: "They can call us Lesbians until such time as there is no stigma attached to women loving women." And with that weapon against feminism gone, the movement could advance unimpeded.

CHAPTER 4

Fiction as a Weapon

Twentieth-century fiction, reflecting society, played a large role in keeping women down through associating feminism with lesbianism and lesbianism with everything horrible. In most of the anti-lesbian novels written in the first half of the twentieth century, the lesbian is a feminist, a woman with a powerful ego, frequently in a position of authority over innocent girls. Almost invariably she is "twisted." While in most cases her perversity has turned her into a vampire, sometimes she is nothing more than a confused sickie. Generally the message is that such women need to be locked up or otherwise put away, either for society's good or their own. Fiction which took this view had been written for decades in nineteenth-century France; in England and especially America, it had been rare in the previous century. But with women's increasing mobility, it became increasingly common.

The most noxious of the lesbian vampire novels, with a predictable girls' school setting, *Regiment of Women* (1915), was written by an Englishwoman, Winifred Ashton, under the name of Clemence Dane. Dane was very possibly a lesbian herself [1]—an interesting commentary on the extent to which love between women was already producing self-loathing as a result of the German and French views on abnormality and decadence. Her novel takes its name from John Knox's *First Blast of the Trumpet Against the Monstrous Regiment of Women*, and, like Knox's work, it warns of the evils that come to pass when a woman rules. The central character, Clare Hartill (heart ill), a senior teacher, who has virtually unlimited power over the girls in her school, is totally self-centered, gratu-

341

itously cruel, emotionally frozen. She is concerned only with using
and deceiving people while she extracts their veneration. She is
extremely bright and talented, but the author suggests that her
excessive gifts are merely a manifestation of what is diseased in her
nature.[2] She reaches the height of evil when she causes an adolescent girl, whom she has made to love her, to commit suicide.

While driving her pupils crazy, Clare, a woman in her mid-
thirties, also conducts an intimate relationship (although there is
no hint that it is sexual) with eighteen-year-old Alwynne, a new
teacher at the school. Before long Alwynne, as a result of Clare's
evil, grows "whitened" and she loses her vitality and the "sparkle
from her eye"—she is the vampire's victim. Clare has made of Alwynne not only an emotional slave but a feminist, so that whenever
she talks to anyone, "all conversational roads led to the suffrage
question." Deep down, however, Alwynne remains, as her aunt Elsbeth describes her, "as sound and sweet as an apple." Therefore,
with the help of a young superman who knows what she is thinking
even before she knows it herself, and who operates with masculine
directness compared with Clare's dishonest female subtleties, she
is able to throw off the older woman's malignant influence. Clare
nevertheless retains her hold on innocent young girls. The book
ends on what the author hoped would be a chilling note as Clare,
pathetic and menacing at once, decides to take the headmistress
position which she has been offered and plots to seduce another
young girl.

The book includes diatribes against all-female schools as well as
the undisputed power of unmarried women teachers like Clare to
mold the women of the next generation. But its particular attack
is on female friendships and their current tendency to take the place
of marriage. In the context of 1915, Clare, who is earning a good
salary and is independent, now has the gall to argue that a young
girl like Alwynne doesn't need to get married because she can spend
her life with another woman and she can work too. "I tell you,"
Clare says to Alwynne's aunt, "we can suffice each other. Thank
God there are some women who can do without marriage—marriage
—marriage!" But Elsbeth replies, ostensibly as the moral voice in
the novel, "Feminine friendship is all very well, very delightful, of
course . . . but when it is a question of marriage—. . . . Surely
you see the difference? How can you weigh the most ideal friendship
against the chance of getting married? . . . When youth is over
what is the average single woman, a derelict, drifting aimlessly on

the high seas of life. . . . she's a failure, she's unfulfilled." Despite the creation of the New Woman, Elsbeth implies, old heterosexual values are unchanged and have the appeal of universal truths. Clare's failure to honor those old values is a sign of her mental disturbance.

In twentieth-century novels of lesbian vampirism, it is not the victim's blood that the villain lives on but her youth and energy, which the modern vampire requires to transfuse her aging, hideous, malcontented self. Such transfusions have only a short-term effect, and soon the vampire is out stalking another victim. The lesbian-teacher-feminist vampire remained a popular image in fiction for decades. Like Clare in *Regiment of Women*, the lesbian headmistress Miss Cash of another English novel, Francis Brett Young's *White Ladies* (1935), is capriciously cruel and ruthless. She seduces her young wards with tenderness and affection, but her tyrannical and "not wholly natural or admirable" instincts are soon visible. Like Clare, she scoffs at marriage and tries to convince her victims that it is "discreditable" and must never happen to them. When Bella, a central character, recovers from her initial infatuation with Miss Cash, she sees her ·for what she is, "a faded, middle-aged woman, of imperious and uncertain temper," feasting on young girls in order to maintain her "illusion of emancipated youth and freedom and daring in what was really the arid life of a confused old maid." After a struggle Bella finally manages to extricate herself. But other girls become Miss Cash's victims. Some time later, Bella is walking with a beau, and they see Miss Cash with another young female. The beau observes that Miss Cash "has the face of an old woman and yet she walks like a girl." "Yes, that's true," Bella replies. "She's quite ageless. You see, she's a vampire. She lives on blood."

Dorothy Baker's *Trio* (1943) follows a pattern similar to Clemence Dane's and Francis Young's novels. The villain, Pauline, is an independent female, a lesbian, a teacher, and a vampire. Her victim is also an unsuspecting student, Janet Logan, who is at least fifteen years younger. Pauline is a French professor who has just published a "decadent and sensational" book on nineteenth-century French poets. She is herself decadent and sensational. While she teaches at Berkeley, campaigns for a promotion to full professorship, and tends to the business of publishing the book (which, it is later discovered, is half plagiarized), she also keeps Janet prisoner, apparently by encouraging her to take dope. She convinces Janet also that the decadence she can furnish for her (we see nothing of this except for a brief reference to a whip that is kept in the bedroom) is tantamount to living life to its fullest. There is not the slightest indication that love or tenderness ever existed between them. Janet is finally rescued by a Hemingway character who, like Alwynne's deliverer in *Regiment of Women,* knows what she is thinking before she thinks it, takes charge of her life, and puts Pauline in her place by characterizing her as "an arty little big-talking professor."

Pauline is condemned from the start of the novel when she is described as being competent, tailored, and brilliant. Once she gets promoted to full professor the game is up. Her capricious nastiness to Janet is almost superfluous. She ends by committing suicide after her plagiarism is discovered, but while she is punished for her dishonesty and her unexplained wicked behavior toward Janet, her crime is also her tailored competence and her cerebral interests. Toward the conclusion of the novel to show that Janet will be a proper female and is fed up with the stifling intellectualism and intellectual pretensions of Pauline, Baker has the young woman burn all her own books and writing.

In all these novels the lesbian is obsessed with a need to control a human life and lead it to destruction, a drive as irrational as that of the worst hell-engendered villains in eighteenth-century gothic novels. In *Trio* the Hemingway character demands of Pauline why she is bent on destroying Janet: "Have you got to have power over somebody? Is that how it is?" he asks. "Do you have to wreck somebody just to show you can do it?" Baker shows she does. But why lesbian villains require such power is never made clear, unless the explanation lies in their sick impulse to be in control in a world where only men should be in control. Once women gain control, the novels say, they wield their power with an evil despotism far surpassing male tyranny. Perhaps the perpetrator of lesbian evil is so often connected with education because that was one of the few professions where women were permitted any power and, as Lundberg and Farnham indicate, such power was threatening even in its limited scope. A woman with authority was unnatural: Her unnatural position, so many novels showed, led to unnatural behavior.

Evil lesbians in twentieth-century fiction did sometimes occupy slots other than pedagogic ones, but they were always shown to crave power and control. In Sinclair Lewis's *Ann Vickers* (1932), the villain, with the Dickensian name of Dr. Herringdean, is a Ph.D. in psychology, an executive in a large store. Like the villains of the Dane and Baker novels, she is condemned for her accomplishments. She is too bright, too authoritative, too smartly dressed. Her victim is a young woman, Eleanor, who has let herself be seduced by feminism. Her seduction by a lesbian is therefore a logical sequence. The executive works to entrap Eleanor and, as soon as her prey is caught, becomes bored and sadistic. But no man comes along to rescue Eleanor as Alwynne, Bella, and Janet were rescued. She ends in suicide, to which she was driven by Herringdean, the fishy woman with authority.

In Arthur Koestler's *Arrival and Departure* (1943), a young woman is ensnared, again by a female who has been permitted academic study of human emotions and who utilizes her knowledge and talent for nefarious purposes. The lesbian villain, Dr. Bolgar (bold and vulgar?), is predictably tall, competent, and authoritative. She has seduced pitiful Odette, who is years younger and emotionally fragile. The nature of Odette's character vis-à-vis Bolgar is described through a mixed metaphor that cannot decide whether she is being eaten or choked, but in any case she is destroyed: "The victim, drowned in the carnivorous flower's embrace."

When the lesbian villain does not have professional dominion, she is at least a carnivorous flower. Mary, the English lesbian villain of Dorothy Sayers' *Unnatural Death* (1927), is a nurse. Naturally she is "tall, handsome, very decided in manner . . . extremely competent" and "beautifully tailored." Lord Wimsey, who dislikes her immediately because of her "masculine mind," suspiciously observes even before he suspects she is a murderer, "I'm perfectly sure she [is] a very capable woman indeed"—that in itself seems to condemn her. Mary kills a woman in a complicated plot to gain an inheritance which she would lose if the woman does not die immediately, and she kills a second time when she fears that Vera, the girl she has seduced, will create problems for her. Vera is seen as a silly young thing who is enamored of whatever is modern and "in," including feminism and antimale attitudes. As Lord Wimsey's assistant, Miss Climpson, observes, Vera is "preyed upon" and used by Mary, whom Miss Climpson calls a "beastly, blood-sucking woman."

Sayers was familiar with Dane's *Regiment of Women*, and in her novel Miss Climpson is also familiar with the book. The assistant writes Lord Wimsey regarding the relationship between Vera and Mary: "I think it rather unhealthy—you may remember Miss Clemence Dane's very clever book on the subject?—I have seen so much of that kind of thing in my rather WOMAN-RIDDEN existence!

It has such a bad effect, as a rule, upon the weaker of the two." Mary was certainly modeled on Dane's Clare. She is as self-sufficient and calculating, she is without scruples, and her interest in the woman to whom she has attached herself is vampirish and loveless.

Vera describes her relationship with Mary in exactly those terms that women used to describe their eighteenth- and nineteenth-century romantic friendships. She compares her friendship with those men have with each other:

> I don't believe they're real friendships at all. Men can go off for years and forget all about their friends. And they don't really confide in one another. Mary and I tell each other all our thoughts and feelings. Men seem just content to think each other good sorts without ever bothering about their inmost selves. . . . [A great friendship must] be just everything to one. It's wonderful the way it seems to colour all one's thoughts. Instead of being centered in oneself, one's centered in the other person.

While few in earlier eras would have disagreed that such views of romantic friendship are noble, in the 1920's those views were seen as foolish or sick at best, and potentially evil. While there is no suggestion whatever that Vera and Mary are having a sexual affair, it is clear that any intimate relations between woman are unnatural.

The carnivorous flower of another English novel, Naomi Royde-Smith's *The Tortoiseshell Cat* (1925), Victoria Vanderleyden, an older woman, actually tells her would-be victim, young Gillian, "You baby, I should like to eat you." V.V. possesses a "haunting physical charm," and exudes a "heavy incense" that all but ensnares Gillian. She is also capriciously cruel. She becomes engaged to a gentle little man in whom she has no interest and causes him to commit suicide. Despite a terrific initial infatuation, Gillian sees V.V. for what she is and saves herself before the affair progresses too far. Gillian comes to understand that V.V.'s soul is "warped" and that she is morally "maimed." There is no explanation of why V.V. is evil. It is enough to know that she is athletic, has an androgynous beauty and cool, strong hands, and is called "Victor" by her friends.

In G. Sheila Donisthorpe's *Loveliest of Friends* (1931), the carnivorous flower is Kim, an "immaculately tailored," "ultra-modern, Eton-cropped, post-War product"—or rather she is an "inevitable advancing tide which, however much you strived to check it, would close around you in the end." Her immediate victim is Audrey, who has been happily, placidly married to a handsome, selfless, totally loving man. But Kim, who feels "regret for all the sins one hasn't committed," seduces Audrey with lavish, exotic gifts and the promise of unknown thrills. Although Audrey puts up a good fight, she loses her battle of resistance to Kim's dark, seductive machinations. She soon realizes, "It was as though she had set out for a walk in the sun and the tide had caught her and there was no turning back. All other paths were closed to her; she must travel on, her feet sinking deeper in at every step." She is not as lucky as Gillian, who extricates herself from V.V. in time. She ends, after enduring Kim's sadistic emotional torture, in terrified loneliness, an attempt at suicide unsuccessful, her life with her husband ruined, and no hope for the future. But why after pursuing Audrey with such great and loving effort does Kim want to make her suffer? Because that is the way of the lesbian, who even in her more benign moments, "like a schoolboy . . . enjoyed piercing the surface of Audrey's happiness to see how far the pin would go in." Sadism is as vital to her as are the "sex adventures" which her "flogged brain" brings "to a pinnacle only met in dreams."

Edouard Bourdet's French play, La Prisonnière (1926), which as The Captive enjoyed some success on the New York stage, was also presented within the same year in Berlin, Vienna, and Budapest. It too portrays a carnivorous lesbian flower, desiring to devour female flesh and succeeding. Brooks Atkinson, in his 1927 introduction to an American translation of the play, creates another metaphor for the lesbian and her evil when he points out that all the characters "have been withered a little by their proximity to the festered one," and he refers to "the blighted fruits of her influence." Atkinson also claims that the play was based on fact. During World War I, Bourdet had met in the trenches a young officer who was deliberately seeking death in battle as an escape from the wretchedness of his home life. His story was, according to Atkinson, the germ of the play.[3]

Irene, the central character, is a twenty-five-year-old woman held captive in her lesbian love for her seductress, an older married woman, Mme. d'Aiguines. Madame's husband has been made old before his time, and at thirty-five he is grey and sickly. He is an inhabitant of hell because of his wife's lesbianism. He tries to escape her, but he too is imprisoned in his love for her. Irene convinces Jacques, who had been her suitor before she met the seductress, to marry her and rescue her from the older woman. Before the marriage Jacques is warned by Mme. d'Aiguines' husband, who happens to be Jacques' old school acquaintance, that women like his wife and Irene, whom she has now infected, are "a menace," that men must not associate with them, that "they must be left to dwell among themselves in the kingdom of shadows." Of course, the marriage does not work. Although Irene does not see Mme. d'Aiguines for a year, she is haunted by her. Irene is in the grip of the carnivorous flower. She tells Jacques that as much as she desires to free herself, she cannot. Madame d'Aiguines is to her "like a prison to which I must return captive, despite myself." She is "fascinated," like the prey of a cobra and cannot move to safety, although she realizes, as she admits to Jacques, "the place I really belong is here against your shoulder." When the other woman summons Irene a year after her marriage, she must go.

Bourdet's story, like Sayers', also makes an interesting comment on romantic friendship in the context of the twentieth century when d'Aiguines warns Jacques that he had once been deceived into viewing the relationship between his wife and other women with complacency. It is dangerous, he suggests, to accept "ardent friendship" and "affectionate intimacy" between women, to say that it is "nothing very serious—we know all about that sort of thing!" Men know *nothing* about it, d'Aiguines protests: "We can't begin to know what it is. It's mysterious—terrible!" Women have an intimacy with each other that men cannot possibly fathom, "a secret alliance of two beings who understand one another because they're alike." And once those female beings get together, man becomes the stranger, the enemy, powerless to separate them because there are no terms on which he can fight them. D'Aiguines' speech is a far cry from the ecstasy of his compatriot St. Preux over the sweet, intimate exchanges between two female friends 150 years earlier.

In a later French work, Françoise Mallet's *Le Rempart des Béguines* (1951; the 1952 English title was *The Illusionist*), the fifteen-year-old victim, Hélène, is as much a captive as Irene. Her tormentor is much less subtle, however, than Mme. d'Aiguines. Tamara, the thirty-five-year-old mistress of Hélène's father and her seducer, is insanely sadistic and receives a "wicked delight" in wielding power over Hélène, literally forcing her on her knees to beg lengthily for forgiveness for the most minor infractions, causing the girl to weep for hours. The sexual aspect of their relationship, which is explicit, is described in French decadent terms: Tamara's face in orgasm, for example, displays "wicked and almost bestial rapture."

These works all adhere to a pattern. The lesbian villain always craves power. Sometimes she receives it through her profession, but always she desires it over her love victims as well. She is usually a feminist, since personal power is so crucial to her. Her victims are generally from ten to twenty years younger than she is. The lesbian *woman* is bent on destroying the innocent *girl*. Why she is evil, why she requires blood, is seldom made clear except by her lesbianism and feminism, which in themselves are supposed to suffice as explanations for her cruelty. Invariably her story is a cautionary tale.

The lesbian who is not a sadist is in any case a sickie in most other lesbian novels of this period. She is often a confused, hysterical personality. When she does not cause others to suffer, she suffers herself and is doomed to be an outcast and lonely. Her existence is sterile not only by virtue of her inability to create life through her sexual pleasures (which are seldom pleasurable), but by her very nature. If the lesbian is not a Clare figure out of *Regiment of Women*, she is a Stephen figure out of *The Well of Loneliness*.

Harvey O'Higgins's novel, *Julie Cane*, which was serialized in *Harper's Magazine* in 1924,[4] is a significant contrast to "The Beautiful House" (see page 305), which appeared in the same publication before the war and before the American popularization of Freud. In this story, as in "The Beautiful House," there is a relationship between an older woman, Martha, and a younger one, Julie Cane. But in contrast to the earlier story, the spinster teacher is neurotic and unhappy rather than productive, content, and dignified. She develops her fixation on Julie, her pupil, as a manifestation of a neurosis that has gotten out of hand. As her "sickness" progresses, she puts herself to sleep at night imagining Julie in her arms. She is obsessive about seeing Julie every day. In the evening she locks herself in the sewing room to sew clothes for the girl: "She kissed the undergarments that were to touch the beloved young body, and when she had made a dress for Julie she caressed it with her hands and hugged it to her breast so that it might, by proxy, be her arms around Julie whenever Julie wore it." When she has the opportunity actually to try clothes on her beloved, "her hands shook, her heart suffocated, and she turned Julie away from her and wept." After the girl leaves the room, Martha "sat with her face in her hands, her cheeks burning against her cold fingers, her mouth aching, seeing still the dimples in Julie's shoulders, kissing them in her imagination and crying weakly, starved." When she thinks that Julie is leaving her school to go away to college, she finally has a "nervous breakdown." Unlike the noble artist in "The Fire" (the 1917 *Century Magazine* story) who teaches her pupil about beauty and courage, the woman here is fatuous and pitiable. Finally she becomes a reconciled old maid once she accepts Julie's forthcoming marriage. She then recovers from her "invalidism."

D. H. Lawrence's *The Fox*, which was serialized in *Dial* magazine in 1922, presents a "clinical" study of lesbian morbidity, according to Edmund Bergler, a psychoanalyst who rose to fame in the 1950's with his homosexual "cures." In his essay "D. H. Lawrence's 'The Fox' and the Psychoanalytic Theory of Lesbianism," Bergler says that "the effectiveness of 'The Fox' derives from Lawrence's predominantly correct . . . observations of a series of clinically verifiable facts on Lesbianism." [5] Bergler neglects of course to see beyond his own Freudian assumptions to the fearful concerns of the novelist with regard to the growing independence of women in the second decade of the twentieth century.[6] *The Fox* is less a "clinically correct" study of lesbianism than a study of Lawrence's worry that women have taken their pursuit of independence too far.

The Fox is set on a farm in the year 1918, toward the end of the war which had taught Englishwomen that they could fend for themselves in the world if need be, and even do the world some good, that they need not be stuck in petticoats and tight corsets, that there was a world outside their insulated communities to which they could even travel alone if they liked. The two women of *The Fox*, March and Banford, decide to live on a farm together and work it by themselves. One learns carpentry and joinery, and goes about in breeches and puttees, belted coat and loose cap. To a reactionary like Lawrence, their notions—which were characteristic of many English and American feminists of his day—were certainly disturbing.[7]

By comparing Lawrence's first version (1918) of *The Fox* [8] with the novel-length version that was published four years later in *Dial* magazine, ones sees his mounting hostility, which appears to be a response to his worry that men are increasingly losing hold over women, who are becoming "self-important." In the first version Henry, a young man who takes it upon himself to break up the lesbian household, marries March, "although to Banford it seemed utterly impossible," but Banford is permitted to live. In the *Dial* version Henry kills her. As her body quivers with little convulsions, he knows that she is really dead, or will be soon: "He knew it, that it was so. He knew it in his soul and his blood. The inner necessity of his life was fulfilling itself, it was he who was to live. The thorn was drawn out of his bowels." This mounting hostility is also evident in passages such as those in which Henry decides to make March his wife. Lawrence added to the *Dial* version a long description in which Henry's pursuit of March is likened to a hunter stalking a deer. "It is a subtle, profound battle of wills, which takes place in the invisible. And it is a battle never finished till your bullet goes home." Lawrence concludes with Henry's realization that "it was as a young hunter that he wanted to bring down March as his quarry."

That two women could mean a great deal to each other while they awaited men to lead them to marriage and the real business of life is negligible; that they could believe that the real business of life is in meaning a great deal to each other and that men are only incidental to their lives—as women could now believe for the first time in history—is of course frightening to a society which prefers to conserve old social patterns. It is probably for this reason that a magazine of the 1920's would publish a story like *The Fox*, which teaches that lesbians are morbid and must either be killed or captured, instead of stories that focus on a woman's love for another woman and her personal growth through that love. There were very few lesbian stories published in magazines after the war that did not carry Lawrence's moral: Women cannot find satisfaction with each other, to try to do so is sick, and some terrible disaster will befall those who test this truth.

A somewhat more sympathetic work, Naomi Royde-Smith's *The Island: A Love Story*, published five years after the author's depiction of lesbian evil in *The Tortoiseshell Cat*, still portrays lesbianism in terms which Bergler and his colleagues would have approved. In *The Island* the lesbian, who is called Goosey because of her childhood timidity in dealing with the facts of life, is a victim of an unscrupulous bisexual woman, Almond, who arouses Goosey's passions only to use her. Goosey, no less than the villains in other novels whose misfortunes are of their own making, is also doomed to loneliness and worse because of her foolish heart. *The Island* too is a cautionary tale.

In contrast to Stephen in *The Well of Loneliness*, which appeared two years earlier, the genesis of Goosey's homosexuality is explained more typically in Freudian casebook terms. She was a motherless child, raised by an old-maid aunt who taught her to be fearful of the biological facts of nature. She is given no confidence in her (very minimal) womanly charms. Her one early attempt at heterosexuality is rebuffed, and because her feelings were so sensual and bare in that incident, her frustration is traumatic. Therefore, she fears and detests men and is open to lesbianism. Her lesbianism is also connected with her feminism—she is shown participating in suffragette demonstrations, carrying "Votes for Women" banners, and handing out leaflets. Royde-Smith implies this is another manifestation of her discomfort with herself as a woman.

Goosey is a gentle character, far more sinned against than sinning, but she is finally destroyed because of her lesbian activities. Her life, taken up with her erratic affair with Almond, is, as one island neighbor correctly characterizes it, "the story of infatuation, of gradually advancing poverty, . . . of loneliness, of jealousy, of quarrels that could be heard from the road, of reconciliations that could be seen at the railway station, sometimes even in the street." Her great crime, and the cause of her suffering, is not simply her susceptibility to lesbianism but her weakness which forced her to give in to that susceptibility. She is plagued by guilt, which is viewed unequivocally as the byproduct of lesbian sex: "Almond's revelation of that dark secret she had never guessed at until Almond, shewing it to her, had made all life a pattern of interlacing wonder and remorse." She realizes that Almond has been her "tempter," and has forced her to eat "the forbidden fruit," which now leaves her desolate. They are both "damned," she announces to Almond, and they are both destined for hell. The author seems to back up this assessment, because a final vignette describes an optical illusion under a sunset in which Almond's house appears to be burning in the fires of hell, with Goosey a monster hovering over it.

Royde-Smith seems to be suggesting that while Goosey was not responsible for her unfortunate upbringing or her heterosexual trauma, she did share responsibility for accepting lesbian sexual knowledge (Gillian in her earlier novel, despite a lesbian infatuation, is exonerated because she frees herself without learning lesbian sex secrets). Royde-Smith shows that Goosey's knowledge has the power to create a hell for her. Victorian antisexuality was not dead in England when Royde-Smith wrote this novel in 1929. Nor was it dead around that time in France apparently. Jacques de Lacretelle in *Marie Bonifas* (1925) presents a character very similar to Goosey. But Marie escapes from hell because, although she has all Goosey's proclivities and cause, she resists sexual knowledge (she also decides that feminism is meaningless to her). Marie is as "plain" and as clumsy as Goosey, and like her is a motherless child who has bad experiences with men. She too is infatuated with women. Her gentleness and generosity to the woman she loves most is repaid shabbily. Like Freud's lesbian, she is attracted to women who need to be rescued from something. She wishes always to offer herself as their protector.

Marie learns literally from the sexologists' books that what she has been feeling for other women is abnormal. De Lacretelle says that "despite the purity of her acts," she could, after reading the literature, trace "the fatal emotion" throughout her life. Once she is warned about the meaning of her emotional attachments, she works to keep a check on herself. Although she sometimes fantasizes wild activities with other women and almost makes a pass at a young woman who is fitting her for a corset, she restrains herself. Finally she is able to drive all the wild thoughts from her brain, and she becomes a true recluse. She is rewarded for her purity by being made the leader of her town during the war. Although at the conclusion of the novel women still have the power to move her, she has grown old with her virtue intact, and so it will remain.

In contrast to most antilesbian novels of the period, both these works written in the 1920's seem to be more concerned with the sexual aspects of lesbianism than with its feminist aspects. But their central characters are independent women anyway, and the authors associate female independence with abnormality, clumsiness, and unhappiness. The social message to the reader remains the same.

When lesbians are not presented as evil or morbid in this literature, they are simply weird. The title of Compton Mackenzie's novel, *Extraordinary Women* (1928), suggests a predominant literary treatment: His lesbians are extraordinary in the sense of abnormal and grotesque. His preface states that they are "the peculiar Aeolian fauna" whose life he ventures to observe. While some of them are extremely attractive, they are all either emotional imbeciles or moral dwarfs. All the clichés of lesbian love are caricatured, including jealousy, promiscuity, impermanence, and the frustration of sterile passions. These women are, Mackenzie says, a casebook of "sexual psychopathy" such as would "make Freud blush, Adler blench, Jung lower his eyes, and Dr. Ernest Jones write his next book in Latin." The novel is, in fact, a *roman à clef* of a lesbian circle on Capri during World War I, made up primarily of wealthy American and English women with whom Mackenzie was acquainted. Natalie Barney, Radclyffe Hall, Una Troubridge, Romaine Brooks, and Renata Borgatti are the most easily identifiable characters.

Mackenzie's intent is to satirize them. Even their acts of goodness are basically foolishness. When they are hurt in an emotional affair, he suggests it is nothing more than they deserve. Their sorrows are not human sorrows such as ordinary people would be credited with; even in their suffering they are ridiculous:

> There is perhaps something a little ludicrous in the sight of a woman with a monocle seated at the table of a cafe and confiding to another woman with a monocle the history of an unfortunate love affair. It becomes even more ludicrous when the monocle of one of the women is continually either blown out like a pane of glass from the tempestuous emotion behind it or sliding down the wearer's cheek on a chute of tears. And it becomes most ludicrous of all when the other woman's monocle thanks to the comparative steadiness of a confidante's nerves magnifies an intensely fixed, slightly malicious, and completely cold eye.

The sufferer's monocle sticks to her eye only after she drops it in her grenadine and cleans it imperfectly.

Mackenzie's message is, finally, that although these women were extraordinary during the war, after the war they became, numerically at any rate, far more ordinary. He points to the "boyishness" of one of the characters, calls her a "precursor," and observes that her uniqueness "would presently be blurred by myriads of post-war girls affecting boyishness." Mackenzie, a Catholic, sees this phenomenon as a threat to the moral order of the universe as well as to the social order. It is his apparent hope to make such women look absurd enough that females of the 1920's would much prefer to scrub floors and kids' faces rather than go to Capri and be like them.[9]

Similar ludicrous depictions of lesbians stocked popular literature of the next few decades, often as walk-on characters who make some point about the decadence or absurdity of society or liberated women. Georgette Heyer, for example, in *Penhallow* (1943) briefly presents a ridiculous lesbian pair consisting of one who "did her best by cutting her strong, wiry hair short and wearing the most masculine garments she could find, to look as much like a man as possible," and another "who resembled nothing so much as pink fondant." Mary Stewart in *Wildfire at Midnight* (1955) also presents two lesbian bit parts. Again, one of the pair has "hair cropped straight and mannishly," and wears only clothes which "exaggerate her masculine appearance." The other, about half her age, is feminine and unhappy-looking. She is bullied by her older friend, who is described by another character as "that impossible female with the moustache."

The paperback-book market, which reached a height during the 1950's and early 1960's, also provided abundant lesbian stories for the masses. Lesbians were not infrequently the central characters in these books, which were designed to titillate while upholding conventional values. With few exceptions, such as Claire Morgan's *The Price of Salt* (1952), in which the attractive lesbian characters end happily together (although one of them must pay a great price), the paperbacks mirrored the familiar images: sadistic and inexplicably evil lesbians, often spouting feminist philosophy and corrupting the innocent; or confused and sick lesbians, torturing themselves and being tortured by others because of their terrible passions, made inescapable by nature or nurture. The novels rely heavily on the lesbian imagery supplied by the French writers and German sexologists, or, rather on those earlier popular authors who were influenced by them and carried their imagery well into the twentieth century.

The lurid covers of these paperbacks, which promised either "a story of twisted passions in the twilight zone" or "the tragedy of those who dwell midway between the sexes," sum up the variety of images of love between women contained in the books. Almost invariably the characters end in violence or suicide if they are not rescued by some strong man. The honest ones admit, as does the woman in Ann Herbert's *Summer Camp* (1966), "I'm a genuine lesbian, truly twisted, and I know it." The dishonest ones do not make such an admission, but it is abundantly clear that they are all more or less "truly twisted." Even the nonfiction paperbacks which pretended to sympathize with the lesbian and called for an end to the persecution against her came to the same conclusion (for example, Ann Aldrich's *We Walk Alone*, 1955; *We, Too, Must Love*, 1958; and *Carol in a Thousand Cities*, 1960; and Donald Webster Cory's *The Lesbian in America*, 1964). Ann Aldrich declares that the lesbian is sick, guilt-ridden, maladjusted, and that "the instability of lesbian life—the jumping from partner to partner" promotes her neurosis, for which she requires a psychoanalyst who can enlighten her "as to the causes, manifestations of, and treatment for homosexuality." [10]

The lesbian image changed significantly in the 1970's because lesbians began to write not to the demands of conventional morality and wisdom, but rather to the demands of the truth and complexity of their own experiences. They were permitted to do this by the growth of the lesbian-feminist movement, which promised them a readership for truthfully portrayed lesbian experiences. And they were encouraged further by the establishment of lesbian-feminist publishing houses, such as Daughters, Inc., Naiad Press, and Diana Press, which guaranteed that the images of the lesbian as human being would not be blue-penciled out or images of the lesbian tormentor or sickie blue-penciled in.[11]

CHAPTER 5

Internalization and Rebellion

Before the 1970's lesbians who read could find few human representations of themselves in fiction. The literary depiction of lesbianism and its effect on public opinion must have been devastating to many young women who preferred to commit themselves to other women. With no other models before them, love between women must have appeared as hell or martyrdom. Women who were isolated in small towns or in rural areas, or even those living in large cities who had no social circle of lesbian friends, must have been terrorized by the literary image. While surely many scoffed at its melodrama and absurdity, it was probably not easy to dismiss what was taken to be a universal truth unless there were powerful counterbalances such as an extraordinary ability to march to a different drummer and block out all discordant sounds, or a close-knit circle of friends to prove to each other that lesbian fiction was nothing but fiction.

While many must have lived out their lives without such counterbalances, some were obviously fortunate enough to have them. *The Stone Wall*, a 1930 biography of a woman who wrote under the name of Mary Casal, was published when the author was in her mid-sixties. It shows that even though some lesbians accepted with one corner of their minds the Freudian explanation of their genesis in penis envy or early traumatic sexual experiences, they nevertheless saw themselves as functioning, quite healthy human beings. They even applied to themselves current theories about the importance of sexual expression, substituting "woman" where the word "man" appeared as lesbians are forced to do if they want to identify with heterosexual characters in movies or books. Casal believes, in keeping with the

357

popular wisdom of her day, that to repress sexual desire is unsalu-
tary, and she proclaims that she and her woman lover "found ourselves far more fit for good work after having been thus relieved." [1]
But while not questioning many of the sexologists' pronouncements,
and even attributing her love for women to childhood trauma, Casal
looks to herself to discover whether or not she was happy, and she
concludes she was. Of her relationship with the great love of her life,
Juno, she states, "We never wavered in our belief that ours was the
very highest type of human love, and our joy in each other grew
greater and greater all the time." In her declining years she still believes that "such a relation is the highest and most complete union
of two human beings." [2] She was not alone among happy lesbians,
even at the height of antilesbian social sentiment. Friendship circles
such as the 1920's and 1930's group of middle-class women in Salt
Lake City, Utah (see page 326), must have provided for many other
women a supportive environment so that they felt that they had an
"ideal" and "happy" life and were "socially accepted," although they
understood that they must be covert about an aspect of their life that
contributed most to their happiness, their lesbianism. [3]

Unlike Mary Casal, most lesbian writers probably believed that
sympathetic or even human representations of lesbians would not get
published, and they seldom tried. The literature written by lesbians
was, for the most part, as much influenced by French and German
models as was the lesbian literature written by heterosexuals. Since
as writers, literature was at least as real to literary lesbians as life,
and being sensitive to the world they were very much affected by
current attitudes which viewed love between women as sickness or
sin, many developed a self-loathing and a weird and exotic self-
image such as would have been entirely appropriate had they
stepped right out of the pages of nineteenth-century German and
French literature. Therefore, they did not consciously lie when
they represented lesbian life as pathetic and terrible.

The nineteenth-century images of decadence and exoticism seem
to have been internalized by many literary lesbians from the end of
the nineteenth century throughout the 1930's. Their preoccupation
with the decadent, with darkness and the lure of the perverse, is explainable perhaps by the fact that independent women and the
aesthete-decadent movement emerged at about the same time. When
the first new breed of females who saw no need to marry, and no
reason not to commit themselves to other women forever, emerged

at the end of the century, they had no models to emulate, and so they sought a style. If they were literary-minded, that style was furnished through French literature, where alone lesbianism was freely discussed in writing available to the masses. The literary young around the turn of the century were especially enamored of literary aestheticism and decadence, and they would have felt little resistance to the images created by the aesthete-decadent writers. Those images thus served as role models, especially to bohemian females who already had rejected convention in wanting to become woman authors and who sought a style that would emphasize their distinctiveness. Through their own writing, they fixed the association of lesbianism with the darker side of experience even more firmly. Although their decadent pose was the result of a search for a style, it became associated with lesbianism as though it were an integral part, and, only much later in the century were other styles born to replace it for literary lesbians.

Auf Kypros,[4] the poems of a German woman, Marie-Madeleine (Baroness von Puttkamer), which were published in 1898, show to what extent women who loved women might by this time see in themselves an embodiment of every sensationalistic attribute French literature gave lesbians. In the poem "Sappho," the poet of Lesbos does not satisfy herself with one girl child—she lusts after "flocks" of them, and she orders each one to "drop your raiments silently" so that she may "drink" the beauty of them all. In "Words of Old Age," the speaker, an old woman, is haunted in her dreams by a young naked blond woman with "wild lust bright in her glances" and with "a mad laugh, a bawdy, echoing peal." In "Vagabonds," the speaker urges another woman to "leave house and heart for the sake of my eyes' dark glow." She realizes that the other woman will be "despised and dishonored," that they will need to become prostitutes together and wander through the streets with "work and sweet sin surging noisily around us, and lust and hunger," and of course they will both get syphilis. But, she concludes, the other woman will undoubtedly follow her anyway:

> And hate and mockery surrounding us,
> and everyone condemning us, and all the preachers
> threatening us with punishment
> and hell-fire, we are
> forever damned!

Marie-Madeleine's obsession with sin and guilt and damnation pervades these poems. So does her ambivalence, which is reminiscent of the earlier aesthete-decadent writers. While her characters are tortured, poisoned, living in hell, they are also beautiful, and their way of life, their bold, impertinent rejection of the bourgeois world, are incredibly exciting. Even her language, full of "wild lust" and "sinful kisses" is reminiscent of French sensationalistic expressions. What is novel, of course, is that perhaps for the first time a woman poet, who has presumably experienced love between women, writes this way and lends authority to a view whose basis was literary to begin with. "Crucifixa" is representative:

> *I saw you tortured on a stake,*
> *high on a dark cross I saw you tied.*
> *The marks of my sinful kisses*
> *glowed on your white flesh like purple wounds.*
>
> *How slender your young limbs are,*
> *and how childish your budlike breasts!*
> *But in your eyes, my blonde child,*
> *burn the torches of wild lust.*
>
> *And yet, you were cool, white velvet,*
> *stainless as a sharpened sword,*
> *when your young innocence enflamed me*
> *and I desired you so boundlessly.*
>
> *I gave you of my own poison,*
> *and I gave you my poison's strength.*
> *And now that you are fully ablaze*
> *my soul shudders at what I have done.*
>
> *I want to kneel before the altars*
> *my own wanton daring destroyed . . .*
> *Madonna with a whore's eyes,*
> *I myself crucified you!*

Once such views were internalized, it was inevitable that self-loathing and guilt would become common in the lives of women who continued to acknowledge their love of other women.

Lesbianism was in high fashion among the literary and the bohemian circles in the early twentieth century, especially in France, but in certain sophisticated milieus in other countries too. According to Hilda Doolittle in her autobiographical novel, *Bid Me to Live*

(1960), it was not unusual for a woman to declare in arty circles in England around the time of World War I, "I think it would be lovely to have a woman lover." Natalie Barney flaunted her lesbian loves in her first book of poems, which appeared in France in 1900; and Liane de Pougy, her lover and one of the most notorious courtesans of Paris, apparently thought that public knowledge of her lesbianism would be good for business when she published the story of their affair, *Idylle Saphique*, in 1901. Even in Imperial Russia after the publication of *Thirty-three Monsters* (1907), a novel by an actress, Annibal Sinowjewa, lesbianism became so fashionable that according to one source many clubs devoted to it sprang up throughout the Empire.[5] The "popularity" of lesbianism increased during the 1920's and 1930's. If there is any truth in Djuna Barnes's depiction in *Ladies Almanack* (1928), lesbianism was the new cosmopolitan chic, which women were not only anxious to experience but delighted to talk about.[6] In the 1930's it was associated with "the beauty of evil, the magic of the lower depths" (*The Secret Paris of the '30's*).[7] The fashionability and excitement of lesbianism together with its sinful connotations must have created a painful ambivalence in many women who chose to be lesbians during those decades.

Renée Vivien (née Pauline Tarn), the Anglo-Amercian poet who settled in Paris at the beginning of the century, appears to have inherited many of her views of lesbian life directly from the poets. Not long after her arrival in Paris, Renée was introduced to Pierre Louys, and, considering him her mentor, began giving him her lesbian poems for criticism. She was influenced by Louÿs even to the extent that she began using the spelling for "Sappho" which he invented—"Psappha" (see "Psappha Revit" and references in her novel, *A Woman Appeared to Me*, 1904, to "Psappha in olden times, who is known by the layman as Sappho").[8]

Louÿs was not her only influence. As Clarissa Cooper has pointed out, Vivien had a "Baudelairean preoccupation with vice."[9] Her lesbian poems, like Baudelaire's, generally deal with the lesbian as social outcast (see especially *A l'heure des mains jointes*, 1906) and the forbidden delights—always outweighed by the torments—of lesbian love (see especially *Sillages*, 1907). Her interest in Swinburne is suggested not only by her adaptation of his poem "Erotion" in "*D'Après Swinburne (A l'heure des mains jointes)*, but also by her unfortunate penchant for imbibing eau de cologne like his heroine, Lesbia Brandon. That habit (complicated by opium in Lesbia's case, and by anorexia and alcoholism in Vivien's) eventually killed both of them. If Colette can be credited, Renée furnished her apartment with Lesbia's trappings. Colette, who had been a frequent visitor in the poet's home, reports that it smelled like a rich man's funeral. Flowers and incense were everywhere, leaded windows were covered always by heavy draperies, and few lamps were permitted (Colette claims she once brought her own candle to dinner).[10] Swinburne's novel sets Lesbia in an almost identical abode, "A funeral fragrance hung about all the air. Close curtains shut out the twilight, and a covered lamp at either end filled the room with less of light than of silver shadow."

While Vivien apparently chose to devote herself to women at least partly because of her strong feminist consciousness, her poetry shows little of her feminism. Her alter ego, San Giovanni, in her autobiographical novel, *A Woman Appeared to Me*, declares that she discovered feminism and love of women together at the age of seventeen, when "a great passion for justice seized me. I was aroused on behalf of women, so misunderstood, so made use of by male tyranny. I began to hate the male for the base cruelty of his laws and the impunity of his morals. I considered his works and judged them evil," and she then sides with female suffering and admires female courage and beauty.[11] But Vivien's poetry has little to do with such insights.

Instead she turns to Baudelaire and his followers for both the language and imagery of lesbianism. Her poetry most often associates lesbian love with vice, artificiality, perfume, and death. In "Chanson" (*Études et préludes*), for example, the beloved, who has "perverse charm," is decked in "gems and perfumery." The speaker laments, "Even the gardenias which winter cannot harm/ Die in your hands of your impure caresses."[12] In a second "Chanson," the beloved is the "dearest despair of my soul," and her kisses are bitter ecstasy."[13] The attraction and repulsion of lesbian sin pervade many of the poems. "Lucidity" begins, "You fill your leisures with the delicate art of vice" and ends "Oh Woman! Only your mouth will quench my thirst."[14] In "Modern Naiad" the speaker states: "You attract and repel me like the unseen abyss/Hidden by the churning waves."[15] "A Cry" ends, "I hate and yet I love you abominably."[16] Most often, like her male predecessors, Vivien sees love between women as "flames of burning desire," "nights of savage desire and fevered helplessness" (*Evocations*),[17] and "cruel pleasure that tears and torments (*À l'heure des mains jointes*).[18]

In her poetry and in much of her life, Vivien seems to have internalized completely the puerile and self-dramatizing aspects of aesthete-decadent literature. Not only did her infatuation with the aesthete-decadent pose contribute to her death quite literally by encouraging her romantic aversion to light and air and supplying her with the idea of drinking eau de cologne, but she even presented herself in nineteenth-century poseur terms in her last statement to the world, her epitaph: "My ravished soul, from mortal breath/ Appeased, forgets all former strife,/ Having, from its great love of Death,/Pardoned the crime of crimes—called Life." [19] Her enchantment with the aesthete-decadent vision in her writing and her life made her inauthentic. She assumed a view of herself as a twilight creature which had less to do with her experiences than with the books she read. That view vitiated her and made her poetry, despite its widely acknowledged technical perfection, irrelevant to contemporary lesbians, who have long since escaped from the spell of aesthete-decadence.

Perhaps it was difficult for any literary lesbian living in France during that era to free herself of that spell, although it is not as marked in most of Colette's lesbian writings as it is in that of her contemporaries. Colette speaks in her memoirs of having become familiar with Pierre Louÿs's *Chanson de Bilitis*,[20] and at the beginning of *Claudine at School*, her fifteen-year-old heroine admits her familiarity with *Aphrodite*, but Louÿs seems to have no effect on Claudine's view of love between women, and little effect on Colette's view. Although during the five or six years she spent in a lesbian relationship she frequented what an outsider would consider to be the exotic haunts of those who walk in shadows, she describes them generally in very different terms than the male writers who depicted such scenes or the lesbians who saw them through the male writers' eyes.[21] In *The Pure and the Impure* she expresses her impatience with the lesbian internalization of aesthete-decadent images and with twentieth-century writers like Marcel Proust, who endowed the lesbian of his Gomorrah "with shocking desires, customs and language, showing how little he knew her." [22] In contrast to Proust and to her neighbor, Vivien, Colette recognizes that the basis of lesbian love is not "bitter ecstasy" or indiscriminate promiscuity but a bond that goes deeper than fleeting sexual passions. She observes, for example, "What woman would not blush to seek out her *amie* only for sensual pleasure? In no way is it passion that fosters the devotion of two women, but rather a feeling of kinship." [23] It is apparent, however, in her preface to *The Pure and the Impure*, which is set in an opium den, and her inclusion of lesbians along with Don Juans and other sexual malcontents, that she too was not entirely free of the lesbian image promulgated by her literary predecessors.

Djuna Barnes seems to have internalized the literary images of lesbianism as much as Renée Vivien, although she did not let them lead to death. Her biographer, Louis Kannenstine, observes in much of her early work "the art-for-art sake detachment of *The Yellow Book*, the mode of the decadents that would render aesthetic all emotions, appearances, and matters of life, including death," [24] but this pose can be found in her later work too. In a 1923 poem, "Six Songs of Khalidine," [25] the beloved's red hair flames and crawls and creeps, as in Verlaine's lesbian poems. Her fallen lids are stained with ebony, she and the speaker are in darkness, there is a thread of fear between them, and they hear a lost bird cry. The speaker exclaims, "It is not gentleness but mad despair/ That sets us kissing mouths, O Khalidine." In "A Little Girl Tells a Story to a Lady" (1929), the setting comes directly out of nineteenth-century French novels of decadence. Inevitably "the room was dark excepting for the moon, and two thin candles. . . . The curtains over the bed were red velvet, very Italian, and with gold fringes." [26]

Barnes's major work, *Nightwood* (1936), was astutely characterized by Theodore Purdy in a 1937 review. He pointed out that the early chapters recall Wilde and Pater, and the rest of the book produces an atmosphere of decay which, despite its Elizabethan pretensions, "stems from the fin-de-siècle Frenchmen." [27] Love of woman for woman in this novel is described as "insane passion for unmitigated anguish." Nora, Robin Vote's lover, says of her love for the other woman, "There's something evil in me that loves evil and degradation." The nineteenth-century views of lesbian narcissism and frustration are delivered up whole here: "A man is another person—a woman is yourself, caught as you turn in panic; on her mouth you kiss your own. If she is taken you cry that you have been robbed of yourself." Faithful to Louys's poem "The Doll," Nora observes, "When a woman gives [a doll] to a woman, it is the life they cannot have, it is their child, sacred and profane." But the nineteenth-century sexologists also make an appearance in this novel: Robin is the true born invert, a member of the third sex, who is distinguished from her lovers, the normal women that fall in love with the invert.

Barnes knew most intimately many lesbians, such as the subjects of her in-joke satire, *Ladies Almanack*, including Natalie Barney, Janet Flanner, and Dolly Wilde, who had absolutely no relationship to the women she describes in *Nightwood*. Insane passion and degradation and doll games and roles had nothing to do with those women's conceptions of lesbianism. Barnes also knew enough to agree with Natalie Barney that Proust's treatment of flighty lesbians who follow gay male patterns of cruising and sexual contacts in *Remembrance of Things Past* was "improbable." [28] Yet Barnes's treatment in her own novel was not much different. It attests to the power of literary images over lesbian writers that, even after criticizing Proust's lies, Barnes called on her knowledge of lesbians in literature rather than in life in order to write her own novel.

Many subsequent lesbian writers before the new wave also went to literature rather than life for their images of love between women. Anaïs Nin, for example, stated that her own "formative roots" as a writer were in Djuna Barnes,[29] and it is not surprising to discover that in her prologue to *Ladders of Fire* (1946), in which the central character, Lillian, is a lesbian, Nin asserts, "This novel deals with the negative pole, the pole of confused and twisted nature." Her images of lesbian love reveal the similarity between her attitude and that of Barnes. For example, Barnes's "a woman is yourself," is echoed in Nin's description of lesbian narcissism in her characters' lovemaking: "Their bodies touched and then fell away, as if both of them had touched a mirror, their own image upon the mirror." In seeming contradiction to the mirror theory of lesbianism, Nin (like Barnes) also sees the necessity for one of the lovers to embody the masculine principle. Thus Lillian is described in her affair as wearing "the man's costume," not literally but rather emotionally in this case.

However, the mirror theory, with the exotic, morbid, destructive implications she invests in it, is her favorite, and it appears in *House of Incest* (1958) as well. The House of Incest, Nin says, is "where we only love ourselves in the other," and that is her explanation of lesbianism. The narrator observes that lesbian loves means "one lies down at peace as on one's own breast" (sic). To Sabina she says, "From all men I was different and myself, but I see in you that part of me which is you," and "Our faces are soldered together by soft hair, soldered together, showing two profiles of the same soul." There is no comfort in their similarities, despite her statement that sometimes the two women lie down at peace. More typically, the narrator declares, "I will let you carry me into the fecundity of destruction. . . . I become you. And you become me." But she never suggests why the love of like beings, two women, should of itself be any more destructive than the love of different beings.

Her vision of lesbian love is melodramatic. It stems from the same attitude which the nineteenth-century French aesthete-decadents displayed: a fascination with the "immoral" and a definition of immorality which differed in no way from the definition of the bourgeoisie against whom they believed they were rebelling. Violette Leduc shows the same kind of ambivalence in her work. She admits in *La Bâtarde* (1965) that she is imprisoned in conventionality: "I was and I always shall be hampered by what people will say." Over and over again in her books she determines to break out of this prison, but society's inculcation acts as jailer. Therefore, while she asks in *Mad in Pursuit,* "Why upset people? . . . Why shock people?" and she says in that book that she believes that homosexuality is "what repelled and will always repel" society, she deals with lesbianism, again in the first person, in the greatest detail. Her desire to *épater le bourgeois* is as confused as it was in the work of nineteenth-century French authors. Her ambivalence is characterized perfectly in a scene in *La Bâtarde* in which Violet and her woman lover go shopping. One asks the other regarding a saleslady, "Do you think she's guessed about us?" and the other replies, "I hope so."

The division of her self not only causes such ambivalence, but it also makes her deny the evidence of her own experience and contradict herself in her depiction of lesbian love. She internalizes her society's view to such an extent that despite her description of Hermine, her lover of ten years, as gentle, generous, and altogether loving, Leduc quite seriously, and with melodrama inherited from Victorian prudery, calls her erotic life with Hermine "the sullies of my flesh."

Those internalized attitudes were by no means limited to French lesbians or to expatriate lesbians who settled in France. The German Baroness von Puttkamer (see page 359) is one case in point. The English Vita Sackville-West is another. Vita, a writer who was Virginia Woolf's sometime lover and the subject of her novel *Orlando* (1928), saw herself, as she said in a 1920 attempt at an autobiography, as a "Dr. Jekyll and Mr. Hyde personality." [30] The good and pure side of herself, she wrote, was her love for her husband. On the other side, she said, "stands my perverted nature," her lesbian self which led her to passionate affairs with women.

In her early twenties, in the midst of an affair with Rosamund Grosvenor, Vita married Harold Nicolson primarily because she enjoyed his company and because women of her upper-class social position married. After their two sons were conceived the marriage seems to have become a matter of companionable friendship, and her sexual life was spent with women. Not long after her marriage, she took up a tempestuous relationship with Violet Trefusis, and both women toyed with the idea of leaving their husbands, as Vita's son reports in *Portrait of a Marriage*. Vita saw her love for women as an "inevitable evil," [31] made inevitable by the androgynous aspect of her personality. Her supposition comes from the sexologists' equation of female "masculinity" with lesbianism: It is her genes or her faulty environment which causes her to seek out women. But even though she cannot help her drive, it is evil.

Her "drive" is, from all the available evidence, a series of poses. Its melodramatic roots are not difficult to discover: Sometimes she is Heathcliffe, sometimes she is a wounded young soldier home from World War I, sometimes she is a gypsy man out of early nineteenth-century English romantic poetry. Perhaps she stared at the picture of Charlotte and Emily Brontë which she kept on her desk as she wrote of Denys Trefusis, Violet's husband (in shameless imitation of Heathcliffe regarding Edgar Linton), "There is no injury I would not do him with the utmost pleasure." [32] Sometimes Violet is her Cathy, at other times she is Isabella Linton: "I took her [to my room], I treated her savagely. I made love to her, I had her, I didn't care, I only wanted to hurt Denys even though he didn't know it." [33] Occasionally, with Violet in tow as her woman, she wears men's clothes with a bandage around her head, allowing others to believe she is a boy who has been wounded in battle: "It was marvelous fun," Vita declares, "all the more so because there was always the risk of being found out." [34] Later she encourages Violet to call her Mitya and Violet becomes Lushka. They are two gypsies, male and female, imprisoned on the estates of the landed gentry when all they want to do is ride around in the caravan with their pots and pans and unmended furniture.

All the while, however, these games taken from literature are interspersed with conventional guilt and shock at the "dark side" of herself. Vita exclaims about leaving Rosamund to marry Harold, "How rescued I felt from everything that was vicious and violent," [35] although in her own account the affair seemed quite tame and neither vicious nor violent by any stretch of the imagination. When Vita's understanding, sympathetic mother-in-law comes to visit her at the height of her affair with Violet, Vita wants to run away because, she says in all seriousness, "I would not pollute their [mother-in-law and husband's] purity any longer." [36] After reading a begging letter Denys sent Violet, Vita tells Violet she would give her up if Violet would go back to him. Vita then declares of that offer, "I did the only thing I am in the very least proud of." [37] There was a split in her personality all right, but not the kind she imagined. Rather it was the split of an individual deceiving herself with a notion of her freedom and bohemianism, entrapped by the moral shibboleths of her day, which limited her perspective as surely as if she had been a model of conformity. Probably it would have taken superhuman strength to escape from that trap.

Since even many lesbians gave credence to the images originally promulgated by men which saw them as sick, confused, violent, and hopeless, love between women lived in disrepute through much of this century. Lesbian writers were trapped by the male-created images for a number of reasons. Since the images were promulgated by "experts," medical men and great writers, who presumably had infinite knowledge of the world, it was difficult to challenge those opinions on the basis of a female's limited contacts. What did it mean if she and a couple of her friends were not sick, confused, and violent when the experts almost invariably said all other lesbians were? Having learned also from the moral spokespersons of society that lesbian love was evil, how is it possible to rid oneself entirely of that indoctrination even when experience belies it? One might live as one chooses, but the suspicion that maybe there is something to what the moralists say continues to lurk, however faintly, when there is no support group to scream just as loudly that the moralists are wrong. And what if a lesbian writer manages to overcome the repeated admonitions of the experts and the moralists? What publisher would print a book which proclaimed the joy of love between women when society was unshakable in its conviction (which it received from the moralists and the experts) that there was only misery in love between women.

Certainly there were oases for many women. Given a cosmopolitan friendship group made up of those with intelligence or talent or wealth that would serve to insulate lesbian life against popular wisdom, the viciousness of antilesbian literature might appear quite laughable (although if there were writers in the group they were seldom willing to make that point in print). Such groups existed in abundance among the expatriate communities in cities like Florence, in New York (Greenwich Village), in London (Bloomsbury), and all over Paris. They permitted those women who were fortunate enough to belong to have confidence in the truth of their own experiences and the experiences of their friends, rather than to examine themselves in the light of literature that told them they were miserable. It is regrettable that their perceptions seldom found their way into literature.

The Paris community which centered on Natalie Barney has received considerable attention particularly in recent years.[38] In the first book to concentrate extensively on Barney's circle, *Ladies Almanack*, Djuna Barnes, who was a member of the group, presents Natalie Barney and her friends in a far different light from that which she casts on the lesbians in her novel, *Nightwood*. Although her primary purpose in *Ladies Almanack* is to satirize the sexual misadventures of her friends, there is no suggestion whatsoever that they are creatures of shadows and tragedy. Perhaps the difference in her perspective in these two works is because *Ladies Almanack* was intended for her friends and printed privately, while *Nightwood* was written for the public, who demanded that their expectations regarding lesbian suffering be fulfilled.

In subsequent books on Barney, the emphasis has been on her role as a seducer of women and a leader of salons attended by male literary and artistic giants such as Paul Valéry, Ford Maddox Ford, Ezra Pound, and George Antheil. What is generally passed over, however, is the extent to which her circle functioned as a support group for lesbians to permit them to create a self-image which literature and society denied them.

The heterosexual males who attended Barney's salons were often annoyed because it was clear that while Barney intended her salons to be cultural events, she also intended them to be lesbian social events. The writer Matthew Josephson, for example, complained that on leaving one of Barney's Friday gatherings his last glimpse was of "some young women, transported by literature and champagne, dancing madly about in each others' arms." William Carlos Williams derided "the women of all descriptions" that he met at Barney's salon, "sneaking off together into a side room while casting surreptitious glances about them, hoping their exit had not been unnoticed." [39] While it is doubtful, especially in view of Barney's criticism of Proust's improbable depictions of lesbian sexual contacts, that sexual games between women were carried on blatantly in these salons as Williams implies, there is little doubt that Barney's lesbian friends believed that she created an environment where they need not hide their preferences nor view themselves as unnatural outcasts. Probably they and Barney would have been surprised to discover that the male writers and intellectuals, whose sexual liberalism they must have taken for granted, were very much products of their time as far as lesbianism was concerned.

As a young woman in 1904, Natalie went to Lesbos with Renée Vivien, hoping to be able to form a colony of women poets in honor of Sappho.[40] The scheme was destined to fail since Natalie, with her love for the here and now and her acute perception of reality, could not long have patience with Vivien, whose reality was based on melodramatic notions she had gleaned from literature. Barney soon returned to Paris and not many years later began her famous salon on 20 Rue Jacob. Among her friends, most of them frequent visitors of her salon, she counted many of the most celebrated and colorful women artists and literati of her day, including Romaine Brooks, Dolly Wilde, Emma Calvé, Colette, Elisabeth de Gramont, Lucie Delarue Mardrus, Radclyffe Hall, Rachilde, Gertrude Stein, Marie Laurencin, Marguerite Yourcenar, Mercedes d'Acosta, Sylvia Beach, Adrienne Monnier, Dorothy Bussy, Wanda Landowska, Mata Hari, Gwen LeGalliene, Edna St. Vincent Millay, Marguerite Moreno, Violet Trefusis, Vita Sackville-West, Edith Sitwell, Ida Rubenstein, and Janet Flanner. Those who were in a position to know—the women regulars at the salon—believed that Natalie had, in fact, established a kind of Lesbos in Paris, that the gatherings were meant for them rather than for the William Carlos Williamses and Ezra Pounds. Janet Flanner's somewhat flippant description must have had considerable truth to it. The parties, she said, consisted of "introductions, conversations, tea, excellent cucumber sandwiches, divine little cakes Berthe [the housekeeper] baked, and then the result: a new rendezvous among ladies who had taken a fancy to each other or wished to see each other again." [41]

The three major studies which deal with Natalie Barney, *Ladies Bountiful, Portrait of a Seductress,* and *The Amazon of Letters: The Life and Loves of Natalie Barney,* all by men, emphasize her lesbianism as a sexual phenomenon and show her avid appetite for sexual conquest. They are fond of repeating shocking little quotations; for example, when a friend asked her if she liked a particular woman, Barney replied, "Like her? Heavens, no, she and I made love, that's all." While Barney may have often chosen to express in that way her liberation as a New Woman in an era in which sex for a woman was like a child's newly discovered, deliciously dangerous, and somewhat prohibited play, there was a good deal more to her than is apparent from her biographers' emphases. First of all, she was a lesbian because she was a feminist. When as a young woman in Washington, D.C., she received a poem from a suitor, John Ellerton Lodge, telling her:

> *Thou canst not stand unsullied and alone, my Sappho*
> *White, in the blackness that the world can give;*
> *Make me the human passion of thy lips. . . .*[42]

Natalie was outraged. She could stand alone, and the world could not sully her because she had the strength and whatever else it took to remain her own person, regardless of what the world tried to heap upon her. When early in life she read Balzac's *Seraphita*, she identified with the heroine's complaint to her would-be fiancé:

> We must always please you, entertain you, always be gay, and only have the caprices that amuse you. . . . Even in our death agony we must still smile at you. You call that, I believe, to rule. Poor women, I pity them.[43]

She determined never to place herself in a situation where she would be at the mercy of men in a world which permitted them to be merciless. She claimed that her feminist awareness dated back even to her childhood when, traveling in Europe, she saw a woman pulling a heavy milk cart while her husband walked along next to her, blithely puffing on a pipe.[44] Taking her response to male-female relationships to a logical conclusion, she chose to relate to women.

As a literate woman of the world who would have been familiar with the sexologists' theories both through their writings and popular opinion, she could not free herself entirely from their explanation of her choice. It is not surprising that she stated in an autobiographical volume, "I consider myself without shame: albinos aren't reproached for having pink eyes and whitish hair, why should they hold it against me for being a lesbian? It's a question of nature: my queerness isn't a vice, isn't 'deliberate,' and harms no one."[45] She also paid occasional lip service to the prevailing views that men alone were intellectually stimulating, while women were important only for their physical beauty and the comfort it could give. It is said that she suggested, long before her death, that her epitaph read: "She was the friend of men and the lover of women, which, for people full of ardor and drive is better than the other way around."[46] But despite her use of the sexologists' theories as an argument for why she should be let alone to live in peace, and despite her wit which accorded with the wisdom of her day, both her youthful responses and her adult concerns indicate that lesbianism was to her an expression of her feminism.

One manifestation of that feminism was her dream of creating an intellectual woman's community, an *Académie de femmes* as she entitles it in Part II of her work, *Aventures de l'esprit* (1929),[47] which she devotes to an examination of her female literary and artistic friends, hoping to call them to public attention and to procure for them the notice which she felt they deserved and generally did not receive. Her real *Académie* was started in 1917 with the primary purpose of bringing together French, English, and American women writers, most of whom were concerned at that time not just with literature but also with putting an end to the war. After the war her efforts to gather female literati together fizzled for a while, but she renewed them. In December 1926 she shared with Gertrude Stein her plan to reestablish an *Académie*, which would include the "femmes de lettres" of the three nations. The following year she changed the format of her salons, in which people generally gathered and amused themselves as they might without a set program. Now many of her salons were devoted specifically to women writers —Colette, Gertrude Stein, Mina Loy, Djuna Barnes, Renée Vivien, etc.—whose works were sometimes presented by the writers themselves, sometimes by others. By this point the *Académie de femmes* became Barney's primary concern, although men were also free to come to many of the salons.[48] Barney's interest in furthering the careers of women in literature and the arts also extended to her financial and emotional support of those who were in need.[49]

Stereotypes of what lesbians were supposed to be had little real effect on her. She must have been an incredible phenomenon, a blessing, to lesbians who were all too conversant with their society's image of them. Radclyffe Hall's picture of her as Valérie Seymour in *The Well of Loneliness* probably reflects much more accurately what she meant to her lesbian friends than those biographies which emphasize her seductive qualities. Hall describes "Valérie's" salons, attended in this scene by both male and female homosexuals, whose social difficulties Hall typically exaggerates but who undoubtedly felt toward Natalie-Valérie just what Hall suggests:

> Valérie, placid and self-assured, created an atmosphere of courage; everyone felt very normal and brave when they gathered together at Valérie Seymour's. There she was, this

charming and cultured woman, a kind of lighthouse in a storm-swept ocean. The waves had lashed round her feet in vain; winds had howled; clouds had spewed forth their hail and their lightning; torrents had deluged but had not destroyed her. The storms, gathering force, broke and drifted away, leaving behind them the shipwrecked, the drowning. But when they looked up, the poor spluttering victims, Why, what should they see but Valérie Seymour. Then a few would strike boldly out for the shore, at the sight of this indestructible creature.

While Natalie Barney is the most famous instance of a lesbian who flourished (and helped others to flourish by her example), she does not stand alone. English, French, and American literary history contains a long roster of such women, including Sylvia Beach and Adrienne Monnier, Margaret Anderson and Georgette LeBlanc, H.D. and Bryher, who generally gave little credence to the absurd images of what lesbians were supposed to be, and made their own lives. Such women were probably everywhere, as the Salt Lake City, Utah, study reminds us. But unless they left some autobiographical record of themselves as the above-mentioned women did,[50] or were the subjects of the few studies conducted outside the dominion of the medical profession, they are hidden from history. If popular literature and the sexologists' writings were our only guide, we would never know they existed or that it was possible to be a lesbian without "living only in twilight," "truly twisted."

PART III

THE TWENTIETH CENTURY

B.
When It Changed

CHAPTER 1

The Rise of Lesbian-Feminism

Those antifeminists who hoped to scare women off from the women's movement by warning them that the movement was composed of lesbians were presenting some glimmer of truth. Their assumption was that the mere term "lesbian" would conjure up visions of such terror—of congenital deformities and vampirish propositions—that "normal" women would steer clear. But the truth of the matter was that women who were concerned about their future as independent beings and the future of other females, women who were "women-identified," [1] women who gave their energy and commitment to women's interests, did love other women. Such a love was weird or evil, however, by male definition. It was women's job to reclaim female same-sex love by redefining it for themselves.

Before 1970 any attempt at redefinition was doomed to failure, since it was drowned out by the writings of medical experts and literary venerables which helped maintain a climate of opinion that affected even those who did not read. One or two or three voices crying in the wilderness, telling other women or society at large that the experts and literature lied, could have little effect. The image of love between women could not begin to change until there were masses prepared to validate the truth of a new image. What was needed was a reawakening of feminism at a period when sexual morality was not rigid. Had there not been a "sexual revolution" about the time feminism was reborn,[2] it is doubtful that attempts at a redefinition would have been successful, not because lesbianism is truly a sexual category but because the association

377

between lesbianism and unorthodox sex was so firmly imprinted on the popular imagination. Since the sexual revolution permitted widespread experimentation, the notion of lovemaking between two women no longer had the power to horrify a priori. Therefore, it was possible to go beyond the old bugaboos to examine what were the real implications of lesbianism. In addition, the (male-dominated) gay movement challenged the public view of homosexuality, forcing old clichés to be questioned, including those about love between women. By the end of the 1960's, the new wave of feminism provided a body of women who had learned not to fear sex outside of marriage, whose society was reexamining old truths about homosexuality, and who had an interest in the welfare of women and an affinity with them. They were ready to begin to reclaim the image.

The emergence of these New Women was initially startling to lesbians who came out in the 1930's or 1940's or 1950's. They had learned to think of themselves, at least in some corner of their minds, as outlaws. Now they were told by the new wave that they were not outlaws at all. They were pioneers. It was demanded of them that they strip away layers and layers of the indoctrination they had received everywhere—from their parents to their college abnormal psychology courses to the paperback literature that most literate lesbians could not avoid reading. The metamorphosis of the old-style lesbian is vividly illustrated in *The Ladder*, a lesbian magazine which was published from 1956 to 1972.

The Ladder began publication as the journal of the newly established lesbian organization, The Daughters of Bilitis (named after Pierre Louÿs's song cycle, which had been dedicated to females of the future and appeared to be a relatively benign treatment of lesbianism). It was also about this time, after the country had gotten over the shock of World War II and after the death of McCarthyism, that male-dominated homosexual organizations such as The Mattachine Society were established in America. The mid-1950's homophile organizations were born into a climate that was to some extent ready for them. The persecution that McCarthy had fostered exhausted itself—nobody was terribly interested in persecuting anybody for a while. Lay interest in psychology was at a peak, and homosexuality was thought to be a problem in psychology. The new civil rights movement, even though it centered primarily on southern Blacks, suggested that minorities had inalienable rights.

In its inception the intent of *The Ladder* and of the organization it represented was no more revolutionary than to take a modest place in an environment that was not unsympathetic to helping the persecuted and the unfortunate. *The Ladder* was not the first effort of its kind. It had had an American precursor, *Vice Versa,* a primarily one-woman operation which ran for nine issues from 1947 to 1948, and a couple of German precursors, *Die Freundin* and *Frauenliebe* (one a section of and the other a supplement to male homosexual journals), which ended with Hitler's rise to power. None of these were radical by contemporary standards.

In 1956 *The Ladder* could expect no large audience to support it in questioning what was thought to be age-old wisdom about lesbianism; and in an age of the "expert," it had great respect for the titles and institutions that produced such wisdom. It argued with the more outrageous homophobes, such as those who saw homosexuals as a "menace," [3] but its list of goals, published on the inside cover of the magazine (which remained the same for about ten years), indicates to what extent *The Ladder* bowed to the knowledge of the "leading members" of the establishment:

1. Education of the variant, with particular emphasis on the psychological, physiological, and sociological aspects, to enable her to understand herself and make her adjustment to society in all its social, civil and economic implications—this to be accomplished by establishing and maintaining as complete a library as possible of both fiction and non-fiction literature on the sex deviant theme; by sponsoring public discussions on pertinent subjects to be conducted by leading members of the legal, psychiatric, religious, and other professions; by advocating a mode of behavior and dress acceptable to society.

2. Education of the public at large . . . leading to an eventual breakdown of erroneous taboos and prejudices. . . .

3. Participation in research projects by duly authorized and responsible psychologists, sociologists, and other such experts directed towards further knowledge of the homosexual.

4. Investigation of the penal code as it pertains to the homosexual, proposal of changes to provide an equitable handling of cases involving this minority group.

In 1967, supported by the infant feminist movement, *The Ladder* made a few changes which indicated that the organization and the magazine's editors were becoming more aware that lesbians were women rather than members of the third sex to be classed with male homosexuals. The word "Lesbian" was generally substituted for "variant" or "homosexual," and a new goal was added—to provide "the Lesbian a forum for the interchange of ideas within her own group." It was not understood until 1970 that "psychologists, sociologists, and other such experts" could usually be depended upon to offer up the established wisdom of their professions, which in most cases had little to do with the realities of lesbian life. Finally, in place of the old list of purposes, the August/September 1970 issue of *The Ladder* carried a new statement which, although it maintained a firm distinction between lesbians and heterosexual women, had its roots in lesbian-feminist consciousness, whose expression the growing women's movement encouraged:

> Initially *The Ladder*'s goal was limited to achieving the rights accorded to heterosexual women, that is, full second class citizenship. In the 1950's women as a whole were as yet unaware of their oppression. The Lesbian knew. And she wondered silently when her sisters would realize that they too share many of the Lesbian's handicaps, those that pertained to being a woman.
>
> *The Ladder*'s purpose today is to raise all women to full human status, with all of the rights and responsibilities this entails; to include ALL woman, whether Lesbian or heterosexual.

Despite its attempts to change, the magazine had to discontinue publication two years later. It had lost its readership because younger women, who would be most likely to subscribe to such a periodical, associated *The Ladder* with the politics of adjustment. The young had also gone a few steps farther: They questioned the view of lesbians as a group with a particular sexual preference. Women are lesbians when they are women-identified, they asserted. Never having had the slightest erotic exchange with another woman, one might still be a political lesbian. A lesbian is a woman who makes women prime in her life, who gives her energies and her commitment to other women rather than to men. Some even proclaimed, "All women are lesbians," by which they meant that potentially all women have the capacity to love themselves and to love other females, first through their mothers and then through adult relationships.

The Ladder's initial conservatism can be explained by the fact that it attempted to represent the views of middle-class, self-identified lesbians whose reference group in those days was the straight world, to which they had to adjust in order to maintain their middle-class status. But it is significant that frequently faint and not-so-faint traces of feminism appeared in the early articles. For example, despite the fact that the popular image of the lesbian couple was, as the Georgette Heyer and Mary Stewart novels suggest (see page 354), a pair divided into "butch" and "femme," a February 1958 article estimated that such women make up "a small minority of the lesbian culture pattern." The author then stated that generally lesbians felt that both women in a relationship should be independent "rather than to have an arrangement more closely approximating husband and wife, because each party to the Lesbian partnership is by her nature a person desiring independence and fulfillment of her own ambitions." [4] A June 1960 report of a reader's survey which asked "Why Am I a Lesbian?" included responses that could have been written at least ten years later. For example, one respondent declared that lesbianism is a "protest against domination by the male . . . a withdrawal from the heterosexual market place of glamor. . . . Emphasis is placed rather upon the independence of the individual and the development of the full personality." Another respondent stated, "I am a lesbian by choice," because that choice (which she said had little to do with a desire for a particular sexual act) permitted her freedom from socially imposed female roles.[5] Early in 1963, immediately upon the release of Betty Friedan's *The Feminine Mystique, The Ladder* recognized that the book would be of great interest to its readership, especially since it could be inferred from the information provided by Friedan that there are numerous social reasons for women to become lesbians; lesbianism permits them "an escape from being cast into a social stereotype which degrades their individuality and limits their activity to the point where it may begin to make an impact on the world outside the home." [6] As early as 1965 readers were demanding that *The Ladder* turn its interests to feminism, and were recognizing the vital link between feminism and lesbianism. For instance, one letter read "Many women who prefer commitment to a career without the responsibilities of wifehood and motherhood would also like to find the kind of emotional satisfaction that is possible only on a sustained basis between equal partners. In today's world this kind of life is open only to the lesbian." [7]

Such articulation of why many women turned to lesbianism in the first place was outweighed however by articles that demonstrated how much lesbians had internalized and been intimidated by the stereotypes about them. Although *The Ladder* was expressly a lesbian journal, it generally included in each issue one or more articles by experts on homosexuality, which almost invariably meant *male* homosexuality. Pages and pages were devoted to authorities like Albert Ellis who told them that homosexuals were "actually emotionally disturbed individuals who are fetischistically attached to some particular type of sex activity—and who usually . . . become fetischistically attached to this form of behavior because of peculiarities or fixations which arouse during their childhood," [8] or to lesser lights who told them that "homosexuality often leads to more violent crimes including homicide," [9] and that homosexuality was a "primary disorder of the divine plan." [10] Even in a magazine published by lesbians presumably *for* lesbians, the writers were allowed to utter paperback inanities such as "I belong to the twilight world —the world of the 'third sex,' neither normal woman nor normal man—a world unexplored like a little known, far-off planet hanging in the darkness of space," [11] and abundant room was given to writers who had so internalized the view of themselves as "emotionally disturbed individuals" that they prayed that "psychiatry could learn enough about the subject to help [them change]." [12]

The metamorphosis the magazine underwent around the late 1960's is representative of the metamorphosis that occurred in many middle-class lesbians who had come out in earlier decades.[13] While many of them had recognized their choice of a lesbian life to have feminist roots, they seldom articulated it because they believed they were unusual. The books said that most lesbians were born or made in childhood, and the world agreed. With the rise of the second wave of feminism, the perception which they had kept virtually a secret was suddenly expounded everywhere, and new feminists recognized that lesbians had much to teach them. As one *Ladder* writer observed of lesbians who chose their life-style before the feminist movement began:

> With the advent of the Women's Liberation movement . . .
> we suddenly find ourselves in demand. We are wanted to be
> living proof that a woman can be a self-realizing human being.
> We are wanted to explain the intricacies of Lesbianism as a

lifestyle. We are wanted to provide a pattern for relationships in which woman is not exploited or demeaned.[14]

Once the connection between lesbianism and feminism was widely acknowledged,[15] older lesbians, whose feminism had up until now been buried under the rubbish of society's views, were able to re-examine in daylight what it was in the first place that made them decide to commit themselves to making women prime in their lives. Now younger women, who became feminists and then chose to become lesbians because of their feminism, reminded the pre-movement lesbian of what she had experienced internally on one level of consciousness or another.

The women who joined the feminist movement first and then chose to become lesbians were not hampered by the weight of all the old images. Generally they did not have to go through the painful coming-out process which the older generations had experienced: the discovery that a woman placed herself beyond the pale if she did not transfer her love and dependence from the mother to the father to the husband, the frantic effort to find out what the experts and the novelists had to say about such women, the agony endured usually alone. These New Women shared their feminism with each other rather than keeping it a sad secret as the older generation had felt compelled to do. Through feminist consciousness-raising they examined why love and passion had to be transferred in girlhood from the female to the male, and they concluded that there was no reason other than heterosexism, which, in an overpopulated world, had absolutely no justification. Many had never read Freud or his predecessors or disciples because psychiatry, psychology, or psychoanalysis had no relevance for them.

While those who came out in the 1950's found themselves in an era when respect for "experts" was at a height, those who did so in the late 1960's or 1970's lived in a society that had far less respect for authority. As conscious feminists they scoffed at the notion of males telling females what they were all about. While their predecessors' literary images of lesbianism came from cheap paperbacks that promised tales of lurid passions, the women who came out later were less burdened with those absurdities—feminism had provided new journals and then new publishing houses in which a new image of love between women could be created. Finally the New Women did not need to come out in isolation. They often had an actual support group of women who would help them validate their choice, or—if they had no physical support group—lesbian-feminist literature, which by 1970 was being published all over the United States in the form of newspapers, newsletters, magazines, pamphlets, and books, provided the support. The distance between these new publications and *The Ladder* (which made every attempt to express its feminist consciousness with the rising women's movement but could not, even in the late 1960's, escape from its awe of the psychiatric and other professions) is characterized by one *Ladder* reader who in January 1968 called the publication an "old conservative rag." [16] In addition to creating new literary images, lesbian-feminists also established by the early 1970's archives of historical documents of love between women, lesbian-feminist record companies, rap groups, therapy, self-help, and community-help clinics—in fact, a whole culture in which women might take care of themselves and each other.

From their very inception the journals of this period presented a great contrast in goals to the original goals of *The Ladder*. *The Lesbian Tide*, for example, an organ of the Los Angeles Daughters of Bilitis, declared in 1971 issues that it was "written by and for" lesbians, and that it would "speak of their numbers, their lives, their ideas, and their pride." *The Furies: Lesbian-Feminist Monthly*, which began in 1972, stated in its first issue: "We call our paper The Furies because we are . . . angry. We are angry because we are oppressed by male supremacy. We have been fucked over all our lives by a system which is based on the domination of men over women, which defines male as good and female as only as good as the man you are with. It is a system in which heterosexuality is rigidly enforced and Lesbianism is rigidly suppressed." [17] *Proud Woman*, which had been a feminist newspaper, asserted in its March/April 1972 issue that it was changing its scope and becoming a lesbian-feminist journal in recognition that the primary feminist goal, "that women should enjoy complete control over their bodies and lives," is also the primary lesbian goal.[18] By the second half of the decade many even more radical journals were established, like the lesbian-separatist *Dyke* and *Tribad*, both of which announced on their front covers that their magazines were to be sold to and shared by lesbians only. A number of specialized lesbian-feminist ¡ournals also began publishing: *Pearl Diver*, a journal concerned with lesbian-feminist music; *Azalea: A Magazine by Third*

World Lesbians; Albatross, a lesbian-feminist satire magazine; and *Focus,* a literary journal.

Out of this culture a lesbian chauvinism developed which replaced the guilt and fear that had been inculcated in lesbians throughout the century. Even older women, who had come out long before the new feminist movement, could now see "Lesbianism as a Liberating Force," as Elsa Gidlow, a poet in her eighties, declared in 1977. While Gidlow may have had such a chauvinistic awareness earlier, it would have been sheer insanity to utter it. In the 1970's a large audience had been created which would agree with her observations that:

> The lesbian personality manifests itself in independence of spirit, in willingness to take responsibility for oneself, to think for oneself, not to take "authorities" and their dictum on trust. It usually includes erotic attraction to women, although we know there have been many women of lesbian personality who never had sexual relations with one another. Even where an erotic relationship exists the sensually sexual may be far from predominant. What is strongly a part of the lesbian personality is loyalty to and love of other women. . . . Every lesbian personality I have knowledge of is in some way creative. To my mind this is because she is freed or has freed herself from the external and internal dominance of the male and so ignored or rejected (usually male prescribed) social assumptions that the constellation of domestic functions are peculiarly hers. The important point is that the lesbian has sought wholeness within herself, not requiring, in the old romantic sense, to be "completed" by an opposite.[19]

And while in other eras women who loved women would often blanch at the word "lesbian," the new chauvinism now permitted women to declare, as a writer did in a 1973 issue of *Sisters,* the journal of the San Francisco Daughters of Bilitis: "Lesbian is a strong, proud word. As women-loving-women, proud of who and what we are, we must think of ourselves in strong, proud terms—as Lesbians —with a capital 'L' " and to say of the word "dyke," "Take the word for your own—instead of cringing when you hear it, make the negative, positive."[20]

Lesbianism had been considered a feminist choice even by some experts before the feminist movement began, but those who took that position were largely ignored. Alfred Adler, for example, who was Freud's contemporary, believed that lesbianism has nothing to do with the traumas that Freud described, and that it is not primarily a sexual phenomenon. Instead, he stated, lesbianism is for some women a means of protest over being accorded an inferior position in society. It is not envy of men's penises that cause women to be lesbians but envy of men's power, advantages, and freedom.[21] Since this view did not fire the popular imagination of his day as did the more dramatic (and male-oriented) penis-envy theory, it was neglected. But women who had lived the experience understood it by themselves, although most did not dare write it, probably believing it would fall on deaf ears. Simone de Beauvoir, however, did write about it as early as 1949. Beauvoir observed that often women choose to become lesbians when they are absorbed in ambitious projects of their own, or when they simply want liberty and decline to abdicate in favor of another human being as the heterosexual relationship generally demands of females. If some women who have made such a choice present themselves as masculine, it is because they have repudiated any appearance of complicity with passive femininity: Their "masculinity" is protection against any potential attempts to transform them into fleshly prey. Beauvoir further points out that most little girls feel outraged at their lack of privilege, at the limitations imposed on them by their sex. The real question is not why some females refuse to accept those limitations (i.e., become lesbians), but rather why most do accept them and become wives. Women conform through docility and timidity, Beauvoir believes, but when their ego sense is too strong or their ambitions too absorbing or the compensations offered by society for being the second sex too inadequate, they refuse to conform and they choose lesbianism.[22]

In earlier eras, when lesbians accepted other people's definitions of them, they often felt compelled to agree that they were men trapped in women's bodies or that they had had traumatic childhood experiences or that they were "truly twisted." When they did not agree they kept silent. With the rise of feminism, when lesbians in large numbers finally defined themselves, their definitions were more like those of Adler and Beauvoir than of the other theorists, as were their explanations of lesbian genesis. Jill Johnston (*Lesbian Nation*), for example, explains of her own choice that she was raised by her mother and grandmother, and the woman-centered life of her childhood gave her an "uninhibited chauvinism" about her identity as a female; she had no "super-ego daddy" in her. As an adult, she found that heterosexuality meant that she would have to sacrifice her female chauvinism to male chauvinism. Lesbianism, on the other hand, meant that she could continue to see femaleness (and herself) as prime, and not be forced to view as secondary what she had always happily viewed as primary.[23] Del Martin (*Lesbian/ Woman*) remembers that when playing "house" in childhood, she chose to be the husband rather than the wife not because she wanted to be a man sexually but because maleness meant being "free to do what one chooses" and femaleness meant having limitations. She knew this both from childhood observations and from concrete minor personal experiences such as being turned down in her request for a local paper route while boys her age were accepted.[24] If she was traumatized, it was not by feeling a genital inferiority but rather by social injustice.

Lesbians now see their lesbianism as a choice they make because they want to be free from prescribed roles, free to realize themselves. Typically, one interviewee in Donna Tanner's sociological study, *The Lesbian Couple*, observes, "I love this relationship for the fact that I don't have to deal in the terms of the culture with what I'm expected to be. A woman who is working who has a husband or children has to keep in mind, whatever she does professionally, and whatever she does socially, that she has to be somebody's wife. This 'wifeness' is prescribed by the culture and the law. I am free from that."[25] The women of Barbara Ponse's sociological study, *Identities in the Lesbian World*, typically remark, "I always had a choice about being a lesbian. It didn't happen to me. . . . I've had relationships with men and think the negativity of those relationships for me was not because I didn't enjoy sex with men but because I didn't like the other expectations that went along with it, the kind of role playing that happens in relationships with men. The kind of thing where his work should come before mine. . . . I wasn't prepared to accept that."[26] While the public in general may continue to hold views of lesbians based on medical or fictional opinions, lesbians no longer internalize those views, since feminism has crystallized for them the meaning of their choice. The reasons for the choice were probably always the same—at the height of Krafft-Ebing's influence, at the height of Baudelaire's influence, at the height of Freud's influence; but because women listened to those who had observed externally and superficially and with male bias, and because they seldom talked to large numbers of other women, they often forgot their original reasons and accepted those of the experts. It was only when they began talking together in large groups, often in feminist consciousness-raising sessions, that they saw that others had made the same choice through the same reasons.

Although the United States has been in the forefront of lesbian-feminism, the movement is almost as strong in many parts of Western Europe. As in the United States, lesbians before the second-wave feminist movement either internalized the stereotype or, for the most part, kept silent. Monique Wittig observes that in France, as in the United States, without feminism, lesbianism as a political phenomenon would not have existed. French lesbian culture and lesbian society, Wittig states, "would still be as secret as they have always been." [27] Many French feminists became lesbians, and many who started as lesbians (whose feminism had been unexamined) became feminists through the new women's movement.[28]

The French *Mouvement des Femmes* grew out of the "1968 French Revolution," which gave birth in France to a number of sociopolitical movements. In general, French feminism has followed the American pattern, including divisions into middle-class-identified feminists who were concerned with issues such as professional equality (for example, despite the fact that France had the second highest number of professional women in Europe after Russia, French women earned about two-thirds the male salaries), and more radical groups. Lesbianism became an issue among French feminists not long after it did in the United States. Beginning in the early 1970's, French lesbian-feminists took on a philosophy and attitudes toward men, toward other women, and toward themselves that were virtually identical to those of their American counterparts.[29]

At the beginning of the twentieth century, lesbians in Germany were more articulate and organized than anywhere else in the world. But while they had made some connection between lesbianism and feminism, many identified primarily with male homosexuals and saw themselves as a third sex. Large numbers of German lesbians belonged to Magnus Hirschfeld's *Wissenschaftlich-humanitäres Kommittee* (Scientific Humanitarian Committee), and argued that they were born different. In the 1920's they joined homosexual men in the *Bund für Menschenrecht* (Society for Human Rights).[30] All such efforts came to an end in the late 1920's and early 1930's with the growth of fascism. The next attempt to revive a German lesbian movement began somewhat weakly in the mid-1950's with the lesbian magazine *Aphrodite*. In 1971, when male homosexuals began organizing at the Berlin preview of Praunheim's film, *Nicht der Homosexuelle ist Pervers, Sondern die Gesellschaft*, lesbians joined them and became the Women's Group of *Homosexuelle Aktion Westberlin*. With the rise of feminism these women too developed a new consciousness. They broke away from the men in 1974 and established the radical *Lesbisches Aktionzentrum*, and a more conservative group of older, middle-class identified women formed the *Gruppe L74*. Each group founded its own lesbian-feminist paper the following year, *Lesbenpresse* and *Unsere Kleine Zeitung*. By 1975 lesbian-feminist groups existed in nineteen German cities.[31] Two years later the May 1977 issue of *Lesbenpresse* listed lesbian-feminist organizations in more than forty German cities.

The influence of American lesbian-feminist theory is apparent in contemporary German feminist fiction. For example, Verena Stefan's *Häutungen* (*Shedding*) [32] might easily have been written by an American woman or—if the explicit feminism and sexual description were removed—by an early nineteenth-century romantic friend in Germany, America, England, or France. The narrator goes through numerous untenable experiences with men, and then finds herself open to women through the feminist movement. The erotic aspect of her impulse is far less sexual than sensual. She rejects the emphasis on genital sex on which men insist. With women it is possible to caress without a goal, she feels, and copulation is not suited to women's more diffuse sexuality. But of greater significance is her political interest in women. She is involved with the feminist group Bread ♀ Roses, and learns to question her previously unquestioned assumption that her place was with a man. It becomes increasingly difficult to reconcile that view with her attachment to the women she works with in the movement. When the narrator's last boyfriend tells her, "I really prefer being together with women," she responds, "Yeah, me too . . . I know what you mean." She can no longer tolerate the unequal demands of a heterosexual relationship. In contrast to loving men, with another woman she discovers that "you have finally met up with that which you have always been giving to men, for the first time it is not only you who is paying attention, offering support and compassion, you are, instead, also the recipient." Despite the twentieth-century context of Stefan's work, loving women means to her primarily what it meant to "normal" women a century or two earlier (and what it means to most self-identified lesbians today): an emotional and sensual attachment to a kindred spirit, with the potential of getting back as much as is given.

England's pre-World War I feminist movement far surpassed that of the United States in drama. Between 1905 and 1914 thousands of suffragists were battered, imprisoned, force-fed when they went on a hunger strike. At least one historian has suggested that the movement was strongly lesbian (see page 337). But English feminism slept a long sleep after the suffrage movement, and organized lesbianism was virtually nonexistent. In the early 1960's the London-based lesbian organizations Minorities Research Group and Kenric were founded. They had goals similar in their conservative nature to the early Daughters of Bilitis. By 1970 many local lesbian organizations sprang up all over England, and lesbianism received media attention such as would have been inconceivable a decade earlier.[33]

Women at that time also joined men in the Campaign for Homosexual Equality, but once the second wave of English feminism was firmly established, many lesbians left the homosexual movement and became involved in organized feminism. In the winter of 1968–1969 equal-pay campaigns were staged in London, and not long after, small women's groups began meeting all over England. The same dynamic that was observed in the United States and elsewhere —lesbians becoming feminists and vice versa—also took place in England. Like N.O.W. in the United States, the English Women's Movement at a national conference adopted a resolution to support lesbianism and to fight the oppression of lesbians. There is the same consensus regarding the meaning of lesbianism among English lesbians. In the introduction to their 1977 book, *We're Here: Conversations with Lesbian Women*, the British editors, Angela Stewart-Park and Jules Cassidy, observe, "We don't see lesbianism as a purely personal issue. It's a political issue for us and for all women. We've made a choice. We've chosen to relate to women sexually and emotionally. We've chosen not to relate to men in these ways. We feel that the choice has made us strong." They connect their ability to make that choice comfortably with their understanding of and association with feminism.[34]

The women they interview speak almost invariably of resenting female dependence and suppression, and of becoming lesbians as a result of their resentment. Consistently they see their lesbianism as a strength in their lives. As one interviewee observed:

If you grow up wanting to be whole as a woman in this society,

then you have to be a feminist. . . . And once you're a feminist it's almost impossible to have any kind of whole relationship with a man because there's all kinds of roles that you're
taught, and even if he's really cool, you know, other people lay
trips on you and it's all so ingrained. That's the only way I can
see myself going really, from a strong person, to a feminist to a
lesbian. It's just a very logical progression.[35]

Certainly there are feminists who have chosen not to make that
"logical progression" in their lives, who prefer either to remain
without close ties to another person or persons, or to attempt to
work out an egalitarian relationship with a man. But there are
probably few feminists who have examined the meaning of lesbianism separated from panic about abnormality and arcane sex practices
who would not agree that there is compelling logic in the progression the Englishwoman described above. And although it might not
be their path for one reason or another, they are able to validate that
choice made by other women.

CHAPTER 2

Writing Lesbian

Before the rise of the lesbian-feminist movement, lesbian writers of popular literature generally depicted one of two types in their works: the lesbian as sickie (for which Clare of *Regiment of Women* was a prototype) and the lesbian as martyr (for which Stephen of *The Well of Loneliness* was a prototype). It is not surprising that those authors who internalized society's views of them (for example, Ann Aldrich and Paula Christian) should write of the lesbian as sickie. Nor should it be surprising that those writers who felt society's homophobia should have latched on to Radclyffe Hall's trick of presenting the lesbian as a poor suffering creature (for example, Gale Wilhelm, especially *We, Too, Are Drifting*, and Ann Bannon). Authors who were more concerned with reflecting diversity and individual truths about lesbian lives felt compelled to veil their subject matter in one way or another. They might, for example, be inexplicit enough about their lesbian subject matter so that it could be argued, before a judge and jury if need be, that the novel was only alluding to a common friendship between females (as in Helen Hull's novels, *Quest*, 1922, and *Labyrinth*, 1923); they might hide their lesbian subject matter by whimsical devices such as Virginia Woolf uses in *Orlando* (1928); or they might hide it by perfunctorily changing the gender of their characters or by encoding their subject matter, as do Amy Lowell and Gertrude Stein.

In 1918 Amy Lowell wrote to D. H. Lawrence, who had been having difficulty finding a publisher for his novels since *The Rainbow* had been suppressed as "obscene" three years earlier:

I know there is no use in counselling you to make any conces-
sions to public opinions in your books and, although I regret
sincerely that you cut yourself off from being published by an
outspokenness which the English public does not understand,
I regret it not in itself . . . but simply because it keeps the
world from knowing what a great novelist you are. I think that
you could top them all if you would be a little more reticent
on this one subject.[1] You need not change your attitude a par-
ticle, you can simply use an India rubber in certain places, and
then you can come into your own as it ought to be . . . When
one is surrounded by prejudice and blindness, it seems to me
that the only thing to do is to get over in spite of it and not
constantly run foul of these same prejudices which, after all,
hurts oneself and the spreading of one's work, and does not do
a thing to right the prejudice.[2]

Lowell actively fought against literary censorship—she demanded
that *Sons and Lovers* and Compton Mackenzie's *Sylvia Scarlett* be
available for circulation in the Boston Atheneum, she supported
Theodore Dreiser's fight against suppression of *The Genius*, and she
argued that "no country can hope to develop itself, unless its authors
are permitted to educate it." [3] But in her own work she took care not
to "run foul" of the public's prejudices. A good many of the poems
in *Sword Blades and Poppy Seed* (1914), *Pictures of the Floating
World* (1919), and two posthumously published volumes, *What's
O'Clock* (1925) and *Ballads for Sale* (1927), concern her lesbian involvement with Ada Russell,[4] with whom she lived for the last
eleven years of her life.[5] Lowell herself did not use the India rubber
which she suggested that D. H. Lawrence employ. But she disguised
her subject matter by omitting gender references and by perfunctorily using a masculine reference even when it might be guessed
from the rest of the piece that the character is a woman.

Amy Lowell first met Ada Russell in 1909 when the actress was
traveling on a New England tour of *Dawn of a Tomorrow*. The two
met again in March 1912, when Russell returned to play in a Boston
theater. They spent part of the summer of 1912 together, and for
the next two years the poet tried to convince the actress to live with
her. This courtship is reflected in approximately twenty poems of
Sword Blades and Poppy Seed. Ada finally yielded to Amy's pursuit
in the spring of 1914. She quit the stage and joined the poet permanently in her Brookline mansion, Sevenels, ostensibly as her

paid companion, but in fact as her mate. The two lived together until Amy's death in 1925.

The usual critical observation that Lowell was overweight and un-married, and that her work is a "knell of personal frustration . . . an effort to hide the bare walls of the empty chambers of her heart . . . ," [6] the exposure of the emotions of "a girlish, pathetic, and lonely woman, underneath [whose] . . . bumptious manner lies disappointment," [7] is not borne out by the body of Lowell's poetry. Starting with her second volume, when her relationship with Ada began, the preponderance of her poems suggests a life and a relationship that were just the opposite of these speculations and that must have been willfully ignored by those who wished to see her through clichés. In "Thorn Piece," Lowell talks about the world being dark and glazed, but another woman gives to her "fire,/And love to comfort, and speech to bind,/And the common things of morning and evening,/And the light of your lantern." In "Christmas Eve" she tells the other woman, "You have lifted my eyes, and made me whole,/And given me purpose, and held me faced/Toward the horizon you once had placed/As my aim's grand measure." "A Dec-ade," the poem that celebrates the first ten years of their acquaint-ance, concludes "I am completely nourished." These poems reflect lesbian life in a way that it could not be depicted in the post-World War I years unless the subject matter were somehow disguised.

It is necessary when studying Lowell's poetry to distinguish be-tween persona poems and personal poems. Several volumes—*Men, Women and Ghosts* (1916), *Can Grande's Castle* (1918), *Legends* (1921), and the posthumously published *East Wind* (1926)—contain virtually no personal poems, and there are many individual persona poems in her other volumes. When a first-person speaker is pre-sented, he or she is characterized so that it is clearly not the poet speaking to us. These compositions may be compared with Brown-ing's "dramatis personae" and Pound's *personae*. In "Appuldur-combe Park" the speaker is an eighteenth-century married woman; in "Sancta Maria, Succure Miseris" it is a poor young orphan boy; in "After Hearing a Waltz by Bartók" it is a madman who kills his sup-posed rival. Much of the misassessment of Lowell's life as reflected in her poetry may be due to a failure to distinguish between per-sona and poet. One critic sees as a confession of her sexual frustration the opening lines of "Appuldurcombe Park": "I am a woman, sick for passion." [8] Another asserts that her "discomfort with herself as a woman" is proven by a poem in which Lowell "pictures herself as the Dean of Rochester." [9] Such works, of course, do not "picture" the poet at all. They picture a characterized persona in a dramatic situation. On the other hand, many of Lowell's poems, particularly her shorter lyrics, contain neither characterized persona nor extended dramatic action. These poems are generally personal, and often reveal the writer's life, although she makes a vague concession to censorship by slight attempts at disguise. The section "Two Speak Together" from *Pictures of the Floating World*, a series of forty-three poems, can be taken as one example. The speaker makes no personal-gender references at all throughout these poems except for the description of one incident in which the word "Sir" is used in relation to the speaker. In the context of the poems which surround that particular lyric, "Sir" can be seen only as a purposely misleading reference.

The autobiographical nature of these poems is evident from the details of Lowell's life and from an admission she made to John Livingston Lowes. Lowes, who had several times been a guest at Sevenels, discerned when he read one of the love poems of "Two Speak Together," "Madonna of the Evening Flowers," that the beloved was Ada Russell. He wrote to Amy on February 9, 1918, praising the poem and its depiction of Ada. Amy responded on February 13, "I am very glad indeed that you liked the 'Madonna of the Evening Flowers.' How could so exact a portrait remain unrecognized?" [10] The images that Lowell uses to describe the beloved in other poems are often almost identical to those in this poem, which suggests that it is the same woman who appears throughout these personal love poems.

In addition to the letter to Lowes, recurrent autobiographical references in "Two Speak Together" support the theory that these are personal poems. In "After a Storm," for example, the speaker refers to her dogs (Amy owned eight English sheepdogs) leaping about the beloved in the garden. In "November" she describes her home, Sevenels, appearing just as it does in pictures, with pine trees and lilacs in the garden, vine leaves against the wall, her cat (which she kept during the war) and herself sitting alone under a lamp, trying to write. In "Penumbra" she confirms that the site of their life together is Sevenels, "the old house which has known me since the beginning."

Despite the title of the series, "Two Speak Together," the beloved only "speaks" by being, by "communing with" the lover. Hers is not the voice in any of the poems. The only speaker is the lover, who is apparently the poet. But while the poet and the speaker appear to be one, in "Preparation," the single poem in which gender is specifically stated, the speaker, purchasing smoke-colored spectacles in preparation for meeting the too-dazzling beloved, is called "Sir" by a shopman. There are perhaps other misleading hints throughout the poems which may confuse the reader as to the gender of the speaker—although gender is never again specified. In "Venus Transiens" for example, the beloved is compared to Botticelli's Venus, and by implication the speaker is compared to the masculine Botticelli: ". . . were the painted rosebuds/He tossed his lady,/Of better worth/Than the words I blow about you/To cover your too great loveliness . . . ?" In "Wheat-in-the-Ear" and "The Weather-Cock Points South," the speaker is the sexual aggressor and the beloved plays a passive role. In "Bullion," "A Shower," and "The Charm," the speaker either is or would like to be protector and giver. Whenever traditionally masculine pursuits are mentioned (for example, driving in "Nerves"), it is the speaker and not the beloved who engages in them.

Despite this masculine characterization, it may be seen that the speaker is in fact a woman. In "The Garden by Moonlight," the speaker suggests her gender by lamenting her childless state and thinking back through the female line of her family:

> *Ah, Beloved, do you see those orange lillies?*
> *They knew my mother,*
> *But who belonging to me will they know*
> *When I am gone.*

In "Autumn," too, she calls herself "[I] who am barren." However, in "April" she employs the language of childbirth to describe creating a poem out of the happiness of her union with her beloved:

> *I will lie among the little squills*
> *And be delivered of this overcharge of beauty,*
> *And that which is born shall be a joy to you*
> *Who love me.*

There are other hints as well that the speaker is really female. For example, "Strain" refers to long fingers being passed "through my drifting hair" at a time when men wore their hair short. In "Interlude" the speaker describes herself figuratively as being engaged in traditionally female tasks such as baking cakes and "smoothing the seam of the linen I have been working" (these are apparently metaphors for writing decorative poetry). It is important to note that the beloved in this poem is compared to the moon, which is always feminine and a frequent metaphor for Ada in Lowell's poetry. "Interlude" is thus the only poem of "Two Speak Together" in which the lover and the beloved are correctly genderized together.

There is no question as to the gender of the beloved. She is almost always depicted in traditionally feminine guise and behavior whenever gender is suggested. In "Mise en Scène" and "Madonna of the Evening Flowers," she is compared to a Madonna. In "Venus Transiens" she is compared to the Goddess of Love. Her garments are always feminine. In "Bright Sunlight" there is a reference to her shawl; in "The Artist" and "The Wheel of the Sun," she wears feminine silks. In "Grotesque" the speaker weaves a garland for her hair. Her occupations are similarly traditionally feminine: In both "Madonna of the Evening Flowers" and "A Sprig of Rosemary," for example, she sews.

We know that "Madonna of the Evening Flowers" is about Ada because of Lowell's 1918 letter to Lowes. A comparison of the images which describe her in this poem with those of the loved woman in other poems will show that Ada is consistently the beloved of "Two Speak Together." In "Madonna of the Evening Flowers," Ada is pictured in the garden at evening. She is directly associated with the colors silver, pale blue, and white—and like the colors which surround her she is described as being cool and pale; but she is also bright, a "white heart-flame of polished silver":

All day long I have been working,
Now I am tired.
I call: "Where are you?"
But there is only the oak-tree rustling in the wind.
The house is very quiet, the sun shines in on your books,
On your scissors and thimble just put down,
But you are not there. Suddenly I am lonely:
Where are you?
I go about searching.
Then I see you,
Standing under a spire of pale blue larkspur,
With a basket of roses on your arm.

You are cool, like silver,
And you smile.
I think the Canterbury bells are playing a little tune.

You tell me that the peonies need spraying,
That the columbines have overrun all bounds,
That the pyrus japonica should be cut back and rounded.
You tell me these things.
But I look at you, heart of silver,
White heart-flame of polished silver,
Burning beneath the blue steeples of the larkspur,
And I long to kneel instantly at your feet,
While all about us peal the loud, sweet Te Deums of the
   Canterbury bells.

Similar imagistic associations with the beloved are contained in almost all the poems of "Two Speak Together" and in numerous other love poems by Lowell.[11] The garden association is perhaps the most prevalent. "Mise en Scène" begins "When I think of you, Beloved,/I see a smooth and stately garden." In "The Weather-Cock Points South," the beloved woman is imagined as an incomparable white flower: "Where in all the garden is there such a flower?" the speaker asks. In "The Garden by Moonlight" the speaker tells the beloved, "You are quiet like the garden,/And white like the alyssum flowers." In "Left Behind" she laments, "Without you, there is no garden."

The paradoxical image in "Madonna of the Evening Flowers" of the beloved as both bright flame and as cool and pale is also explored in a number of other poems in "Two Speak Together." In "July Midnight" Ada is "moon-white," but she is surrounded by "sparkles of lemon-green flame." In "Wheat-in-the-Ear" she ignites the speaker. In "After a Storm" the beloved is seen walking in the garden "under the ice trees/But you are more dazzling than the ice flowers,/And the dogs' barking is not so loud to me as your quietness." "Opal" begins "You are ice and fire,/The touch of you burns my hands like snow./You are cold and flame."

The speaker's worship of the beloved, which is suggested in the central religious image of "Madonna of the Evening Flowers," also appears in many other Lowell love poems, both outside *Pictures of the Floating World*[12] and in this volume. "Mise en Scène," for example, concludes with an image of the beloved's shawl which "Flares out behind you in great curves/Like the swirling draperies of a painted Madonna."

D. H. Lawrence's major complaint about Lowell's poems has since been echoed by almost every Lowell critic. "Why don't you always be yourself?" he asked with regard to her writing. "Why do you take a pose?" [13] and "Do write from your *real* self, Amy, don't make up things from the outside, it is so saddening." [14] Lawrence's criticism was directed primarily at Lowell's long persona poems, which comprised the bulk of her work. She may have written so much persona poetry because she felt it constituted her best work, since she accepted T. S. Eliot's aesthetic that poetry was not an expression of personality, but an escape from personality. Perhaps she really believed her own pronouncement on Edna St. Vincent Millay, who, she said, "attempted nothing beyond the personal, which is the hallmark of minor poetry." [15] But it is at least as likely that Lowell avoided the personal because of the taboos of her day which surrounded the subject matter that was most personal to her: lesbian love, and which forced her to disguise her theme—even though it was awkward and absurd, like the "Sir" of "Preparation." She was not alone among lesbian writers who made perfunctory disguises which weakened their work (compare Willa Cather, page 201), and who often directed themselves away from the subject they knew best because they could not be entirely honest.

Like Amy Lowell, Gertrude Stein was happy to offer her writer friends advice on how to avoid censorship. When young Ernest Hemingway showed her his story, "Up in Michigan," Stein warned him that although the story was good, it contained too much graphic sexual detail, which made it impractical: it was *inaccrochable*, Stein said, like a painting with salacious subject matter, which one could never exhibit. "There is no point" in such a work, she insisted, because nothing could be done with it.[16] But Stein's favorite subject was much more *inaccrochable* in the post-World War I years than Hemingway's reference to the size of his hero's penis.

Stein's awareness of the threat of censorship probably accounts for her adoption of an unconventional style. Edmund Wilson suggested in 1951 that the vagueness and the unexplained metaphors which began to blur Stein's writing from 1910 were only partly the result of an effort to emulate modern painting; they were just as much due to "a need imposed by the problem of writing about relationships between women of a kind that the standards of the era would not have allowed her to describe more explicitly." [17] Wilson retracted this assessment later after reading a posthumously published volume written between 1908 and 1912, *Two: Gertrude Stein and Her Brother*, which has nothing to do with lesbianism.[18] More recently, however, James R. Mellow has pointed out in *Charmed Circle: Gertrude Stein and Company* (1974) that while *Two* has no lesbian references, it does contain a portrait of male homosexuals called "Men":

> Sometimes men are kissing. Men are sometimes kissing and sometimes drinking. Men are sometimes kissing one another and sometimes there are three of them and one of them is talking and two of them are kissing and both of them, both of the two of them who are kissing, are having their eyes large then with there being tears in them.

Mellow thus revives Wilson's theory that it was Gertrude Stein's predominant subject matter, homosexuality, which largely determined her style.[19] If she is difficult and often impossible to read, it is because she felt that one could not write clearly about homosexuality and expect to be published.

The subject matter of many of Stein's works is her love affair and daily life with Alice B. Toklas, who was her mate for thirty-eight years. The two women met in Paris in 1907 through Sarah Stein, who was Gertrude's sister-in-law and an acquaintance of Alice's traveling companion, Harriet Levy. Alice became a part of the Gertrude and Leo Stein household in 1909. In 1914 Leo moved out, and the women's lives together, through which they created Gertrude Stein as a force in letters and art, began in earnest. The minutest and most personal details of their shared existence are described in Stein's hermetic poetry.

Stein's interest in lesbian subject matter antedates her meeting with Alice B. Toklas. Her first novel, *Q.E.D.*, which remained unpublished for years after her death, was written in 1903 and concerned a triangular relationship in which she became involved during her student days. Early subsequent works such as *Fernhurst* (1904) and portions of "Melanctha" (1910), and later works such as "Miss Furr and Miss Skeene" (1922), also concern lesbians, although the subject matter is not autobiographical.

But in much of the work she produced after she met Alice ("Ada," "Bonne Année," "Sacred Emily," "I Love my Love with a V," "A Third," "Didn't Nelly and Lilly Love You," "In this Way, Kissing," "The Present," "Lifting Belly," "A Sonatina Followed by Another,"

"Here: Actualities," "Pay Me," "Water Pipe"), all or part of the subject matter deals with her "marriage" to Alice. Often it appears to be written with Alice as the sole audience. Until abundant biographical information about them became available in recent years, Alice was the only one who might be expected to understand many of Gertrude's inside jokes. Her focus is frequently on the humdrum aspects of their daily life together, incidents that had significance only for them, and, very often, their sex life. In "All Sunday," for example, Gertrude asks Alice, "What are you doing my precious?" and her friend replies, "Taking grease off my face my love." Intimate details such as their secret, teasing pet names for each other are revealed. In "Lifting Belly," for instance, Alice is "pussy," Gertrude is "Mount Fatty." Their sexual relationship is explicitly described (Alice is often seen as "wife," but there is no attempt to hide her identity). In "A Third," for example, orgasms are a major focus:

Climax no climax is necessary
And so near soon.
What and what wives.
Please and pleases.
Extra for them.
Now they have mountains.
She came easy. . . .
It is a very great pleasure altogether.
Softly in a hotel, softly and in a hotel softly in a hotel
  softly in a hotel.
Next.
Softly in a hotel softly.
When she is through there is nothing more to do when she is
  through everything is done.

"In this Way, Kissing" is also explicit about their sexual behavior:

> *Next to me in me sweetly sweetly*
> *Sweetly Sweetly sweetly sweetly.*
> *In me baby baby baby.*
> *Smiling for me tenderly tenderly.*
> *Tenderly sweetly baby baby*
> *Tenderly tenderly tenderly tenderly.*

"Lifting Belly" devotes most of its sixty pages to sexual exchanges between the two, employing a secret language to describe the most intimate details (for example, the word "cow" means orgasm here as well as in "A Sonatina Followed by Another" and "As a Wife Has a Cow: A Love Story").

Stein presents herself in many of her autobiographical works as a sensual, humorous lesbian lover who relishes lesbian life and lesbian sex. She could write as positively and explicitly as she did because she disguised her subject matter. Like many other lesbian writers, she often changed the gender of her characters. Not infrequently she refers to the Alice figure as her wife and she gives herself masculine pronouns. But she also uses other devices: She invents a secret sexual language which can be decoded only through familiarity with the body of her work; she includes incidents from her daily life with Alice which, on the surface, are irrelevant to the focus of the work; and she uses repetition and frequent deletion of crucial subject or verb, which serve to obfuscate the subject matter. The reader needs considerable biographical information in order to decipher the meaning of most of these works. Gertrude may have assumed that many contemporary readers, who had little access to such information, would believe that her writing was about heterosexuals.

Like Lowell, however, she is often perfunctory in her attempt to disguise gender. In "Didn't Nelly and Lilly Love You" (1922), the story of her "marriage" proposal to Alice, Part One, begins, "He prepared in that way./What did he say." But despite the masculine gender which is attributed to the proposer, "he" asks the woman as an entrée into "his" proposal, "Didn't Nelly and Lilly love you?" Gertrude is "he" and Alice is "she." The respective genders are used consistently throughout the poem, but it is never explained why "he" feels encouraged in his proposal because "she" has had two previous women lovers. The poem is, in fact, strictly autobiographical and is representative of Gertrude's explicit treatment of lesbian subject matter disguised by stylistic devices.

The title refers to the fact that through a mutual friend, Annette Rosenshine, whom Gertrude had attempted to psychoanalyze before Alice came to Europe, Gertrude learned that Alice had had close attachments to Eleanor Joseph (Nelly) and Lily Anna Hanson (Lilly). Knowing that Alice had experienced love between women before, Gertrude was confident that whether or not Alice accepted her proposal, she would not be shocked by it. In Gertrude's description of her proposal in this work, she has the two women wander over the hills of Fiesole, where they had gone with Harriet Levy and Leo, while Gertrude gathers the courage to ask the crucial question about Nelly and Lily:

We were on a hill and he was very still, he
settled to come and tell whether, would he could he
did he or should he, and would he, she wound around
the town. She wound around the town and he was nervous.

Typically Stein does not relate the incidents of the day in chronological order. Details of the proposal are brought in intermittently, often through stream of consciousness and flashback. For example, she depicts their 1922 relationship at one point: "My darling wife may all that's good in life be yours . . ." and later goes back to her 1907 proposal: "Can you be fairly necessary to me. Didn't Nelly and Lilly love you." Gertrude shows herself in retrospect, feeling silly about the manner in which she proposed, and thinking now that she would have deserved to be turned down by Alice: "And was I ever ridiculous. I am afraid I could merit chastity." She depicts what appears to be their private wedding ceremony: "Now say to me. I have always had a great many responsibilities. Now say to me I am prepared to be prepared." She dramatizes her concern about the extent of Alice's sexual involvement with "Nelly" and "Lilly":

Have you been at all interfered with.
Have you been at all interfered with. The meaning
of this is have you been at all interfered with.

Another theme of "Didn't Nelly and Lilly Love You," related to that of the proposal, is the establishment of "positions" in the marriage of Gertrude and Alice. The use of the terms "he" to represent Gertrude and "bride" to represent Alice was not only an attempt to deceive the censors. It also suggests that the union was patterned after a heterosexual model. Gertrude must have outlined their roles very carefully if her text gives us an accurate picture:

May I say, I passionately may say, can you obey.
Remember the position. Remember the attention that
you pay to what I say.

Later she suggests an appropriate role for a wife (with some humor, one hopes):

A wife hangs on her husband that is what Shakespeare
says a loving wife hangs on her husband that is what she does.

The episodic account of their lives prior to the Italian vacation begins with information about their childhood. Gertrude "was born in Allegheny in the state of Pennsylvania the seventh child of a father and mother" and lived when she was young in California and Europe. Alice, who was born in California, "went north to Seattle" at about the same time that Gertrude "went back to the petted section of France Austria and arithmetic." Stein reiterates that although they both lived in California, "We never met. No, we never have met." When they finally do meet alone in Paris, without Gertrude's relatives and Harriet Levy who were present at the first meeting, the event begins with some awkwardness because Gertrude is peremptory and impatient:

> She came late I state that she came late and I said
> what was it that I said I said I am not accustomed to
> wait.

As the union progressed, Stein implies, her brother Leo's position in the rue de Fleurus household changed from a central one to one that was clearly peripheral. Gertrude became aware that she no longer needed Leo, or anyone other than Alice. The two women, having taken over the apartment and the Saturday evening salons, then plan the permanence of their *ménage à deux*:

> We find that there was really no need of men and women.
> Sisters. What are sisters, and sisters and brothers. What are
> sisters and brothers . . . And I said I wish to stay and she said
> I stay and they said how can you delay and we said it is better
> to be settled than not and we said go away and he said I can
> easily go on that day.

And, of course, Leo left the ménage and never came back.

Details of their private and public life together emerge, such as their confidence in the success of their union, the development of the famous logo "Rose is a rose is a rose" which appeared on many of their personal belongings, and the fame of Alice's cooking:

> We also did know that we had not undertaken sheets and
> initials and illustrations unnecessarily. We surmised that we
> were equally to be measured by the rose and by the table.

The sexual nature of their relationship is also revealed here, sometimes in veiled language (for example, the use of the word "cows" with the same sexual denotations found in other Stein works), and sometimes in fairly open allusions:

I am being led I am being led I am being gently led to bed.

"Didn't Nelly and Lilly Love You" is especially remarkable as one of the first twentieth-century lesbian love stories with a happy ending. But Stein would not and could not have written it had she not first come upon the idea of masking her subject matter through her stylistic obscurity.

The work helps to confirm Edmund Wilson's 1951 guess that Stein's stylistic experimentation is at least in part explainable by her interest in presenting her own experience of love between women at a time when it could be dealt with only through stereotypes or not at all. She wished to create a record of the history of the day-to-day life of two women lovers, perhaps not unlike the record left by Eleanor Butler in the eighteenth century. But she wrote in the first half of the twentieth century and was entirely aware of her society's view of love between women. Such love was essentially the same to her as it was to Eleanor (although she could not escape her twentieth-century sexual consciousness), but it could not be committed guilelessly to paper as it could in Eleanor's day. Gertrude probably knew, even before she began her stylistic experiments, that Natalie Barney, Renée Vivien, and Liane de Pougy all treated lesbian subject matter openly; that while it was not possible in her native America to publish such material, it was in France. But she did not see herself in their—or rather in their male predecessors' exotic terms. She really believed, as she has her autobiographical character, Adele, say in *Q.E.D.*, "the middle class ideal which demands that people be affectionate, respectable, honest, and content, that they avoid excitements and cultivate serenity is the ideal that appeals to me, in short, the ideal of affectionate family life, of honest business methods." But she knew that the public was not ready to grant such possibilities to lesbians. Her material was *inaccrochable* unless she could disguise it. She was determined to tell the truth, but willing to compromise enough to "tell it slant."

It was not until the early 1970's, with the establishment of lesbian-feminist journals and presses, that all the truth could be told without indirection and that love between women could be presented in a positive light.[20] The feminist movement, and the lesbian-feminist movement which grew out of it, comprised a readership which demanded that its own experiences be reflected in literature. Since the questioning of male authority and omniscience with regard to women is basic to feminism, women who became lesbians through the movement were never deceived into internalizing the concept of lesbian exoticism or morbidity; instead they began their lesbianism with the view that love between women was an expression of sisterhood and health, that lesbianism was generally a cause for celebration. A survey of the literature that has emerged from the lesbian-feminist movement is beyond the scope of this chapter, but it is revealing to note some of the major concepts that have developed in lesbian writing as a result of the movement.

In lesbian-feminist journals and in many novels, the "given" is that lesbian-feminism is the norm, not an abnormality—and that other sociosexual orientations are indicative of a neurotic view of one's womanhood. Lesbian-feminist readers of the 1970's did not demand that all literature written for them reflect a utopian lesbian society. But they wanted and needed depictions of revolutionary cultures, lesbian heroes, and lesbian lives lived outside of the stereotypes.

Lesbian-feminist prose style is often nonlinear, but not for Gertrude Stein's reasons of obscuring the meaning. Many lesbian-feminist writers have rejected a traditional style as being an arbitrary invention of the patriarchal culture. Since they refuse the other limits of patriarchy, they see no reason to accept its narrow literary forms. Having no vested interest in the literary establishment, and little hope of becoming part of that male-dominated institution, many of them feel free to create their own stylistic experiments.

Earlier writing, if it treated lesbianism openly, focused on explaining the "problem" to heterosexuals, or it showed the lesbian characters trying to adjust, with varying degrees of success, to the demands of the straight world. Lesbianism was the major conflict of the story. In the writing which began to emerge with the lesbian-feminist movement, the "problem" is never one's lesbianism but it might be the stupidity of a society that can react to lesbianism only through prejudices. The lesbian hero's task is generally not to adjust to the heterosexual world, but to create herself in her lesbian world.

The most popular of the lesbian-feminist novels, Rita Mae Brown's *Rubyfruit Jungle* (1973), presents the central character, Molly Bolt, as a combination female Tom Jones and a crusader for justice. She is in all ways outstanding—a straight A student, a fine athlete, an effective leader, and absolutely beautiful. But unlike the polished, superior women of the antilesbian novels of earlier decades, Molly's perfection is just that. And it is connected with her lesbianism because she is much too good to form a subservient alliance with any of the males around her. The villain of this piece is never of course the central lesbian character, but rather heterosexually identified females who experiment with lesbianism, lesbians who hide their lesbianism, the rich who use their money to buy the poor, the straights who relate to lesbians through stereotypes. Molly battles their ignorance and hypocrisy, knowing always that she has truth and justice on her side. She goes through one picaresque adventure after another; she always comes out on top, always maintains her essential innocence, and always sees herself and demands that the reader see her as a hero. Unlike the one earlier comic novel about lesbians, Compton Mackenzie's *Extraordinary Women*, it is never Molly the lesbian who is laughable but rather all the fools she meets on her odyssey. The novel is so popular among lesbian-feminists because it gives them what they have long awaited: a character with whom they can identify, who is bold, brave, always in the right, an avenger of all the wrongs done to lesbians in twentieth-century life and literature.

The growth of lesbian-feminism also provided a readership for the kind of popular literature that lesbians in earlier eras could identify with only by doing mental gymnastics with the gender pronouns. Sensing the demand for such "leisure-time" reading, Barbara Grier and Coletta Reid collected stories with lesbian heroes from the defunct periodical, *The Ladder,* and published them in an anthology with the-not-entirely-tongue-in-cheek title, *The Lesbian's Home Journal* (1976). Similarly Judy Grahn edited a collection of lesbian stories entitled *True to Life Adventure Stories* (1978), with the express goal of providing fiction that was morally useful to her lesbian-feminist readers. Mary F. Beal's *Angel Dance* (1977), a thriller in the mode of hard-boiled detective fiction, substitutes for the macho Humphrey Bogart protagonist a Chicana lesbian-feminist detective while maintaining the traditional idiom of the genre. In these works lesbian sexual orientation is very often a given and quite beside the point of the central problem of the story. It is assumed that the reader is lesbian, understands the virtues of love between women, and has no internal conflict over her choice.

The same assumptions are generally made in more serious lesbian-feminist fiction. The drama never centers around the usual explanations of lesbian genesis (hereditary defect or early trauma), although sometimes genesis is explored in political terms as the protagonist becomes a lesbian through feminism. Nor does the conflict focus on adjusting to the world as a lesbian, as it did even in the most sympathetic earlier novels like Claire Morgan's *The Price of Salt* (1951). Instead, the main emphasis is on the central character's finding herself—apart from her sexual orientation, which usually she has long since found. In Sharon Isabell's *Yesterday's Lessons* (1974), the protagonist's problems arise not particularly from being a lesbian but from the narrowness of her lower-class life. Her quest is not for adjustment but for happiness, which, she declares, "doesn't have anything to do with being straight or gay." Elana Nachman's *Riverfinger Woman* (1974) begins with the problems of being lesbian and young in the 1960's, but the protagonist quickly realizes that she must redefine her own reality, which is totally separate from the heterosexist world to which she ceases to relate. Her task is not to adjust her lesbianism to the larger world but to adjust her life to a society she and her friends have created which has little reference to the straight world. In June Arnold's *The Cook and the Carpenter* (1973), the characters' sexual orientation is incidental to their search for how to live. It is seemingly so incidental that all gender pronouns are neutralized, although the characters discover before the end of the novel that while their sexual orientation does not create a great problem when they relate to the outside world, the fact that they are women does. In June Arnold's later novel, *Sister Gin* (1975), the sexual orientation of the protagonist, a journalist, is significant in that she must learn to be publicly honest about it in order to write honestly. But the novel is really about dealing with middle age, developing courage, learning to live one's life better. In many lesbian-feminist novels the women invent themselves anew. They re-create society, choosing often to form a communal society with new rules. The patriarchy hardly exists for them.

Lesbian-feminist literature often concerns itself with universal human experiences: the difficulty of opening oneself to another person, the search for a constructive way of being, the fear of growing old—but the writers generally have no interest in claiming that their characters are just like heterosexuals except for the slight difference of sexual orientation. Although that difference is seldom a major focus in lesbian-feminist literature, the writer and the reader can never forget that it exists and that the "universal" experiences are somehow filtered through the protagonist's sexual orientation, if only because the heterosexist world outside (even if she has ceased to relate to it) has insisted on the lesbian's difference and has at some time or another impressed that difference on her. Usually she has consciously rebelled against that world, and although her rebellion may not be foremost in her mind always, it has nevertheless helped to form her.

The poet Adrienne Rich suggests that when readers ignore the protagonist's sexual orientation and see only the universals, they willfully misread; they simplify the work and strip it of its essential meaning; they refuse to understand its deepest implications. She admits to being angered when two women friends wrote her about reading her lesbian volume, *Twenty-One Love Poems* (1976), with their male lovers and feeling how "universal" the poems were. Rich resents the attempt to defuse her meaning by invoking "androgyny" or "humanism," the attempt to assimilate lesbian experience by saying that relationships are really all the same, that love is always difficult. "I see that," Rich says, "as a denial, a kind of resistance, a refusal to read and hear what I've actually written, to acknowledge what I am." [21] The position of the lesbian-feminist writer is often that only the lesbian-feminist reader can truly understand what she has written, even if her subject is a seemingly universal human experience, because it has been filtered always through her life as a lesbian in a heterosexual world. For that reason she directs her work to a lesbian-feminist audience, usually through a lesbian-feminist press.

The interest of commercial presses in publishing lesbian literature by lesbians or feminists, which began early in the 1970's and grew throughout that decade, indicates that there must be a considerable interest among heterosexual readers in lesbian experiences.[22] This increasing acceptance of lesbian literature by commercial houses may be partly responsible for what appears to be some slowing down of production among the lesbian-feminist presses. Their output was greater in the mid-1970's than at the end of the decade. They cannot hope to compete in terms of advances and advertising with the big New York houses. The danger of such cooption, of course, is that the strongest messages will be toned down by commercial publishers who are not entirely understanding of or sympathetic to lesbian-feminism. It is possible, too, that knowing that some of her readers will be heterosexual, the lesbian-feminist author will feel compelled (as Paula Christian says lesbian authors did in the 1960's) to explain what a strictly lesbian-feminist readership would have understood without explanation and to focus less on the "universals" as they apply to lesbian life and more on genesis or whatever else the heterosexual reader requires in order to understand lesbian characters. But regardless of the problems commercial houses may impose on lesbian writing, a crucial step toward honesty appears to be irreversible. The need to disguise gender, to encode messages, to hide from the censors, which influenced so much of Amy Lowell's and Gertrude Stein's writing and that of their contemporaries no longer exists, nor does the need to assume the stance of moral spokesperson for the establishment such as many covert lesbian writers took in the decades before the 1970's.

CHAPTER 3

Romantic Friendship and Lesbian Love

Passionate romantic friendship between women was a widely recognized, tolerated social institution before our century. Women were, in fact, expected to seek out kindred spirits and form strong bonds. It was socially acknowledged that while a woman could not trust men outside her family, she could look to another female for emotional sustenance and not fear betrayal. Had a woman of an earlier era *not* behaved with her intimate friend as the two Palo Alto high school girls did in their 1973 experiment, she would have been thought strangely cold. But her relationship to another female went beyond such affectionate exchanges. It was not unusual for a woman to seek in her romantic friendship the center of her life, quite apart from the demands of marriage and family if not in lieu of them. When women's role in society began to change, however—when what women did needed to be taken more seriously because they were achieving some of the powers that would make them adult persons—society's view of romantic friendship changed.

Love between women—relationships which were *emotionally* in no way different from the romantic friendships of earlier eras—became evil or morbid. It was not simply that men now saw the female sexual drive more realistically. Many of the relationships that they condemned had little to do with sexual expression. It was rather that love between women, coupled with their emerging freedom, might conceivably bring about the overthrow of heterosexuality—which has meant not only sex between men and women but patriarchal culture, male dominance, and female subservience. Learning their society's view of love between women, females were compelled to

411

suppress natural emotion; they were taught to see women only as rivals and men as their only possible love objects, or they were compelled to view themselves as "lesbian," which meant "twisted" either morally or emotionally. What was lovely and nurturing in love between women, what women of other centuries clearly understood, became one of the best-guarded secrets of the patriarchy.

In the sophisticated twentieth century women who chose to love women could no longer see themselves as romantic friends, unless they enveloped themselves in a phenomenal amount of naïveté and were oblivious to modern psychology, literature, and dirty jokes. If they persisted in same-sex love past adolescence, they would at least have to take into account what society thought of lesbians, and they would have to decide to what extent they would internalize those social views. If they were unusually strong or had a strong support group, they might escape regarding themselves as sick sinners. For many of them, without models to show that love between women was not intrinsically wrong or unhealthy, the experts' pronouncements about lesbianism worked as a self-fulfilling prophecy. They became as confused and tormented as they were supposed to be. But it was only during this brief era in history that tragedy and sickness were so strongly attributed to (and probably for that reason so frequently found in) love between women.

This changed with the rise of the second wave of feminism. Having made a general challenge to patriarchal culture, many feminists in the last decade began to challenge its taboos on love between women too. They saw it as their job to divest themselves of all the prejudices that had been inculcated in them by their male-dominated society, to reexamine everything regarding women, and finally to reclaim the meaning of love between women. Having learned to question both the social order which made women the second sex and the meaning behind the taboos on love between women, they determined to live their lives through new definitions they would create. They called themselves women-identified-women, or they consciously attempted to lift the stigma from the term "lesbian" and called themselves lesbian-feminists, by which they meant that they would put women first in their lives because men had proven, if not on a personal scale then on a cultural scale, that they were not to be trusted. Lesbian-feminists see men and women as being at odds in their whole approach to the world: men, as a rule, are authoritarian, violent, cold, and women are the opposite. Like romantic friends before them, lesbian-feminists choose women, kindred spirits, for their love objects. Unlike most romantic friends, however, they understand through feminist doctrine the sociopolitical meaning of their choice.

Lesbian-feminists differ from romantic friends in a number of ways. Most significantly, the earlier women generally had no hope of actually spending their lives together despite often reiterated fantasies that they might; but also romantic friends did not have an articulated doctrine which would help them explain why they could feel closer to women than to men. And the primary difference which affected their relationship to the world is that romantic friends, unlike lesbian-feminists, seldom had reason to believe that society saw them as outlaws—even when they eloped together like the Ladies of Llangollen did. Lesbian-feminists understand, even when they are comfortable within a large support group, that the world outside views them as criminal and reduces their love to a pejorative term. Whatever anger they began with as feminists is multiplied innumerable times as lesbian-feminists as soon as they experience, either in reality or by observation, society's hostility to what is both logical and beautiful to them. Even if they do not suffer personally— if they do not lose their children in court or if they are not fired from their jobs or turned out by their families because of their political-sexual commitments—lesbian-feminists are furious, knowing that such possibilities exist and that many women do suffer for choosing to love other women. Romantic friends never learned to be angry through their love.

There is a good deal on which lesbian-feminists disagree, such as issues concerning class, whether or not to form monogamous relationships, the virtues of communal living, whether separatism is necessary in order to live as a lesbian-feminist, the nature of social action that is efficacious, etc. But they all agree that men have waged constant battle against women, committed atrocities or at best injustices against them, reduced them to grown-up children, and that a feminist ought not to sleep in the enemy camp. They all agree that being a lesbian is, whether consciously or unconsciously perceived, a political act, a refusal to fulfill the male image of womanhood or to bow to male supremacy. Perhaps for romantic friends of other eras their relationship was also a political act, although much more covert: With each other they could escape from many of the externally imposed demands of femininity that were especially stringent throughout much of the eighteenth and nineteenth centuries. They could view themselves as human beings and prime rather than as the second sex. But they did not hope that through their relationship they might change the social structure. Lesbian-feminists do.

They see their lesbian-feminism not just as a personal choice regarding life-style, even though it is certainly a most personal choice. But it is also a political choice which challenges sexism and hetero-sexism. It is a choice which has been made often in the context of the feminist movement and with an awareness of the ideology behind it. It has seemed the only possible choice for many women who believe that the personal is political, that to reject male supremacy in the abstract but to enter into a heterosexual relationship in which the female is usually subservient makes no sense. Contemporary lesbianism, on the other hand, makes a great deal of sense. It is a combination of the natural love between women, so encouraged in the days of romantic friendships, with the twentieth-century women's freedom that feminism has made possible.

While romantic friends had considerable latitude in their show of physical affection toward each other, it is probable that, in an era when women were not supposed to be sexual, the sexual possibilities of their relationship were seldom entertained. Contemporary women can have no such innocence. But the sexual aspect of their lesbian-feminist relationships generally have less significance than the emotional sustenance and the freedom they have to define themselves. While many lesbian-feminist relationships can and do continue long after the sexual component has worn off, they cannot continue without emotional sustenance and freedom of self-definition. Romantic friends of other eras would probably have felt entirely comfortable in many lesbian-feminist relationships had the contemporary label and stigma been removed.

But many women today continue to be frightened by love between women because the pejorative connotation of the contemporary label and the stigma are still very real for them. Such fear is bound to vanish in the future as people continue to reject strict orthodoxy in sexual relationships: Women will be less and less scared off by the idea of same-sex love without examining what it entails beyond "sexual abnormality." The notion of lesbianism will be neutralized. As females are raised to be more independent, they will not assume that heterosexual marriage is necessary for survival or fulfillment; nor will they accept male definitions of womanhood or non-woman-hood. They will have no need to repress natural feelings of affection toward other women. Love between women will become as common as romantic friendship was in other eras. The twentieth-century combination of romantic friendship and female independence will continue to yield lesbian-feminism.

In an ideal world lesbian-feminism, which militantly excludes relationships with men, would not exist. And, of course, the romantic friendships such as women were permitted to conduct in other centuries—in which they might be almost everything to each other but in which a male protector was generally needed in order for them to survive—would not exist either. Instead, in a utopia men would not claim supremacy either in social or personal relationships, and women would not feel that they must give up a part of themselves in order to relate to men. Women with ambition and strength and a sense of themselves would have no reason to see men as the enemy out to conquer and subdue them. Nor would there be any attempt to indoctrinate the female with the notion that to be normal she must transfer the early love she felt for her mother first to her father and then to a father substitute—a man who is more than she is in all ways: older, taller, better educated, smarter, stronger. Women as well as men would not select their love objects on the basis of sexual politics, in surrender or in reaction to an arbitrary heterosexual ideology. They would choose to love another only in reference to the individual needs of their own personalities, which ideally had been allowed to develop untrammelled and free of sex-role stereotyping. Potential or actual bisexuality, which is today looked on by lesbian-feminists as a political betrayal and by heterosexuals as an instability, would be normal, both emotionally and statistically. But until men stop giving women cause to see them as the enemy and until there ceases to be coercion to step into prescribed roles without reference to individual needs and desires, lesbian-feminists will continue to view their choice as the only logical one possible for a woman who desires to be her own adult person.

Notes

Introduction

1. See, e.g., Edward Shorter, *The Making of the Modern Family* (New York: Basic Books, 1975), especially chapter III.

2. John Kantner and Melvin Zelnik, "Sexual Experience of Young Unmarried Women in the United States," *Family Planning Perspectives*, IV, 4 (Oct. 1972), 9–19.

3. Shorter, *The Making of the Modern Family*, p. 114.

4. See, e.g., Emil Lucka, *The Evolution of Love*, trans. Ellie Schleussner (London: George Allen and Unwin, 1922); Gordon Rattray Taylor, *Sex in History* (New York: Harper and Row, 1954); A. J. Denomy, "Fin' Amors: The Pure Love of the Troubadors, Its Amorality, and Possible Sources," *Mediaeval Studies*, vol. III (1945), 139–207.

Part IA. *Chapter 1.* LESBIANISM AND THE LIBERTINES

1. Brantôme, *Lives of Fair and Gallant Ladies* (first complete edition, 1665), trans. A. R. Allinson (New York: Liveright Publishing Corp., 1933), p. 33.

2. Ibid., p. 131.

3. Ibid.

4. Ibid., p. 134.

5. In *Le Cabinet secret du Parnasse: Théophile de Viau et les libertins*, ed. Louis Perceau (Paris: Au Cabinet du Livre, 1935), Vol. IV, p. 139.

6. In *Le Cabinet secret du Parnasse: Pierre Ronsard et la pleiade*, ed. Louis Perceau (Paris: Au Cabinet du Livre, 1928), Vol. I, pp. 182–87.

7. Brantôme, *Lives of Fair and Gallant Ladies*, p. 134.

8. In *Le Cabinet secret du Parnasse: François Malherbe et ses escholiers*, ed. Louis Perceau (Paris: Au Cabinet du Livre, 1932), Vol. III, p. 183.

9. In *Le Cabinet secret du Parnasse: Mathurin Regnier et les satyriques*, ed. Louis Perceau (Paris: Au Cabinet du Livre, 1930), Vol. II, p. 36.

10. Giacomo Girolamo Casanova de Seingalt, *The Memoirs of Jacques Casanova* (n.p., n.d.), Vol. IV, p. 26.

417

11. Ibid., pp. 92–94. Cf. the *Memoirs* of Alexandre de Tilly, trans. Françoise Delisle (1800; reprinted New York: Farrar, Straus, 1952), p. 145, in which a young man tells the Comte de Tilly of a woman's involvement with another woman: "I confess this sort of rivalry gives me no ill humor, on the contrary, it amuses me, and I am so lacking in morals as to laugh at it."

12. Casanova, *Memoirs*, Vol. IV, pp. 51–52.

13. Ibid., p. 97.

14. *The Ladies' Dispensatory; or Every Woman her Own Physician* (London, 1740), p. 10.

Part IA. *Chapter 2.* WHAT DO WOMEN DO?

1. Brantôme, *Lives of Fair and Gallant Ladies* (first complete edition, 1665), trans. A. R. Allinson (New Lork: Liveright Publishing Corp., 1933), pp. 132–33.

2. Sir Philip Sidney, *The Countess of Pembroke's Arcadia*, ed. H. Oskar Sommer (London: Kegan Paul, 1891), p. 119. Mistaken sexual identity is common in the plots of English, French, and Italian works from the sixteenth through the eighteenth centuries. Cf. the Princess Amany story in *La fleur lascive Orientale*, Honoré d'Urfe's *Astrée*, Ariosto's *Orlando Furioso* (discussed below), Shakespeare's *Twelfth Night*, Helen Marie Williams's *Anecdotes of a Convent*, etc. In all these works either a woman falls in love with another "woman" who is actually a man in disguise, or a woman falls in love with a "man" who is in fact a woman.

3. *Sexual Life in England: Past and Present*, trans. William H. Fostern (London: Francis Aldor, 1938), p. 422.

4. *Sex Variant Women in Literature* (1956; reprinted Baltimore: Diana Press, 1975), p. 38.

5. Robert James, *Medicinal Dictionary* (London, 1745), Vol. III.

6. John Cleland, *Fanny Hill* (1749; reprinted New York: G. P. Putnam's Sons, 1963), p. 229.

7. Samuel Tissot, *Onania: A Treatise Upon the Disorders Produced by Masturbation*, trans. A. Hume (London: J. Pridden, 1766).

8. *The Ladies' Dispensatory; or Every Woman Her Own Physician* (London, 1740).

9. Philip Massinger, *The Bondman* (1623; reprinted Princeton: Princeton University Press, 1932), Act II, Scene 2, p. 104.

10. See Henri Estienne, *Apologie pour Hérodote* (1566; reprinted Paris: Isidore Liseus, 1879), Vol. I, p. 175; Anonymous, *Satan's Harvest Home* (London, 1749), pp. 45–61; Tobias Smollett, *The Adventures of Roderick Random* (1748; reprinted London: Gibbings Co., 1895), Vol. III, p. 44; Giacomo Girolamo Casanova de Seingalt, *Memoirs*, trans. Arthur Machen (New York: Regency House, 1938), Vol. VI, pp. 237, 251.

11. Ludovico Ariosto, *Orlando Furioso*, trans. Sir John Harrington (1591; reprinted London: Oxford University Press, 1972), p. 280ff.

12. Ibid.

13. Lodovico Maria Sinistrari, *Peccatum Mutum: The Secret Sin*, ed. Montagu Summers (New York: Le Ballet des Muses, 1958), paragraph 7ff. (Pages are not numbered.)

14. Prospero Farinacci (Farinaccius, 1554–1618) and Antonio Gomez (1501–?) also made distinctions between mere rubbing and penetration with regard to appropriate punishments; and their distinctions had great influence on later theologians and lawmakers. In Spain, Gomez declared that if a woman used a dildo she was to be burned. If she indulged in lesbian sex without a dildo, her punishment was arbitrary: She might, for example, be beaten as delinquent women were in Granada. Farinaccius decreed that if a woman behaves "like a man with another woman she will be in danger of the penalties for sodomy and death," but he goes on to make some distinctions: If she only makes overtures, she is to be publicly denounced; if she "behaves corruptly with another woman only by rubbing," she is to be "punished," but if she "introduces some instrument into the belly of another," she is to be put to death (quoted in *Miss Marianne Woods and Miss Jane Pirie Against Dame Helen Cumming Gordon*, New York: Arno Press, 1975, "Authorities," pp. 4–5). Louis Crompton in "The Myth of Lesbian Impunity: Capital Punishment from 1270 to 1791," *Journal of Homosexuality* (forthcoming), includes similar distinctions made by other Renaissance theologians.

15. Sinistrari, *Peccatum Mutum*, paragraph 47.

16. Even in our own sex-conscious age, women who identify themselves as lesbians are, according to numerous studies, less interested in sex with other women than in a life commitment with them. For example, J. H. Gagnon and W. Simon in *Sexual Deviance* (New York: Harper and Row, 1967) point out that a female homosexual's "discovery" of love relationships usually precedes her "discovery of sexuality." In an article entitled "Femininity in the lesbian community" (*Social Problems*, 1967, 15:2, pp. 212–21), the same authors show that for most women the pursuit of sexual gratification without emotional and/or rational involvement is unattractive and often even unthinkable. R. R. Bell confirms this in *Social Deviance* (Homewood, Ill.: Dorsey Press, 1971), p. 292, suggesting that for lesbians, sexual interest is generally only a part of a broader, interpersonal interest. Mary Riege Laner in " 'Personals' Advertisements of Lesbian Women" (*Journal of Homosexuality*, Fall 1978, Vol. 4, No. 1, pp. 41–61) demonstrates that unlike the "personals" advertisements of both heterosexual and homosexual men, lesbians expressed almost no interest in sex as a goal. They were more concerned with compatible aspects of personality, and were interested in establishing stable, permanent relationships.

Part IA. *Chapter 3.* EIGHTEENTH-CENTURY FANTASY AND THE LESBIAN IMAGE

1. Mathieu François Mairobert, *L'Espion Anglois* (1777–1778; reprinted London: John Adamson, 1851), Vol. X, pp. 218–333. Jeannette Foster says that Mayeur de Saint-Paul may have written the lesbian portions of this work, *Sex Variant Women in Literature* (1956; reprinted Baltimore: Diana Press, 1975), p. 48.

2. See *La Secte des Anadrynes* by Jean Hervez (Paris: Bibliothèque des Curieux (c. 1910) for his "explanation" of the eighteenth-century lesbian psyche, based entirely on Mairobert; and Jean de Reuilly, *La Raucourt et ses amies: étude historique des moeurs saphiques au XVIIIᵉ siècle* (Paris: Bibliothèque du Vieux Paris, 1910) which for two entire chapters adopts the description of "The

Sect of the Androgynes" from Mairobert's book and presents it as fact. Later scholars relied heavily on the accounts of Hervez and de Reuilly for their discussions of the extent of lesbianism in eighteenth-century France: see Georges May, *Diderot et La Religieuse* (New Haven: Yale University Press, 1954); Raymond de Becker, *The Other Face of Love* (trans. Margaret Crosland and Alan Daventry, New York: Bell Publishers, 1964); and Jacob Stockinger, "Homosexuality and the French Enlightenment" (in *Homosexualities and French Literature*, eds. George Stambolian and Elaine Marks, Ithaca, New York: Cornell University Press, 1979).

3. Quoted in Iwan Bloch, *Sexual Life in England: Past and Present,* trans. William H. Forstern (London: Francis Aldor, 1938), pp. 345–46. Bloch also refers to *La galerie des femmes* (1799), which "contains an artistic representation of these facts, true in the main," but this work too seems to have been influenced by Mairobert.

4. This kind of fantasy about flagellation in lesbian sex seems to appeal much less to females than to males, as Emily Sisley and Bertha Harris point out in *The Joy of Lesbian Sex* (New York: Crown Publishers, 1977). They note that flagellation and sado-masochism are extremely rare in lesbian sex, and that women, except in male fantasy, "tend to recoil at equating eroticism with playing rough." Although a rare exception modelled on gay sado-masochism has recently emerged in the small Samois Club in San Francisco (see Pat Califia, "A Secret Side of Lesbian Sexuality," *The Advocate,* December 27, 1979), it is doubtful that a "sexual" act so rarely occuring in our liberated times would have existed in such proportions two centuries ago that clubs were formed especially to practice it.

The continued appeal of flagellation in male fantasies about sex between women is evident in the number of contemporary pornographic novels and "studies" of putative lesbian sado-masochism: Hodge Evans, *Lash of Lust,* 1961; Don Holliday, *Flesh Flogger,* 1965; Edward Marshall, *Discipline Hour,* 1966; Nicholas Strange, *Sado-Masochistic Lesbians,* 1968; and more recently (1980), books published by the Lesbos Library such as *The Woman Slave* and *Eve's Lesbian Hell.*

5. Quoted in Henry Ashbee (Pisanus Fraxi), *Centuria Librorum Absconditorum* (1879; reprinted New York: Documentary Book Co., 1962), pp. 467–68.

6. The imputation of pan-sexuality to eighteenth-century actresses in the following 1736 poem about a dancer in the Opéra is typical:

> *The critic is perplexed about Salle:*
>   *Some believe that she has made many happy;*
> *Others claim that she prefers her own sex.*
> *A third party replies that she tries both.*
> *But it's an injustice that everyone debases her.*
> *As for me, I'm certain of her virtue;*
> *Resnel* [her supposed male lover] *tells us that she's a tribade,*
> *Gronet* [another female dancer who accompanied her on a trip
>   to England] *tell us she's not a w . . .*

in *Chansonnier historique du XVIIIe siecle,* ed. Émile Raunié (Paris: Quantin, 1879–1883), Vol. V, pp. 163–64.

7. Mairobert provides a list of the "leading" lesbians of the day, *L'Espion Anglois*, Vol. X, pp. 266–67. Jean de Reuilly offers a key to those names in *La Raucourt et ses amies* (Paris: Bibliothèque du Vieux Paris, 1910), pp. 114–15n.

8. "By-ways of History: History of an Unreadable Book," *Bentley's Miscellany*, 1857, pp. 616–25. See also Pisanus Fraxi, *Centuria Librorum Absconditorum* (1879; reprinted New York: Documentary Books, 1962), pp. 320–22, which provides a key to the characters in *The Toast* and other information from marginal notes in the copy that King presented to John Gascoigne in 1749.

9. William King, *The Toast* (1736; reprinted New York: Garland Publishers, 1974), p. 2n.

10. It is significant that many of her sexual sins have racial and class overtones; not only does she have a lesbian affair but the other woman is a "jewess"; not only does she go to bed with scores of men but they are of the lower class, "Hired from the Scum of the People" (page 231). King describes in particular detail on p. 72n her "well known Amour with a common soldier":

> Myra, as she went into the Castle an Evening, fell in Love with a tall Grenadier, who stood Sentinel at the Gate. The force of this new Passion was so sudden and violent, that having dismissed her Attendants, she made no Scruple of stepping into the Sentry Box for immediate Relief. . . . She afterwards allowed the good Soldier a weekly Pension: till his Strength failing him, he became unfit for her Ladyship's Service.

In this heterosexual incident Myra has behaved as a man would with a mistress. She is doubly damned, both for her libido and her class-mixing, which was common enough among upper-class men and their lower-class mistresses but unforgivable for an upper-class woman. The social aspect of the sexual act outweighs in importance the sexual aspect.

11. Count Anthony Hamilton, *Memoirs of the Count de Gramont: An Amorous History of the English Court Under the Reign of Charles II*, Vol. II, pp. 88–120, 162–64.

12. The pamphlets are reprinted in *Les pamphlets libertins contre Marie-Antoinette* (Paris: Bibliothèque des Curieux, 1910); *Les maîtresses de Marie-Antoinette* (Paris: Les Éditions des Bibliophiles, n.d.), and *Madame de Polignac et la cour galante de Marie-Antoinette* (Paris: Bibliothèque des Curieux, 1910), all edited by Hector Fleischmann.

13. In *Les maîtresses de Marie-Antoinette*, pp. 50–51.

14. Ibid., pp. 245–46.

15. Georges May, "Le modèle inconnu de "La Religieuse" de Diderot: Marguerite Delamarre," *Revue d'histoire littéraire de la France*, Vol. LI (1951), pp. 273–87.

16. See the Italian work by Aretin, *Ragionamenti*, in which young Nanna peers through a hole in a convent wall to watch the nuns in sexual dalliance with each other. See also the poem by Clémont Marot, "La vierge méprisant mariage," *Oeuvres*, ed. George M. Guiffrey (Paris: Quantin, 1875–1881), Vol. II, pp. 235–36, in which the speaker tries to convince a young woman wishing to become a nun in order to remain celibate that convent life does not permit celibacy:

422 ❖ SURPASSING THE LOVE OF MEN

> *Among these virgins*
> *There are quite a few*
> *Who in morals resemble Sappho*
> *More than in sense.*
>
> *Ho! Ho!*

17. Georges May, for example, in the chapter "Diderot sexologue" in his book-length study of *The Nun*, attempts to prove that Diderot, who had a great interest in medicine, has produced a medically accurate picture of "the lesbian," a composite which is "objective, sympathetic, scientific, and precise," *Diderot et la Religieuse: étude historique et litteraire* (New Haven: Yale University Press, 1954), p. 119. Vivienne Mylne agrees that Diderot's portrayal of lesbianism "springs from a genuine and informed scientific interest," *The Eighteenth Century French Novel* (New York: Barnes and Noble, 1965), p. 201. Leonard Tancok remarks that Diderot has succeeded in this novel in treating lesbianism "objectively" and with "sympathy" and "understanding," introduction to *The Nun* (Baltimore: Penguin Books, 1974), p. 16. Even Jeannette Foster claims that "for clinical accuracy of detail it had no equal until Westphal's scientific case study of a homosexual woman was published in 1870," and she calls it "a landmark in the literature of female sex variance," *Sex Variant Women in Literature* (1956; reprinted Baltimore: Diana Press, 1975), p. 55.

18. Arthur Wilson, *Diderot: The Appeal to Posterity* (New York: Oxford University Press, 1972), pp. 388–89. See also Georges May, *Quatre Visages de Diderot,* pp. 80–83.

19. *Correspondance,* ed. Georges Roth, Vol. II (April 1, 1759), p. 125 and Vol. III (September 17, 1760), pp. 74–75.

20. Georges May also hypothesizes several associations between the sisters and the novel—e.g., Diderot believed that Mme. le Gendre was once in love with a nun; since he was forced to separate from Sophie during the summer when she was "locked up" with her family on vacation, in his writing he connected her with Suzanne, who was also "locked up"; and he was especially upset because "Madame le Gendre was near Sophie as the Superior of Saint-Eutrope was near Suzanne." May thus concludes, *"The Nun* is a novel nourished in the private life of its author. Certainly Suzanne Simonin is primarily Marguerite Delamarre, but . . . she is also sometimes Sophie Volland." *(Diderot et la Religieuse,* pp. 145–46).

21. See, for example, Georges May, *Diderot et la Religieuse,* Chapter V.

22. Ibid., p. 11.

23. Diderot, Sur les femmes," *Oeuvres Choisis* (Paris: Garnier, n.d.), p. 252.

24. Ibid., p. 257.

25. *The Nun,* p. 149.

Part IA. *Chapter 4.* Transvestism: Persecution and Impunity

1. Pierre Bayle, "Sappho," *Dictionary Historical and Critical* (1710), Vol. V (translation of Ovid's poem is by Alexander Pope).

2. William Harrison, *Description of England* (1587; reprinted Ithaca, N.Y.: Cornell University Press, 1968), pp. 147–48.

3. Cited in Carroll Camden, *The Elizabethan Woman: A Panorama of*

English Womanhood, 1540–1640 (London: Cleaver-Hume Press, 1952), pp. 264–66.

4. See Pearl Hogrefe, *Tudor Women: Commoners and Queens* (Ames: Iowa State University Press, 1975).

5. Dorothy Lyle, "Masquerade: Women in Drag," *Lesbian Lives*, eds. Barbara Grier and Coletta Reid (Baltimore: Diana Press, 1976), pp. 117–18.

6. *Huon of Bordeaux*, trans. Lord Berners (London: Trubner and Co., 1884). Ovid's story of Iphis is in *Metamorphoses*: Iphis, a girl whose gender had been disguised since birth by her mother to save her from the female infanticide to which her father had condemned her, is betrothed to another female when she grows up. Iphis loves her future bride but, like Philoclea and Fiordispina, grieves at her impossible predicament. At the zero hour, however, she is fortuitously changed into a male by a divine power.

7. It is at first glance surprising that there were so few accusations of lesbian sexual activity directed against witches during the sixteenth, seventeenth, and eighteenth centuries, when the hysteria over witches and particularly their supposed sexual orgies was raging. Perhaps this is because a principal fear of the witch hunters was that through sexual intercourse with Satan or one of his manifestations, witches would conceive his progeny and thereby re-populate the world, replacing the children of God with the Children of the Devil. Since such conception was not possible through lesbian sex, it was not to be feared. See, for example, James Springer and Heinrich Kramer, *Malleus Maleficarum* (c. 1490; reprinted, London: Pushkin Press, 1951), trans. Montague Summers, pp. 21–28. The authors of this, the most important text to the whole witch craze, seem to discount the possibility of lesbianism among witches entirely, in stating that nowhere in the Scriptures "do we read that incubi and succubi fell into vices against nature," (p. 30). See also Lodovico Maria Sinistrari, *Demoniality* (c. 1700; reprinted London: Fortune Press, n.d.), pp. 21–24.

Some scholars have suggested that lesbianism, or even membership in some Dianic witch cult, was a major factor in Joan of Arc's condemnation and burning in 1431. See Margaret Murry, *The Witch Cult in Western Europe* (London: Clarendon Press, 1921); and Arthur Evans, *Witchcraft and the Gay Counterculture* (Boston: Fag Rag Books, 1978). But while it is true that Joan's transvestism was extremely important to her prosecutors' case and was even perhaps essential to her condemnation, there is scant evidence in her trial record that she had ever had any love relationship with another woman or that lesbianism was ever an issue in the case.

8. "Evangelium Lucam" in Vern L. Bullough, *Sexual Variance in Society and History* (New York: John Wiley and Sons, 1976), p. 379.

9. In Derrick Sherwin Bailey, *Homosexuality and the Western Christian Tradition* (1955; reprinted Hamden, Conn.: Archon Books, 1975), p. 142.

10. Magnus Hirschfeld, *Die Homosexualität des Mannes und des Weibes* (Berlin: Louis Marcus, 1925), p. 822.

11. Meg Bogan, *The Woman Troubadours* (Scarborough, England: Paddington Press, 1976), pp. 132–33.

12. *Records of the Colony of New Plymouth*, ed. Nathaniel Shurtleff (Boston: Published by the Order of the General Court, William White, Printer, 1855–1861), Vol. II, p. 137.

13. Unpublished chronology, compiled by Louis Crompton, University of Nebraska, Lincoln. There is no evidence that any transvestite woman was brought before the law or that there were transvestites who tried to pass as men in seventeenth-century Colonial America. It would have been hard to hide one's sex through male garb in the small communities of the Colonies. As far as the law was concerned, when in 1636 John Cotton was asked by the General Court of Massachusetts to draw up legislation for the Colony, and he placed, for legal purposes, sexual relations between women on a par with those between men, his proposal was rejected. In fact, the only Colonial law which seems to mention sexual relations between women was passed in 1655 in New Haven Colony, and even that law, based on the ambiguous Biblical injunction in Romans I: 26, may refer only to a woman practicing fellatio or permiting a man to perform anal intercourse on her. See Jonathan Katz, *Gay American History: Lesbians and Gay Men in the U.S.A.* (New York: Thomas Crowell, 1976), pp. 20, 23.

14. *Apologie pour Hérodote* (1566; reprinted Paris: Isidore Liseus, 1879), Vol. I, p. 178. It is interesting to note that Estienne believed that an attempt by a woman to pass as a man, both socially and sexually, was unique to his wicked era. He made firm distinctions between the sins of this woman—wearing male disguise, employing a dildo—and lesbian behavior, which is relatively harmless. Sex with a dildo, in which the lesbian transvestite engaged, he says, "has nothing in common with the sexual acts of naughty girls who were called in former times 'tribades.' " He explains that the latter used only the rubbing technique. Since they did not imitate men and their lesbianism, like Sappho's, was presumably transitory (the transvestite's clearly was not), they could not be considered wicked.

15. Montaigne, *Journal de Voyage,* ed. Charles Dedeyan (Paris: Belles- Lettres, 1946), pp. 87–88.

16. "Another Case of Contrary Sexuality," F. C. Mueller, in *Friedreich's Series for Forensic Medicine: Criminal Investigation* (Nuremberg, 1891). Although there is no record of lesbian execution in France as late as the eighteenth century, ecclesiastic law continued to demand the death penalty up until the dawn of the Revolution. Daniel Jousse in his work of the 1770's, *Traite de la justice criminelle de France,* devotes a chapter to the punishment of "Sodomy and other crimes against nature," in which he states: "The crime of women who corrupt one another is regarded as a kind of sodomy, if they practice venereal acts after the fashion of a man and a woman, and is worthy of capital punishment according to the law 'on abominations,' " quoted in Louis Crompton, "The Myth of Lesbian Impunity," *Journal of Homosexuality* (forthcoming).

17. Quoted from Busbequius's *Travels in Turkey,* pp. 146–47, in Anonymous, *Satan's Harvest Home,* (London, 1749), pp. 60–61.

18. Louis Crompton cites several other cases of lesbian execution in "The Myth of Lesbian Impunity," op. cit., but not enough evidence is available regarding those cases to determine whether or not the women executed were transvestites. See also Chapter 2, footnote 14 in this book regarding executions.

19. Henry Fielding, *The Female Husband* (1746; reprinted England: Liverpool University Press, 1960).

20. Cited in Paolo Mantegazza, *The Sexual Relations of Mankind,* trans.

Samuel Putnam (New York: Eugenics Publishing Co., 1935), p. 83.

21. Robert James, *Medicinal Dictionary* (London, 1745), Vol. III, "tribades."

22. In O. P. Gilbert, *Women in Men's Guise*, trans. J. Louis May (London: The Bodley Head, 1932), pp. 36–140.

23. Margaret Goldsmith, *Christina of Sweden* (Garden City, N.Y.: Doubleday, 1935), pp. 204–08.

24. Ibid., pp. 69–70.

25. But the Princess Palatine saw homosexuality everywhere. She also complained of the lesbian activities of Mme. de Maintenon, Henriette d'Angleterre, and Mme. de Monaco. Henry Vizetelly, in his introduction to Anthony Hamilton's *Memoirs of the Count de Gramont: An Amorous History of the English Court Under the Reign of Charles II* (London: Vizetelly and Co., 1889), points out that such accusations were entirely common during Louis XIV's day, and they were also hurled at two of the Regent's daughters, the Abbess of Chelles and the Princess of the Asturias, the Duchess of Mazarin, and her intimates, including Lady Harvey, and Mlle. Beverweert-Nassau, Vol. I, p. 89. See also Georges May, *Diderot et La Religieuse: étude historique et litteraire* (New Haven: Yale University Press, 1954), pp. 91, 107–08; Vincent Buranelli, *Louis XIV* (New York: Twayne Publishers, 1966), pp. 47–48; and Nancy Mitford, introduction to *The Princess of Cleves* (New York: New Directions, 1951), pp. xvi–xvii.

26. The story was originally reported in *Gentleman's Magazine* in 1776. A very sympathetic treatment of Mary East later appeared in an American magazine, *Fincher's Trade Review*, Vol. I, No. 8 (July 25, 1863), p. 29. Bram Stoker, in *Famous Imposters* (London: Sidgwick and Jackson, 1910), pp. 241–64, also refers to a written discussion of the case in 1825, in which Mary East is again treated very sympathetically.

27. Havelock Ellis, in *Studies in the Psychology of Sex* (Philadelphia: F. A. Davis, 1900), Vol. I, Pt. 4, p. 245, remarks that although there are no facts to prove that she was homosexual, "we see clearly what may be termed the homosexual diathesis."

28. Stoker, *Famous Imposters*, pp. 235–41.

29. Charlotte Charke, *A Narrative of the Life of Mrs. Charlotte Charke (Youngest Daughter of Colley Cibber, Esq.)*, ed. Leonard Ashley (1755; reprinted Gainesville, Fla.: Scholar's Facsimiles and Reprints, 1969).

30. Arno Karlen, *Sexuality and Homosexuality: A New View* (New York: W. W. Norton, 1971), p. 141.

31. There are a number of works dealing with female transvestites of this period and other eras. See, for example, Stoker, *Famous Imposters*, op. cit.; Oscar Paul Gilbert, *Women in Men's Guise* (London: The Bodley Head, 1932); Charles J. S. Thompson, *Mysteries of Sex* (London: Hutchinson, 1938); and Jonathan Katz, *Gay American History* (New York: Thomas Crowell, 1976).

32. Herbert Mann, *The Female Review: Life of Deborah Sampson* (1797; reprinted New York: Arno Press, 1972), p. 250. This is reprinted from the 1866 edition, edited by John Adams Vinton.

33. Ibid., p. xxii.

34. Ibid., p. 124n.

35. Ibid.

36. Ibid., p. xxviii.

37. Ibid., p. 121n.

38. Ibid., p. 131n.

39. Ibid., p. 134.

40. Ibid., p. 225n.

41. Ibid., p. 225.

Part IB. *Chapter 1.* THE REVIVAL OF SAME-SEX LOVE:
SIXTEENTH AND SEVENTEENTH CENTURIES

1. Michel de Montaigne, "On Friendship," in *Montaigne's Essay on Friendship and XXIX Sonnets by Éstienne de la Boëtie*, trans. Louis How (Boston: Houghton Mifflin Co., 1915).

2. Chapters VII, IX, and XXII in *Cicero's Essays on Friendship and Old Age*, trans. Cyrus R. Edmunds (New York: Translation Publishing Co., 1922).

3. L. J. Mills, "The Renascence Development in England of the Classical Ideas About Friendship," dissertation, University of Chicago, 1925, p. 9.

4. Baldassare Castiglione, *The Book of the Courtier*, trans. Thomas Hoby (London: J. M. Dent, 1944), Book II, p. 137ff.

5. *Flovvers of Epigrammes* (1577; reprinted London: Spenser Society, 1874), p. 286.

6. Ed. Joseph Jacobs (1566; reprinted London, 1890), Vol. II, p. 104.

7. *The Complete Works of Thomas Lodge* (reprinted London: The Hunterian Club, 1883), Vol. II.

8. Ibid., Vol. I, pp. 34–35.

9. Henrietta Maria Bowdler, *The Proper Employment of Time, Talents, and Fortune* (London: T. Cadell, 1836), p. 37.

10. Quoted in Jane Aldis, *The Queen of Letter Writers: Marquise de Sévigné* (London: Methuen Co., 1907), p. 304.

11. *Mademoiselle de Scudéry: sa vie et sa correspondance*, eds. Rathery and Boutron (Paris: Léon Techener, 1873), p. 162.

12. While it is probable that such a relationship had a source in a philosophic ideal with which these educated women would have been familiar, the evidence shows that it took on a power of its own in practice. Although there is very little proof that romantic friendships existed in the lower classes during the seventeenth century, since women who were not literate did not leave many records, it is likely, for reasons to be discussed in Chapter 3, that the institution of romantic friendship spread to classes other than the intellectually elite.

13. Katherine Philips, *Poems* (London, 1667), prefacing poem, "On the Death of Mrs. Katherine Philips."

14. Katherine Philips, "To Berenice," *Familiar Letters* (London, 1697), Vol. I, p. 147.

15. Katherine Philips, "Orinda to Lucasia on Parting 1661 at London," *Poems*, pp. 139–40.

16. Ibid., pp. 51–52.

17. Ibid., pp. 82–83.

18. Ibid., p. 107.

19. Ibid., p. 48.

20. Ibid., pp. 53–55.

21. Thomas Heywood, *Tunaikeion: or Nine Bookes of Various History Concerninge Women* (London, 1624), pp. 323–24.

22. *The Poems of Edmund Waller* (1686 edition), ed. G. Thorn Drury (London, 1893), pp. 60–61.

Part IB. *Chapter 2.* THE "FASHION" OF ROMANTIC FRIENDSHIP
IN THE EIGHTEENTH CENTURY

1. Iwan Bloch, *Sexual Life in England: Past and Present*, trans. William H. Forstern (London: Francis Aldor, 1938), pp. 176, 395.

2. Elizabeth Mavor, *The Ladies of Llangollen: A Study of Romantic Friendship* (1971; reprinted New York: Penguin Books, 1973), p. xvii.

3. *The Hamwood Papers of the Ladies of Llangollen and Caroline Hamilton*, ed. Mrs. G. H. Bell (London: Macmillan, 1930), p. 27.

4. Anonymous, *Satan's Harvest Home* (London, 1749), pp. 51–52.

5. Obrien is depicted as being villainous in every way. His negative assessment of female friendship is therefore immediately discredited, as are the negative assessments of most of the men in these novels. Jane Austen was one of the few women writers who seemed to scoff at the excesses of romantic friendship. In *Love and Freindship* [sic], a juvenile satire, she has Louisa, who has been deprived of a "real" friend for three entire weeks, finally able to exult, "imagine my transports at beholding one, most truly worthy of the name. . . . We flew into each others arms and after having exchanged vows of mutual Freindship for the rest of our Lives, instantly unfolded to each other the most inward secrets of our Hearts."

6. Edmond and Jules de Goncourt, *The Woman of the Eighteenth Century*, trans. Jacques le Clercq and Ralph Roeder (1862; reprinted London: George Allen and Unwin, 1928), pp. 91–92.

7. Ibid., pp. 92–93. The exchange of locks of hair in trinkets such as these described by the Marquise's maid was also a custom in England. In 1751, Elizabeth Carter wrote to Catherine Talbot, sending her "a thousand thanks" for her lock of hair, "which certainly need not the decoration of gold and crystal to heighten my estimation of its worth." *A Series of Letters Between Mrs. Elizabeth Carter and Miss Catherine Talbot*, ed. Montagu Pennington (London: E. C. and J. Rivington, 1809), Vol. II, pp. 36–37.

Of course, not all women could lend themselves to passionate friendship with such enthusiasm. Madame de Genlis seemed to find the institution laughable. In one of her comedies she parodied Marie Antoinette's intimate circle of women friends and what she saw as their fashion of having an "inseparable" friend from whom they separated at the slightest quarrel, Violet Wyndham, *Madame de Genlis: A Biography* (New York: Roy Publishers, 1958), p. 91. There was considerable hostility between Mme. de Genlis and Marie Antoinette, which may help to explain her parody. Madame de Genlis, who was the governess to the sons of the Duc de Chartres and an intimate friend of this nobleman, had been referred to by Marie Antoinette as "the governess of Monsieur le Duc de Chartres."

But Genlis's lack of enthusiasm for romantic friendship seems to have been based also on her conviction that if, unlike those of the queen's circle, romantic friendships were indeed permanent and profound, they would interfere with the creation of offspring, which was one's insurance against loneliness in old age. When Mme. de Genlis stayed for a night in the home of the Ladies of Llangollen she was, she wrote later, awakened by the mournful notes of an Aeolian harp, which filled her with gloom. The next morning she reflected on how lonely the friend who survived the other would be without children or grandchildren to console her in old age. However, she seems to have been ambivalent about the relationship of her hostesses. She made their romance even more romantic than it was by adding to the myth that they were born on the same day and the same year (Eleanor was born in 1739, Sarah was born in 1755), and that when they reached the age of seventeen they decided to dedicate their lives to each other (Eleanor was thirty-nine when they ran off together, Sarah was twenty-three), ibid. p. 444 and *The Hamwood Papers*, p. 371.

8. See, for example, Lester G. Crocker, *Jean-Jacques Rousseau: The Prophetic Voice (1758–1778)* (New York: Macmillan, 1973), Vol. II, p. 61.

9. Juliette Récamier's heterosexual "affairs" seem to have been largely asexual. Louis Gillet speculates with regard to Chateaubriand's connection with her: "He was obliged, for all his stormy protests, to wear the yoke of friendship," and that "even her husband had been that in name only, . . . she simply had no sexual passion and was ignorant as a nun of the humiliating laws of the senses." Her love relationship with Chateaubriand was thus not essentially different from the one she had with Mme. de Staël, in Louis Batiffol, et al, *The Great Literary Salons: XVII and XVIII Centuries*, trans. Mabel Robinson (London: Thornton Butterworth, 1930), pp. 22–23.

10. Maurice Levaillant, *The Passionate Exiles* (French title, *Une Amitié Amoureuse*), trans. Malcolm Barnes (New York: Farrar, Straus, and Cudahy, 1958), p. 4. See also the correspondence between Mme. de Staël and Mme. Récamier cited in Amelie Lenormant, *Madame de Staël and the Grand Duchess Louise* (London: Saunders, 1862) and Mme. de Boigne's novel about them, *Une Passion dans le Grand Monde* (Paris: Michel Lévy Frères, 1866).

11. Levaillant, *The Passionate Exiles*, pp. 137, 182, 183–84.

12. *Letters from the Duchess de Crui*, by a Lady (London, 1776), Vol. II, p. 91.

13. In Mavor, *The Ladies of Llangollen*, p. 95.

14. See, for example, John Ciardi, "Review of Rebecca Patterson's *The Riddle of Emily Dickinson*," *New England Quarterly*, Vol. XXV (1952), pp. 93–98, and Grace B. Sherrer's review of Patterson's thesis in *American Literature*, Vol. XXIV (1952), pp. 255–58.

15. By the end of the eighteenth century, sentimentality was in great vogue in England and, partly through the influence of Samuel Richardson's novels, soon spread to France. Regarding the term "sentimental," Lady Bradshaigh observed in 1749, "Everything clever and agreeable is comprehended in that word," quoted in Walter Francis Wright, "Sensibility in English Prose Fiction," dissertation, University of Illinois, Urbana, 1935, p. 30. The eighteenth-century vogue of sentimentality was a reaction to the dryness of "The Age of Reason." "Sensibility" (Wright says that was the most commonly used noun, and "senti-

mental" the most commonly used adjective) did not of course always encourage superficial or artificial feeling. It often permitted people to express emotions that other eras would have preferred to repress, to "get in touch with one's feelings," in the contemporary phrase.

16. Mavor, *The Ladies of Llangollen,* p. 95.

17. *Letters of Anna Seward Written Between the Years 1784 and 1807,* ed. Sir Walter Scott (Edinburgh: Constable and Co., 1811), Vol. I, p. xlvi.

Part IB. *Chapter 3.* THE BATTLE OF THE SEXES

1. Elizabeth Mavor, *The Ladies of Llangollen: A Study of Romantic Friendship* (1971; reprinted New York: Penguin Books, 1973), p. 80.

2. *The Autobiography of Anne Lady Halkett,* ed. John Nichols (New York: Johnson Reprint Co., 1965), p. 3. Throughout the eighteenth century also, men and women in France, England and America inhabited separate spheres. See, for example, Rousseau's *Emile,* Dr. Gregory's *Legacy to His Daughters,* and also Mary Wollstonecraft's objections to sexually segregated functions in *A Vindication of the Rights of Woman.* Mary Sumner Benson in *Women in Eighteenth-Century America: A Study of Opinion and Social Usage* (1935; reprinted Port Washington, N.Y.: Kennikat Press, 1966), discusses American sex segregation. Males and females were separated on almost all occasions; e.g., "Women like men were expected to attend church regularly, [but] the sexes were usually seated separately in church. . . . In Hadley there were even separate stairs for the galleries occupied by young men and women," p. 262. By the end of the eighteenth century, American girls were permitted more freedom, at least in comparison to their French counterparts. La Rochefoucauld observed in *Travels Through the United States,* 4 vols. (London, 1799), Vol. IV, pp. 591–92: "The young women here enjoy a liberty which to French manners would appear disorderly; they go out alone, walk with young men, and depart with them from the rest of the company in large assemblies; in short, they enjoy the same degree of liberty which married women do in France, and which married women here do not take." But, La Rochefoucauld states, an American girl dares not abuse her liberty, because she understands that if her virginity is lost, or even if she is innocent and her reputation is besmirched, she will not get a husband.

3. Quoted in Emily James Putnam, *The Lady: Studies of Certain Significant Phases of Her History* (1910; reprinted The University of Chicago Press, 1970), p. 264.

4. See Pearl Hogrefe, *Tudor Women: Commoners and Queens* (Ames: Iowa State University Press, 1975), and Bartlett Burleigh James, *Women of England* (Philadelphia: George Barrie and Sons, 1908).

5. Quoted in Hugo P. Thieme, *Women of Modern France* (Philadelphia: George Barrie and Sons, 1907), p. 190.

6. Literary salons were conducted by women as early as the sixteenth century. The poet of Lyons, Louise Labé (1525–1566), held elaborate salons in her upper-middle-class home. Her collected poems of 1555 were dedicated to another woman poet of Lyons, Clémence de Bourges, and a number are addressed directly to women readers, sometimes specifically to the "Dames Lionnoises," suggesting that it was with them that she hoped most to communicate in her

writing. See Frederic Prokosch, introduction to Louise Labé's *Love Sonnets* (New York: New Directions, 1947), and Fernand Zamaron, *Louise Labé: Dame de Franchise* (Paris: A-G Nizet, 1968). Occasional salons in sixteenth- and seventeenth-century England, such as those conducted by the Countess of Pembroke in Spenser's day and by Lucy, Countess of Bedford, in Ben Jonson's, had some influence on literary taste. But it was not until the eighteenth century with the rise of the bluestocking that the salon became an institution in England.

7. In *Le cabinet secret du Parnasse: Théophile de Viau et les libertins*, ed. Louis Perceau (Paris: Au Cabinet du Livre, 1935), Vol. IV, p. 162.

8. Quoted in *Mrs. Montagu: Queen of the Blues, Her Letters and Friendships from 1762–1800*, ed. Reginald Blunt (London: Constable and Co., n.d.), Vol. II, p. 7.

9. William Kenrick, *The Whole Duty of Women* (London, 1753), pp. 5, 17.

10. Benson, *Women in Eighteenth-Century America*, p. 39.

11. See, for example, *A Series of Letters Between Mrs. Elizabeth Carter and Miss Catherine Talbot*, ed. Montagu Pennington (London: Rivington, 1809); *Letters of Anna Seward: Written Between the Years 1784 and 1807* (Edinburgh: Constable and Co., 1811); *Letters from Mrs. Elizabeth Carter to Mrs. Montagu between the years 1755 and 1800*, ed. Montagu Pennington (London: Rivington, 1817); *The Autobiography and Correspondence of Mrs. Delany (Revised from Lady Llanover's Edition)*, ed. Sarah Chauncey Woolsey (Boston: Roberts Bros., 1882); *Elizabeth Montagu: The Queen of the Blue-Stockings: Her Correspondence from 1720 to 1761*, ed. Emily J. Climenson (London: John Murray, 1906); *Mrs. Montagu: Queen of the Blues—Her Letters and Friendships from 1762 to 1800*, ed. Reginald Blunt (London: Constable and Co., n.d.).

12. Abbe de Pure, *La Prétieuse*, ed. Emile Magne (Geneva: Droz, 1939), Vol. II, p. 113.

13. *Mrs. Montagu: Queen of the Blues*, Vol. II, pp. 356–57.

14. *The Poetical Works of Anna Seward with Extracts from Her Literary Correspondence*, ed. Walter Scott, 3 vols. (Edinburgh: John Ballantyne and Co., 1810), Vol. I, p. lxi.

15. See Keith Thomas's discussion in "The Double Standard," *Journal of the History of Ideas*, Vol. 20 (1959), pp. 195–216.

16. *Miscellanies by the Right Noble Lord, the Late Marquis of Halifax* (London, 1700), pp. 17–18.

17. "Ev'ry Woman is at Heart a Rake," *Eighteenth-Century Studies*, Vol. 8 (1974), pp. 27–46.

18. Sheila Rowbotham, *Hidden from History: Rediscovering Women in History from the Eighteenth Century to the Present* (New York: Pantheon Books, 1974), p. 15.

19. Ruth Kelso, *Doctrine for a Lady of the Renaissance* (Urbana: University of Illinois Press, 1956), pp. 23–25.

20. *Life of Johnson*, ed. John Murray (London, 1835), Vol. IV, p. 219.

21. Quoted in Robert Palfrey Utter and Gwendolyn Needham, *Pamela's Daughters* (1936; reprinted New York: Russell and Russell, 1972), p. 289.

22. *The Complete Letters of Lady Mary Wortley Montagu*, ed. Robert Halsband (Oxford: Clarendon Press, 1965), Vol. I, May 5, 1710, p. 35.

23. Diderot, "Sur les femmes," *Oeuvres Choisis* (Paris: Garnier, n.d.), p. 261.

24. Diderot reported to Sophie Volland in a letter dated November 22, 1768, that he had recently made such admonishments to the girl.

25. Benson, *Woman in Eighteenth-Century America*, Chapters I–III.

26. In her study of magazine-fiction heroines from 1750 to 1974, Mirabel Cecil shows that eighteenth-century writers were preoccupied with one theme alone: "How their heroines *avoided* sex—the pursuit, the flight, the closing in, the fighting off, and, just occasionally, the perpetration of the horror." In story after story the eighteenth-century male uses the most underhanded techniques in his attempt to get what the eighteenth-century female must fight to the death to deny him. *Heroines in Love* (London: Michael Joseph, 1974), pp. 25ff.

27. Edward Shorter, *The Making of the Modern Family* (New York: Basic Books, 1975), pp. 50–51.

28. Anonymous, *Satan's Harvest Home* (London, 1749), pp. 1–12. Peter Laslett, *Family Life and Illicit Love in Earlier Generations* (Cambridge, England: Cambridge University Press, 1977), pp. 115–17, records a steady increase in illegitimate births in England from the post-Puritan period to the end of the eighteenth century. Laslett refers to a "sub-society" of the "bastardy-prone," suggesting that many lower-class women had illegitimate children repeatedly, but if the author of *Satan's Harvest Home* can be believed, they did not do so with impunity. Milton Rugoff observes that in eighteenth-century America, country families were lenient toward an unwed daughter who bore a child, since all children were welcome because numbers were important in the business of conquering and peopling the wilderness. As long as the burden of supporting the child did not fall on the community, the authorities often winked at illegitimate births. Nevertheless, the legal penalty for fornication was usually a public whipping and a fine, despite the fact that it was not often enforced. *Prudery and Passion* (New York: G. P. Putnam's Sons, 1971), p. 21.

29. Edmond and Jules de Goncourt, *The Woman of the Eighteenth Century: Her Life, Her Love and Her Philosophy in the Worlds of Salon, Shop, and Street*, trans. Jacques le Clercq and Ralph Roeder (London: George Allen and Unwin, 1928), p. 105.

30. Choderlos de Laclos, *Les liaisons dangereuses*, trans. Richard Aldington (London: George Routledge, n.d.), p. 105.

31. Ibid., p. 341.

32. See, for example, *Justine* (1791) and *Juliette* (1797).

33. Nicolas Restif de la Bretonne, *Pleasures and Follies of a Good-Natured Libertine: or l'Anti-Justine*, trans. Pieralessandro Casavini 1798 (Paris: Olympia Press, 1955), preface.

34. Ibid., Chapter XV.

35. *A Treatise on the Use of Flogging* appeared in England in 1718, and by the end of the eighteenth century, whipping was called on the Continent "the English vice," but the English had few exquisite refinements comparable to Sade in this area.

36. See, for example, *The Yorkshire Tragedy* and George Wilkins's *The Miseries of Enforced Marriage*, both of 1607.

37. Thieme, *Women of Modern France*, pp. 294–97.

38. The Goncourts, *The Woman of the Eighteenth Century*, p. 16. Cf. *Les liaisons dangereuses*, in which the fifteen-year-old Cecile Volanges is removed from a convent by her mother and learns only by the bustle of wedding preparations that it is because her mother has found a husband for her. Other fictional works confirm that well-born women had little to say in the choice of their life partners, and that they were usually obedient to their parents' wishes. For example, in Rousseau's *La nouvelle Héloise*, Julie determines not to marry St. Preux, despite her overwhelming love, because her father disapproves of him and wishes her to marry another. Parental choice of the daughter's mate seems to have been customary well before the eighteenth century. Molière, in *Les Précieuses ridicules* (1659), makes Gorgibus appear ridiculous, and his daughter and orphaned niece also appear spoiled and foolish because they disobey his wish that they marry two rich men he has selected for them.

39. The Goncourts, *The Woman of the Eighteenth Century*, p. 172. Edward Shorter suggests that the marriage of convenience made by parental arrangement was frequent among the middle classes as well, especially the land-holding peasantry of France; see *The Making of the Modern Family*, Chapter 2.

40. Abel Hugo, *France Pittoresque* (Paris, 1839), Vol. II, p. 29.

41. Mirabel Cecil, *Heroines in Love* (London: Michael Joseph, 1974), p. 27.

42. Quoted in Rosamond Bayne-Powell, *Eighteenth-Century London Life* (London: John Murray, 1937), p. 70. Lawrence Stone, *The Family, Sex and Marriage in England: 1500–1800* (New York: Harper & Row, 1977), shows in his chapter "The Companionate Marriage" (pp. 325–405) that there were attempts by numerous seventeenth- and eighteenth-century writers to encourage matrimony based on love, but the weight of evidence indicates that the wealthier classes generally continued to marry for practical considerations. Christina Simmons argues that romantic friendship fell into social disfavor when companionate marriage became widespread; however, that was not until the 1920's, "Companionate Marriage and the Lesbian Threat," *Frontiers*, Vol. IV, 3 (Fall, 1979), pp. 54–60.

43. Reprinted in *A Series of Letters on Courtship and Marriage* (Springfield, 1796). Fiction of the period demonstrates that young women generally accepted without question their parents' right to select their spouses. For example, in Charles Brockden Brown's fragment of Jessica and Sophia, written about the time Franklin's letters were published, Jessica expresses shock that her friend should ever question the appropriateness of her father's choice of a husband for her; in *The Life of Charles Brockden Brown, Together with Selections from the Rarest of His Printed Works, from His Original Letters, and from His Manuscripts Before Unpublished*, 2 vols. (Philadelphia: James P. Parke, 1815), Vol. I, p. 119. Mary Sumner Benson in *Women in Eighteenth-Century America* writes that it was not always parental coercion but often a young woman's practicality that caused her to marry without love, p. 76.

44. *The Autobiography and Correspondence of Mrs. Delany*, Revised from *Lady Llanover's Edition* (Boston: Roberts Brothers, 1882), Vol. I, p. 24.

45. J. M. S. Tompkins, *The Popular Novel in England, 1770–1800* (1932; reprinted Lincoln: University of Nebraska Press, 1961), p. 147.

46. Putnam, *The Lady*, p. 274.

47. Ibid.
48. Bayne-Powell, *Eighteenth-Century London Life*, pp. 54–55.
49. Quoted in the Goncourts, *The Woman of the Eighteenth-Century*, p. 19.

Part IB. *Chapter 4*. ROMANTIC FRIENDSHIP IN
EIGHTEENTH-CENTURY LITERATURE

1. Quoted in Walter Crittendon, introduction to *A Description of Millenium Hall* (New York: Bookman Associates, 1955), p. 13.
2. *The Ladies of Llangollen: A Study of Romantic Friendship* (1971; reprinted New York: Penguin Books, 1973), p. 83.
3. Elizabeth Carter records an attempt by three women to establish their own Millenium Hall in Hitcham in 1770. Because of some disagreements among them, the scheme failed, and Carter fears that its failure would "reflect on female friendship," but she asserts to her correspondent, "people do not disagree either because they are men, or because they are women, but because they are human creatures," *Letters from Mrs. Elizabeth Carter to Mrs. Montagu, Between the Years 1755 to 1800*, ed. Montagu Pennington (London: F. C. and J. Rivington, 1817), Vol. II, p. 16. It does not appear that the relationship between any of the women in the Hitcham undertaking was "romantic," unlike that of two of the couples of Millenium Hall, but the novel seemed to provide a blueprint, idealized and difficult to match as it was, for female communal living.
4. Anonymous, *Female Friendship, or The Innocent Sufferer: A Moral Novel*, 2 vols. (London, 1770).
5. *The Autobiography and Correspondence of Mrs. Delany (Revised from Lady Llanover's Edition)*, ed. Sarah Chauncey Woolsey (Boston: Roberts Bros., 1882), Vol. I, pp. 11–12. The friend mentioned here was Hester Kirkham, who later became the writer Mrs. Chapone, so much admired by Mary Wollstonecraft for her understanding of girls. Mrs. Chapone devoted half a volume of her letters to discussing with a fifteen-year-old girl the subject of romantic friendship. She advised young women to select a worthy female friend and attach themselves eternally, and she encouraged fidelity and devotion in "two hearts desirous to perpetuate their society beyond the grave."
6. J. M. S. Tompkins, *The Popular Novel in England, 1770–1800* (1932; reprinted Lincoln: University of Nebraska Press, 1961), p. 146n.
7. *Moreau de St. Méry's American Journey, 1793–1798*, trans. and ed. Kenneth Roberts and Anna M. Roberts (Garden City, N.Y.: Doubleday, 1947), pp. 285–86.
8. *The Life of Charles Brockden Brown, Together with Selections from the Rarest of His Printed Works, from His Original Letters, and from His Manuscripts Before Unpublished*, ed. William Dunlap (Philadelphia: James P. Parke, 1815), Vol. I, pp. 107–69.
9. He shared the views of his countrymen. Male homosexuality had been punishable by death in the colonies. In 1777 Thomas Jefferson pleaded for "liberalizing" Virginia law, making sodomy punishable by castration, in Jonathan Katz, *Gay American History* (New York: Thomas Crowell, 1976), p. 24.
10. *The Life of Charles Brockden Brown*, Vol. II.

11. Constantia's reunion with Sophia is described in terms of "the impetuosities of a master passion," Robert Rigby Hare, "Charles Brockden Brown's *Ormond*: The Influence of Rousseau, Godwin, and Mary Wollstonecraft," dissertation, University of Maryland, 1967.

12. That notion seems hard for many twentieth-century critics to accept since contemporary women are more guarded in their expressions of affection toward other women. Since modern scholars have so little chance to witness actual romantic friendships, they generally assume that it is a literary convention with strictly literary models or that the author was making some subtle remark about his characters' "abnormality." See Ernest Marchaud, introduction to *Ormand* (New York: American Book Co., 1937), p. xxxii, who calls the relationship between the two girls in Brown's novel "almost unnatural"; and Harry R. Warfel, *Charles Brockden Brown: American Gothic Novelist* (Gainesville: University of Florida Press, 1949) p. 132, who suggests it is an "abnormal relationship." Donald A. Ringe, *Charles Brockden Brown* (New York: Twayne Publishers, 1966), pp. 60–61, attempts to explain the girls' closeness by the fact that they "were reared together" which would "understandably bind them to one another" but still finds something uncomfortably sapphic about it and concludes that "at best, the relationship is not one to increase the stature of Constantina as the heroine of the novel." Those twentieth-century critics who see Constantina as the ideal woman often have a difficult time when they attempt to reconcile her perfection with her passion for another woman; thus they tend to ignore the intense love relationship which is central to the novel, or they defensively assert, as David Lee Clark does, that there is no evidence that Constantina is a "victim of homosexuality" and drop the subject at that.

One of the most blatant examples of a critic's inability to distinguish between his own expectations and those of a reader from another century is found in Leslie Fiedler, *Love and Death in the American Novel* (1952; revised edition New York: Stein and Day, 1966). Fiedler states that Brown's contemporaries did not like the novel because they did not know what to make "of such a perverse reversal of the expected terms of affection" and that while they could have understood and responded to love between the Pure Maiden and her brutal Seducer, they could not have been sympathetic to love "between the Maiden and an old girl friend." But if reading audiences were so confused and upset by the depiction of romantic friendship the theme would not have appeared so frequently in the most commercially intended novels. Nor is there any reason to believe that *Ormond* was as unsuccessful as Fiedler implies: the first edition sold out completely in England within the first year and a second edition was brought out almost immediately (1800). A short time later it was translated into German and published in Leipzig (1802). While *Ormond* did not go into a second printing in America, neither did any of Brown's other novels.

13. See, for example, Brown's *Alcuin*, a dialogue about the rights of woman; David Lee Clark, "Brockden Brown and the Rights of Women," *University of Texas Bulletin*, No. 2212 (March 22, 1922); and Augusta Genevieve Violette, "Economic Feminism in American Literature Prior to 1848," *University of Maine Studies*, Second Series, No. 2 (Orono, 1925).

14. Twentieth-century critics, however, have not been so satisfied with this

ending. Robert Hare, "Charles Brockden Brown's *Ormand*," pp. 216–18, for example, protests, "If, as Brown seems to say, the sum of all Constantina's virtues leads to spinsterhood, the confrontation seems hardly worthwhile. . . . She certainly deserves better than spinsterhood."

Part IB. *Chapter 5*. ROMANTIC FRIENDSHIP IN
EIGHTEENTH-CENTURY LIFE

1. *The Complete Letters of Lady Mary Wortley Montagu*, ed. Robert Halsband (Oxford: Clarendon Press, 1965), Vol. I, p. 4.

2. Iris Barry, *Portrait of Lady Mary Wortley Montagu* (Indianapolis: Bobbs-Merrill, 1928), pp. 61, 54. Robert Halsband similarly emphasizes that Mary's friendship with Anne was based on Anne's role as a go-between for Mary and Edward. He does not even seem to notice, as Barry did, the romantic language in the letters that passed between the two women, *The Life of Mary Wortley Montagu* (New York: Oxford University Press, 1956). Anne died shortly after these letters were written, and Mary and Edward shared their grief together. Their correspondence continued over several years in generally lukewarm and argumentative terms. Mary married Edward, primarily it seems to escape from the confines of her father's home. They seldom lived together, although they never attempted to seek a divorce. Alexander Pope (who translated Ovid's poem about Sappho), an admirer-turned-calumniator, called Lady Mary "Sappho" to insult her. She had close relationships with women throughout her life. Her one traceable passionate involvement with a man occurred when she was middle-aged. She fell in love with a young Italian poet, Francisco Algarotti, who was in his twenties, homosexual, and the lover of Lord Hervey and King Frederick of Prussia, among others. Voltaire described Algarotti's sexual activity with the French ambassador's young male secretary in a poem: "But when . . . /I see the tender Algarotti/Crush with passionate embrace/ The handsome Lergeac, his young friend,/ I imagine I see Socrates fastened/Onto the rump of Alcibiades," in Robert Halsband, *Lord Hervey: Eighteenth-Century Courtier* (London: Oxford University Press, 1974), p. 272. See also *The Complete Letters of Lady Mary Wortley Montagu*, passim.

3. Louis Kronenberger, *Marlborough's Duchess: A Study in Worldliness* (New York: Alfred A. Knopf, 1958), p. 57n.

4. Their story is told at length in two works in print, Mary Gordon, *Chase of the Wild Goose* (1936; reprinted New York: Arno Press, 1975) and Elizabeth Mavor, *The Ladies of Llangollen: A Study in Romantic Friendship* (1971; reprinted New York: Penguin Books, 1976). The latter is by far the more detailed and scholarly. Colette devotes fifteen pages to the Llangollen Ladies in *The Pure and the Impure* (1932; reprinted New York: Farrar, Straus, and Giroux, 1967).

5. Mavor, *The Ladies of Llangollen*, pp. 69, 138.

6. Quoted in *The Hamwood Papers of the Ladies of Llangollen and Caroline Hamilton*, ed. Mrs. G. H. Bell (London: Macmillan, 1930), p. 354. The sonnet was published in 1827. Wordsworth referred to the two women in his correspondence as "dear friends of mine."

7. *The Poetical Works of Anna Seward with Extracts from Her Literary*

Correspondence, ed. Walter Scott (Edinburgh: John Ballantyne and Co., 1810), Vol. III, pp. 107–08.

8. Reverend J. Pritchard, D.D. (c. 1856), quoted in Mavor, *The Ladies of Llangollen,* pp. 203–04.

9. See *The Hamwood Papers,* Sarah Tighe to Sarah Ponsonby, August 28, 1798, p. 304.

10. See *The Hamwood Papers,* p. 321.

11. Ibid., passim.

12. Quoted in Mavor, *The Ladies of Llangollen,* pp. 97, 98 from the Ormonde manuscript. Mavor suggests that "such meticulous recordings of migraines and vomits could be read as more significant than the roboust interest taken by contemporaries in such matters; more significant than the unsophisticated acknowledgement of '. . . purest kindness and most endearing love.' They could be read as a code; as the only permissible expression of a yet more intimate relationship; or as the unconscious expression of the desire for such a relationship," p. 98.

13. See Nancy F. Cott, "Passionlessness: An Interpretation of Victorian Sexual Ideology, 1790–1850," *Signs,* Vol. 4 (1978), pp. 219–36.

14. As they grew older both women assumed a quasi-transvestite appearance.

15. Quoted in *The Ladies of Llangollen,* pp. 73–74.

16. Claire Tomalin, *The Life and Death of Mary Wollstonecraft* (London: Harcourt Brace Jovanovich, 1974), pp. 71–72.

17. While Eleanor records having read *Les mémoires du Comte de Grammont* on September 16, 1788 (*The Hamwood Papers,* p. 133), she makes no mention whatever of the Miss Hobart incident described at length in that work (see page 42 here). It is probable that one who was concerned with the difficulties that female homosexuals might encounter would have noted the case, especially since such detailed descriptions of accusations against lesbians were rare in literature at that time.

18. *The Hamwood Papers,* p. 257.

19. *Thraliana: The Diary of Mrs. Hester Lynch Thrale (Later Mrs. Piozzi): 1776–1809,* 2 vols., ed. Katharine C. Balderston (Oxford: Clarendon Press, 1942), Vol. II, pp. 740, 786, 949. Observing the existence of lesbianism in London and Bath, Mrs. Thrale called the first, "A Sink for every Sin" and the second, "a Cage of these unclean Birds," *Thraliana,* Vol. II, p. 949.

20. *The Intimate Letters of Hester Piozzi and Penelope Pennington,* ed. Oswald G. Knapp (London: John Lane, 1914). Twenty-four of her letters to Sarah and Eleanor are preserved, *Thraliana,* Vol. II, p. 957n.

21. In fact, it would not be easy to find a less retiring couple than these two. While they may originally have sought to avoid the world, the world soon sought them out. On one not-atypical day (August 5, 1821), Eleanor records they were visited by "Mr. Loyd of Rhagatt, Mr., Mrs., Miss and Mr. Augustus Morgan in the morning, then Lord Ormonde and Lord Thurles, then Lord Maryborough and Lord Burguish to Luncheon, then Lord, Lady Ormonde and Lord Thurles to dinner. Then Lady Harriet, Lady Anne, Lady Louisa, Mr. Walter, Mr. James, Mr. Richard, Mr. Charles Butler to Supper. Prince Paul Esterhazy for a short time in the evening, and Lord and Lady Ormonde slept in our State

Apartment," *The Hamwood Papers,* p. 377. Visitors seemed to be attracted especially by Eleanor's sharp wit and entertaining conversation, and to the superb housekeeping of the cottagers. Their life-style had a good deal in common with that of Gertrude Stein and Alice B. Toklas in the twentieth century.

22. *Thraliana,* Vol. II, p. 949.

23. *A Series of Letters Between Mrs. Elizabeth Carter and Miss Catherine Talbot,* Vol. I, p. 309. N.b., "Mrs." was a title of respect given to any woman over thirty in the eighteenth century and did not indicate marital status.

24. Ibid., Vol. II, p. 29.

25. See, for example, *Letters from Mrs. Elizabeth Carter to Mrs. Montagu Between the Years 1755 and 1800,* 3 vols., ed. Montagu Pennington (London: E. C. and J. Rivington, 1817), Vol. I, p. 25, a letter dated 1759; and *A Series of Letters Between Mrs. Elizabeth Carter and Miss Catherine Talbot,* Vol. III, p. 204, a letter dated November 13, 1769.

26. *A Series of Letters Between Mrs. Elizabeth Carter and Miss Catherine Talbot,* Vol. I, pp. 2–3.

27. Ibid., p. 4.

28. Ibid., p. 6.

29. Ibid., p. 9.

30. The letters suggest that Catherine consistently tried to calm Elizabeth's passion toward her, whenever it reared its head: see, for example, the letters of June 25, 1751 (Vol. II, pp. 36–37) and August 12, 1752 (Vol. II, pp. 90–91). Catherine seems to have been embarrassed by any great tribute given her, but there is absolutely no indication that this stemmed from the fact that her lover was a woman.

31. *A Series of Letters Between Mrs. Elizabeth Carter and Miss Catherine Talbot,* Vol. I, pp. 12–13, 189, and Vol. II, pp. 36–37.

32. Ibid., Vol. III, p. 51.

33. Ibid., pp. 57–58.

34. Ibid., pp. 55–56.

35. The only record that exists of heterosexual attachment for her outside of her unhappy marriage is her correspondence with Lord Bath, begun when she was in her forties and he was in his eighties. According to her biographer, Reginald Blunt, the intensity of the relationship, which lasted for four years until Lord Bath's death in 1764, was enough to cause people to talk and Elizabeth to defend angrily the "purity" of her reputation. Her other intense relationships were with women; see *Mrs. Montagu: Queen of the Blues, Her Letters and Friendships from 1762–1800,* ed. Reginald Blunt (London: Constable and Co., n.d.), Vol. I, p. 108.

36. Ibid., pp. 297–98.

37. Ibid., Vol. II, pp. 363–64.

38. *Letters from Mrs. Elizabeth Carter to Mrs. Montagu,* Vol. I, p. 184.

39. Ibid., p. 195.

40. Ibid., p. 210.

41. Ibid., p. 229.

42. Ibid., p. 241.

43. Ibid., p. 243.

44. Ibid., pp. 279–80.

45. *Letters of Anna Seward: Written Between the Years 1784 and 1807*, 6 vols., ed. Walter Scott (Edinburgh: Constable and Co., 1811), Vol. III, pp. 29–30.

46. Frederick A. Pottle, in preface to Margaret Ashmun, *The Singing Swan: An Account of Anna Seward and her Acquaintance with Dr. Johnson, Boswell and Others of Their Time* (New Haven: Yale University Press, 1931), pp. x–xi.

47. Ashmun, *The Singing Swan*, pp. 17–18.

48. *Letters of Anna Seward*, Vol. IV, p. 217.

49. Ibid.

50. *The Poetical Works of Anna Seward*, Vol. III, p. 134.

51. Ibid., p. 135.

52. Ibid., p. 140.

53. Ibid., p. 133.

54. Ashmun, *The Singing Swan*, pp. 28–29.

55. *The Poetical Works of Anna Seward*, Vol. I, pp. 76–77.

56. Ibid., pp. 82–83.

57. It is equally doubtful that Anna Seward had a sexual relationship with John Saville, to whom she gave in her middle-age, according to a twentieth-century scholar, "the passionate and unremitting devotion of her heart." Anna's letters often refer to her "pure and disinterested attachment to his worth," and there is no reason to disbelieve her. She praised him openly and did what she could do to further his career as a church singer. They seem to have been exceptionally devoted platonic friends. But during all that time, Anna's obsession with the long-dead Honora continued.

58. *The Poetical Works of Anna Seward*, Vol. III, p. 152.

59. Ibid., p. 153.

60. Ibid., Vol. I, pp. 100–03.

61. Ibid., Vol. III, p. 401.

62. *Letters of Anna Seward*, Vol. I, p. 6.

63. Ibid., Vol. VI, p. 7.

64. Anna Seward had several other romantic attachments to women, among them Elizabeth Cornwallis, Mrs. Mompesson, Penelope Weston, and Miss Fern, with whom she lived in the early nineteenth century, and to whom she wrote in February 1806, "My health and my heart have need of you." But none of these passions was as intense and enduring as her love for Honora.

65. *Letters of Anna Seward*, Vol. IV, p. 164.

66. Ibid., pp. 16–17.

67. *The Poetical Works of Anna Seward*, Vol. III, pp. 70–80.

68. Ibid., p. 107.

69. *Collected Letters of Mary Wollstonecraft*, ed. Ralph Wardle (Ithaca, N.Y.: Cornell University Press, 1979), p. 62.

70. Ibid., p. 67.

71. *Memoirs of Mary Wollstonecraft* (1798; reprinted London: Constable and Co., 1927), ed. W. Clark Durant, p. 19.

72. *Collected Letters of Mary Wollstonecraft*, p. 73.

73. *Memoirs of Mary Wollstonecraft*, pp. 30–31.

74. See, for example, Eleanor Flexner, *Mary Wollstonecraft: A Biography*

(New York: Coward, McCann, and Geoghegan, 1972), p. 39.

75. *Memoirs of Mary Wollstonecraft,* pp. 18 and 35.

76. Ibid., p. 72.

77. Ibid.

78. *Letters Written During a Short Residence in Sweden, Norway, and Denmark* (London, 1796), p. 203.

79. *Collected Letters of Mary Wollstonecraft,* pp. 90–91.

80. Ralph M. Wardle, *Mary Wollstonecraft: A Critical Biography* (Lawrence: University of Kansas Press, 1951), p. 41.

81. Ibid., pp. 41–42. Wardle admits that "on the surface Waterhouse seems like the last man in the world who would have attracted Mary Wollstonecraft," but since he was the only man around, Wardle concludes, "apparently he did," p. 37. Godwin does not mention a relationship with Waterhouse. Since Mary told him the most intimate and embarrassing details of her other affairs, it is unlikely that she would have kept from him an affair with Waterhouse which supposedly accounted for a deep depression lasting for years. Furthermore, as Wardle himself characterizes her correspondence with George, Mary inundated him "with advice against prodigality, homilies on the ardors of the true Christian life, and assurances that she had 'a motherly tenderness' for him" (ibid., p. 40). That being the case, it is unlikely she would have confessed to him an affair so spicy that a later hand expunged all references to it in order to save her reputation.

82. Tomalin, *The Life and Death of Mary Wollstonecraft,* p. 18.

83. While this chapter concentrates on eighteenth-century England, recent examinations of the letters and diaries of eighteenth-century American women verify that romantic friendships were conducted with the same intensity and passion across the ocean. See, for example, Laurie Crumpacker, "The Journal of Esther Burr Addressed to Miss Prince of Boston," Ph.D. dissertation, Boston University, 1976; and Nancy Cott, *The Bonds of Womanhood: "Woman's Sphere" in New England, 1780–1835* (New Haven: Yale University Press, 1977).

Part IIA. *Chapter 1.* THE ASEXUAL WOMAN

1. Transcripts of the trial are collected in *Miss Marianne Woods and Miss Jane Pirie Against Dame Helen Cumming Gordon* (New York: Arno Press, 1975). Lillian Hellman based *The Children's Hour* on a recounting of the trial she had read in William Roughead, *Bad Companions* (New York: Duffield and Green, 1931), pp. 111–46.

2. *Miss Marianne Woods and Miss Jane Pirie . . . ,* "Speeches of the Judges," p. 94. (Note that each section of this text is numbered separately.)

3. "Leana and Clonarium," *The Works of Lucian,* trans. M. D. MacLeod (Cambridge: Harvard University Press, 1961), Vol. III, pp. 379–85.

4. *Miss Marianne Woods and Miss Jane Pirie . . . ,* "State of the Process," p. 14.

5. Ibid., "The Additional Petition of Miss Marianne Woods . . . ," p. 38.

6. Ibid., "Speeches of the Judges," p. 12.

7. Ibid., p. 20.

8. Ibid., p. 41.

9. Ibid., pp. 55–57.

10. Ibid., p. 59.

11. Ibid., "The Additional Petition of Miss Marianne Woods . . . ," pp. 152–53.

12. Ibid., "State of the Process," p. 27.

13. Recent scholarship attempts to contradict these assumptions about Victorian sexuality, but the evidence offered is generally too narrow to convince the reader that most middle-class women were any more sexual than they have been depicted as being in Victorian literature. See, for example, introduction to *The Mosher Survey*, eds. James MaHood and Kristine Wenburg (New York: Arno Press, 1980), a nineteenth-century study of the sexual attitudes of forty-five women who were all self-selected, many of them wives of Stanford University faculty members; and Carl N. Degler, "What Ought to Be and What Was: Women's Sexuality in the Nineteenth Century, *American Historical Review*, Vol. 79 (December 1974), pp. 1467–90.

14. Ibid., "Speeches of the Judges," p. 60.

15. Ibid., "The Additional Petition . . . ," p. 28. This view also prevailed in more sophisticated places and times. In Daniel Defoe's *Roxana, or the Fortunate Mistress* (1724), for example, Roxana's lover arrives unexpectedly late at night, and finds her in bed (lacking her shift) with Amy. He indicates his relief that " 'tis not a Man-Bedfellow" and thinks nothing of her being naked with a woman bedfellow. It appears that Defoe himself thought nothing of such a situation!

16. *Miss Marianne Woods and Miss Jane Pirie . . .* , "Speeches of the Judges," p. 2.

17. Ibid., p. 92.

18. Cited in Henry Spencer Ashbee (Pisanus Fraxi), *Index Librorum Prohibitorum* (1877; reprinted New York: Documentary Books, 1962), pp. 340–42.

19. *The Phoenix of Sodom, or The Vere Street Coterie* (London, 1813).

20. Cited in Ashbee, *Index Librorum Prohibitorum*, pp. 334–38.

21. Gordon Rattray Taylor's *The Angel-Makers: A Study in the Psychological Origins of Historical Change, 1750–1850* (London: Heinemann, 1958) demonstrates that the extreme, straitlaced view of sex we associate with Queen Victoria's era had long been prevalent among the middle classes but became even more dominant in the nineteenth century as the middle classes became more influential in all areas of public life that create public opinion.

22. Cited in André Breton, "Lettres inédites de Flora Tristan," *Le surréalisme même*, Vol. 3 (Autumn 1957), p. 7.

23. John Morley, "Mr. Swinburne's New Poems: *Poems and Ballads*," *Saturday Review*, August 4, 1866.

24. Allan McLane Hamilton, "The Civil Responsibility of Sexual Perverts," *American Journal of Insanity*, Vol. 52 (April 1896), pp. 503–09.

Part IIA. *Chapter 2.* KINDRED SPIRITS

1. See Barbara Welter, "The Cult of True Womanhood, 1820–1860," *Dimity Convictions: The American Woman in the Nineteenth Century* (Athens: Ohio University Press, 1976), pp. 21–41.

2. Ronald Pearsall, *The Worm in the Bud: The World of Victorian Sexuality* (Toronto: Macmillan, 1969), p. 227.

3. G. J. Barker-Benfield, *The Horrors of the Half-Known Life: Male Attitudes Toward Women and Sexuality in Nineteenth Century America* (New York: Harper and Row, 1976). See also a discussion of this male-female division in Ann Douglas, *The Feminization of American Culture* (New York: Alfred A. Knopf, 1977).

4. Thomas Branagan, *The Excellence of Female Character Vindicated* (Philadelphia, 1808), p. 161.

5. John Ellis, *Marriage and its Violations* (New York, 1860), p. 21.

6. Henry N. Guernsey, *Plain Talk on Avoided Subjects* (Philadelphia: F. A. Davis, 1882), p. 103.

7. Nancy F. Cott, "Passionlessness: An Interpretation of Victorian Sexual Ideology," *Signs: Journal of Women in Culture and Society*, Vol. IV, No. 2 (Winter 1978), pp. 219–36.

8. See, for example, Douglas, *The Feminization of American Culture*, and Nancy F. Cott, *The Bonds of Womanhood: "Woman's Sphere" in New England, 1780–1835* (New Haven: Yale University Press, 1977).

9. Henry David Thoreau, *Friendship* (reprinted New York: Thomas Crowell, 1906). The term "romantic friendship" was apparently used to describe male-male relationships as well as female-female relationships in mid-nineteenth century America. See Francis Parkman, *The Oregon Trail* (1846), quoted in Jonathan Katz, *Gay American History: Lesbians and Gay Men in the U.S.A.* (New York: Thomas Crowell, 1976), pp. 303–04.

10. *New England Quarterly*, Vol. XXXVI, No. 1 (March 1963), pp. 23–41, and *Signs: Journal of Women in Culture and Society*, Vol. 1, No. 1 (Autumn 1975), pp. 1–29.

11. See, for example, Judith Becker Ranlett, "Sorority and Community: Women's Answer to a Changing Massachusetts, 1865–1895," Ph.D. dissertation, Brandeis University, 1974 (especially the discussion of the views of female superiority, pp. 41–42 and pp. 120–21).

12. Margaret Fuller Ossoli, *Women in the Nineteenth Century and Kindred Papers Relating to the Sphere, Condition and Duties of Women* (Boston, 1855), pp. 342–43. Fuller's love of other women is discussed at greater length in my review of Bell Chevigny, *The Woman and the Myth: Margaret Fuller's Life and Writings* in *Journal of Homosexuality*, Vol. IV, No. 1 (Fall 1978), pp. 110–12.

13. Anna Cogswell Wood, *The Story of a Friendship: A Memoir* (New York: Knickerbocker Press, 1901), p. 4.

14. Ibid., p. 22.

15. Ibid., p. 311.

16. William Rounseville Alger, *The Friendships of Women* (Boston: Roberts Brothers, 1868); see, for example, pp. 346–58. These expressions of trust were common in love letters between women. See, for example, Helen Morton to Mary Hopkinson, July 24, 1872: "I, the inside I, am at home, at ease, and clear with you, as if heart and soul had found blue sky and sunshine" (Radcliffe Women's Archives, Schlesinger Library, Radcliffe College, Cambridge, Mass.).

17. Ibid., p. 364.

18. Ibid., p. viii.

19. Ibid., p. 365.

20. See John Ruskin, "Of Queen's Gardens," in *Sesame and Lilies: Three Lectures* (1865) for one of the most popular nineteenth-century English discussions of what that sphere was.

21. Meredith's contemporary, Edith Arnold (a niece of Matthew Arnold) also wrote about love between women which is complicated by the "natural force" of heterosexuality, but female love wins out in the end. In her novel *Platonics: A Study* (1894), two romantic friends, Kit and Susan, become interested for a time in a man. Kit, the younger of the two, marries him after Susan refuses his first proposal. But for these women the heterosexual passion is transitory or unsatisfactory, while their love for each other is immutable. Kit realizes, "There are some women whom no man's love can compensate for the loss of a woman's and Kit was one of them." Susan, too, comes to acknowledge her own priorities. During a fatal illness, she writes to Kit of her brief heterosexual interest, "All that has faded away. Passion has died as it must always die, and at the end of it all I am only conscious of my love for you. The past is all lit with it—I cannot realize the time when it was not; it holds a torch up to the future—for its cessation is unthinkable."

22. In K. A. McKenzie, *Edith Simcox and George Eliot* (New York: Oxford University Press, 1961), p. 102.

23. Ibid., p. 38.

24. Unpublished paper, 1979, Women's Studies Program, San Diego State University, Calif.

25. *Selections from the Letters of Geraldine Endsor Jewsbury to Jane Welsh Carlyle*, ed. Mrs. Alexander Ireland (London: Longmans, Green and Co., 1892), p. 22. Jane Carlyle's letters to Geraldine Jewsbury were destroyed by Geraldine just before her death. See also Virginia Woolf's discussion of their relationship in "Geraldine and Jane," *Times Literary Supplement* (February 28, 1929).

26. *Selections from the Letters of Geraldine Endsor Jewsbury* . . . , p. 38.

27. Ibid., p. 58.

28. Ibid., p. 88.

29. Ibid., pp. 333–34.

30. Ibid., p. 43.

31. See, for example, a letter to Mrs. Russell, January 16, 1858, referring to Geraldine's involvement with a Mr. Mantell: "She has been making a considerable fool of herself, to speak plainly, and has got estranged from me utterly for the time being," quoted in Susanne Howe, *Geraldine Jewsbury: Her Life and Errors* (London: George Allen and Unwin, 1935), p. 162.

32. Ibid., p. 57.

33. *Selections from the Letters of Geraldine Jewsbury* . . . , pp. 347–49.

34. See a more extensive discussion of this work in my article, "Female Same-sex Relationships in Novels by Henry Wadsworth Longfellow, Oliver Wendell Holmes, and Henry James," *New England Quarterly*, Vol. LI, No. 3 (September 1978), pp. 309–32.

35. Edward Carpenter, *The Intermediate Sex: A Study of Some Transitional Types of Men and Women* (New York: Mitchell Kinnerley, 1912), p. 18.

36. Martha Dickinson Bianchi, *The Life and Letters of Emily Dickinson* (Boston: Houghton Mifflin and Co., 1924).

37. Martha Dickinson Bianchi, *Emily Dickinson Face to Face: Unpublished Letters with Notes and Reminiscences* (Boston: Houghton Mifflin and Co., 1932).

38. I discuss at greater length Dickinson's emotional involvement with Sue Gilbert and other women in my articles, "Emily Dickinson's Letters to Sue Gilbert," *Massachusetts Review*, Vol. XVIII, No. 2 (September 1977), pp. 197–225 and "Emily Dickinson's Homoerotic Poetry," *Higginson Journal*, Vol. 18 (June 1978), pp. 19–27.

39. *The Letters of Emily Dickinson*, eds. Thomas H. Johnson and Theodora Ward (Cambridge: Harvard University Press, 1958), letter 73.

40. Bianchi, *Emily Dickinson Face to Face*, p. 184.

41. Ibid., p. 216.

42. Johnson and Ward, *The Letters of Emily Dickinson*, letter 94.

43. Bianchi, *Emily Dickinson Face to Face*, p. 218.

44. Johnson and Ward, *The Letters of Emily Dickinson*, letter 96.

45. Clement Wood, for example, argued in a study published one year after Lowell's death that she was not a good poet because many of her poems were homosexual and therefore did not "word a common cry of many hearts." Thus he concluded that she may qualify "as an impassioned singer of her own desires; and she may well be laureate also of as many as stand beside her," but nonlesbian readers will find nothing in her verse, *Amy Lowell* (New York: Harold Vinal, 1926), pp. 13, 173.

Part IIA. *Chapter 3.* NEW WOMEN

1. Andrew Sinclair, *The Better Half: The Emancipation of the American Woman* (New York: Harper and Row, 1965), suggests that the English women's movement was more militant earlier because many "ladies" made up its ranks: "The sense of superior birth often frees people to act against convention. Some of the militancy of the English lady can be explained by her pure knowledge that she was a lady—while her American sister was often not sure enough of her status to behave unlike a lady," p. 284. However, by virtue of their numbers alone, English aristocratic women could not have made a movement. They needed the voices of the middle class.

2. Troy Female Seminary opened in 1821 for "higher education," but its program was not largely academic.

3. Duncan Crow, *The Victorian Woman* (London: George Allen and Unwin, 1971), p. 326.

4. Sinclair, *The Better Half*, pp. 119–20.

5. Frances M. Trollope, *Domestic Manners of the Americans* (1832; reprinted New York: Howard Wilford Bell, 1964), pp. 54–55, 135.

6. *The Industrial and Social Position of Women in the Middle and Lower Ranks* (London, 1857), pp. 21–22.

7. Edward Shorter, *The Making of the Modern Family* (New York: Basic Books, 1975), pp. 55–62.

8. John Boyd-Kinnear, "The Social Position of Women in the Present Age," in *Woman's Work and Woman's Culture: A Series of Essays*, ed. Josephine E. Butler (London: Macmillan and Co., 1869), p. 335.

9. Even mid-nineteenth-century women writers, whose fortunes were made advocating that the only female organs worth cultivating were heart and womb, understood that women of the middle classes needed more to do for their own sakes and for the well-being of society. See, for example, Sarah Stickney Ellis, *The Women of England: Social Duties and Domestic Habits* (New York: D. Appleton, 1839), pp. 265ff, and Dinah Maria Mulock Craik, *A Woman's Thoughts About Women* (New York: Rudd and Carleton, 1858), pp. 14–15.

10. Sinclair, *The Better Half*, pp. 280–81. In the decade immediately preceding 1848, there was much ferment of feminist ideas, although little semblance of organization. In America, for example, Sarah Grimke published *Letters on the Equality of the Sexes and the Condition of Women* in 1838. The 1841 *Edinburgh Review* (Vol. 73, pp. 189–209) lists six British books on women's rights published between 1839 and 1840.

11. Werner Thönnessen, *The Emancipation of Women: The Rise and Decline of the Women's Movement in German Social Democracy, 1863–1933*, trans. Joris de Bres (Frankfurt am Main: Pluto Press, 1969), p. 16.

12. Evelyne Sullerot, *Histoire de la presse féminine en France des origines à 1848* (Paris: Armand Colin, 1966). French feminist groups also emerged through the socialist movement beginning in the 1830's; see Marguerite Thibert, *Le féminisme dans le socialisme français, 1830–1850* (Paris: Marcel Giard, 1926), Sylvie Weil-Sayre and Mary Collins, *Les Femmes en France* (Paris: Des Femmes, 1977); and Maïté Albistur and Daniel Armogathe, *L'Histoire du féminisme français* (Paris: Des Femmes, 1977).

13. Simone de Beauvoir discusses the comparative timidity of the French feminist movement in *The Second Sex* (1949; reprinted Vintage Books, 1974), pp. 137–39.

14. Anna Rueling, "Welches Interesse Hat die Frauenbewegung an der Loesung des Homosexuellen Problems?" *Jahrbuch für Sexuelle Zwischenstufen*, Vol. VII (Leipzig, 1905), p. 137, translated in Lillian Faderman and Brigitte Eriksson, *Lesbian Feminism in Turn-of-the-Century Germany* (Weatherby Lake, Mo.: Naiad Press, 1980).

15. Ibid., p. 132.

16. Wanda Fraiken Neff, *Victorian Working Women: An Historical and Literary Study of Women in British Industries and Professions, 1832–1850* (New York: Columbia University Press, 1929), p. 12.

17. J. A. and Olive Banks, *Feminism and Family Planning in Victorian England* (Liverpool, England: Liverpool University Press, 1964), p. 27.

18. Ibid.

19. Clara E. Collet, *Educated Working Women: Essays on the Economic Position of Women Workers in the Middle Classes* (London: P. S. King and Son, 1902), p. 30.

20. See, for example, Andrew Ure, *Philosophy of Manufactures* (London,

1861), p. 475, who justifies the lower wages paid to women workers by asserting that if they made too much money, they would turn their backs on wifely and motherly duties, and Mrs. Lynn Linton, *The Autobiography of Christopher Kirkland* (1885; reprinted New York: Garland Publishing Co., 1976), p. 11, in which she states that women who demand equal work opportunities will "break up the cradles for firewood."

21. Caroline Dall, *"Woman's Right to Labor": or, Low Wages and Hard Work* (Boston, 1860), p. 104.

22. Middle-class women elsewhere had not much better choices. When George Sand left her husband in 1831 and hoped to become financially independent, she realized that the only jobs open to her were that of governess, actress, or writer. She chose the latter because the first meant that at best her children would be treated as poor relations in the family in which she worked, and she did not feel she could succeed on the stage because most actresses were high-priced courtesans too, and her age (late twenties) would have hampered her ability to compete in that area; see Samuel Edwards, *George Sand: A Biography of the First Modern, Liberated Woman* (New York: David McKay, 1972). Lower-class Frenchwomen had many more choices than their middle-class counterparts, although all their job opportunities were, of course, very low paying. In a mid-nineteenth-century article in *Household Words*, "More Work for the Ladies," the author points to the diversity of employments for Frenchwomen: ticket sellers at the railroad, telegraphers, baggage inspectors, attendants at theaters, produce sellers—and argues that the limited job opportunities for Englishwomen of a comparable class should be likewise expanded; quoted in Neff, *Victorian Working Women*, p. 111.

23. Reverend G. Butler, "Education as a Profession for Women," in Butler, *Woman's Work and Woman's Culture*, p. 56.

24. Crow, *The Victorian Woman*, pp. 250 and 327.

25. Mary Kathleen Benét, *The Secretarial Ghetto* (New York: McGraw-Hill, 1972), p. 35.

26. Anna E. Dickinson, *A Ragged Register* (New York: Harper and Bros., 1879), p. 186.

27. Collet, "Through Fifty Years: The Economic Progress of Women," in *Educated Working Women*, p. 137.

28. Many professions continued to create barriers throughout the nineteenth century. For example, women could not practice law in England until 1919; they were forbidden to become engineers until 1899.

29. See, for example, Charles McCool Snyder, *Dr. Mary Walker: The Little Lady in Pants* (New York: Vantage Press, 1962).

30. Sophia Jex-Blake, "Medicine as a Profession for Women," in *Woman's Work and Woman's Culture*, pp. 78–120.

31. Crow, *The Victorian Woman*, p. 327.

32. *A Woman of the Century*, eds. Frances Willard and Mary Livermore (Buffalo, N.Y., 1893).

33. Amanda Carolyn Northrop, "The Successful Woman in America," *Popular Science Monthly*, Vol. LXIV (1904), pp. 239–44.

34. Emilie Hutchinson, "Women and the Ph.D.," *American Association of*

University Women Journal, Vol. XXII (1928), pp. 19–22.

35. Letter to her sister, 1846, quoted in Judith Becker Ranlett, "Sorority and Community: Women's Answer to a Changing Massachusetts, 1865–1895," Ph.D. dissertation, Brandeis University, 1974, p. 32.

36. Louisa May Alcott, "Happy Women," *The New York Ledger*, Vol. XXIV (April 11, 1868).

37. *Charlotte Cushman: Her Letters and Memories of Her Life*, ed. Emma Stebbins (Boston: Houghton Mifflin and Co., 1881), pp. 182–83.

38. Manuscript collection of Harriet Levy, Chapter XX, unpublished stories, Bancroft Library, University of California at Berkeley, pp. 54–56.

39. Edward Carpenter, *The Intermediate Sex: A Study of Some Transitional Types of Men and Women* (New York: Mitchell Kennerley, 1912), pp. 72–73. A number of contemporary historians have speculated about the high degree of lesbianism in the nineteenth-century women's movement, but they have not generally understood its significance as a step toward female independence. Thus they reduce it to its most obvious and trivial terms, e.g., Susan B. Anthony writing Anna Dickinson on March 18, 1868, that she has a *"double bed*—and big enough and good enough to take you *in"*; see, for example, Sinclair, *The Better Half*; Crow, *The Victorian Woman*; and George Dangerfield, *The Strange Death of Liberal England* (London: MacGibbon and Kee, 1968).

Part IIA. *Chapter 4.* Boston Marriage

1. Helen Huntington Howe, *The Gentle Americans: Biography of a Breed* (New York: Harper and Row, 1965), p. 83.

2. *The Notebooks of Henry James*, eds. F. O. Matthiessen and Kenneth R. Murdock (New York: Oxford University Press, 1947), p. 47.

3. I comment on these points further in my article, "Female Same-sex Relationships in Novels by Henry Wadsworth Longfellow, Oliver Wendell Holmes, and Henry James," *New England Quarterly*, Vol. LI, No. 3 (September 1978), pp. 309–32.

4. F. W. Dupee, *Henry James* (New York: William Sloane Associates, 1951), p. 152.

5. Louis Auchincloss, *Reading Henry James* (Minneapolis: University of Minnesota Press, 1975), p. 42. See also Robert McLean, *"The Bostonians*: New England Pastoral," *Papers in Language and Literature*, No. 7 (1971), p. 374, and Theodore C. Miller, "The Muddled Politics of Henry James's *The Bostonians*," *Georgia Review*, Vol. XXVI, p. 338.

6. Auchincloss, *Reading Henry James*, p. 76.

7. McLean, *"The Bostonians*: New England Pastoral," p. 381.

8. Ibid., p. 376.

9. Michael Egan states that James did not become interested in Ibsen until 1889, four years after the publication of *The Bostonians*. But Egan uses as evidence for this date a letter that James wrote to his friend Edmund Gosse, requesting more information about Ibsen after Gosse's article on the playwright in the *Fortnightly Review*; see *Henry James: The Ibsen Years* (London, 1972), pp. 37–38. However, Gosse had been for twenty years previous Ibsen's most

vocal advocate in England. In view of the friendship between James and Gosse, it is likely that James would have been familiar with Ibsen well before he made his request for more information.

10. McLean, "*The Bostonians*: New England Pastoral," p. 381.

11. "*The Bostonians*" in *The Air of Reality: New Essays on Henry James*, ed. John Goode (London: Methuen and Co., 1972), p. 76.

12. James was sympathetic to male homosexuality. Writing to Edmund Gosse about John Addington Symonds's defense of homosexuality in *A Problem in Modern Ethics*, he thanks Gosse for "bringing me those marvelous outpourings," [quoted in Leon Edel, *Henry James: The Treacherous Years: 1895–1901* (Philadelphia: Lippincott, 1969), p. 124]. When Symonds died in 1893, James referred to him as a "much-loved, much doing, passionately out-giving man" (ibid., p. 127). In 1895 he protested against Oscar Wilde's imprisonment for homosexuality, and he appealed to a member of Parliament to ease Wilde's prison conditions (ibid., pp. 128–30). In the last volume of his James biography, *Henry James: The Master* (London: R. Hart-Davis, 1972), Leon Edel also shows that James himself was in love with at least two young men.

13. *The Diary of Alice James,* ed. Leon Edel (New York: Dodd, Mead and Co., 1964), p. 10.

14. Ibid., pp. 10–11.

15. Ibid., p. 13.

16. Ibid., p. 181.

17. Ibid., p. 13.

18. Gay Wilson Allen, *William James: A Biography* (New York: Viking Press, 1967), p. 227.

19. Mark A. DeWolfe Howe, *Memories of a Hostess: A Chronicle of Eminent Friendships Drawn Chiefly from the Diaries of Mrs. James T. Fields* (Boston: Atlantic Monthly Press, 1922), p. 283.

20. Helen Howe, *The Gentle Americans,* p. 84.

21. Ibid., pp. 83, 185ff.

22. Francis Otto Matthiessen, *Sarah Orne Jewett* (Boston: Houghton Mifflin and Co., 1929), p. 72.

23. In Sarah Orne Jewett, *The Mate of Daylight* (Boston: Houghton Mifflin and Co., 1883).

24. Sarah Orne Jewett, *A Country Doctor* (Boston: Houghton Mifflin and Co., 1884), pp. 336–37.

25. Sarah Orne Jewett Manuscript Collection, Houghton Library, Harvard University, Cambridge, Mass. I wish to acknowledge Glenda Hobbs, who called my attention to the Jewett material at Harvard University through a paper she delivered at the Modern Language Association Convention, December 1977.

26. Sarah Orne Jewett's diary for May 24, 1871, Houghton Library, Harvard University, Cambridge, Mass.

27. "Love and Friendship," second (untitled) draft is dated August 23, 1880, Sarah Orne Jewett Manuscript Collection, Houghton Library, Harvard University, Cambridge, Mass.

28. See my article, "Emily Dickinson's Homoerotic Poetry," *Higginson Journal,* No. 18 (First half, 1978), pp. 19–27.

29. *Letters of Sarah Orne Jewett,* ed. Annie Fields (Boston: Houghton Mifflin and Co., 1911), p. 11.

30. Ibid., pp. 16–17.

31. Ibid., pp. 17–18.

32. Ibid., pp. 246–47.

Part IIA. *Chapter 5.* LOVE AND "WOMEN WHO LIVE BY THEIR BRAINS"

1. E. Krause, "The Truth About Me," *Jahrbuch für sexuelle Zwischenstufen,* Vol. III (Leipzig, 1901), pp. 292–307, reprinted in Lillian Faderman and Brigitte Eriksson, *Lesbian-Feminism in Turn-of-the-Century Germany* (Weatherby Lake, Mo.: Naiad Press, 1980).

2. E. O. Somerville and Martin Ross, *Irish Memories* (New York: Longmans, Green and Co., 1917), p. 326.

3. Christopher St. John, *Ethel Smythe: A Biography* (London: Longmans, Green and Co., 1959), p. 193. Somerville's claims were so convincing to Ethel Smythe, the composer, that she too began trying to contact her beloved dead.

4. Somerville and Ross, *Irish Memories,* p. 309.

5. In Geraldine Cummins, *Dr. E. O. Somerville: A Biography* (London: Andrew Dakers Ltd., 1952), pp. 180–86.

6. Ibid., p. 7.

7. Maurice Collis, *Somerville and Ross* (London: Faber and Faber, 1968). Collis could not find even a hint of a similar interest in Somerville's life. According to him, her only passion before meeting Ross was for another female cousin, whose death cast her into despondency for some time.

8. Somerville, *Irish Memories,* p. 133.

9. In Cummins, *Dr. E. O. Somerville,* p. 185.

10. Somerville, *Irish Memories,* p. 125.

11. Cummins, *Dr. E. O. Somerville,* p. 104.

12. Quoted in Betty Askwith, *Two Victorian Families* (London: Chatto and Windus, 1971), p. 192.

13. Mary Sturgeon, *Michael Field* (London: George G. Harrap, 1922), p. 27.

14. T. and D. C. Sturge Moore, Introduction, *Works and Days: From the Journal of Michael Field* (London: Murray, 1933), p. xvi.

15. Michael Field, *Underneath the Bow* (1893; third edition, Portland, Me.: Thomas B. Mosher, 1898), p. 50.

16. See, for example, Sturgeon, *Michael Field,* pp. 75–78.

17. Sturge Moore, *Works and Days,* p. 16.

18. Quoted in Sturgeon, *Michael Field,* p. 47.

19. See, for example, the letter to Miss Louie Ellis, quoted in Sturgeon, *Michael Field,* p. 75.

20. See, for example, Sturge Moore, *Works and Days,* p. 57.

21. Michael Field, *Long Ago* (1889; reprinted, Portland, Me.: Thomas B. Mosher, 1907), p. xxv.

22. *The Wattlefold: Unpublished Poems by Michael Field,* ed. Emily C. Fortey (Oxford: Basil Blakwell, 1930), p. 69.

23. Ibid., p. 193.

24. Michael Field, *Mystic Trees* (London: Eveleigh Nash, 1913), p. 146.

25. Sturgeon, *Michael Field*, p. 61.

26. Her novels are romantic and soppy, but, surprisingly, despite the fact that they were consciously responsive to the demands of popular fiction (which meant that the female characters' most important pursuit was love), they were also filled with feminist sentiment. Corelli claimed that women were equal to any task men might perform, she denounced women's sufferings under tyrant subjugators, and she depicted wives who were forced into martyrdom by their husbands' wrong doings.

27. Bertha Vyver, *Memoirs of Marie Corelli* (London: Alston Rivers, 1930), p. 97.

28. William Stuart Scott, *Marie Corelli: The Story of a Friendship* (London: Hutchinson, 1955), p. 93.

29. Vyver, *Memoirs of Marie Corelli*, p. 97.

30. Eileen Biglund, *Marie Corelli: The Woman and the Legend* (London: Jarrolds, 1953), p. 218.

31. Vyver, *Memoirs of Marie Corelli*, pp. 96–97.

32. Scott, *Marie Corelli*, pp. 198–99.

33. The most complete biography of Octave Thanet is George McMichael, *Journey to Obscurity: The Life of Octave Thanet* (Lincoln: University of Nebraska Press, 1965). Thanet's short story, "My Lorelei," in *The Western*, New Series, VI (Jan. 1880), 22, contains her most extensive literary discussion of romantic friendship.

34. *Reminiscences of Rosa Bonheur*, ed. Theodore Stanton (1910; reprinted New York: Hacker Art Books, 1976), p. 7.

35. Ibid., p. 33.

36. Ibid., pp. 97–98.

37. Ibid., p. 102.

38. Ibid., p. 269.

39. Ibid.

40. Louisa May Alcott, untitled romance, unfinished manuscript, Alcott Papers, Houghton Library, Harvard University, Cambridge, Mass. The work has recently been made available through Arno Press under the title *Diana and Persis*.

41. Hosmer, who spent most of her professional life in Rome was, nevertheless, a strong role model for American girls. Jeannette Gilder, for example, writes of reading an article about her during the early 1860's in a popular periodical, *The Ladies Repository*, and vowing immediately to cut her hair short like Hosmer's and become a sculptor. See *The Autobiography of a Tomboy* (New York: Doubleday, Page and Co., 1900), p. 183.

42. *Harriet Hosmer: Letters and Memories*, ed. Cornelia Carr (New York: Moffat, Yard and Co., 1912), p. 35.

43. Hosmer's letters as well as biographies of friends like Charlotte Cushman (e.g., Joseph Leach, *Bright Particular Star: The Life and Times of Charlotte Cushman*, New Haven: Yale University Press, 1970), suggest that she probably had romantic friendships with Annie Dundas, Matilda Hays, and possibly Charlotte Cushman and a Mrs. Sartoris.

44. Quoted in *Charlotte Cushman: Her Letters and Memories of her Life*,

ed. Emma Stebbins (Boston: Houghton Mifflin and Co., 1881), pp. 12–13.

45. Charlotte Cushman's diary for 1844–1845, Charlotte Cushman manuscript collection, Butler Library, Columbia University, New York, N.Y.

46. Ibid.

47. Leach, *Bright Particular Star*, p. 157.

48. W. T. Price, *A Life of Charlotte Cushman* (New York: Brentano's, 1894), p. 61.

49. Quoted in Leach, *Bright Particular Star*, p. 158.

50. Cushman's diary for 1844–1845, Butler Library, Columbia University, New York, N.Y.

51. Susanne Howe, *Geraldine Jewsbury: Her Life and Errors* (London: George Allen and Unwin, 1935), p. 23. Jewsbury met Charlotte in 1846. Shortly thereafter she made her the prototype of her feminist heroine in *The Half Sisters*.

52. Leach, *Bright Particular Star*, pp. 217–18.

53. Ibid., p. 234.

54. Ibid., p. 210.

55. Ibid., p. 271.

56. Stebbins, *Charlotte Cushman*, p. 21.

57. Cushman's diary, January 11, 1845, Butler Library, Columbia University, New York, N.Y.

58. Leach, *Bright Particular Star*, pp. 311–12.

59. *Correspondence of Fraülein Günderode and Bettine von Arnim*, trans. Margaret Fuller (1842; reprinted, Boston: T. Burnham, 1861), p. 83.

60. Ibid., p. 293.

61. Ibid., p. 2.

62. Ibid., p. 47.

63. Elaine Kendall, *Peculiar Institutions: An Informal History of the Seven Sister Colleges* (New York: G. P. Putnam's Sons, 1976), pp. 127–28.

64. Anna Mary Wells, *Miss Marks and Miss Woolley* (Boston: Houghton Mifflin and Co., 1978), p. 9.

65. Jeannette Marks, *Gallant Little Wales* (Boston: Houghton Mifflin and Co., 1912), p. 168.

66. Wells, *Miss Marks and Miss Woolley*, p. 67.

67. Ibid., p. 252.

68. Such relationships have been discussed at length in several books. See Edith Finch, *Carey Thomas of Bryn Mawr* (New York: Harper and Bros., 1947), which deals with the first woman president of Bryn Mawr and the two major relationships of her life, one with English professor Mamie Gwinn (which is also the subject of Gertrude Stein's short 1904 novel, *Fernhurst*) and one with Mary Garrett. See also Vida Dutton Scudder, *On Journey* (New York: E. P. Dutton, 1937). Scudder, a Wellesley professor, had a lifelong romantic friend in another professor and author, Florence Converse. Katharine Lee Bates and Katharine Coman, also a Wellesley faculty pair, are the subjects of Dorothy Burgess's *Dream and Deed: The Story of Katharine Lee Bates* (Norman: University of Oklahoma Press, 1952), and of a more recent article by Judith Schwarz, "Yellow Clover: Katharine Lee Bates and Katharine Coman," *Fron-*

tiers, Vol. IV, No. 1 (Spring 1979), pp. 59–67. Mary Garrett, the only non-academic woman in the group, was a very wealthy woman. While she did not share with Carey Thomas the struggles of academia, she was able to offer her support that would have been quite improbable had she been a husband rather than a romantic friend. For instance, when Carey was in the running for the presidency of Bryn Mawr in 1893, Mary wrote to the board of trustees, promising, "Whenever Miss M. Carey Thomas should become President of your College, to pay into her hands the sum of ten thousand dollars yearly, so long as I live and she remains President, to be used at her discretion, for the English Department in the first instance, and then for the other departments of the College . . . ," Finch, *Carey Thomas,* p. 209. Whether or not the trustees were influenced by Mary's pledge, her friend became president in 1894. Mary kept her promise until her death in 1915.

69. Jeannette Marks papers, "Unwise College Friendships," Williston Memorial Library, Mount Holyoke College.

70. Jeannette Marks, *A Girl's Student Days and After* (New York: Fleming H. Revell and Co., 1911), pp. 36–37.

71. Jeannette Marks papers, unpublished correspondence with Dr. Arthur Jacobson, Williston Memorial Library, Mount Holyoke College.

Part IIB. *Chapter 1.* The Rise of Antifeminism

1. Elizabeth Lynn Linton, preface, *The Girl of the Period and Other Social Essays* (London: R. Bentley, 1883).

2. G. J. Barker-Benfield, *The Horrors of the Half-known Life: Male Attitudes Toward Female Sexuality in Nineteenth Century America* (New York: Harper and Row, 1976).

3. Mrs. E. Sandford, *Woman in Her Social and Domestic Character* (London: 1831), p. 13.

4. Sarah Stickney Ellis, *The Woman of England: Social Duties and Domestic Habits* (New York: D. Appleton, 1839), p. 14. Over the next few years, distinguished male writers in England began to join the protest against the exercise of intellect in women. See, for example, Benjamin Disraeli, *Sybil* (1845), Chapter VI, and William Thackeray, *Pendennis* (1848–50), Chapters XXII and XXXIX.

5. Even the most committed feminists, such as Margaret Fuller, did not dare to challenge that view completely. Fuller is careful never to suggest that women should cultivate their intellect instead of their domestic virtues—although she says that domestic "functions must not be drudgery or an enforced necessity, but a part of life," *Woman in the Nineteenth Century* (1843; reprinted Boston, 1855), p. 44.

6. "Female Orators," *The Mother's Magazine,* Vol. VI (1838), p. 27.

7. Henry F. Harrington, "Female Education," *Ladies Companion,* Vol. IX (1838), p. 293.

8. Colesworth Pinckney, *The Lady's Token, or Gift of Friendship* (Nashua, N.H., 1848), p. 119.

9. Henry James, Sr., "Woman and the Women's Movement," *Putnam's Magazine,* Vol. I (1853), pp. 279–88.

10. Edward H. Clarke, *Sex in Education, or, A Fair Chance for Girls* (Boston: J. R. Osgood, 1873).

11. A. Hughes Bennett, "Hygiene in the Higher Education of Women," *Popular Science Monthly*, February 1888.

12. Quoted in Duncan Crow, *The Victorian Woman* (London: George Allen and Unwin, 1971), p. 166.

13. Dinah Maria Mulock Craik, *A Woman's Thoughts About Women* (New York: Rudd and Carleton, 1858), pp. 12–13.

14. Horace Bushnell, *Women's Suffrage: The Reform Against Nature* (New York: C. Scribner, 1869).

15. Mrs. Lynn Linton, *The Autobiography of Christopher Kirkland* (1885; reprinted New York: Garland Publishing Co., 1976), p. 9.

16. "Women's Votes," *Saturday Review*, May 6, 1871.

17. See Marguerite Thibert, *Le féminisme dans le socialisme français, 1830–1850* (Paris: Marcel Giard, 1926) and Maïté Albistur and Daniel Armogathe, *L'Histoire du féminisme français* (Paris: Des Femmes, 1977).

18. Quoted in Edna L. Steeves, "Pre-Feminism in Some Eighteenth Century Novels," *Texas Quarterly*, Vol. XVI, No. 3 (Autumn 1973), p. 49. In Balzac's work *La physiologie du mariage pré-originale* (1826), he reminded husbands that they were the governors of their small estates, i.e., their families, and that if they did not maintain dominance over their wives, their states would fall apart.

19. Werner Thönnessen, *The Emancipation of Women: The Rise and Decline of the Women's Movement in German Social Democracy, 1863–1933*, trans. Joris de Bres (Frankfurt am Main: Pluto Press, 1969), p. 15.

20. See Elaine Kendall, *Peculiar Institutions: An Informal History of the Seven Sister Colleges* (New York: G. P. Putnam's Sons, 1976), pp. 127–28.

21. See Crow, *The Victorian Woman*, p. 274.

22. For example, in England, Alexander Walker, *Intermarriage; or the Natural Laws by Which Beauty, Health, and Intellect Result from Certain Unions, and Deformity, Disease, and Insanity from Others* (London: John Churchill, 1841), pp. 86–87; in America, Henry N. Guernsey, *Plain Talk on Avoided Subjects* (Philadelphia: F. A. Davis, 1882), pp. 82–83.

23. Allan McLane Hamilton, "The Civil Responsibility of Sexual Perverts," *American Journal of Insanity*, Vol. LII, No. 4 (April 1896), pp. 503–09.

Part IIB. *Chapter 2*. THE CONTRIBUTIONS OF THE SEXOLOGISTS

1. Carl von Westphal, "Die Konträre Sexualempfindung," *Archiven für Psychiatrie und Nervenkrankheiten*, Vol. II (1869), pp. 73–108.

2. Jeannette Foster suggests that the French writer Adolphe Belot, author of the homophobic *Mlle. Giraud, Ma Femme*, who alludes in this 1870 novel to the serious concern prevalent in Germany with regard to love between women, was probably familiar with Westphal; see *Sex Variant Women in Literature* (1956; reprinted Baltimore: Diana Press, 1975), p. 81. Bonnie Zimmerman speculates that George Eliot may have been reluctant to encourage Edith Simcox's romantic friendship because she had become familiar with Westphal's theories through George Lewis, who had extensive discussions with him in Germany in 1870 while researching his book, *Problems of Life and Mind*. Eliot

thus may have learned to view love between women as a sign of congenital taint; "My Whole Soul is a Longing Question: Edith Simcox and George Eliot," unpublished paper, Women's Studies Program, San Diego State University, San Diego, Calif.

3. See, for example, Ferdinand Lundberg and Marynia Farnham, *Modern Woman: The Lost Sex* (New York: Harper, 1947).

4. Havelock Ellis, *Studies in the Psychology of Sex: Sexual Inversion* (1897; reprinted Philadelphia: F. A. Davis, 1911), p. 120.

5. A year before his death, Krafft-Ebing wrote "Neue Studien auf dem Gebiete der Homosexualität, which was published in *Jahrbuch für Sexuelle Zwischenstufen*, Vol. III (1901): pp. 1–36. In this article Krafft-Ebing reversed his lifelong stress on homosexual "degeneracy" and "taint," and conceded that although many deviants had mental disorders and were neuropathic, homosexuality was not a disease but rather a congenital anomaly that was not necessarily incompatible with mental health. But *Psychopathia Sexualis* (1882; reprinted, New York: Surgeons Book Co., 1925) is of course a far better-known work than this article. Many readers who were familiar with his book and his theories probably did not know about the subsequent essay, and its impact on popular notions regarding homosexuals was minimal.

6. Iwan Bloch, for example, asserts that "*genuine homosexuality . . .* occurs in perfectly *healthy* individuals quite independently of degeneration" and is the result of "*congenital* conditions" (italics are Bloch's); *The Sexual Life of Our Time*, 6th ed. (New York: Allied Book Co., 1908), p. 456.

7. Others who held views similar to Krafft-Ebing were Paul Moreau (*Des aberrations du sens génésique*, Paris: Librairies de la Faculté de Médecine, 1887); B. Tarnowsky (*Die Krankhaften Erscheinungen des Geschlechtssinnes*, Berlin: A. Hirschwald, 1886); and Cesare Lombroso (*The Female Offender*, London: T. F. Unwin, 1895).

8. John Addington Symonds, the author of *A Problem in Modern Ethics*, collaborated with Ellis on *Sexual Inversion* but died before the work was published, and his family demanded that his name as coauthor be removed from the text. There are significant differences in the two works regarding the view of homosexuality as being pathologically based. In his book Symonds argued that ancient Greece, where homosexuality was a cultural custom and even an institution, "offers insuperable difficulties to the theorists who treat sexual inversion exclusively from the point of view of neuropathy, tainted heredity, and masturbation" (1896; reprinted New York: Benjamin Blom, Inc., 1971), pp. 36–37. He specifically criticized Krafft-Ebing, suggesting that at that moment in Europe there was probably not a single person who had inherited no neuropathic stain whatsoever. If that be true, Symonds argued, everybody is liable to sexual inversion, and so the principle of heredity becomes purely theoretical (ibid., pp. 48–49). Symonds did believe, however, that the true homosexual was a person born with sexual instincts that are improperly correlated to his/her sexual organs, and he emphasized that no inherited or latent morbidity is (necessarily) involved. He granted that many homosexuals evince "nervous anomalies," but these, he said, are "not evidence of an originally tainted constitution, but the consequence of the unnatural conditions to which [they have]

been exposed from the age of puberty," *A Problem in Modern Ethics,* p. 74.

9. Ellis, *Sexual Inversion,* p. 132. I discuss these points at greater length in my article, "The Morbidification of Love Between Women by Nineteenth Century Sexologists," *Journal of Homosexuality,* Vol. IV, No. 1 (Fall 1978), pp. 73–90.

10. *Sexual Inversion,* p. 132. Germaine Greer in *The Female Eunuch* (New York: McGraw-Hill, 1971), p. 75, offers an example from her own life of how girls are taught to develop a distaste for same-sex love, and of how that cultivated distaste has nothing to do with natural feeling.

11. He does admit that "it frequently happens" that a young woman may experience "periods of intimate attachment to a friend of her own sex," but he refuses to recognize that those attachments and the attachments of his inverts are essentially the same, though the reader can see the similarities through the material he presents.

12. Ellis, *Sexual Inversion,* pp. 147–48.

13. Ibid., p. 30.

14. See footnote 8.

15. Ellis, *Sexual Inversion,* pp. 133, 140.

16. Ibid., pp. 136, 137.

17. Ibid., p. 134.

18. Ibid., pp. 134–37.

19. Ellis's wife, Edith Lees, seems to have been a victim of those theories. From his own account Ellis apparently convinced her that she was a congenital invert, while she had believed herself to be only a romantic friend to other women. He relates in *My Life* that during the first years of their marriage, she revealed to him an emotional relationship with an old friend who stayed with her while she and Ellis were apart. Ellis, on the basis of that, identified all her problems as stemming from inversion:

> . . . she had told me everything of the sentimental and sometimes passionate attraction which from early school life up to a few years before marriage she had experienced for girl friends. I knew that when a school girl the resulting relationships had sometimes possessed a slight but definite sensuous character, though it had not found that expression in later adult friendships with women. I knew that such feelings were common in young girls. But at that time I had no real practical knowledge of inborn sexual inversion of character. . . . I was not yet able to detect all those subtle traits of an opposite sexual temperament.

They were, he says, the roots "of the disharmonies which tortured her." He thus encouraged her to see herself as an invert and to regard her subsequent love relations with women as a manifestation of her inversion; Havelock Ellis, *My Life: Autobiography of Havelock Ellis* (Boston: Houghton Mifflin and Co., 1939), pp. 308–09 and passim. Françoise Delisle, Ellis's second wife, also hints that Ellis encouraged Edith's "inversion," see *Friendship's Odyssey* (1946; reprinted London, 1964), p. 220.

20. Ellis, *Sexual Inversion,* p. 140n.

21. Ibid., p. 254.

22. Other writers had commented on such relationships much earlier, although their studies had not been systematic. See, for example, Charlotte Brontë's *Jane Eyre*, 1847 (Chapter IX, the love between Jane and Helen Burns); William Alger's *The Friendships of Women*, 1868, in which Alger observes of such school friendships: "In their mental caresses, spiritual nuptials, their thoughts kiss each other. . . . Keener agonies, more delicious passages, are nowhere else known than in the bosoms of innocent school-girls, in the lacerations or fruitions of their first consciously given affections." Alger ends this section with a story of two sixteen-year-old schoolgirls who committed suicide when a parent tried to separate them (pp. 270–71); see also the German novel by Gabriele Reuter, *A Girl from a Nice Family*, 1895, in which she describes a school love affair between Eugenie and Agathe: "Agathe immediately was seized with a passionate love for her. She now could think of no greater pleasure than to be with Eugenie Wintrow, to snuggle up to her and to kiss her."

23. Ellis, *Sexual Inversion*, p. 243.

24. Ibid.

25. Ibid., p. 244.

26. Ibid., p. 245.

27. Ibid., pp. 250–56.

28. Ibid., pp. 256–57.

29. Ibid., p. 252.

30. Ibid., p. 244.

31. Ibid., p. 248.

32. See Arno Karlen, *Sexuality and Homosexuality: A New View* (New York: W. W. Norton, 1971), p. 195. In fact, if Ellis's colleague, the English sex researcher J. A. Hadfield, can be believed, Ellis himself saw flaws in his congenital theory, but adhered to it for political purposes only. Hadfield wrote in the *British Medical Journal*, Vol. II, 1323, in 1958, "Havelock Ellis maintained that homosexuality was of a constitutional type, but he admitted to me in person that he made this statement only because he wanted to emphasize that the individual could not help being what he was."

33. See Magnus Hirschfeld, "Homosexuality," *The Encyclopaedia Sexualis: A Comprehensive Encyclopaedia-Dictionary of the Sexual Sciences*, ed. Victor Robinson (New York: Dingwall-Rock, 1936), p. 222.

34. See discussion of such groups in Lillian Faderman and Brigitte Eriksson, *Lesbian-Feminism in Turn-of-the-Century Germany*, introduction (Weatherby Lake, Mo.: Naiad Press, 1980).

35. G. J. Barker-Benfield discusses the brutalities nineteenth-century male doctors perpetrated on women in *The Horrors of the Half-Known Life: Male Attitudes Toward Women and Sexuality in Nineteenth Century America* (New York: Harper and Row, 1976).

36. James D. Steakley hypothesizes that in Germany urbanization, first experienced by the generation of the 1860's, was also responsible for the creation of an invert society. Prior to that time most Germans lived in villages, and it would have been impossible for the "eccentric bachelor and spinster" to imagine themselves as a group with shared interests. Steakley comments with respect to

men that "urban homosexuals developed the ritualized forms of interaction which would facilitate mutual recognition, and effeminate behavior on the part of males first became a caste mark in the city," *The Homosexual Emancipation Movement in Germany* (New York: Arno Press, 1975), pp. 14–15. Women who saw themselves as inverts probably also took on certain identifying characteristics (for example, "butch" mannerisms) for the first time in this late nineteenth-century urban environment.

37. Xavier Mayne, *The Intersexes: A History of Similisexualism as a Problem in Social Life* (1908; reprinted New York: Arno Press, 1975), pp. 150–51, 521.

38. See Elisabeth Dauthendey, *The Uranian Question and Women* (Leipzig, 1906) and the introduction and selections in Faderman and Eriksson, *Lesbian-Feminism in Turn-of-the-Century Germany.*

39. John Lauritsen and David Thorstad, *The Early Homosexual Rights Movement (1864–1935)* (New York: Times Change Press, 1974), pp. 15–16.

40. See, for example, Anna Rueling, "Welches Interesse hat die Frauenbewegung an der Loesung des homosexuellen Problems?" *Jahrbuch für Sexuelle Zwischenstufen,* Vol. VII (Leipzig, 1905), trans. in Faderman and Eriksson, *Lesbian-Feminism in Turn-of-the-Century Germany.*

41. Vida Dutton Scudder, *On Journey* (New York: E. P. Dutton and Co., 1937), p. 224.

42. Ibid., p. 226.

43. Ibid., pp. 211–12.

44. *Whose Fault Is It?*, a 1901 Danish novel by Richard Meienreis, excerpted in *Jahrbuch für Sexuelle Zwischenstufen,* Vol. V (Leipzig, 1903).

45. *The Disinherited of Love's Happiness,* discussed in "Wie Ich Es Sehe," *Jahrbuch,* Vol. III (Leipzig, 1901).

46. In *Jahrbuch,* Vol. III (Leipzig, 1901), trans. in Faderman and Eriksson, *Lesbian-Feminism in Turn-of-the-Century Germany.*

Part IIB. *Chapter 3.* LESBIAN EXOTICISM

1. Havelock Ellis, *Studies in the Psychology of Sex: Sexual Inversion* (1897; reprinted Philadelphia: F. A. Davis, 1911), p. 119.

2. John Stewart Collis, *Havelock Ellis, Artist of Life: A Study of His Life and Work* (New York: William Sloane Associates, 1959), p. 65.

3. See Chapter 3, Part IIA, "New Women," footnote 12.

4. Mario Praz, *The Romantic Agony,* 2nd ed. (New York: Oxford University Press, 1970), p. 201.

5. Ibid., p. 333.

6. Her fantasy letter to Marie Dorval, written in 1833, suggests a very sensual but not unambiguously sexual relationship between them. The letter pictures George in bed, awaiting Marie; but when the beloved arrives, she *sits* by George's bed*side*. The two exchange kisses and gentle caresses, and Marie steals away as lithely as she came. It is possible, however, that the flower references in the letter are meant to symbolize an interlude more specifically sexual; for example, "What flowers are those on your forehead, in your hands? Flowers unknown. . . . Their perfume is intoxicating, my angel, spread them over me,

cover me with leaves from your dewy crown," in Joseph Barry, *George Sand: In Her Own Words* (Garden City, N.Y.: Anchor Books, 1979), pp. 429–30. Whatever the nature of their relationship was, Alfred de Vigny, the romantic poet who had been Marie's lover when she met George Sand, feared that it was threatening to his status and demanded in two letters that Marie have nothing more to do with "that damned Lesbian"; quoted in Samuel Edwards, *George Sand: A Biography of the First Modern, Liberated Woman* (New York: David McKay Co., 1972), pp. 5–6.

7. Menken wrote Gautier about Sand, "She so infuses me with the spirit of life that I cannot bear to spend an evening apart from her," quoted in Edwards, *George Sand: A Biography . . .* , pp. 248–49. George Sand's *Intimate Journal*, ed. Marie Jenny Howe (New York: Haskell House Publishers, 1976) implies that she also had passionate attachments to Marie d'Agoult (the novelist "Daniel Stern," who was the mistress of Franz Liszt) and to the singer Pauline Garcia, who became the title character in Sand's 1842 novel, *Consuelo*). While recent Sand biographies do not ignore her relationships with women, older works almost invariably do, even those with such provocative titles as *George Sand and Her Lovers* [Francis Gribble (New York: Charles Scribner's Sons, 1907)].

8. Quoted in Edwards, *George Sand: A Biography . . .* , p. 4.

9. A. E. Carter, *The Idea of Decadence in French Literature, 1830–1900* (Toronto, 1958) discusses Gautier's central role in the development of aesthete-decadent ideas in literature and his influence on subsequent writers.

10. The French aesthetes of the 1830's sought any and every method to separate themselves from the bourgeoisie and, in effect, to declass themselves, including outrageous dress and absurd behavior. Gautier, for example, paraded about in a medieval red doublet, Jehan du Seigneur in a black velvet tunic with a taffeta tie. Théophile Dondey claimed that he kept his glasses on all night because he was too nearsighted to see his dreams without them. Gerard de Nerval used to bring his own drinking mug to parties—a skull which he claimed was his father's—and he went walking in public parks leading a live lobster on a pale blue leash. See Enid Starkie's discussion of the Bouzingo artists in *Baudelaire* (New York: New Directions, 1958), pp. 82–83.

11. About the sexual possibilities of lesbianism, Gautier and/or his characters seem to be entirely in the dark. Neither D'Albert (a man of the world who has experienced all manner of sexual debauchery), nor Rosette, nor Maupin herself have any conception of the ways in which a woman can make love to a woman. Maupin wishes repeatedly that she were a man so that she might enjoy Rosette's ardor, and she suffers in her frustration. After D'Albert initiates Maupin into heterosexuality, she knows what a man does with a woman and then goes to Rosette's room aparently to do the same—but the narrator does not say with what equipment. Gautier is as coy as Lucian: the narrator remarks that what Maupin said and did in Rosette's room, "I have never been able to ascertain," but the maid told him that Rosette's bed "was disturbed and tossed, and bore the impress of two bodies." From a male perspective, a woman could not figure out by herself what to do with another woman, and required the instruction of a man and the model of heterosexuality.

12. In a later novel, *Cousin Bette* (1846), which begins in Paris of the 1830's,

Balzac also complains of how society had changed and become more corrupt since 1830 (reprinted New York: Random House, 1958), p. 95.

13. Isabelle de Courtivron, "Weak Men and Fatal Women: The Sand Image," in *Homosexualities and French Literature*, eds. George Stambolian and Elaine Marks (Ithaca, N.Y.: Cornell University Press, 1979), p. 221. Courtivron cites as her source for the early Balzac-Gautier relationship, R. Bolster, *Stendhal, Balzac, et le féminisme romantique* (Paris: Lettres Modernes, 1970), p. 152; but at least one scholarly work speculates that Gautier and Balzac did not meet until Balzac had published *The Girl with the Golden Eyes* and then read *Mademoiselle de Maupin*; Alfred de Spoelbergh de Lovenjoul, *Les lundis d'un chercheur* (Paris: Calmann Lévy, 1894), p. 11.

14. In an 1829 review of *Fragoletta* for *Le Mercure du XIXᵉ Siècle* Balzac asserted that Latouche's novel was destined to be a "brilliant hit." in an 1831 article he spoke of Latouche as one of the men in whom profound reason is united with a great power of imagination. In *Lettres sur Paris* (1831) he referred to the "ravishing pages" of *Fragoletta*. Quoted in Randolph Hughes, commentary on *Lesbia Brandon* by Algernon Charles Swinburne (London: The Falcon Press, 1952), pp. 402–03.

15. Gonzague de Reynold, *Charles Baudelaire* (Paris, 1920), p. 225, and Georges May, "Diderot, Baudelaire, et les Femmes Damnées," *Modern Languages Notes*, LXV (June 1950), 395–99, suggest that as a young man Baudelaire greatly admired Diderot's *The Nun* and even borrowed the title of one of his lesbian poems, "Femmes Damnées," from the lesbian Mother Superior's cry in *The Nun*, "Je suis damnée." But Gautier was to him "The Master and my Master" and "the great poet of the century," quoted in Starkie, *Baudelaire*, p. 472.

16. Starkie, *Baudelaire*, p. 18.

17. Ibid., pp. 80–82.

18. Ibid., pp. 318, 406.

19. Baudelaire's need to declare his right to freedom as an artist also compounded his confusion regarding his "slavery to his baptism": Although his notes to his lawyer repeatedly insist that the lawyer emphasize in the obscenity trial that *Les Fleurs* shows a Catholic "HORROR OF EVIL" [sic], he also wants him to argue that "there are several kinds of morality. There is the positive and practical kind which everyone must adhere to. But there is also an artistic morality. This is quite different, and since the beginnings of society, the arts have proved it," in *Baudelaire: The Flowers of Evil and All Other Authenticated Poems*, trans. Dr. P. J. W. Higson and Elliot R. Ashe (Cestrian Press, 1975), pp. 190–91.

20. Ibid., p. 25.

21. Ibid., pp. 150–53.

22. Ibid., pp. 122–23.

23. Ibid., pp. 153–56.

24. Courbet would certainly have been familiar with "Doomed Women." In 1855 he completed a canvas entitled "The Painter's Studio," in which his enemies are placed on the left and his friends on the right. Baudelaire, whom he considered among his closest friends, is placed in a prominent position on the right.

25. The May 1, 1883, Italian bimonthly, *Cronaca Bizantina*, hints that during the reign of Empress Eugènie in France (1853–1870), lesbianism flourished in fact as well as in fiction, particularly at court. The author of the article on Eugènie, P. Petraccelli della Gattina, states that the empress was not only a seducer of young girls (although she liked men too), but she also encouraged the women at all the Napoleon III residences to indulge in lesbian practices. However, the tone of della Gattina's article is sensationalistic and appears to be based more on what he read in Gautier and Balzac than on reality. Very possibly he attacked Eugènie's sexuality for the same reasons that Marie Antoinette's enemies had attacked hers: Eugènie had been altogether too powerful in political matters for a woman, and she was instrumental in the failure of a proposed alliance between France and Italy in 1868, *Cronaca Bizantina*, Vol. I, No. 1, columns 3–7.

26. *A Summer in the Country*, trans. Donald Thomas (1867; reprinted London: Odyssey Press, 1970), p. xxv.

27. Paul Verlaine, *Oeuvres Libres* (1868; reprinted Switzerland, 1975), p. 17.

28. Quoted in Starkie, *Baudelaire*, pp. 498, 523.

29. See especially the Poems of the "Amies" section in *Oeuvres Libres*, p. 7ff.

30. See especially in *Poems and Ballads: First Series* (1866; reprinted London: Chatto and Windus, 1911), "The Masque of Queen Bersabe," "Anactoria," "Sapphics," and "Faustine"; in *Poems and Ballads: Second Series* (1878; reprinted New York: Hurst and Co., n.d.), "Fragoletta," "Hermaphroditus," "Memorial Verses on the Death of Théophile Gautier," "Obitum Theophili Poetae," "Le tombeau de Théophile Gautier," and "Ave Atque Vale."

31. Quoted in Hughes, commentary on *Lesbia Brandon*, p. 418.

32. Ibid., p. 419.

33. Ibid., pp. 402–05.

34. H. P. Clive discusses Louÿs's great interest in Gautier, Baudelaire, Verlaine and Swinburne; *Pierre Louÿs (1870–1925): A Biography* (Oxford: Clarendon Press, 1978), pp. 5, 16, 31, 56–57.

35. Pierre Louÿs, *The Songs of Bilitis* (1894; reprinted n.p., 1919), p. xii.

36. See, e.g., "The Wedding," "The Doll," "The Silence of Mnasidika," and "Absence." There is no concrete evidence to prove that Louÿs was familiar with Krafft-Ebing and other sexologists who published before *The Songs of Bilitis* was written, but it is noteworthy that the "butch-femme" theme is stronger in his work than that of his immediate predecessors, and may have been influenced by the sexologists' idea that true inverts were generally masculine women, i.e., "butches." In his novel *Aphrodite*, Louÿs also uses a heterosexual model for lesbianism. He describes an ancient (fictional) lesbian marriage rite at Ephesus: Two adolescent virgins who are in love with each other go to the temple of Dionysus, "where the more virile of the two is given a little sharp-edged gold knife and a white cloth to stanch the blood" from the more feminine one's hymen. In the evening "whichever of the two is the fiancée is led to her new home in a flowered chariot," seated near her "husband." Presumably, if the two were equally feminine or equally androgynous, they had a big problem. Perhaps Louÿs believed they would not have "married" at all, since in his heterosexual view only opposites attract. Of two young women in his novel,

Myrto and Rhodis, he has a third character say, "I don't need to ask which of you is the husband. I know that Myrto has everything necessary to create the illusion. You are lucky to have such a friend, Rhodis. They are rare, let me tell you," trans. Lewis Galantière (1896; reprinted New York: Modern Library, 1933), pp. 62–63.

37. Louys, *The Songs of Bilitis*, p. 50.

38. Ibid., p. 52.

39. Ibid., p. 67.

40. Ibid., p. 95.

41. Adah Isaacs Menken, "Answer Me," *Infelicia* (1868; reprinted Philadelphia: Lippincott Co., 1902), pp. 119–22.

Part IIB. *Chapter 4.* LESBIAN EVIL

1. Macvey Napier, *Hypocrisy Unveiled and Calumny Detected* (London, 1818), p. 50.

2. Roy Basler, *Sex, Symbolism and Psychology in Literature* (New Brunswick, New Jersey: Rutgers University Press, 1948), was one of the first to suggest that "Christabel" was a poem about lesbianism. Basler points to Coleridge's apostrophe to shame and sorrow, and infers from that specific lesbian implications. However, Geraldine's mark of shame and seal of sorrow may be seen as a physical deformity which is a manifestation of her general evil as a bad spirit.

3. See, especially, Coleridge's statement that William Hazlitt "spread about the report that Geraldine was a man in disguise," in *Unpublished Letters of Samuel Taylor Coleridge, Including Certain Letters Republished from Original Sources,* ed. Earl Leslie Griggs (London, 1932), Vol. II, p. 247, letter to Robert Southey, February 1819; see also the review in *The Champion,* Sunday, May 26, 1816, p. 166, which speculates in shocked seriousness that Geraldine was probably a man; and David Macbeth Moir (pseud. Morgan Odoherty), *Blackwoods,* Vol. V (April–September 1819), pp. 286–91, a satirical conclusion for "Christabel" in which nine moons had "waxed and waned and Christabel is about to give birth to a child. Coleridge's confidant, Dr. James Gillman, with whom the poet lived for a number of years while he was being treated for drug addiction, indicated that Coleridge's intent was much closer to what his contemporaries had guessed than to what ours have. According to Gillman, Geraldine was, in fact, not really a woman, but a disembodied evil spirit who could climb into a male or female body at will, and Coleridge planned to show that spirit at the conclusion of the poem changing itself into the guise of Christabel's knight and marrying Christabel, who has developed an unaccountable abhorrence for her betrothed; James Gillman, *The Life of Samuel Taylor Coleridge* (London, 1838), pp. 301–02. It is curious that Basler uses Gillman's statement to prove his assertion that "Christabel" is a poem about lesbian evil *(Sex, Symbolism, and Psychology in Literature,* pp. 48–50). If "Geraldine" is a disembodied spirit who can change gender at will, "it" is not a woman (and thus not a lesbian) any more than "it" is a man. "It" takes a female form in the part of the poem Coleridge completed because only in that guise could the spirit have had access to Christabel. She would have run from a man that she met in the woods at midnight. The poet's son, Derwent Coleridge, argued that his father had told him that Geraldine was

not intended to be a malignant being of any kind, but rather a good spirit, executing her appointed task with the best good will. Derwent Coleridge, "Introductory Essay," *The Poems of Samuel Taylor Coleridge* (London: E. Moxon, 1870), p. xlii. See also some twentieth-century discussions of this point of view: Norman Fruman, *Coleridge, The Damaged Archangel* (New York: George Braziller, 1971), pp. 357–58; T. R. Preston, "Christabel and the Mystical Tradition," *Essays and Studies in Language and Literature,* ed. Herbert H. Petit (Pittsburgh, Pa.: Duquesne University Press, 1964), pp. 138–57; and Gerald Enscoe, *Eros and the Romantics: Sexual Love as a Theme in Coleridge, Shelley, and Keats* (The Hague: Mouton, 1967), pp. 44–52.

4. Foster, *Sex Variant Women,* p. 81.

5. Adolphe Belot, *Mademoiselle Giraud, My Wife* (1870; reprinted Chicago: Laird and Lee, 1892), trans. "A.D.", publisher's announcement.

6. Ibid., pp. 342–48.

7. William Rounseville Alger, *The Friendships of Women* (Boston: Roberts Bros., 1868), p. 269.

8. Belot, *Mademoiselle Giraud,* p. 217.

9. Ibid., p. 389.

10. Charles Baudelaire, "Doomed Women: Delphinia and Hippolyta," *The Flowers of Evil and All Other Authenticated Poems,* trans. Dr. P. J. Higson and Elliot R. Ashe (Cestrian Press, 1975), p. 156.

11. Belot, *Mademoiselle Giraud,* pp. 253–54.

12. Ibid., p. 394.

13. Catulle Mendès (*Méphistophéla,* 1890) shows that lesbianism causes his character, Sophie, to perpetrate the worst horrors. She gives up the daughter she bore while married, has only lecherous feelings for the girl, slips so far into debauchery that she frightens even the women of Paris lowlife, and as the novel ends is seen injecting morphine into her veins, on her way to an inevitable tortured death.

14. Joséphin Péladan (*La Gynandre,* 1891) presents a peripatetic male hero, Tammuz (named after the Babylonian equivalent of Dionysus), who examines various levels of lesbian society and ends by matching all the salvageable lesbians with eligible bachelors, feeding them aphrodisiacs, lowering the lights, and thus instantly converting the lesbians to the joys of marriage and motherhood.

15. Quoted in H. P. Clive, *Pierre Louÿs (1870–1925): A Biography* (Oxford: Clarendon Press, 1978), p. 169.

16. In *La décadence latine,* Péladan also identifies lesbianism as a malaise of the past few years, but he implies it is due to the dangerous flexibility of sex roles—neither men nor women seem to understand that it is crucial for society that they strictly maintain the role appropriate to their gender. He complains, "The number of women who think they are men increases daily and the masculine instinct leads them to violent action, in the same proportion as the number of men who think they are women give up their gender and, becoming passive, move into a negative plane," quoted in Mario Praz, *The Romantic Agony,* trans. Angus Davidson (1933; reprinted Cleveland, Ohio: Meridian Books), p. 334.

17. Quoted in Ronald Pearsall, *The Worm in the Bud: The World of Victorian Sexuality* (Toronto: Macmillan, 1969), p. 475. Writing in 1908, Xavier Mayne (Edward Stevenson) remarked that in many of the large cities of Europe—Paris, Berlin, Vienna, London—lesbian practices among prostitutes were common, *The Intersexes: A History of Similisexualism as a Problem in Social Life* (1908; reprinted New York: Arno Press, 1975), p. 523. August Bebel observed in 1884 that a quarter of the prostitutes in Berlin indulged in lesbianism, *Women and Socialism*, trans. Meta Stern (reprinted New York: Socialist Literature Co., 1910), p. 205. Twenty years later the number was 20 percent, according to Anna Rueling, "What Interest Does the Women's Movement Have in the Solution of the Homosexual Problem?" in Lillian Faderman and Brigitte Eriksson, *Lesbian-Feminism in Turn-of-the-Century Germany* (Weatherby Lake, Mo.: Naiad Press, 1980).

18. Cited in Praz, *The Romantic Agony*, pp. 319–20.

19. Bernard Talmey, *Love: A Treatise on the Science of Sex Attraction* (New York: Practitioners Publishing Co., 1919), p. 285.

20. Introduction, *Mademoiselle Giraud*, pp. 12–13.

21. In Guy de Maupassant, *The Complete Short Stories*, Vol. I (London: Cassell and Co., 1970).

22. Alphonse Daudet, *Sappho* (reprinted Chicago: Franklin Publishing Co., n.d.).

23. Praz, *The Romantic Agony*, p. 332.

24. August Strindberg, *A Madman's Manifesto*, trans. Anthony Swirling (University, Ala.: University of Alabama Press, 1971), p. 197. The book was written in 1887 but was not published until 1893 in Berlin. Strindberg and Siri are called Axel and Maria, but he published this book to vindicate himself when their divorce became messy, and he intended that everyone understand who the principals were in real life.

25. Ibid., p. 212.

26. Ibid., p. 165.

27. Ibid., p. 209.

28. Ibid., p. 219.

29. Ibid., p. 212.

30. Ibid., p. 166. Siri's innocence becomes somewhat believable when she proclaims her amorous sentiments for her female cousin in the midst of a gathering, "without blushing, without even being aware she was making a mistake," and she naïvely tells Strindberg that she herself is astonished at the depth of her love for the young woman, since she had not believed "that it was possible for a woman to fall in love like that with another woman with such madness," ibid., p. 165.

31. Ibid., p. 58.

32. Ibid., p. 75.

33. Ibid., p. 146.

34. Ibid., p. 214.

35. Ibid., p. 193.

36. Ibid., p. 168.

37. It is possible that LeFanu read Coleridge's poem "Christabel" as a lesbian story in the light of his more knowledgeable time, and was then inspired to ex-

pand on the lesbian vampire portions, at which Coleridge may have (or may not have) hinted. There are, in any case, numerous superficial similarities between the two stories: both Christabel and Laura come from ancient noble families and live on grand estates; the "vampire" character in both stories claims some long standing connection to the heroine's family, and both gain entrance into their victim's homes by pretending to be dazed and in dire straits; the heroine's father in each case takes responsibility for the "vampire," and the heroine's dead mother tries to come to her defense from the other world. Carmilla's actions, however, can by no stretch of the imagination be interpreted as ultimately beneficial to Laura, as so many scholars have argued with regard to Geraldine's actions *vis à vis* Christabel. Carmilla is out to get Laura's blood and to turn her into a companion vampire.

38. Peter Penzoldt, *The Supernatural in Fiction* (1952; reprinted New York: Humanities Press, 1965), p. 75. Penzoldt says that although LeFanu did not know he was writing about lesbianism, "his description of the mental attitudes of the seducer and the seduced in the following example is psychologically perfect." He then quotes the passage in which Carmilla tells Laura, "I live in your warm life, and you shall die—die, sweetly die into mine." Obviously the legacy of French literature regarding lesbian love continued to be powerful in the 1950's.

39. Nelson Browne, *Sheridan LeFanu* (New York: Roy Publishers, 1951), p. 8.

40. "Inversion" and sexual ambiguity seem to have intrigued Moore throughout his long career. In *Pagan Poems* (1881) he included "The Hermaphrodite," inspired by Gautier and Swinburne. In 1927, he wrote a short story about a female transvestite who spends her life passing as a male, "Albert Nobbs," *Celibate Lives* (London: Chatto and Windus, 1927). As well as being familiar with the sexologists and the French writers, Moore was also very interested in the effects of feminism on women's views of themselves. He explores this topic to some extent in *A Drama in Muslin* (London: Vizetelly, 1886).

41. Irving C. Rosse, "Sexual Hypochondriasis and Perversion of the Genesic Instinct," *Journal of Nervous and Mental Disease*, Vol. XVII, No. 11 (November 1892), p. 805.

42. Ibid., p. 807.

43. F. L. Sim, "Forensic Psychiatry: Alice Mitchell Adjudged Insane," *Memphis Medical Monthly*, August 1892, quoted in Jonathan Katz, *Gay American History: Lesbians and Gay Men in the U.S.A.* (New York: Thomas Crowell, 1976), pp. 53–58.

44. Dr. F. E. Daniel, "Castration of Sexual Perverts," *Texas Medical Journal* (August 1893), quoted in Katz, *Gay American History*, pp. 135–36.

45. "The Trial of Josephine Mallison Smith," *Alienist and Neurologist* (July 1893), quoted in Katz, *Gay American History*, p. 577. See also Mary Wood Allen, *What a Young Woman Ought to Know* (Philadelphia: 1898), pp. 148, 173–76, one of the first American books intended for the lay reader of the late nineteenth century to warn girls against "sentimental friendships" with other women.

46. Paul Popcock, *Commercial Appeal*, quoted in Katz, *Gay American History*, p. 576.

47. Quoted in Katz, *Gay American History*, p. 576.

48. Some decades later, after the publication of Krafft-Ebing's work, Lobdell was committed to an insane asylum and diagnosed by the attending doctor in terms he acknowledged to have learned from Krafft-Ebing. The doctor closes his 1883 report saying, "the subject possesses little forensic interest, especially in this country, and the case herewith reported is offered as a clinical curiosity in psychiatric medicine," P. M. Wise, "Case of Sexual Perversion," *Alienist and Neurologist* (January 1883), quoted in Katz, *Gay American History*, pp. 221–23.

49. See, for example, S. Emma E. Edmonds, *Nurse and Spy in the Union Army: Comprising the Adventures and Experiences of a Woman in Hospitals, Camps, and Battle-Fields* (Hartford, Conn.: W. S. Williams and Co., 1865); Sylvia Dannett, *She Rode with the Generals: The True and Incredible Story of Sarah Emma Seelye, Alias Franklin Thompson* (New York: Thomas Nelson and Sons, 1960); *Personal Memoirs of Philip Henry Sheridan, General, United States Army* (New York: 1888), Vol. I, pp. 253–55; a series of articles in *Fincher's Trades' Review* for 1863 and 1864; Charlotte Clark, *Three Score Years and Ten* (Minnesota: Harrison and Smith, 1888); and George Washington Adams, *Doctors in Blue; the Medical History of the Union Army* (New York, 1952), which estimates that four hundred female transvestites fought in the Civil War.

50. See Charles McCool Snyder, *Dr. Mary Walker: The Little Lady in Pants* (New York: Vantage Press, 1962).

51. Mary E. Wilkins Freeman, "The Long Arm" (1895; reprinted in *American Detective Stories*, ed. Carolyn Wells, Oxford University Press, 1927), pp. 134–78.

52. F. L. Sim says "Nothing coarse or immoral is known of Alice or Fred," quoted in Katz, *Gay American History*, p. 58.

53. Mrs. Mary R. P. Hatch, *The Strange Disappearance of Eugene Comstock* (New York: G. W. Dillingham, 1895).

54. For example, Alice Mitchell had once planned to elope with Freda Ward and, disguised as a man, get married to her (Katz, *Gay American History*, p. 55). The lesbian villain of Hatch's novel actually does elope with a woman and marry her in male guise.

Part IIIA. *Chapter 1.* THE LAST BREATH OF INNOCENCE

1. Margaret Constance Dubois, "The Lass of the Silver Sword," *St. Nicholas: An Illustrated Magazine for Young Folks*, December 1908–October 1909.

2. See Chapter 1, Part IIB, "The Rise of Antifeminism," footnote 22.

3. Thomas Washington Shannon, *Perfect Girlhood* (Marietta, Ohio: S. A. Mullikin Co., 1913).

4. See p. 27, Chapter 1, Part IA, "Lesbianism and the Libertines."

5. Not only did American women volunteer for defeminizing war service on a large scale in 1917, but in the same year they also wrested the right to vote in New York, Rhode Island, Michigan, and Nebraska. There was at this time a tremendous influx of women into government service and jobs hitherto reserved for men. What had been "manpower" in industry became "womanpower." See, for example, Mary Van Kleeck, *Suffragists and Industrial Democracy* (New York: National Women's Suffrage Publishing Co., 1919).

6. After the war, popular magazines began to carry frequent articles with such titles as "Freud and Our Frailties," "A New Diagnosis for Hidden Mental

Taint," and "How it Feels to Be Psychoanalyzed." Freud's "The Psychogenesis of a Case of Homosexuality in a Woman" was published in English in 1920. The American medical profession had taken an interest in female homosexuality years previous to the popularization of Freud. For example, the second series of the *Index Catalogue of the Library of the Surgeon General's Office, U.S. Army* (1896–1916) lists almost a hundred books and over five hundred articles relating to lesbianism. But those works were intended for professionals and the masses would have had virtually no access to them.

7. Mary MacLane, *The Story of Mary MacLane by Herself* (Chicago: Herbert S. Stone and Co., 1902), p. 38.

8. Ibid., pp. 38–42.

9. Ibid., p. 100.

10. Ibid., p. 135.

11. Ibid., p. 182.

12. Mary MacLane, *I, Mary MacLane: A Diary of Human Days* (New York: Frederick A. Stokes Co., 1917), pp. 276–78.

13. As discussed in the previous chapter, although sophistication came earlier in England, a number of English novels written in the first decades of the twentieth century indicate that there were still pockets of "naïveté" regarding love between women. In Ellen Thorneycroft Fowler's *The Farringdons* (1900), for instance, the narrator states in all apparent innocence: "There are two things which are absolutely necessary to the well-being of the normal feminine mind—namely, one romantic attachment and one comfortable friendship." She then depicts Elisabeth's romantic attachment to Anne and her comfortable friendship with Christopher. In John Masefield's *Multitude and Solitude* (1909), Agatha develops from a brittle person to a sympathetic one through her love of and loss of another woman. She vows in memory of Ottalie to start a school for poor girls, and she sees life as being more serious and bigger than it had been in her former vision. In Ethel Sidgwick's *A Lady of Leisure* (1914), one character matter-of-factly observes of the passion between two women in their twenties, "Girls at school get enthusiasms for one another. . . . Violet never was at school, so I suppose she never worked off that phase and is going through it now." The narrator explains the "torrential force" of this passion: "The revelation of woman to woman is often just as remarkable, for all the truisms on the subject, as the revelation of woman to man."

14. Josephine Dodge Daskam, *Smith College Stories* (New York: Scribner's, 1900).

15. Jennette Lee, "The Cat and the King," *Ladies' Home Journal*, October 1919, pp. 10, 67–68, 71.

16. There is some evidence that the taboo has recently begun to lift. See R. R. Knudson, *You Are the Rain* (New York: Delacorte, 1974), a novel about a constructive and entirely admirable romantic friendship of two young girls intended for adolescent girl readers, and Sandra Scoppettone, *Happy Endings Are All Alike* (New York: Harper and Row, 1978), an even more surprising novel about two popular, well-adjusted, intelligent, and attractive teenage lesbian lovers aimed at readers "twelve years and up."

17. Reprinted in William Sidney Porter, *The Trimmed Lamp* (New York: Doubleday, Page and Co., 1914).

18. Catherine Wells, "The Beautiful House," *Harper's Magazine*, Vol. 124 (1912), pp. 503, 511.

19. Helen Hull, "The Fire," *Century*, Vol. 95 (November 1912), pp. 105–14. This and the other short stories discussed above are the subject of my article, "Lesbian Magazine Fiction in the Early Twentieth Century," *Journal of Popular Culture*, Vol. XI, No. 4 (Spring 1978), pp. 800–17.

20. See, for example, Os-Anders, "Karen: A Novel," *The Little Review* (Spring 1922), pp. 22–28, and Bryher, "Chance Encounter," *The Little Review* (Autumn and Winter, 1924–1925), pp. 35–39.

21. Ann Cheney, *Millay in Greenwich Village* (University, Ala.: University of Alabama Press, 1975), p. 20.

22. Elizabeth Atkins, *Edna St. Vincent Millay and Her Times* (Chicago: University of Chicago Press, 1936), pp. 37–38.

23. Vera Brittain, *Testament of Friendship: The Story of Winifred Holtby* (New York: Macmillan, 1940), p. 1.

24. Ibid., p. 243.

25. Ibid., pp. 159–60.

26. Ibid., p. 111.

27. Ibid., p. 306.

28. Ibid., pp. 1–2.

29. See discussion in Chapter 2, Part IIA, "Kindred Spirits," p. 161.

30. Winifred Holtby, *Letters to a Friend*, eds. Alice Holtby and Jean McWilliam (New York: Macmillan, 1938).

31. Brittain wrote one of the first reviews of Hall's novel ("Facing Facts," *Time and Tide*, August 1928), and about forty years later she did an entire study of *The Well of Loneliness* and its legal problems, *Radclyffe Hall: A Case of Obscenity?* (New York: A. S. Barnes, 1969).

32. Doris Faber, *The Life of Lorena Hickok: E.R.'s Friend* (New York: William Morrow and Co., 1980), p. 152.

33. It is doubtful that before the twentieth century anyone would have bothered to write as Xavier Mayne did in 1908, "In speaking of love, we must differentiate in it certain strong affections often called love [e.g., fraternal love]. . . . Such sentiments, however spontaneous, deep, and pure, are not love, as that sentiment really is, and as it should be distinguished from all non-sexual phases of our regard. . . . However beautiful they are far less certain, less genuine, less obscure and less mysterious than love." He then attempts to "grade" the human sentiments, giving love (i.e., sexual attraction) the top place. Xavier Mayne, *The Intersexes: A History of Similisexualism as a Problem in Social Life* (1908; reprinted New York: Arno Press, 1975), p. 24.

34. "Gay Experiences—The Sisters Speak Out: High School," *Ain't I a Woman*, June 24, 1970, reprinted in *Lesbians Speak Out*, eds. Carol Wilson et al. (Oakland, Calif.: Women's Press Collective, 1974).

35. Sidney Abbott and Barbara Love, *Sappho Was a Right-on Woman* (New York: Stein and Day, 1972), p. 19.

36. "Girl Love Test Gets Barbs," *Sacramento Bee*, May 15, 1973.

Part IIIA. *Chapter 2*. THE SPREAD OF MEDICAL "KNOWLEDGE"

1. Cf. Xavier Mayne, *The Intersexes: A History of Similisexualism as a Prob-*

lem in Social Life (1908; reprinted New York: Arno Press, 1975): The male homosexual "refers back . . . to a vigorous, well-balanced human type, not to speak of higher suggestions," p. 129. He later does "speak of higher suggestions," for example, "We have cause to believe that Christ was a Uranian," p. 259.

2. Elisabeth Dauthendey, The Uranian Question and Women (Leipzig, 1906).

3. Excerpted and reviewed by Magnus Hirschfeld, Jahrbuch, Vol. V, No. 2 (1903). It is revealing to compare Hirschfeld's discussion of Georg Keben's story "Impossible Love," from Amongst Women, which was published at the same time as the Danish novel and is reviewed in the same issue of Jahrbuch. Keben's story is in the French mode: The lesbian character is perverse and immoral by choice, and she delights in corrupting other women. Hirschfeld thinks Keben achieves nothing but "claptrap," and he laments because "the shortcomings and improbabilities of the story won't prevent those who know about homosexuality only from literature and who deny that it is congenital from discovering in Keben's protagonist an example of their theories."

4. Auguste Forel, The Sexual Question: A Scientific, Psychological, Hygienic, and Sociological Study, trans. F. Marshall, 2nd ed. (New York: Physicians and Surgeons Book Co., 1925), preface.

5. Radclyffe Hall papers, Humanities Research Center, University of Texas Library, Austin, Texas.

6. Forel, The Sexual Question, p. 484.

7. I discuss this novel and The Well at greater length in "Radclyffe Hall and the Lesbian Image," Conditions, Vol. I, No. 1 (April 1977), pp. 31–41.

8. Unpublished letter to Havelock Ellis, December 2, 1928, Humanities Research Center, University of Texas, Austin, Texas.

9. That the book was intended primarily for heterosexual readers is evidenced in the December 2, 1928, letter to Havelock Ellis cited above, in which Hall assures him that The Well is explicitly nonproselytizing, and that because it points out "the pitiful plight of inverts who form a sexual union," she believes "it would really act as a warning to any young and thoughtless girl— a warning to think seriously before she threw in her lot with an invert."

10. Vera Brittain, "Facing Facts," Time and Tide, August 1928, quoted in Vera Brittain, Radclyffe Hall: A Case of Obscenity? (New York: A. S. Barnes and Co., 1969), p. 49.

11. James Douglas, Sunday Express, August 19, 1928, quoted in Brittain, Radclyffe Hall, p. 9, and Lovat Dickson, Radclyffe Hall at the Well of Loneliness: A Sapphic Chronicle (New York: Charles Scribner's Sons, 1975), p. 148.

12. Brittain, Radclyffe Hall, p. 138.

13. Del Martin and Phyllis Lyon, Lesbian/Woman (New York: Bantam Books, 1972), p. 17.

14. Vern Bullough and Bonnie Bullough, "Lesbianism in the 1920's and 1930's: A Newfound Study," Signs: A Journal of Women in Culture and Society, Vol. II, No. 4 (Summer 1977), p. 897.

15. Quoted in Meryle Secrest, Between Me and Life: A Biography of Romaine Brooks (Garden City, N.Y.: Doubleday, 1974), p. 291.

16. Quoted in Philippe Julian and John Phillips, The Other Woman: The Life of Violet Trefusis (Boston: Houghton Mifflin, 1976), p. 228.

17. Quoted in *Carol in a Thousand Cities*, ed. Ann Aldrich (Greenwich, Conn.: Fawcett, 1960), correspondence section, p. 253.

18. Ibid., p. 231.

19. In Sigmund Freud, *Three Contributions to the Theory of Sex* (1905), *The Basic Writings of Sigmund Freud*, trans. A. A. Brill (New York: Modern Library, 1938).

20. Sigmund Freud, "The Psychogenesis of a Case of Homosexuality in a Woman" (1920), *The Standard Edition of the Complete Psychological Works of Sigmund Freud*, Vol. XVIII (London: Hogarth Press, 1955).

21. Sigmund Freud, "Historical Notes: A Letter from Freud" (1935), *American Journal of Psychiatry*, Vol. 107 (April 1951), pp. 786–87.

22. Some early examples of such promises are found in A. Sadger, "Welcher Wert Kommt der Erzählungen und Autobiographien der Homosexuallen zu?" *Archiv für Kriminalanthropologie und Kriminalistik von Gross*, Vol. 53 (1913), and in Isodor Coriat, "Homosexuality," *New York Medical Journal* (1913), pp. 589–90. These promises continued to be made by Freud's disciples for decades.

23. Wilhelm Stekel, "Is Homosexuality Curable?" trans. Bertrand Frohman, *Psychoanalytic Review*, Vol. 17 (1930), pp. 443–51.

24. Ibid., p. 446. See also R. de Saussure, "Homosexual Fixations in Neurotic Women," *Revue française psychoanalytique*, Vol. 3 (1929), pp. 50–91, and Ernest Jones, "The Early Development of Female Sexuality," *International Journal of Psychoanalysis*, Vol. 8 (1927), pp. 59–472, in which the author attributes lesbianism to "very strong sadism."

25. Robert Latou Dickinson and Lura Beam, *The Single Woman: A Medical Study in Sex Education* (New York: Reynal and Hitchcock, 1934), p. 203.

26. Bullough and Bullough, "Lesbianism in the 1920's and 1930's," p. 903.

27. Katharine Bement Davis, *Factors in the Sex Life of Twenty-two Hundred Women* (New York: Harper and Row, 1929), p. 247.

28. Ibid., pp. 270–71.

29. Ibid., p. 260. Despite Davis's statistics, which showed that the majority of the women studied had loved other women, and her picture of the glowing health of those who identified themselves as having had lesbian experiences, some of her contemporary commentators on the study did not hesitate to apply to her subjects the language of abnormal psychology. Joseph Tenenbaum, for example, after pointing out that about 50 percent of Davis's subjects had had intense emotional relations with other women and 26 percent had had sexual relations, then comments, "There is a large scale of imponderables in sex inversion. Most intimacies do not transgress the boundaries of the permissible. Some crave psychic contact rather than physical or psychophysical. In a minority, actual perversion may accompany inversion," *The Riddle of Women: A Study of the Social Psychology of Sex* (New York: Lee Furman, Inc., 1936), pp. 71–72.

30. Davis, *Factors in the Sex Life*, p. 311.

31. Ibid., p. 308.

32. Mayne, *The Intersexes*, p. 408.

33. Dr. Maurice Chideckel, *Female Sex Perversion* (New York: Eugenics Publishing Co., 1935).

34. Aron Krich, *The Sexual Revolution: Seminal Studies into Twentieth Century American Sexual Behavior* (New York: Dell, 1964).

35. Donna M. Tanner, *The Lesbian Couple* (Lexington, Mass.: D. C. Heath, 1978), p. 82.

36. Barbara Ponse, *Identities in the Lesbian World: The Social Construction of Self* (Westport, Conn.: Greenwood Press, 1978), p. 148. See also Alice E. Moses, *Identity Management in Lesbian Women* (New York: Praeger Pubs., 1978) and Sasha Gregory Lewis, *Sunday's Women: A Report on Lesbian Life Today* (New York: Beacon Press, 1979).

37. Martin and Lyon, *Lesbian/Woman*, p. 71. In her study of English lesbians, Charlotte Wolff, a British psychiatrist, comes to the same conclusion. She cites a case of a woman who has never had any kind of physical relationship but identifies herself as being exclusively lesbian, and she also states, "There have been and there are many lesbians, particularly in the older age-groups, who have lived happily with their beloved friends over the years without any sexual acts." She concludes that homoemotional is a more accurate description of lesbianism than homosexual. *Love Between Women* (New York: Harper and Row, 1971), pp. 125–33, 16–17.

38. Sally Gearhart and William R. Johnson, *Loving Women/Loving Men* (San Francisco, Calif.: Glide Pubs., 1974), pp. 132–33.

39. Judy Grahn, "Lesbian as Bogey Woman," *Gay Women's Liberation*, January 1970, reprinted in *Lesbians Speak Out*, ed. Carol Wilson et al. (Oakland, Calif.: Women's Press Collective, 1974).

40. Nina Sabaroff, "Lesbian Sexuality: An Unfinished Saga," in *After You're Out: Personal Experiences of Gay Men and Lesbian Women*, eds. Karla Jay and Allen Young (New York: Harcourt Brace Jovanovich, 1975).

41. Mary Daly, "Sparking: The Fire of Female Friendship," *Chrysalis: A Magazine of Women's Culture*, Vol. 6 (1978), pp. 27–35.

42. Alfred Kinsey et al., *Sexual Behavior in the Human Female* (Philadelphia: Saunders, 1953), p. 447.

43. Albert Ellis, Introduction to Donald Webster Cory, *The Lesbian in America* (New York: Citadel Press, 1964), p. 11.

44. Frank Caprio, *Female Homosexuality: A Psychoanalytic Study of Lesbianism* (New York: Citadel Press, 1954). Incredible as it may seem, Caprio based many of his assertions on stories which he discovered in "true confession" magazines and shamelessly offered up as fact.

45. Edmund Bergler, *Homosexuality: A Disease or a Way of Life?* (New York: Hill and Wang, 1956).

46. Robert C. Robertiello, *Voyage From Lesbos* (New York: Citadel Press, 1959).

47. Benjamin Karpman, *The Sexual Offender and His Offenses* (New York: Julian Press, 1954).

48. See, for example, Dr. Mark Freedman, "Homosexuality Among Women and Psychological Adjustment," reported in *The Ladder*, Vol. II, No. 2 (January 1968), pp. 2–3; June Hopkins, "The Lesbian Personality," *The British Journal of Psychiatry*, Vol. 115, No. 529 (December 1969); Jack Hedblom, "The Female Homosexual: Social and Attitudinal Dimensions, in *The Homosexual Dialectic* (Englewood Cliffs, N.J.: Prentice-Hall, 1972); W. L. Cotton, "Social and Sexual

Relationships of Lesbians," *The Journal of Sex Research*, No. 11 (1975), pp. 139–48; Andrea Oberstone and Harriet Sukoneck, "Psychological Adjustment and Life Style of Single Lesbians and Single Heterosexual Women," *Psychology of Women Quarterly*, No. 2 (1976), pp. 172–88; and Alan P. Bell and Martin S. Weinberg, *Homosexualities: A Study of Diversity Among Men and Women* (New York: Simon and Schuster, 1978).

Part IIIA. *Chapter 3.* KEEPING WOMEN DOWN

1. Otto Weininger, *Sex and Character* (London, 1906), p. 292.

2. Auguste Forel, *The Sexual Question: A Scientific, Psychological, Hygienic, and Sociological Study* (1906; reprinted New York: Physicians and Surgeons Book Co., 1925), p. 67.

3. Godfrey Leland, *The Alternate Sex: or, The Female Intellect in Man, and the Masculine in Woman* (New York: Funk and Wagnalls, 1904), pp. 58–59.

4. H. L. Mencken, *In Defense of Women* (1922; reprinted New York: Time Inc. Book Division, 1963), p. 151.

5. Andrew Sinclair, *The Better Half: The Emancipation of the American Woman* (New York: Harper and Row, 1965), pp. 331–32.

6. Sidney Ditzion, *Marriage, Morals, and Sex in America: A History of Ideas* (New York: Bookman Associates, 1953), pp. 371–72.

7. Dr. E. F. W. Eberhard, *Feminismus und Kul016uruntergang: Die Erotischen Grundlagen der Frauenemanzipation* (Leipzig: Wilhelm Braunmüller, 1927), Chapter 6, especially pp. 372–81.

8. See, for example, Victor Margueritte, *La Garçonne* (Paris: Ernest Flammarion, 1922); Charles-Etienne, *Inassouvie* (Paris: Editions Curio, 1927); André Gide, *Genevieve* (1936; reprinted New York: Alfred Knopf, 1950).

9. Edward Carpenter, *Love's Coming of Age* (London: Mitchell Kennerley, 1911), p. 72.

10. The 1911 British census shows, for example, 383,000 women in professions and their subsidiary service; 50,000 women in public administration; and about 200,000 women in commerce, Kate Caffrey, *The 1900's Lady* (London: Gordon and Cremonesi, 1976), p. 87.

11. George Dangerfield, *The Strange Death of Liberal England* (London: Constable and Co., 1936), pp. 141–43.

12. Xavier Mayne, *The Intersexes: A History of Similisexualism as a Problem in Social Life* (1908; reprinted New York: Arno Press, 1975), pp. 147, 182, 401.

13. Phyllis Blanchard, "Sex in the Adolescent Girl," in *Sex in Civilization*, ed. V. F. Calverton and S. D. Schalhausen (Garden City, N.Y.: Garden City Pubs., 1929), pp. 538–61.

14. Floyd Dell, *Love in the Machine Age* (New York: Farrar and Rinehart, 1930), pp. 304–05. Nalbro Bartley's portrayal of Harriet's relationship with Leila in *A Woman's Woman* (1919) and the central character's observations of her classmates in Wanda Fraiken Neff's *We Sing Diana* (1928) illustrate the fears that were rampant regarding female education and lesbianism. In Sherwood Anderson's *Poor White* (1920), Clara goes to a state university rather than a women's college, but she meets Kate Chancellor, a feminist (the namesake and spiritual sister of Olive Chancellor of *The Bostonians*), who "had the body

of a woman," yet "was in her nature a man." Although their relationship is given no overt sexual expression, it is highly charged emotionally. It ruins Clara for marriage for a while: On her wedding day she remembers "something very like lovemaking" that had occurred between herself and Kate, and she thinks, "What I want above everything else is a woman." Marion Patton's novel about a girls' school, *Dance on the Tortoise* (1930), shows that such all-consuming relationships are inevitable even in lower institutions where females congregate to get educated.

15. See, for example, M. Vaerting, "Dominant Sexes," in *Our Changing Morality: A Symposium*, ed. Freda Kirchwey (New York: Boni, 1924), pp. 147–63, and John Erskine, *The Influence of Women and Its Cure* (Indianapolis: Bobbs-Merrill, 1936), p. 65.

16. William Carlos Williams' lesbian story entitled "The Knife of the Times," in *Knife of the Times* (Ithaca, N.Y.: Dragon Press, 1932). Williams was a close friend of some of the most illustrious lesbians of his era: H.D., Gertrude Stein, Margaret Anderson, Jane Heap, but they apparently made him nervous. He reported, for example, that he used to visit the apartment that Anderson and Heap shared: "There was a huge swinging bed suspended from the ceiling. We poor males would look timidly at it and marvel," in *I Wanted to Write a Poem*, ed. Edith Heal (Boston: Beacon Press, 1958), p. 33. He was also uncomfortable in Natalie Barney's lesbian-dominated Paris salon. He observed with disgruntlement that Barney "could tell a pickle from a clam any day of the week," and he went on savagely to deride the shocking lesbian goings-on he saw there. (See Chapter 5, Part IIIA, "Internalization and Rebellion," p. 369).

17. Elaine Kendall, *Peculiar Institutions: An Informal History of the Seven Sister Colleges* (New York: G. P. Putnam's Sons, 1976), p. 204.

18. Ferdinand Lundberg and Marynia Farnham, *Modern Woman: The Lost Sex* (New York: Harper and Row, 1947), p. 143.

19. Ibid., p. 296.

20. Ibid., pp. 365–66.

21. See, for example, Talcott Parsons and R. F. Bales, *Family, Socialization, and Interaction Process* (New York: Free Press, 1955).

22. Kendall, *Peculiar Institutions*, p. 219. See also Betty Friedan's discussion of the successful conspiracy to return women to the home in the 1950's, *The Feminine Mystique* (New York: Norton, 1963).

23. "Women's Lib: A Second Look," *Time Magazine*, December 8, 1970, p. 50.

Part IIIA. *Chapter 4.* FICTION AS A WEAPON

1. Violet Trefusis, the lover of Vita Sackville-West, was apparently close friends with Ashton around 1920 and used her to make Vita jealous; Philippe Julian and John Phillips, *The Other Woman: A Life of Violet Trefusis* (Boston: Houghton Mifflin, 1976), p. 200.

2. The association of brilliance and talent with a masculine, evil, invariably neurotic or psychotic woman is common in antilesbian and antifeminist literature. It appeared in fiction at the beginning of the century and continued for decades. One of the first examples, Mizpra, the Ph.D. feminist of William Lee Howard's *The Perverts* (1901), is "clever, talented almost to the heights of

472 ❖ SURPASSING THE LOVE OF MEN

genius in her mental attainments," but she is also a born criminal and "to kill, destroy, cause misery, and produce unhappiness was her life."

3. Brooks Atkinson, Introduction to Edouard Bourdet, *The Captive*, trans. Arthur Hornblow, Jr. (New York: Brentano, 1927), p. x. Shortly after the play opened in the United States, efforts were underway to suppress it; see Jonathan Katz, *Gay American History: Lesbians and Gay Men in the U.S.A.* (New York: Thomas Crowell, 1976), pp. 82–91.

4. Harvey O'Higgins, *Julie Cane, Harpers*, Vol. 148; the serial began February 1924.

5. In Harry T. Moore, *D. H. Lawrence: A Critical Survey* (London: Forum House, 1969), pp. 49–55; originally published in *Journal of Nervous and Mental Disease* (Baltimore), 1958. Bergler enumerates these observations in scientific terms: "1. Lawrence describes the typical husband-wife camouflage of Lesbians, and at the same time stresses the psychic-masochistic substructure of the camouflage. . . . 2. Lawrence correctly describes March's constant 'injustice collecting,' hence her hidden psychic-masochism. . . . 3. Lawrence accurately depicts the two sets of identification in March: the 'leading' masochistic identification with the victim, and the 'misleading' masculine identification, deposited in the Oedipal camouflage of her relationship with Banford. . . . 4. Lawrence ingeniously hints that the fox, the devourer of chickens, symbolizes the 'devouring' mother; we know that the fear of being devoured has priority in the 'septet of baby fears.' . . . 5. Lawrence describes the unvarying inner defense of his masochistic heroine: the search for love, which these sick women can find neither in the Lesbian nor in the connubial bed since 'injustice collecting' is the real aim. 6. Finally, Lawrence presents with clinical correctness the defensive pseudo-aggression so predominant in Lesbians."

6. As Frank Kermode (*D. H. Lawrence*, New York: Viking Press, 1973, p. 116) observes, Lawrence began his "career of male chauvinism" in his "Preface" to *Sons and Lovers*, written in 1913, and such chauvinism appears consistently in all his later works. However, in the years immediately following World War I, he seems to have reached a sort of apogee, perhaps because it was becoming shockingly clear to him that women were moving in the direction of freedom— a direction opposite to what he saw as necessary if the world was to right itself— more rapidly than ever at this time. His letters of this period suggest a hostility to "self-important" and "bullying" females, both in his own life and in the world in general. For example, writing to his Russian translator friend, S. S. Koteliansky, on March 14, 1919, Lawrence complained of his wife, "She really is a devil— and I feel as if I would part with her forever—let her go alone to Germany, while I take another road. For it is true, I have been bullied by her long enough. I really could leave her now, without a pang, I believe. The time comes, to make an end, one way or another." (*The Collected Letters of D. H. Lawrence*, Vol. I, ed. Harry T. Moore, New York: The Viking Press, 1962, p. 581). A couple of months later (May 7, 1919) he complained to Koteliansky of Margaret Radford, a writer and casual acquaintance, "I wish one could exterminate all her sort under a heap of Keating's powder. I feel utterly 'off' the soulful or clever or witty type of female—in fact, the self-important female of any sort." (*Collected Letters*, Vol. I, p. 585.) His work is full of assertions that women must concern

themselves not with "thinking" and "abstracting" but with their womanly activities, "the immediate personal life" ("Education of the People," 1918, in *Phoenix: The Posthumous Papers of D. H. Lawrence*, New York: Viking Press, 1936, p. 664), that the final destruction of the evil power of women is mandatory for the progress of mankind (*The Sea and Sardinia*, New York: T. Seltzer, 1921) and that the "intelligent" woman is a perversion of the "true" woman, whose business is at night. During the day she must remain "half in fear" of the male. Always she must submit to a purpose which is "beyond her" (*Fantasia of the Unconscious*, New York: T. Seltzer, 1922).

7. Lawrence's annoyance is also reflected in an earlier novel, *The Rainbow* (1915). Winifred Inger, a feminist school teacher and an older woman who seduces sixteen-year-old Ursula, provides another commentary on his view of independent females as well as love between women. The chapter which deals with their affair at length is entitled "Shame."

8. In Moore, *D. H. Lawrence: A Critical Survey*, pp. 28–48.

9. Dorothy Parker uses a similar ploy in a short story, "Glory in the Daytime," in *After Such Pleasure* (1933). Her impressionable central character, Mrs. Murdock, who is married to a stodgy husband, becomes excited by Hallie Noyes, a glamorous, independent woman who wears black velvet trousers and tailored paraphernalia. Hallie kisses Mrs. Murdock on the lips and lets her know she is having an affair with an exciting actress. Mrs. Murdock soon sees that Hallie's existence is as sterile as her glass and chrome furniture, and that the actress is pathetic, filthy, and faded. Mrs. Murdock finally wants only to return to her humdrum existence.

10. Ann Aldrich, *Carol in a Thousand Cities* (Greenwich, Conn.: Fawcett, 1960), p. 121.

11. Maureen Brady and Judith McDaniel show in their article, "Lesbians in the Mainstream: Images of Lesbians in Recent Commercial Fiction," *Conditions* (forthcoming), that commercial publishing houses are generally still unwilling to publish and promote fiction presenting healthy and happy lesbians. Although melodramatic images of lesbian evil and sickness seem to be a thing of the past, in their study of about twenty novels published by commercial houses during the last half of the 1970's, Brady and McDaniel conclude that almost all the lesbian characters are in some way disempowered or punished, and often they are filled with self-hatred.

Part IIIA. *Chapter 5*. INTERNALIZATION AND REBELLION

1. Mary Casal, *The Stone Wall: An Autobiography* (1930; reprinted New York: Arno Press, 1975), p. 185.

2. Ibid., p. 165.

3. Quoted in Vern Bullough and Bonnie Bullough, "Lesbianism in the 1920's and 1930's: A Newfound Study," *Signs: Journal of Women in Culture and Society*, Vol. II, No. 4 (Summer 1977), p. 897.

4. Marie-Madeleine, *Auf Kypros* (Berlin: Vita, 1898). I wish to thank Brigitte Eriksson and Frankie Hucklenbroich for their assistance in translating these poems.

5. Joseph Tenenbaum, *The Riddle of Woman: A Study in the Social Psychology of Sex* (New York: Lee Furman, Inc., 1936), p. 74.

6. Djuna Barnes, *Ladies Almanack* (1928; reprinted New York: Harper and Row, 1972), p. 34.

7. Brassaï [Gyula Halasz], *The Secret Paris of the 1930's*, trans. Richard Miller (New York: Pantheon Books, 1976), preface.

8. At least one lesbian poet continues to use Louÿ's spelling today: See Elsa Gidlow's "Invocation" to the Greek poet in *Motive*, Vol. 32, No. 1 (1972), p. 47. According to Mitchell Starrett Buck, translator of the 1919 edition of *Songs of Bilitis*, "no authority is evident for the statement that Sappho was known in Lesbos under the name of Psappha," p. 172. Vivien, and probably Gidlow too, found the name in *Songs of Bilitis* only. Twentieth-century male authors have also been influenced by Louÿs's lesbian fiction. Richard Aldington, for example, attempted to emulate him in a series of poems about Myrrhine and Konallis, two Mytilenean lovers, which he pretended, as did Louÿs, to have translated from the Greek. Most of the poems appeared in *Little Review*, August 1915, November 1916, and March 1917. They were later revised, more poems were added, and they were published as *The Love of Myrrhine and Konallis and other Prose Poems* (Chicago: Covici, 1926).

9. Clarissa Burnham Cooper, *Women Poets of the Twentieth Century in France* (New York: King's Crown Press, 1943), p. 301.

10. Colette, *The Pure and the Impure* (1932; reprinted, New York: Farrar, Straus, and Giroux, 1967), p. 81.

11. Renée Vivien, *A Woman Appeared to Me* (1904), trans. Jeannette Foster (Reno, Nev.: Naiad Press, 1976), pp. 21–22.

12. *The Muse of the Violets: Poems by Renée Vivien*, trans. Margaret Porter and Catherine Kroger (Bates City, Mo.: Naiad Press, 1977), p. 23.

13. Ibid., p. 24.

14. Ibid., p. 26.

15. Ibid., p 28.

16. Ibid.

17. Ibid., p. 32.

18. Ibid., p. 70. The one lover who has left a record of their affair, Natalie Barney, claims that she was frustrated in their relationship because all of Vivien's passion went into words and she had little sexual desire. The "words" were, of course, from Vivien's literary predecessors.

19. Quoted in "The Amazon of Letters," *Adam: International Review*, Vol. XXIX, No. 299 (1962), p. 104.

20. Colette, *L'Étoile Vesper: Souvenirs* (Paris, 1946), p. 131.

21. See, for example, Colette, *Earthly Paradise*, ed. Robert Phelps (New York: Farrar, Straus and Giroux, 1961), pp. 144–50, and *The Pure and the Impure*, pp. 69–78.

22. Colette, *The Pure and the Impure*, p. 131.

23. Ibid., p. 111.

24. Louis F. Kannenstine, *The Art of Djuna Barnes: Duality and Damnation* (New York: New York University Press, 1977), p. 10.

25. Djuna Barnes, *A Book* (New York: Boni and Liveright, 1923), pp. 145–46.

26. Djuna Barnes, "A Little Girl Tells a Story to a Lady," *A Night Among the Horses* (New York: Horace Liveright, 1929), pp. 238–39.

27. Theodore Purdy, Jr., review of *Nightwood*, in *Saturday Review*, March 27, 1937, p. 11.

28. Natalie Clifford Barney, *Aventures de l'esprit* (1929; reprinted, New York: Arno Press, 1975), p. 74, and George Wickes, *The Amazon of Letters: The Life and Loves of Natalie Barney* (New York: G. P. Putnam's Sons, 1976), p. 179.

29. Quoted in Kannenstine, *The Art of Djuna Barnes*, p. xi.

30. Quoted in Nigel Nicolson, *Portrait of a Marriage* (New York: Atheneum, 1973), p. 35.

31. Ibid., p. 106.

32. Ibid., p. 108.

33. Ibid., p 114.

34. Ibid., p. 110

35. Ibid., pp. 38–39.

36. Ibid., p. 118.

37. Ibid., p. 119.

38. Two books as well as numerous articles appeared about Barney during the late 1970's. See especially Wickes, *The Amazon of Letters*, and Jean Chalon, *Portrait of a Seductress: The World of Natalie Barney* (1976), trans. Carol Barko (New York: Crown Publishers, 1979).

39. Quoted in W. G. Rogers, *Ladies Bountiful* (New York: Harcourt Brace and World, 1968), pp. 44–45.

40. "The Amazon of Letters," *Adam*, p. 11.

41. Quoted in "A Natalie Barney Garland," ed. George Wickes, *The Paris Review* (Spring 1975), p. 131.

42. John Ellerton Lodge, unpublished poems, in Natalie Barney collection, Beinecke Rare Book and Manuscript Library, Yale University, New Haven, Conn.

43. Quoted in Chalon, *Portrait of a Seductress*, p. 14.

44. Quoted in Wickes, *The Amazon of Letters*, p. 26.

45. Quoted in Chalon, *Portrait of a Seductress*, p. 47.

46. Quoted in Rogers, *Ladies Bountiful*, p. 45.

47. Natalie Clifford Barney, *Aventures de l'esprit* (1929; reprinted New York: Arno Press, 1975).

48. I wish to thank Virgil Thomson who met Barney through Gertrude Stein for sharing this information with me in conversation, January 3, 1976.

49. Mr. Thomson mentioned that Barney offered support to at least two women he knew of, Djuna Barnes and Gwen LeGalliene.

50. See especially Margaret Anderson, *My Thirty Years War* (New York: Covici, Friede, 1930), *The Fiery Fountain* (New York: Hermitage House, 1951), and *The Strange Necessity* (New York: Horizon Press, 1969); Sylvia Beach, *Shakespeare and Company* (New York: Harcourt Brace, 1959); Bryher, *The Heart to Artemis: A Writer's Memoirs* (New York: Harcourt Brace, 1962); *The Very Rich Hours of Adrienne Monnier*, trans. Richard A. McDougall (New York: Charles Scribner's Sons, 1976).

Part IIIB. *Chapter 1.* THE RISE OF LESBIAN-FEMINISM

1. The term was coined in a May 1970 essay by New York Radicalesbians, "Woman-Identified-Woman" (reprinted in *Lesbians Speak Out*, Oakland, Calif.: Women's Press Collective, 1974, pp. 87–89).

2. Edward Shorter shows the statistical extent of the "sexual revolution" of the 1960's, not only in America but throughout Western Europe as well; *The Making of the Modern Family* (New York: Basic Books, 1975), pp. 164–65.

3. "Are Homosexuals a Menace?" *The Ladder*, Vol. I, No. 8 (May 1957), pp. 3–5.

4. "Homosexuality, A Way of Life," *The Ladder*, Vol. II, No. 2 (February 1958), pp. 18–19.

5. "Why Am I a Lesbian?" *The Ladder*, Vol. IV, No. 9 (June 1960), pp. 20–24.

6. Review of *The Feminine Mystique*, in *The Ladder*, Vol. VII, No. 6 (March 1963), p. 9.

7. "Readers Respond," *The Ladder*, Vol. IX, No. 9 (June 1965), pp. 25–26.

8. *The Ladder*, Vol. I, No. 10 (July 1957), pp. 3–5, 21–23.

9. Ibid., Vol. III, No. 4 (January 1959), p. 14.

10. Ibid., Vol. IV, No. 9 (June 1960), p. 5.

11. "The Experiment that Failed," *The Ladder*, Vol. IV, No. 9 (June 1960), pp. 7–14.

12. Paula Christian, *The Ladder*, Vol. V, No. 5 (February 1961), p. 20.

13. See, for example, "Notes of an Old Gay," *Motive: Lesbian/Feminist Issue*, Vol. 32, No. 1 (1972), pp. 16–18. The author states that feminism has permitted lesbians to understand on a "head level" what they had understood only on a "gut level." "When I review my childhood again," she says, "as I did so many times before in a desperate search for the thing that 'went wrong,' I find that the facts have not changed, but my reading of them has changed dramatically. What seemed before to have been a perverse tendency to view my situation in a 'distorted manner' and to adopt 'immature' solutions, seems now to have been an essentially accurate comprehension of what lay in store for me as a woman and a willful resistance along the only route that lay open to me."

14. Ann Hayley, "Why Women's Liberation Would Like to Like Lesbians," *The Ladder*, Vol. XV, Nos. 7 and 8 (April/May 1971), pp. 4–6.

15. The acknowledgment did not take place everywhere without a struggle. For years many feminists, led by Betty Friedan, the founder of the National Organization for Women, were terrified that N.O.W. would be accused of harboring lesbianism, and lesbian purges were not uncommon in feminist groups. The two major events which brought lesbianism and feminism together were the feminists' support of Kate Millett after the 1970 *Time* attack on her as a bisexual and the 1971 N.O.W. resolution to support lesbians. But lesbianism and feminism might have been brought together without those events, with only an examination of the issues, freed of the fear of unorthodox sexuality, such as had been taking place in consciousness-raising groups all over the country. By 1970 many feminist writers began to declare lesbianism to be a logical extension of feminism.

16. "Readers Respond," *The Ladder*, Vol. XII, No. 2 (January 1968), pp. 28–29.

17. Ginny Berson, *The Furies: Lesbian-Feminist Monthly* (January 1972), p. 1.

18. Editorial, *Proud Woman*, Vol. II, No. 1 (March/April 1972), p. 2.

19. Elsa Gidlow, "Lesbianism as a Liberating Force," *Heresies: A Feminist Publication on Art and Politics*, Vol. I, No. 2 (May 1977), pp. 94–95. See also the statement in this issue on lesbian artists: "Being a lesbian allows my womanness to be all mine. I have all that force behind my work. And that's what makes a difference," in "The Tapes," ed. Louise Fishman, pp. 15–21.

20. Sharon Crase, *Sisters*, Vol. IV, No. 6 (June 1973), pp. 18–19.

21. Alfred Adler, "Sex," in *Psychoanalysis and Women*, ed. Jean Baker Miller (London: Penguin Books, 1973). Some subsequent psychoanalysts came to the same conclusions, but they were often muddied by a devotion to Freudianism. Charlotte Wolff, for example, in *Love Between Women* (New York: Harper and Row, 1971), saw a "tinge of tragedy" resulting from the "impossibility of complete sexual fulfillment" in lesbianism (pp. 12–13), believed that lesbians were fixated on an early stage of the Oedipus Complex (p. 24), and stated with absolutely no proof and counter to a number of studies, "the incidence of neurosis and psychosis is significantly higher in homosexual than heterosexual women" (p. 66). But she also recognized that lesbians had no desire to be men, and if in childhood they wanted a penis, "it was not because they envied the male organ itself, but because to them it symbolized freedom" (p. 59). She recognized, too, that a woman becomes a lesbian in "rejection of female inferiority and masquerade," and that "the lesbian was and is unquestionably in the avant-garde of the fight for equality of the sexes, and for the psychical liberation of women" (p. 79).

22. Simone de Beauvoir, *The Second Sex* (1949; reprinted New York: Vintage Books, 1974), pp. 456–58.

23. Jill Johnston, *Lesbian Nation: The Feminist Solution* (Simon and Schuster, 1973), pp. 72, 64–65.

24. Del Martin and Phyllis Lyon, *Lesbian/Woman* (New York: Bantam Books, 1972), pp. 22–23.

25. Donna M. Tanner, *The Lesbian Couple* (Lexington, Mass.: D. C. Heath, 1978), pp. 90–91.

26. Barbara Ponse, *Identities in the Lesbian World: The Social Construction of Self* (Westport, Conn.: Greenwood Press, 1978), p. 177. See also Dolores Klaich's interviews with lesbians, whose statements about why they are lesbian are almost identical to these, *Woman + Woman: Attitudes Toward Lesbianism* (New York: William Morrow and Co., 1974), especially pp. 22, 36, 114, 245–46.

27. Monique Wittig, "Paradigms" in *Homosexualities and French Literature*, eds. George Stambolian and Elaine Marks (Ithaca, N.Y.: Cornell University Press, 1979), p. 118.

28. Hélène Cixous, in a 1976 interview, claimed to see no connection between feminism and lesbians who came out before the movement. She apparently believed that those lesbians, if they were political, had closer ties to the French male homosexual movement, and that they modeled their relationships on heterosexual dichotomies. However, the introduction to this interview in Stambolian and Marks, *Homosexualities and French Literature*, indicated that Cixous later repudiated her earlier views. Possibly in the three years between

the interview and the book's publication, older French lesbians made their position on feminism more clear, "Rethinking Differences," pp. 70–86.

29. See, for example, Bonnie Charles Bluh, *Woman to Woman: European Feminists* (New York: Starogubski Press, 1974) pp. 162ff, and Hélène Cixous, "The Laugh of the Medusa," trans. Keith Cohen and Paula Cohen, *Signs: Journal of Women in Culture and Society*, Vol. I, No. 4 (Summer 1976), pp. 875–93.

30. *Die Freundin*, Vol. V, No. 12 (September 18, 1929), p. 2, and Vol. VI, No. 22 (May 28, 1930), p. 6.

31. Ursula Linnhoff, *Weibliche Homosexualität: Zwischen Anpassung und Emanzipation* (Köln: Kiopenhour und Witsch, 1976).

32. Verena Stefan, *Shedding*, trans. Johanna Moore and Beth Werkmueller (1975; reprinted New York: Daughters, Inc., 1978).

33. Val Vanderwood, "Lesbian Life in England," *The Ladder*, Vol. XIV, Nos. 7 and 8 (April/May 1970), pp. 6–9.

34. Angela Stewart-Park and Jules Cassidy, *We're Here: Conversations with Lesbian Women* (London: Quartet Books, 1977), pp. 2–3.

35. Ibid., p. 140.

Part IIIB. Chapter 2. WRITING LESBIAN

1. *The Rainbow* was suppressed because of two erotic passages in particular: a heterosexual love scene between Ursula and Anton Skrebensky, and a lesbian love scene between Ursula and Winifred Inger. While the heterosexual scene was unchanged in later editions, the lesbian passage was modified. Harry T. Moore, *D. H. Lawrence: His Life and Works* (New York: Twayne Publishers, 1964), p. 120. The following discussion of Lowell is adapted from my article, "Warding Off the Watch and Ward Society," *Gay Books Bibliography*, Vol. I, 2 (Spring 1979).

2. S. Foster Damon, *Amy Lowell: A Chronicle, with Extracts from her Correspondence* (Boston: Houghton Mifflin, 1935), pp. 482–83.

3. Letter to H. L. Mencken, September 18, 1916, in Foster Damon, *Amy Lowell*, p. 372. Although Lowell was publicly opposed to censorship, in her letters to personal acquaintances she expressed her distaste for the unbridled works of Ezra Pound, James Joyce, Richard Aldington, and even Lawrence, whom she always championed in print and in her lectures.

4. Lowell's first volume, *A Dome of Many Coloured Glass* (1912), also contains a number of seemingly homoerotic poems, addressed apparently to two other women.

5. Jean Gould's *Amy: The World of Amy Lowell and the Imagist Movement* (New York: Dodd, Mead, 1975) is the first to deal in depth with the specific nature of the relationship between Lowell and Ada Russell. In a scurrilous study published one year after Amy Lowell's death, Clement Wood argued that Lowell was not a good poet because many of her poems were homosexual; therefore, they did not "word a common cry of many hearts." Lowell, he concluded, may qualify "as an impassioned singer of her own desires; and she may well be laureate also of as many as stand beside her," but nonlesbian readers will find nothing in her verse; *Amy Lowell* (New York: Harold Vinal, 1926), pp. 13, 173. Perhaps because Ada Russell was still alive when Wood published his study, he uses almost no biography to support his thesis. G. R. Ruihley, in

his introduction to *A Shard of Silence: Selected Poems of Amy Lowell* (New York: Twayne Publishers, 1957) and in his critical study, *The Thorn of a Rose: Amy Lowell Reconsidered* (Hamden, Conn.: Archon Books, 1975), discusses the "powerful attachment" between Amy Lowell and Ada Russell, but he characterizes the relationship as being on "a rare and platonic plane." Other biographers have referred to Ada Russell as Lowell's "companion" or "dear friend," and have ignored the intensity that inspired the poet to write hundreds of love poems to the other woman.

6. Hervey Allen, "Amy Lowell as a Poet," *Saturday Review of Literature*, Vol. 3, No. 28 (February 5, 1927), pp. 557–58, 568.

7. Winfield Townley Scott, "Amy Lowell Ten Years After," *New England Quarterly*, Vol. 8 (June 1935), pp. 320–30.

8. Ruihley, *A Shard of Silence*, p. xvii.

9. Wood, *Amy Lowell*, p. 151.

10. Damon, *Amy Lowell: A Chronicle*, p. 441.

11. These Ada images appear not just in the volume under consideration, but in earlier and later volumes as well. For example, in "In a Garden" (*Sword Blades and Poppy Seed*) the speaker would love to watch the other woman bathing, "white and shining in the silver-flecked water/While the moon rode over the garden," surrounded by cool-colored lilacs. In "The Giver of Stars" from the same volume, the beloved is associated with both coolness and "flickering flame." In "Twenty-Four Hokku on a Modern Theme" (*What's O'Clock*), the beloved is compared to "a cloud of lillies" (number 22) and the "sweet smell of wet flowers/Over an evening garden" (number 23). In the same volume she is compared to a white flower—she is "bright as a clematis at the touch of night" ("Song for a Viola D'Amore"). Her shadow is "sunlight on a plate of silver," her footsteps "the seeding-place of lillies" ("In Excelsis"). In "Afterglow," as in "Madonna of the Evening Flowers," she is associated specifically with the "pale blue larkspur." In "Paradox" (*Ballads for Sale*), she is associated with gardens, things quiet and pale, twilight, and "splendid flashing." In "Heraldic" from the same volume, she is again seen through images of whiteness and a garden.

12. In *What's O'Clock*, for example, the lover observes, "Last night, at sunset,/The foxgloves were like tall altar candles./Could I have lifted you to the roof of the greenhouse, my Dear,/I should have understood their burning" ("Vespers"). In "In Excelsis" the beloved is presented in Christ imagery—the speaker is awed by the miracle of this other woman and proclaims:

I drink your lips,
I eat the whiteness of your hands and feet . . .
How have you come to dwell with me,
Compassing me with the four circles of your mystic lightness,
So that I say "Glory Glory!" and bow before you
As to a shrine?

In *Ballads for Sale* the speaker compares the beloved's garment to a cardinal's and declares: "I kneel at the trace of your feet in the grass" ("Thorn Piece").

13. Letter to Lowell from D. H. Lawrence, November 18, 1914, Damon, *Amy Lowell: A Chronicle*, pp. 277–79.

14. Letter to Lowell from D. H. Lawrence, March 23, 1917, ibid., p. 405.

15. Letter from Lowell to May Lamberton Becker, July 7, 1923, ibid., p. 635.

16. Quoted in Ernest Hemingway, *A Moveable Feast* (New York: Bantam, 1969), p. 15.

17. Edmund Wilson, "Books," *The New Yorker*, Vol. XXVII, No. 31 (September 15, 1951), pp. 124–31.

18. Edmund Wilson, *The Shores of Light* (New York: Farrar, Straus, and Young, 1952), pp. 581–86.

19. James R. Mellow, *Charmed Circle: Gertrude Stein and Company* (New York: Praeger Publishers, 1974), p. 134. Later in her career Stein felt she could deal with male homosexuality with impunity. She did a blurb for the book jacket of *The Young and Evil* (1933) by her friends Parker Tyler and Charles Henri Ford.

20. The lesbian writer's awareness of the restrictions conventional publishers placed on her—their insistence that she keep the clichés alive and make the lesbian characters suffer—is reflected in an article by one of the most prolific writers of lesbian fiction during the 1950's and 1960's, who later became an editor, Paula Christian. "Through my own experience at Fawcett," Christian observed, "it should be understood that a publisher (with the moral character of a nation in mind) cannot allow this theme to be promoted as something to be admired and desired. Nor can a publisher in the paperback field expect the general public to accept a truly sophisticated treatment where there is no justification for the 'deviation' with a great deal of why's, wherefore's and 'we hate ourselves but what can we do,' " *The Ladder*, Vol. V, No. 5 (February 1961), p. 19.

21. In "An Interview With Adrienne Rich," Part II, *Conditions: Two* (Fall 1977), p. 58.

22. In recent years virtually every major house has published at least one novel or nonfiction work about lesbians by a lesbian or a feminist writer, including Harcourt Brace, Bobbs-Merrill, Doubleday, Houghton Mifflin, Viking, Holt Rinehart, Simon and Schuster, Random House, Alfred Knopf, William Morrow, Norton, E. P. Dutton, Macmillan, and Prentice-Hall.

INDEX